WINN
2017 NATIONAL BOOI

THE HELEN BERNSTEIN вии, ...
FOR EXCELLENCE IN JOURNALISM

FINALIST FOR THE NATIONAL BOOK CRITICS
CIRCLE AWARD

Praise for

THE FUTURE IS HISTORY

"Ambitious, timely, insightful, and unsparing. . . . By far Gessen's best book, a sweeping intellectual history of Russia over the past four decades, told through a Tolstoyan gallery of characters. . . . What makes the book so worthwhile . . . are its keen observations about Russia from the point of view of those experiencing its return to a heavy-handed state. It helps that Gessen is a participant, and not just an observer, able to translate that world adeptly for Western readers. . . . You feel right there on the streets." —*The Washington Post*

"Fascinating and deeply felt." —*The New York Times Book Review*

"Forceful and eloquent on the history of her native country, Gessen is alarming and pessimistic about its future as it doubles down on totalitarianism."
—*Los Angeles Times*

"A remarkable portrait of an ever-shifting era . . . Gessen weaves her characters' stories into a seamless, poignant whole. Her analysis of Putin's malevolent administration is just as effective . . . a harrowing, compassionate, and important book." —*San Francisco Chronicle*

"Masterful . . . as fascinating as it is urgently relevant today."
—*The Boston Globe*

"Gessen is an exemplary journalist who knows when to sit back and let facts speak for themselves . . . [and] *The Future Is History* just might be the culmination of [her] life's work. . . . If you've been confused by all the talk about 'Russia stuff,' this might be the most important book you'll read all year."
—*The Seattle Times*

"One of Putin's most fearless and dogged critics tracks the devastating descent of post-Soviet Russia into authoritarianism and kleptocracy through the lives of four disillusioned citizens."
—*Esquire*

"Essential reportage."
—*O, The Oprah Magazine*

"Brilliant and sobering . . . with formidable powers of synthesis and a mordant wit, Gessen follows the misfortunes of four Russians who have lived most of their lives under Putin . . . [and] vividly chronicles the story of a mortal struggle."
—*Newsday*

"Gessen outlines the failure of Russia's reform with precision and humanity, thoroughly explaining the strength of an authoritarian government's hold on its citizens' psyche. It's not just history; it is an urgent awakening."
—Buzzfeed

"Gessen, the sterling Russian-American journalist and activist, has been outspoken in recent press articles about the threat of totalitarianism in America. But in her latest book, *The Future Is History*, she never mentions America's problems. Here, instead, she examines what is wrong in her native country and lets readers, wide-eyed, draw the parallels."
—*The Christian Science Monitor*

"Starting with the decline, if not the disintegration, of the Soviet regime, Masha Gessen's *The Future is History* tracks totalitarianism through the lens of a generation raised in post-Communist Russia."
—*Vanity Fair*

"Remarkable . . . Gessen's deft blending of . . . stories gives us a fresh view of recent Russian history from within, as it was experienced at the time by its people. It is a welcome perspective."
—*The New York Review of Books*

"Excellent . . . Gessen's cast of characters tell a powerful story of their own, giving us an intimate look into the minds of a group crucial to understanding the country's brief experience of democracy and of the authoritarian regime that follows." —*The New Republic*

"One of our most urgent and iconoclastic journalists. . . . Few . . . are better placed to understand the parallels between the two egomaniacs who now dominate world affairs." —*Out* magazine

"Impressive . . . *The Future Is History* warns us of what will become of the United States if we don't push against our burgeoning authoritarian government and fight for democracy. . . . A chilling read, but a necessary one." —Bitch Media

"A lively and intimate narrative of the USSR's collapse and its aftershocks." —*Bookforum*

"A thoroughly reported history of a dismal sequence of events with a strong, engaging narrative and central set of characters." —*The Forward*

"Gessen makes a powerful case, arguing that Putin reconstituted the political and terror apparatus of the Soviet state and that ideology was the last block to fall into place." —*Financial Times*

"A devastating, timely, and necessary reminder of the fragility and preciousness of all institutions of freedom." —*Booklist* (starred review)

"Brilliant . . . A worthwhile read that describes how Putin's powerful grip on Russia developed, offering a dire warning of how other nations could fall under a similar spell of state control." —*Library Journal*

"An intimate look at Russia in the post-Soviet period, when the public's hopes for democracy devolved within a restricted society characterized by 'a constant state of low-level dread' . . . a well-crafted, inventive narrative." —*Publishers Weekly*

"Masha Gessen is humbly erudite, deftly unconventional, and courageously honest. At this particular historical moment, when we must understand Russia to understand ourselves, we are all very lucky to have her."
—Timothy Snyder, author of *On Tyranny*

"A fine example of journalism approximating art. Necessary reading for anyone trying to understand the earthshaking events of our time: how in one country after another individual aspirations for wealth and power mutated into collective cravings for strongmen."
—Pankaj Mishra, author of *An End to Suffering* and *Age of Anger*

"A beautifully written, sensitively argued, and cleverly structured journey through Russia's failure to build democracy. . . . It is a story about hope and despair, trauma and treatment, ideals and betrayal, and above all about love and cynicism. If you want to truly understand why Vladimir Putin has been able to so dominate his country, this book will help you."
—Oliver Bullough, author of *Let Our Fame Be Great* and *The Last Man in Russia*

THE FUTURE
IS HISTORY

ALSO BY MASHA GESSEN

Dead Again: The Russian Intelligentsia After Communism

Ester and Ruzya: How My Grandmothers Survived Hitler's War and Stalin's Peace

Blood Matters: From Inherited Illness to Designer Babies,
How the World and I Found Ourselves in the Future of the Gene

Perfect Rigor: A Genius and the
Mathematical Breakthrough of the Century

The Man Without a Face: The Unlikely Rise of Vladimir Putin

Words Will Break Cement: The Passion of Pussy Riot

Gay Propaganda: Russian Love Stories (editor)

The Brothers: The Road to an American Tragedy

Never Remember: Searching for Stalin's Gulags in Putin's Russia
(with photographer Misha Friedman)

THE FUTURE
IS HISTORY

HOW TOTALITARIANISM
RECLAIMED RUSSIA

MASHA GESSEN

RIVERHEAD BOOKS NEW YORK

RIVERHEAD BOOKS
An imprint of Penguin Random House LLC
375 Hudson Street
New York, New York 10014

Copyright © 2017 by Masha Gessen
Penguin supports copyright. Copyright fuels creativity, encourages diverse voices, promotes
free speech, and creates a vibrant culture. Thank you for buying an authorized edition
of this book and for complying with copyright laws by not reproducing, scanning, or
distributing any part of it in any form without permission. You are supporting
writers and allowing Penguin to continue to publish books for every reader.

Anna Akhmatova's publishing rights are acquired via FTM Agency, Ltd., Russia.

Verses from *Requiem* by Anna Akhmatova are quoted from
Anna Akhmatova: Selected Poems Including 'Requiem' by A.S. Kline,
translator. Copyright © 2005, 2012. All rights reserved.

Verses from "Snow-Clad Is the Plain" by Sergey Yesenin
are translated from the Russian by Alec Vagapov.

The Library of Congress has catalogued the Riverhead hardcover edition as follows:

Names: Gessen, Masha, author.
Title: The future is history : how totalitarianism reclaimed Russia / Masha Gessen.
Other titles: How totalitarianism reclaimed Russia.
Description: New York : Riverhead Books, 2017. Includes bibliographical references and index.
Identifiers: LCCN 2017014363 (print) | LCCN 2017034714 (ebook) |
ISBN 9780698406209 (ebook) | ISBN 9781594634536 (hardcover)
Subjects: LCSH: Russia (Federation)—Politics and government—1991– | Russia
(Federation)—History—1991– | Moscow Region (Russia)—Intellectual life. |
Russia (Federation)—Biography.
Classification: LCC DK510.763 (ebook) | LCC DK510.763 .G48 2017 (print) |
DDC 947.086—dc23
LC record available at https://lccn.loc.gov/2017014363
p.   cm.

First Riverhead hardcover edition: October 2017
First Riverhead trade paperback edition: October 2018
First Riverhead trade paperback ISBN: 9781594634543

Printed in the United States of America
1   3   5   7   9   10   8   6   4   2

Book design by Lauren Kolm

While the author has made every effort to provide accurate Internet addresses
at the time of publication, neither the publisher nor the author assumes any
responsibility for errors, or for changes that occur after publication.
Further, the publisher does not have any control over and does not assume
any responsibility for author or third-party websites or their content.

■

IN MEMORY OF SVETLANA BOYM

CONTENTS

DRAMATIS PERSONAE

SEVEN PEOPLE ACT as the main characters of this book, making appearances throughout the narrative. I have used a modified Russian convention to refer to them. As anyone who has ever read a Russian novel knows, Russians have numerous names. A person's legal name is the full first name plus a patronymic—a form of the father's name. In contemporary life, however, the name/patronymic combination is generally reserved for formal occasions and for older people. At the same time, most full names have a variety of diminutives that derive from them. Most Russians have a diminutive that was chosen for them in childhood and continue to use it throughout their lives; most, though not all, diminutives derive clearly from their full name, which can be reverse-engineered from the diminutive. For example, all Sashas are Alexanders; most Mashas are Marias. Children are almost always addressed by their diminutive.

In this book, those who first appear in the story as children are called by their diminutive throughout (e.g., Masha, Lyosha). Those who first appear as adults are called by their full names (e.g., Boris, Tatiana). Those who first appear as older people are introduced by their name and patronymic and referred to by these names for the duration of the book. Below is a list of the main characters. Dozens of other people are mentioned in this book; their names are not on this list because their appearances are episodic.

Zhanna (b. 1984)
Boris Nemtsov, father
Raisa, mother
Dmitry, husband
Dina Yakovlevna, grandmother

Masha (b. 1984)
Tatiana, mother
Galina Vasilyevna, grandmother
Boris Mikhailovich, grandfather
Sergei, husband
Sasha, son

Seryozha (b. 1982)
Anatoly, father
Alexander Nikolaevich Yakovlev, grandfather

Lyosha (b. 1985)
Galina, mother
Yuri, biological father
Sergei, stepfather
Serafima Adamovna, grandmother

Marina Arutyunyan, psychoanalyst
Maya, mother
Anna Mikhailovna Pankratova, grandmother

Lev Gudkov, sociologist

Alexander Dugin, philosopher, political activist

PROLOGUE

I HAVE BEEN TOLD many stories about Russia, and I have told a few myself. When I was eleven or twelve, in the late 1970s, my mother told me that the USSR was a totalitarian state—she compared the regime to the Nazi one, an extraordinary act of thought and speech for a Soviet citizen. My parents told me that the Soviet regime would last forever, which was why we had to leave the country.

When I was a young journalist, in the late 1980s, the Soviet regime began to teeter and then collapsed into a pile of rubble, or so the story went. I joined an army of reporters excitedly documenting my country's embrace of freedom and its journey toward democracy.

I spent my thirties and forties documenting the death of a Russian democracy that had never really come to be. Different people were telling different stories about this: many insisted that Russia had merely taken a step back after taking two steps toward democracy; some laid the blame on Vladimir Putin and the KGB, others on a supposed Russian love of the iron fist, and still others on an inconsiderate, imperious West. At one point, I was convinced that I would be writing the story of the decline and fall of the Putin regime. Soon after, I found myself leaving Russia for the second time—this time as a middle-aged person with children. And like my mother before me, I was explaining to my children why we could no longer live in our country.

The specifics were clear enough. Russian citizens had been losing rights and liberties for nearly two decades. In 2012, Putin's government began a full-fledged political crackdown. The country waged war on the enemy within and on its neighbors. In 2008, Russia invaded Georgia, and in 2014 it attacked Ukraine, annexing vast territories. It has also been waging an information war on Western democracy as a concept and a reality. It took a while for Western observers to see what was happening in Russia, but by now the stories of Russia's various wars have become familiar. In the contemporary American imagination, Russia has reclaimed the role of evil empire and existential threat.

The crackdown, the wars, and even Russia's reversion to type on the world stage are things that happened—that I witnessed—and I wanted to tell this story. But I also wanted to tell about what did not happen: the story of freedom that was not embraced and democracy that was not desired. How do you tell a story like that? Where do you locate reasons for the absences? When do you begin, and with whom?

Popular books about Russia—or other countries—fall into two broad categories: stories about powerful people (the czars, Stalin, Putin, and their circles) that aim to explain how the country has been and is run, and stories about "regular people" that aim to show what it feels like to live there. I have written both kinds of books and read many more. But even the best such books—perhaps especially the best such books—provide a view of only one part of the story of a country. If we imagine reporting, as I do, in terms of the Indian fable of six blind men and an elephant, most Russia books describe just the elephant's head or just its legs. And even if some books supply descriptions of the tail, the trunk, and the body, very few try to explain how the animal holds together—or what kind of animal it is. My ambition this time was to both describe and define the animal.

I decided to start with the decline of the Soviet regime—perhaps the assumption that it "collapsed" needed to be questioned. I also decided to focus on people for whom the end of the USSR was the first or one of the first formative memories: the generation of Russians born in the early to middle 1980s. They grew up in the 1990s, perhaps the most contested decade in Russian history: some remember it as a time of liberation, while for others it represents chaos and pain. This generation have lived their entire adult lives in a Russia led by Vladimir Putin. In choosing my subjects, I also looked for people whose lives changed drastically as a result of the crackdown that began in 2012. Lyosha, Masha, Seryozha, and Zhanna—four young people who come from different cities, families, and, indeed, different Soviet worlds—allowed me to tell what it was to grow up in a country that was opening up and to come of age in a society shutting down.

In seeking out these protagonists, I did what journalists usually do: I sought people who were both "regular," in that their experiences exemplified the experiences of millions of others, and extraordinary: intelligent, passionate, introspective, able to tell their stories vividly. But the ability to make sense of one's life in the world is a function of freedom. The Soviet regime robbed people not only of their ability to live freely but also of the ability to understand fully what had been taken from them, and how. The regime aimed to annihilate personal and historical memory and the academic study of society. Its concerted war on the social sciences left Western academics for decades in a better position to interpret Russia than were Russians themselves—but, as outsiders with restricted access to information, they could hardly fill the void. Much more than a problem of scholarship, this was an attack on the humanity of Russian society, which lost the tools and even the language for understanding itself. The only stories Russia told itself about itself were created by Soviet ideologues. If a modern country has no sociologists, psychologists, or philosophers, what can it know about itself? And what can its citizens know about themselves? I realized that my mother's simple act of categorizing the Soviet regime and comparing it to another had required an extraordinary measure of freedom, which she derived, at least in part, from having already decided to emigrate.

To capture the larger tragedy of losing the intellectual tools of sensemaking, I looked for Russians who had attempted to wield them, in both the Soviet and post-Soviet periods. The cast of characters grew to include a sociologist, a psychoanalyst, and a philosopher. If anyone holds the tools of defining the elephant, it is they. They are neither "regular people"—the stories of their struggles to bring their disciplines back from the dead are hardly representative—nor "powerful people": they are the people who try to understand. In the Putin era, the social sciences were defeated and degraded in new ways, and my protagonists faced a new set of impossible choices.

As I wove these stories together, I imagined I was writing a long Russian (nonfiction) novel that aimed to capture both the texture of individual tragedies and the events and ideas that shaped them. The result, I hope, is a book that shows not only what it has felt like to live in Russia over the last thirty years but also what Russia has been in this time, what it has become, and how. The elephant, too, makes a brief appearance (see page 386).

PART ONE

BORN IN THE USSR

one

BORN IN 1984

MASHA

ON THE SEVENTIETH ANNIVERSARY of the Great October Socialist Revolution, Masha's grandmother, a rocket scientist, took Masha to the Church of St. John the Warrior in Central Moscow to be baptized. Masha was three and a half years old, which made her roughly three years older than all the other children in the church that day. Her grandmother Galina Vasilyevna was fifty-five, which made her roughly the age of most of the grownups. They were old—fifty-five was the retirement age for Soviet women, and you could hardly have found a fifty-five-year-old who was not yet a grandmother—but not so old that they remembered a time when religion was practiced openly and proudly in Russia. Until recently, Galina Vasilyevna had not given religion much thought. Her own mother had gone to church, and had had her baptized. Galina Vasilyevna had studied physics at the university and, though she graduated a few years before a course on the "foundations of scientific atheism" became a graduation requirement at all colleges, she had been taught that religion was the opium of the people.*

---

*English-language readers are generally more familiar with a different version of the phrase: "Religion is the opiate of the masses." The Russian translation is closer to the original but was usually learned out of context, just as it was in Western popular culture. The passage from which the phrase

Galina Vasilyevna had spent most of her adult life working on things that were the very opposite of religion: they were material, not at all mystical, and they flew into space. Most recently, she had been working at Scientific Production Unit Molniya ("Lightning"), which was designing the Soviet space shuttle *Buran* ("Blizzard"). Her task was to create the mechanism that would allow the crew to open the shuttle's door after landing. Work on the shuttle was nearly finished. In another year, *Buran* would take flight. Its first test flight would be unmanned, and it would be successful, but *Buran* would never fly again. Funding for the project would dry up, and the mechanism for opening the space-shuttle door from the inside after landing would never be used.[1]

Galina Vasilyevna had always been extraordinarily sensitive to the subtle changes in the moods and expectations of the world around her—a most useful quality in a country like the Soviet Union, where knowing which way the wind was blowing could mean the difference between life and death. Now, even though all things appeared to be on track in her professional life—it was still a year until *Buran* took flight—she could feel that something was cracking, something in the very foundation of the only world she knew—the world built on the primacy of material things. The crack was demanding that other ideas, or better yet, another foundation, appear to fill the emptiness. It was as though she could anticipate that the solid and unmystical thing she had spent her life building would fall into disuse, leaving a metaphysical void.

Galina Vasilyevna may have learned that religion was the opium of the people and she may have been told, along with the rest of the country and the world, that the Bolsheviks had vanquished organized religion, but, having lived in the Soviet Union for more than half a century, she knew that

is culled reads as follows: "Religious suffering is, at one and the same time, the expression of real suffering and a protest against real suffering. Religion is the sigh of the oppressed creature, the heart of a heartless world, and the soul of soulless conditions. It is the opium of the people. The abolition of religion as the illusory happiness of the people is the demand for their real happiness. To call on them to give up their illusions about their condition is to call on them to give up a condition that requires illusions. The criticism of religion is, therefore, in embryo, the criticism of that vale of tears of which religion is the halo." Karl Marx, *Critique of Hegel's Philosophy of Right*, trans. Joseph O'Malley (Oxford: Oxford University Press, 1970), p. 3.

this was not entirely true. Back in the 1930s, when she was a child, most Soviet adults still said openly that they believed in God.[2] The new generation was supposed to grow up entirely free of the superstitions of which religion was merely a subset and of the heartache that made religion necessary. But then, when Galina Vasilyevna was nine, the Second World War began. The Germans were advancing so fast, and the Soviet leadership appeared so helpless, that there was nothing left to believe in but God.[3] Soon enough, the Soviet government seemed to embrace the Russian Orthodox Church, and from that point on, the Communists and the clergy fought the Nazis together.[4] After the war, the church went back to being an institution for the older generation, but the knowledge remained that in times of catastrophic uncertainty it could be a refuge.

Grandmother told Masha that they were going to church because of Father Alexander Men. Men was a Russian Orthodox priest for people like Galina Vasilyevna. His parents had been natural scientists, and he had a way of talking to people who did not grow up in the church. He had been ordained by the Russian Orthodox Church, which ever since the war had served at the pleasure of the Kremlin, but he had his own ways of learning and teaching, and these had brought him to the brink of being arrested.[5] Now that things were opening up slightly, Men was on the verge of becoming spectacularly popular, gathering a following of thousands and then of hundreds of thousands, though it would still be a few years before his writing could be published in the Soviet Union. Masha did not understand much of what her grandmother told her about Father Alexander or the light in the teachings of Jesus Christ, but she did not object to going to church. November 7* was always her favorite holiday, because on that day, the anniversary of the Great October Socialist Revolution, her grandmother, who for 364 days a year was a reluctant and subcompetent cook, baked pies that Masha liked to eat.

---

*The anniversary of the October Revolution falls on November 7 because czarist Russia had kept its own calendar, one devoid of leap years. By the year 1917, it had fallen thirteen days "behind" the Western calendar—and once the days were adjusted by the Bolsheviks, the latter part of October became November.

"What the fuck did you do that for?" Masha's mother asked when she came to pick up her daughter and discovered her wearing a tiny cross around her neck. That, however, was the extent of the discussion. Tatiana did not have much use for conversation: she was a woman of action. When she had discovered that she was pregnant, she went to the Party Committee at her graduate school in the hope that the authorities would compel the future baby's father, who had at least one other girlfriend, to marry Tatiana. This was not an unusual request and would not have been an unusual intervention for the Party Committee to stage, but in Tatiana's case it backfired. Masha's father lost his spot in graduate school and, consequently, his right to live in Moscow, and had to return home to the Soviet Far East, thousands of kilometers from his girlfriends.

New motherhood brought further unpleasant surprises. It made Tatiana dependent on her parents. Virtually everyone in her generation used parents as a source of free childcare:[6] the only alternatives were state-run neighborhood-based nursery schools, which were a cross between baby prisons and warehouses, or prohibitively expensive and questionably legal private nanny services. Tatiana had won unusual independence from her parents—unlike most other people her age, she lived separately from them, in a communal apartment she shared with just one family—but the baby tethered her anew to her parents' apartment a few blocks away. With two rooms and a kitchen, Galina Vasilyevna and Boris Mikhailovich had the space to care for little Masha, and with both of them working as senior scientists in the space industry, they had more time than their graduate-student daughter. Tatiana figured that to escape her parental home for good, she needed to make money and pull strings. None of what she had to do was exactly legal under Soviet law, which restricted all activities and banned most entrepreneurship, but much of what she did was quietly tolerated by the authorities in a majority of the cases.

At age three, Masha was admitted to a prestigious, highly selective, virtually inaccessible residential preschool for the children of Central Committee members. (In fact, by the time Masha was born, the average age of a Central Committee member was approaching seventy-five,[7] so the school served their grandchildren and great-grandchildren as well as the children of a few extraordinarily enterprising Soviet citizens like Tatiana.) Here is how a writer from a previous generation of students described the preschool:

> Inside, everything reeked of prosperity and just-baked pirozhki. The Lenin's Corner was particularly resplendent, with its white gladioli arrangements beneath Ulyanov family photos arranged like icons on a crimson velvet bulletin board. On a panoramic veranda facing the haunted woods, *nomenklatura* offspring snoozed al fresco, bundled like piglets in goose-feather sleeping bags. I had arrived during Dead Hour, Soviet for afternoon nap.
>
> "Wake up, Future Communists!" the teacher cried, clapping her hands. She grinned slyly. "It's fish-fat time!" . . . A towering nanny named, I still recall, Zoya Petrovna approached me with a vast spoon of black caviar in her hand.[8]

By the time Masha enrolled in school, the Lenin Corner had lost some of its luster and the teachers had toned down some of their rhetoric, rarely roaring the word "Communists" at their charges. But the daily rations of caviar remained, in even starker contrast to the world outside, where food shortages were the determining factor of everyday life. Still there, too, was the ubiquitous Soviet-preschool-issue single-lump farina, which could be stood vertically upon a plate. The school maintained a five-day-a-week boarding schedule, an unsurpassed Soviet luxury. On weekends, Masha, like many Soviet children, generally stayed with her grandparents. Trying to make enough to sustain this life kept Tatiana busy seven days a week.

When Masha was four, her mother taught her to tell counterfeit dollars from genuine currency. Being caught with either real or fake foreign money would have been dangerous, punishable under Soviet law by up to fifteen years behind bars,[9] but Tatiana seemed incapable of fear. At any rate, this was her livelihood. She also ran a tutoring business: she had started out as a tutor herself, but soon figured out that she needed volume to make real money. She began matching clients—mostly high school students readying to face the grueling oral exams for university admission—with her fellow graduate students, who could prepare them. In her own tutoring, she now stuck to a highly profitable and rare specialty she had developed: she prepared young people to face the "coffins."

"Coffins" were questions specially designed for the Jewish applicants. Soviet institutions of higher learning generally fell into two categories: those that admitted no Jews at all and those that admitted a strictly limited number of Jews. The rules of non-admission were not, of course, publicly posted; rejection was administered in a peculiarly sadistic way. Jewish applicants usually took entrance exams along with all the other aspiring students. They pulled examination tickets from the same pool as everyone else. But if they succeeded in answering correctly the two or three questions on the ticket, then, alone in the room with the examiners, they would be casually issued an extra question, as though to follow up on the answers given. This would be the "coffin." In mathematics, this was usually a problem not merely complex but unsolvable. The applicant would falter and founder. The examiners would then nail the cover of the coffin shut: the Jewish applicant had failed the exam. Unless, that is, the applicant had had Tatiana for a tutor. She perfected the art of teaching her clients not merely specific "coffins," which she had somehow managed to procure, but the general algorithm for recognizing them and proving them to be unsolvable. This bucktoothed blonde in aviator glasses could teach Soviet Jews to beat the antisemitic machine, and this kept Masha in caviar and disgusting Central Committee farina.

ZHANNA

TO ACHIEVE ANYTHING even resembling a level playing field, one had to not be Jewish. One's "nationality"—what Americans would call "ethnicity"—was noted in all important identity documents, from birth certificate to internal passport to marriage certificate to personnel file at work or school. Once assigned, "nationality" was virtually unchangeable—and it was passed on from generation to generation. Zhanna's father, Boris, had somehow—most likely through the foresight and effort of his parents—lucked into documents that identified him as ethnically Russian. With his dark brown eyes and dark hair in tight curls, and his parents' identifiably Jewish first names, Dina and Yefim, he was not fooling anyone, but he managed to short-circuit most inquiries by claiming, illogically, to be "half Jewish." This skill, his ethnically correct documents, and top high school marks enabled him to get admission to university. There had been one major obstacle: unlike the overwhelming majority of Soviet high school students, Boris had not joined the Komsomol, the Communist Youth League, and his graduation documents consequently identified him as "politically unreliable." His mother, Dina Yakovlevna, lobbied the high school to change the wording. It seemed like an impossible undertaking, but it had to be done. In this family, which consisted entirely of natural scientists and medical doctors, everyone was brilliant and everyone was accomplished. The wording was changed. Boris was admitted to the Department of Radio Physics of Gorky State University. He would graduate with top honors and would complete his PhD dissertation by the time he was twenty-four. Consensus among his family and friends was that he would eventually win the Nobel Prize for his work in quantum physics.

Zhanna was born in 1984, the year Boris finished his dissertation. Her mother, Raisa, was a teacher of French. In Soviet terms, they were a *bogema*—bohemian—family, which meant that they organized their life in accordance with ideas that seemed Western and in ways that continuously expanded their social circle. They rented a house, while Boris's older sister and her child lived with Dina Yakovlevna, as was the norm. The house, in the dilapidated center of town, was old and wooden and had no bathtub or shower, only a toilet. The family made do—they heated water on the stove and washed over a basin, or showered at friends' houses—and anyway, they were not so Western that they had to shower every day. They were, however, so Western as to play tennis, a rarefied sport that landed the family a photo spread in the city paper when Zhanna was a toddler. All three of the people in the picture had dark hair and white-toothed smiles as wide as their cheekbones. They stood out in their gray city.

The city was named Gorky, after the Russian writer Alexei Peshkov, who, as was the Revolutionary fashion, had taken a tearjerker pen name: it meant "bitter." When Zhanna was first becoming aware of her surroundings, she had no idea that a writer named Gorky had ever existed: she thought the name was a literal description of her town. The Soviet government seemed to agree: four years before Zhanna's birth, it had chosen Gorky as the place of exile for the physicist Andrei Dmitrievich Sakharov, the 1975 Nobel Peace Prize laureate and the country's best-known dissident. Sakharov's last name meant "sugar," and from the way Zhanna's father said his name, Zhanna knew there was something magical about him. She begged her father to take her with him when he said he was going to "Sakharov's building"—she did not realize that he was not actually visiting the great man, just keeping a sort of occasional vigil—but he would not take her. She named her kitten Andrei Dmitrievich Sakharov.

Here is how Sakharov's wife, Yelena Bonner, described the city in the spring of 1987, when Zhanna was not quite three years old:

> You would think it's not early April but late autumn or the onset of winter. . . . I see pedestrians pulling their feet up out of the puddles as they walk: heavy, enormous clumps of dirt cling to their shoes. The wind bends treetops right down to the ground. A mix of snow and rain is falling from a dim sky, laying dirty-white stains on the surface of something that I'm not sure deserves to be called "earth."[10]

Zhanna was pretty sure hers was the worst city on earth and its bitter name described the lives of those forced to live there, especially her mother. Raisa had to spend most of her time hunting for food. Sometimes she took the train to Moscow—a night to get there, then she would spend the day standing in line, and the next night on the train back. Most often Moscow yielded processed meats, which had not been seen in Gorky in years. Moscow had shortages of its own, but compared with Gorky, where a store might be selling nothing but unidentifiable dark juice in three-liter glass jars with tin covers, Moscow was the land of promise if not of plenty. One time Raisa returned with candy, a clear plastic bag full of sloppily wrapped grayish-brown cylinders. They were soy mixed with sugar, crushed peanuts, and a sprinkling of cocoa powder. Zhanna thought she had never tasted anything better. Another time a friend of Raisa's brought bananas in a gym bag. They were green and hard, and Raisa—who, unlike her daughter, had seen bananas before—knew that they should be kept in a dark cupboard, where they would ripen. Boris did not share in the responsibilities of daily procurement, but occasionally he shone with something he had "reached"—the Soviet term for getting hard-to-find food, and Zhanna thought that her father could "reach" things because he was so very tall. Basically, he was a superhero.

Zhanna had no set bedtime, and since there were always people at the house, sitting around the table and talking, she stayed up with them, until midnight or later. Her father, who had no set office hours, would drop her off at the neighborhood preschool on his way to the lab. This usually coincided with the beginning of Dead Hour—nap time—which was convenient, since Zhanna had not had enough sleep at home.

When Zhanna was about three, conversations around the table at the old wooden house began to change. They shifted away from the anomalous Doppler effect or whatever theoretical issue had been on Boris's mind to the fact that a nuclear-powered heating plant was about to be built in Gorky. Ground had been broken.[11] It had been only a year since the catastrophic accident at the Chernobyl nuclear power plant in Ukraine; the government had tried to keep information about the disaster from getting out but had succeeded only in slowing it down. By now, the magnitude of the loss and danger had seeped in. Dina Yakovlevna, a pediatrician, was badgering her son: "How can you, a physicist, stand idly by when something like that is about to be built within city limits?"

For as long as Zhanna, Raisa, Boris, and even Dina Yakovlevna had been alive, Soviet people had stood idly by while the government willfully put their lives in danger, but something had changed. In 1985, the new secretary-general of the Communist Party—the Soviet head of state—had declared what he called "a new course." He was not the first secretary-general to say those words or even the word *perestroika*, which means "restructuring," but now something was indeed changing. Dina Yakovlevna went to a rally at which she protested the planned nuclear plant; just a year earlier, a rally that had not been sanctioned by the Party would have been seen as a crime against the state, and participants would have been arrested and tried. Sakharov was allowed to leave Gorky after seven years and move back to Moscow. A physicist, an inventor of the Soviet hydrogen bomb, he had long become a crusader for nuclear safety. Boris went to visit him at his Moscow apartment and recorded an interview in which the great man spoke out against the nuclear plant, and the interview was published in the city paper *Gor'kovskiy rabochiy* ("The Gorky Worker"). Sakharov had concluded by saying, "I hope that you succeed in changing the flow of events. I am fully on your side."[12]

In the end, plans for the nuclear-powered plant were scrapped and Boris had found something that engaged him as much or more than physics. The word *politika* sounded around the table more and more often, eventually joined by the word *vybory*—"elections."

BOTH MASHA AND ZHANNA were born in the Soviet Union, the world's longest-lasting totalitarian state, in 1984, the year that in the Western imagination had come to symbolize totalitarianism. George Orwell's book could not be published in a society that it described, so Soviet readers would not have access to it until 1989, when censorship constraints had loosened sufficiently to enable the country's leading literary journal to print a translation.[13] But in 1969 a journalist named Andrei Amalrik had published—that is, typed up and distributed among his friends—a book-length essay titled *Will the Soviet Union Survive Until 1984?*, arguing that the regime was headed for an implosion.[14] Amalrik, who had already served time as a political prisoner, was arrested, along with a man accused of having distributed the book, and both were sentenced to prison terms. In his closing statement in court Amalrik said, "I realize that trials such as this one are intended to frighten the many—and many will be frightened—but I still think that a process of liberation of ideas has begun and is irreversible."[15] He spent more than three years behind bars, followed by another three of internal exile, and was then forced to leave the Soviet Union. In 1980 he died in a car accident in Spain, on his way to a human rights conference.[16] The Soviet regime lived on, surviving even 1984.

But the very next year, something began to crack. Was it launched by the new secretary-general, Mikhail Gorbachev, when he called for changes and declared glasnost and perestroika? Or was he merely giving voice to the process Amalrik had attempted to describe a decade and a half earlier? Amalrik had argued that Marxist ideology had never had a firm grip on the country, that the Russian Orthodox Church had lost its own hold, and that without a central unifying set of beliefs, the country, pulled in opposite directions by social groups with different desires, would eventually self-destruct.

Amalrik was one of a very few Soviet citizens who saw the system as essentially unstable—most others thought it was set in stone or, rather, in Soviet-style reinforced concrete, and would last forever. The year Amalrik stood trial, another dissident writer, Alexander Galich, authored a song in which he described a small group of friends listening to one of his recordings. One of the listeners suggests that the singer is taking too great a risk with his anti-Soviet jokes. "The author has nothing to fear," responds the host. "He died about a hundred years ago."[17] (Galich was forced to emigrate in 1974 and died in his Paris apartment three years later as a result of an electrical accident.[18])

All who were thinking about the Soviet Union, inside the country and outside, shared two handicaps: they had to base their conclusions on fragmentary knowledge and phrase them in language inadequate for the task. Not only did the country shield all essential and most nonessential information behind a wall of secrets and lies, it also, for decades, waged a concerted war on knowledge itself. The most symbolic, though by no means the most violent, battle in this war was fought in 1922, when Lenin ordered two hundred or more (historians' estimates vary) intellectuals—doctors, economists, philosophers, and others—deported abroad on what became known as the Philosophers' Ship (in fact, there were several different ships). The deportations were framed as a humane alternative to the death penalty. Future generations of intellectuals were not as fortunate: those deemed disloyal to the regime were imprisoned, often executed, and almost always separated from their chosen discipline.[19] As the regime matured, restrictions on the social sciences grew broader and, by virtue of the sheer passage of time, more profound. While the arms race spurred the Soviet government to rejuvenate and nurture the exact sciences and technology, there was nothing—or almost nothing—that could motivate the regime to encourage the development of philosophy, history, and the social sciences. These disciplines atrophied to the point where, as a leading Russian economist wrote in 2015, the top Soviet economists of the 1970s could not understand the work of those who had preceded them by a half century.[20]

In the 1980s, social scientists working in the Soviet Union lacked not only the information but also the skills, the theoretical knowledge, and the language necessary to understand their own society. Very few of them were trying, against all odds and obstacles, and these people were groping in the dark.

two

LIFE, EXAMINED

DUGIN

ON NEW YEAR'S EVE 1984, Evgenia Debryanskaya was hosting a party. Evgenia was a thirty-year-old single mother from Sverdlovsk, the largest city in the Urals. She thought of herself as provincial and undereducated—she had never gone to college—but she had money, connections, and beauty, which significantly boosted her ambition of becoming someone in Moscow. Her money came from playing cards: she was a shark, and thus an outlaw. Her connections came from an unlikely fact of provenance: she was the out-of-wedlock daughter of the longtime Moscow Party boss.[1] Her beauty was unconventional: she was extremely thin, with a prominent nose and short dark hair cut asymmetrically to fall over half of her chiseled face; and she spoke in a deep, smoke-filled baritone. Some combination of these unusual traits secured for Evgenia the use of a very large nomenklatura apartment on Gorky Street, Moscow's central avenue.

On New Year's Eve, people kept coming, to stay until the Metro reopened early in the morning—or to keep drinking and smoking and talking well into the next day and the day after. This was Moscow's *bogema*, the hard-partying, black-market-trading, intellectually edgy crowd. Some of them were writers or artists, and others claimed membership simply by living outside the official economy or by hosting good parties. Some of them would have read or heard of Orwell's *1984* or Amalrik's *Will the Soviet Union Survive Until 1984?*, and this added an extra note of recklessness to the mood. A very young aspiring actress arrived with an entourage of male admirers. One of them split off from the group as soon as they walked in. Instead of continuing to the kitchen, he sat down on an orphaned chair in the hallway. He looked like he was barely out of his teens. He asked the hostess for water.

Evgenia brought him a glass. He took a sip and asked, "Do you know when violets bloom on the lips?" She had no idea what that meant, and she loved it. She loved him for being able to say something that was so clearly beautiful and so utterly incomprehensible. He stayed the next day and the day after that, for three years, until she stopped loving him.[2]

His name was Alexander Dugin. He came from what they both thought of as the dullest type of Soviet family: his father, who was educated as an engineer, worked for the KGB in some secret but unglamorous capacity. His mother was a bureaucrat at the health ministry. His grandmother was a dean at the Higher Party School, an apparatchik factory that took up several city blocks just a few minutes from the apartment Evgenia and Dugin now shared. Their love was not the only emotion that united them: a shared hatred of the Soviet regime brought them even closer. In 1985, Dugin, whose imagination took more risks than Evgenia's, said that the Soviet Union was ending. This was after Gorbachev had declared perestroika. They had a son that year and named him Artur, in honor of Rimbaud.

Evgenia learned French and English from Dugin, who insisted that books must be read in the original. When they met, Dugin was twenty-two and had been expelled from a technical university, but he could already read in French, English, and German. Now it took him two weeks at a time to acquire a new European language. He learned by reading books, and Evgenia learned by reading with him, taking turns sounding out the sentences. As long as she loved him, she never tired of hearing words she could not understand. The first book she read in English with him was *The Picture of Dorian Gray*.

Evgenia continued to bring in the money, but both agreed that Dugin was the one who worked. He rose early, ate whatever he could scavenge in the kitchen, and sat down at his desk to read for the next eighteen hours. The void he sought to fill by reading was vast. His focus was philosophy. He spent months explaining Nietzsche's concept of the Dionysian to Evgenia; she loved the idea of embracing chaos—it seemed the perfect antidote to the stifling regimented boredom that surrounded them. Then Alexander told her that he had found a philosopher no one had ever heard of, one who had taken Nietzsche so much further. The philosopher's name was Heidegger.

The first translation of Heidegger's writing—just twenty pages of it—would not be published in Russian until 1986.[3] Nor could Dugin, who had no affiliation with any Soviet institution and as a result no access to any but the smallest neighborhood libraries, find any of Heidegger's books in the original German. He finally procured a copy of *Being and Time* on microfilm. In the absence of a microfilm reader, he rigged up a diafilm projector—a Soviet technology for using thirty-five-millimeter film to show cartoons or short films at home using a hand-crank—to project the book onto the top of his desk. By the time he was done with *Being and Time*, Dugin needed glasses. He had also read the foundational text of his thinking and of the rest of his life.

ARUTYUNYAN

THE PHRASE A RUSSIAN INTELLECTUAL is probably most likely to use when talking about the early 1980s is *bezvozdushnoye prostranstvo*—"airless space." The era was stuffy like the Russian *izba*, a log cabin, when its windows are caulked for the winter: it keeps out the cold, but also the fresh air. The windows will not be opened even a crack until well into spring, and as time goes on, smells of people, food, and clothing mix into one mind-numbing undifferentiated smell of gigantic proportions. Something similar had happened to the Russian mind over two generations of Soviet rule. At the time of the October Revolution, the Russian intellectual elite had been both a part of and a partner to the European conversation about God, power, and human life. After fifty years of purges, arrests, and, most damaging, unrelenting pressure on what had become an isolated thought universe, the Russian intellectual landscape was populated by barely articulated ghosts of once vibrant ideas. Even Communist ideology was a shadow of its former self, a set of ritually repeated words that had lost all meaning. Lenin had long ago dispensed with most of what Karl Marx had to say, enshrining a few of his selected ideas as überlaw.

"As the time passed, Marx's successors revealed a tendency to present his teachings as a finite and all-inclusive concept of the world, and to regard themselves as responsible for the continuation of all of Marx's work, which they considered as being virtually complete," wrote Yugoslav Marxist dissident Milovan Djilas. "Science gradually yielded to propaganda, and as a result propaganda tended more and more to represent itself as science."[4]

Marina Arutyunyan enrolled in Moscow State University's psychology department in 1973, when she was seventeen. The department was new, the subject and purpose of study were not entirely clear—what, after all, could and would a psychologist do in Soviet society?—but it drew young people like Arutyunyan: cerebral and romantic in comparable measure, and driven to learn the secrets of the human soul. Arutyunyan knew that "psyche" meant "soul."

For the first two years at the psychology department, Arutyunyan was in hell. Endless hours were devoted to a subject called Marxist-Leninist Philosophy. This was a clear case of propaganda masquerading as scholarship, and while the young Arutyunyan might not necessarily have phrased it this way, she cracked the propaganda code. She developed a simple matrix on which any philosophy could be placed and easily appraised. The matrix consisted of two axes on a cross. One ran from Materialism (good) to Idealism (bad) and the other from Dialectics (good) to Metaphysics (bad). The result was four quadrants. Philosophers who landed in the lower left quadrant, where Metaphysics met Idealism, were all bad. Kant was an example. Someone like Hegel—Dialectics meets Idealism—was better, but not all good. Philosophical perfection resided in the upper-right-hand corner of the graph, at the pinnacle of Dialectical Materialism. Arutyunyan shared this matrix with several classmates, and now they had Marxist-Leninist Philosophy down.

History of the Party proved a much more difficult subject. "Look at yourself," the professor said to her derisively. He used a Russian word—*taz*—that could mean either "hips" or "basin." There was apparently something wrong with Arutyunyan's *taz*. She looked around, confused, wondering if she had somehow besoiled a laboratory basin in a History of the Party classroom. The professor, it turned out, was referring to her hips, which he deemed too narrow to produce quality Party progeny.

In addition to the various propaganda sciences, psychology department students received hands-on instruction in the natural sciences. They dissected frogs, and were expected to proceed to dissect rats, but Arutyunyan rebelled when it came to that and her group was, blessedly, exempted from having to kill mammals. There was a subject called Anthropology, but this area of study in its Western understanding was disallowed in the Soviet Union, so the course would more accurately have been called Theory of Evolution. It included the study of genetics, banned for decades but recently redeemed, and this was interesting.

Physiology of Higher Nervous Functioning featured human brains in formaldehyde, which were brought in for every class and set on each table. Arutyunyan was too squeamish to use her finger—gloves, in short supply all over the country, were not an option—so she stuck it with a pen, earning the professor's wrath. "You are damaging the brain!" he bellowed.

For the purpose of legitimizing their peculiar area of inquiry, psychology students were also required to undergo detailed and rigorous training in statistical and data analysis. As for the psyche, it was conspicuously absent. If Arutyunyan learned anything in her first couple of years at university, it was only the basic logic behind this absence.

Marxism in the Soviet Union had been boiled down to the understanding that people—Soviet citizens—were shaped entirely by their society and the material conditions of their lives. If the work of shaping the person was done correctly—and it had to have been, since by now Soviet society claimed to have substantially fulfilled the Marxist project by building what was called "socialism functioning in reality"—then the person had to emerge with a set of goals that coincided perfectly with the needs of the society that had produced him. Anomalies were possible, and they could fall into one of two categories: criminality or mental illness. Soviet society had institutions to handle both. No other kind of disharmony was conceivable. Inner conflict was not an option. There was really no reason to take up the subject of the psyche.

To this day, the website of the psychology department of Moscow State University bears the traces of Russia's disjointed history with the study of the psyche. A Psychological Society was established at Moscow State University in 1885 and, the site states proudly, "became the center of Russia's philosophical life."[5] In 1914 the society became a full-fledged institute, with teaching and research functions. Then the narrative on the site becomes suddenly depersonalized: "During the years of acute ideological struggle for the construction of a Marxist psychology, the institute's leadership changed." In fact, the institute itself was abolished in 1925. Six years later, the university shut down all departments dedicated to the humanities and social sciences. Ten years after that, the humanities returned, but psychology was now subsumed by the department of philosophy. Only in 1968 did the Soviet government recognize psychology as a discipline in which degrees could be awarded—and the country's leading university resumed, at least on paper, the study and teaching of the psyche—after a break of nearly half a century.[6] The new students could hardly have known that less than a century ago Russian thinkers had been reading Nietzsche and arguing with him, or that Lou Andreas-Salomé, who popularized the great philosopher's ideas in Russia and broke his heart, was a native of St. Petersburg. She went on to become one of Sigmund Freud's early and close students and to work as a psychoanalyst in Germany almost up until her death in 1937, at the age of seventy-five, but her ties to Russia had been severed by the Revolution nearly twenty years earlier.[7]

The Bolshevik state set out to create a New Man. The project contained an echo of Nietzsche's Übermensch idea, but now it was a practical task rather than a philosophical exercise. For a time, it seemed that Freud's teachings could help bridge the gap between theory and practice. His writing had been widely translated before the Revolution, and he and his students had taught a number of Russian psychoanalysts.[8] At one point, not long before the Bolsheviks came to power, psychoanalysis seemed to be gaining a foothold in Russia faster than in Western Europe.[9] After 1917, the new regime set out to transform Freud's theories into dogma on which massive institutions could be based, much as it was doing with Marxism. In its simplified form, Freudism—a term coined by analogy with Marxism—"was seen as a scientifically valid promise of an actual, rather than fictional, transformation of man, to be carried out on the basis of his consciousness," wrote Alexander Etkind, a historian of psychoanalysis in Russia.[10]

A newly formed state publishing house put out a three-volume edition of Freud's *Introduction to Psychoanalysis* in 1922, and twenty thousand copies— a large press run, considering the era and the topic—were snapped up within a month.[11] The Russian Psychoanalytic Society was formed the same year, under the auspices of the state.[12] Between 1922 and 1928, state publishers put out an entire library of translations of foundational works by Freud, Jung, and other early psychoanalysts.[13] A psychoanalytic preschool opened in Moscow, drawing the children of the newly minted Bolshevik elite. It was a pilot project, the prototype of an imagined future factory for the production of New Man.

It did not work. Not only was psychoanalysis particularly unsuited for reproduction on an industrial scale, but even in the confines of a single elite preschool it had a way of producing discomfort and discontent. The experimental psychoanalytic preschool was shut down in 1925, amid vague fears of precocious sexuality.[14] Over the following five or six years, the Russian Psychoanalytic Society ceased functioning, Freud was depublished, and Freudians fell into disfavor or worse. Freud's most important Russian student, Sabina Spielrein, a patient, student, colleague, and lover of Carl Jung, a teacher of Jean Piaget, and a co-discoverer of countertransference, had returned to Soviet Russia from Germany in 1923 and soon, it seems, faded from view. She died in 1942 in the southern Russian city of Rostov, shot as a Jew by the occupying Nazi troops.[15]

The demise of Russian psychoanalysis spelled the near-total end of any study of the psyche—in part because psychoanalysis had so dominated psychology and in part because the new state was now rejecting any explanation of human behavior that was not both material and simple. Ivan Pavlov's straightforward theories of cause and effect fit this approach perfectly; it remained only to condition the entire population, rendering it pliant and predictable. Etkind writes of a psychoanalyst in Odessa who installed a portrait of Pavlov on the flip side of a likeness of Freud that hung in his office: Pavlov would face visitors during the day, when an official might happen by, and Freud greeted his clandestine psychoanalysis patients in the nighttime.[16]

Only a few of the early Soviet psychoanalysts remained in Russia and lived. One long-term survivor was Alexei Nikolaevich Leontiev, who narrowly escaped official censure or worse in the 1930s[17] and went on to have a long academic career, venturing into psycholinguistics late in life. But the work that had allowed Leontiev to continue research during the darkest Soviet decades was his activity theory, which viewed human beings exclusively through the lens of behavior and any human action as part of a larger process of communal action.[18] When Arutyunyan was a student at Moscow State University, Leontiev's course represented the sum total of psychological theory taught in the first few years. His lectures were boring, painful, and infuriating. It made Arutyunyan angry that Leontiev's theory recognized only the conscious part of being human, leaving no room for metaphysics. Leontiev taught by feeding his students uncatchy phrases that summed up counterintuitive theories. One such mantra was "shifting motive onto the goal." For instance, if the student's goal is to pass his exam and he develops interest in the subject matter, then his motive will have shifted onto his goal. This never seemed to happen for Arutyunyan.

She became seriously ill after her second year. Her medical leave lasted another two years. She came back older and perhaps smarter, and after passing exams for one year, was allowed to resume learning as a fourth-year student. This was the year students chose their specialty and began research projects. Arutyunyan landed in social psychology, and a new life began. Graduate students led seminars, including one on attraction. The young instructor talked about the threat of castration that men perceived as emanating from highly attractive women, and his students went wild. This was no "activity theory," this was sex and the psyche and everything they had dreamed of thinking about when they applied to the psychology department. Gradually, Arutyunyan and some of her classmates discovered that the space around them was not entirely airless. Russian architecture, created as it was for a very cold climate, contains a peculiar invention called the *fortochka*. It is a tiny window cut inside a larger pane. Even when windows have been sealed for the long winter, the *fortochka* can remain in use, being opened regularly to allow air to circulate. The Soviet university, as it turned out, had its *fortochka*s, and the way to learn was to hunt for them and then to stick your whole face in them and breathe the fresh air as though one's lungs could be filled up with reserve supplies.

One such *fortochka* was the thinker Merab Mamardashvili, who lectured in the philosophy department. He talked about Marx and Freud as intellectual revolutionaries, which was akin to heresy since Arutyunyan and her friends thought that Freud was something like God and Marx more like the Devil, but witnessing someone thinking—actually thinking—out loud proved exhilarating. Another *fortochka* was Alexander Luria, who lectured in the clinical psychology specialty. Luria had served as chairman of the Russian Psychoanalytic Society in the 1920s,[19] had survived by going into neurology, and had become a great storyteller of the mind. Across a generation, an ocean, and the Iron Curtain, he managed to inspire Oliver Sacks, who considered Luria his teacher in the art of the "neurological novel."[20] The most important *fortochka* of all was found in the university library, which contained the *spetskhran*, a restricted-access collection to which a resourceful student or researcher could gain access. The *spetskhran* contained Freud's case studies. It was the most compelling, most engrossing, most mind-shattering thing Arutyunyan had ever read. Only years later, long after the last of the old Russian psychoanalysts had died, did she realize that what tied all the *fortochka*s together was not just that they gave her new knowledge and that they contrasted markedly with the mind-numbing recitations that filled the university, but that they all saw and described human beings the way she wanted to understand them.

Every school of psychology has its own concept of the person. Carl Rogers's sees people as basically good but often unlucky: they must be tended to better. The cognitive behaviorists imagine imprints that interfere with the functioning of otherwise serviceable human beings. The human being of psychoanalysis is a complicated creature, a creature capable of reflection but doomed to make mistakes in the process of reflecting, a creature endowed with huge, destructive energies. It is by no means an innocent creature, born good and merely handicapped by external forces. This was the creature Arutyunyan wanted to study. It would be years before she was able to articulate this, but for now she was writing her thesis on cognitive dissonance, thereby creating her own little *fortochka*. It turned out you could do that—write about Soviet people as though they could contain contradictions and inner conflicts—as long as you framed the story in requisite meaningless phrases lifted from one of the approved textbooks.

GUDKOV

WHAT WAS ARUTYUNYAN GOING TO DO with all the knowledge she was hoarding? Being able to apply one's theoretical expertise was an unimaginable luxury in the airless space—if one was a psychologist or social scientist, that is, rather than a rocket one. Intellectuals aspired to and prized luxuries of a different order: an unburdensome job in a nontoxic environment that left time for thinking and breathing some *fortochka* air. This was a lot to want, and getting it required luck, brains, and connections. Arutyunyan, both of whose parents were sociologists, got a job at the Institute of Sociology, and this was virtually a dream setup.

An odd feature of the time—most likely an intended result of the system's highly developed ability to suppress those with deep expertise or excessive passion—was that people often had to work in fields that ran parallel to their primary interests. Ten years before Arutyunyan graduated from the department of psychology and went to work at the Institute of Sociology, a young man who wanted nothing more than to be a sociologist was writing a term paper on Freud's concept of defense mechanisms. Lev Gudkov had set out to be a journalist like his own father. Two years in a row he tried to gain entrance to Moscow's exclusive Institute of Foreign Relations, which trained diplomats and foreign correspondents, a high percentage of them fated to work for intelligence services. Both times Gudkov failed the essay portion of the entrance exams, which was graded on a dual scale: one mark for form and one for content. Both years, his form was deemed excellent and his content got a failing grade. He was not well-versed enough in what he was supposed to think. A criticism that would haunt his early career was that he lacked "critical thinking"—meaning, he was not sufficiently critical of anything that diverged from the current Party line.

Gudkov gave up and enrolled as an evening student at the journalism department of Moscow State University. This was one of the university's least challenging branches, and evening students, especially, were left to their own devices. For many of them, the department offered a nearly painless way to obtain a university diploma after six years of attending some lectures after work (the program was longer than normal because of its light course load). Gudkov realized that if he did not seek out knowledge himself, it would never find him. He looked, and eventually stumbled upon an elective lecture course offered by sociologist Yuri Levada.

The year was 1968, and the fact that thirty-eight-year-old Levada called himself a sociologist, and his subject sociology, was almost revolutionary. Sociology was not exactly banned in the Soviet Union, but the name of the discipline had been reduced to something like a curse word. Lenin himself had inaugurated it as a Soviet insult. The problem with sociology was much the same as with psychoanalysis: the field of study refused to be a "science" that could be used to create a new society of new men. A year before the Philosophers' Ship sailed, one of Lenin's closest allies, Nikolai Bukharin, published *The Theory of Historical Materialism*, an attempt at a sort of Marxist textbook of everything, written in a folksy language intended for the proletariat. Three things that Bukharin did in this textbook proved deadly for Soviet sociology: he included new ideas that he believed advanced Marxist theory, he subtitled it *A Popular Textbook of Marxist Sociology*, and he proclaimed the supreme importance of sociology among the social sciences because it "examines not some one aspect of public life but all of public life in all its complexity."[21] Lenin hated the book, and the word "sociology" took the brunt of his rage. He underlined it throughout the book and supplied a small variety of comments in the margins: "Haha!" "Eclectic!" "Help!" and the like.[22] In another eight years, when Bukharin was deposed in a Party power struggle, Stalin recalled Lenin's skepticism by describing Bukharin's work as possessed of "the hypertrophied pretentiousness of a half-baked theoretician."[23] Bukharin was eventually executed. Much earlier, sociology had had to go into hiding.

A cautious excavation began after the Second World War. The Institute of Philosophy in the Soviet Academy of Sciences was allowed to acknowledge the existence of a discipline called "sociology." The primary context in which the word appeared was criticism of Western sociological theories, which provided scholars with an excuse for studying them.[24] The Soviet academics took care not to call their own work "sociology": in 1968, a unit within the Academy of Sciences was allowed to graduate to being an institute, but it would be called the Institute for Concrete Social Studies. Levada, who had been trained as a philosopher, would head up the theory department of the new structure.

The Politburo resolution establishing the Institute for Concrete Social Studies was marked "top secret," as was a later document outlining the new institute's scope of work.[25] The secrecy, along with the institute's name—"social" instead of "sociological"—suggested that the Politburo thought it was stepping into sensitive and even dangerous territory. The potential benefits, however, outweighed the risks. The new structure was charged not only with criticizing bourgeois theory but also with studying Soviet society. The Central Committee itself was to approve studies and to receive their results. It was 1968, the year of the Prague Spring, when the Czechoslovak Communist Party attempted to split off from the Soviet Union and pursue its own, comparatively liberalized version of socialism. The Politburo was worried about similar ideas circulating in the Soviet Union. Indeed, in the summer, after Soviet tanks rolled into Prague, eight extraordinarily brave people staged a protest in Red Square; all were arrested. The following year, Amalrik would write his essay asking if the Soviet Union would last until 1984. The Politburo wanted to know the answer to that question too, and it ordered the Institute for Concrete Social Studies to be fully staffed, with 250 researchers, by 1971. Of course, there were no trained sociologists in the Soviet Union, so the new institute received special dispensation to hire researchers without advanced degrees. Levada was one of a handful of Soviet citizens who had trained themselves in sociology. He had graduated from Moscow State University with a degree in philosophy, studied sociology theory that he had found in *spetskhran*, and had then gone to Communist China to do research there: the system was always more tolerant of inquiry directed at other societies. Now Levada was virtually legitimized as a sociologist, and he was lecturing in the journalism department.

Levada was frighteningly intelligent, unabashedly passionate, and most important, he had mastered the art of thinking out loud during a lecture. He suggested that the peculiarities of everyday life in the Soviet Union could be observed, examined, and understood. In one lecture, for example, he analyzed a short story in which collective-farm workers are sitting around waiting for a Party meeting to start, complaining about their unreasonably demanding bosses and terrible work conditions. Then the meeting commences and the workers take turns lauding their collective farm's accomplishments and boasting of their own contributions to the Soviet cause. Once the meeting is over, they go home, where they return to complaining of their senseless work and miserly pay. Levada showed that the public-private behavioral divide, instantly recognizable to all his listeners, could be understood not just as hypocrisy but as a social and cultural institution.[26]

Fourth-year student Gudkov fell in love. Now he wanted to be a sociologist and work for Levada. There were no job openings, so he would wait. An assistant's position finally opened up in September 1970. Who knew that work could be so enjoyable? Everyone was constantly joking, telling stories, and everyone seemed to be in love with everyone else, through some sort of multiplier effect produced by everyone's crush on Levada himself.[27] The best part, though, were the discussions. Each staff member had an ongoing assignment to read a Western sociologist and prepare presentations and discussion questions for the rest of the group. Gudkov got Max Weber. He felt like an ugly duckling, not nearly as smart as his new colleagues, but the thrill and sense of privilege far outweighed his discomfort.

Within two years, it was all over. Levada's problems began after he published his university talks in two tiny books titled *Lectures on Sociology*. The books passed the censors, who allowed a thousand copies out into the world, but once they were published, they were condemned for not relying on concepts of historical materialism in all their statements, and, worst of all, for "allowing for ambiguous interpretations"—in other words, for being the opposite of dogma, forcing listeners and readers to think.[28] Levada publicly admitted his mistakes but was still stripped of one of his advanced degrees and eventually forced to resign from the Institute. All his staff lost their jobs.

Levada's people struggled to find work: being purged for ideological reasons and their very affiliation with Levada marked them as dangerous. Within a year, though, all had settled somewhere, but often doing nothing beyond the empty imitation of activity that Soviet academic institutions had become so good at producing. What mattered was that Levada assembled his group into a seminar that met every couple of weeks in the evenings. They met wherever Levada was working at the time, and even when they got kicked out and had to move to another institute and had to change the seminar's name (following especially acrimonious evictions), for the next quarter century they never stopped meeting[29] and their mode of work and mission remained constant. It was, as the participants put it, "to assimilate Western sociology." They read twentieth-century theory, talked, and wrote papers that could never be published. In order to write a dissertation that he could defend, Gudkov had to recast his reading of Weber as criticism of Weber, and still it took him years to get his doctorate—he was once again criticized for insufficiently critical thinking, as well as for "bourgeois objectivity," the thought crime of failing to recognize the inevitability of capital-ism's demise.

———

WESTERN VISITORS to the Soviet Union who lucked into Moscow's insular intellectual circles were usually taken with the luxurious sense of timeless-ness in which they existed. With careers almost entirely lateral and ambi-tions, if they ever existed, generally shelved, people like Arutyunyan, Gudkov, and even Dugin seemed to study solely for the sake of learning, rarely even entertaining the possibility that theory could be put to work in any way. But in 1984 Arutyunyan learned that the government was launch-ing psychological "consultation" services, to provide something like family therapy. They were to be called Family and Marriage Centers, and their task was to try to stem the tide of divorces. Party committees had apparently despaired of their ability to manage and shore up the Soviet family: in the 1970s the number of divorces in the country had nearly doubled while the number of marriages barely grew.[30]

A session with a psychologist at one of the new centers would cost three rubles if the psychologist had the equivalent of a master's degree; a doctorate holder's hour ran five rubles and fifty kopecks. This was a fraction of the cost of a black market pair of jeans, but one could buy dozens of loaves of bread with such a sum. Arutyunyan held a doctorate in philosophy by now, but her first client was disappointed to discover that he had just paid top-shelf rate for a meeting with a skinny young woman. She showed him her degree. He still wanted his money back because he had come for help talk-ing sense into his teenage son but the boy had taken off on the way to the appointment. Arutyunyan was firm: there would be no refunds.

They met weekly for about six months. The son never showed, but judg-ing from the father's reports, their relationship gradually evened out. As for the father himself, at his last session he told Arutyunyan, "All this time I have simply been living my life when I should really have been thinking about life."

three
PRIVILEGE

SERYOZHA

FOR SERYOZHA, 1985 was the year his family was reunited.* Seryozha was three years old, and for as long as he had known, his family had been divided: he had an older sister, whom his parents missed very much, and so Seryozha missed her too, though he was not sure he had ever seen her. She lived very far away, in Canada, with Seryozha's grandfather. Seryozha's parents had chosen to send her to Canada; it was an opportunity for a better life for her, but the separation seemed to weigh heavily. Now she would come home, because Seryozha's grandfather was being allowed to return to the Soviet Union. He had been living in Canada as the Soviet ambassador. For someone like Seryozha's grandfather, this was exile. That is what he called it: "political exile."

Alexander Nikolaevich Yakovlev was a strange Communist bird. Raised in rural central Russia outside the city of Yaroslavl, he first learned of the Party as the all-powerful monster that punished the needy and the hungry:

---

*In fact, it appears that Alexander Nikolaevich Yakovlev returned from Canada in 1983, a time Seryozha cannot remember. His recollection, however, is a family reunion occurring simultaneously with the beginning of perestroika.

women in his village were jailed for digging potatoes out of the already frozen soil of collective farm fields, where they had been abandoned after a poorly managed harvest. He was not yet eighteen when he was drafted in August 1941. At the front he saw that the Communists were the bravest, most dedicated soldiers. He joined the Party. He was severely wounded and survived. Before the war was over, he was given an opportunity to go to college. He shared a dorm room with four other disabled veterans. One of them had books of poetry by Sergei Yesenin, who had once written of the beauty of the countryside not far from where Alexander Nikolaevich had grown up. Then Yesenin had led a life of glamour and debauchery, marrying the American dancer Isadora Duncan, traveling to the United States with her, and finally committing suicide in a Leningrad hotel in 1925. His books went out of print shortly after, and for the next quarter century were circulated only surreptitiously. He was too lyrical, too reckless, too human to be Soviet.

> *Snow-clad is the plain, and the moon is white*
> *Covered with a shroud is my country side.*
> *Birches dressed in white are crying, as I see.*
> *Who is dead, I wonder? Is it really me?*[1]

he had written in the year of his death.

Alexander Nikolaevich was struggling, in a way he could not yet put into words, with the idea of what—and who—was and was not Soviet. Yesenin, who had so eloquently written about his love of Russia and his childhood in its beautiful and impoverished countryside, was somehow not Soviet. Now, as the Red Army was liberating its own citizens from Nazi camps, they were condemned as traitors for having allowed themselves to be captured. Alexander Nikolaevich went to the railroad station to see the cattle cars carrying these inmates from the Nazi camps to the Soviet camps, and he saw women who went there in the hopes of seeing their missing men, if only for a second, and he saw hands throwing crumpled-up pieces of paper out of the cattle cars—these contained their names and addresses and the hope that someone would let their loved ones know they were alive.

Alexander Nikolaevich wondered how this could possibly be right. But the Party was very good to him. It gave him an education and started rapidly pulling him up the career ladder. Alexander Nikolaevich set his doubts aside. By the time Stalin died in 1953, Alexander Nikolaevich was a member of the Central Committee. As soon as the leader died, some of his most recent decisions were reversed: a giant planned show trial was scrapped, and the relatives of some of the members of the Party elite were released from the Gulag. In 1956, at the twentieth congress of the Soviet Communist Party, the new Party secretary, Nikita Khrushchev, condemned Stalin as an unworthy successor to Lenin, applied to his rule the damning Marxist term "cult of personality," and disavowed mass arrests and executions.[2] This was when Alexander Nikolaevich lost his ability to reconcile the Party line and his long-shelved doubts. He asked to be released from the Central Committee in order to study Marx and Marxism—first in Moscow and then for a year at Columbia University in New York. The exercise worked, both because he found Marx profoundly compelling and because the United States on the cusp of the McCarthy era and the Cold War hardly seemed like an appealing alternative to the Soviet system. He returned to the Soviet Union to rejoin the Marxist-Leninist effort.

Still, he remained, in increasing contrast to most of the nomenklatura, a thinker. In 1972, Alexander Nikolaevich published an article titled "Against Ahistoricism." To those who could fight their way through its turgid Soviet language, the article delivered a radical message of protest against what Alexander Nikolaevich saw as the Soviet Union's growing nationalist conservatism based on the glorification of some imaginary peasant class's traditional values.[3] "Political exile" to Canada was his punishment for publishing it.[4] He returned more than a decade later, to become idea man to the new general secretary, Mikhail Gorbachev, in his project of reforming the Party and its country. In December 1985, Alexander Nikolaevich authored a document that proposed radical change:

The main components of perestroika are:

1. A market economy in which market rates are paid for labor.
2. The property owner as the agent of freedom.
3. Democracy and glasnost, which bring with them information accessible to all.
4. A system of feedback.[5]

To be sure, his idea of democracy was limited: in a letter to Gorbachev he suggested splitting the Communist Party in two—the Socialist Party and the People's Democratic Party—that would make up an entity called the Communist Union, which would run the country. He proposed creating the office of a president, who would be nominated by the Communist Union and voted by the people for a ten-year term. He argued that all this needed to be done because the Soviet government needed to try to stay ahead of the curve.[6] Alexander Nikolaevich predicted the general vector of events accurately. The Communist Party was never split in two, but in a few years, the Soviet Union would hold a series of hybrid elections: nominations were handled from above, and the resulting legislative bodies had a convoluted structure designed to ensure the primacy of the Communist Party, but for the first time in seven decades, Soviet citizens had some choice at the polls. Gorbachev would indeed become the first president of the Soviet Union. He would also be the last, because the project of staying ahead of the curve failed.

It must have been the summer of 1985 or 1986 that Alexander Nikolaevich and Gorbachev spent together at a Party dacha in the Crimea. Seryozha met Ksenia, Gorbachev's granddaughter, and in another year or two they would spend the summer together at a nomenklatura children's camp on the Black Sea, but this summer, as the two men talked endlessly about what to do with their country, Seryozha was largely left to his own devices. He roamed the fenced-in grounds, which seemed boundless. He explored buildings that were designed to look like castles and had underground tunnels connecting them. He climbed down into the tunnels. Only later would it occur to Seryozha that the grounds had been heavily guarded and he had been watched at all times. Much later he would wonder, he would obsess, about how much of what he remembered of his childhood was real—whether he was ever really alone, and whether he was ever really loved by the people who surrounded him. Like the cook at his grandfather's dacha, who seemed to adore little Seryozha—later Seryozha's sister told him the cook had been a KGB colonel, and this made Seryozha wonder whether the love had been a part of his assignment.

SERYOZHA WAS A GRANDCHILD, not a child, of a top Party functionary, so some of his early life passed in what he thought, then and later, were regular Soviet conditions. His family, like other families, faced shortages of food and other consumer products, from toilet paper to wall paint. Little Seryozha took his turn standing in line with his number written in ballpoint pen on his palm—when lines went on for hours and days, assigning numbers became an additional measure for maintaining self-organization and what passed for fairness. But the place where Seryozha lived with his parents was known in the vernacular as *tsarskoye selo*—"the Czars' Village." The original Tsarskoye Selo—a real place that was officially named the Czar's Village—was the site of Peter the Great's summer residence in the early eighteenth century. Under the Soviets, Tsarskoye Selo was renamed Pushkin, for the poet who had been educated there, but the name "the Czars' Village" began attaching itself to blocks and small neighborhoods that housed the Soviet elites.

The stores here were better stocked, even though they were affected by the shortages. The buildings were better designed and constructed.[7] The air was better than anywhere else in the city: the neighborhood in the west of Moscow contained less industry and more parks than any other.[8] A state born of protest against inequality had created one of the most intricate and rigid systems of privilege that the world had ever seen. It began when the first Bolsheviks moved themselves into the palaces and the luxury hotels.

Within the first few years of Bolshevik Russia's existence, the main mechanisms of privilege were defined and created. Even before the October Revolution—a few months before—Lenin had written that "the first phase of Communism" would not bring equality for all: "differences in wealth will remain unjust differences." Just a week after the Revolution, Lenin wrote that highly qualified professionals would need to retain their privileged position "for the time being." While the idle rich had to be stripped of their possessions, the highly trained had to be enticed to work for the new regime. The Marxist principle of "from each according to his ability, to each according to his need" was replaced with the more pragmatic approach of paying what the state could pay for extracting the maximum from those with high ability. Over the next few years, the list of those whose labor the state valued most highly was established, as were the mechanisms of compensation. The Bolsheviks placed a premium on the "creative intelligentsia," as it was termed—writers, artists, and, especially, filmmakers—as well as scholars and scientists. Military officers ranked even higher. But most of all, the Bolsheviks valued themselves: privileges and benefits for "political workers" exceeded those of all other groups.

The reasons were not only pragmatic but also ideological. "The leadership of the Soviet Communist Party has, from its early days, been profoundly elitist in its attitudes," Mervyn Matthews, a British scholar of Soviet society, wrote in the 1970s. "It has regarded itself as an enlightened band which understands the march of history and is destined to lead the Russian people—indeed the whole world—to communism. In daily life it has always ensured for itself and its close associates privileges commensurate with these awesome demands."[9]

The Soviet privileged were entitled to higher salaries and a set of additional financial rewards; bigger and better apartments; favored access to consumer goods; and certain education and travel privileges.[10] The privileges grew in value and scope during the three decades of Stalin's rule, as did the wealth gap. In the Khrushchev decade, which saw a giant residential construction push, the gap narrowed slightly, but when Leonid Brezhnev came to power in 1964, the old tendency of growing differentiation resumed.[11]

Paradoxically, the peculiarities of the Soviet economic system made the borders between differently valued groups of citizens only starker and harder to penetrate. Taxation was minimal, and redistribution of wealth was not its goal.[12] Because most of the extra compensation for the privileged was non-monetary, and because all of it was centrally administered, members of a given caste were grouped together socially and geographically. Members of the Politburo lived in the same building as other members of the Politburo, procured consumer goods at the same distribution centers, sent their children to the same schools, got treated at the same clinics, were given plots of land on which to build a wooden dacha—a weekend or summer house—in the same area, and took the waters in the same sanatoriums. The same was true for members of the Academy of Sciences, who had their own special infrastructure, and for members of any of the "creative unions," such as those of the writers, artists, or cinematographers.

The quality of the construction and the comfort level of apartments varied from building to building: members of the Politburo were granted more square meters per family member but also larger windows, higher ceilings, and flooring made of harder wood. Academics got less, "creatives" less than that, engineers less still. Menial laborers often lived in dormitory rooms with linoleum flooring and shared bathroom facilities.

Those at the very top, whether out of a sense of shame or a residual longing for the security of a fortress, shielded their lives behind tall solid fences. Alexander Galich, the dissident singer-songwriter, had a song called "Beyond Seven Fences." Its narrator, an ordinary Soviet citizen, encounters the fences that surround the Communist leaders' estates and begins to fantasize about what the fences conceal: fresh, untrampled grass, clean air, hard-to-find chocolate-mint candy, birds of different kinds, shish kebab consumed in the security of knowing the fence is guarded, and at night, to top it all off, "they show films about whores." The narrator cannot take it anymore, heads back to the city, and the whole way back, he is subjected to a lecture extolling Soviet egalitarianism, broadcast over the train's radio system. He thinks of the leaders again: "Back there, beyond the seven fences, / Behind the seven locks, / they don't have to listen to this lecture, / they can just eat their shish kebab." The imagination painted a picture of the ultimate Soviet privilege: living in material comfort—and watching Hollywood films instead of listening to the leaders' own propaganda.[13]

Much of Seryozha's life passed behind the fences. On weekends, a black government Volga—the top model among Soviet-made cars—equipped with flashing lights that entitled it to ignore traffic regulations carried Seryozha's family out of the city. They took Rublyovskoye Shosse, a smooth and narrow road effectively reserved for use by the Soviet elites. The Volga turned off at Kalchuga, a village of solid fences. An automatic gate would open in one of them, and the car would drive onto the grounds of a government dacha reserved for the use of Alexander Nikolaevich. On weekdays, a similar Volga carried Seryozha to a different fence along the same road. This was a preschool for the offspring of the very top of the Soviet elite—a cut above the Central Committee preschool to which Masha's mother had bought access. In the city, the building in which Alexander Nikolaevich lived served as its own fence: it was a city block in which all entrances faced a large courtyard. Uniformed men guarded the gates between the building and the outside world. Seryozha found the men interesting and tried to charm them by talking to them. He knew he was charming—everyone said so, everyone agreed that he was wonderfully cute and fat and blond. But he could never get so much as a smile out of the men.

LYOSHA

LYOSHA GREW UP not quite at the opposite end of the Soviet class spectrum from Seryozha but at a great, unbridgeable remove. His family, too, had privilege, and Lyosha was aware of this growing up. His grandfather, a collective farmer, had had a local Party career. This would have meant several years of added pay for serving a term in the regional Soviet, a putative legislative body, and, later, some informal privileges of access. When he died in 1978, at the age of sixty or so, he had a bit more than others in the village: he left his family a cow. His widow, Lyosha's grandmother, sold the cow a couple of years later so that one of her five children could go to university in

Perm, the nearest big city. Higher education in the Soviet Union was free, and students who had consistently high grades received a monthly stipend, yet with the food shortages, and the shortages of most other things one needed for living, no young person could reasonably expect to survive without help from home.

Lyosha's mother, Galina, the fourth-born and the smartest of her siblings, was lucky to get the help. Her older brother had gone to a military college after his compulsory service, but their mother had not had the money to send any of the rest to university or even so much as to help them leave the village. Two sisters married out, though both would soon be widowed. Then there was the cow, and the sale of the cow, and Galina went to Perm. After university she became a history teacher. She did not have to move back to the village: she was assigned to work in the town of Solikamsk, where, as a teacher, she qualified for a room and later even a small apartment of her own.

Solikamsk was one of the oldest settlements in the Urals: salt was mined there starting in the fifteenth century. In the 1930s and 1940s the town swelled with labor camps: tens of thousands of inmates were brought in from elsewhere in Russia and, later, from the occupied Baltic states and from defeated Germany.[14] By the time Galina came here in the late 1970s, the camps were gone but the town, like so many Soviet towns, seemed bloated: many of its roughly hundred thousand residents lived like temporary settlers, in makeshift accommodations.

By the age of thirty-one, Galina was working as the vice-principal of a trade school and seeing the principal of another trade school in town. He was married. She became pregnant and planned to have an abortion. It would not have been her first, and this was normal: in the absence of methods for pregnancy prevention—hormonal contraceptives were unavailable in the Soviet Union and condoms were of abominable quality and in short supply—abortion was a common contraception method. In 1984, the year Galina became pregnant, there were nearly twice as many abortions in Russia as there were births.[15] There was nothing shameful about having an abortion, so there was no reason to keep the plan secret: Galina's family knew, and her brother-in-law talked her out of it. He pointed out the obvious: she was over thirty, still unmarried, and if she had an abortion this time, she might never have a child at all. Statistically speaking, he was right: more than 90 percent of Russian women were married by age thirty,[16] and few had children after that age.[17]

Galina agreed. She would keep the baby and raise him alone. This, too, was an ordinary path. For decades now, the Soviet Union had been trying, and failing, to recover from the catastrophic population loss caused by the Second World War and the Gulag extermination system. The thrust of the population policies initiated by Khrushchev was to get as many women as possible to have children by the comparatively few surviving men. The policies dictated that men who fathered children out of wedlock would not be held responsible for child support but the state would help the single mother both with financial subsidies and with childcare: she could even leave the child at an orphanage for any length of time, as many times as she needed, without forfeiting her parental rights. The state endeavored to remove any stigma associated with resorting to the help of orphanages, or with single motherhood and having children out of wedlock. Women could put down a fictitious man as the father on the child's birth certificate—or even name the actual father, without his having to fear being burdened with responsibility. "The new project was designed to encourage both men and women to have non-conjugal sexual relationships that would result in procreation," writes historian Mie Nakachi.[18] When Galina's son was born on May 9— Victory Day—1985, she gave him her own last name, Misharina, and the patronymic Yurievich, to indicate that his father's name was Yuri. Lyosha's full official name was thus Alexei Yurievich Misharin.

Galina became the principal at what was called a "correctional school." The name was misleading: the school was less a correctional facility than the state's attempt to compensate for any number of things that had gone terribly wrong with its students. Correctional schools were created to serve children deemed incapable of succeeding in mainstream schools. Most of these schools provided boarding during the week or year-round; some had special services for children with disabilities.

Galina worked at a correctional school of the most common type—the type for children whose parents failed to take care of them, often because they drank. Her students came from the neighborhood that lay between Lyosha's childhood block and the school: while he and Galina lived in a regular concrete-block building, this neighborhood was made up of wooden barracks left over from when the Gulag exploded Solikamsk's population. They called it the *barachnyi* district. Walking through it, as Galina did on her way to and from work six days a week, was considered dangerous; she carried a knife to protect herself. Sometimes she had to take Lyosha with her to the *barachnyi* district, usually when she was looking for a student who had gone missing. Lyosha found the barracks impressive and terrifying. The ceilings looked like they might cave in. There was a stench that was stronger and more offensive than anything he had ever smelled. Most of the inhabitants, including the parents with whom Galina occasionally had long conversations, were drunk. Lyosha was aware that this was somehow a function of poverty. He also made a mental connection between poverty and the word "suicide," which Galina used with some regularity when talking about her students. Other words included "pregnancy" and "alcohol" and, later, "drugs." These were children—older than Lyosha but children nonetheless, she made this clear—who drank, got pregnant, and killed themselves. Lyosha understood that the fact that these words did not apply to his and Galina's world was a function of privilege.

One did not have to go to the *barachnyi* district to see extreme poverty: it was found on Lyosha and Galina's block as well. A woman who lived one door down drank heavily, and her kids went to the correctional school. Some nights she passed out and the kids were locked out. Those nights, they often slept on Galina's landing—Lyosha figured they chose it because they knew she would not hurt them. Unfortunately, this meant that some mornings when Galina opened the door to take Lyosha to preschool the landing stank: the children went to the bathroom there. Eventually, in the 1990s, the building's residents installed a lock on the front door, to keep these and other interlopers out.

Lyosha's preschool days were long: he was dropped off at six, before his mother walked the half hour to her own school, and was often not picked up until ten, when only the night guards remained on the grounds. This was just the way it had to be, because Galina was raising Lyosha alone, she had a demanding job, and her own mother lived too far away to help on a daily basis. Galina told Lyosha that his father lived in the big city of Perm, where she had gone to university. Perm was 120 kilometers* away, but for how often people went there, it may as well have been a thousand miles. Sometimes, a nice man stopped by and spent time with them. Galina told Lyosha to call him Uncle Yura.

When Lyosha was about three, Galina started to have the television turned on at all times. Sometimes she sat down in front of the black-and-white set and watched for hours as gray men on the screen did nothing but talk, occasionally raising their voices. Galina talked to Lyosha about the men—she seemed to have personal relationships with them—and there was tension in what was happening on-screen, a sense of earnestness and importance, so it was not boring. Lyosha learned some names, including Gorbachev, who was the most important. He had a large mark on his forehead, and Lyosha's cousin, who was quite a bit older, told Lyosha that it was a map of the USSR because Gorbachev was the president. When Lyosha told Galina that, she laughed and said it was just a birthmark. She had to be right, but the cousin would not hear of it. Galina took Lyosha to the polls, explaining that it was their "civic duty." What exactly their civic duty was, was unclear, but Lyosha liked voting because the precinct was decorated with red cloth and there were open salami sandwiches for sale.

In the summers, Lyosha stayed in the village with his grandmother. Assorted cousins were sent there as well, and their parents floated in and out, sometimes spending a week or two and sometimes staying just the weekend. One day when he was five, his aunt said, "Let's go get baptized," and they all went to another village, where there stood a church in a profound state of decay that was only accentuated by some recent spot repairs. A man in a dress took Lyosha by the hair and dunked his face in a vat of water. At that

---

*About seventy-five miles.

moment Lyosha hated the man and his own aunt, but a few minutes later he liked the bread and the wine the man put on his tongue, and he loved the little cross the man put around his neck. When they got back to their own village, Lyosha ran up to his mother shouting, "Look what I have"— meaning the little cross. Galina took a step back, looking like she might faint. She later explained to him that she was an atheist, and what that meant.

Lyosha loved to hear Galina explain things, especially when they had to do with history. She had many history books at home, and Lyosha worshipped these, particularly the ones about the Great Patriotic War. He read *The Wreath of Glory*, a set of heavy books in red leatherette covers. The giant anthology collected works of fiction and nonfiction, with each volume devoted to one aspect of the war: a book on the defense of Moscow, a book on Leningrad, a book on victory itself.[19] He listened to vinyl records of war songs—the great march songs calling on people to rise up, the lyrical ballads about missing loved ones and fighting for them, and the heartbreaking postwar songs about lost comrades. Lyosha was convinced that his birth date was no accident: he was not just born on Victory Day—he was born on the fortieth anniversary of the end of the greatest war ever fought. When relatives came over on his birthday, he would grill them on their knowledge of war history. Once he was older, he turned the ritual into a quiz, putting days into preparing questions about the great battles at Stalingrad and Kursk. He did his best to play war songs on the piano. One of his cousins had given him a collection of Great Patriotic War sheet music for one of his birthdays. Lyosha took lessons in playing accordion, not piano, but he could read music, and he had intense determination. He played using one finger.

four

HOMO SOVIETICUS

PERESTROIKA WAS AN IMPOSSIBLE IDEA on the face of it. The Party was setting out to employ its structures of command to make the country, and itself, less command-driven. A system whose main afflictions were stagnation and inflexibility was setting out to change itself. Worst and probably intractable was the fact that people who had spent their lives securing power and individual leverage were expected to devise change that would dismantle the hierarchy of levers and might dislodge them. The system resisted change instinctively, and a great number of individuals plotted consciously to sabotage the change.

As the man appointed by Gorbachev to think through perestroika, to design it and guide it, Alexander Nikolaevich was confronted daily with the futility of the task. Much of the Party's leadership rejected change for fear of losing power. Those who appeared to welcome change, like, most notably, the head of the Moscow Party organization, Boris Yeltsin, were ultimately also driven by the desire for power, and this made them unreliable allies. The leaders of many of the Soviet Union's constituent republics were becoming lax in monitoring and containing nationalist forces: for decades the country had prosecuted local nationalist activists as enemies of the state, but perestroika loosened talk of self-determination in the Baltic republics, Ukraine, Georgia, and even in places that were nominally part of the Russian republic within the USSR. It was beginning to pull the country apart, creating tension and instability when the USSR could least afford it. The media, which were now—in large part thanks to Alexander Nikolaevich's efforts—granted greater freedom and even encouraged to tackle difficult subjects, were by turns too passive and too conservative, even reactionary. The public, to the extent that Alexander Nikolaevich could track what the public was thinking, also seemed torn between inappropriate passivity and equally inappropriate action: those who began speaking out seemed invariably to choose extreme positions, whether they were speaking in favor of democratization or in favor of cracking down to preserve the Soviet order. Alexander Nikolaevich took to calling all of them "extremists."

As a man who had struggled to educate himself, who had had to teach himself to think, Alexander Nikolaevich was sympathetic to the great number of people resisting change simply because they had never been exposed to anything outside the Party's dogma. In May 1988 he convinced the Central Committee to approve a concerted effort to restore thought and knowledge to the land. "It has come to the point where the West now has scholars who are better versed in the history of our own homegrown philosophy than we are," he wrote in the draft of an address to the Central Committee. "Twentieth-century Western philosophy contains a number of ideas that are avidly debated in books, at conferences, and so on. But many of these ideas were originally articulated by our thinkers. This is not surprising, for the *tension* [his italics] of the spiritual quest in Russia in the years leading up to the Revolution exceeded that of any European country." Alexander Nikolaevich suggested creating a team of five or six editors who would put together a library of Russian philosophers, between thirty-five and forty volumes that would include works by depublished nineteenth-century thinkers as well as those who had sailed on the Philosophers' Ship. He compiled his own list of thirty-nine thinkers to be restored to the Russian canon. And if this went well, he wrote, then books on history and economics (which he still called "political economy") could follow. The Central Committee said yes.[1]

BEFORE THE PLANNED COLLECTION could materialize, journals began publishing previously silenced philosophers. Even Heidegger could now see print. For someone like Dugin, this was a confounding moment. On the one hand, he no longer had to spend his days hunting down copies of banned books or hurting his eyes by trying to read the microfilm projected onto his wooden desktop. On the other hand, his entire life was constructed around just this: fighting his way to difficult ideas, becoming one of the few people in the country to understand them, and continuing his process of self-education, knowing that he had all the time in the world, his hated static world. If the world was no longer static, and if the knowledge was no longer banned, who was Dugin now?

Evgenia left him. She joined a group of people who coalesced around a strange woman, Valeria Novodvorskaya. She was in her late thirties, and she had been in and out of punitive psychiatric clinics since she was a teenager—she was a radical lone-wolf dissident. Now, for the first time, she was assembling like-minded people. They began with a seminar, held in Moscow and Leningrad, for about eighty participants—a number that would have been unthinkable just a few months earlier. Even now, in April 1987, the organizers were terrified. They started with studying Soviet history—Novodvorskaya, who was a walking encyclopedia, lectured more often than anyone else—and soon began to organize protests on every topic they studied. They held tiny rallies to commemorate events that Soviet citizens had not been allowed to know about. Evgenia started getting detained on a regular basis. She seemed to enjoy it, and the publicity that accompanied it as Soviet papers began to cover what was happening in the streets. She was no longer living in the apartment she had shared with Alexander—she had managed to be allotted a place of her own, one room plus a kitchen in a

1970s concrete-block tower a short subway-plus-tram ride from the center. Dozens of people would cram into this space now, all of them rebel freaks, and as many as a dozen KGB cars were keeping vigil at the front door on any given day.[2] Their son, Artur, was living with Alexander's mother now, and Evgenia took him on weekends when she was not busy protesting or being held at a precinct.

Novodvorskaya's group began calling itself a political party—this in a country where for seven decades there had existed only one Party. The new party was founded in May 1988 in the course of a three-day "congress" with about a hundred attendees. Some of the sessions were held in Evgenia's apartment. Participants were harassed, some were detained, some roughly. A dacha where the third day's meetings were scheduled to convene was raided by KGB agents who turned the place upside down, rendering it unusable. Only about fifty of the participants dared sign their names to the new party's platform.[3] It was an outrageous document, which called for the dissolution of the Warsaw Pact and referred to the Baltic states—Latvia, Lithuania, and Estonia—as "occupied," demanding that they, along with any other constituent republic that so wished, be allowed to secede from the Union. It abolished the KGB, the death penalty, and the draft. Novodvorskaya and Evgenia would have gone even further—their views were a combination of libertarianism and anarchism, both of which seemed to them, at that point, the ultimate in Western thought—but the rest of the group held them back. As it was, several of the old dissidents who had served time for their anti-Soviet activities thought the document was too confrontational.[4] This was not even what Alexander Nikolaevich meant when he used the term "extremists": it was a caricature of what he meant. A prosecutor threatened Novodvorskaya with charges of high treason, which carried the potential of the death penalty. But the activists responded in an utterly un-Soviet way: they did not stop in fear, and they did not fight the prosecutor—they just paid the threat no mind. All the organizers received summonses, and all ignored them. They proceeded with their congress, even though several people were detained in the process and held for about a week. The first political party in the Soviet Union that was not the Communist Party would be called Demokraticheskiy Soyuz, the Democratic Union.[5]

Novodvorskaya would later write that Evgenia was not so much anti-Soviet, like Novodvorskaya herself, as un-Soviet.[6] Evgenia was having the time of her life—she was engaged, she was performing, she was admired, and she was also in love. She was having such a good time, in fact, that she was proving too much even for the Democratic Union, which kicked her out for talking out of school, often while drunk. In 1989, when founding a new political party no longer seemed radical in itself, she cofounded the Russian chapter of the Transnational Radical Party, a pacifist non-electoral political group with headquarters in Italy. The Italians gave Evgenia her first computer, but then the Radicals, too, kicked her out, for oversleeping on the day of a demonstration in front of the Romanian embassy. She decided that she was more interested in capitalism than in politics and started the Russian Libertarian Party. She also came out as a lesbian—the love that had been fueling her political life was the love of a woman—and launched the first queer organization in the country, the Association of Sexual Minorities (more specific terms of identity, like "gay" or "lesbian," were not yet familiar to the Russian ear).[7]

AMONG THE MANY THINGS that grew confusing in the late 1980s was the left-right dichotomy. The way Alexander Nikolaevich used the word "right," it was but a stand-in for "conservative" in the most basic sense of the word: just wanting things to stay the way they were. But the way they were, nominally, was "left"—the most conservative force was the Communist Party. Few people, therefore, wanted to call themselves "left." That made everyone "right," or something closer to "radical" or "democratic" as opposed to conservative. Evgenia's Radical Party, which would have been far left in Europe, and her Libertarian Party were roughly equidistant from the Communist Party, which made the leap from one to the other seem like a small step. In fact, all her views shared a category much more important than the familiar and therefore suspect—political divisions: they were Western. Before finding Novodvorskaya, Evgenia was briefly involved in an effort called the Group for Trust Between East and West, whose sole agenda was to counter the most basic premise of Soviet propaganda: the idea that the West was a threat. Even in Alexander Nikolaevich's rhetoric, if not necessarily in his thinking, this premise appeared inviolate: almost any time he wrote a letter or gave a speech on the state of things in the Soviet Union, he made note of Western efforts to undermine the country and Western plots to sabotage perestroika itself. So if one strove to be, first and foremost, un-Soviet, as Evgenia did, one did well to embrace any number of political positions, from libertarianism to pacifism, one more Western than the next. Gay rights, the legalization of drugs, and the abolition of the death penalty, the lifting of all state controls in favor of the reign of the unfettered free market—everything fell naturally into line.

As for Dugin, who had lost the woman he loved, his son, and his life of intensive open-ended learning, he was bound to look for and find the position that was the opposite of everything. First he drifted into Pamyat ("Memory"), an organization that in the mid-1980s was emerging from the underground. It had long trafficked in antisemitic rhetoric, from *The Protocols of the Elders of Zion* to contemporary world-Zionist-conspiracy theories. Now it allied itself with Gorbachev's perestroika on the one hand and with an imagined Russian nationalist revival on the other.[8] The combination was fairly intuitive: Soviet internationalist rhetoric was just one of the aspects of hollow ideology that were being deflated. While official Soviet media pre-glasnost doled out their own regular servings of antisemitism framed as anti-Zionism, the system had generally subdued outright Russian-nationalist voices. Now this lid was lifted and hatred emerged in many stripes, of which Pamyat was the brightest. The Soviet leadership was either unsure about how best to react or unwilling to react, but Alexander Nikolaevich raged privately and publicly. "I am not Jewish," he said during a talk at the Higher Party School in March 1990, "yet every day I get fliers from Pamyat in which I am called 'the head of the Judeo-Masonic lounge of the Soviet Union.' There is only one reason for this, as far as I can tell: I really do speak out publicly, in writing and in speaking, everywhere and anywhere I can, against all manifestations of nationalism, including antisemitism. And I consider it to be the shame of any member of the Russian intelligentsia and any Russian person at all who subscribes to this kind of ideology of racial hatred.”[9]

After decades of amorphousness underground, Pamyat had acquired a charismatic leader, a former photographer named Dmitry Vasilyev, who railed against all the world at once: the Holocaust was a Jewish conspiracy (Eichmann was a Jew); rock music was a Satanist plot (slowed-down vinyl records sounded out chants to Satan); and yoga was a Western scourge (all the West wanted to do was contaminate Russian culture).[10]

Between its Soviet conservatism, as manifested by its avowed allegiance to Gorbachev, and its anti-Western, anti-everything-foreign stand, Pamyat was indeed the perfect opposite to the Democratic Union. Like Evgenia, though, Dugin soon parted ways with his first political organization. But while she became, briefly, a serial founder of radical groups, Dugin set out on a new intellectual project.

He now found inspiration in the writing of René Guénon, a long-dead Frenchman who had published more than a dozen books on metaphysics. A couple of volumes focused on Hindu beliefs, but he also wrote on Islam, cosmism, and “the esoterism of Dante.” Dugin perceived a coherent worldview in this eclectic collection, or at least a coherent quest: the search for a tradition, or, rather, Tradition. He wrote a book—his first—*The Ways of the Absolute*. It was a dense text, parts of which no one but Dugin himself would be able to understand, but it contained one clear proposition: put aside all existing belief systems, all things learned, in favor of what he called “total traditionalism,” a sort of meta-ideology that contained the cosmos. Indeed, it contained so much that it was probably better defined by what it decisively rejected: “the ‘modern world’ as such.” Modernity was the opposite of Tradition, so the essential tradition Dugin was seeking could be located only by stripping away all views and things contemporary and working backward. Another word for “modern” might be “Western.” By using a French philosopher obsessed with Hinduism and Islam to get at this idea of Tradition,

Dugin was coming full circle to an earlier, newly forgotten idea held by Russian thinkers who argued that their country should be turned away from Europe and toward Asia.[11]

Dugin made his own pilgrimages to Western Europe. In 1990 he went to Paris, where he met Belgian New Right thinker Robert Steuckers. Here was an intellectual from the West who was as radical in his thinking as Guénon, but he was living right now and speaking to Dugin. Steuckers introduced him to the concept of geopolitics and, more broadly, the concept that Dugin's ideas could have practical implications in a changing world. He also suggested to Dugin that his ideas might combine into something called National Bolshevism. Within a year, Dugin met a number of other Western European New Right intellectuals, was welcomed to the conferences of the ethno-nationalist think tank Groupement de Recherche et d'Études pour la Civilisation Européenne in Paris, and was published by an Italian New Right house.[12]

Dugin's book about Guénon was published in Russia in 1990, among many books—some of them better-written, but few by a better-read person—that attempted to find a metaphysical, esoteric, supernatural, or, on the contrary, ultrarational, mathematically argued way of explaining all of life and the world, which had so suddenly become so complicated. Dugin himself, meanwhile, found the Tradition he wanted in the Orthodox faith—not in the contemporary church but with the Old Believers, a faction that split off in the seventeenth century and had since attempted to maintain its ways in spite of the modern world.

THE CLICHÉ OF THE ERA was "floodgates." Everyone in every field was claiming that the floodgates had opened. To Arutyunyan, it felt more like the *fortochka* opened wider, then wider still, and then the entire window swung open. A friend who worked at the Moscow cardiology center told Arutyunyan that a doctor there was teaching a seminar on administering the Minnesota Multiphasic Personality Inventory. The world's most popu-lar personality test, in use since the 1930s, had been studied by a few Soviet psychiatrists and psychologists in the 1970s.[13] They had tried to adapt it to Russian, which proved an infinitely difficult task. For one thing, Russian is a thoroughly grammatically gendered language: most first-person state-ments have a feminine and a masculine form. The MMPI consisted of 566 first-person statements. The first adaptation efforts, therefore, created two versions of the test—one for women and one for men.

More important, the original test was rooted in American reality—and had been empirically tested for years before it was finalized and came into wide use. The Soviet psychiatrists and psychologists had very little oppor-tunity to test their clinical reality. Now, in the late 1980s, one of them was allowed to include outsiders in his work, turning them into students, col-laborators, and testers at once. How were they going to apply this foreign test? The Russian language, gendered or not, was the least of their prob-lems. The test contained statements like number 58: "Everything is turning out just like the prophets of the Bible said it would." The Soviet person's reality included no prophets, and no Bible. The original adapted version of this statement read, "A person's future has been predetermined."[14] Testing showed this to be a poor substitute, though. A better fit, as it turned out, was, "I am more cheerful when the weather is good." Question 255, "Some-times at elections I vote for men about whom I know very little," became "Sometimes I positively appraise people about whom I know very little," and question 513, "I think Lincoln was greater than Washington," sidestepped possible disagreements about history by turning into "I prefer working with a supervisor who gives clear instructions to working with one who gives me greater freedom."

By 1989, the original MMPI was being retired in the United States in favor of an updated version, adjusted for changes in American society and clinicians' understanding of it. The "men" in the elections question became "people," and Lincoln and Washington were dropped altogether.[15] In the Soviet Union, the adapted version of the first test was coming into use just as the reality to which it had been adapted was changing drastically—possibly making the effort to delete from the test all references to elections not just superfluous but counterproductive. Still, the very fact that more than a few psychologists, newly trained in using the MMPI, were going to start administering the test to a large number of apparently regular people—not psychiatric patients or criminals but previously unpathologized, untreated, and unstudied ordinary Soviet citizens—was groundbreaking.

Whatever its limitations as a diagnostic tool in the USSR, the MMPI proved invaluable for inspiring trust in psychologists: the strange trick of being able to draw convincing conclusions about someone's personality—being able to point to such traits as excitability, cynicism, or a proclivity for developing unexplained symptoms of physical illness—on the basis of a series of apparently unrelated questions struck the perfect balance between magic and science. It showed that, despite lacking a medical doctor's white coat, psychologists knew something the subjects did not. Even better, they knew things about the subjects that the subjects themselves did not know—at just the time when so many Soviet people were starting to sense that they knew less about themselves and their world than they had thought.

The psychologists, meanwhile, started to learn to be clinicians. Moscow State University's psychology department abandoned most caution and launched a series of workshops for and by practicing psychologists. Self-styled shrinks emerged from their apartments, where they had been seeing clients without a permit or permission, or from the library, where they had been reading Freud in the *spetskhran*, and began helping one another systematize their knowledge. There were workshops on family therapy, Gestalt therapy, and psychoanalysis.

As the Iron Curtain began to open a crack—a byzantine visa system was still in place, and the activities of visiting foreigners were highly restricted, but some people were now welcome to come in for some reasons—Western psychotherapists began to visit and teach. Carl Rogers came in 1987. It was both bizarre and earth-shattering that Rogers, a founder of humanistic client-centered therapy and the pioneer of nondirective counseling, would be the first major Western psychologist to lecture in the Soviet Union: his approaches rested first on placing the person at the center of things, and, second, on not telling the person what to do. An organizer of his visit recalled that Rogers himself pointed this out, saying, "What you have asked us to do here is dangerous . . . because if people learn to empower themselves, they may not do what you want them to do. It may not fit in this culture."[16]

Rogers proceeded to lead some of the strangest groups he had ever encountered. Following a large lecture at Moscow University, he planned to spend four days working with a group of no more than thirty people. The roughly fifty people who crowded into the room and another dozen who congregated outside the door spent the first day screaming and fighting one another for a spot in the group. Rogers was, he wrote later, "horrified"—he italicized the word. "Rarely, if ever, have I heard such vicious hostility directed personally toward present members of the group."[17] On day two, he noted, "It became evident that many of their personal problems relate to the great frequency of divorce. In this educated and sophisticated group, it is similar to the United States. One woman spoke of the way in which she and her husband had gradually worked toward a better and seemingly more permanent relationship. She was definitely the exception. Nearly everyone else spoke of 'When I left my first husband'; 'I have a problem with my child by my second marriage'; 'If I leave my second wife.' There was talk of the insecurity and estrangement of children of previous partnerships; the difficulty of maintaining relationships with one's children when they are at a distance; the interference of ex-wives and ex-mothers-in-law—the whole gamut."[18] Even after the room had settled down, Rogers continued to be taken aback by his students' inability to listen to one another. Yet the formal debriefing several days later convinced Rogers that as therapists his students had been deeply affected by the suggestion that they should hold back judgment and even guidance. Indeed, they attempted to conduct what should have been a formal and formulaic meeting of an "academic council" in Rogerian fashion, a feat Rogers himself called "extravagant." As people, though, the Russian participants seemed to sadden the great therapist: he and his co-facilitator noted "a certain 'lostness' . . . a pervading sense that there should be more to life, a deep despair about ever finding it."[19]

Virginia Satir, the world's most famous family therapist, came the following year. Pulling people one by one onto the stage from a crowded auditorium, she explained the most basic tenets of her approach, her belief in the fundamental goodness of every person: "I know he is a wonderful man. Why do I know this? Because he is a man at the station of life, and he is the only one exactly like him in the whole world."[20] Viktor Frankl came and lectured on existential therapy. The psychologists of Moscow were catching a glimpse of the twentieth century's professional conversation before the last of its great participants were gone. Rogers died in 1987; Satir in 1988; Frankl lived for another decade, but by the time he visited Moscow he was already in his eighties.

Arutyunyan tried to hear and learn all of it, all at once, before she came to the realization that to help a human being, she had to choose a single framework for understanding him. This was when she concluded that the flawed, complicated, and sometimes frightening human of psychoanalysis was her choice. It would be a while before she knew that psychoanalysis, too, had its different schools, each of which represented a different vision of the person.

GUDKOV'S SECOND INVITATION to work with Yuri Levada was twenty years in coming. After two decades of home-based seminars, Levada was reassembling his team as part of an official Soviet institution. In July 1987 the Central Committee decreed that "in order to study and deploy the public opinion of the Soviet population on the most pressing socioeconomic issues" a new center would be created under the auspices of the trade union authority and the labor ministry. This and subsequent documents made it clear that the future All-Union Public Opinion Research Center would not in fact be merely a research institution: it was expected to actively devise and implement strategies for shaping public opinion.[21] The choice of overseeing agencies was logical: centrally controlled trade unions and the labor ministry were in charge of the human resource that was all the Soviet people—who, the thinking went, would now be properly monitored and directed.

The new center began in chaos and confusion. The trade unions allocated half a million dollars—hard currency—to buy the latest computer equipment, and the sociologists were promptly swindled out of the entire sum by a con man posing as a Canadian technology supplier.[22] On the bright side, there was the staffing: Levada knew exactly what needed to be studied, and he had all his people with him to conduct the research.

Levada's hypothesis, formed over the course of more than three decades working not only in the Soviet Union but also, in the 1950s, in newly communist China, was that every totalitarian regime forms a type of human being on whom it relies for its stability. The shaping of the New Man is the regime's explicit project, but its product is not so much a vessel for the regime's ideology as it is a person best equipped to survive in a given society. The regime, in turn, comes to depend on this newly shaped type of person for its continued survival.

Levada hypothesized a detailed portrait of Homo Sovieticus. The system had bred him over the course of decades by rewarding obedience, conformity, and subservience.[23] The successful member of Soviet society, suggested Levada, believed in self-isolation, state paternalism, and what Levada called "hierarchical egalitarianism," and suffered from an "imperial syndrome."[24] Self-isolation was a key strategy for both the state and the individual: as the Soviet Union sealed itself off with the Iron Curtain, so did the Soviet citizen separate himself from everyone who was Other and therefore untrustworthy. Ideology supported these separations by stressing "class enmity," but keeping one's social circle small was also a sound survival strategy during the era of mass terror, when excessive trust could prove deadly.[25] The belief in a paternalistic state, and an utter dependence on it, were bred in Homo Sovieticus by the very nature of the Soviet state, which, Levada wrote, was not so much a complex of institutions, like the modern state, but rather a single superinstitution. He described it as a "universal institution of a premodern paternalistic type, which reaches into every corner of human existence."[26] The Soviet state was the ultimate parent: it fed, clothed, housed, and educated its citizen; it gave him a job and gave his life meaning; it rewarded him for doing good and punished him for doing wrong, no matter how small the transgression. "By its very design, the Soviet 'socialist' state is *totalitarian* because it must not leave the individual any independent space," wrote Levada.[27] This description of totalitarianism echoed Hannah Arendt's explanation of how totalitarian regimes employ terror: "It substitutes for the boundaries and channels of communication between men a band of iron which holds them so tightly together that it is as though their plurality had disappeared into One Man of gigantic dimensions."[28] Robbed of his individuality and therefore the ability to interact meaningfully with others, she wrote, man became profoundly lonely, which made him the perfect creature and subject of the totalitarian state.[29]

Since the state controlled every thing and every person, Soviet society had a simple vertical structure, rendering the Soviet citizen's thinking fundamentally hierarchical. Even though the exact systems of rank and privilege were secret, the basic logic according to which the state doled out goods and comforts in exchange for valued services ruled every person's life. At the same time, official ideology extolled equality and the state punished those who had, or wanted to have, too much. For Homo Sovieticus this translated into the value of equality within groups—a strictly enforced conformity at one's station in life. This was what Levada termed "hierarchical egalitarianism."[30] This term was an example of what Levada called "antinomies"—a philosophical concept that refers to the contradiction between statements either of which appears reasonable. Homo Sovieticus's world, according to Levada, was shaped by pairs of antinomies. The most important of these may have been what Levada called "the imperial syndrome." On the one hand, the USSR, like the Russia that preceded it, was incontrovertibly an empire. Its strength, breadth, and size were all sources of citizen pride. Every schoolchild knew that the Soviet Union occupied the largest territory of any country in the world—one-sixth of the Earth's landmass.

Broad is my native land
Many there are forests, fields, and rivers.
I know of no other country
Where man breathes so freely

This was a popular patriotic song that clearly made the connection: the Soviet person's wonderful life was a function of the very size of his country. On the other hand, every Soviet citizen was constantly made aware of his ethnic origin, which was immutable and contained on every document that referred to him. Only members of the single largest ethnic group—the Russians—could occasionally forget who they were. "So Homo Sovieticus is by his very nature, genetically, frustrated, faced with the impossible choice between an ethnic and a superethnic identity," wrote Levada.[31]

The antinomies required Homo Sovieticus to fragment his consciousness to accommodate both of the contradictory positions. Levada borrowed George Orwell's term "doublethink." Homo Sovieticus, like the characters of *1984*, could hold two contradictory beliefs at the same time. These beliefs ran on parallel tracks, and so long as the tracks indeed did not cross, they were not in conflict: depending on the situation, Homo Sovieticus could deploy one or the other statement in the antinomic pair, sometimes one after the other, in quick succession.

But the most important thing Levada believed about Homo Sovieticus was this: his was a dying breed. He had been formed by the one-two punch of the Revolution and the Great Terror: the first event brought its ideals and values, and the second taught Homo Sovieticus to conform in order to survive. But now, thirty years after the death of Stalin, the people so shaped were dying off. Their children and grandchildren would be different. That, in turn, would mean that the regime could no longer rely on them to ensure its survival through their behavior. And that would mean that the regime— the USSR as it existed—would collapse. This was a far cry from what the trade union authority, the labor ministry, and the Central Committee had in mind, but this was what Levada wanted his team now to prove: that Homo Sovieticus conformed to his description and that the phenomenon of

Homo Sovieticus was bound to an older generation, which would mean that Homo Sovieticus would soon cease being the dominant social type in the Soviet Union, which would mean the end of the Soviet Union itself.

THE TASK OF PROVING that a certain social type existed, was dominant, and would soon die off was so circular that it verged on impossible. But this was not the biggest problem with the study. The biggest problem was that none of Levada's sociologists had ever done anything like this before. They had faithfully attended the seminar for twenty years. They had read their Western sociologists. Some of them, like Gudkov, had been lucky enough to work with some data in their official jobs. But none of them had ever done a survey, a poll, or any kind of field research.

They were theoreticians, so they had an idea of how a questionnaire ought to be designed. They were certainly well-versed in choosing samples—and for the first time ever, they would be allowed to do this. But what would they do with the data? None of them had been trained in statistical analysis: they would have to train themselves. The lack of computers made the setup look more farcical than tragic. It took them two years to be able to design and implement their study. On second look, the idea that they knew how to design a survey also seemed suspect. In Western sociology, which they had been studying, surveys inevitably built on earlier surveys, and, more important, on the terms of long-running public conversations. The problem was similar to the challenge of adapting the MMPI, except in this field there was no MMPI to adapt. In the Soviet Union, there had been no public, precisely because there had been no conversation: "One Man of gigantic dimensions" must speak with a single voice, and only when called upon.

How do you bring up a topic that has never before been discussed? How do you elicit the opinions of people who have not been entitled to hold opinions? How do you have conversations for which there is no language? Gudkov began to think of their group as a geological expedition setting out to determine the makeup of a monolith. They would have to begin with an exploratory explosion, a man-made disturbance that would expose the nature of Soviet society. Gudkov invented a tool for doing just this. Ask people "what should be done" with certain deviant groups. It was not hard to be a deviant in Soviet society, and many people were—people who listened to rock music, for example (they were generally referred to as "rockers"), and hippies (the term was still in circulation in the late 1980s because there was still a subculture of people wearing long hair and singing to acoustic guitar). Offer respondents a range of options, from "leave them alone" to the Leninist "liquidate." Gudkov figured that such questions would tease out the limits of tolerance and, more to the point, help measure the levels of underlying aggression.

The results of this part of the questionnaire surprised the group. Homo Sovieticus was clearly opening up to the world, feeling reasonably peaceful toward even the most deviant of groups, like the homosexuals: fully 10 percent believed that homosexuals should be "left to their own devices," another 6 percent thought they should be "helped" (the questionnaire did not specify what kind of help they should receive), and a third thought that homosexuals should be "liquidated."[32] Considering that homosexual conduct was a crime punishable by up to three years in prison, Gudkov thought this level of aggression was low. More than 20 percent of respondents wanted to "liquidate" rockers, and nearly 8 percent wanted to "liquidate" alcoholics. But then a whopping 27 percent wanted rockers to be left alone, and more than 50 percent wanted to see alcoholics get help. In the absence of any data that could be used as reference, the researchers concluded that these results reflected a trend toward greater tolerance. The highest proportion of those who wanted to "liquidate" homosexuals was found in respondents older than fifty and younger than twenty: adults of working age were markedly less aggressive.[33]

There was a lot of other good news. First, Levada's Homo Sovieticus hypothesis was largely borne out. The survey found the traits Levada had described, and it fleshed out the way Soviet doublethink functioned in daily life. Orwell had described doublethink as follows:

To know and not to know, to be conscious of complete truthfulness while telling carefully constructed lies, to hold simultaneously two opinions which cancelled out, knowing them to be contradictory and believing in both of them, to use logic against logic, to repudiate morality while laying claim to it, to believe that democracy was impossible and that the Party was the guardian of democracy, to forget whatever it was necessary to forget, then to draw it back into memory again at the moment when it was needed, and then promptly to forget it again: and above all, to apply the same process to the process itself. That was the ultimate subtlety: consciously to induce unconsciousness, and then, once again, to become unconscious of the act of hypnosis you had just performed. Even to understand the word "doublethink" involved the use of doublethink.[34]

The study showed how doublethink kept doubling back on itself. What Soviet people were required to believe and proclaim was counterfactual, and the requirement itself was but a mechanism of control, precisely because it contained its own negation. Homo Sovieticus lived a life of constant negotiation with the omnipotent state, and the negotiation itself was both the individual's sole survival strategy and an instrument of control. The sociologists identified several key areas of negotiation that they called "games."

There was a game called "Work," and one of the most-often-repeated Soviet jokes described it perfectly: "We pretend to work, and they pretend to pay us." There was a game called "Care," in which "they"—the state—pretended to take care of the citizenry, which pretended to be grateful. What made this simple-sounding game instantly complicated was that it was not all pretense: the state indeed controlled the citizen's fate, and the citizen could be said to owe his continued survival to the state. In this sense, the game of "Complicity" was similar: Homo Sovieticus pretended to participate in the affairs of the state, and this made him complicit in everything the state did. The game of "Agreement," on the other hand, was a straightforward negotiation: pledging support for the state bought the citizen a modicum of privacy (and privacy was often the first thing dissidents were forced to sacrifice). The game of "Consensus" was a corollary of "Agreement": it allowed Homo Sovieticus's private self to be indifferent to and even dismissive of the state—as long as the public, collective citizenry demonstrated its loyalty to and enthusiastic support for the state.[35]

The group administered its hundred-question survey to 2,700 people of various ages and backgrounds in different parts of the USSR, and here is what they did not find: people who believed in a radiant communist future, true Marxists, ideologues. The survey provided many opportunities for a true believer to manifest his convictions. But when answering the question "Where do you think a person can find answers to questions that concern him?" only 5.6 percent chose "In the teachings of Marx and Lenin," which would have been the "correct" answer in a different setting. About half chose the option "My own common sense." Asked whether they would prefer a supervisor who was a member of the Party, only 10.3 percent said yes, 21.5 percent said they would prefer to report to someone who was not a member of the Party, and the rest said they did not care.[36]

Homo Sovieticus was not indoctrinated. In fact, Homo Sovieticus did not seem to hold particularly strong opinions of any sort. His inner world consisted of antinomies, his objective was survival, and his strategy was constant negotiation—the endless circulation of games of doublethink.

But the researchers saw hope. Younger people seemed less "Soviet." Asked to define a festive occasion, for example, respondents over the age of fifty were most likely to name official holidays, beginning with the days of military glory (Soviet Army Day and Victory Day) while the younger ones would say, "when you've gotten lucky" or "when you can get together with friends and have a drink." Asked to describe their greatest fear, the older people would say "war" while the younger ones said "humiliation." Asked to name the most significant event of the twentieth century, the older respondents most often said "victory in the Great Patriotic War" while the younger ones mentioned Stalinist Terror more often than anything else.[37]

Levada concluded that the second part of his hypothesis, which held that Homo Sovieticus was dying off, was correct, and that this was inevitable. "One of the outcomes of these deals with the devil," he wrote, referring to the constant "games" Homo Sovieticus played, "is the disintegration of the structure of personality itself." Homo Sovieticus was caught in an infinite spiral of lies: pretending to be, pretending to have, pretending to believe, and pretending not to. The fakery concerned the most basic of facts and the most fundamental of values, and what lay at the bottom of the spiral was an absence: "even to understand the word 'doublethink' involved the use of doublethink." The system destroyed the individual and the fabric of society: nothing was possible in the absence of everything, resulting, wrote Levada, in "the falling standards of education, culture, morality, in the degradation of all of society." If the Soviet person was ultimately an absence, then he could not reproduce. "Therefore we can view the Homo Sovieticus as a transient historical event," concluded Levada. The Soviet man would go extinct, and so would the USSR.

PART TWO

REVOLUTION

five

SWAN LAKE

IN LATE DECEMBER 1991, Masha was on a train with her mother. They were going to spend New Year's in Poland. Tatiana had been going there for a couple of years: since the stores in Moscow had emptied out completely and tutoring could no longer buy them a semblance of comfort, she had become one of Russia's first *chelnoki*—"shuttles," people who made their living by importing goods in quantities small enough to be carried as personal luggage. Tatiana trafficked in wares that had just last year been exotic but were now consumer goods: feminine pads, erotic magazines, and other intimate items everyone needed and no one had. The journey from Moscow to Warsaw took twenty-one comfortable hours: the train left in the afternoon and arrived the following morning. A few hours after pulling out of Moscow's Belorussky Station, the train crossed an invisible border.

"Belorussia," said Tatiana. "Here it is. Yesterday it was still ours. Today, it's a separate country."

Masha, who was in second grade, was not sure what this meant.

"Is Poland still ours?" she asked.

"Shush," snapped Tatiana, and looked at the two Polish women who shared their compartment, to make sure they had not been paying attention.

That discussion was over. On other occasions that year, Tatiana had tried to explain things to her daughter, generally confounding her further each time. In January, she told Masha that they would never again travel to Lithuania, where they had spent the previous August at the Baltic seaside resort of Palanga. Now, she said, "we" had done something terrible there and the people of Lithuania would forever hate Russians. Masha had never really thought of herself as a part of some "we" who were Russians. At the Central Committee preschool the teachers had talked of "us" being "the Soviet people." The Soviet people had, for example, defeated the German fascists in the Great Patriotic War. Actually, it was difficult to think of another example of something "the Soviet people" had done, but then, the Great Patriotic War was enough—to know who the people were, and who Masha was.

In first grade, Masha's teacher also talked about the Great Patriotic War and the Soviet people, but added a children's subset to the category: the first-graders would be joining the Little Octobrists, the Communist Party's wing for seven-to-ten-year-olds. Over the decades, the Little Octobrists followed the Party's broadening trajectory: the organization had started out as small and voluntary, drawing politically motivated children, but by the 1960s all primary school children were inducted, wholesale, in first grade.[1] The ceremony usually took place in the fall, and from that point on every child wore a Little Octobrist pin on the lapel of his uniform. It was a red metal five-pointed star, with a picture of a toddler-age wavy-haired Vladimir Lenin in gold in the circle in the middle. Once inducted, Little Octobrists would be organized into "little stars"—groups of five, each with its own leader who reported to the class leader, who, in turn, reported to a mentor from within the school's Young Pioneer organization—the ten-to-fourteen-year-olds' segment of the Communist Party.

In Masha's year, the ceremony had to be postponed due to a shortage of Little Octobrist pins, so she spent months in anticipation. All the wide-ruled and large-graph green primary school notebooks had the bylaws of the Little Octobrists printed on the back cover. There were five of them:

Little Octobrists are future Young Pioneers.

Little Octobrists are studious kids. They study hard, love school, and respect their elders.

Little Octobrists are honest and truthful kids.

Little Octobrists are fun-loving kids. They read and they draw, they play and they sing, and they stick together.

Only those who work hard and persist earn the right to be called Little Octobrist.[2]

While they waited, the children learned the mythology of Communist-leader childhoods. They read Mikhail Zoshchenko's *Stories About Lenin*, written in 1940, a few years before Zoshchenko was condemned as an anti-Soviet writer and his short stories for adults were banned. The Lenin stories stayed in the curriculum, however, with the authorship de-emphasized. The stories portrayed Lenin as an extraordinary student and a loyal friend, but the story that made the biggest impression on Masha was the one called "Vase." In it, little Volodya accidentally breaks a vase while frolicking with his brothers and sisters at their aunt's house. He then lies about it and suffers pangs of conscience until, two or three months later, he makes a tearful confession to his mother, who then gets him absolved by the aunt. The story, ostensibly based on the recollections of Lenin's older sister, Anna, adds the apparently fictional detail that the other children had been so busy playing that they had not noticed who broke the vase—this serves to excuse their un-Soviet failure to denounce their little brother to the authorities.[3]

Masha also learned that another top Bolshevik, Sergei Kirov, was orphaned at an early age and spent part of his childhood in an orphanage. She did not learn that Kirov was assassinated in 1934 and that his death served as the pretext for one of the deadliest waves of Stalinist terror. She learned of a different set of deaths, though. The Bolsheviks—Lenin, Kirov, and others whose names she did not yet know—had killed the czar. There was scant mention of the czar's name, or of his wife and children, who perished with him. The killing of the czar was presented in a nondramatic, neutral manner, as an event that had been dictated by the laws of history.

Tatiana said this was wrong. Lenin had been no hero. He was bad. Did this mean that the czar was good? No, not really.

In fact, no one in the family shared Masha's joy when she finally became a Little Octobrist in March 1991. Her grandparents said it was nothing to be proud of. Yes, they affirmed, Lenin was bad. He had instigated something they called the Red Terror. The Chebotarev family did not do the Communist Party. Galina Vasilyevna's father had been a highly placed Party apparatchik who failed to stand up for his Jewish wife during Stalin's antisemitic purges of the late 1940s. His had been a fairly typical predicament. Most famously, Stalin's foreign minister, Vyacheslav Molotov, had seen his Jewish wife arrested. Masha's grandfather Boris Mikhailovich had his own reasons to dislike the Party, though he never mentioned them directly. He had been drafted into the Red Army in 1945, at the age of eighteen, and shipped directly to the front line, which by then was in Germany. He spent the next six years in Berlin, where he served in what he invariably called "the occupying army." He deflected any questions about his time in the service with a statement of unparalleled bitterness: "I hate German women and Jews." If pressed, he would add only that he hated the Jews because they invented Communism.

A dozen years earlier, before Masha was born, Tatiana, then a student, had been told to join the Party. A representative at the university told her that the physics department had been instructed to admit one top student to the Party, and Tatiana was it. At twenty-four, Tatiana was a samizdat-reading Soviet cynic, and joining the Party appeared to her as an opportunistic, morally indifferent option. Her parents surprised her with their principled opposition. "This is not a done thing," they said. The university's Party organization would not take no for an answer: it had quotas to fill. Galina Vasilyevna and Boris Mikhailovich started getting phone calls at work: "Why doesn't your daughter want to join the Party?" The threat was hardly veiled: both Boris Mikhailovich and Galina Vasilyevna were non–Party members working for secret Soviet institutions. Theirs were exceptions of long standing, negotiated thanks to Galina Vasilyevna's father's Party status and Boris Mikhailovich's six-year military service, but they could be revoked. In the end, Tatiana managed to secure her own exception: she had been tutoring a classmate who had entered the department after his military service, as a standing Party member, and with his own exceptions made to the competitive admissions process. The department needed him, he needed Tatiana to continue his studies, and she needed him to make the Party organization leave her alone.

Galina Vasilyevna retired from her space-shuttle job in 1990. Alexander Men, the intellectual priest who had brought her to the Church, was murdered in 1990, but Galina Vasilyevna's spiritual quest had already taken her away from religion, to the TV, where a hypnotist by the name of Anatoly Kashpirovsky was making frequent appearances. As his live shows demonstrated, he had healing powers, so Galina Vasilyevna, like millions of other Soviet citizens, was holding widemouthed glass jars of tap water up to the television set to obtain a healing charge. Masha's grandfather also spent an inordinate amount of time in front of the screen, though he had no use for Kashpirovsky. For the first time in his life, he was interested in something other than his work and his bitter feelings about the Great Patriotic War: politics. He loved what he called "the democrats." This was a relatively small group, no more than 300 out of the 2,249 delegates to the periodic Congresses of People's Deputies of the USSR. It included, most notably, the dissident physicist Sakharov, along with a number of newly politicized academics and professionals and a few unorthodox Communist Party functionaries. Very little united them, except all were able to get behind Sakharov's opposition to the primacy of the Communist Party in Soviet politics and affairs of state. After Sakharov died in December 1989, Boris Yeltsin, the head of the Moscow Party organization, became the sole leader of the "democrats." Boris Mikhailovich loved Yeltsin like he had perhaps never loved anyone. Yeltsin was locked in mortal combat with Gorbachev, who oscillated on reform and would not cede the Communist Party. In 1990, Yeltsin resigned from the Party. Within a year, so did roughly four million other people—more than a fifth of the Party's total membership.[4]

In March 1991, the month Masha was inducted into the Little Octobrists, Gorbachev banned street protests in Moscow, in an effort to silence Yeltsin and his supporters. There were tanks in the streets, but the protests went ahead anyway, and Boris Mikhailovich went with hundreds of thousands of others and chanted "Yel-tsin!" In June, with millions of others, Boris Mikhailovich voted to elect Yeltsin president of Russia—no one was quite sure what this meant, considering that Russia was a part of the USSR, but it was an important part of the struggle.

SERYOZHA'S GRANDFATHER, Alexander Nikolaevich, did not want to leave the Communist Party. In the end, the choice was made for him. In a couple of years, he had gone from being one of the most powerful men in the Politburo (which numbered between twelve and fourteen members out of the more than four hundred people on the Central Committee[5]) to a pariah within the Party.

For over a generation before Gorbachev came to power, Politburo membership had generally been a lifetime appointment. When a member died, he was mechanically replaced by a candidate long held in reserve, often scarcely younger than the departed. Gorbachev started reshuffling the Central Committee's leadership several times a year, in an uphill battle to bring in fresh blood and shore up his own position at the same time. In his memoirs he notes, for example, that he chose to replace one Politburo member after he started nodding off during meetings—and the tone of the description makes clear this was a familiar symptom.[6] When Alexander Nikolaevich first joined the Politburo as a full member in June 1987, Gorbachev put him in charge of ideology. In September of the following year, Gorbachev undertook one of his largest shake-ups of the bureaucracy. He brought in Vladimir Kryuchkov, a top state security officer who came highly recommended by Alexander Nikolaevich. Kryuchkov would now run the KGB. Gorbachev also freed up the post of the Politburo member in charge of foreign affairs—and he decided to move Alexander Nikolaevich into that role.[7] Now he had his own handpicked people in the most sensitive posts.

Over the next year and a bit, Alexander Nikolaevich oversaw the rapid disintegration of the Eastern Bloc. Historian Stephen Kotkin has called the Bloc the Soviet Union's "outer empire," like the "outer party" in Orwell's *1984*.[8] If the Soviet Union, with its fifteen constituent republics, was the inner empire, then the other countries of the Warsaw Pact—Bulgaria, Czechoslovakia, East Germany, Hungary, Poland, and Romania—formed the outer empire. The Soviet Union gained dominion over these six countries in the post–Second World War negotiations with the Allied Powers. Initially, the arrangement also included Yugoslavia and Albania, but they wrestled free of Soviet influence in the 1940s and the 1960s, respectively. Each pursued its own leaders' version of socialism—a freer version of Soviet society in the case of Yugoslavia, and hard-line Stalinism in the case of Albania. Hungary, Czechoslovakia, and, to some extent, Poland attempted to break ranks over the years, but the Soviet Union brutally repressed these efforts—with military action in Hungary in 1956 and in Czechoslovakia in 1968, and a sort of preemptive imposition of martial law in Poland in 1981. Now Alexander Nikolaevich's mandate was inaction. He received an unending stream of visitors, representatives of those he called "friends" in his reports—the Communist parties of each of the satellites, who by turn tested the waters, asked for support, guidance, and permission. They were able to secure more permission than anything else.

One after another, the Eastern European states allowed protests, which quickly grew massive, and opened borders and attempted some measure of free elections with the participation of rapidly forming parties that were not Communist. Most places, the ruling party sat down with the opposition in what were called "round tables" and then exited the scene peacefully if not gracefully, leaving the ad hoc groups of former dissidents, academics, student activists, and trade union organizers to sort out the mess of turning a Soviet-style state with a command economy and a one-party system into a functioning democracy. In Romania, where the Party would not budge, a rebellious army seized and executed the Communist dictator and his wife. But the revolutions elsewhere were described by both local and Western press as "velvet."

The soft luxurious texture of these transformations was guaranteed by the passivity overseen by Alexander Nikolaevich. After regime change in its satellites, the USSR began pulling its military, secret police, and political personnel out of these countries. This was a complicated, expensive, and ill-prepared operation that often added homegrown insult to the moral injury of the personnel being decommissioned in a turnaround no one had bothered to warn them about. A KGB agent who was stationed in the East German city of Dresden would later describe the experience as frightful and humiliating.[9] The agent's name was Vladimir Putin.

In the logic of perestroika, the pullout from Eastern Europe was inevitable: the "outer empire" was costing the Soviet Union too much, and the continued occupation of these countries could not be justified in the new ideology of openness. But Gorbachev, and Alexander Nikolaevich, imagined that the chain reaction would somehow stop at the Soviet border and the "inner empire" would remain intact.

ALEXANDER NIKOLAEVICH had never thought of the USSR as an empire. No one did, not even the Soviet Union's foes—even when Ronald Reagan called the country "the evil empire," his emphasis fell solely on "evil," by which he meant godless.[10] Czarist Russia had been an empire, and during the civil war of 1918–1922, the Red Army took on a number of different national-liberation armies that were fighting the center more than they were fighting Bolshevism. Large chunks of the empire broke off and established independent nation-states: Armenia, Azerbaijan, Georgia, Finland, Estonia, Latvia, Lithuania, Poland, and Ukraine. Of these, only five countries around the Baltic Sea—Finland, Estonia, Latvia, Lithuania, and Poland—got to keep their independence while Moscow reconquered the rest. Over the next several years, the Soviet government developed an entirely novel method of managing potentially troublesome regions. Historian Terry Martin has called the resulting system an "affirmative action empire."

At the basis of the affirmative action empire lay the belief that nationalism was a "masking ideology"—the need for national identity would fall away as class consciousness took hold and a stronger, socialist identity developed. National interests would naturally be superseded by class interests. Until that happened, however, national identities and national interests had to be acknowledged—but only insofar as they did not threaten the unity of the Soviet state. The Bolsheviks created a maze of national republics—starting with four (Russia, Ukraine, Belorussia, and the Transcaucasian Republic) and then subdividing them and conquering new territories for a total of eleven. Education and cultural production in the national language were encouraged in the republics. The largest, Russia, was an exception: both the expression and cultivation of a Russian national identity were strongly discouraged. Other ethnic groups living on the territory of the Russian republic were, however, pressed to assert themselves. Indeed, tiny ethnic groups were "discovered" and the number of ethnicities in Soviet Russia kept growing—for a time. In the 1930s the policy was rolled back, whether because of Russians' resentment, Stalin's paranoia (he feared subjects who might have connections to members of their ethnic groups living elsewhere in the world), or because the contradictions between the policy and its theoretical underpinnings had become too glaring—or for all these reasons. The practice of fostering national education and culture was scaled down. The Russian ethnicity was officially redeemed, and indeed the leading role of the Russian people began to be emphasized in most propaganda. The official expression of this new approach was "friendship of the peoples." The affirmative action empire was over. All peoples were equal, but the Russian nation was "first among equals." The phrase first appeared in a *Pravda* front-page editorial:

> All the peoples [of the USSR], participants in the great socialist construction project, can take pride in the results of their work. All of them from the smallest to the largest are equal Soviet patriots. But

the first among equals is the Russian people, the Russian workers, the Russian toilers, whose role in the entire Great Proletarian Revolution, from the first victory to today's brilliant period of its development, has been exclusively great.[11]

This was 1936—about a decade before Orwell's *Animal Farm*, with its principle that "some animals are more equal than others."

A campaign of concerted promotion of the Russian language, culture, art, and people began. The language was anointed the greatest of all the languages of the USSR. A 1937 editorial proclaimed: "In the center of the mighty family of peoples of the USSR stands the great Russian people, passionately loved by all the peoples of the USSR, the first among equals."[12] The constitution adopted in 1936 stated that the USSR was a "state union formed on the basis of the voluntary unification of equal Soviet Socialist Republics," each of which had the right to secede.[13]

In 1939–1940, in accordance with a pact Stalin signed with Hitler, the Soviet Union annexed some of the territories of the former Russian Empire, including a part of Poland (which was integrated into Ukraine and Belorussia), a chunk of Romania (which became Moldavia), a part of Finland (which eventually became a part of the Russian Republic), and the Baltic states of Estonia, Latvia, and Lithuania, which became republics within the Soviet Union—with the theoretical right to secession. The constitution adopted in 1977, which Alexander Nikolaevich helped draft, added that the USSR was "multinational" and a federation. At the same time, the constitution gave the central government complete control over policy, including the command economy, and provided no guarantees of representation of the republics in the central government.[14] Each of the constituent republics had its own cookie-cutter constitution, which gave it virtually no control over law, policy, or budget, even on paper. Yet every republic was, on paper, a "sovereign state." The Russian Republic itself was a federation that contained sixteen different "autonomous republics" that were also "states," plus dozens of other territorial units. None of these, however, had the right to secede from the Russian Soviet Federated Socialist Republic.[15]

In the daily experience of the Soviet citizen, living in one or another constituent republic meant little. Quality of life was determined by individual privilege and, to a lesser extent, by proximity to the center. For visitors from other republics, life in the Baltics appeared strikingly different—in large part because these republics were annexed later and retained some of their pre-Soviet infrastructure and culture; fewer people there spoke Russian, while other republics had been subjected to decades of learning the greatest of all languages. All Soviet citizens, however, were aware of their ethnicity, which was never neutral information—it could confer advantages where vestiges of affirmative action remained, or open one up to official discrimination or persecution if one's ethnic group was currently suspect. Policies and practices regarding different Soviet ethnicities shifted shapes frequently, and one had to be alert to successfully navigate the terrain of the "friendship of the peoples."

In other words, the Soviet system of managing both the republics and the various ethnic groups who populated them was inherently contradictory. Soviet Russia had once declared itself to be the world's first multiethnic anti-imperial state, yet its practices were imperial. It was another of the games the Soviet state played, much like the "We pretend to work and they pretend to pay us" game.

PERSONAL

Mikhail Sergeevich,

Some mathematical problems have no solution. They cannot be solved. Mathematics has methods for proving that a
problem is unsolvable.

Karabakh is such a problem. It cannot be solved. There is
no optimal solution. Any conceivable solution will be
unacceptable to one of the two sides.[16]

Alexander Nikolaevich wrote this note to Gorbachev in January 1988. For months, tension had been building between the republics of Armenia and Azerbaijan in the Caucasus concerning Nagorny Karabakh, an ethnic Armenian enclave that was part of Azerbaijan. This was the first region in the Soviet Union to cry foul in the nationalism/internationalism game. The impossibility of a solution was obvious: Azerbaijan was never going to cede the territory to Armenia, and Armenia was never again going to be satisfied with Armenians living in Azerbaijan on what it thought of as historic Armenian land. One could, of course, have argued that it did not matter where a Soviet citizen lived, since republics had no real authority. But the fragile balance between symbolism and lived experience, identity and perception, had been shattered.

The Armenians appealed to Moscow for help. Alexander Nikolaevich was shocked by the depth of the conflict. He had always thought of nationalism as a retrograde ideology whose adherents were a priori in the wrong, making their opponents, invariably, right. Now he saw the face of ethnic conflicts the world over: no one was in the right. "It's time to stop wasting time and effort looking for a *solution* and, instead, look for *a way out* of the predicament in which we find ourselves," he wrote to Gorbachev. Alexander Nikolaevich proposed imposing direct Moscow rule in the region and, in the interests of lowering tensions, reintroducing full censorship in both Armenia and Azerbaijan. He proposed to "abstain completely from using any visual information (televised images, photographs, documentary film footage etc.) other than precleared materials of a positive nature."[17]

It did not work. About a month after Alexander Nikolaevich wrote the letter, the Nagorny Karabakh regional council, until then a ceremonial body, resolved to secede from Azerbaijan and join Armenia. Two days later, fighting broke out. The Politburo attempted to intervene by removing the head of the Nagorny Karabakh Party organization. Anti-Armenian pogroms broke out in Azerbaijan. Moscow removed Party bosses of both Armenia and Azerbaijan. Each republic voted to consider Nagorny Karabakh its own. Moscow sided with Azerbaijan. More anti-Armenian pogroms followed. Armenia expelled ethnic Azeris. Gorbachev had the Nagorny Karabakh secessionist movement leaders arrested (they were released six months later). Azerbaijan's Supreme Soviet voted to secede from the USSR. Anti-

Armenian pogroms broke out in the Azerbaijan capital, Baku, a large, opulent city—one of the world's first oil capitals, where Azeris, Armenians, Jews, and assorted others had thrived for over a century. Now ninety Armenians were dead and the rest of the Armenians of Baku became refugees. Chess champion Garry Kasparov, a Baku native of Armenian-Jewish descent, chartered a plane to evacuate his family and as many other Armenians as the vessel could fit. Soviet troops entered Baku a week after the pogroms began and killed about 130 people. Armenia voted to secede from the USSR.[18] It was now August 1990—two and a half years after Alexander Nikolaevich wrote the letter urging Gorbachev to seek a way out rather than a solution.

The Soviet Union was splitting along all of its seams. Gorbachev, though he may not have followed Alexander Nikolaevich's recommendations precisely, had been doing nothing but looking for a way out instead of solutions. Organizations that called themselves "popular fronts"—a term coined in Nagorny Karabakh—appeared, one after another, in Lithuania, Latvia, and Estonia, as well as Ukraine and Belorussia. All proclaimed support for perestroika as their goal, but it quickly emerged that their goals did not match Gorbachev's.[19] The Baltic republics, where there was still a living awareness that there had been a life before the Soviets, wanted their independence back. On August 23, 1989, as many as two million people formed a human chain connecting Vilnius, Riga, and Tallinn, the capitals of the three republics. If this count is correct, then one in four residents of the region participated in the peaceful protest, called the Baltic Way. The date was the fiftieth anniversary of the signing of the Hitler-Stalin pact that had granted the Baltics to the USSR. These people did not want to secede: they wanted an end to the occupation.

Five days earlier, Alexander Nikolaevich had given perhaps the most difficult interview of his life: he told the *Pravda* that the pact, known as the Molotov-Ribbentrop Pact, and the secret protocols that divided Europe, existed. The USSR had denied the existence of the protocol for five decades. Just ten weeks before the fiftieth anniversary of the signing, Alexander Nikolaevich had hastily convened a commission to formulate a new, glasnost-appropriate stance on the pact. He was ill prepared, and he was not even entirely sure, at the start, that the secret protocol existed: the USSR had not preserved an original copy. Still, he felt, it was essential for official Moscow to say something to distance Gorbachev from Stalin, on the one hand, and on the other, to de-escalate tensions with the Baltics.[20] The line he took in the *Pravda* interview was to acknowledge the protocols but not the occupation: Moscow would still claim that the Baltic states had voluntarily joined the empire. The hedge failed. Alexander Nikolaevich dealt a blow to the all-important myth of the infallibility of Soviet action in the Second World War, but from the point of view of the Baltics, his revelation was painfully insufficient. In a few months, Lithuania took a declaratory step toward independence: its Communist Party decided to sever ties with the Soviet Party organization. This was a double blow—to the Soviet Union and to the Party.

ARTICLE 6 of the Constitution of the USSR stated, "The Communist Party of the Soviet Union is the leading and directive force of Soviet society and the nucleus of its political system." In other words, it had the monopoly on everything. Two bureaucracies existed—the Party one and the state one—but a single career ladder fed both, and Soviet bosses moved between Party and state jobs, often combining them.

In June 1989, during the first Congress of People's Deputies of the USSR, as the entire country watched, glued to the television, the recently elected Sakharov called for the abolition of Article 6. If the country failed to distribute power, he warned, perestroika would fail.[21] What he was proposing sounded impossible even to Sakharov's allies at the Congress. But in just six months, when the pro-democracy faction formed a movement they called Democratic Russia, they proclaimed the fight against the Communist Party's monopoly their top goal.[22] Sakharov had died a week earlier. Yeltsin became the singular leader of Democratic Russia. He had come up through the Party's hierarchy, but his views were changing faster than those of any other top-level Communist.

In the spring of 1990, Estonia and Latvia declared null and void all documents that made them a part of the USSR. In June, the Russian Republic, which now had its own parliament—chaired by Yeltsin—voted to assert "state sovereignty," though no one knew what that might mean. The following month, Yeltsin resigned from the Communist Party, and this meant that the largest Soviet republic, the first among equals, now had a leader who was not a member of the Party.

Alexander Nikolaevich disliked Yeltsin, his naked populism and his unabashed ambition. Alexander Nikolaevich was committed to reforming the system rather than destroying it, but as perestroika progressed, the distinction proved increasingly fuzzy. Sometimes, reform, as opposed to destruction, looked simply impossible. By late 1989, Alexander Nikolaevich came to the conclusion that the Soviet Union needed to be transformed into a federation, each of whose members would have tangible legislative independence and economic responsibility.[23] But he expected patience and trust from the republics. In October 1989, Zbigniew Brzezinski, the Polish-born former national security adviser and scholar of totalitarianism who had counseled a succession of American presidents, came to Moscow and, among other questions, asked Alexander Nikolaevich what would happen if the Baltics ratcheted up their calls for independence. Alexander Nikolaevich said that this would be the end of perestroika because Gorbachev needed everyone to try to ride things out as a union.[24] Brzezinski was unimpressed. He titled his next book *The Grand Failure*, and in it he condemned not only the Soviet experiment but also Gorbachev's efforts at reform. He predicted that only Poland and Hungary might have a shot at a peaceful transition and a post-Communist future. For the Soviet Union, he laid out five pessimistic scenarios, two of which involved coups, either by the military or by the KGB, and one, the outright collapse of the regime.[25]

Alexander Nikolaevich feared the failure of perestroika perhaps more than anything else. He kept lashing out at the Party's conservatives for holding the process back, and at times it seemed like Gorbachev had stopped listening to him altogether: all he was doing at any given point was looking for a stopgap measure, a way to balance the teetering union at the edge of a precipice. In the summer of 1990, following Russia's declaration of sovereignty (whatever it meant), the conservative wing pressured Gorbachev to introduce a state of emergency. He went halfway: he abolished the deliberative top government bodies of the USSR in favor of a cabinet and a security council under direct presidential control, but he refused to declare a state of emergency. But in January 1991, without any formal declaration, he allowed his ministers of defense and of the interior and the head of the KGB to try to retake the Baltics. This was exactly two years after the bloodshed in Baku, on a different edge of the empire. This time, nineteen people died: fifteen in Vilnius and four in Riga.[26] This was why Masha's mother told her they would never be welcome in Lithuania again.

Alexander Nikolaevich had known nothing of the planned intervention, and he did not know what to say to journalists who questioned him about the killings in Vilnius. He had not spoken to Gorbachev in days. He was not even sure he had a job any longer. One thing he knew for certain now, though, was that he had changed his mind about the nature of the Union: he decided that "friendship of the peoples" had been, at best, a delusion.[27]

For a few days after Vilnius, some Soviet citizens assumed and others feared that the conservatives had taken over, perestroika had ended, and the only remaining question was how fast, and how far, reforms would be rolled back. But Gorbachev continued his balancing act, over a precipice that seemed to grow only deeper: both sides were now sure at all times that he was unduly favoring the other. Gorbachev scheduled a referendum on the future of the country. The single question citizens of the USSR were asked to consider: "Do you believe it is necessary to preserve the Union of Soviet Socialist Republics as a renewed federation of sovereign republics with equal rights, where the rights and freedoms of people of all nationalities will be fully guaranteed?" It was not clear what the legal and practical consequences would be, or even what the question meant, since, with the exception of the words "renewed federation," it said the same thing as the existing Soviet constitution. Really, it was not so much a referendum as an opinion poll, with one poorly designed, overburdened question.

The Central Referendum Commission of the USSR reported that nearly 150 million people, or 80 percent of all eligible voters, took part in the referendum and that they overwhelmingly voted to preserve the Soviet Union: 76.4 percent said yes. Trouble was, all of these voters lived in nine of the fifteen republics. The Baltics and Armenia did not vote at all. In Georgia and Moldavia, the vote took place only in a couple of outlier regions. Kazakhstan offered an edited version of the referendum question, without the word "federation" or any reference to human rights.[28] The center no longer wielded sufficient power to compel different republics to coordinate efforts and questions on a referendum. There was little basis for concluding that a majority of citizens of the Soviet Union wanted the same thing, but Gorbachev interpreted the results as a mandate to draft a renewed union treaty. Yeltsin pressed on with the business of state-building in Russia. In late March—just ten days after the referendum—Gorbachev banned demonstrations in Moscow, to prevent a Yeltsin rally. Tanks blocked some of the streets in the center of the city. Demonstrators came out anyway, and no blood was shed. Once again, no one had won: the struggles between Yeltsin and Gorbachev, between the conservatives and the democrats, between the unionists and the pro-independence forces continued, almost ploddingly. On June 12, Yeltsin was overwhelmingly elected president of the Russian Republic. The new union treaty was scheduled to be signed on August 20.

Alexander Nikolaevich was, by turns, terrified, dismayed, and angry. In late April he wrote Gorbachev a letter warning him that conservative forces were gaining the upper hand. The only way forward was to stop Gorbachev's incessant political zigzagging. If Gorbachev was not going to lead decisive political and economic reform, then Alexander Nikolaevich would try to do it himself. "I must be, I absolutely must be, honest before my country, before my people, before my self!" he wrote. "I shall seek dignified ways to fight incipient fascism and the Party's reactionism, to fight for the democratic transformation of our society. I don't have that much time left."[29] Alexander Nikolaevich was speaking not so much about the time he personally had left—he was sixty-eight, just eight years older than both Gorbachev and Yeltsin—as about the country, where, he felt, the window of opportunity for change had nearly closed.

Alexander Nikolaevich decided to help form a new political movement, the Movement for Democratic Reform. It had three foundational principles. Politically, it would renounce the vision of the USSR as a unitary state in favor of creating a federation with a clear division of rights and responsibilities between members and the center. Economically, it would set out a clear program of transition to a market system, in which, for the interim period, the state would retain only a third of all property. Most important, it would create a safety net for those who would be hardest-hit by economic reform.[30] The difference between a "movement" and a "party" was as confusing as everything else in the USSR. A movement exists to create change while a party strives to govern. But in the new Soviet reality a movement could include several parties. But then, a megaparty—*the* megaparty—was starting to include different movements. For Alexander Nikolaevich, it was key that he did not need to leave the Communist Party to become one of the leaders of the new movement. He was still hoping that the massive weight of the Party could be tilted in favor of reform. On July 20, 1991, he delivered an inspired speech at the founding congress of his new movement. He spoke of the painful discoveries that he had made, most of them in the six years since perestroika began:

> We have fallen two epochs behind. We have missed the postindustrial era and the information era. As a result, our society is deeply ill. Our souls are permanently empty. We have grown to presume everyone guilty at all times, thus creating hundreds of thousands of guards watching over our morality, conscience, purity of world view, compliance with the wishes of the authorities. We have turned truth into a crime. We have robbed nature to within a breath of its life. We have created crime, queues, rudeness, corruption that goes all the way up from a store's truck unloader to a government minister. We have ostracized intellectualism and fostered a regime of the ignorant. . . .

Today we are living as though in two worlds at once. The old Stalinist world does not want to leave, and it is holding on to everything that can still prop it up. The new world is struggling to stay afloat within the old structures and often begins to act in accordance with their rules. . . .

Over the last seventy years the Communist Party of the Soviet Union has been not a party but an organization of administrative command, integrated into the structures of state as its primary Legislator, Distributor, Controller, and Monopolist on the Truth. . . . None of this is said by way of reproach. These are lessons. Marx never imagined that his analysis of early capitalism would be transformed into an ideological weapon in the struggle for power. Nor is our great people to blame for having followed its trusting nature and its passionate faith in a better life, making it vulnerable to manipulation. It would not be right to direct this criticism at the millions of ordinary Communists who have been dominated by a caste of Party bosses.[31]

This was war. Party leadership began talking about expelling Alexander Nikolaevich. A top-level member had not been expelled since the Stalin era: this seemed a fate worse than death. Death was another option. Alexander Nikolaevich got word that he might be assassinated. He drafted a letter to be opened in case of his death and then sought out the head of the KGB, his old protégé Kryuchkov, in the Kremlin corridor. "Tell your people that they've miscalculated," he said. "I've drafted a letter, and three different outlets will publish it if something happens to me."[32] On August 15, the Party Control Committee—which was precisely what its name suggests, a committee created for the control of Communists and the disciplining of any who strayed—voted to recommend Alexander Nikolaevich's expulsion.[33] Alexander Nikolaevich heard about it on the radio. On August 16, he wrote two letters. The shorter one, marked with his Party membership number—00000051—tendered his resignation.[34] The longer one was titled "An open letter to Communists on the danger of revanchism." Alexander

Nikolaevich had been working on it for over three months, but it so happened that he finished it the day the Party expelled him. Two days later, on August 18, he showed the draft to one of the other founders of the Movement for Democratic Reform, Leningrad mayor Anatoly Sobchak. Alexander Nikolaevich wanted to ensure it was clear and well-argued before sending it out. "Tragedy is possible," warned the letter, "for changes have affected the interests of the ruling elite." The letter was never sent.[35]

ON AUGUST 18, Masha's mother came to pick her up from her grandparents' dacha. She said she needed her daughter in Moscow to apply for a new foreign-travel passport for her. Three months earlier, Gorbachev had signed a new law concerning entering and exiting the USSR. The Iron Curtain was being lifted in stages. At the beginning, only a very few people were allowed to travel out of the Soviet Union, and only if they had a compelling reason and a slew of sterling character references from their place of work, their place of residence, and, preferably, the Party too. Foreign-travel passports were kept under lock and key, released only for the duration of the approved trip—no one got to keep his passport around the house. Starting in the mid-1980s, the vetting process gradually relaxed. Now the new law would make it possible for ordinary Russians to obtain five-year travel passports and even, if the law was followed to the letter, release them from the obligation to apply for an exit visa every time they wanted to travel.[36] Tatiana, whose business often took her to Poland, had long used her connections to secure a foreign-travel passport with a long-term exit visa, but with the new law, she figured she would get one for her daughter.

On August 19, Tatiana and Masha took the commuter train into the center of Moscow, then the Metro, and then an aboveground tram to their neighborhood. When the tram was passing through a tunnel at Volokolamskoye Roadway, Masha saw two tanks moving in the opposite direction.

"Wow! Cool!" said Masha.

"Fuck," said Tatiana.

She thought for a moment.

"We have to leave the country," she said. "We are getting off the tram." Her plan was to go directly to the passport office and, rather than apply for a new passport for Masha, have her name added to Tatiana's passport. Then they would go directly to the American embassy, where, rumor had it, anyone could get a visa just for showing up. Then they would leave the country.

The woman at the passport office refused the request and refused a bribe too. Her boss said, "Come back in a week." It was all over: there was no point in even applying for a passport for Masha. They left.

They could not go home. It had been nearly two years since Tatiana managed to get rid of their flatmate, so the apartment was no longer a communal one; Tatiana and Masha had its two rooms and a kitchen all to themselves, but now Tatiana was being harassed by the *reketiry*—a new Russian word that meant "racketeers"—a mafia in the making that was trying to ride on the coattails of private enterprise in the making. Most of these guys ran primitive protection rackets, promising to be the *krysha*—cover—that would shield you from others like them. Lately they had established a permanent post outside Tatiana's apartment door. She did not want to go there with her child, so they went to Tatiana's parents' apartment instead.

In the empty apartment, Tatiana turned on the television. *Swan Lake*, the ballet, was on. She changed the channel. *Swan Lake*. This was boring. Masha went outside into the courtyard and played with a boy named Vitalik.

AT SIX AND AT EIGHT THAT MORNING, when the radio and television channels resumed programming after their nightly break, a familiar male voice had come on the air and said, "A decree of the vice-president of the USSR. In light of the inability, for health reasons, of Mikhail Sergeevich Gorbachev to carry out his duties as president of the USSR . . . the vice-president of the USSR, Yanaev, has taken over the duties of the president of the USSR as of August 19, 1991." Then the anchor read two addresses to the people of the

USSR from people who called themselves "the Soviet leadership." First came a dry one, announcing a state of emergency effective at four that afternoon. Then came an impassioned one:

> Countrymen! Citizens of the USSR!
> It is at a critical hour for the fate of the Motherland and our peoples that we address you! A deadly danger is looming over our great Motherland! Reforms initiated by M. S. Gorbachev . . . have hit a dead end. Enthusiasm and hope have given way to distrust, apathy, and despair.

It blamed the reforms for inter-ethnic strife that had killed hundreds and turned half a million into refugees.

> Every citizen feels a growing uncertainty about what tomorrow may bring and a deep worry for the future of his children.

It blamed the reforms for the country's economic crisis.

> It is long past time to tell people the truth: failing urgent and decisive steps to stabilize the economy, the very near future will inevitably bring famine and a new wave of impoverishment.

It blamed the reforms for rising crime rates.

> The country is sinking into a quagmire of violence and lawlessness.

It promised to restore the pride, safety, and integrity of the USSR—that is, on the eve of the planned signing of the union treaty, to restore the empire to its former self. Read on the air and published in the morning's newspapers, the address was signed by the State Committee on the State of Emergency in the USSR, which numbered eight people, including Gorbachev's vice-president, Gennady Yanaev; and the head of the KGB,

Kryuchkov; as well as the prime minister and the ministers of defense and the interior—the entire conservative cadre with whom Gorbachev had recently surrounded himself.[37] It took ten minutes to read all three documents. After that, *Swan Lake* came on.

Zhanna was in the countryside outside Gorky with her grandmother. Her parents had gone to Moscow the day before—they had planned only to pass through on their way to vacation on the Black Sea. Now, with nothing but *Swan Lake* for news, Zhanna's grandmother was sure that her son was in the thick of whatever was happening in Moscow, and she was worried sick. So was Zhanna.

They were right to be worried. Raisa, Zhanna's mother, was in front of the White House, the massive high-rise of white concrete that housed the Russian Supreme Soviet. Yeltsin had declared it the headquarters of resistance to the coup, and hundreds of people gathered there. After a bit of consideration, they started building barricades. Zhanna's father, Boris, was inside the building.

IN SOLIKAMSK, where Lyosha's mother had been watching politics on television for two years, everyone was now watching the ballet on television. The grown-ups seemed subdued. In the days before *Swan Lake*, Galina's coworkers had been coming by the apartment to discuss lesson plans: the school year was starting in less than two weeks and history, it seemed, had changed again, so teaching it had to change too. The same thing had happened the summer before, and the summer before that. Now they were silent. At some point the ballet stopped and a gray picture with six old men wearing suits of different shades of gray appeared. One of them introduced the rest, and each of the men half stood at the sound of his name. Lyosha remembered the name of one of the men in the middle: Yanaev. He said that Gorbachev could no longer work as president and he, Yanaev, was taking over. Lyosha also remembered the word "Foros"—it was the name of the place where Yanaev said Gorbachev was lying ill.[38]

Then there was a man on a tank, a big man surrounded by many smaller men. He held a piece of paper in his hand, and he said that something was illegal.[39] Lyosha asked his mother who it was. "That's our president," Galina said.

Then there was an airplane on the TV, against a dark sky, the sound of its engines winding down, and Gorbachev descending the stairs wearing a light casual jacket and smiling. His granddaughter followed, draped in a blanket, and Gorbachev's wife, Raisa, her arm around the girl. Gorbachev shook hands with several men, and then his face came fully into focus and a voice said, "Mikhail Sergeevich, for three days the country has been living in terrible tension, in awful worry for its president, for its future, for the fate of democracy. . . ."[40] Lyosha started crying. He loved Gorbachev so much, and he really had been so worried and so tense ever since he heard that Gorbachev was sick.

Soon it began to seem to Lyosha that all of it had happened in one day—the ballet, the three presidents on TV one after another, then Gorbachev's granddaughter with the blanket, and the tears. In fact, it had taken three days. On August 18, four men dispatched by the leaders of the coup flew to Gorbachev's dacha in Foros, in the Crimea, and effectively took Gorbachev hostage. The following morning, television broadcasts began with the state-of-emergency announcement and transitioned to *Swan Lake*. Yeltsin and his closest supporters took up their post inside the White House and his more distant supporters began to gather around the building while troops entered the city. Around noon Yeltsin climbed atop a tank parked outside the White House and declared the state of emergency illegal—but this would not be shown on television that day or the next. Instead, the gray men held their televised press conference. The people outside the White House, who now numbered in the thousands, built barricades that never could have stopped a tank, and handed out gas masks, falling far short of being able to equip everyone. The following day passed in nervous anticipation outside the White House and negotiations inside: the general who would have to lead the attack on the White House was unwilling to obey that order if it came but was not going to switch sides either. In the early-morning hours of August 21, three young men died trying to stop armored personnel carriers headed in the direction of the White House but still nearly a mile from it. By mid-afternoon six men, including the minister of defense and KGB director Kryuchkov, flew to the Crimea. A couple of hours later three men from among the coup's opponents followed them. Around two o'clock the following morning Gorbachev's plane landed in Moscow. Kryuchkov, who flew on the same plane, was immediately taken into custody: the Russian prosecutor general had already ordered the arrest of all the coup organizers. At noon on August 22 a Russian flag—white, blue, and red stripes—was raised over the White House for the first time. That afternoon Gorbachev held a press conference in which he said, "I have come back to a different country." He said that there had been an attempt to return the country to a totalitarian state and it had failed. At some point, Gorbachev had started using the word "totalitarian" to describe the regime that now seemed, finally, to have toppled. With that out of the way, he said, he would now press ahead with a new union treaty. He had already appointed ministers to replace the rebels in the Soviet government.[41]

FOR SERYOZHA, who had spent a summer in the castle-like dacha where Gorbachev was held hostage, the failed coup offered an unremarkable spectacle. He knew the girl whom the entire country watched coming out of the airplane draped in a blanket. He was used to seeing his intimates on television. What struck him more was the short conversation his father had with him. Anatoly said that he had spent the three days in front of the White House. He said it with disgust: he had hated feeling helpless, unarmed in the face of tanks.

Seryozha's grandfather Alexander Nikolaevich had been at the Moscow City Council building, where the local government was organizing its own resistance effort. He had addressed the crowd. "The most frightening thing that could happen, has happened," he said. "Never before has our land seen days so tragic."[42] But while Gorbachev thanked Yeltsin and his allies for their help in resisting the coup, he had no words of gratitude for Alexander Nikolaevich. He did not see his old ally when he returned to Moscow, and when questioned during his press conference, he reproached Alexander Nikolaevich for having caved in to the hard-liners and resigned from the Party. It seemed there might not be a place for Alexander Nikolaevich in the leadership of this new country to which Gorbachev claimed to have returned.

But what country was this? "Does the Soviet Union still exist?" became the conversation opener of the day, the week, and the autumn. The Soviet Union seemed to exist, but its form was elusive. Yeltsin's Russian Republic summarily subsumed some of the Union's governing mechanisms. Yeltsin also plainly strong-armed Gorbachev into canceling some of his first post-coup appointments. Most important, he made Gorbachev appoint an outsider of Yeltsin's choosing to run the Soviet KGB and then added the dismantling of the agency to the man's job description.[43] On August 23 and August 25, Yeltsin signed decrees that suspended the activities of both the Communist Party of the Soviet Union and the Russian Republic's own Communist Party.

On August 27—five days after the coup—Yeltsin appointed Boris Nemtsov, Zhanna's father, to run the Nizhny Novgorod region. Only three of Russia's eighty-nine regions had leaders who had been elected, their posts newly created during perestroika: the mayors of Moscow and Leningrad and the president of Tatarstan. The rest of the regions were still run by Party structures, which were now literally, physically being abandoned. Yeltsin began appointing presidential "representatives" to these regions, signing off on dozens of names a day—mostly people he did not know, who had been hurriedly recruited by his staff. Nemtsov was an exception. Yeltsin knew him and liked him, and after spending three days in the besieged White House together, they started playing tennis with each other whenever they could. Nemtsov was thirty-one, and he would now be running Russia's third-largest city and the surrounding area. This was one of Yeltsin's more considered appointments.[44]

The union treaty, meanwhile, was crumbling. Gorbachev continued negotiating, but so did Yeltsin. The Russian president pressured the Soviet one finally to recognize the independence of the Baltic states. Even the republics that had seemed to favor the Union before the coup now declared independence. Gorbachev, however, kept trying to convene meetings on the treaty. But Ukraine, the second-largest republic, now boycotted them. Finally, on December 7, the leaders of Russia, Ukraine, and Belarus convened a meeting at which they devised the formal dissolution of the USSR and invented a consolation prize, a vague entity called the Commonwealth of Independent States. Gorbachev was not invited, and was not even the first to know: he was informed by the Belorussian leader only after Yeltsin had called the American president, George H. W. Bush, to notify him. Gorbachev raged to reporters a few days later: "I don't think our people understand yet that they are losing the country. The country will not exist!"[45]

Less than two weeks later, on December 25, Gorbachev addressed his countrymen as president for the last time: "In light of what's happened, with the foundation of the Commonwealth of Independent States, I am resigning my post as president of the USSR."[46] The Soviet Union ceased to exist.

Masha and her mother were on the train to Poland, valid passports of a nonexistent country in Tatiana's bag.

six

THE EXECUTION OF THE WHITE HOUSE

SERYOZHA REMEMBERED THIS. He was on a Metro train, on his way home from school, and when the train emerged from the tunnel onto the bridge over the Moscow River, Seryozha saw tanks. He got off at the next stop to board the train going in the opposite direction so that he could ride over the bridge again and look at the tanks. Then he did it again, and again, and again, until it was dark.

When he was an adult, he wondered whether this was a memory from 1991 or 1993. He checked Wikipedia, but then he forgot. He checked again, and searched for a mnemonic device, but then forgot again. Eventually he resigned himself to looking it up every six months or so.

SERYOZHA COULD BE FORGIVEN for being perpetually unable to pin down what had happened to the country in which he was born: much older people, learned observers and passionate participants in the events alike, had similar difficulties. Several narratives finally emerged. Harvard historian Serhii Plokhy has argued that the USSR collapsed because it was an empire in the century that ended empires: the process may have taken longer and looked different from the deaths of other empires because of the peculiarities of Soviet state-building and ideology, but that did not change the forces that pulled the Soviet Union apart.[1] Zbigniew Brzezinski, who predicted the Soviet collapse—and the 1991 coup—wrote that a basic paradox would bring the country down: its economy had dead-ended, and to survive economically it would have to reform politically, which would inevitably destroy the state's entire system. But if, he posited, the country wanted to preserve its political system, it would fail economically.[2]

More than a decade later, Princeton historian Stephen Kotkin wrote the story of the Soviet collapse as precipitated by Gorbachev himself, by oscillating between pursuing reform and not, constantly trying to fight a process he had set in motion.[3] In other disciplines, University of California at Berkeley anthropologist Alexei Yurchak has also written that the Soviet Union was brought down by its own paradoxes, falling into the gap between the governing ideology and lived reality—a gap that exists and can produce a crisis in any society.[4] And, of course, Yuri Levada and his team of sociologists predicted that the Soviet Union would die off because Homo Sovieticus, who held up all of its institutions, would go extinct.

With the exception of Brzezinski, who was a student and theorist of totalitarianism, and Levada, who proposed the Homo Sovieticus model, all these explanations try to make sense of the demise of the USSR in terms imported from very different societies. The loss of the social sciences in the Soviet Union made this inevitable: Soviet society had been forbidden to know itself, and had no native language to describe and define what had happened. The occasional *fortochka*s that opened up the possibility of self-examination were usually too small to allow scholars to adjust and adapt imported models, or to invent their own. Yurchak, who grew up in the Soviet Union but received his graduate education in the United States in the 1990s, provides probably the most obvious example of the ill fit of foreign models. He lacks the tools to explore the ways in which the gaps between ideology and reality in the Soviet Union differed from the gaps in Western countries, for which his model was devised. In functioning democracies the contradictions between avowed ideals and reality can be and often are called out, causing social and political change. That does not eliminate the built-in gap, but it has a way of making societies a little more democratic and a little less unequal, in spurts. Totalitarian ideology allows no such correction. Hannah Arendt maintained that any ideology can become totalitarian, but for that to happen it needs to be reduced to a single simple idea, which is then turned into a single simple idea from which the ostensible "laws of history" are derived—and enforced through terror.[5] What distinguishes a totalitarian ideology is its utterly insular quality. It purports to explain the entire world and everything in it. There is no gap between totalitarian ideology and reality because totalitarian ideology contains all of reality within itself.

That quality of Soviet ideology is also the problem with Plokhy's argument that the USSR fell apart because it was an empire. Not only did the Soviet state not consider itself an empire, it claimed to be the opposite of one. That self-concept did not change during the Soviet dismantling or later, when Russia became its own federation of different territories, cultures, and ethnic groups. Of course, one can argue that an empire does not stop being an empire just because it says it is not one—a dog does not stop being a dog just because it identifies with its friend the cat—but an empire is unarguably a sociopolitical construction, and what it thinks of itself matters. To pass, like other empires in the twentieth century, into a post-imperial future, Russia would have had to reform its identity accordingly. But not even Yeltsin, who played perhaps the most important role in taking the Soviet Union apart, thought of it, or of Russia, as an empire.

Kotkin's explanation for the disintegration of the Soviet state is, essentially, mismanagement: Gorbachev flailed until nothing worked. Kotkin's is a view from the top of the process of institutional collapse that Levada had predicted from the bottom. But neither man focused on the connections between persons and institutions, the glue that holds societies together.

When the word "totalitarianism" is used in casual Western speech, it conjures the image of a monstrous society in which force is applied to every person at all times. Of course, that would be impossibly inefficient, even for an extremely inefficient state such as the Soviet Union. The economy of force in totalitarian societies is achieved through terror. Totalitarianism establishes its own social contract, in which most people will be safe from violence most of the time, provided they stay within certain boundaries and shoulder some of the responsibility for keeping other citizens within the same boundaries. The boundaries are ever-shifting—Arendt described totalitarian societies as producing a state of constant flux and inconsistency[6]— and this requires the population to be ever-vigilant in order to stay abreast of the shifts. A hypersensitivity to signals is essential for survival.

ONE AREA in which Soviet citizens learned to be hypersensitive to signals was the regulation of private life. The party line on the family kept changing over the course of Soviet history. Right after the 1917 Revolution, marriage was abandoned and the family was willed to wither away. Less than twenty years later, the family was officially redeemed and even consecrated as the "nucleus of Soviet society."[7] In the years immediately following the Revolution, homosexuality was tolerated (but, contrary to myth, not celebrated or even really accepted), but in 1934 it was recriminalized.[8] As the pendulum swung back, divorce was made prohibitively difficult, and abortion, legal and common in the 1920s, was outlawed.[9] Faced with a crisis of depopulation after the Second World War, the Soviet Union first made divorce even more difficult and then reversed direction, taking measures, instead, to encourage single motherhood by legitimizing, in effect, multiple relationships.[10] In the mid-1950s, however, abortion was again legalized.[11]

The legal shifts demanded that Soviet citizens change not only their behavior but also their very outlook on life—and the social contract dictated that the state send out reasonably clear signals and the population react accordingly. Signals were sent through propaganda in newspapers, movies, and books; through legal changes; and through enforcement, with demonstrative punishment of the few keeping the many in line (the proportion of those being punished to those observing shifted after the death of Stalin, and this solidified the principle of teaching by frightening example). It was this system of signaling and response that broke down by 1991.

The milestones of the breakdown were large and small. In 1988, Gorbachev released all political prisoners. The same year, Novodvorskaya and her allies held that outrageous congress founding the country's first alternative political party, the Democratic Union, and ignoring the threats and summonses from the KGB (which their party proposed to abolish). The way Gorbachev was zigzagging, the release of all political prisoners did not mean that dissidents would never again be jailed—it was the Democratic Union's rejection of the KGB's signals that made the secret police powerless against them. In March 1991, Gorbachev used tanks in the streets of Moscow to signal his resolve to put an end to pro-Yeltsin demonstrations—and hundreds of thousands of Muscovites ignored this signal. That month, as the country prepared for the referendum on the Union, Central Committee functionaries were frantically trying to keep the country in check. They banned a women's forum planned in Dubna, a nuclear-science town a couple of hours outside Moscow, after a newspaper reported that among the young academics now hungrily cramming gender theory, older dissidents who had been publishing underground feminist journals, labor activists focusing on women's rights, and a dozen foreign dignitaries, there would be two out lesbians from the United States. But one of the foreign guests—Colette Shulman, a New York journalist and academic who had long cultivated relationships among the Soviet elite—intervened, and the organizers' arrangements were reinstated even though the newspaper, and the lesbians, rejected the request for a retraction.[12]

The Russian politician Yegor Gaidar described similar incidents in his memoir. In the late 1980s he served as economics editor at *Kommunist*, a journal of the Central Committee.

> *Kommunist* pages now contained words that had been unthinkable as applied to a socialist economy: inflation, unemployment, poverty, social inequality, budget deficit. We published the first realistic

estimates of military spending. . . . Periodically a call would come in from the Central Committee's headquarters.

"What are you doing? Since when is this issue subject to public discussion?"

Such calls were generally easy to handle. I would ask in response, "Don't you know?" The caller, a bureaucrat who could not be sure of what the latest party line was, would shrink back and leave me alone.[13]

The Party's signaling system had ceased functioning, and this in turn rendered the ideology no longer hermetic—in effect, no longer totalitarian.

Four months after the women's forum, the two American lesbian activists and their Soviet partners held a gay and lesbian film festival and a series of workshops, first in Leningrad and then in Moscow. Mindful of the feminists' experience, they made backup arrangements in case they lost their venues. But the festival proceeded without incident, in a centrally located "house of culture" in Leningrad and a similarly central movie theater in Moscow. Both venues belonged to the state, but by now they could be rented for a few hundred dollars. The organizers were able to bring into the country reels with gay-themed films, though neither censorship nor criminal penalties for homosexual conduct had been abolished. At the end of the festival, they even rented a restaurant in central Moscow and held the country's first nonclandestine gay party. By this time, Moscow had a few "cooperative" restaurants—a perestroika-era euphemism for newly legalized private businesses—but this was not one of them: the gay party was held at the Central House of the Workers of the Arts, which for six decades had served the elite who serviced the ideology.

In the four months between the feminist forum and the gay festival the government had not shifted its stance on homosexuality or on private life more generally, but between rapid political change and new economic exigencies—every venue needed hard currency—the system of signaling and response, the very social contract of Soviet society, lay in ruins. At one point during the Moscow leg of the festival, the police meekly tried to seal off the movie theater from the street by stringing construction-site flags around it. The gays cut these down with scissors, and the shows went on. In another three weeks, many of the people who had attended the gay festival were in front of the Moscow White House, preparing to push back the tanks. The American activists had given the Moscow gay group a photocopier, and it was now put to work printing Yeltsin's address to the people.

The tanks were there but never moved in on the protesters. Gaidar later described what happened as follows:

> As of August 19, 1991, there was nothing in Russian or Soviet history to give one hope that the resistance would not be brutally suppressed. The coup leaders were clearly prepared to do just that. All that was needed was someone willing to accept immediate responsibility for large-scale bloodshed and mass repressions, someone who would organize and demand action from the troops, someone who would identify the most reliable, trustworthy, and decisive of generals and place him on the leading tank, assigning to him personally the task of crushing the resistance. In other words, there had to be a person who would overcome the military's natural inertia and reluctance to accept blame. As it turned out, there was no such person among the coup plotters. Hence the back-and-forth, the inconsistency of action, the will to shift responsibility onto others, and the military's wheel-spinning.[14]

The coup organizers, in other words, tried to will the signaling system back into existence simply by issuing several decrees—and by placing the country's president under house arrest, which has to rank near the top in the hierarchy of signals—but the social contract could not be resuscitated. The army did not respond to the hard-liners' signals, but it did not pick up on signals from Yeltsin's White House either, and did not side with the resistance: it simply did not act.

FOR THE POST-SOVIET INTELLIGENTSIA and Western journalists and politicians, the most important moment in August 1991 came after the coup failed, when a giant statue of Felix Dzerzhinsky, founder of the Soviet secret police, was removed from its pedestal in the middle of Lubyanka Square, a short walk from the Kremlin, a block from the Central Committee, and right in front of KGB headquarters and the Children's World department store, which stood kitty-corner to each other. The toppling, mandated by the Moscow City Council, which wanted to beat the jubilant crowds to it for safety reasons, symbolized the simultaneous dismantling of the two pillars of totalitarianism: ideology and terror. As it was lifted by a crane, the giant monument was revealed to be hollow.

Neither Masha nor Lyosha nor Zhanna nor Seryozha remembered the toppling of Dzerzhinsky—which was televised—as the defining moment of the coup. They remembered the tanks in the streets, the ballet on television, Yeltsin on the tank, and Gorbachev on the plane. Lyosha also thought he remembered footage of Gorbachev under house arrest, but that was probably an acquired memory rather than a true one. In general, they remembered the coup not as the end—or the beginning—of an era, with a strong symbolic finale, but as one in a chain of confusing and exciting and sometimes frightening events that engaged the adults in their lives. Another such event for Lyosha was the murder, later in 1991, of Igor Talkov, a young bearded singer who performed heartrending pop songs of a new patriotism— Russian rather than Soviet. Lyosha's mother had a boyfriend now—she would marry him before the year was out—and he followed newly emerging popular culture. Like everyone else in Russia, Sergei loved Talkov. He was watching the Song of the Year contest on television when the announcer said, "Talkov has been shot." Sergei and Lyosha, sitting next to each other on the couch, saw the singer's body being carried on a stretcher; he was wearing only his underwear. Sergei cried, and so did Lyosha. It was the most frightening thing he had ever seen.

The August coup looked like only one in a chain of important events from at least one other vantage point: that of Yeltsin. He spent all that year waging his war for Russia. He was fighting on at least two fronts simultaneously, against the Party conservatives, who opposed all reform, and against Gorbachev, who wished to rein in Russia's and Yeltsin's own political ambitions. Yeltsin won several battles that year: in March he defeated Gorbachev in the battle for the streets of Moscow; in June, when Russia declared sovereignty, he won a battle against both of his opponents—a battle for the hearts of Russians. When Yeltsin triumphed over the coup in August, he eliminated one of the fronts in his war. With hard-liners no longer a force, it was just him against Gorbachev. On this front, victory was virtually assured.

In the intelligentsia's mythology, 1991 was the year of Russia's bloodless revolution. But it was not bloodless: its victims included the three men who died in Moscow in August and the nineteen people killed in Vilnius and Riga in January, and the hundreds who had died in Azerbaijan since 1988 and during the brutal breakup of a demonstration in Tbilisi, Georgia, in 1989.[15] Nor was it a revolution. For the remainder of 1991 Yeltsin focused not on destroying the institutions of the Soviet state but on taking them over. He claimed, for his newly independent Russia, the army, the central bank, and the Soviet seat in the United Nations. Wisdom in the West was that this was a good thing: most of the Soviet nuclear arsenal would be in one place, and Russia would not renege on its predecessor's foreign debt, as the Bolsheviks had done in 1917.

To a very hopeful, very anti-Soviet eye, Yeltsin might have appeared to be tackling the pillars of the totalitarian system, its machines of ideology and terror. He banned the activities of the Communist Party and he tasked his (nominally, Gorbachev's) new head of the KGB with dismantling the organization. But on closer inspection, the Party ban concerned economic activity—Yeltsin feared, with good reason, that the Party apparatus would siphon off what remained of its wealth. The dismantling of the KGB was actually its partitioning into fifteen constituent parts among the republics of the USSR, which ensured that Russia inherited a functioning Soviet-style secret police.[16]

By the end of 1991, Yeltsin had a country to run. But even with the former institutions of the Soviet state under his control, he faced a dire deficit of instruments of governance, and of people to use them. He appointed leaders of the constituent members of the Russian Federation—in some cases, leaders who had already emerged locally, whether they called themselves "governor," "mayor," or "president." Only a few of them were, like Boris Nemtsov, loyal to Yeltsin personally and committed to his political agenda, with its focus on the immediate introduction of the market. Nemtsov set about privatizing stores and other property in Nizhny Novgorod. An endless stream of foreigners—potential investors, Western advisers, journalists, and dignitaries—flowed into the city to talk to him. Yeltsin did not have other regional leaders to show them.

In several regions, especially Chechnya and Tatarstan, the local leader had been brought to power by a movement for national independence. Elsewhere, like in Yakutia in the far north, home to Russia's diamond mines, the push to secede was framed in terms of economic self-interest. Even a group in St. Petersburg proclaimed independence as the region's goal, only half in jest. The constitution of the Russian Republic, unlike the constitution of the USSR, did not guarantee the right to secession, but that seemed irrelevant now.

The forces pulling at Russia now were eerily similar to those that had torn apart the Soviet Union. There were also new, confounding problems. Russia was a country nearing economic ruin, surrounded by other countries nearing economic ruin. It shared a currency with them and its borders with them were porous, yet Russia held next to no political sway over them. One of these countries—Georgia—was sinking into civil war, and the neighboring regions of Russia—North Ossetia and Chechnya—were already involved in the conflict. The South Ossetians, on Georgian territory, were fighting to secede and join Russia. Over to the west, a small part of Moldova called Transdniester was fighting to join Russia, from which it was now separated by a narrow strip of independent Ukraine. Russian troops were mired in the conflict there. Russia now also acquired an exclave: Kaliningrad, the former Prussian city of Königsberg, which had been annexed and Russified by the

USSR after the Second World War and now had independent Lithuania between it and the Russian mainland.

The legal and political foundations of the new state were not entirely clear. It had a parliament of sorts, the Congress of People's Deputies, which had been elected in 1990, before Russia declared sovereignty. At its first session, in May 1990, 920 of its 1,068 members belonged to the Communist Party of the Soviet Union. A year later, only 767 Congress members remained in the Party. But even after Yeltsin banned the Communist Party's activities, a majority—675 people—maintained their Party affiliation. The Congress could pass legislation, including amendments to the constitution. The president had the right to veto legislation, but his veto could be overcome with a simple majority of the Congress.[17]

There were laws. Like every other former Soviet republic, Russia inherited criminal and civil procedure codes that banned private enterprise in nearly any guise, operations with hard currency, and being unemployed, among other things. Russia also inherited a constitution that contained virtually no information about the country's structure, principles, and identity. This was an issue common to all former Eastern Bloc countries, with the exception of East Germany: all they knew about themselves at first was that they were not what they had been. The peaceful-revolution narrative (which was more accurate in most of the other countries) compelled them to start their new state on the old legal foundation. Their success depended largely on implied political understandings. Countries amended their old Communist constitutions to make them workable, and lived with the resulting patchwork for years. But here, as in other areas, Russia's problems ran deeper because its inherited constitution did not aim to create even an illusion of statehood.

In the late fall of 1991, Yeltsin scrambled to create a functioning cabinet. He most urgently needed someone to take charge of the economy, which after the coup went from bad to dead. Both trust in and fear of command-economy authorities had evaporated, and collective farms halted grain deliveries to the centralized distribution centers: rather than fulfill their socialist obligations in exchange for worthless rubles, they would barter their goods locally. Russia's biggest cities, where the military-industrial complex dominated the economy, were hit the hardest, for they had little that could be bartered. "The country was in a state of high anxiety," Gaidar the economist wrote in his memoir. "Autumn 1991 was filled with anticipation of catastrophe, hunger, and the paralysis of transportation and heating systems. Portable coal stoves were in high demand. The dominant topic of conversation was survival."[18] Ration cards had long been introduced throughout the country, but local authorities could no longer guarantee a supply of even minimal rations.

Yeltsin asked Gaidar to figure out how the country was going to survive. Gaidar was the thirty-five-year-old scion of a privileged Soviet family, grandson of two of the country's most venerated writers and husband of the daughter of a third.* Save for a short stint as an editor, he had worked only at research institutions. He assembled a team of like-minded economists, starting with half a dozen and later adding a few more. All of them were roughly the same age and came from academia. They had no experience in government or administration of any sort, and with the exception of a few recent short trips to the West, they had never seen a market economy outside of a textbook. Their predicament was not unlike that of Levada's sociologists trying to devise their first actual survey, except this group of theoreticians was asked to prevent famine and a total collapse of the infrastructure while also reinventing the country's economy.

The group spent the fall of 1991 holed up at a government dacha outside Moscow. In the first few weeks they learned that the situation was even more dire than they had imagined. The country had no currency or gold reserves—most had been spent and the rest appeared to have been plundered. Because consumer goods had been in short supply for years, and also because prices for all goods were set by the government without regard for cost or demand, people had accumulated a lot of unspent rubles—there was no telling exactly how many. Between that and the inability of the Russian

---

*Yegor Gaidar's grandfathers were Arkady Gaidar, author of Communist children's literature, and Pavel Bazhov, a collector and reteller of fairy tales. His widow, Maria Strugatskaya, is the daughter of science fiction writer Arkady Strugatsky.

government to control the supply of rubles in the economy—because the neighbors could print them too—there was little to no hope of being able to stem inflation if consumer goods became available and price controls were lifted. But the only way to make consumer goods available seemed to be to lift price controls. "It became clear that the situation was mercilessly dictating only one option: the most conflict-ridden and riskiest scenario of starting reform," wrote Gaidar.[19]

In November 1991, Yeltsin appointed Gaidar his minister of the economy and finance with the rank of vice-premier. Yeltsin decided to run the cabinet himself, without appointing a prime minister—in no small part because no one wanted to accept a suicide mission—and this meant that Gaidar would in effect run the government. To ensure that reform could go forward, Yeltsin secured the right to issue decrees that contradicted existing law, provided the Congress signed off on them.

ON JANUARY 2, 1992, the government lifted price controls on consumer goods, with the exception of bread, milk, and alcohol. In a couple of weeks, goods began showing up on store shelves. Within a month, prices had gone up 352 percent and the money that Russians had thought of as savings and Gaidar had thought of as a dangerous cash surplus had been spent.[20] In an effort to avoid continued hyperinflation, the government pursued a stringent monetary policy. For most Russian citizens, this meant that on the one hand they were paid in large wads or small bags of cash, and on the other hand they could not afford most of the goods that were now accosting them everywhere. In January 1992, Yeltsin signed a decree legalizing private commerce, and private citizens began trading. They stood on the sidewalks holding their wares—sometimes a single raw steak or a fried chicken, exposed, because wrapping supplies were a deficit and a luxury. Many of them had clipped Yeltsin's decree out of the newspaper and pinned it to their jackets to protect them from the police. The orderly gray streets of Soviet cities came alive, vibrating with the sight of varied goods, the voices of people hawking them, and the overwhelming sense of uncertainty. Gaidar's reforms may have averted famine and total infrastructural collapse, but the anxiety they produced far exceeded anything that had come before. By the end of the winter, Yeltsin's honeymoon with the Congress was over.

A majority of the people's deputies adopted a stance familiar from the perestroika era, when the parliament's main task was to challenge central authority. The Congress wanted reforms stopped or even reversed, and it wanted Gaidar out. Yeltsin would not budge, and his cabinet continued along its path. Where local authorities cooperated, stores and services were privatized. By the summer, the government discontinued all subsidies of consumer goods, including bread, milk, and alcohol. Inflation stabilized at levels well below hyperinflation. From the point of view of Gaidar and his team, this was success. From the point of view of many Russians, this was unemployment, no longer hidden, as it had been under the old regime, with its pretend work for pretend pay. Not only had it been exposed, it was growing, thanks to falling production, and wages that had become laughable. The Congress began blocking presidential decrees—for example, one that would have introduced bankruptcy as an option and a procedure. Wrote Gaidar:

> As we moved forward, more and more obstacles presented themselves. Our progress felt strange. It did not resemble climbing a mountain: however steep and dangerous it may be, the end result depends only on you, your strength, and your perseverance. It was more like trying to make one's way through a tar pit: the path is unstable beneath your feet, sedge is cutting your skin, mosquitoes are getting in your eyes, and a single misstep can plunge you into the liquid blackness.[21]

In other areas, Yeltsin was walking a similarly uncertain path. In March, almost exactly a year after Gorbachev's referendum on the Soviet Union, Yeltsin organized the signing of the Federation Treaty, the founding document of the new Russian union. This was not a promising beginning for the country: the document was hazy, and the signing was rocky. The federation included three different categories of members, with different degrees of independence from the center. Two republics—Tatarstan and Chechnya—refused to sign; both considered themselves independent states. The otherwise unremarkable Kaluga region, just a couple of hours from Moscow, signed but added a caveat. St. Petersburg added three—among other things, it refused to recognize Moscow's right to declare a state of emergency in the region.[22] The imposition of a state of emergency followed—not in St. Petersburg, but in North Ossetia and Ingushetia, where armed conflict over territory erupted in 1992.[23]

By the fall of 1992, even Nemtsov, the poster boy for economic reform, was begging the cabinet to slow down.[24] But the cabinet pressed on with ever greater urgency. By the end of the year, it approved a privatization plan for Russia, according to which every one of the country's 148 million citizens would receive a voucher that could be turned into shares of any newly non-state-owned enterprise. The Congress generally hated the idea, but agreed to let it proceed. Soon after, the people's deputies demanded that Yeltsin get rid of Gaidar: until he did, they would block every one of the president's initiatives.

The new Russian prime minister, Viktor Chernomyrdin, looked much more the part of a Russian, or, rather, Soviet official. He was fifty-four, came from a working-class family in a small town in the steppes, and had risen through the ranks of the Communist Party, from which he never resigned. He had been a member of the Central Committee, and his last job before joining the cabinet had been as head of the state's natural-gas monopoly.[25] He promised the Congress to stem the fall of production and to keep the population from growing poorer. "A market system need not be a bazaar," he said.[26]

Chernomyrdin failed. He tried to reverse some of Gaidar's policies, but he lacked the cooperation of most of the cabinet. Russian politics had returned to its pre-coup state: the president and his cabinet, hardly a united front, were in an all-out war with the Congress. The hastily patched and repatched old Soviet-Russian constitution made matters worse because it did not delineate the responsibilities and powers of the branches of government. As large industrial plants began privatizing, corruption became a major force once again, with officials scrambling to apportion property, whether or not they had the right to do so.[27] With the president and Congress at war, there was no chance of adopting a new constitution. Instead, the Congress began to discuss, ad nauseam, impeaching Yeltsin. In a televised address on March 20, 1993, Yeltsin declared that the country's political crisis stemmed from "a deep contradiction between the people and the old Bolshevik anti-people system that still has not fallen and that now aims to restore the power it has lost."[28] Yeltsin said he was revoking the Congress's power to block his decrees and was scheduling a referendum for April 25. Russian citizens would be asked to affirm their confidence in the president and to vote on the draft of a new constitution.

It did not work. Yeltsin's move itself was unconstitutional, and the Constitutional Court invalidated it. Yeltsin got his referendum, but only on the following four questions:

1. Do you have confidence in the president of the Russian Federation, B. N. Yeltsin?
2. Do you approve of the social and political policies pursued by the president and cabinet of the Russian Federation since 1992?
3. Do you consider it necessary to hold early elections to the office of the president of the Russian Federation?
4. Do you consider it necessary to hold early elections of people's deputies of the Russian Federation?[29]

Leading up to the vote, Yeltsin's supporters flooded the airwaves with a chant: *Da-Da-Nyet-Da*, "Yes-Yes-No-Yes." Flyers with the same rhythmic sequence were handed out on every corner. This was, in essence, the first election campaign in post-Soviet Russia. Yeltsin got nearly the vote he wanted: Russians answered "Yes" to all four questions, but the margin on question 3 was very small. The Constitutional Court had ruled that early elections would require a majority of all eligible voters, not merely those who had gone to the polls, and question 4 did not get that despite the fact that the number of those who said "Yes" was more than twice that of voters who said "No." Yeltsin declared victory, but he did not have legal grounds to schedule a new parliamentary election.

In the days immediately following the referendum, Yeltsin fired his vice-president, General Alexander Rutskoi, who had taken to siding with the Congress, and began to push measures that the cabinet considered important. One was a set of changes to Russian criminal and procedure codes that brought them into line with minimal European standards. These included penalties for the use and mishandling of biological weapons, the criminalization of kidnapping, and the decriminalization of consensual homosexual intercourse.[30] All of these changes were required for membership in the Council of Europe. This legislation went largely unnoticed, including by the prison authority, which neglected to instruct wardens to release men convicted of sodomy. There had been bigger news that day: Yeltsin unveiled the draft of a new constitution and invited the federation's constituent republics to start submitting amendments.[31]

Within a week, Russia's political setup reverted to its pre-referendum state of ongoing, slow-burning crisis. The people's deputies produced their own draft constitutions, at least two of them. None of these documents had a chance of garnering enough support from all branches of government to begin the process of shaping the law of the land.

ON SEPTEMBER 21, 1993, Yeltsin issued a decree dissolving the Congress and scheduling a new election for December 12. The Congress refused to recognize the decree and instead anointed General Rutskoi the country's new president. Just two years after the coup that finished the Soviet Union, history was repeating itself in a B-movie version. Now it was the opposition to Yeltsin that barricaded itself in the White House—several hundred men and a few women—their supporters gathering outside. The country once again had two men who called themselves president. This time, again, the people who thought of themselves as proponents of democracy were supporting Yeltsin, who they thought had waited too long to take action against his political enemies. If they feared anything, it was that he would not carry through. Veronika Kutsyllo, a young journalist for the leading newspaper *Kommersant*, which positioned itself as the voice of the new entrepreneurial class, was inside the White House along with a group of other reporters:

> Before the clock struck midnight, we got a chance to grab some coffee in the cafeteria and discuss the situation. We concluded that the thing everyone had been wishing for, long and passionately, had happened. The president had finally violated the Constitution ("He has stomped on it," I added as a point of clarification), and this meant that in accordance with Amendment 6 to Article 121, the president is automatically removed from power. That makes Rutskoi president and the parliament happy. Yet it's clear that Yeltsin is not about to retreat. That creates a stalemate. He needs to take the next step, it needs to be decisive, but what will it be? Our peace-loving leader surely won't want to use force to get the deputies out of the White House.[32]

The 1991 coup had exposed the collapse of the Soviet social contract. That void had not been filled. Russian citizens still carried Soviet passports with a hammer and sickle on the cover, paid for food with Soviet rubles decorated with profiles of Lenin and the Soviet state seal, and could not even be sure of the name of their country. Was it Russia? The Russian Federation? The constitution still called it the Russian Soviet Federated Socialist Republic, but the constitution was a thing to be stomped on, and Yeltsin's most important supporters—the new journalists—thought he was not doing it with enough force.

Even though Yeltsin had spent months considering his move to dissolve the Congress, he was no better prepared than the coup plotters two years earlier. He had no plan of action in case the people's deputies, in full accordance with the constitution, refused to disband. Worse, his opposition had stronger evident ties to the military, the police, and the KGB than he did. And unlike Yeltsin in 1991, the men—and a few women—who had now barricaded themselves in the White House had access to weapons. They began handing them out to their supporters in the street. At the same time, the Congress voted to institute the death penalty for Yeltsin's key supporters. In response, the cabinet had the phones in the White House turned off.[33]

The standoff, punctuated by ever more virulent public statements on both sides, lasted nearly two weeks. The heads of the Constitutional Court and the Russian Orthodox Church brokered negotiations, and these failed. On October 3, armed supporters of the Congress stormed the Moscow mayoralty and the federal television center. For a time, TV screens went blank—or, rather, gray—with an announcement in white type: "Broadcasting on Channels 1 and 4 has been disrupted by an armed mob that has forced its way into the building." Nearly a hundred people died during the attack on the television center. The armed mob, directed by General Rutskoi, went on to storm the Ministry of Communications, the customs office, and other federal buildings. Gaidar, who was now back in the cabinet, serving as minister of the economy, issued a radio address in which he once again called on civilians to come out and protect Yeltsin, as they had done two years earlier. In the evening of October 3, Muscovites began coming out into the streets. The cabinet was mobilizing civilians because it could not be sure that the armed services would side with it: there was no law and no force that could compel them to do so.

This time, though, the military chose sides, and it picked Yeltsin. By the morning of October 4, tanks had pulled up to the White House. At seven, they began firing, aiming at the upper floors, apparently to provide the people's deputies and their supporters the option of evacuating the building. Still, when soldiers finally forced their way in, they found about forty bodies. Twenty military men died during the storm. The White House burned into the night, visible for miles around: it was by far the tallest building in the neighborhood. In the morning, it looked like a giant decayed tooth. The casualty total was 146 dead, over a thousand injured, and at least two thousand arrested.[34]

Yeltsin scheduled a parliamentary election for December. A referendum on his draft of the new Russian constitution would be held the same day.

There would be no parliamentary discussion of the document, because until then, there would be no parliament. For the first time in a year and a half—virtually for the first time since the end of the Soviet Union—Yeltsin had a firm hold on power. The hold was based not on law but on force. But the fact that Yeltsin had been able to resort to force stemmed from a new understanding in Russian society, though the nature of that understanding could not be clear to anyone in the immediate aftermath of what became known as "the Execution of the White House."

ARUTYUNYAN NOTICED THAT very soon after the Execution of the White House people began conflating the events of 1991 and 1993. The two sets of barricades, two sets of politicians holed up in the White House, two television gray-outs, and two sets of deaths and arrests melded into one. All of it settled in memory as "politics," and the charred remains of the White House stuck out in the Moscow landscape as a daily reminder that in politics, anything is possible. Looking at it, one wanted to stay as far away from politics as possible.

Masha's grandfather, who had been such an ardent Yeltsin supporter, had had a political change of heart. He now spent his days reading the emergent ultranationalist press, newly known as the red-brown part of the political spectrum for its combination of Communist and brownshirt fervor. Boris Mikhailovich took to reading antisemitic passages out loud. Tatiana diagnosed this as senility and told her daughter that such was the tragedy of old age: Boris Mikhailovich, who had been an articulate, if generally quiet, opponent of the Communists his entire life, was now aligning himself with people who were not only brown but also red. More to the point, after his brief love affair with politics, Boris Mikhailovich was angry and disillusioned, and the "red-brown" press was the vehicle most immediately available for the expression of his disgust with politics.

Evgenia was no longer involved with any political party. Gay activism had also suddenly lost its way after Yeltsin repealed the sodomy law for no reason that had anything to do with actual gays and lesbians in Russia. She decided to boycott the December 1993 election: the idea was, clearly, to create a pliant parliament and to ram through a constitution drafted behind closed doors, and she wanted nothing to do with either. But if she was going to vote for anyone, she would pick Vladimir Zhirinovsky and his Liberal Democratic Party.[35] Its platform, and Zhirinovsky's public statements, were anything but liberal or democratic. The Western media called him an ultranationalist. Russians were more likely to see him as either a clown or a truthsayer.

> Unless we get back the historical borders of Russia, at least those that existed before the 1917 Revolution, or those that corresponded to the 1977 [Soviet] Constitution, we are slowly going to degrade and die out. . . . That is what the West wants. The West is afraid of us, and this circumstance must be made use of in the resurrection of Russia. When I speak of this, I am accused of being a "fascist," a "Hitler scaring other people." We have been feared for a millennium. That is our capital.[36]

That passage from a 1993 speech, and many others like it—Zhirinovsky was a prolific speaker—certainly sounded like ultranationalism. But his speeches were both more and less than that. They promised a return to simplicity after years of the soul-searching that perestroika had demanded, and the mind-numbing economic and legalistic debates of the Yeltsin years. They were triumphantly anti-political.

If Evgenia and Boris Mikhailovich were merely listening to people who were flirting with ultranationalist and fascist rhetoric, then Dugin was going to the source. He had grown fascinated with Hitler's philosophy and system of governance. He produced and narrated a documentary movie series called *The Mysteries of the Century: The Mysticism of the Third Reich*, a close study that mixed archival research and rumor. The first episode asked whether it might be true that Hitler had access to "ancient knowledge" that led to the invention of the atomic bomb. Dugin also wondered aloud whether it was possible that evidence of the Nazis' satanic practices had been elided from the transcripts of the Nuremberg trials. The film hinted at a Western conspiracy to conceal the true nature of Hitler's power, and also promised perhaps to show how a disillusioned society could be brought to cohesion. "The streets are filled with the Brownian motion of disappointed Germans," explained the voice-over to footage of early 1930s Berlin. "But a drop of some magical catalyst has already fallen into this mass and chaos will soon turn to order. Every loser in this desolate world of profit-driven decisions and outdated religious dogma will be transformed. He will follow a Holy Grail that will grant him power over all the world." Cut to footage of Germans marching in formation and throwing their hands up in the Hitler salute.[37] The three-part miniseries was broadcast on Russia's two leading federal channels in the fall of 1993, and Dugin, who was on-screen for minutes at a time, leafing through what looked like archival documents and telling a story of mysticism and world domination, became famous.

On election night, the country's leading television channel was broadcasting the returns live. Sixty percent of voters approved of the new constitution—enough to make it the country's foundational document in accordance with the very low bar set by Yeltsin's September decree. Of the thirteen parties that had succeeded in getting on the ballot during the very short campaign, eight got enough votes to sit in parliament. Zhirinovsky's Liberal Democrats were firmly in the lead with 23 percent. Russia's Choice, the government's party, led by Gaidar, got 15.5 percent. The Communist Party came in third with 12.4 percent. "Russia, you have lost your mind!" shouted a well-known writer, Yuri Karyakin, who had been invited as a guest commentator. Then he stormed out of the studio.[38]

seven

EVERYONE WANTS TO BE A MILLIONAIRE

FOR ZHANNA, politics ended in 1991. Until that fall, everything that happened on television had also happened in the Nemtsov family kitchen—first in the strange wooden house in central Gorky, and then in the two-rooms-plus-a-kitchen they had been granted a few bus stops from the center of town. When conversation did not concern elections and reforms, it centered on food and shortages, which led right back to reform, and elections.

But when Boris was appointed governor in 1991, they moved to a dacha in a village created for the Party elite just outside the city—which, much to Zhanna's relief, was no longer called Gorky, or "bitter," but had recovered its pre-Soviet name, Nizhny Novgorod. The village was designed to feel like a piece of heaven that could exist anywhere, so it seemed as if the Nemtsovs had left familiar space and time altogether. Zhanna spent most of her time biking around the village, collecting berries in the lush surrounding woods, and playing with the cat, Andrei Dmitrievich Sakharov. Food was no longer an issue of importance, because there was plenty of it. Politics, which had been the subject of animated conversation at the kitchen table, turned into a set of incomprehensible words, which Boris recited like a mantra: "privatization," "investment," "infrastructure." These magic words seemed to transform Zhanna's father into a celebrity. The foreign advisers who flocked to town took up residence in the Nizhny Novgorod Kremlin, a medieval fortress where Boris now had his office; World Bank economists and Peace Corps advisers were quartered there side by side.[1] Journalists and foreign officials came to see what Moscow was advertising as the Nizhny Novgorod miracle.

"So what, then, is the situation in this ancient city of merchants, a place that has declared itself unabashedly open for business, a genuine enterprise zone where local officials are pushing ahead with real economic reforms faster than anywhere else in the country?" asked a *Chicago Tribune* correspondent in September 1992. His report was mixed. Nizhny had held the first public auction of grocery stores just five months earlier and had also since privatized 22 percent of the three thousand small businesses in the city. Nemtsov had devised an ingenious plan for solving the most vexing problems of privatizing enterprise: the shops and restaurants were sold free of debt and also free of the obligation to retain old employees—but some of the proceeds from each auction were deposited in a fund for those who lost their jobs as a result. At the same time, the privatization was temporary: in most cases, the new storekeepers could secure only five-year leases, because their businesses were located in large apartment buildings that would not be privatized until the following year. Worse, the storekeepers' ability to do business was impeded by infrastructural obstacles old and new: a Soviet-era trucking monopoly that controlled deliveries, and tax rates that changed from month to month, at one point rising to some 85 percent of profits.

And then there was the American who opened a restaurant only to be denied access to the city's water system, and the hotel whose manager "delights in gouging his foreign guests, barring them from the restaurant and, often, simply refusing to rent them rooms." This happened to be the city's only hotel in a state of reasonable repair, so most of the foreign visitors tried to stay there, opening themselves up to humiliation.[2] Still, the reporter found one example of spectacular positive change: what had been Municipal

Cheese Shop Number 11 was bought by employees at the city's very first auction, cleaned up, restocked, and rechristened Dmitrievsky. It even stopped shuttering for lunch in the middle of the day.

Margaret Thatcher, the retired British prime minister, came to visit in 1993. As she later wrote in her memoirs, rumors of Nemtsov's commitment to a "radical programme that some called Thatcherism" had reached her back in London:

> Nizhny Novgorod's saviour was, I found, frighteningly young (in his mid-thirties), extraordinarily good-looking and gifted with both intelligence and shrewdness (which do not always go together). . . .
>
> The Governor and I took a walk down Bolshaya Pokrovskaya Street. All the stores were privately owned. Every few yards we stopped to talk to the shopkeepers and see what they had to sell. No greater contrast with the drab uniformity of Moscow could be imagined. One shop remains vivid in my memory. It sold dairy produce, and it had a greater selection of different cheeses than I have ever seen in one place. I ate samples of several and they were very good. I also discovered that they were all Russian, and considerably cheaper than their equivalents in Britain. I enthusiastically expressed my appreciation. Perhaps because as a grocer's daughter I carry a conviction on such matters, a great cheer went up when my words were translated, and someone cried, "Thatcher for President!"[3]

From that point on, Dmitrievsky's director kept three pictures on her desk: Jesus, Mary, and Margaret Thatcher.[4]

The visiting foreigners included a young American who seemed to follow Nemtsov everywhere and whom Zhanna liked because he was always cracking jokes. On the whole, though, she resented her father's new job, because he was coming home late and no longer had time to help her with her homework. He asked a physicist friend who often stayed at the dacha to help her instead, but Zhanna found his explanations confusing and unsatisfying. She took to begging Boris to take her to work with him, but soon realized that she hated it: her father's workday seemed to consist of driving from one town or collective farm to the next, stopping every time the car crossed an invisible border between districts and having a full banquet served on a tablecloth spread on the hood of the car. With vodka the most important element of each of these feasts, Zhanna's father's conversation grew duller with each passing hour and dried up completely by mid-afternoon.

In a memoir Nemtsov wrote much later, he explained the origins of his strange banquet habit. When he was first appointed, his deputy, an older and more experienced politician, told Nemtsov that if he wanted to be taken seriously, he would need to drink with every local boss in his region, including the directors of some five hundred factories and the heads of about 750 collective farms. Nemtsov whittled the list down to four hundred and set about the project of sharing a bottle of vodka with each of them. In about a year he realized that his health had deteriorated, his body had become permanently swollen, and he was generally exhibiting the symptoms of alcoholism familiar to most Russians. He also noticed that he had assimilated attitudes typical of the Soviet political establishment, which was suspicious of any man who did not drink.[5]

In some ways, Nemtsov proved more adaptable than his young daughter. She got used to the dacha easily, but she could not make peace with the black Volga, the perennial nomenklatura car, that now took her to school in the mornings. She asked to be dropped off about five hundred yards from the entrance, even though everyone knew she was the governor's daughter and expected her to be chauffeured. And though she liked that her mother no longer had to spend her days struggling to procure food, the way foodstuffs now showed up at their dacha made Zhanna uneasy. At holiday time—New Year's, Victory Day, and the anniversary of the Great October Revolution every November—something frighteningly extravagant, like an entire roasted baby pig, would show up on the doorstep, as though placed there by the invisible and indestructible hand of the Soviet privilege machine.

WHILE ZHANNA WAS STRUGGLING to accept the cars and roast piglets, Seryozha had woken up one day to their absence. His grandfather still led a political party, still served on commissions—but in 1991, along with the entire Gorbachev establishment, he was rendered irrelevant to the machinery that ran the country. Seryozha's parents divorced that year. His father moved out. Everything was different now.

Seryozha changed schools. His old school was in the neighborhood, and his classmates there were other children from the Czars' Village, plump and blond. Multiple black Volgas pulled up to the building in the morning to deposit them in an environment that, from the start, reminded Seryozha of the way he had seen prison shown in films. During breaks between classes, the children walked around the school vestibule in a circle, in different-sex pairs, holding hands. If a child asked to be allowed to go to the bathroom during class, he was likewise paired with a student of the opposite sex, who had to stand guard outside the lavatory. This system of opposite-sex pairing was one of peer control: that the children could not actually enter the bathroom together ensured there would be no collusion and truancy; making children walk in circles with someone of the opposite sex—someone who, at that age, could not possibly be a friend—bored them into passivity.

Seryozha's new school was in a dilapidated building in the messy center of Moscow. Children did not wear uniforms, march in formation, or in any other way resemble Seryozha's old classmates. School Number 57 had long been an oasis of freethinking in Moscow: it was a math-and-science high school under the old regime, a place where ideological controls were slightly relaxed to facilitate the production of minds useful to the Soviet military-industrial complex. During perestroika, the school was allowed to start offering primary-level education. Seryozha now joined the children who had been the first entering first-graders. Their parents—linguists, writers, and one psychoanalyst—tensed up at the appearance of a child of the nomenklatura who would now be studying alongside their offspring, but grew to accept him, because the times were meant to be changing.

To Seryozha, entry to School Number 57 felt a bit like the Russian bathhouse where his grandfather so liked to go: a jarring sequence of warm comfort, extreme overstimulating heat, and dips in an ice-cold pool. He liked the lessons—most of them centered on an experimental classification of all worldly phenomena as either "bags" or "chains," meaning sets and sequences, and this made good sense. The school's social world, however, was harsh and convoluted. The class was divided into castes, with four extremely bright and charismatic boys at the top. They made up games that were worlds unto themselves, governed by rules and plots accessible only to their authors and their handpicked playmates. Seryozha was rarely invited. When he was allowed a peek into their world, he saw ghosts, spirits, and cosmic vampires. The second social tier consisted of boys and girls whose parents belonged to the same circles as the parents of the boys at the top—the Moscow intelligentsia that was now feeling confident and free. Seryozha was generally accepted by this second caste, but he felt a bit different from them, perhaps because his language and habits came from another world, or because their parents viewed him with suspicion. In his mind, Seryozha belonged to a third caste, in which he was perhaps alone. Still, he was not one of the kids at the bottom—the misfits, whom the rest of the class called "the untouchables" when they were not calling them something far more insulting, like *bomzh*, a new acronym for a new phenomenon: someone who was homeless.*

So rigid and cruel were the divisions these ten-year-olds created that one day their teacher canceled a regular biology class in order to teach them the plot of *Lord of the Flies*. Everyone was deeply impressed, and nothing changed in the way the class dynamics operated. Seryozha had a sense that what happened in class mirrored the new ways of life for the adults. He had been born into a small world where everyone stood on equal footing and was affirmed and appreciated simply for being, not for doing anything in particular. Adults were talking about this a lot now, and their words— "snobbery" and "inequality"—described his experience too.

Bomzh stands for *bez opredelyonnogo mesta zhitel'stva*—"without a definite place of residence"— invented by Soviet law and order when the system of residence registration began to disintegrate.

Perhaps it was because the other children had not spent their childhoods behind tall fences that Seryozha also felt like a bigger child—or, to be more precise, like a smaller child—than everyone else. Soon after he finally became close friends with two boys in his class, both of his friends developed crushes on the same girl and fought about it, and Seryozha went home and cried himself to sleep over the fact that his friends felt pain and caused each other pain and he could do nothing to alleviate this pain or even to understand it.

Seryozha's mother, who taught at Moscow State University, could not have made ends meet on her salary (which, in the past, had been largely irrelevant because the nomenklatura distribution system had provided a safety net). Unlike other professors, though, she had their large Czars' Village apartment, and she took a boarder, a Belgian man. He had a car, and he paid Seryozha a dollar to wash it. That bought a couple of cans of Coca-Cola at a new kiosk right in Red Square, a ten-minute walk from School Number 57. What had been sacred ground was now home to commerce. The honor guard still goose-stepped to their post at the entrance to the Lenin Mausoleum and stood there perfectly motionless, but there was no longer a giant line of people waiting to see the leader of the Bolshevik Revolution in his glass coffin. After the Execution of the White House, Yeltsin ordered the honor guard removed, and on October 6, 1993, the last two soldiers to have had that duty departed with a casual wave.[6] In 1990 Seryozha and his classmates from his old school were inducted into the Little Octobrists at the History Museum at the entrance to Red Square. Now he treated his new classmates to Coca-Cola here. It felt like freedom.

It seemed that Seryozha's grandfather was experiencing something similar. Alexander Nikolaevich no longer had his Central Committee dacha behind the tall solid fence but he had been granted a dacha in an Academy of Sciences village, just one rung lower on the ladder of privilege. The house was opulent by Soviet standards and most of the world's standards, but Seryozha had never seen a smaller house. Still, it sat on a plot filled with century-old pines, and the trees, combined with the size of the yard, made it feel like the only house for miles. Alexander Nikolaevich had always wanted a yard with a pond with fish in it, and now his son and his grandson were endlessly pushing wheelbarrows of soil off his property as what would one day be the pond grew deeper. In the old days, there would have been conscripts around to do the digging and push the wheelbarrows, but now, Seryozha understood, the Yakovlevs lived like regular people, the way his grandfather had always preferred.

When Seryozha was in eighth grade, his father and a couple of friends decided to organize a home school for their children. Seryozha lost touch with children from School Number 57. He spent the next four years speaking only to members of his family and the other two teenagers at the home school. They did not become friends. He had no friends, or people, other than his grandfather, who understood him in this world.

FOR LYOSHA, economic reform began with soap. Lyosha's mother amassed scores of what was called "household soap"—hard, sharp-edged bars that looked like greenish-brown bricks. When none of the imported better-smelling and nicer-looking alternatives were available, the highly alkaline soap could be used to wash clothes, dishes, skin, and hair, and even to make a nasal rinse that was said to cure a cold. Teenagers said it killed acne. Some claimed it could burn off a wart. It probably killed everything in its path—to keep hair from falling lifelessly after washing with "household soap," one had to rinse it with vinegar. "Household soap" was the only thing Galina could get for her ration cards in 1991, so she stocked up. The bars formed a fifth wall in their bathroom.

The same year, Lyosha saw something he had never seen before: a chicken that consisted only of legs and thighs. Until then, "buying a chicken" meant bringing home a bluish rubbery-looking thing that Galina held over the flame of the gas stove to singe the copious remnants of feathers before cooking. Now she brought home leg quarters, each of them nearly as large as a whole chicken. She said that these were "Legs of Bush" and then explained that Bush was the name of the American president and he and

Gorbachev had struck an agreement to send to Russia the dark-meat parts of chickens, which Americans happened to dislike. This was the story generally told about "Legs of Bush," and it was only slightly inaccurate. In 1990, Bush and Gorbachev finally signed a trade agreement that had languished for years. This allowed United States producers to sell to the Soviet Union grain and the dark-meat parts of chicken that Russians, indeed, prefer and American consumers disproportionately shunned. But the Soviet Union had no money to pay for the grain and the chicken quarters, so in December 1990 President Bush arranged for loans to the Soviet Union, and this ensured that the dark meat of chickens, in Russia, bore his name for years after his presidency ended.[7]

"Legs of Bush" signaled the beginning of a better time. Before they appeared, there had come a point when preserved cabbage was the sole grocery item available in Solikamsk, and the lines to buy it stretched for blocks. After "Legs of Bush," other food items began to materialize, and Lyosha's mother could afford some of them. When Galina's school stopped paying its employees, she found a job at a different school. By this time, she had married Sergei, her boyfriend, and his salary tided them over. Sergei worked as a miner. Many miners did not get paid because, like teachers, they were employed by the state, and the state, in accordance with Gaidar's policies of monetary austerity, had no cash. Sergei's mine was privatized early, and this meant that he had a salary—as long as he could stay sober long enough to go to work.

It was the drinking families in Lyosha's building that seemed to hit the point of utter despair. Some were hunting stray dogs to eat them. The kids who used to sleep on Lyosha's landing were trying to make their own money. The two brothers, aged about five and six, were serving local teenage boys, who paid them a ruble, then ten rubles at a time, for performing oral sex on them. There was little you could buy with that.

The secret of plenty lay in private enterprise, this much was clear. When Galina's school ran out of cash, it simply stopped paying, but when his stepfather's mine ran low, it found ways to pay employees in kind. Sergei brought home odd-tasting Swedish candy—it must have been licorice—and metal cans containing tiny little sausages in brine. A friend of Galina's, a fellow history teacher, quit the school to go to work as manager at the Solikamsk Pulp and Paper Mill, which was among the first Russian companies to be privatized.[8] The company was one of the country's largest producers of newsprint during a newspaper renaissance. Its building was soon lavishly renovated for all to see. Galina's former colleague became a rich man. Every time Lyosha's family went to his house for dinner, they saw food and things—pens, notebooks, dishes, and other objects Lyosha generally thought of as souvenirs—unlike any they saw elsewhere.

Like all Russians, in 1992 Lyosha's family got privatization vouchers, watermarked certificates roughly five by three inches in size, with a picture of the Moscow White House in an elliptical frame in the middle. They had a little over a year to decide what to do with the vouchers: sell, invest, or ignore. They exchanged their three vouchers for shares of Doka Pizza, a new restaurant that advertised on billboards all over town. They never saw any dividends. Some of Galina's friends told her she should have done what they did: bought shares in one of the newly privatized oil companies. These would indeed be worth money in a few years.

In the new world of vouchers, private companies, and investments, one story caught Lyosha's attention. A company called MMM saturated the airwaves with thirty-second TV spots devoted to the financial life of a dowdy middle-aged man named Lyonya Golubkov. At first Lyonya did not know what to do with his rubles, which were losing purchasing power so rapidly. Then he figured out that he could convert his worthless cash into MMM shares and live off dividends. This allowed him to buy a new pair of black leather cowboy boots for his wife, then a full-length fur coat for her, then a car and a house. The wife, who in the early ads seemed too young and tall for Lyonya, was now sitting in a chair in her pink housecoat, eating bonbons, looking less glamorous and perfectly domesticated, while Lyonya swelled with newfound financial confidence. Lyonya's brother, a miner, criticized Lyonya for doing nothing, but Lyonya found the words to argue that, far from being a sloth, he was a shrewd investor who made money with hard-earned money. When Lyonya bought tickets to the United States to see a soccer match between the Russian and Brazilian national teams, his brother, seated next to him in the stands, had to concede his point, tearfully.[9]

Like any pyramid scheme, MMM collapsed. It happened in the summer of 1994. People who had handed over their savings to the company numbered in the millions. When the founder of MMM was arrested for tax evasion, hundreds of these investors camped out in front of the company's headquarters in Moscow demanding his release and the return of a company in which they continued to have faith. In Solikamsk, nine-year-old Lyosha was devastated: he realized he was in love with Lyonya Golubkov, who was now gone from TV.

PYRAMID SCHEMES ABOUNDED. A company called Hoper-Invest ran a fifteen-second spot that showed a cheerful military officer walking into a modern-looking office where two nearly identical women in feminine business attire poured him a cup of tea while they handed him his shares.[10] Millions of people bought Hoper shares at two dozen branches across the country.[11] A Ponzi scheme that called itself Chara Bank eschewed television advertising in favor of word of mouth, and members of the urban educated classes entrusted it with their savings—in exchange for handsome monthly dividends—because they felt they were in the know. The companies issued watermarked certificates that looked no less or more official than the state's privatization vouchers and supported them with assurances that sounded no less or more credible than the government's. MMM promised boots, a car, and a trip to America; Hoper dangled the prospect of looking and acting like imaginary Western office workers; Chara guaranteed a worry-free future in an uncertain world; and the government said that everyone would be rich. In August 1992, introducing the voucher program, privatization chief Anatoly Chubais claimed that with time each certificate would be worth as much as two Volgas.[12] All these promises sounded equally new and bizarre.

In the early 1990s, Lev Gudkov was trying to make sense of Russians' emerging relationship to wealth. Adjusting expectations was a traumatic process, he found, one that opened up chasms between generations. In the postwar Soviet Union, each successive generation had lived moderately better than the last. Aspirations were passed on from parents to children with only minor adjustments. Most Soviet citizens had hoped that they, or their grown children, would be able to graduate from a room in a communal apartment to a one-room-plus-a-kitchen apartment of their own, and then to two rooms and a kitchen. With luck, they would eventually add a dacha and a Soviet-made Fiat. No one except the elites dreamed of palaces or Volgas—and the elites were safely hidden from view by their seven fences and seven locks. Now most of what Russians saw on television—commercials, government announcements, and even the sets of the Latin American soap operas everyone seemed to be watching—told them to aspire to more. Only the Soviet movies, which the television also still showed, allowed the weary eye and mind to rest on the reassuringly modest decorations of the bygone era.

Gudkov and his team began asking survey respondents not only how much they made but also how much they needed to survive and how much they needed to live well. An extremely large study—nearly seventy-five thousand respondents in all—showed that real income grew consistently, but so did everyone's idea of what it would take to live well. Later, two American economists who mined Russian statistical data came to the same conclusion: in the course of the 1990s, average living space increased (from sixteen to nineteen square meters per person), the number of people traveling abroad as tourists more than tripled, the percentage of households that owned televisions, vacuum cleaners, refrigerators, and washing machines increased, and the number of privately owned cars doubled.[13] Compared with life in the Soviet Union in the 1980s, Russians were better off—but they *felt* poor.

Conventional wisdom was that some people were getting very rich while others sank into poverty, but Gudkov's data did not bear this out: it looked like the wealth gap was remaining steady or even shrinking slightly. True, some of the screens shielding the structural inequalities of Soviet society had been lifted, allowing people to observe others being rich—if only because, with most of the old secret distribution centers closed, the rich were now much more likely to do their shopping in plain view. But this exposure could hardly explain what Gudkov was seeing. He focused on the millions of people who had now traveled abroad: by 1995 nearly 17 percent of adults had been outside Russia. The experience had not made them feel like life had gotten better. They had seen something more devastating than the fact that some of their compatriots were better off: they saw that, beyond the country's western borders, virtually everyone was better off than virtually everyone in Russia. They had felt themselves to be not just poor individuals but people from a poor country. As this self-perception solidified, so did some of the results of Gudkov's surveys: the gap between answers to the questions "How much do you earn?" and "How much do you need to earn to survive?" closed. This did not mean that people felt like they had enough; they felt like things could hardly get worse. Their idea of how much they needed to live well continued to be out of reach.

Even as the country seemed to be in the throes of romance with private enterprise, one of Gudkov's stock questions—"Who is living well and happily in Russia?"—continued to elicit a stock, Soviet-era answer: crooks, con men, bureaucrats, criminals, and entrepreneurs. Happiness and wealth belonged to the Other. Asked if they thought they earned more or less than other people of comparable skill and experience, two-thirds of respondents answered "less"—a statistical impossibility that doomed Russians to jealousy.[14]

In late 1994, when MMM collapsed, Hoper-Invest also stopped paying out, and the ruble lost nearly a quarter of its value overnight. All three events were to some extent related to something that had happened earlier in the year: the government relaxed its monetary policy and began printing rubles—this was a boon to the pyramid schemes, and it also doomed the ruble to fall.[15] Many Russians' core beliefs were thus confirmed: the government was no more trustworthy than the self-anointed investment kings, and economic hardship and injustice were life's only certainties.

ARUTYUNYAN WAS NOW ATTENDING training seminars abroad: Western psychoanalysts continued to give generously of their time and expertise to help their less experienced colleagues. At one of these seminars, conducted in English, she noticed that she could now tell the difference between the meanings of two words: "envy" and "jealousy." The former was a way of desiring something that someone else had and you lacked; the latter was resenting someone's taking possession of something that was yours. Envy was what you felt when someone had more money than you did. Jealousy was what you felt when you thought that the money was or should be yours. Either emotion could be awful to experience, but envy could also be constructive—it could spur you to action—and even benevolent, like when you envied someone his ability to be generous or productive. It stood to reason that the distinction was lacking in contemporary Russian: for three generations everything had been said to belong to everyone, and having more was said to be shameful. Jealousy was the only relevant emotion.

Human beings are perhaps born jealous—the emotion stems from a basic survival instinct. Now it was like Arutyunyan's clients had been stripped to their bare selves and could feel only that most basic, most painful, most burning of emotions. Everyone felt like he had been robbed. The visual symbols of wealth were raspberry-colored sport coats that someone must have glimpsed at a private school abroad—and they, complete with a gold-embroidered emblem on the breast pocket, became the uniform of the emerging flaunting class. The other symbol was the Mercedes. Both signs of extreme wealth, like extreme wealth itself, were so rare as to be almost phantoms, but the mere shadow of a sighting gave rise to furious jealousy. It had never before been acceptable to show wealth. Arutyunyan's mother remembered having studied, at Moscow State University, alongside Stalin's daughter. The first daughter, she said, was the worst-dressed girl in their year, and the chauffeur had always dropped her off two blocks away from the school. Such was the Soviet ethos of demonstrative asceticism, which Zhanna must have absorbed as a toddler, before privilege happened to her. Newly visible wealth was doubly insulting because it violated aesthetic conventions and because the newly wealthy, unlike the old nomenklatura, had no claim to entitlement: Who were they to be rich?

The fact that the very rich were vanishingly few exacerbated things. The only thing worse than feeling like a loser was feeling like a member of an entire society of losers. The jealousy rarely manifested as jealousy: before it reached the surface it was usually transformed into a different sentiment—feeling used, feeling angry, feeling fear.

Some people had good reason to feel fear. The new entrepreneurs, it was said, were murdering one another left and right. For most people, the violence was as much an abstraction as was big money, but the fear of being caught in the cross fire was not entirely unfounded. A friend of Arutyunyan's once stumbled onto a shootout in the street in Moscow in broad daylight. Arutyunyan's office mate, a cognitive behavioral therapist—they rented a small apartment together and took turns seeing clients there—took months to work up the nerve to ask a client, an entrepreneur, to stow his gun in the coat closet when he arrived for his session.

Arutyunyan's first client from the new world of entrepreneurship did not carry a gun. He was, contrary to stereotype, a cultivated young man from a professor's family not unlike Arutyunyan's own. He would not say what exactly he did, but Arutyunyan surmised that it had to do with oil. He sought help because he had started flying into rages. It took only a few sessions—too few, Arutyunyan later realized—to conclude that the rages stemmed from repressed anxiety. Shortly after, the man decided to stop therapy. Getting in touch with his feelings was too risky a proposition. "I am a tightrope walker," he explained. "Imagine what can happen to me if I pause to think." He might look weak. He might even cry. Flying into a rage and, say, beating someone to a pulp was an altogether safer option. Neither Arutyunyan nor the client broached the idea that he could change his line of work to something less evidently dangerous: in the new reality, everyone was assumed to want to be an entrepreneur.

———

MASHA'S MOTHER had long since stopped importing intimate essentials from Poland. She now made frequent trips to China to buy patent-leather handbags. They looked distinctive and, Masha thought, hideous, but some quirk of fashion fortune made them the "it" bag for Russian women in 1993–1994. Tatiana now had her own kiosk on Kalininsky Prospect, a wide central avenue lined with high-rises that had looked chic in the 1960s. She sold the bags at the kiosk, and also supplied them to other vendors.

There was a day when Masha entered a Metro car and noticed that every woman in it had one of those bags that her mother—and no one else—imported. Every single woman in the subway car. "We must be rich," thought Masha. But the image of what it was to be rich in no way jived with how she and Tatiana lived. They still had their two-rooms-plus-a-kitchen rather than a palace. They washed their clothes by hand in the bathtub. Masha still got bullied at school: for being younger than all her classmates, for the clothes she wore, but most of all, for being somehow different. That would not happen if they really were rich, would it?

PART THREE

UNRAVELING

eight

GRIEF, ARRESTED

IN THE MID-1990s the Western psychoanalysts who had sporadically been traveling to post-Soviet countries launched a formal training program for their colleagues from countries where the psychoanalytic tradition had been interrupted. Arutyunyan attended a series of training sessions held in Poland. She had been working as an analyst for about a decade, give or take a flailing year or two. For years now she had enjoyed free access to psychoanalytic literature. She had also been studying psychodrama at a school started in Russia by Swedish therapists. She was a well-educated, well-rounded psychoanalyst, no longer a beginner, so she had a phrase to call what she experienced when she started at the new program: it was a narcissistic blow. She observed masters at work, and she realized that she could not work half that well—not because the instructors were innately so much more talented or intelligent but because they stood on the shoulders of their predecessors, who stood on the shoulders of their predecessors, who stood on the shoulders of giants. Arutyunyan, on the other hand, stood on emptiness, and she herself felt empty. Her ideas were archaic at best, naive at worst. What she felt was that burning, destructive jealousy: this mastery, this fluidity, this depth should have been hers.

The post-Soviet psychoanalysts lacked the central qualification of their profession: they had not themselves gone through analysis. A number of psychoanalysts in Germany, the Czech Republic, and the Netherlands began taking on the role of analyst and supervisor for the Russians, who would travel to their supervisors' cities for a few weeks at a time to undergo analysis, while their own patients were on hold, to return and pick up their work and receive supervision over e-mail. Some of their colleagues pointed out that this was not how it was done, but the participants recalled that the early Freudians had shuttled much the same way. Arutyunyan began traveling to Germany for three-week stints of daily analysis. The language of her sessions was English, the mother tongue for neither analyst nor patient. Sometimes the work of expressing feelings in a language to which these feelings were foreign seemed impossible. Other times, Arutyunyan was grateful for the task of simplification and explication English forced upon her: it made obfuscation more difficult. As she went deeper into analysis, she observed the unconscious playing tricks with language—like when her dreams contained German phrases that she thought she could not understand—but she could remember them and, translated, they unmistakably revealed their meaning.

Shuttle analysis worked on a rigid schedule with long gaps, hardly suited to work so delicate and unpredictable. Arutyunyan often left her clients in Moscow at the least opportune moment in their own analytic processes and then compounded the problem by returning in a changed and vulnerable state. Weekly e-mail sessions with a supervisor called her to order. "Where did that come from?" he would write, challenging her interpretation of a particularly difficult moment. "Could it be that you are frustrated at being torn away from your own analysis and you are taking revenge on the person who caused the separation?" That would be her patient, who was utterly defenseless in this situation. Arutyunyan felt defenseless. All of Russia felt defenseless, it seemed. Pressing on with her own analysis, and her patients', was a way to hang on, by the skin of her teeth, to who she was.

LYOSHA'S MOTHER ENCOURAGED HIM to enter a citywide history essay contest. It was the sort of thing she did—she was, after all, a history teacher, and she expected her only son to do much better than she had, just as she had done so much better than her own illiterate-peasant mother. The essay topic was "My Family Story in the History of the Twentieth Century." Lyosha had a sense that this was a trendy topic—the heady days of media revelations about Stalin and the Gulag were over, long since overshadowed by economic reform and political conflict, but recently people all around Lyosha and Galina seemed to be talking about their family histories. The teachers at school had also suggested that researching one's roots was a good pathway to winning student competitions. Except Lyosha had hardly any family and certainly no history. He did not even carry the family name anymore: when his mother married Sergei, in December 1991, she had changed Lyosha's last name from Misharin to Gorshkov, and his patronymic from Yurievich to Sergeevich, as though Lyosha had always been his new stepfather's son. It had been a horrible wedding, during which Lyosha was told not to get in the way of the adults while they celebrated, and he had decided then and there that he hated marriage and would never marry as long as he lived. His stepfather, who had seemed so fun before the wedding, when he would spend hours watching pop music performances on television with Lyosha, now appeared to be a quiet, lazy alcoholic who simply vegetated in front of the television. Lyosha decided that he hated everything about him, especially the way he ate—as though he would never eat again. Lyosha hated his new patronymic and surname too.

Galina said that she could tell him a bit about family history. Lyosha's great-grandparents, she said, were part of a large German-speaking community that had settled along the Volga River in the late eighteenth century.[1] By the standards of the Revolution, the family were *kulaks*—peasants who owned land and livestock, which made them class enemies. Lyosha's great-grandfather was stripped of his belongings and disappeared. His great-grandmother and her children lived in abject poverty as members of a newly formed collective farm. Two years after the disappearance of the husband and father, Lyosha's great-grandmother and her children were loaded into a cattle car, along with other ethnic Germans, and shipped off to the Urals, to a remote rural area outside Solikamsk. Here, reunited with Lyosha's great-grandfather, they had to start from scratch at a new collective farm, on previously uncultivated land. Lyosha's grandmother was ten years old. When the family was being herded onto the train, a soldier had taken away her only toy, a wooden doll. In the Urals, authorities changed her name from Emma to Serafima. She received no schooling after the deportation, which was why she was functionally illiterate: before the disaster, the family had spoken German exclusively, and the girl had learned to read using the German Bible.

Everyone in the new village was German. This sounded familiar to Lyosha—there was a part of Solikamsk that was called the German Settlement, though the ethnic Germans who lived there had all emigrated during perestroika. They left behind neat little village-style houses they had built themselves, and a ghost of clean and ordered living that Lyosha found seductive. When Serafima was eighteen, a young man from a neighboring village decided to make her his. In Galina's telling, his resolve was unilateral and final. He was Russian. He moved Serafima to his village, where she was hated for being a German and a Catholic. Her new husband was an atheist and a Communist, but his own mother was Russian Orthodox, and she refused to accept Serafima as her daughter-in-law in the absence of a church wedding. There was no wedding at all, in fact—this was the early 1930s, and marriage was still a bourgeois anachronism.

Serafima's new husband drank, had numerous affairs and relationships—at least one other woman considered herself his wife—and built a career in the Party and on the collective farm. He would eventually become chairman of the collective farm and a member of the Supreme Soviet. In 1935, a *voronok*—a black prisoner-transport car—pulled up to the house: someone had denounced Serafima's husband for stealing the bricks he had used to build his house. Fortunately, it was Serafima's habit to maintain order in all things, including receipts for the purchase of bricks, and her husband escaped being jailed.

In 1941, Serafima's husband went off to war to fight the Germans, and Serafima herself, left alone with a small baby—her first son—went from being an outcast to being the enemy. Her own brother-in-law came around, drunk, in the middle of the night, to smash all her windows, screaming, "German!"

In the late 1940s, years after the Soviets had resanctified marriage, as Lyosha's grandfather made his way up the Party ladder, he finally registered his marriage to Lyosha's grandmother. Serafima took her husband's Russian surname, Misharina. The last people to carry the German family name, Klauser—Lyosha's great-grandparents—died long before he was born. Lyosha had seen photographs of their funerals and he had asked about their coffins, adorned with what looked to him like a very strange Christian cross, but no one had answered his questions. Now his mother explained that her grandparents had been Catholic, and her sister recalled that as children, Serafima's two daughters and three sons would spend summers in the German-speaking village and their grandfather would ply them with candy to persuade them to agree to speak a little German or to read from his German Bible. When Serafima's parents died, the German stopped—none of her children remembered it now—and so did the connection with family on the Klauser side, who had once written Lyosha's great-grandfather letters, some from Kazakhstan, where they had also been exiled, and others from Germany and New York, where they had escaped during the war.

Serafima confirmed the story for Lyosha and added personal details about her five children. Two of her daughters—Lyosha's aunts—had been left alone with their children because, like Serafima, they had married alcoholics. One of the husbands drowned while drunk, the other died of alcohol poisoning. As for Galina, said Lyosha's grandmother, she had been lying to him when she told him that his father lived in Perm. Lyosha's father was right there in Solikamsk—he was "Uncle Yura," who had stopped visiting when Lyosha's stepfather came on the scene. Unlike the stepfather, Yuri was an educated man who did well for himself in the new economy, rising to the position of director at a manufacturing company. He came from a family of Polish Jews who had also been exiled to these parts. He was married and had a daughter, about ten years Lyosha's senior, who worked at the local children's library. Lyosha started going to the library even more frequently. He fantasized about inserting a note to his half sister into one of the books he was returning. "You don't know me, but we have something important in common." Or, "I see you several times a week, and I wonder if you ever notice our likeness." The logistics of the plan were unclear—what if someone else found the note?—and the consequences were unpredictable, so Lyosha never followed through.

When he was not thinking about being his father's son, he thought about being German. It all made sense now: his punctuality, his obsessive neatness, his love of all things that made sense, and his inability to tolerate the sounds Sergei made when eating. Lyosha was no Alexei Sergeevich Gorshkov or even Alexei Yurievich Misharin: he was Alexei Klauser. He won the history essay contest.

Meanwhile, Galina sent a query to the state archives in Saratov, the major city in the Volga region from which she understood her family to have been exiled. You could do this now—ask for information on family who had been declared traitors, criminals, or enemies by the Stalin state. The archives confirmed that Lyosha's great-grandfather had, in the language of the authorities, "been repressed." As for Lyosha's great-grandmother, her file had been misplaced and no information was available.

"TO LEARN ABOUT ONESELF is the toughest among the challenges of learning," wrote Alexander Etkind, one of the most perceptive scholars of the post-Soviet cultural experience. He was writing about the particular horror of the Soviet legacy:

> Victims and perpetrators were mixed together in the same families,
> ethnic groups, and lines of descent. . . . If the Nazi Holocaust exter-

minated the Other, the Soviet terror was suicidal. The self-inflicted nature of Soviet terror has complicated the circulation of three energies that structure the postcatastrophic world: a cognitive striving to learn about the catastrophe; an emotional desire to mourn for its victims; and an active desire to find justice and take revenge on the perpetrators. . . . The suicidal nature of the Soviet atrocities made revenge all but impossible, and even learning very difficult.[2]

Before perestroika, dissident historians had been trying to do the work of learning in the near-complete absence of information. Even after mass terror ended with the death of Stalin, even after Nikita Khrushchev chose to speak out about the terror, he first doctored the information and then made the redacted story secret. When Mikhail Gorbachev, as Party leader, looked at some of the secret archives for the first time in the 1980s, he felt shock, disgust, and disbelief—not only because of what had been done but because it had been done by his own Party and in its name.[3]

In 1989, Gorbachev made Alexander Nikolaevich chair of a newly created Rehabilitation Commission, in charge of reviewing archival documents and clearing the names of those who had been unjustly punished in the Stalin era. Alexander Nikolaevich was better prepared than Gorbachev to start learning about the terror, both because he was old enough to have heard Khrushchev deliver his secret speech to the Party Congress and because he had seen the cattle cars carrying Soviet prisoners of war to the Gulag after the Great Patriotic War. But what he saw when he studied the archives during perestroika made his stomach turn. He saw that Stalin personally had signed execution orders for forty-four thousand people, people he did not know and whose cases he had not read, if the cases even existed— he had simply signed off on long lists of names, apparently because he enjoyed the process.[4] He saw evidence of secret-police competitions, formal ones—like when different departments within the NKVD (the precursor agency to the KGB) raced one another to highest number of political probes launched—and informal ones, like when three of the NKVD brass took three thousand cases with them on a train journey, got drunk, and engaged in a speed challenge: Who could go through a stack of cases fastest, marking each with the letter *P*. They were not reading the cases. The letter *P*—pronounced *r* in Russian—stood for *rasstrel*, "execution." He saw evidence of specific days on which the fate of thousands was decided. On November 22, 1937, Stalin and two of his closest advisers, Vyacheslav Molotov and Andrei Zhdanov, approved twelve lists submitted by the NKVD, containing 1,352 people who would be executed. On December 7, they signed off on thirteen lists for a total of 2,397 people, 2,124 of whom were to be executed. On January 3, 1938, they were joined by two other top Bolsheviks, Kliment Voroshilov and Lazar Kaganovich, and together they signed off on twenty-two lists with 2,547 names, 2,270 to be executed.

June 10, 1938: twenty-nine lists, 2,750 people, 2,371 to be executed.

September 12, 1938: thirty-eight lists, 6,013 people, 4,825 to be executed.

There were too many such dates and figures to make them commemorative or otherwise meaningful. Some lists had a specific makeup. On August 20, 1938, Stalin and Molotov together signed off on a list of fifteen women who were classified as "wives of enemies of the people." Ten of them were housewives and two were students. All were executed. Their husbands, who had been arrested earlier, were executed later.[5] Other lists looked altogether random, though the mind scrambled each time to make sense of them.

Lidiya Chukovskaya, a writer whose husband, a physicist, was executed in 1938 at the age of thirty-one, raged against this habit of attempting to make sense of the absurd:

> The truth was too primitive and too bloody. The regime had attacked its citizens for no imaginable reason and was beating them, torturing them, and executing them. How were we to understand the reason for such whimsy? If you let it sink in that there is no reason, that they were doing it "just because," that killers killed just because it is their job to kill, then your heart, though no bullet has pierced it, will be torn apart, and your mind, in its intact shell of a head, will grow shaky. Looking at the truth would have been akin to staring down the barrel of a gun, so one tried to steal oneself away.[6]

Alexander Nikolaevich had not read these lines: Chukovskaya drafted and redrafted this book for decades, perhaps still hoping to land on a narrative. It was published by Chukovskaya's daughter only in 2001, five years after its author's death. The book was called *The Elision*.

Alexander Nikolaevich ultimately concluded that the terror could not be understood. The explanations offered by his colleagues and any number of historians—that Stalin was mentally ill, that he suffered from paranoid delusions—explained nothing. The tyrant had had any number of his relatives, and the relatives of his wives, executed. One time, Alexander Nikolaevich discovered, Stalin invited an old friend back in Georgia to Moscow for a reunion. They dined and drank—Stalin took pride in his hospitality and his menus, which he personally curated.[7] Later the same night, the friend was arrested in his hotel room. He was executed before dawn. This could not be explained with any words or ideas available to man.[8]

Alexander Nikolaevich could not understand it, but he could try to describe it. The Soviet state was based on punishment. As Young Pioneers, children were taught to criticize one another and themselves in a group setting, reveling in the details of their shortcomings, the intricacies of blame, the ecstasy of repentance, and the imagined precision of the penalties. The Komsomol and the Party itself were also enforcement organizations, as was the "labor collective"—Sovietspeak for "workplace"—where meetings were regularly convened to "expose" fault and to "take measures."[9]

In 1989, its first year in existence, the Rehabilitation Commission reviewed about 280,000 court cases and cleared 367,690 names.[10] This was, by Alexander Nikolaevich's estimate, about 2 percent of the job. From what he could tell now that he had full access to existing documents, casualties of mass terror numbered about twenty million. That was just Stalin's part of it: more people had died in the collectivization campaign that preceded his rise to power, and the punishment machine had continued to work, albeit at a greatly reduced pace, after Stalin's death.[11] Even if the group continued to review cases at the same rate as in its first year, it would not complete the job in Alexander Nikolaevich's lifetime.

The Rehabilitation Commission had been formed under the auspices of the Central Committee. This meant that Yeltsin's 1991 decree halting all economic activity of the Communist Party turned the commission into a nongovernmental organization with no funding, and Alexander Nikolaevich into its unpaid coordinator. He decided to ensure that the documents to which he had access were at least published. He planned to put together volumes on the secret police and on Stalin's chief henchmen, and a series on the Party's foreign activities, including a book on the crushing of the Prague Spring in 1968. If everyone had access to the facts on paper, it would be harder to lie about history, he reasoned. The documents might also make it possible to tell the truth—if anyone ever did find a way to begin making sense of the past. He assembled a team of ten people, if you counted the administrative assistant, the accountant, and the typist, and began the work of sorting, verifying, and cross-referencing.[12] The first volume, on a failed 1921 military rebellion against Bolshevik rule, was published in 1997. Seryozha began helping too, first with the typing, then with some of the more complicated tasks. His grandfather was in a hurry—he said that he had to publish as much as possible before he, and the country, lost access to the documents.

By law, information about mass terror had to be publicly available: Yeltsin had issued a decree to that effect in June 1992.[13] Early on, even some of the dissident historians had favored a cautious approach. Some of what they had glimpsed in the archives, they argued, could not be released to the public without further analysis. Take, for example, a report submitted by a little-known writer on her much more famous friend. The report's author wrote that the other woman had praised Stalin in superlative terms. It appeared likely that the lesser-known writer had made the claim—and, indeed, had agreed to be an informant—solely to protect her friend from suspicion and persecution. But if the document were released uncritically, it might sully a great writer's name. Or take another case: a low-level KGB operative reports that he has met with a dissident who has been consigned to internal exile and the man has agreed to cease all anti-Soviet activity. It is known, however, that after his term in exile the man continued to be active in the dissident movement. How is the report to be interpreted? Was the KGB officer lying, was the dissident telling him what he wanted to hear just to end the conversation, or is there reason to believe that after his exile the dissident had become a mole? Something similar had happened in Poland, where the secret-police archives turned up a dossier on Lech Wałęsa, founder of the Solidarity movement, Nobel laureate, and the country's first post-Communist president. If the dossier was to be believed, Wałęsa had been a paid secret-police informant. Wałęsa's stature and popularity outweighed the damage the dossier could have done, but the paper trail continued to haunt him for years.[14]

There was a deeper reason Russia did not throw open the door to its secret-police archives. The Eastern Bloc countries that took this step—Poland, Germany, and the Czech Republic among them—treated the documents as having been left behind by an occupying power. But Soviet institutions had become Russian institutions after 1991, and soon the Russian bureaucracy began to guard many Soviet secrets like its own. Following the logic of institutions rather than the law, a government commission was formed to review archival documents one by one and decide whether they could be declassified. As time went on, fewer and fewer documents made it into the open. A variety of institutions, ranging from the KGB to the foreign ministry to the Cartographic Service, all of which used to be "all-Soviet" and became "all-Russian," stopped releasing any part of their archives to authorities that could theoretically declassify them. Soviet secrets ossified.[15]

Alexander Nikolaevich concentrated on publishing the documents to which he had already secured access—those would be enough for a lifetime and more. The inability to make sense of tragedy continued to plague him: not only was there no identifiable reason for what had happened, there was no clear border between the victims and the executioners. He had decided early on that he would focus on victims on a case-by-case basis, regardless of who the victims had been before. But what if a person was victimized by becoming the executioner? Take Stalin's last wave of terror, euphemistically called "the anti-cosmopolitan campaign." Blatantly anti-semitic in nature, it had hinged on a conspiracy ostensibly discovered among the country's most prominent doctors—most of them Jewish—who were accused of poisoning their patients among the Party elite. When the smear campaign against the doctors kicked into gear in January 1953, the nation learned of a Russian doctor who had apparently exposed the Jewish bastards. Her name was Lidia Timashuk, and she was promptly, amid much fanfare, awarded the Order of Lenin for her vigilance. The campaign claimed thousands of victims in the Soviet Union and the Eastern Bloc before it was halted abruptly following Stalin's death in March 1953. The doctors were presently exonerated, and the Order of Lenin was quietly rescinded—so quietly, though, that Timashuk remained forever associated with the plot to frame the Jews.[16]

As late as 1966—thirteen years after Stalin's death—Timashuk wrote to the Party leadership asking for her good name back. She had never claimed the doctors were enemies of the state, much less killers, she wrote. All she had done was, years earlier, disagree with an older colleague on the course of treatment chosen for a top member of the Politburo. It had emerged that she had been right to disagree—the older doctor had misdiagnosed a heart attack as a chronic condition—but she was remembered as the woman who had launched the hideous campaign against Soviet Jews, not as the doctor who had the right diagnosis.[17] Timashuk may or may not have been telling the truth when she wrote that she never, not even when questioned by the secret police, cast aspersions on the Jewish doctors. She had certainly suffered less than the other doctors, who had been jailed and tortured and one of whom had died in pretrial detention: Timashuk complained that she had been forced to retire a decade after the Doctors' Plot because those who had been targeted by the campaign refused to work side by side with her. Surely, as executioners went, she was not in the major leagues. Neither was she unequivocally a victim. When she wrote her letter in 1966, the post-Stalin Thaw was over and her appeal was ignored. By the time Alexander Nikolaevich read the letter, Timashuk was dead. He decided to publish the letter.

The cases of other, more obvious executioners presented legal conundrums but not moral ones. Stalin's terror machine executed its executioners at regular intervals. In 1938 alone, forty-two thousand investigators who had taken part in the great industrial-scale purges were executed, as was the chief of the secret police, Nikolai Yezhov. The last of the top-level killers, Lavrentiy Beria, was executed after Stalin's death—but he was convicted not of murder, torture, and abuse of power but of having spied for fourteen different foreign countries. Other executioners had also been punished for imaginary crimes. Legally, this was grounds for rehabilitation. Morally, Alexander Nikolaevich decided that as long as he headed the Rehabilitation Commission, honor would not be restored to a single executioner. He also decided that he would run the commission as long as he lived and was able. Under Yeltsin, the commission was taken back into the fold of the state, with the heads of all federal law-enforcement agencies joining as members, though Alexander Nikolaevich continued to serve in an unpaid capacity. Clearing the names of tens of millions of Soviet citizens was his volunteer job.[18]

A WOMAN CAME to see Arutyunyan about her eleven-year-old daughter, an otherwise lovely girl who kept having strange accidents that her mother suspected were not entirely accidental. Once, for example, she accidentally set the curtains on fire. Another time she accidentally locked the door to the balcony when her own grandmother—the woman's mother—was outside, stranding the older woman in the brutal cold without a coat. The family dynamics were clear enough: three generations of women were living together as an insular family unit—a fairly typical setup. The grandmother ruled the family like a tyrant. The mother carried out all the grandmother's orders, no matter how unreasonable, and tolerated all interventions, no matter how cruel. One time, for example, the mother had the apartment renovated—an expensive and arduous task. When the job was completed, the grandmother demanded a change of wallpaper, and the mother complied. Another time the older woman showed up at her granddaughter's school to denounce the girl for being insufficiently conscientious about homework.

Clearly, the girl's "accidents" were outward expressions of aggression that her mother was stifling. Arutyunyan and her patient began working through it. The woman's pain was immense: she was facing the apparent facts that she, a loving daughter, secretly wished her mother dead, and, even worse, that she, a loving mother, had saddled her own daughter with unmanageable feelings. Then the mother made a discovery: the grandmother had once worked as a guard in the Gulag.

The family was now recast as a camp, complete with dead-end makework, the primacy of discipline, and the total abolition of personal boundaries. The balcony incident looked particularly eerie in this light: it reproduced a common torture technique, when inmates were forced to stand in the freezing cold just outside their barracks. Arutyunyan remembered reading—back when she had access to only some of Freud's writing—that humans play out that which they cannot remember.

A man came seeking help for problems that clearly resided in his relationship with his father. The man's life looked like an unfunny caricature of Soviet culture. He had grown up in a bedroom where the walls were entirely covered with slogans. He went to bed and woke up to "Man! The word has a proud sound!" (a quote from the writer Maxim Gorky), "Courage lies not in a lack of fear but in one's ability to suppress one's fear" (a quote from educator Alexei Makarenko), and the like. Not an inch of space was left vacant, and the message of all these pronouncements together was that not a fraction of the little boy's soul or body should remain unoccupied. When he broke both of his arms, he dared not tell his father, because he was afraid to admit that he had engaged in disorderly play. Nor could he admit to feeling pain—the slogans had taught him that would be weakness—so he never cried. The boy's father had no room for thoughts and perceptions in his mind either, so he made no notice of his son's injuries. The man who came to Arutyunyan now had limited mobility in both of his arms because they had healed without the aid of casts.

Arutyunyan worked with the man to reconstruct a family story: whatever had hurt him so profoundly had clearly traumatized his father first. The father, as the man described him, was a man who had no inner world whatsoever. His single greatest fear seemed to be that of having a thought of his own. It eventually emerged that an earlier generation had greatly feared arrest and had devised a strategy of extreme mimicry: they would be more Soviet than the Soviets who might arrest them for not being Soviet enough. The strategy may have worked—or the man's relatives may simply have been among the tens of millions who happened not to be arrested—but by the time Arutyunyan's patient was born, the Soviet masks had been pulled on so tight for so long that the people behind the masks were frozen in immobility.

As extreme as the case was, the way forward was fairly clear. When the patient's main fear is that of simply engaging in reflection, the presence of an uncritical other can help him realize that he will not destroy the world with his thoughts. The journey is extremely painful, but at the end of it lies freedom.

THROUGHOUT THE 1990S, Robert Jay Lifton, an American psychiatrist known for his work on trauma and on the traumatic effects of totalitarian ideologies, convened a group of Eastern European psychotherapists to try to understand the particular problems they and their patients faced. The essential story revolved around people discovering their histories in family secrets. "Often, parents hide facts because they don't want to endanger their children," wrote Fyodor Konkov, the Russian contributor to the resulting collection.

> They reason that ignorance of a parent who has been purged or marginalized will protect their children from having problems with the regime. But what I understand happens in such situations from the child's point of view is that an empty space, a void develops in their identity.[19]

The strategy had two protective goals, practical and psychological:

The parent thinks, if I deny that something bad has happened to us and I deny and prevent myself from showing the feelings I have about the trauma, I will save my child the pain of these feelings. But the surviving parent also prevents himself from the potential closeness with the child which comes from sharing the pain. By behaving in this manner, the parent trains the son to deny the clues he has already perceived. . . . It is not hard to understand that children raised in this way experience gaps in their emotional life which affect their ability to make and keep intimate relationships. Many layers of understanding are missing.[20]

"Dr. Konkov describes a specific affective state, one of inner emptiness, which children experience during arrested grief, when they feel they have been lied to about the life and death of their parents or grandparents," Lifton and his coeditor, psychoanalyst Jacob D. Lindy, added in their comments.[21] Perhaps this was the nature of the emptiness that had so struck Carl Rogers when he visited the Soviet Union—when he also observed that none of his interlocutors seemed to have been able to keep an intimate relationship going.

Lifton and Lindy also noted a particular problem these therapists faced, one that they had seen in other psychologists working with traumatized populations: a certain kind of countertransference. "In each case, this intense reaction was a clue to ways in which the patient's wound—a legacy of the Communist era—connected with the therapist's wound of the same traumatic history."[22]

ARUTYUNYAN WAS CERTAIN that wounds formed when something was missing, willfully unremembered. Her own family had made the unusual choice to maintain its story, and this gave her an advantage. She had learned the story in stages. It must have been in fourth or fifth grade when she asked her mother why the family album contained no photographs of Arutyunyan's grandfather. The absence was conspicuous: the life of the family was otherwise solidly visually documented, or so it seemed to Arutyunyan. There was a photograph of her mother, Maya, as a baby, in 1925. There were numerous photographs of Maya's mother, Anna Mikhailovna, as she made her way up to the very top of the Soviet ladder, becoming a member of the Academy of Sciences and the Central Committee, collecting honors and awards along the way, looking stern yet inspired every time. And not a single photograph of Anna Mikhailovna's husband, Maya's father, Grigory Yakovlevich Yakovin. Arutyunyan knew that he had died long ago, before the war, and even that he had been executed. But surely there had to be pictures?

"They feared for me," said Maya. "So they destroyed the photographs."

"They" were Maya's mother and grandmother, but what did this mean?

"You see, there was a time when innocent people could be condemned. And if their families did not reject them, then children could be in danger." Maya got out a volume of the *Great Soviet Encyclopedia*, a tome in blue-black cloth. This was volume five, which began and ended with perfectly incomprehensible words: "Berezna" and "Botokudy." Maya opened the book to a full-page portrait of a middle-aged, mostly bald man with a round face, perfectly thin lips, and a pince-nez with round rimless lenses. This was Lavrentiy Beria, whom the accompanying four-page article described as "one of the most outstanding leaders of the All-Soviet Communist Party of Bolsheviks and of the Soviet state, a loyal student and comrade of J. V. Stalin," and so forth. This was not Arutyunyan's grandfather—this was Stalin's chief executioner. After he himself was executed, subscribers to the *Great Soviet Encyclopedia* received a letter that Maya was now showing her:

> The state scholarly publishing house of the Great Soviet
> Encyclopedia recommends that pages 21, 22, 23, and 24,
> as well as the portrait bound in between pages 22 and 23,
> be removed and replaced with new pages, enclosed with this
> letter.

Use scissors or a razor blade to remove the above-mentioned pages, taking care to retain inner margins to which new pages are to be glued.

The replacement pages contained an article on the Bering Strait.[23]

"You see, this is the sort of thing that would happen," explained Maya. "And if it was a close relative, you had to be really careful."

This was a fascinating answer. It had a tinge of adventure to it. The physical and figurative disappearance of Grigory Yakovlevich Yakovin registered as mystery rather than tragedy.

Then, in high school, Arutyunyan read *A Steep Road*,* a memoir by a woman, a historian and a loyal Party member, who was falsely accused of being a Trotskyist and spent a decade in the Gulag, followed by another in internal exile. The book was a clear-eyed catalog of human suffering:

When I was young, I liked to repeat the phrase, "I think, therefore I am." Now I could say, "I hurt, therefore I am." . . .

Back in 1937, when I first admitted my share of responsibility for all that had happened, I dreamed of redemption through pain. By 1949, I knew that pain works only for a time. When it stretches for decades and becomes a part of the everyday, it is no longer redemptive. It is simply something that turns you into a block of wood.

Physical suffering drowns out the pain of inner torment.

This is a horror theater in which some of the actors have been assigned to play victims and others, the executioners. The latter have it worse.[24]

The book was published in the West and smuggled into the Soviet Union, and Arutyunyan had simply found it sitting on the desk of one of her parents. Now she could not put it down. She could not sleep. She could not stop crying. She summoned her closest friends from school. They spent

---

*The title of the book is usually translated into English as *Into the Whirlwind*.

the night—the book could not be taken out of the apartment—reading and crying.

"Why didn't you tell me?" Arutyunyan demanded of her parents.

"But we did," they said.

"Not like this!"

She came back to them after this conversation, asking for details about her grandfather. After a few queries, Maya handed her a copy of a poem typed, in the samizdat fashion, on what was called "cigarette paper"—it was thin as rolling papers, and this allowed as many as four copies to be produced through the use of carbon paper and a manual typewriter.

"Here, read this," Maya said. "The facts don't match, but this is your grandmother's story."

It was a long piece by the émigré poet Naum Korzhavin. It was written in the second person, addressed to a woman who, if the poem was to be believed, was wholeheartedly, slavishly devoted to the Party.

> *You lied in the name of ideals,*
> *but the tradition of lying*
> *Was continued by those*
> *better suited for purposeful lies.*
> *We are all mortal beings.*
> *Our passions express who we are. . . .*
> *You rejected your love*
> *in the name of a higher desire.*
> *But was there love,*
> *was there love even once in your life?*

No, said the poem, the woman had never loved. Yes, it contradicted itself, once she did fall in love, with a fellow Party intellectual, a skinny bespectacled Jew. His views were to the right of the protagonist's—which meant that they were to the right of the Party line—and they argued the issues, until he got arrested. She was asked to testify, and she did not hesitate.

The work of the Party is sacred,
no room for emotions.
Stick to the substance.
Discard everything else.

She "told them everything." It was the right thing to do, but when she found out that he had died, she spent all night crying. By this time, according to the poem, she was in the Gulag herself. By the end of the poem it becomes clear that the heroine survived—and, in spite of all that happened to her, remained a true believer. The author despairs of reasoning with her.

You gave it all to the fight,
including that which cannot be given.
All of it:
the ability to love,
to think, and to feel.
All of you, nothing spared—
But how
do you live without your self?[25]

If this was the story of her grandmother—a claim Arutyunyan instinctively doubted—then her grandfather had once again been elided. The poem described the betrayal, but not the man who was betrayed. Maya finally told her daughter what she knew. Both of her parents had been revolutionaries, underground organizers in czarist Russia, fighters during the Civil War, and scholars after. They had met as students at the Institute for Red Professors, which had been formed to create a cadre of university instructors to replace those who were being exiled or arrested. This was around the time of Lenin's death and Stalin's rise to power. When Maya was a newborn, her parents were dispatched to Germany for a year to further their studies. When they returned, the Party assigned them to teach history in Leningrad. Soon after, Maya's mother, Anna Mikhailovna, denounced her husband publicly for his Trotskyist views—Arutyunyan had no idea what that meant, and Maya explained that he was opposed to Stalin, who he feared would establish the rule of terror. Then Anna Mikhailovna left for Moscow, taking little Maya with her. Maya never saw her father again, though he lived for another dozen years. He was arrested, exiled, arrested again, and finally executed, and in all that time he never named a name, never signed a false confession, and never wavered in his beliefs.

All of this sounded, suspiciously, like the sort of story Arutyunyan would have learned in school when they studied the lives of the Bolshevik quasi-saints: all heroism and no human. Maya spoke about her mother in similarly epic terms. She was pure. She loved the Party and she loved her husband, and later, when she was a powerful woman, she always stood up for people who fell out of favor, always defended their Leninist credentials. Back in the 1920s, Maya said, her mother had been granted a visit with her jailed husband. Maya was unclear about whether the initiative had been her mother's or the Party's, but she knew that the goal of the visit was to tear Grigory Yakovlevich from his mistaken beliefs and return him to the fold of the Party of Stalin. He had been elated to see his wife, but the moment he realized what her true objective was, he asked her to leave.

Thus had Anna Mikhailovna lost her one true love among men. From that point on, she belonged to the Party only, body and soul. But in the mid-1930s, when Maya was about ten, Anna Mikhailovna was herself expelled from the Party, for mentoring a student whose dissertation was perceived to contain nationalist notes inconsistent with the then current post-anti-imperial line. She made a suicide pact with her best friend, who had also fallen into disfavor. She left a note: "The Party can live without me, but I cannot live without the Party." The maid walked in on her, spoiling the suicide attempt; the best friend was already dead. After that, a senior scholar stepped in, arranging for Anna Mikhailovna to teach history at a provincial secondary school. For years after that, it was Maya's grandmother who took care of her. After the war, however, Stalin decided that he needed a woman in the Central Committee, and Anna Mikhailovna was not only reinstated in the Party but flown right up the career ladder to the top.

Arutyunyan found this narrative unsatisfying. It sounded to her like not one but two bad plays: one about star-crossed lovers, the other about a man so heroic he could not be imagined. She had read enough by now to know that the system of torture, humiliation, and threats broke the best of the best and that the current generation was in no position to judge them.

This was the early 1970s, years before Arutyunyan became a professional psychologist, but she needed no special training to see through the family myth. It was all compensation. Maya loved her mother, and she needed a story grand enough to make up for her betrayals. Anna Mikhailovna had taken Maya's father away—twice: first by denouncing him and again by destroying all traces of him. She had also abandoned Maya repeatedly, first as a baby: that beautiful picture from 1925 had been taken in a Berlin children's home, where the little girl was kept while her parents were off uniting the world's proletariat in revolt. The calligraphically perfect caption on the back of the photograph said, *"Liebe Mutter, liebe Tochter,"* and this broke Arutyunyan's heart. When Anna Mikhailovna went off to teach school in a remote city, she did not even say goodbye—she simply disappeared. There were no letters, only an anonymous message that Maya's mother was "well and living in a different city." Wounds that large required equally large myths, which was why Maya had had to conjure a father so heroic and a mother so long-suffering that they could exist only in her imagination. This explained why Maya chose to believe, too, that Korzhavin's tragic, romantic poem had something to do with her mother even though the plot details did not match: if the poet had such compassion for his protagonist, then she must have deserved it. Arutyunyan was a loving daughter too, so she kept her doubts to herself.

TWENTY YEARS after that conversation, in a friend's kitchen in Munich, of all places, Arutyunyan met a historian of the samizdat, the keeper of the largest known collection of self-published Russian writing. She did not even know why she felt compelled to mention the family legend according to which Korzhavin's poem "Tan'ka" had been written for and about her grandmother. The archivist became curious. A day later he returned to that kitchen to tell Arutyunyan that he had located an early manuscript of the poem and it contained a dedication to A. M. Pankratova, her grandmother. He suggested that the dedication had been omitted from later iterations to avoid endangering Anna Mikhailovna's family—Arutyunyan and her parents.

Maya was not a sentimental person, but when Arutyunyan told her that she had confirmed the legend of the poem, she teared up—perhaps because her daughter had remembered what she had told her so many years earlier, or perhaps because she had finally believed her.

Maya died in 1999. In her papers, Arutyunyan found Anna Mikhailovna's journals. Maya had quoted lines from them to her daughter but had never let her see them: she said that they were too intimate. They were.

> 1 November 1923 (night)
> We have just parted, and I have flown back to my room like a bird, so incredibly, insanely, unconscionably happy.
> "Why do I love you so?" he asked. "Why does it make me so happy to see you?"
> "Is that true?" I asked. I could not yet believe it, but I could feel the fire engulfing me.
> We were standing on the stairs and discussing Party business.

Anna Mikhailovna carried this love through the rest of her life, just as Maya had said. Her later notes contained a chronology of nonstarter romances. "Gr. would never do a thing like that," she would write, damning a potential suitor with this comparison to her late husband. "No, he is no Gr.," she would write, dismissing another.

Arutyunyan asked a close friend, a historian well-versed in Stalin-era archives, to look up her grandfather's case files. She gave him power of attorney for the purpose—by this time, access to archives was restricted to family members.

It all checked out. Grigory Yakovlevich was every bit the hero from

Maya's stories. He never named a name, never lost his dignity, never gave an inch to his tormentors. Transcripts of his interrogations were repetitive:

"I consider it inappropriate to name people."

"I deny that."

"Prosecutors and investigators may be concerned with actions, not opinions and intentions. . . . I do not see a need to testify with regards to opinions."

"I don't recall."

"I will not name anyone."

"That's a falsehood. I am aware of no such group."

The unbelievable story of Anna Mikhailovna's failed redemptive visit also proved true. She had been dispatched by the Party to try to lure her estranged, ideologically wayward husband back into the fold. He was released into her custody. They spent three or four nights together at a hotel before irreconcilable ideological differences separated them forever. Arutyunyan's friend was even able to make copies of photographs—two sets of mug shots, taken at two arrests. Grigory Yakovlevich was handsome, with strong features and a full head of dark wavy hair. He looked tall, if one can look tall in a mug shot. His likeness had nothing in common with the "skinny, bespectacled Jew" from the Korzhavin poem. There had been other scant but more accurate descriptions of him, including this from the memoir of revolutionary expat Victor Serge:

> Grigory Yakovlevich Yakovin, aged thirty, had returned from Germany, on which country he had just written an excellent book. A sporting enthusiast with a constantly alert intelligence, good looks, and a spontaneous charm . . .[26]

The Chilean writer Roberto Bolaño gave Grigory Yakovlevich a three-line cameo in his epic novel *2666*: "Grigory Yakovin, a great expert in contemporary Germany history."[27] Several years after Maya, the last person to have seen Grigory Yakovlevich alive, had died, Arutyunyan was finally able to see a clear picture of her grandfather—in an academic paper her historian friend wrote after researching the case.[28]

———

ARUTYUNYAN FOUND HERSELF regretting that her mother did not live to read her own father's court documents—and then she wondered why Maya had not used the brief window of openness in the early 1990s to look for the case herself (a history professor, she would have been confident undertaking that kind of research). Had Maya harbored her own doubts? Her information had, after all, come solely from her mother, who had idolized her late husband and whose authority Maya would have feared undermining even decades after her death.

There was something extravagantly old-fashioned about the way Anna Mikhailovna and Grigory Yakovlevich's generation had carried its beliefs. "In the disillusioned world of post-Stalinism, maintaining the values of the revolutionary years was perceived as personal vanity," wrote Etkind, the cultural historian.[29] In the post-Stalin era, scaling desires and ambitions from universal down to petit-bourgeois was seen as a virtue, a sign of humanity that was being gradually restored. That made it complicated to admire Grigory Yakovlevich and empathize with Anna Mikhailovna, and it made it difficult to mourn them. The tools of mourning are epic and profound, but after Stalin, people trusted only small emotions and soft categories. "Now, Shakespeare seemed too earnest, austere, stiff; his gravity seemed laughable," Etkind wrote.[30]

The people who most clearly opposed the Soviet regime were, at least in Arutyunyan's generation, the ones who were most suspicious of grand gestures and big pronouncements. Perhaps this was one of the reasons people stopped removing Soviet monuments within a couple of days of the August 1991 coup. The toppled Dzerzhinsky, along with a Stalin, a head of Khrushchev, and a couple of very large Old Bolsheviks, were delivered to a vast vacant lot in the back of a recently constructed House of the Artists in central Moscow. But hundreds, if not thousands, of Lenins, Bolsheviks, obscure heroic Young Pioneers, and disembodied hammer-and-sickles and five-pointed stars continued to dot Moscow parks, public squares, and building facades. Alexander Nikolaevich suggested removing the largest Lenin monument in the city, in Oktyabrskaya Square, and replacing it with a monument to all victims of Soviet terror—but retaining the name of the square "as a lesson to our descendants."[31] Instead, Lenin kept standing, roughly as tall as a three-story building, but the square was renamed.

In November 1996, on the seventy-ninth anniversary of the Great October Revolution, Yeltsin renamed the holiday that was always celebrated on November 7. From now on, it would be called the Day of Agreement and Reconciliation. The following year, the eightieth since the Revolution and the sixtieth since the year of the Great Terror—the most brutal year of Stalinism—would become an entire Year of Agreement and Reconciliation.[32] The same year, post-apartheid South Africa established its Truth and Reconciliation Commission, which harked back to a number of "truth commissions" that had functioned in countries such as Argentina, Chile, Nepal, and others. But Yeltsin was omitting the fact-finding component of the process, focusing solely on reconciliation, or at least agreement. Indeed, Yeltsin was proposing to dispense with all three of the "energies" that Etkind has described as components of postcatastrophic recovery—knowledge, grief, and justice—and proceed directly to some imaginary future in which reckoning had been left behind.

Yeltsin no longer had the strength, or the popular support, to continue fighting against the Communist Party. If he went ahead with a planned trial of the Party, he risked losing—if not in Constitutional Court then in the court of public opinion. With resentment the dominant emotion in the land, Yeltsin could afford no public confrontation with the past. The eighty-volume case against the Communist Party, and the argument for a permanent ban on its existence, were now shelved. The organizers of the 1991 coup and the leaders of the armed uprising of 1993—three dozen people in all—were pardoned by the Russian parliament in its very first amnesty, in February 1994—not because the two conflicts had melded into one in the minds of Russian parliament members but because both conflicts had to be retired and forgotten.[33] Even Alexander Nikolaevich's quiet and plodding work on the Rehabilitation Commission came to seem too confrontational. In 1997, Alexander Nikolaevich submitted two rehabilitation decrees—one concerning children who had been incarcerated in the Gulag and the other concerning members of non-Bolshevik socialist parties who had been executed in the terror—and Yeltsin ignored them.[34]

Yeltsin, who had always had an infallible sense of the public mood, was increasingly distancing himself from the young radical reformers in favor of many of the old guard. He seemed willing to forget and forgive everything, including personal insults and state treason. "He is making himself a laughing stock with the Communists!" said Alexander Nikolaevich. In April 1997, in the spirit of reconciliation, Yeltsin sent greetings to the annual congress of the Russian Communist Party. The hall whistled and booed when the address was read from the stage. Then they laughed.[35]

nine

OLD SONGS

NEW YEAR'S EVE 1994 was depressing. Like most of his acquaintances, Lev Gudkov was feeling shell-shocked—or simply shocked. Russia had gone to war against a part of itself. After months of rumors, threats, and several botched covert operations, Yeltsin had decided to put an end to a forceful separatist movement in Chechnya, a small republic in the North Caucasus, on the border with Turkey and Georgia. He would use the army to dislodge the local government. But the Chechen resistance was well armed and possessed of ten times the resolve of the Russian troops, along with familiarity with the terrain and the support of the local population. What had been planned as a fast attack, essentially a police operation, turned into an all-out military offensive. On December 31—twenty days after the operation began—Moscow staged a series of bombing raids that reduced Grozny, one of the country's own cities, to a smoking ruin. Several of the old dissidents— men who were well past middle age, and who had seen prison but never armed battle—were now down in Chechnya, documenting the atrocities and trying to use their own bodies to draw the world's attention to the war. The entire Moscow press corps, it seemed, was also there. Information was flowing from Chechnya like blood from a broken artery. The effect of the glut of macabre detail was as terrifying and depressing as anything Gudkov had ever experienced.

This effect was exacerbated by the results of a survey the public opinion center had just completed. Five years after the original Homo Sovieticus study, Levada's team decided to check in. It was another difficult survey to design: the country's borders, its name, and its system of government had changed since the first study. Some questions had to be discarded, and some of the others were reworked. A few new ones had to be devised.

There was good news in the survey: when people were asked Gudkov's "dynamite" question—what ought to be done with various deviant groups—their responses generally expressed more tolerance than they had five years earlier. The overall share of those who favored "liquidating" deviants went down from 31 to 23 percent, and those who supported the idea of "leaving them to their own devices" went up from 12 to 29 percent. Those who would "liquidate" the disabled decreased from 25 to 18 percent while those who would "help" the disabled grew from 50 to 56 percent. By Western standards, these were frightening figures, but those were not the standards to be applied here: the sociologists wanted to know only how much attitudes were changing, and in which direction. But even such scant optimism as was engendered by this approach was dampened by responses to other questions. The share of those who would "leave alone" members of religious cults dropped from 57 to 51 percent while the proportion of those who would "liquidate" or "isolate" them grew noticeably. The same thing happened with "rockers": 26 percent wanted to "liquidate" them, up from 20. This issue was a bit of a Rorschach test: no one could be quite sure what "rockers" meant. It had once referred to those who played or listened to forbidden Western music, but the days when the state banned rock music were long over. If there was no marginalized or indeed identifiable group that was called "rockers," whom were the respondents wanting to "liquidate," and why? The sociologists concluded that the word had become a stand-in for "other," or "strange," and elicited an aggressive reaction precisely because—unlike homosexuals or the disabled—"rockers," whoever they were, were not the subject of any public discussion.

The rest of the survey left little room for hope. The percentage of people who said they were unhappy had more than doubled in five years—from 14 to 34 (though the share of those who said they were happy stayed steady at 46). A clue to what had made so many people so unhappy showed up in answers to another question, in which respondents were asked to rank the importance of changes that had occurred in the country. Barely half named things that could be considered accomplishments, such as political freedoms, the ability to travel, work, and study abroad, the right to open one's own business, and the "option of living without regard for the authorities," as the sociologists phrased it. An overwhelming majority saw the state's failures as the most significant changes: the rise of unemployment, the "impoverishment of the people," and a "weakening of Russian unity." Asked to name the most important events in the entire history of the country, people resorted to Soviet historiography, pointing to the Great October Revolution and the Great Patriotic War, which seemed to have lost none of its symbolic sheen despite a wealth of newly available information, starting with the Stalin-Hitler military alliance. In general, people seemed to have lost interest in learning more about Stalin, his rule, and his terror. Twenty-five percent of respondents now saw his role in history as positive (there was no benchmark to compare this response with, because five years earlier, at the height of the public conversation about Stalinist terror, the question itself would have been inconceivable). He ranked not far below Gorbachev and Yeltsin, whose "positive" ratings were 33 and 30 percent, respectively. These reflected a newly dim view of perestroika, which, people overwhelmingly said, had led to the regrettable breakup of the Soviet Union. The democratic revolution of 1991—the defeat of totalitarianism—was an event that existed in the sociologists' minds but not in the minds of their respondents.

Gudkov recalled going to a celebratory rally immediately after the failure of the August 1991 coup. A German friend had come along. "Long live great Russia!" chanted the crowd, and Gudkov sensed his friend tensing up. He noted that Germans are hypersensitive to expressions of nationalism, but Gudkov himself was unconcerned about the crowd's sentiment. Now he wondered if he should have paid more attention to the tone, and to the linguistic sleight of hand of the slogan. It had started as "Long live democratic Russia," but in the course of a few hours the word "democratic" had been dropped in favor of "great." Had the ideas of freedom and democracy really been forgotten no sooner than they had apparently won?

Asked, in 1994, which of the major changes of the last five years had brought the country more harm or more good, Russians were lukewarm on freedoms: only 53 percent thought that freedom of speech had been a positive change, and other new freedoms ranked lower. Only 8 percent thought that the breakup of the Soviet Union had been a positive development. Seventy-five percent thought it had caused more harm, and this was the single highest figure in the entire survey, the thing Russians agreed on over any other.

Respondents did not exactly want to return to the Soviet Union, from what Gudkov could tell: the memory of food shortages, poverty, and airlessness was still raw. What Russians wanted was certainty, a clear sense of who they were and what their country was.

The sociologists tried to tease out what ideas of national identity there were. All individuals and societies define themselves, to some extent, in opposition to others, and for the Russians in 1994 this jumping-off image was a generalized stereotype of the European. This imaginary person was rational, cultivated, active—and Other. Russia was coming off a period of concerted self-denigration, when society was processing the shock of seeing firsthand what it had been told was the "rotten West." It had turned out to be shiny, happy, and also ordinary and law-based. For years, newspapers had used the phrase "the civilized world" to refer to that which Russia was not. Now Russians were distinctly tired of thinking of themselves, and their country, as inferior. So what did they see as the innate positive qualities of Russians? This open question elicited, on the basis of 2,957 surveys, three leading qualities: "open," "simple," and "patient." The ideal Russian, it seemed, was a person without qualities. It was clear to Gudkov that this was the blank mirror of the hostile and violent regimes under which Russians had long lived.

Hannah Arendt had written about the way totalitarianism robs people of the ability to form opinions, to define themselves as distinct from other members of society or from the regime itself.[1] Now this hollowed-out person was holding up the emptiness as his greatest virtue. If "open" and "simple" described the undifferentiated nature of a Russian, then "patient," as Gudkov read the responses, referred to Russians' tolerance for violence. In contrast to the imaginary European, all of whose qualities described agency, the respondents saw themselves as subjects of a regime that ruled by force. This made it seem that the war in Chechnya, which most of Gudkov's circle saw as a tragic anomaly, was actually a logical expression of the people's expectations.

The worst news in the survey, though, was that it contradicted Levada's original concept of Homo Sovieticus: back in 1989, he had predicted that as the subjects of totalitarianism died off, Soviet institutions would crumble. But this survey suggested that Homo Sovieticus was not going anywhere: there was no clear evidence that this sociological type was less prevalent among young people than in their parents' generation. Homo Sovieticus's central trait—doublethink—was in full display across age groups. Respondents continued to think in antinomies. A central one was this. A majority of respondents agreed with the following statement: "Over the seventy-five years of the Soviet regime our people have become different from people of the West, and it is too late to change that." A slightly larger majority agreed with the statement "Sooner or later Russia will follow the path that is common for all civilized countries." Most people agreed with both statements at the same time, and the fact that they did seemed to affirm the former and make the latter seem vanishingly unlikely.[2]

If Levada's original hypothesis was wrong, then the sociologists' interpretation of the collapse of the Soviet Union needed to be revised. Levada had long ago suggested that Soviet society moved, pendulum-like, between periods of extreme oppression and relative liberalization, as under Khrushchev and early on under Gorbachev, and that these cycles followed a pragmatic logic. The periods of liberalization allowed pent-up frustrations—and, more important, the people who would articulate them—to bubble to the surface. With the potential troublemakers visible and active, the crackdown that inevitably followed eliminated them. In the long run, the cycles ensured the stability of the regime. The sociologists called the crackdowns "periodic castration."

Perestroika had seemed to begin as yet another period of a temporary loosening of the reins, but then the pendulum appeared to swing too far, bringing the entire edifice down. But what if that was not what happened? What if, in fact, it had swung just as far as it needed to go to maintain the cycles? What if the changes in borders, state structure, and laws did not actually reflect or cause profound changes in the structure of society?

ON DECEMBER 31, 1995, Channel 1, the main television broadcaster, aired a wholly new type of show. The New Year's Eve tradition had been in flux since perestroika. In 1986, Gorbachev, speaking at the twenty-seventh Party Congress, condemned Soviet television for being dull. In response, broadcast executives rushed to reformat their programming, scrapping, among others, *The Blue Flame*, the New Year's Eve variety show that had been in existence for a generation. Now Channel 1, which reached about 93 percent of Russian households, showed a film that sounded remarkably like the old show.[3] Called *Old Songs About the Most Important Things*, it was billed as a musical. The cast of characters harked back to the propaganda musicals of the 1930s and 1950s. These generally featured collective-farm workers, friendly competitions, and innocuous love interests that spurred self-improvement in the less perfect of the pair. Often, there was class conflict that presented the opportunity for mild ideological critique, which invariably ended with the victory of communism over evil.

Old Songs featured collective-farm workers, a truck driver, a recently decommissioned soldier, a teacher, a bourgeois, a recently released convict, a "rocker" (one could tell because he had long hair and wore fancy city clothes), and a "virgin ready for marriage" (this was the role as listed in the credits), among others. The plot, such as it was, provided opportunities for this ensemble to sing twenty-one Soviet songs, most of them lyrical but many with references to the Great Patriotic War. This was no remake of a Soviet movie, though. In this film, the classes lived in peace. Indeed, there was no conflict of any kind. There was a lot of pursuing of love interests, interspersed with the women's insistence that there be no premarital sex, but there was no culmination: no one got married, no one had sex, and nothing triumphed over anything else. The only person clearly marked as Other in the film—the "rocker"—sang a song in Ukrainian, a language not yet perceived as foreign but rather as a difficult-to-decipher dialect of Russian. In fact, nothing happened in the film, and this seemed to be the heart of its nostalgic message: against the backdrop of post-Soviet Russia, where the war in Chechnya was entering its second year, where newspapers reported endlessly on crime, conflict, and constant economic concerns, it imagined a past straight out of Soviet newspapers, where nothing ever happened unless it was in the West. In *Old Songs*, people happily consumed Soviet-made products such as hollow-filter Belomorkanal cigarettes (so named for the Gulag's largest project) and a rubbery processed cheese called Druzhba ("Friendship"), but they bought them willingly, and without having to stand in line, from a well-stocked shop where male customers were cheerfully served by busty saleswomen decked out in evening gowns. The Soviet era was recast as romantically placid and the Soviet regime as benevolent. In the film's most bizarre moment, a man and a woman huddle in a tiny rowboat.

"Do you know why your feet are so adorable?" he asks her.

"I do," she responds. "It is because our Soviet regime is so wonderful."

"That's correct," he says, and rises from kissing her feet to kissing her face—or so we assume, for the camera shyly pans away. The scene referenced Soviet-era spoofs of Soviet propaganda, which ascribed to the regime both unlimited powers and boundless magnanimity. But if the Soviet-era spoofs, which circulated in samizdat or simply as jokes, were edgy, this spoof of a spoof was soft and rounded. At the end of the film the entire cast, including the "rocker," the bourgeois, and the convict, gather around a giant table at the center of which sits one of the unique edible symbols of Soviet privilege, a roast suckling pig just like the ones Zhanna's father started receiving on New Year's Eve once he became governor. In the reimagined Soviet past, everyone got a piece of the pig.[4]

Created by two men who were about to become the most influential people in Russian television,* *Old Songs* was a huge hit. The new renditions of the old songs could, for the next year and beyond, be heard on street corners all over the country, where kiosks were briskly selling two-cassette audio sets. There would be sequels: *Old Songs About the Most Important Things* 2, 3, and 4. The following year, the other major federal broadcast channel resurrected *The Blue Flame*, the Soviet New Year's Eve show, to compete for what was turning out to be a giant nostalgia audience. Once cable and satellite television took hold a few years later, an entire channel was launched to show Soviet television twenty-four hours a day. It was called Nostalgia, and its logo, shown in a corner of the screen, contained a red hammer and sickle.

Television producers were tapping into the moods Gudkov and his colleagues had documented in their survey. In the years between the 1989 and 1994 studies, Russians had grown tired of thinking about the future. They were drawing their sense of identity from the past, and they were imbuing this past with an additional air of wholesome conservatism.

THE "OPEN," "SIMPLE" quality-less Russian outsourced his agency to something or someone more powerful. An element of the nostalgia that was becoming evident by the end of 1995 was the longing for a strong leader, capable of exerting the force for which Homo Sovieticus was ever prepared. Yeltsin no longer seemed suited for the role: he was passive, often absent, always embroiled in yet another tussle with the parliament, though these had long since stopped seeming fateful. His army was fighting a hopeless,

---

*The film was produced by Konstantin Ernst, who went on to head Channel 1, and Leonid Parfenov, who became probably the best-known and best-loved post-Soviet television host and filmmaker.

protracted war against Russian citizens in Chechnya, and Yeltsin himself, who had once seemed larger than life, was fumbling even this opportunity to demonstrate his resolve. On two occasions Chechen insurgents took large groups of hostages on territories adjacent to Chechnya, in an effort to force Russia to negotiate. The first time, Yeltsin went missing and his prime minister had to handle the negotiations; the second time, Yeltsin made incoherent televised comments.[5] The war had lost him the support of the old dissidents and many of the new liberal economists who had worked in his government, but this served only to reinforce a tendency that had been evident for a couple of years: Yeltsin was increasingly surrounding himself with old Soviet hands. In the population at large, the war was unpopular but not so unpopular that it could arouse protests of any scale—after a few attempts, efforts to organize demonstrations devolved into a weekly miniature rally, more of an information session held by a few activists staffing a table in central Moscow. The war did not arouse passions, but in 1995 Yeltsin's popularity plummeted into the single digits.[6] In 1996, as he approached the end of his first term, his political life seemed to be over.

Yeltsin, democrat though he was, had a distinctly monarchical obsession with choosing a successor. In August 1994 he cruised into Nizhny Novgorod on a river liner sailing down the Volga and, stepping ashore to speak to the crowds, announced that he had settled on a successor: Boris Nemtsov. "I just want to say that he has grown so much that we can now set our sights on his being president," said Yeltsin. The awkward phrasing showed that the decision was Yeltsin's, not the younger man's.[7] Nemtsov remained the heir apparent until he began voicing his opposition to the war in Chechnya. In 1996 the people of Nizhny Novgorod collected a million signatures against the war—with a population of 3.7 million, this meant that nearly all adults in the region signed. Nemtsov rode in a Nizhny Novgorod–made van to deliver the signatures to the Kremlin. He had the driver stop just outside the fortress and marched straight into Yeltsin's office, one of the fat cardboard binders with petitions in his hands.

"What do you think," asked Yeltsin, addressing him in the familiar, as one might address a child. "Are these signatures for me or against me?"

"If you stop the war, they will be for you, and if you don't, they will be against you."

When Nemtsov left, he assumed he was no longer Yeltsin's chosen successor. He did not hear from the president for months.[8]

In March 1996, Yegor Gaidar, the former prime minister, came to Nizhny Novgorod to ask Nemtsov to run for president. He joined Nemtsov on a visit to one of the collective farms, and what he saw only affirmed his resolve. Nemtsov, who had been governor during four and a half years of struggle and extremely complicated reforms, was genuinely beloved in his region. Unlike Gaidar, whose name was associated with every unpopular move made by the Russian government and whose manner and looks made him seem aloof and condescending, Nemtsov was a natural politician, charismatic and attractive in an approachable way. Gaidar argued that Nemtsov could become the true democratic candidate and beat both Yeltsin and the resurgent Communists in the election. Nemtsov said that he could not betray Yeltsin. Gaidar argued in favor of principle over personal loyalty, and failed.[9]

In the end, it looked like it would be Yeltsin against the Communists and he would lose. But the country's newly rich rallied behind the president, as did the politicians he had patronized—including, in the end, the majority of the antiwar bureaucrats—and as did the newly free press. But most of all, it was Yeltsin himself who rallied. After a couple of years when he seemed to oscillate between depression and binge-drinking, the president mobilized to campaign. "The people suddenly saw an entirely different president, one they had forgotten: it was Yeltsin as he had been in 1991, with his unique ability to talk to people, to attract support through his energy and drive," Gaidar wrote later.[10]

Surveys conducted by Levada's center showed that Russians wanted three things in this election cycle: an end to economic instability; an end to the war in Chechnya; and the restoration of their country to greatness. Among themselves, the sociologists began talking about the trauma caused by the collapse of the Soviet Union. For the Kremlin, they wrote memo after memo. Gudkov wrote one in which he claimed to prove that if Yeltsin did not find a way to end the war in Chechnya, he would lose the election.

Yeltsin called Nemtsov to summon him to a government airport in Moscow: they were going to Chechnya, together, to signal the beginning of the end of the war.[11] Yeltsin dispatched a negotiation team to Chechnya with the mandate to broker peace at any cost. Watching television reports on negotiations that quickly proceeded from ceasefire to treaty, Gudkov marveled at the real-life consequences of sociology.

If peace in Chechnya was a difficult goal, the other two—ending economic hardship and restoring Russian grandeur—were impossible. Yeltsin opted to fight directly against the rising wave of nostalgia. His campaign endeavored to drown out *Old Songs About the Most Important Things* with a barrage of messages, most of them frightening. Cartoons imagined a future under the Communists, with nothing in the refrigerator and only one program on television. A rock star implored his fans to vote for Yeltsin because "I don't want my country to turn into a communist concentration camp again." A clip composed of black-and-white footage from the 1918–1922 civil war said, "It's not too late to prevent civil war or famine."[12] In July 1996, Yeltsin won the election.

YELTSIN WAS APPARENTLY AWARE THAT he had won by promoting an emotion rather than a program. Ten days after the election, he created a commission to look for a new Russian national idea. He appointed a close aide, Georgy Satarov, to run the commission, and gave it a year to produce a result. The government newspaper *Rossiyskaya gazeta* announced an essay contest with a handsome top prize—10 million rubles, or about $2,000, for the best national idea in seven pages or less. Satarov, an intellectual and a liberal, rushed to reassure the public that the commission would not be crafting an ideology and forcing it on the population, Soviet style. Rather, it would aim to help articulate an idea on which the nation could agree, and perhaps already agreed on. Satarov himself proposed to the commission that it could borrow a page from West Germany's post-Nazism playbook, combining a program of economic healing with what he called "national penitence." The proposal flopped. The essay contest fizzled, and the grand prize was never awarded.[13]

"Rumor has it, government dachas outside Moscow are filled with dozens of Russia's 'best minds,'" wrote the leading nationalist magazine, *Nash sovremennik* ("Our Contemporary"), in May 1997. "They've wasted tons of paper trying to formulate the idea. But it seems something is not working."[14]

Rumor in the Kremlin press pool in the fall of 1997 was that Yeltsin would unveil the Russian national idea during a visit to Nizhny Novgorod, which remained a post-Communist transition success story. Word was, Yeltsin would say that Russia was now a capitalist country working toward the glorious future of a "people's capitalism." The construction paralleled the old Soviet propaganda paradigm, when the country was said to be "socialist," working toward a glorious communist future. A catchphrase had apparently been coined to express the essence of the new national idea: "equal-opportunity capitalism," as opposed to what much of the population perceived to be Russia's current state of enrichment for the well-connected.

The rumor may have been false, in whole or in part, or Yeltsin may have thought better of the plan. On the visit to Nizhny Novgorod he did make liberal use of the phrase "equal-opportunity capitalism," but he did not present it as the new Russian idea. The press pool concluded that conservatives in the Kremlin had scuttled the proposal, once again winning at palace intrigue.[15]

GUDKOV'S AND HIS COLLEAGUES' RESEARCH suggested that no message about the present and the future could capture the hearts and minds of Russians, who now had their eyes set firmly on the past. A year after failing to produce an idea for the future, Yeltsin addressed the past, finally introducing the concept of national penitence. On July 17, 1998, he took an apparently impulsive, unplanned trip to St. Petersburg to speak at the reburial of the remains of Russia's last czar and his family. It was the eightieth anniver-

sary of the day when Czar Nicholas II, his wife, Alexandra, their five children, and four other people had been executed in the basement of a house in
Yekaterinburg, where they had been held for several months.

After the execution, the house had served as a museum of the Revolution, and later as a minor administrative building. Details of what had happened to Nicholas and his family were never made public. No one knew
where they were buried. Soviet schoolchildren learned only that the last
Russian czar had abdicated and the October Revolution had triumphed. To
ensure that all memory of the execution was erased, in the 1970s the Party
ordered the house razed, and Yeltsin, then the local Party boss, made sure
the order was carried out. Local lore maintained an uncertain memory
of the execution, however, and in 1991 remains that were thought to belong
to the czar and his family were exhumed. Genetic analysis took seven
years—the science of testing remains was just then coming into being—but
in the end the remains were positively identified as belonging to the czar,
his wife, and three of the five children. Now they would receive a proper
Russian Orthodox burial.

Yeltsin entered a St. Petersburg cathedral, flanked by the local governor
and Nemtsov, who had last chaired the government commission on identifying the remains. "Esteemed countrymen," said Yeltsin,

> today is a historic day for Russia. It has been eighty years since the
> day the last Russian emperor and his family were killed. For many
> years we concealed this horrific crime, but the time has come to tell
> the truth. The Yekaterinburg massacre is one of the most shameful
> pages of our history. As we bury the remains of these innocent vic-
> tims, we seek redemption for the sins of our fathers. The blame be-
> longs with those who committed this act of violence and with those
> who, for decades, justified their actions. The blame belongs with all
> of us. We have no right to lie to ourselves, using political adjectives
> to justify senseless cruelty. The execution of the Romanov family
> resulted from an irreparable split in Russian society, into "us" and

"them." We are still suffering from the consequences of that split. By burying the remains of the victims of the Yekaterinburg tragedy we commit, first and foremost, an act of *human* justice. It symbolizes the unification of our people and the redemption of our shared guilt. We are all responsible for preserving the historical memory of our people. That is why I had to be here today. It is my duty as a man and as the president to be here. I bow my head before the victims of merciless killing.

Yeltsin lowered his head, and after a moment of silence the church choir stepped in. Rather, this was what happened on national television.[16] In reality, Yeltsin continued for another two minutes:

As we build a new Russia, we must find our footing in its history. The Romanov* name is written on some of the glorious pages of our fatherland's history, but this name is also connected to one of history's most bitter lessons: any attempt to change our life through violence is doomed. It is our duty to bring closure to this century, which for Russia became a century of blood and lawlessness, through repentance and reconciliation, regardless of our political views, religious belief, and membership in an ethnic group. History is giving us a chance. As we enter the third millennium, we must do this, for the sake of those alive today and for the sake of the generations to come. Let us remember the innocent victims of hatred and violence. May they rest in peace.[17]

Whether in its truncated or full version, it was a magnificent speech, all the more striking because Yeltsin, for all his charisma, had never been a particularly inspiring speaker.

Lyosha was thirteen when the czar and his family were reinterred. Four

---

*The dynasty of the czars.

years earlier, he had read a book about the family and the execution and had decided that he hated the Bolsheviks for killing children. His mother had hidden away her desktop bust of Lenin a couple of years earlier, and had started bringing home books like this one. When school started again in September 1998, Lyosha's entire class discussed Yeltsin's speech. They concluded that now, after the ceremony, the Soviet era was finally over.

But what did that mean? Solikamsk began rebuilding a cathedral destroyed by the Bolsheviks. A men's monastery, which had been repurposed as a Soviet jail, reopened as a monastery. Somehow, these events seemed to Lyosha to connect directly to Yeltsin's speech in the glorious St. Petersburg cathedral, under an elaborate dome and majestic chandeliers to which the camera had panned after the president bowed his head.

Yeltsin's brief speech contained two key messages: the need for national unity and the need for national penitence. Only the unity part had traction, though, perhaps because it had been heard before, paired with "agreement and reconciliation." The ideas of redemption and of accepting the blame for Soviet-era crimes sounded from the national pulpit only once, on that day in St. Petersburg, and they remained suspended somewhere under the beautiful painted dome. Nemtsov, who wrote a detailed memoir of his political career in the 1990s, made no mention of his role as chairman of the commission that identified the remains. Yeltsin, for his part, left the entire subject of the "national idea" out of his memoirs. In a book published in 2000—barely two years after the ceremony—Yeltsin quoted his own speech at the reburial as follows:

> For many years we concealed this horrific crime, but the time has come to tell the truth. The Yekaterinburg massacre is one of the most shameful pages of our history. As we bury the remains of these innocent victims, we seek redemption for the sins of our fathers. The blame belongs with those who committed this act of violence and with those who, for decades, justified their actions. . . . I bow my head before the victims of merciless killing. . . . Any attempt to change our life through violence is doomed.[18]

In this version of the speech, blame was entirely externalized. The theme of shared responsibility, as well as the idea of the historic significance of the moment, was omitted. Both sets of omissions—Nemtsov's and Yeltsin's—showed the extent to which, for both politicians, the symbolic sphere took a backseat to the material. Yeltsin's elisions also suggested that he had thought better of his one attempt to accept, on behalf of his nation, the weight of responsibility for its "century of blood and lawlessness."

BY THE TIME Lyosha was a teenager, he was familiar with the Soviet film canon—the small number of movies that had been produced in the Soviet Union, and the fact that they kept being shown on television made this possible. He liked the propaganda musicals of the 1930s and 1950s, which he watched with his mother, and the slightly bitter comedies from the 1970s—mild, wink-and-a-smile satires of the Brezhnev era—but his favorites were the films about the Great Patriotic War. He liked all of them: the melodramas from the 1950s, the treacly portrayals of heroism from the 1970s, and the singular 1970s film that carried a heavy undertone of complexity (it was called *Twenty Days Without War*). Basically, he loved the Great Patriotic War.

So did most Russians. The 1994 survey showed that, after all the upheavals of the 1980s and 1990s, they clung stronger than ever to the one event that seemed to occupy an unambiguous place in the nation's memory. Reading survey responses, Gudkov imagined this war as an ideal vehicle. The vehicle had headlights, which illuminated the Soviet Union's future as a superpower. The vehicle also had rear lights, which cast a beatifying glow on the crimes of the regime that preceded the war. The vehicle's heft conveniently obscured the outsize losses of the Soviet military and the disregard for human life that had made them, and the Soviet victory, possible. What Gudkov could not yet quite imagine were people like Lyosha, born in the year perestroika began but identified entirely with a war that had ended forty years to the day before he was born.

Masha loved the war too. As she entered her preteen years, she and her mother began an asymmetrical argument. Tatiana became more explicit about why they continued to live amid peeling plaster: life in Russia was no kind of life, she said, and it would never be any kind of life. She did not mean that they did not live well, exactly—by this time it was clear that they were some kind of well-off—but she meant that life that required paying a bribe to do anything was a life of daily humiliation, and in protest she continued willfully failing to repaint, re-wallpaper, or buy a washing machine; instead, they gave their washing to a new wash-and-fold place called Diana, which had pickup and drop-off spots all over town. The implication was that someday they would go somewhere else to live a life worth living, and this life was a life beyond Russia.

In protest against her mother's protest, Masha joined the Young Seamen Club, which somehow deigned to accept a girl. The club offered target practice, endless talk of Russian military greatness, and computer-programming lessons, which were the reason Tatiana allowed Masha to join up. As soon as the ice broke at the Khimki Reservoir, a short tram ride from Tatiana and Masha's dilapidated apartment, the Young Seamen would start practice—paddling around the reservoir in small rowboats. They sailed to St. Petersburg to tour a real navy yard, but Masha was excluded because the ship could not accommodate a female.

As the only female Young Seaman, though, Masha was given a ticket to attend the festivities on May 9, 1995, the fiftieth anniversary of the great victory. World leaders were coming, though this had not been easy to arrange. Yeltsin was facing international criticism for the war in Chechnya, and American president Bill Clinton was wavering as late as March. As a concession, or a lure, Yeltsin promised to forgo a military parade with tanks and rockets in Red Square. Such parades had been conducted before the Second World War to frighten potential opponents and after the Second World War to celebrate victory, but none had been held since 1990. A chapel had even been constructed at the entrance to Red Square in the exact spot where a chapel had stood until 1931, when it was razed to make way for military equipment on parade days. For the half-century jubilee, a parade was planned again, but Yeltsin volunteered to hold it elsewhere, allowing foreign leaders to attend a veterans' procession in Red Square but avoid the military.

Clinton came, as did the United Kingdom's John Major, France's François Mitterrand, Germany's Helmut Kohl, and many others—the first meeting of the Allies on Russian soil since 1945, and one of the largest gatherings of dignitaries in Moscow, ever.[19] Military bands from all over the world paraded just next to Red Square, in front of the History Museum, and this was the part of the festivities that Masha got to attend. She thought it was awesome. Even Tatiana admitted reluctantly that she could see its appeal. Masha, triumphant, clutched an iron-on patch given to her by one of the members of the American brass band.

THE HISTORY MUSEUM, which still told a story that spanned from the Stone Age to the USSR and had left more than a few Little Octobrists with the impression that prehistoric man had developed directly into Lenin, had, on days when there was no Victory Day parade, become a magnet for Russian nationalists of all kinds. Men and occasionally women milled around on its porch, giving speeches aimed at the thousands who filed by daily, convening improvised discussion groups, handing out flyers, and, most important, selling books and periodicals. One came here to buy the journal *Nash sovremennik* and other publications that advertised themselves as "patriotic." Folding tables buckled under the weight of books on Russia and the Russians, which ranged from works by men who had left on the Philosophers' Ship to *The Protocols of the Elders of Zion.*

By far the most prominent and most numerous were books by Lev Gumilev, a prolific ethnographer whose work had been inaccessible to the general public during the Soviet era. Gumilev was the son of Anna Akhmatova, one of the greatest Russian poets of all time, and Nikolai Gumilev, a poet and an officer in the czar's army who was executed by the Bolsheviks. Lev Gumilev was arrested for the first time, briefly, in 1933, when he was barely twenty-one, then again two years later. That time he was held for a couple of months and, upon his release, expelled from the university. In 1938 he was arrested again. He spent the following five years in the Gulag. Almost as soon as he was released, he was conscripted. After the end of the Second World War he was finally allowed to return to his studies, and, at the age of thirty-six, to defend his doctoral dissertation. Then he was arrested again, and sentenced to ten years. He served seven—his release came after Khrushchev condemned Stalin's political prosecutions—and finally obtained his first research position at the age of forty-four. He claimed, however, to have conceived his most important ideas while he was in the camps.[20]

Gumilev's central idea was the concept of ethnogenesis, a process by which, according to his theory, different ethnic groups came into being and acquired distinct characteristics that were passed on from generation to generation. An ethnic group, or an *ethnos*, as Gumilev called it, was shaped by two major forces: the geographic conditions in which they lived, and radiation from outer space. In his works on ethnogenesis, Gumilev detailed his ideas on radiation and the resulting genetic mutations, while in his works on history he pursued the geographic-determinist line and drew on the ideas of Eurasianists, a school of thought—born around the time of, and apparently in reaction to, the Bolshevik Revolution—that held that Russia's unique course was set by its predicament of straddling the two continents.[21]

Gumilev was barely tolerated by the Soviet academic establishment after he was released and his name was cleared, and his ideas were largely shunned. But he enjoyed a year or two of popularity and even celebrity before his death in 1992: he recorded a series of lectures that millions saw on television, and later the press runs of his books, originally written for an academic audience, beat all conceivable records. He was the perfect post-Soviet intellectual hero, a victim of the regime whose mind seemed to have triumphed over unconscionable adversity. His famous mother's best-known work, a heartbreaking cycle of poems called *Requiem*, which circulated underground in the Soviet Union, told the story of his imprisonment.

They took you away at dawn,
As though at a wake, I followed,
In the dark room weeping children,
Among icons, the candle guttered.
On your lips, the chill of a cross,
On your brow a deathly pall.
I'll be, like a woman to be shot,
Dragged to the Kremlin wall.[22]

Gumilev's intellectual quest could be seen as the essence—or as a caricature—of the fate of the social sciences in the Soviet Union: decades spent working in a hostile environment, isolated from the ideas of others, struggling to invent the wheel in the dark. Working on his own, Gumilev had had to create his own theory of the universe, complete with radiation from outer space. The totality of his theory and its scientific sheen had to appeal to post-Soviet minds, which had just lost another totalizing explanation of the world. *Ethnos* entered everyday Russian speech, as did other concepts of Gumilev's coinage, such as *passionarnost'*, a measure of the degree to which an *ethnos* was initially receptive to radiation and eventually possessed of *ethnos*-specific powers.

Other schools of thought that offered totality and scientific language were also gaining a foothold in Russia. Scientology, for example, was particularly popular among small-business men and bureaucrats in smaller cities. But two attributes made Gumilev's ideas perfect for the historical moment. His insistence on the essential nature of ethnic groups helped explain the agony of the empire. His geographic determinism fit well with the idea of Russia's unique destiny, which the Levada survey had shown to be so important for Russians.

Masha's grandmother was taken with Gumilev's theories. Masha's mother objected. She chose a different all-encompassing revisionist theory, one invented by Anatoli Fomenko, a mathematician who claimed that his calculations recast all of world history. In his story, history was shorter and more accessible: in the Middle Ages, the world was a giant empire with Russia at its center; before that, there was hardly anything. Conventional history was fiction, concocted by the Russians-who-ruled-the-world for their own entertainment. Fomenko was a classic conspiracy theorist: he proved his assertions by way of relentlessly logical constructions based on random mathematical assumptions, and he dismissed all contrary evidence as falsification by his enemies. Fomenko was particularly popular with the exact-sciences crowd, including the chess champion Garry Kasparov, who for a time became a vocal adherent.[23] The head of Moscow State University, also a mathematician, idolized Fomenko and by the mid-1990s had promoted him to the top of the university's mathematics hierarchy, lending his theories ever more credibility.[24] This was yet another reason for family fights: Masha's grandmother held forth on ethnogenesis, Masha's mother screamed at her about the math that proved that everything was something else, and Masha's grandfather shouted the loudest that all of it was a Jewish conspiracy. Sometimes he also mentioned the queers, but then Masha's mother invariably pointed out that Tchaikovsky had been a homosexual and yet a great Russian composer. To Masha, she added that Freddie Mercury had been gay too.

DUGIN ABSORBED ALL of Gumilev as his foundational science. Gumilev's language became his language, and he used Gumilev's premises to launch his own new ideas. He was writing nearly as fast as he was reading, firing off articles for the patriotic press and then compiling them into books at the rate of one or two every year. Now that he had access to a nearly unlimited number of publications, he was finding ideas he could use everywhere. The German theorist Carl Schmitt, Hitler's favorite legal scholar, became a source of inspiration, but so did Karl Popper, the Austrian-British philosopher who created the concept of an "open society." George Soros, the Hungarian-born American billionaire who was opening foundations and learning institutions throughout the disintegrating Eastern Bloc, had been taken with Popper for decades and included the words "open society" in the names of most of his organizations. Popper's ideas represented everything that Russia was now declaring it wanted to be, and the philosopher himself had once suggested a dichotomy: the open society on one hand, and its enemies on the other. Dugin wanted to be the enemy of the open society.

In 1994, Dugin published *The Conservative Revolution*. In this book, he envisioned a movement that would resist what he called "extremist humanism"—the idea that all humans everywhere have rights—and the concept of a law-based society. He explained that these ideas, imported from the West, were wrong precisely because they were fundamentally foreign to Russians, whose *ethnos* developed in accordance with its own destiny and whose geography made it the natural enemy of the United States and Britain.[25]

Dugin teamed up with two men who were older and much better-known than he: a rock star named Yegor Letov and a writer named Eduard Limonov. Both were leather-jacket-wearing bohemians who had spent their lives in opposition to any establishment they encountered. Limonov had been an underground poet in the Soviet Union, a gay-identified hobo in 1970s New York, an avant-garde writer in 1980s Paris, and he had returned to Russia by way of Yugoslavia, where he had spent time traveling with the Bosnian Serb leader Radovan Karadžić and firing at Bosnian Muslims for fun. Now Limonov was looking for a way to be heard in the cacophony of post-Soviet Russia. Together, the three men took the idea proposed to Dugin by Robert Steuckers, the Belgian, three years earlier, and launched the National Bolshevik Party. For Limonov, Letov, and another avant-garde musician who immediately joined the group with the shocking name, the National Bolshevik Party was primarily an artistic exercise. Dugin took it more seriously as a long-term project, both a political and a philosophical one. After nearly four years of shuttling back and forth to Europe to take part in New Right gatherings, Dugin stopped traveling to concentrate on working in Russia. He penned the party's manifesto, which read in part:

The best and most complete definition of national-bolshevism would be the following: "National-bolshevism is a superideology common to all enemies of open society." It is not merely one of the ideologies hostile to an open society but specifically its complete conscious total and substantive opposite. National-bolshevism is a worldview that is built on the total and radical negation of the individual and his centrality.[26]

Neither the Bolsheviks nor the Nazis had stated it quite so explicitly.

ten

IT'S ALL OVER ALL OVER AGAIN

AFTER WINNING THE ELECTION, Yeltsin again began casting about for a successor. The task was now less symbolic and more urgent. The 1993 constitution dictated that his second term would be his last. Though he could easily have made the legal argument that he had first run for office in a different country, this would have gone against his own principles. And in the autumn of 1996 Yeltsin had multiple-bypass heart surgery, which, combined with the enormous battle he had had to wage to remain in office, must have made him aware of his own vulnerability. At the same time, the 1996 presidential election—the first to have been conducted in post-Soviet Russia—did not convey the sense that the country would now be governed by men chosen on their merits by the public. It had the opposite effect, that of showing that the battle for power in Russia was waged between clans, a war in which victory depended on the effectiveness of mobilization on either side.

Gudkov spent much of his time trying to make sense of this effect, and also of the fact that this description could certainly be applied to the functioning of some Western democracies, most notably the United States. The difference lay in the historical contexts. The Russian clans were direct descendants of the Soviet nomenklatura system. In the five years that had passed since the collapse of the Soviet Union, no new institutions for producing leaders, public politicians, or even government bureaucrats had emerged. If anything, the opposite had happened: younger people, like Gaidar and the members of his cabinet, who had come to government from structures adjacent or tangential to the Party, had been pushed out of government and had mostly gone into private business.[1] Old government, Party, and KGB hands had filled the many voids at all levels of the bureaucracy and had resumed their ascent up the power ladder, as though the end of the Soviet Union had caused just a temporary layoff. Among these old faces, there were just a handful of exceptions—a few elected governors and a couple of prominent generals who had gone into politics—and it so happened that Yeltsin disliked most of them.

That left Boris Nemtsov. His designated-successor status had been suspended after his protest against the war in Chechnya, but now that the war had ended, Nemtsov could be restored to favor. Yeltsin's attitude toward the younger Boris had always been paternal—caring and condescending at the same time—and this made it easier to return Nemtsov to favor. The thirty-seven-year-old Nemtsov was appointed one of two first vice-premiers—the number-three position in the cabinet—and brought to Moscow, with all the media reporting that the appointment was an anointment.

To Zhanna, the move was yet another step in her father's love affair with himself in politics. After he became governor, he had developed a taste for watching himself on television. When he was on the news—as he often was, being an active and supremely popular governor—the whole family had to watch. He teased Zhanna for loving a soap opera called *Santa Barbara*: he joked that he could be dying and if *Santa Barbara* was on she would not notice. This made him sound jealous of a television show, but Zhanna was, even more absurdly, jealous of her father's infatuation with his own televised likeness. At the end of the year, the local station usually prepared a two-hour year-in-review special that effectively starred Boris Nemtsov, and he would be glued to the set for the entire two hours. To Zhanna, this was what politics now meant: her father's insatiable taste for himself on the screen. Now this drive was taking the family from the dacha Zhanna loved, from the forest and her bike, to Moscow.

Boris promised that in Moscow they would also live at a dacha in the woods. This was not a lie, but it also was not true. There was a dacha, in an old nomenklatura village, outfitted with dusty, impersonal furniture. Zhanna's school was in the very center of Moscow, and the drive there, even with a cabinet member's traffic privileges, felt interminable. The school, which had once been reserved for the Soviet elite, was now inhabited by the children of the new rich, drawn by the school's reputation for good English-language instruction. The students were the daughters of an aluminum king, a game-show host, a media magnate. Zhanna was thirteen, awkward, and provincial. Her clothes were ordinary, and she knew nothing about luxury brands. She also did not know anything about expensive cars. She did not vacation abroad and had given no thought to a future at some fancy Western school. She did not belong.

After one quarter at the school, Zhanna declared that she was returning to Nizhny Novgorod. Her parents knew better than to argue. Her teacher said, "You are making the biggest mistake of your life." Whatever glorious future she might be forfeiting, as her teacher implied, Zhanna wanted no part of it. She returned to Nizhny Novgorod, took up residence with her grandmother, and resumed studies at her old school.

Back in Moscow, her father was experiencing frustrations and humiliations similar to her own. Around the time of his arrival in Moscow, Nemtsov published a book he had written over the preceding year. The slim volume was called *The Provincial*, but if the title promised some ironic distance, the book delivered none. It exposed an overconfident young man who was dazzled by his own standing in the world. The book's meaty middle was a series of capsule descriptions of all the famous men—and one woman, Margaret Thatcher—whom Nemtsov had been lucky enough to meet, from Boris Yeltsin to Richard Gere. These included miniature profiles of some of the men with whom Nemtsov would now be working in Moscow, and an unflattering description of their progress so far:

We are living in shapeless times. What reforms are there to talk about? There have been no real reforms! So consumer prices have been deregulated. Freedom for all has been declared. What kind of reforms are those? Reforms involve a leash that is being let out gradually, with constant control exercised over the level of tension. You have to be able to tell the difference between freedom and total lack of oversight![2]

Not only was the government neglecting its oversight function, wrote Nemtsov, but it was letting itself be manipulated by the newly moneyed class. He compared their influence to that exerted by the mystic Grigory Rasputin over Russia's last czar in the 1910s.

Russia has always had its official authorities, who had the job titles and the status, and its unofficial ones. There was, for example, Grishka Rasputin. Now we have a sort of group Rasputin. There are many of them, but they are nobodies. Grishka was an extraordinary man who had his talents. You can't really say that about the people who surround the czar we have today.[3]

Nemtsov coined two terms: "oligarchs" and "robber-baron capitalism"; the usages stuck.[4] He conjured a plan for getting the rich in line once he arrived in Moscow. After five years of wielding power effectively in Nizhny Novgorod, he was sure that in his new post getting the federal government's house in order would be a simple matter of will.[5] He wrote a memo to Yeltsin outlining his program for what he called "nationalizing the Kremlin." The memo explained that the Kremlin—by which Nemtsov and the rest of Russia meant "political authority in the country"—had been privatized in much the same way as shops and oil companies had been, and now had to be reclaimed by its rightful, elected occupants. Nemtsov's "nationalization" involved measures big and small. The oligarchs' Kremlin-issued identification cards, which allowed unrestricted entrance to the fortress, must be taken away, along with their Kremlin-issued license plates and flashing blue lights, which made them exempt from traffic rules. Privatization, going forward, should be transparent, creating a level playing field for all potential investors. The practice of loans-for-shares auctions must be discontinued. These auctions allowed investors to take possession of large companies by granting them credit guaranteed by a majority of the shares, knowing that the companies would be unable to repay; the auctions themselves were generally organized by the prospective lender.

Yeltsin liked the plan—Nemtsov later wrote that the part about the oligarchs' access privileges must have been particularly appealing to the president because it reminded him of the old Party system of apportioning and regulating perks, a system Yeltsin had once railed against. But as soon as the government tried to implement plans for leveling the privatization playing field, the oligarchs went to war. Nemtsov had misjudged the situation badly: he thought that he could use against the ascendant oligarchs the tools he had honed at home, dealing with old Soviet-style bosses whose power had waned. He had also banked on his authority as a government official, not realizing that in Moscow power was never fixed but always contingent on one's proximity to Yeltsin, and on his favor. The president continued to support Nemtsov's plan in theory, but he grew irritated with the public battles and Nemtsov's lack of skill in handling them.[6]

Nemtsov had insulted the oligarchs by calling into question their legitimacy and their talents, and now he wanted to take away their political influence and their prospective wealth. They owned the media. They often used it to fight one another, but now they united against him. Moscow journalists ridiculed him for the same reasons the rich girls at her school bullied Zhanna: his cluelessness about clothes and cars. He had worn white trousers to the airport on a hot summer day to greet the president of Azerbaijan, who had arrived for a state visit. This disgraceful breach of protocol was shown on television over and over.[7] As for cars, Nemtsov was lobbying to require that the government use only Russian-made cars to chauffeur its bureaucrats around. By this time, the officials in Moscow were used to Mercedes-Benz S-Class cars, and Nemtsov was portrayed as not only ignorant about cars but also possibly corrupt, because the Volga, for which he was lobbying, was made in Nizhny Novgorod. One of the country's most popular television anchors, Sergei Dorenko, reported that Nemtsov had taken part in a sex party with strippers hired for the occasion—and failed to pay them.[8] Nemtsov later wrote that after a few years Dorenko told him that he himself had hired the sex workers to defame Nemtsov on camera.[9]

Nemtsov's nationwide popularity rating, which had been around 50 percent when he arrived in Moscow, dropped to an undetectable level.[10] He was no longer the president's heir apparent.

IN 1995, Masha's mother quit the retail business. She stopped shuttling back and forth and importing the hideous Korean handbags. With the money she had made, she bought a dacha on the Istra River, northwest of Moscow, and went back to college. She wanted to use her mind again, but physics was clearly never going to bring her any money. Someone had told Tatiana about a new field called "actuarial science"—it was new for Russia, that is: the market was ushering it into existence, but very few people were qualified to work in this area. Tatiana figured that with her background in statistical physics, she could succeed, fast. Then, through her studies, she met a man from the Military Insurance Company, and he gave her a job.

Like so many new businesses, the Military Insurance Company was born out of a combination of a new need and old resources and access. Tatiana's new bosses were retired military brass, and they created a company from expertise and connections: much of their business early on exploited legal loopholes to allow clients to use what appeared to be payments on insurance policies to avoid paying taxes. Some of their business was actual insurance, though, and Tatiana's newly acquired actuarial skills proved invaluable. The retired colonels liked her. It was as alien an environment as any she had ever encountered, but they were kind to her and to Masha, who spent some time around the office that Tatiana never seemed to leave.

Tatiana had not exactly changed her view on the subject of a future in Russia—she had simply adjusted her expectations by one generation. She herself would never make a life elsewhere, but her daughter would. To that end, she not only secured a decent and stable income but spent most of her money on tutors for Masha, whose job it now was to gain admission to Moscow State University and later parlay that degree into a ticket to graduate school abroad.

Then, one day in August 1998, Tatiana's bank card stopped working. All the money they had in the world was in that account. The word was "default." Russia had stopped paying its bills, and this meant that the ruble tumbled, prices skyrocketed, panic set in, people ran to the banks to get their money, and the banks cut off clients' access to their own accounts. In several cases, this still could not keep the banks from collapsing.

Masha's tutoring had to be suspended, as did the sending out of the wash. But what really frightened Masha was the prospect of having to go without sanitary pads. She had recently started menstruating, and Tatiana had told her that back in the USSR, they had had to use cotton during their periods (she omitted the fact that even cotton was not reliably available). What if Masha's next period came before Tatiana could get cash, and Masha had to resort to cotton? What if "default" meant that sanitary pads would disappear from the stores altogether? The thoughts were too much to bear. Someone they knew, who worked for Procter & Gamble, had just been paid in products—toothpaste and pads—and Masha convinced her mother to barter something, anything, for an industrial-size box of maxipads.

This panic did not last. Within a couple of months, Tatiana was getting paid regularly and they were sending out the wash again. They owed their family's speedy recovery to the improved fortunes of the Military Insurance Company, which had just secured a lavish new contract with the Federal Security Service, the FSB, where Yeltsin had just appointed a new boss. He was a colonel from St. Petersburg, by the name of Vladimir Putin.

FOR A TEACHER living in Solikamsk, recovery took much longer. Lyosha's mother, like other teachers she knew, worked for no pay for the entire 1998–

1999 school year. Her husband was still drawing a salary at the mine, but it was Lyosha's mother's potato garden that kept them going. When they were not eating potatoes, it was pasta with sugar—a stomach-fooling dish from Galina's childhood. They forgot about meat for months.

IN THE SUMMER OF 1998, Zhanna agreed to return to Moscow, on one condition: she would go to a regular-people school. Secondary School Number 312 was so regular that students who did not drink and smoke stood out, uncomfortably. But even before school began in September, there came a day Zhanna would always remember.

They were living on the Garden Ring, the wide circular avenue that circumscribed central Moscow. Yeltsin had granted Nemtsov his own apartment there—it was very much the done thing at all levels of government now: a judge would get an apartment from the mayor, a regional legislator from the governor, and a member of the cabinet, like Nemtsov, from the president himself. The difference between this reward system and the old Soviet one of assigning privilege was that the new approach was more personalized and less systematized—each apartment was gifted on its own terms, at the discretion of the boss. Also, unlike the Soviet apartments, which nominally belonged to the state, these new ones became the property of the recipient, whether he stayed in his post for many years or for a few months.

An apartment on the Garden Ring was a mark of privilege and prestige. It was also a very convenient and very uncomfortable place to live: you could get anywhere in the city fast from there, but the Garden Ring itself was so heavy with traffic at all times that one could not even open the front-facing windows, so much noise and filth would burst in. They kept the windows shut, and watched an ever thicker layer of black film coat them on the outside.

But that day in August, Zhanna went up to the window and saw nothing. Where a solid flow of cars should have been, only a few could be seen—

they looked like stragglers from some great escape. Something terrible must have happened. Her father had for months been talking about a looming economic crisis. This must be what that looked like.

Nemtsov had been sounding the alarm about the Russian state's mounting debt. The government's misleading laissez-faire attitude, which masqueraded as freedom, was, Nemtsov believed, simply failure to accept responsibility for an economy headed for implosion. Alexander Nikolaevich Yakovlev, looking at the issue through the prism of his own experience as a member of the Soviet leadership, saw the triumph of the group he had found most intractable during the perestroika era. These were the heads of Soviet industry, who, in the central-planning system, held the posts of government ministers, but whom Alexander Nikolaevich called simply the Mafia.[11] He believed that they had once again contrived to receive—and loot—giant sums of money. Clifford Gaddy, an economist at the Brookings Institution in Washington, D.C., made the radical claim that all of Russia's reforms of the early 1990s had failed to budge the behemoths of the command economy, which continued, in all their illogical and profoundly unprofitable ways, to dominate the Russian economy. All the trappings of the new economy—the supposed market-based prices, the competitive salaries, and the taxes—were, according to Gaddy, nothing but illusions. He called it the "virtual economy," coining the term long before the word "virtual" took on a different and more appealing meaning. He meant that the country pretended to have entered a new economic age but in reality traded through barter and never fully met any of its monetary obligations. He, too, placed the blame on the unreformed, and politically powerful, core of the command economy: the enormous inefficient companies run by the very Mafia that worried Alexander Nikolaevich. The "robber barons" who concerned Nemtsov were kings of the "virtual economy."[12]

Whether one focused on debt, on the remaining influence of the Soviet economic lobby, or on the imaginary nature of the new Russian economy, these critics—who included a number-three member of the cabinet—agreed that the situation was untenable and the government was in denial. Nemtsov had been proposing monetary reform, which would have included dropping the value of the ruble—thereby perhaps making the entire monetary system a little less "virtual"—but these proposals were rejected. Instead, Russia borrowed more and more heavily, to prop up the currency. The debt became a pyramid, which collapsed in August 1998. This was "default"—a word Boris Nemtsov read on the newswires and Zhanna heard on the radio. Russia stopped servicing its debt, the people went into a panic, the banks stopped giving out cash, and cars stopped running up and down the Garden Ring.

Nemtsov wanted to resign from the cabinet but Raisa said, "You were not the one who defaulted, and you shouldn't be the one who resigns." Yeltsin said something essentially similar: he fired much of the rest of the cabinet, but kept Nemtsov. But, weakened politically by the crash, Yeltsin could not hope to push a premier of his own choosing through parliament. A seventy-year-old veteran of the foreign intelligence service who embodied the crumpled-gray-suit ethos of the Soviet bureaucrat, Yevgeniy Primakov, was finally confirmed to run the government. Nemtsov resigned: there was nothing he was going to be able to do in a Primakov cabinet.

Time slowed instantly. After New Year's, the family flew to America. They stayed at Harvard for a month. Nemtsov lectured on the Russian economy, arguing that it was in need of a profound restructuring and a deep cleansing.[13] The family was given a room in a university residence hall. It had cracking plaster on the ceiling, creaky bunk beds, and, as it turned out, bedbugs. Boris complained, and a professor set them up in his own apartment, which he was not using. Zhanna was allowed to attend classes at a nearby private school in Cambridge. She was happy. Things were better than they had been in years. After Harvard they went to New York, where the slow, intimate life of temporary exiles continued.

BACK IN RUSSIA, politics was speeding up. On March 24, 1999, NATO forces began bombing Serbia in response to the Yugoslav army's actions in Kosovo. Prime Minister Primakov happened to be on his way to the United

States when the bombing began. The insult and the injury were on display. Russians had long considered the Orthodox Serbs to be their existential allies. Kosovo was, legally, a part of Serbia—a secessionist, Muslim part—and the parallels to Chechnya were obvious. Primakov was mere hours from arriving in the United States, where President Bill Clinton might at least have paid lip service to consulting him, and not doing so was an affront. Primakov turned his plane around and returned to Russia.

The following day, Masha's class had a field trip to the Lev Tolstoy Library on Lev Tolstoy Street. They had recently read Lev Tolstoy's novel *Anna Karenina*, at the end of which Anna's love, the endlessly desirable Vronsky, volunteers to fight on the side of the Serbs against the Ottoman Empire. As they walked down Lev Tolstoy Street, the tenth-graders discussed the NATO bombings of Serbia. It was an outrage, they agreed, a betrayal, and practically an American attack on Russia. For Masha, this was a moment when the two most authoritative and passionate voices in her head—the one of the militarized sailing club and the one of her cinephile mother—finally came together in a single fervor. The Americans were bombing Masha's Serbian brethren in the land of the great director Emir Kusturica.

In a survey conducted by Gudkov's colleagues, a majority of the respondents—52 percent—said they felt "outrage" at the bombing, and 92 percent said they believed the bombing campaign was illegal. Twenty-six percent said they felt "anxiety," and 13 percent confessed to feeling "fear."[14] Gudkov sensed that all three emotions—outrage, anxiety, and fear—were stand-ins for "humiliation," the sense that Russia's loss of status in the world had just been shoved in the country's face. Primakov's dramatic sulk over the Atlantic had reinforced this sentiment.

On May 9—a month and a half after the start of the bombing campaign—Red Square saw its first Victory Day military parade in a decade. There was no heavy equipment—no tanks and rockets, like in days past, only a march of men in uniform—and they moved through the square in the opposite direction to that taken in Soviet times, before the chapel at the entrance to the square had been restored. But the four men goose-stepping in front of the procession—one leader and three young officers behind him—carried a red flag with a hammer and sickle, like the one that had been placed on the Reichstag in 1945. Yeltsin did not take the Soviet secretary-general's conventional place atop the Lenin Mausoleum, but he assumed the traditional role of overseeing the parade, from a podium set up just in front of the granite building, where the Bolshevik leader's body was still on display after seventy-five years. It was the fifty-fourth anniversary of victory in the Great Patriotic War, but the television voice-over pronounced that figure as though it had particular symbolism and went on to stress, "Whoever might be trying today to diminish the significance of our victory, for the people it will forever remain great."[15] There was no need to spell out that it was NATO, with its bombing campaign, that was attempting retroactively to "diminish the significance of our victory."

Yeltsin, thought Gudkov, was finally playing the card he had resisted using for so long: staking his own legitimacy on the mythology of the Great Patriotic War.

THREE DAYS after the Victory Day parade, Yeltsin set in motion a parade of successors. Primakov, whom he distrusted and plainly disliked, was out. He appointed a new prime minister, forty-seven-year-old Sergei Stepashin, who had been serving as minister of the interior. A career law-enforcement officer, Stepashin had been in and out of the government for a decade, so his was a familiar face—even if he lacked the force of personality to elicit any particular emotional response. Now, by dint of being appointed prime minister, he was Yeltsin's new heir apparent.

The NATO bombing of Serbia ended in May, with a negotiated agreement that turned Kosovo into a de facto protectorate of the Western powers. Peacekeeping troops began moving into position in the area, for what would clearly be a long stay. On June 12—which happened to be Russian Independence Day—British peacekeepers were slated to secure the airport in

Pristina, the capital city. But the night before, two hundred Russian peace-keepers stationed in Bosnia suddenly marched across the border to Pristina and seized the airport. The operation seemed to have no strategic objective, or even a plan—the Russian troops had not made arrangements for supplies, and were ultimately fed by NATO troops who took pity on them. Back in Russia, the demonstration of pointless and unopposed military power played well. Masha and her friends cheered the siege of the airport in much the same way as they cheered a Russian soccer victory over Holland. After a week, Russia agreed to send about 3,600 troops to Kosovo to work along-side Western peacekeepers, effectively renewing its relationship with NATO—which had been severed when the bombing began—without accepting NATO command.[16]

In less than three months, Yeltsin once again changed his mind regarding his successor, fired Stepashin, and appointed another gray, unremarkable man. This time, however, the heir apparent was a virtual unknown, the colonel Yeltsin had recently chosen to run the secret police, Vladimir Putin.

That summer, before Masha's last year of high school, she went to Crimea with a friend and the friend's mother. They rented a single room in Alushta. They went to the beach and watched television. Masha read romantic poetry by Anna Akhmatova and Maximilian Voloshin. They met teenagers from Ukrainian cities—Dnepropetrovsk and Kiev—who told them that they spoke with a Moscow accent. Masha objected that she did not have an accent: they did. They laughed. They drank together, a lot. After the friend's mother left, trading places with Tatiana, they had even more freedom. They had no curfew. They drank on the piers at night. One night, a freak wave covered all of them and pulled them off the pier, but they got out and laughed.

"I'm sick of Crimea," Masha said at one point. "I want to go back to Russia. You know, birch trees, mosquitoes, the nostalgia."

Tatiana thought this was funny—who gets sick of the sea? Masha thought it was funny too. But they went to the dacha for the rest of the summer. It was early August.

"So he'll be our prime minister now?" asked Tatiana. "Weird." She had negotiated insurance contracts with this man, and she was unimpressed.

Masha was impressed, though. He was an intelligence officer. Soviet intelligence officers were a special breed. Masha had binge-watched films about them when she was sick one time, at her grandmother's apartment. There was the miniseries *TASS Is Authorized to Declare*, in which a flawless and brilliant KGB officer exposes an American spy in Moscow. The spy's handler, an American called John Glabb, is pure evil: not only does he organize pro-American military coups in small African countries, but he also traffics in heroin, which he packs into the bodies of infants purchased from impoverished families and killed for this purpose. He is also married to the scion of a Nazi fortune.[17] Another film was *Dead Season*, in which a Soviet intelligence officer working deep undercover captures a former Nazi doctor now working for one of the Western powers. The doctor has developed a potion that turns off individual will.[18]

Masha had also read a lot of books of the sort on which these films were based. Her grandmother had an endless supply of them. The glossy jackets had all been lost, so the books were plain brown or gray. The aesthetic uniformity of the outside matched the contents, which reliably delivered a light thrill followed by a sense that all was right with the world. Around eighth grade Masha graduated from the gray and brown books to black hardcovers with red letters, the complete translations of Arthur Conan Doyle in eight volumes. Here the thrill was greater but the moral-satisfaction quotient lower. Masha missed that feeling.

"I hope he is our next president," she said of Putin.

LIKE MOST PEOPLE HE KNEW, Gudkov assumed that Putin would be a temporary figure, a placeholder picked by a leader who was feeling disoriented. Unlike most people he knew, though, Gudkov was painfully aware of the expectations most Russians were placing on the country's next president: they wanted a savior, a leader who would be not merely decisive but dominating. Putin hardly seemed suited for that role: he had no history and no presence.

What happened over the next few months looked unbelievable. From August to November 1999 the number of those who answered "Yes" to the question "Do you think that Vladimir Putin is, on the whole, doing a good job?" shot up from 31 to 80 percent, and the number of those who answered "No" dropped from 33 to 12. On a graph, it looked like two vertical lines, a blue one going up and a red one shooting down.[19] It looked like nothing Gudkov had ever seen.

Deeper questioning revealed a process akin to magic. Russia had been in a state that Gudkov could only describe as depression—more a psychological than an economic one. The financial crisis of 1998, coming as it did just when life was starting to seem normal again and when hope had seemed warranted, had plunged people into the darkest darkness—precisely because it crushed the very fragile fresh sprouts of hope. Economically, people regained their footing relatively fast, but emotions did not follow—until Putin came along and eight out of ten Russians miraculously regained hope just by looking at him.

Politically, on the face of it, things looked anything but hopeful. In August and September the country was shocked by a series of apartment-building explosions that killed 293 people and injured more than a thousand. The government used the bombings as a pretext to launch a new offensive in Chechnya, reigniting the war that had once nearly cost Yeltsin the presidency. This time, though, Gudkov observed that while Russians' hearts ached for the young men being sent to fight the war, virtually no one seemed to feel sympathy for the civilians in Chechnya, their ostensible countrymen who were once again being bombed. Another thing made this war different from the first Chechen one: this time the Russian offensive was seen as spearheaded by a leader. If Yeltsin came across as desperate and flailing when he began his war in 1994, then his own prime minister, restarting the war five years later, came across as brave, and as a defender of ordinary Russians. This impression was based primarily on a single utterance Putin made in response to the apartment-building bombings: "We will pursue terrorists wherever they are. At the airport, if they are at the airport. And that means, I apologize, that if we catch them going to the bathroom, then we will rub them out in the outhouse, if it comes to that. That's it, the issue is closed."

A majority saw courage and determination in Putin's phrasing, and this distinguished him from Yeltsin. Some were charmed by his hint at modesty and reason—"I apologize" and "if it comes to that" played to this audience. On the whole, he came off as being one of the people, and yet ready to lead the people.

Who were "the people"? Levada's team had conducted its third Homo Sovieticus survey, and the results were devastating. Ten years after the original study, the hypothesis had been fully invalidated. Homo Sovieticus was not, as Levada had suggested, dying off. He was not only surviving but reproducing—and this meant that he was reclaiming his dominant position in the population.

According to the results of the 1999 survey, Russians were ever more nostalgic. "Would you prefer that things return to the way they were before 1985?"—before perestroika—drew a clear majority of respondents who agreed: 58 percent, up from 44 in 1994. The proportion of people who viewed the changes of the early 1990s as positive continued to shrink, while the percentage of those who said they could not cope with the changes grew noticeably. The more distant past became ever more appealing: now 26 percent believed that Stalin's rule had been good for the country, up from 18 percent in 1994. Those who held a negative view of the Soviet dictator were now in the minority. Russians continued to think of themselves mostly as "open" and "patient"—the percentage of people who cited these qualities had grown. At the same time, respondents seemed to become more open-minded with regard to "deviants": only 15 percent now wanted to "liquidate" homosexuals, down from 22 percent in 1994. But the number of those who would "leave them to their own devices" dropped too, from 29 to 18 percent. Russians now overwhelmingly wanted to "help" their homosexuals—an option that implied a sort of medieval model of helping the afflicted. Viewed in the context of epidemic nostalgia for the Soviet past, these results made sense: they represented yet another way of returning to the paternalistic state.[20]

In December 1999, Russia held its third post-Soviet parliamentary election. This seemed like one of the new era's few indisputable accomplishments: a number of different parties competed in what could reasonably be called a fair and open process. They split the popular vote in ways that pointed to the existence of large distinct groups that favored particular parties. There were features, however, that made this election very different from one you might observe in a functioning democracy. The leading parties had been formed just weeks or months before the election. This had been the case in the first two post-Soviet elections as well, but that had seemed understandable in the early stages of Russia's self-reinvention. Now, though, Gudkov found himself trying to understand what caused political parties to be discarded between elections.

The other troublesome feature in this election was a change in public etiquette. Local and federal government officials made an effort to appear on television more often than during the off-season—this was normal. But this time they did not appear solicitous of their voters: they consistently expressed certainty in their victory, making the election sound like a ritual rather than a contest. Their tone reminded Gudkov of the bureaucratic entitlement of the Soviet period.

Looking at the data, Gudkov and his coauthor, Boris Dubin, concluded that these two traits of the parliamentary election were symptoms of a single problem: the election had all the trappings of a political contest but lacked the substance of one. Democratic procedure, which had seemed a revolution in itself, was now the political equivalent of the "virtual economy" described by Gaddy—a mask pulled over a structure that refused to change.

Russia's current nominal multiparty system had grown out of the collapse of the Party state. The process was not unlike what Alexander Nikolaevich had proposed more than a decade earlier when he suggested to Gorbachev that the Communist Party should be split into two, in order to launch political competition. The suggestion might have looked naive but well-intentioned back then: Alexander Nikolaevich was trying to bridge the gap between a totalitarian system and a democratic one. Now it appeared that the gap had been unbridgeable: the old system's institutions had reconstituted themselves in a new guise. Gudkov and Dubin found that Russians—both the candidates and the voters—believed that political power rightly belonged to bureaucrats, whose chief qualification was experience in the bureaucracy. If a party advanced an agenda that diverged widely from existing policy, this party was viewed a priori as marginal. Elections became a popularity contest in a very small political field, where the leading candidates, by definition, agreed with one another. Of course, to some extent this could be said of many, possibly any, Western democracy. But Western democracies did not inherit their narrow political field from a seventy-year period of totalitarianism, and their future did not depend on their ability to advance fundamental social change.

It was now clear that even back in 1996, when the contest between Yeltsin and his Communist challenger, Gennady Zyuganov, was filled with desperate rancor, the two candidates' political platforms were interchangeable: both contained vague promises of building a market economy with a human face. Now, in a country united by two waves of strong emotions in one year—first in response to the NATO bombing of Serbia and then, more profoundly, in reaction to the apartment-building explosions and the war in Chechnya—there was no room at all for difference. Two new political parties appeared just before the election. One, Yedinstvo ("Unity"), was formed by the Kremlin for the express purpose of supporting Putin's ascendancy to the throne. The other, the Union of Right Forces, was its nominal liberal opponent, but it too supported Putin and the war in Chechnya. They differed mostly in style, with the Union of Right Forces—which included Nemtsov among its five leaders—appealing to a younger, more educated audience, the same people who had most vocally opposed the first war in Chechnya. In Solikamsk, fourteen-year-old Lyosha was observing this neat nondivision division clearly: his aunts, who had supported the Communists as long as he could remember, were now in favor of Unity, while his mother's more sophisticated friends donned T-shirts brought to town by the Union of

Right Forces; they were emblazoned with the phrase "You Are Right." There was no disagreement among his mother's friends and her family, though, because all of them were positively in thrall to Putin.

Gudkov started thinking that "political party" and "election" were just two more Western terms that could not be used in Russian—except to mislead. A more precise term could be borrowed from Max Weber, whom Levada had had Gudkov study all those years ago. The term was "acclamation," a process by which the governed affirm a choice already made for them.[21]

But Russians were acclaiming not only the candidates chosen for them by the bureaucracy—Putin chief among them—but also themselves, reaching for a sense of belonging, a sense of being with the majority that had been lost with the Soviet Union. What was felt as a void in the early 1990s had gradually been transformed into nostalgia, and now it could be focused on one person. It was precisely Putin's lack of distinction, which had made Gudkov think that he was a temporary figure, that in fact made him the perfect embodiment of the Soviet leadership style. In his person, charisma met bureaucracy.

Gudkov and Dubin included these observations in their article about the December 1999 parliamentary election, which they titled "The Time of the 'Gray People.'" They meant that the distinction between supposedly competing parties was as minor as the difference between gray and black—specifically that the so-called reformers had diluted their agenda to such an extent that they could stand out only against the pitch-black background of total Soviet nostalgia. The headline also contained a literary reference, to a novel called *Hard to Be a God*, a piece of science fiction by brothers Arkady and Boris Strugatsky, which the Soviet intelligentsia of the 1980s read and quoted like the Bible. The novel described a future academic-history experiment involving an artificially assembled civilization from the human Middle Ages. "The Gray Ones" in the novel are the shock troops of a man who appears to be an interim ruler, someone dispatched by stronger—and darker—forces to clear the land. The Gray Ones wage war on what they see as dangerous liberal ideas and on enlightenment as such. The Gray Ones, and their gray cardinal of a leader, appear inept, and come off as saboteurs rather than statesmen, yet they turn out to have infinite staying power.[22] Gudkov and Dubin were thinking of no such scenario, though: when they chose the title for their article, they had in mind only the image of gray against black.[23]

PART FOUR

RESURRECTION

eleven

LIFE AFTER DEATH

ON DECEMBER 31, 1999, Lyosha, his mother, his stepfather, his aunt, and her son all drove out to the countryside to celebrate New Year's with Lyosha's grandmother. Serafima Adamovna greeted them on the porch. She looked devastated.

"Yeltsin is leaving," she said.

All of them stood there, stricken by this news. They had been abandoned. How was this even possible?

In the house, the television was on. Yeltsin had already announced his resignation, and now the news anchors were talking about it, showing clips of Yeltsin's speech—he looked like he was crying—and other footage that showed that while Lyosha and his family were driving, the country had moved on.

"I have fulfilled my life's mission," Yeltsin had said in his address. "Russia will never go back to the past. From now on, Russia will be moving forward. I should not stand in the way. I should not spend another six months holding on to power when the country has a strong man who deserves to be president—and on whom virtually every Russian today is pinning his hopes for the future."[1]

Then there were two men in a Kremlin office, one wearing a Navy uniform and the other in a gray civilian suit. Yeltsin shook both their right hands. In their left hands, each held a hard-sided briefcase and something that looked like a camera case. There was no voice-over—only the sound of the Russian national anthem playing—but it was obvious that the four objects together constituted what was known in the vernacular as the "nuclear suitcase." The men shook Putin's hand next. Then he stepped closer to Yeltsin. Putin was holding a red file folder under his arm. Yeltsin wiped a tear from his left eye. He looked like he had limited mobility now—he seemed bloated—and he had only three fingers on his left hand because of a childhood accident, and all that together made him look awkward and vulnerable, like a giant toddler. Putin, Lyosha thought, looked disoriented and unsure of himself. Lyosha's grandmother was disoriented too, and scared, though in the months leading up to this day she had been quoting Putin copiously and gleefully, mostly his line about the terrorists in the outhouse. On the television, the patriarch of the Russian Orthodox Church, in his tall white hat topped with a golden cross, was watching over the transfer of power.

Then there was Yeltsin wearing an overcoat, opening a door for Putin, who was dressed only in a suit. "Here is your office," said Yeltsin, gesturing with his three-fingered hand. The camera panned to the presidential desk, with a small decorated New Year's tree next to it.*

And then there was Yeltsin out on the porch, in his overcoat and fur hat, with Putin next to him, still wearing only a suit, like a host who has stepped outside for a moment to say goodbye to a departing guest. Yeltsin got into a Mercedes stretch limo and drove off the premises as Putin, flanked by several other men, waved to him from the porch.[2]

———

SOMETIMES SERYOZHA THOUGHT THAT he was crazy—or everyone else was. This whole setup with the transfer of power struck him as bizarre, possibly

———
*In the 1930s, when the Soviet government reinstated many of the traditions of pre-Revolutionary life, the Christmas tree was reincarnated in the secular tradition of a New Year's tree, decorated for a celebration on December 31. The tradition survives to this day.

even unreal. On New Year's night, he asked, "Is he putting us on?" But even his grandfather, who was usually Seryozha's political ally and guiding light in the family, said that Putin was saying some reasonable things, making points that Alexander Nikolaevich himself had long been making. He heard Putin speaking about the social responsibility of government—health care, education, culture, words that Yeltsin had never seemed to utter—and this gave him some hope. He was cautious—he said that he feared seeing Putin fall into a trap set by the resurgent bureaucracy, what he called "the nomen-klatura monster," and when he heard Putin speak of the need to strengthen the state, his concern grew. Still, he thought the new president deserved a chance.[3] And Putin, to him, certainly seemed saner than the outgoing Russian president.

The way everyone seemed to be acting like this was normal, to take this gray little man, announce that he would be president, and watch him ascend to the throne three months later—the way everyone was unfazed by this, made Seryozha feel crazy. He had been feeling that way more and more often.

At Moscow State University, where Seryozha was now studying computer programming, everyone seemed to have been waiting for Putin to come along. Seryozha did not even notice when his portraits began appearing, along with patriotic paraphernalia he had not noticed before: flags, flyers for Putin's Unity Party, posters calling on everyone to vote in the hastily scheduled presidential election. This pretend election of a barely perceptible candidate who was the preordained winner made Seryozha feel like he barely existed himself. It was probably a good thing that his field required virtually no social contact with his fellow students: he could not have grasped their reality if he had wanted to.

IN AUGUST 2000, Lyosha went to the Black Sea coast with his mother. They spent their days at the beach, which was so crowded that they had to get there early to find a place to throw down a towel on the sand, and their evenings in the kitchen of a rented apartment, eating sickly sweet local grapes and listening to the radio. The news was as slow as the southern air, until something inconceivable happened. According to the radio, a Russian nuclear submarine, the *Kursk*, had sunk off the coast of Murmansk. Some of the crew were still alive, but trapped at the bottom of the Barents Sea. The radio was saying that Russian rescue crews could not get to the submarine. The radio was also saying that Norway had offered to help but Russia had declined. The radio was saying that President Putin had decided not to interrupt his vacation in Sochi.

The days slowed even more. In the fog of his sleepless nights and his circular daydreams, Lyosha kept imagining the sailors, boys a few years older than he was, at the bottom of the cold sea, waiting for help that could not get to them, and the president—the little man to whom Yeltsin had handed his office—somewhere quite near here, lying on a stretch of the Black Sea beach that was pristine and uncrowded, reserved for Putin's uninterruptible vacation.

Thinking about all this was a relief, because Lyosha's thoughts before the submarine disaster had been even worse. Something had happened to Lyosha his first day at the beach. When he saw other boys, teenagers like himself or young men, dressed, like he was, in only a pair of small black bathing trunks, he felt heat shoot excruciatingly through his body and a thrilling invisible shiver set in. It happened every day after that first time. The thoughts it brought were unthinkable. I am a pervert, he thought. I am sick. I am the only person in the world who feels this way. Now these awful phrases floating in his mind mixed with images of the sailors dying at the bottom of the sea.

Rationally, Lyosha knew that there were homosexuals in the world. In seventh grade his class had made a weekly visit to a family-planning center where a psychologist talked to them about things their parents did not. The program was funded by American billionaire George Soros, the school had a contract with the center, and parents of the seventh-graders had to sign consent forms to allow their children to attend. The psychologist happened to be the mother of Lyosha's friend, a girl with whom he shared a desk in every one of his classes. She was as unpopular as he was, not just with other children but also with teachers, who seemed to suspect her of being smarter than they were. Lyosha, for his part, had somehow earned the nickname "faggot" among fellow students. One day at the center, the psychologist said that in addition to "heterosexual" families there were also "homosexual" ones. The idea was sudden, exciting, and as foreign as Soros, the American billionaire.

The following year—eighth grade—an older girl stormed into their class one day and asked loudly, "Did you know you had a prostitute in your grade?" She explained that thirteen boys had locked the girl in question in a cellar and had taken turns having intercourse with her. "She couldn't get out," said this accuser, "and she liked it." Over the course of the next few days, the story was recounted many times, as the male participants boasted of their roles in it. Their victim stayed out of school for a few weeks, and when she returned, she and Lyosha became friends. They were now a group of three: the Faggot, the Prostitute, and the Snob.

As they got older, some of their classmates seemed to develop respect for their intelligence and their ability to learn, explain, and argue about things. In tenth grade—the penultimate year of high school—Lyosha studied harder than ever before, because this seemed the only way to chase away the thoughts that had begun tormenting him in August on the Black Sea. Toward the end of the school year, he was elected class president: whatever some of his classmates thought of him, whatever led them to call Lyosha "faggot," they agreed that he was the best person to represent their interests before the school administration.

In May 2001, toward the end of tenth grade, Lyosha and his two friends were hanging out at the playground behind his building. They were too old for playgrounds, of course, but in the absence of other public spaces all young people in Solikamsk hung out in playgrounds, especially when the weather was good. A girl strolled by—she was one of the kids who used to sleep in Lyosha's stairway, except she was not a kid anymore. She called out to someone else who happened to be walking by, a man of about thirty. He sauntered over. She pointed at Lyosha.

"Faggot," she said.

The man took a short running start and kicked Lyosha in the lower back. Then again. His eyes were crazy, empty and furious at the same time, and Lyosha knew that he was about to be beaten to death.

Lyosha's stepfather happened to come out on the balcony just then. This gave him a clear view of the playground.

"Get out of here," barked the girl.

Lyosha ran.

At the emergency room he was told that there was bleeding and that he now had a condition called a "floating kidney"—literally, one of his kidneys was no longer securely attached by surrounding tissue. The pain was excruciating, and to relieve it—and to avoid surgery—he would have to stay in bed for two weeks. Lyosha's mother wanted to go to the police, but Lyosha was terrified that the reason for the beating would then be revealed. Because if he had to explain what had happened to him, he would have to say, "I am gay."

"I am gay," he said to himself. He had learned the word from films on the cable channel. The beating convinced him that the word applied to him.

There was a new counselor at school, a recent college graduate who had made it clear that she wanted to be Lyosha's friend. He dialed her number now, from his sickbed, while his mother and stepfather slept in the next room. Lyosha's courage ran out once she picked up the phone, though. They stayed on the line for five hours, alternating between filler chatter and awful silences.

"Is this about something illegal?" she asked.

"Drugs?" she asked.

"Are you trying to tell me that you are gay?" she asked.

"I am gay."

She was fine with it—more than fine. Lyosha was suddenly spilling his thoughts and feelings, and she sighed and laughed in all the right places. He was even able to talk to her about sex, or what he imagined sex to be. After that, he told his cousin, who was now a military-school cadet. The cousin said that he could not accept the homosexual lifestyle but he still loved Lyosha.

Lyosha decided not to tell his two school friends, but even so, things did not look nearly so desperate as they had a year ago, on the Black Sea. He had stopped being afraid of his stepfather since the time Sergei got drunk and nasty and Lyosha hit him over the head with a kitchen stool. He had only one year of high school left. After that, he would leave Solikamsk for good and go to university. He studied harder than he ever had before, entering every conceivable student competition to maximize his chances of university admission.

By May 2002, it was clear that Lyosha would be graduating with a silver medal, a scholastic distinction that would entitle him to skip general-knowledge university entrance exams: he had to sit only for the exam in whatever subject he chose to study. On the eve of graduation, Lyosha bleached one half of his bangs. At the breakfast table, his stepfather, wearing his perennial wife-beater undershirt, took a break from making his disgusting eating noises to ask:

"Are you a faggot or something?"

"None of your business," said Lyosha.

AFTER GRADUATION, one of the boys in the class threw a party at his parents' dacha, and about fifteen people went. They danced and drank. By five in the morning, a couple of the guests had passed out in an alcoholic stupor. The rest gathered in the kitchen to eat ice cream. Lyosha stood up and said, "I am gay."

"Why?" asked one of the girls. She seemed upset.

"I knew it," said someone else.

Then the conversation moved on. Lyosha had his high school diploma. In five days' time he would go to the mayor's office to pick up his silver medal. He would be out of there.

Then it dawned on him that there was no turning back. Soon enough, the news of his coming out would spread through town. His life now depended on getting into university.

———

MASHA WANTED A CAREER in the military. There were a few problems with this, of which Tatiana's shock and horror at the idea was perhaps the least. Masha wanted to be an officer in an army that was not the Russian army but a glorious army of some strong and proud country. She sometimes thought of herself as a sort of extraterritorial patriot: given a country, she would be proud, and given a uniform, she would serve. Instead, she was given Russia, which filled her heart with despair and her mind with the idea that life was not worth living.

With an empty mind like that, Masha would never get into university, said Tatiana. By "university" she meant Moscow State, where everyone in the family had gone. Everything else was not really higher education. And everything that was not the sciences was not really knowledge. Meanwhile, Masha was barely passing chemistry. She started cramming, and discovered that she actually liked chemistry. She declared her intention to apply to the chemistry department of Moscow State. This would be a lot better than a military academy, said Tatiana, if only Masha had a prayer of getting in.

Masha graduated from high school in May 2000, a month after her sixteenth birthday. She took the Moscow State entrance exams and fell just one point short of full admission to chemistry. In the post-Soviet setup, state universities now had two tracks: tuition-free admission for the top students and paid for those who scored slightly lower. Tatiana could afford to pay for Masha to attend, but she refused, citing a central rule of her own life: "Never put yourself in a situation where you will be the smartest person in the room." Masha would have to push papers at the Military Insurance Company for a year and then try for admission to the tuition-free track again.

In June 2001, she was accepted. This was the beginning of real life, and

Masha was starting out with success. Tatiana was now talking about buying an apartment where they would live for the next five or six years, before Masha went off to graduate school abroad. They went to look at some of the more promising apartment towers going up in the neighborhood. Masha said she wanted a bedroom with a view of the Moscow River. They would start apartment-shopping in earnest in the fall, after Masha got some well-deserved rest on the Black Sea. She was going with her aunt; Tatiana was staying in Moscow, at work, where she was now a senior executive in charge of rates.

Masha and her aunt returned on August 25, a week before classes would start. Masha was seventeen, tall and tan, and her hair was the whitest shade of blond it had ever been. That evening Tatiana told her that she had breast cancer, stage IV.

In the months that followed, Masha went to class and Tatiana went to work and to get chemo. Sometimes she went into the hospital. At the end of May 2002, the hospital told her to go home: there would be no more chemo. She lost weight. Then she gained weight, because her liver grew and grew. In mid-June she stopped going to work.

At the apartment, women kept ringing the doorbell, saying they were faith healers sent by Masha's aunt. Masha's grandmother pushed an inexhaustible supply of books with titles like *Cancer Can Be Cured*. Everyone was insisting that Tatiana be baptized. It was a hot summer in Moscow. It got dark late, and cooled down even later. Only at night did Masha get to be alone with her mother, in a sort of peace.

On June 30, Tatiana asked Masha to pick up a morphine prescription at the neighborhood polyclinic, which still, eleven years after the end of the USSR, had a monopoly on prescribing controlled substances, which could be dispensed only to citizens officially residing in the clinic's catchment area.

"It's not time yet," said the doctor.

"Well, when it is time, why don't you just let me know," said Masha.

"Since when are you allowed to speak to me like that?" asked the doctor.

"Since my mother is dying," said Masha.

The doctor called the chief of the polyclinic, who had Masha removed from the premises.

THAT NIGHT, Tatiana fell asleep in the armchair. When it finally got dark, Masha lifted her mother out of the chair and laid her on the couch. She was about to get some sleep herself, on a cot set up in the same room, when a flock of pigeons landed on the windowsill outside. Tatiana said something. Masha got up and turned on the light. Tatiana was staring out the window. Masha picked up and held her mother's body in her arms.

She called her aunt, told her, and put down the phone. She wanted to sit there for a bit and maybe learn to understand what had happened. But her aunt must have gotten on the phone, because an ambulance came, a policeman, then someone from the morgue. They said that Masha had to wake up the neighbors because someone had to witness the removal of the body. It was three in the morning, and Masha felt bad about waking people up, but she was worried that soon it would get hot again and things would start happening to the body. While she was trying to decide what to do, the morgue's driver left. The policeman remained and was now demanding money, a bribe, though Masha could not quite understand what for. She called her aunt again. She came, and so did Masha's grandparents. The body was now cold and the skin had started changing color. It will be hot soon, Masha said.

Her grandfather shouted at her, something about how the smell was the only thing she was worried about, and why was she not crying?

Why was she not crying? Because she needed to be alone to cry, and she also needed a cigarette, she wanted to smoke more than anything in the world right now, but she had only recently turned eighteen and she still did not feel that she could smoke in front of her grandparents.

Someone from the Military Insurance Company came, took a look at the family, and said that Masha would need help. The company's logistics director was dispatched to deal with the arrangements. Together with Masha's grandparents and aunt, he organized a memorial service at a church. Masha tried to tell them that this was a bad idea, but she did not know how to explain it. They asked her if she believed in God, and she said that she did but she also loved and respected her mother, who had been an atheist, and they should respect her too. They said Tatiana was with God now.

Somewhere along the way Masha learned that some hours after Tatiana died, a Russian passenger plane had collided with a cargo plane over southern Germany, killing seventy-one people, including more than fifty children.[4] From that point on, she would tell people that her mother died on the day of the Überlingen catastrophe. That way the day meant something to other people too.

LYOSHA APPLIED to the history department at Perm State University. With his silver medal, all he had to do was get a top score on an oral history exam. He pulled what they call a "ticket"—a card with a topic printed on it:

The Battle on Ice and Soviet Culture of the 1920s and 1930s

Lyosha talked. He knew his subject, but he sensed that he did not do as well as he should have. His score was five/four when what he needed was five/five.

So much for the history department. The political science department was examining applicants the next day. He called his mother, and she said that he would find political science boring. But he could not go back to Solikamsk. He carried his application over to political science and went to the library to study for another oral exam.

He went about studying in the most stubborn and counterproductive way possible, and he knew it. He wanted to figure out what he had been missing during the exam he had just taken. He pulled out Mikhail Pokrovsky's *Russian History Beginning in Ancient Times*, a classic tome, and started reading. He knew this was the book he should have referenced, just as he knew it was too late to fix the omission.

The examiners were the same two professors as the day before. Lyosha pulled his ticket, turned it over, and read:

The Battle on Ice and Soviet Culture of the 1920s and 1930s

"Do you have anything to add?" asked one of the examiners.

Lyosha did. He got a five/five. He would be studying political science.

Political science turned out to have its own language, which made Lyosha understand things differently—both the events he was now witnessing and ones he had largely ignored when his body and mind were overwhelmed with other concerns two years earlier, on the Black Sea. In that time, as he now read in an article by Moscow political scientist Olga Kryshtanovskaya, Putin had reshaped the government and now a quarter of all top posts were held by military officers. Kryshtanovskaya wrote that this was called a militocracy.[5] Back in the dorm, talking to young women who were his new friends, Lyosha said, "Putin reminds me of some sort of miniature military dictator." The women agreed.

When he said "miniature," Lyosha did not really mean Putin's size—more the general sense that whatever frightening words his new books offered, the phenomena they were describing did not feel quite real. Lyosha, for one, did not have the sense of living in a military dictatorship, or a military anything, or any kind of dictatorship. He was a student at a very politically liberal department, where instructors ridiculed Putin mercilessly, as though engaged in some sort of competition for the wittiest put-down. The facts were there—in just two years, Putin had greatly weakened the power of elected officials by creating federal oversight over governors and giving the federal center the right to fire elected governors; reversed judicial reform; and monopolized national broadcast television in the hands of the Kremlin. So while his regime could not yet be called authoritarian, that seemed to be the direction in which it was headed. This transitional state,

Lyosha learned, was called an "authoritarian situation"—meaning, authoritarianism could happen here.

In October of Lyosha's first year at university, a group of armed men and women who said they were Chechen seized a theater in Moscow during the performance of a musical, taking more than nine hundred hostages. The standoff lasted three days, and then federal troops stormed the theater, killing the terrorists and freeing the hostages. Lyosha was on his way to Solikamsk for the weekend when the storm began, and when he got to his mother's apartment all that the television would show him was footage of the theater hall, empty but for the bodies of the terrorists slumped over some of the seats. The chairs were a plush red, the terrorists were all dressed in black, and the scene reminded Lyosha somehow of a game of checkers. He learned from the radio that 129 hostages had died in the storming of the theater, which sounded like it had been botched—the sleeping gas that had been pumped into the space to disable the terrorists had ended up killing many of the hostages, although there were no pictures of those other bodies. So this is what an authoritarian situation looks like, thought Lyosha. A checkerboard.

SOME DISASTERS COME SUDDENLY and proceed in tedious slow motion. Gudkov was not a member of the executive board of his center, so he was not privy to some of the early discussions, but once he knew, it seemed obvious: they were in big, inexorable trouble. There was a rumor that Putin had seen Levada make an inappropriate face at some official function and had taken offense. The new president was getting a reputation for being thin-skinned and vengeful, and the old sociologist, for all his Soviet experience, had never had much of a poker face. The rumor may or may not have been true, and it was ultimately unnecessary for explaining what was happening to the center.

They had begun as the All-Soviet Center for Public Opinion Research, under the auspices of the trade union authority and the Soviet labor ministry. It was the Soviet Union, and every institution was an institution of the state, and this seemed no more absurd in the case of the public opinion research center than it did in the case of the trade unions. Then the Soviet Union collapsed and the center became the All-Russian Center for Public Opinion Research, under the auspices of the Russian Labor Ministry and the state property authority. This conformed entirely to the logic by which institutions passed from the old empire to the new Russian state. Like many other state institutions, the center received no direct government funding but was able to rent office space from the government at a fixed rate that seemed laughably low as Moscow real estate prices grew. The nominal founders of the center—the ministry and the property authority—had the power to appoint the director, but had no other way to exert control over the center's work or staffing; they lacked even the power to fire the director before his five-year term was up. If anyone who worked at the center were to claim that this seemed like sufficient protection from government interference, that would be a lie: in fact, no one at the center was at all concerned with protecting it from government interference.

But it was the sociologists' job to observe shifts in the logic and culture of institutions, and they saw it clearly soon after Putin took office. He moved to reassert executive-branch control not only over the media but also over the judiciary and, broadly, the economy. He instituted tax reform that was widely praised by liberal economists for the introduction of a flat income tax but whose other provisions served to push smaller businesses into the shadow; at the same time, Putin started placing his own people at the helm of large corporations that were owned by the state—and some that were not. His relationship with the oligarchs seemed to follow the logic of Nemtsov's idea of "nationalizing the Kremlin": he directed the very rich to forfeit their political power—and sometimes the assets that ensured this power. Two of the oligarchs who owned national television companies, Vladimir Gusinsky and Boris Berezovsky, were forced into exile, but not before giving up control of their media outlets. And it was clear that in Putin's Russia ownership would mean active control: the tenor and content of the television broadcasts were changing rapidly. The first thing to go was any programming that poked fun at the Kremlin.

The All-Russian Center for Public Opinion Research did not ridicule the Kremlin or its new inhabitant. For the most part, the news it produced was flattering to Putin: people liked their new president and their life with him. When Levada wrote his traditional year-end summary for 2000, he noted that it had felt to Russians like the easiest year in a long time. They had hope. They had little or no concern for the issues that disproportionately worried the liberal intellectuals, like the state takeover of broadcast media or the fact that Russia had now restored the old Soviet national anthem as its own, with the lyrics changed slightly, to omit references to Lenin and the glorious communist future. Still, the *Kursk* nuclear submarine disaster ranked as the most important event of the year by far, and support for the second war in Chechnya, now a year and a half old, was clearly waning.[6]

Two years later, after the theater siege in Moscow, the center reported that 81 percent of Russians believed they were not being told the whole truth of what had happened, and 75 percent thought the leadership of Russian security ministries had to be held responsible for letting the hostage-taking occur in the first place.[7]

Then an election year began. It would not be the entire parliament—Putin had reinterpreted a vaguely worded provision in the 1993 Constitution to turn the upper house into an appointed body—but the 450 seats in the lower house would come up for a vote in December 2003 (and Putin himself would face reelection in March 2004). The ruling party was now called United Russia, and at the start of the election year the center's polls showed its ratings dropping precipitously.[8]

Levada was summoned to the ministry. His contract would not be up for another two years, but he now faced a small group of bureaucrats, one of whom said to him, "You are not a young man." They said that he needed a successor and they had someone for him. In fact, this proposed successor was there, in the next room, waiting to be introduced to Levada. He entered presently. He was all of twenty-nine, and his experience was limited largely to working for one of the groups that had created Putin's political persona for the presidential election. Levada was instructed to appoint this youth as his deputy for about six months and then retire. Without waiting for a response, Levada's interlocutors told him what would happen if he failed to comply: he would face criminal charges. Surely a tax or other financial irregularity could be found, given a careful-enough examination of the center's records.

Levada refused, and the center's death watch commenced. Gudkov dreaded seeing Levada charged with a crime or dragged into the media. Levada, meanwhile, tried to petition the state to allow the staff to buy out the center and transform it into a joint-stock company. The petition was rejected. Everyone on staff who had ever been friendly with or done a survey for a highly placed official in the government now appealed for help. These people promised to try but then invariably confessed that they had failed.

In the end, Levada was fired. It was against the law, but this no longer mattered. If he sued, he would lose. Every single person on the center's staff—more than a hundred people—tendered a resignation. One of them, an older woman from accounting, decided to retire. The rest set about creating a new company. It was no longer the All-Russian Center for Public Opinion Research—that name now belonged to other people. This one would be called simply the Levada Center. Compared with the times Levada had been forced out of jobs back in the Soviet Union, this experience was an improvement: the team could stay together now. All they had to do was start from scratch.

A month after Levada was forced out of the center he had built, the richest man in Russia, Mikhail Khodorkovsky, was arrested. He had failed to observe the new rules of the game. He was not staying out of politics—he was giving money to political parties and civil-society organizations—and at a meeting at the Kremlin, called to give the wealthy an opportunity to pledge allegiance to Putin, he had spoken about growing corruption. Soon after, the state takeover of his business ensued, playing out just like the earlier purges of the oligarchs Gusinsky and Berezovsky—or like the purge of Levada, except that there was a lot more money involved. Khodorkovsky got his warnings and failed to heed them. Now he was arrested and charged with tax evasion. In short order his company—the world's largest oil producer—would be expropriated by the Putin clan. Gudkov observed with bitter satisfaction that although the Khodorkovsky arrest was different from the others only in the scale of his business, at least it had gotten some of his acquaintances finally to start expressing reservations about Putin.

In December 2003, United Russia won the election with 37 percent of the vote,[9] which would give it an absolute majority in parliament. For the first time since the end of the Soviet Union there would be no party in parliament that positioned itself as liberal, pro-reform, and generally post-Soviet: the other three parties that won enough votes to be seated were the Communists, the misnamed Liberal Democratic Party, which had been running on radical nationalist rhetoric for more than a decade, and a new Kremlin-backed party, Rodina ("Motherland"). Nemtsov spent election night getting drunk with his friends and allies and trying to enumerate the reasons for the disastrous showing of the Union of Right Forces. He thought they had run bad campaign ads, advanced the wrong candidates, and failed to form a coalition with another right-liberal party.[10] But if he had read Gudkov's analysis three years earlier, he might have noticed that the reason for the party's failure was different, and simpler: this time it was not the one positioned by the Kremlin as the "other" party of power. He also might have noticed that something basic had changed in the way the two-party game was played. In 1996 and 2000, the foil to the ruling party was more liberal and advocated for greater economic and social reform. Motherland, the party that played the role of foil this year, staked out a more nationalist, more socially conservative position than the official political mainstream. The differences continued to be ever more subtle—gray against black—but the country had reversed political direction.

FOR THE FIRST SIX MONTHS after Tatiana's death, Masha slept with the lights on. Everything that had ever happened in the apartment now came back to her as a frightening memory, even if she had been too young or had felt too safe to be scared when it first happened. The time the local authorities sent them new flatmates, an ethnic Russian couple who had fled Chechnya. The time after the couple moved out and Tatiana was waging her battle to keep the apartment for herself and Masha, when the residential authorities broke down the door; Tatiana replaced it with an unbreakable steel one. The two times, in 1995 and 1997, when Masha's former classmate, now a heroin addict, climbed in through the window to steal something he could sell. In the harsh electrical light at night the apartment looked worse than ever: peeling wallpaper, cracked plaster, every color a faded copy of itself. It occurred to Masha that Tatiana's perennial idea that life was elsewhere really meant that she had expected life to happen later. Now she was dead at forty-three.

Tatiana had saved some money for that apartment she was going to buy—it was in her debit-card account, but when she was dying, she could not remember her PIN. She left no will. Convoluted Russian law granted priority inheritance rights to veterans of the Great Patriotic War—and anyway, it was not like eighteen-year-old Masha was going to fight her relatives. The money was gone. Masha's aunt claimed the dacha. Masha got the apartment. There went Masha's relationship with her aunt, too. The Military Insurance Company never abandoned Masha—she got a small monthly payment from it—and that amount, combined with her university stipend, added up to about two hundred dollars a month. After she paid all the apartment bills, Masha had enough left to buy buckwheat and butter to last her a month. After the 1990s, she felt she had a clear idea of what poverty looked like, and now she was staring it in the face. She had a boyfriend who came from a well-to-do family, and his relatives made comments about Masha's cheap clothes.

In March 2003, after one semester of this existence, Masha took a leave of absence from the university. She got a job as a "consultant," which really meant salesperson, at a shop called Digital Foto. Now she spent her days with people her age who lived with their parents and for whom Moscow State University was as foreign a phenomenon as, say, England.

Masha realized that the only way she would ever rid herself of her fear of the dark was to just plunge in. One night she flipped the switch.

By summer, Masha had saved enough money to hire a crew to make her apartment "pretty." That was the word she used, and the workers understood what she wanted. Money was beginning to flow in Moscow and everyone was beautifying their apartments: putting in new double-pane windows in plastic housing, painting the kitchens yellow, and buying fuzzy rugs for the bathroom at the newly opened IKEA just outside the city (it ran a free shuttle from the Metro). Masha got a cat.

She needed to return to her world. She went back to university. She posted her résumé on a new site called job.ru and got calls from two companies. She took a job with the one that imported chemicals for the cosmetics industry, which was taking off because everything was taking off. Thanks to the skyrocketing price of oil, Russia was having a consumer boom on a scale the reformers of the 1990s could not have imagined. Large shiny well-lit shopping malls were opening all over Moscow, stalling traffic, and all of them had one or two makeup department stores stocked with products both real and counterfeit, and vast quantities of chemicals were required to produce them. These chemicals had to be imported, and it was Masha's job to organize the process. She negotiated—she learned to use her English on the phone—and she arranged, and she cleared customs: she learned to give bribes. She also looked stunning at meetings with suppliers, and once she had a drink in her, she could tell jokes in English.

The chemistry department had an unofficial online home called chemport.ru. Among other things, it hosted anonymous reviews of department faculty. This meant a captive audience: undergraduates, graduate students, and professors. This, as far as Masha was concerned, meant that the site should be making money. Anyone who was not making money these days was an idiot. She found the guy who had started the site. His name was Sergei Baronov. He was a graduate student, recently divorced, and therefore living in the dorms. She told him about her scheme: they had to create a subscription service for sales managers for chemical companies. All they had to do was think of a service these people would get in exchange—they were just looking for a way to spend their companies' money. Sergei asked if she knew why countries had given up the gold standard in favor of gold-and-currency reserves. Why? Masha asked—she had a slightly hostile way of asking that she never could quite modulate—and he started explaining. He was not an idiot at all. She liked someone who could tell her something she did not know. As it turned out, he had started his dissertation at a university in Florida and was teaching radiochemistry. They became a couple, and chemport.ru started making money.

Sergei said they should have children. It sounded reasonable. Masha was not exactly in love with him, but they did have a business together. Money was raining down on them, and there was no reason to think it would stop. Other things, though, might be short-lived. By "things," Masha meant people. She was twenty, he was twenty-five, and they might as well have children now. He moved into her pretty apartment. They started trying to conceive, but it did not work. They tried assisted insemination, and that did not work. They gave up, got drunk, and it worked.

When Masha was eight weeks pregnant, the doctor said that the fetus had no heartbeat and handed her a referral for a D&C. She went home, cried her eyes out, and then googled "fetal heartbeat." She went back to the doctor and told her that the heartbeat can show up later than eight weeks.

"What are you, the smartest one here?" asked the doctor.

"Yeah," said Masha.

twelve

THE ORANGE MENACE

BORIS NEMTSOV WORRIED THAT his daughter would not make it in the world. He was convinced that, stern and uncompromising as she was, she would never find a husband. That meant that she would have to be self-sufficient—but as far as he could tell, she lacked ambition. He was right about that: in her lack of ambition, Zhanna was like her mother, but Raisa, unlike Zhanna, was pliant and easy to live with. Boris said that was fine: he did not want his women too smart or too active—except his daughter, who was so headstrong that she needed a Plan B. When she tagged along with him one day to an interview at Echo Moskvy (Echo of Moscow), the big pro-democracy radio station, he had a sudden inspiration.

"Hey," he said to the editor in chief in the overly familiar tone he assumed when the situation called for underscoring his influence. "Why don't you take my girl on as an intern here?"

Why not, indeed. The fact that Zhanna was fifteen, too young legally to work full-time, was of little concern. She had a famous name and she knew people—or, more accurately, many people knew her as her father's daughter. Zhanna was hired. Her job was to call Yeltsin's press secretary and inquire after the president's health. Rather than brush her off rudely, as he would have another reporter, the press secretary dutifully allowed her to record a sentence or two to the effect that the president's health was just fine.

When Zhanna was not calling Yeltsin's press secretary, she was fetching, xeroxing, and performing other typical intern duties. The point was, she was developing a work ethic that would allow her to survive in spite of her insufferably unaccommodating personality. She started school at nine in the morning, rushed directly from her last class to the radio station to be at work by four, and finished at midnight. It was hell, but she was able to buy herself a black-and-gray cropped cardigan sweater at Benetton. It cost a lot of money, and it was money she had earned.

Then Yeltsin quit—the phone call came on New Year's Eve, a couple of weeks after Boris had won his parliamentary election, when the family was on vacation at a ski resort in France. Soon after, the leadership of his new party, the Union of Right Forces, gathered to discuss their position on the presidential election. Would they field a candidate? Yeltsin's resignation had been timed to render such an attempt futile—he had effectively moved the vote up by four months, to March. The traditional New Year's and Christmas holidays, when no one was in Moscow (except, as it turned out, Yeltsin and Putin), had already bitten another two weeks off the lead time. Putin's popularity rating was sky-high. The rational thing to do under the circumstances, argued former prime minister Gaidar and two other members of the party's leadership, was to fall in line behind Putin. Boris argued that as long as the presumptive president had no political platform—which Putin did not—there was nothing to get behind. He was outvoted.

On March 26, 2000, Vladimir Putin was elected president of Russia, and Zhanna turned sixteen. She was nearly indifferent to both events. In the preceding months, she had quit her job at Echo Moskvy and found ambition. Her life's goal now was to gain admission to an American university. This was not at all what Boris had had in mind when he told her that she needed to be self-sufficient. It would not be a good look for a parliament member to have a daughter studying in America. But he said that he would not stand in her way.

He was not helping her either. Zhanna got all the textbooks and study aids and proceeded in a self-sufficient manner. She got the highest possible score on the Test of English as a Foreign Language and very high SAT scores as well. She was accepted to Fordham University in New York City. She was aiming higher, of course, but now she had a plan: a year or two at Fordham, then she would transfer to Columbia and finish up there. In August 2001 she said goodbye to the apartment on the Garden Ring and moved to America.

She could not have imagined what it would feel like to be alone in New York City. She was living near the Manhattan branch of the university, amid the skyscrapers of Midtown and next to the edgy neighborhood she learned was called Hell's Kitchen. The only person she knew was the daughter of a Russian oligarch who had just graduated from a New York college and was now working for a consulting company. Her work week averaged eighty hours, and she told Zhanna that this was her future too. Then, within two weeks of Zhanna's arrival, the city's streets filled with cars with blaring sirens, people in respirator masks, panic. Zhanna walked downtown, as far as she could before hitting a police cordon, and saw the second of the two towers crumple. Then there were flyers everywhere, with addresses where people could go to donate blood. Zhanna walked to one of those addresses.

She called her grandmother, the pediatrician. The call would cost ten dollars, maybe more, so she had to make it fast.

"Grandma, tell me quickly, what's my blood type?"

"O negative."

Zhanna hung up. On the other end of the line, Dina Yakovlevna imagined unimaginable things happening to her granddaughter in the city seized by terror. In New York, Zhanna stood in line for four hours to give blood. She was told that hers was a precious, much-needed type of blood and the maximum allowable amount would be drawn. She left the hospital woozy, dragged her body to a deli, and sat there for an eternity, eating herself back to her feet.

She asked Boris not to tell anyone about the blood donation—she could tell over the phone that he was bursting to—but he was so proud of her that he told the story anyway. *Komsomolskaya Pravda*, the propaganda broadsheet turned tabloid, carried the headline "Zhanna Nemtsova Shed Blood for America."[1]

After September 11, the solitude of the foreign college freshman in New York proved intolerable. Zhanna managed another month before she asked Boris to book her a ticket back to Moscow. He was thrilled. He also pulled some strings to get Zhanna admitted to the Institute of International Relations, home to the children of the nomenklatura headed for careers in diplomacy and international trade. *Komsomolskaya Pravda* reported that in the wake of the terrorist attacks Zhanna had been shunned by her classmates for being a foreigner.[2]

Her first evening at home, an oligarch friend of Boris's, Mikhail Fridman, was visiting. Father and daughter's joy at their reunion made him furious. "Idiots," he sputtered. "You are insane." Meaning, anyone who forfeited the chance at an American future in favor of a Russian one had to be crazy.

THERE WAS SOMETHING DISTURBING in the way Russians were reacting to the terrorist attacks in America. Gudkov had long been thinking about the way Russia's self-concept was reflected in its attitudes toward the United States, and now he watched all the resentments and anxieties about America come to the surface. The wave of intense hatred with which Russians had reacted to NATO's Kosovo bombing campaign of 1999 had died down within a few months, returning the country to a sort of baseline level of anti-American sentiment, but now Gudkov was seeing it return, incongruously, in the wake of the September 11 attacks. Initially, the polls showed, Russians had reacted with sympathy and compassion, but very soon those feelings gave way to something else: the search for a way to blame the Americans themselves for the tragedy.

Part of this surely had to do with a sort of habitual insensitivity Russians as a society had developed in response to the wars, the terror, the violence, and poverty of its own twentieth century. This insensitivity, in turn, was tied, as both cause and effect, to the lack of social or cultural institutions that help process feelings. All of this was equally true of the ways Russians reacted to their own grief: they dulled it and moved on. But the resentment coming to the fore now was specific to the way Russians felt about Americans.

The Soviet Union had historically defined itself in opposition to the United States. The century of identification consisted of several distinct periods. First, early Soviet Russia based its revolutionary push to industrialize on the American model and on American machinery. During the Great Depression, American-made industrial equipment became affordable—American tragedy worked in synergy with Russian need. Stalin said, *"Dogonim i peregonim Ameriku"* ("We shall catch up to America and overtake it") and Soviet factory machines were often inscribed with the letters *DIP* in honor of this aspirational slogan.

During the Second World War the competition was set aside in favor of military cooperation. The two countries were allies. But with the beginning of the Cold War the United States had ceased being a partner or even a rival: it became the enemy—indeed, an existential threat. This image had shaped the final four decades of the Soviet Union's existence, had been the bedrock of its system of mobilization and control.

When the Soviet Union collapsed, Russians did not stop looking into the American mirror. What they saw now was humiliating: the United States was giving Russians handouts, sending them "Legs of Bush" and other food that Americans themselves did not want to eat. America was not just wealthier than Russia—so were many other countries, and some of them, like Switzerland or Saudi Arabia, were wealthier than the United States itself. But unlike an old European country, America did not apportion its wealth according to an entrenched class structure: it was a country of achievement and possibility for all—or so it claimed, and Russians believed this part. Nor was it a tiny oil dictatorship like the Saudis. America was the very definition of modernity; it was the country that Russia had failed to become. Here was a sterling example of Soviet-style doublethink: America was attractive and threatening at the same time, worth emulating and eminently hateable.

Hatred for the United States had become a Soviet political and social tradition. And now Russia's search for its own traditions infused this hatred with new potency. "I hate, therefore I am," Gudkov wrote, trying to describe the driving force behind this new anti-Americanism. September 11 fueled the hatred because it engendered anxiety. Surveys were showing that Russians feared that a third world war would result from the attacks, though there was no consensus as to who the parties in this war might be. It was nonetheless—or all the more—a terrifying prospect, and it was America's fault.

More than half the respondents said that the time had come to increase defense spending, even if this meant that cuts had to be made elsewhere. For a country that was barely—almost imperceptibly for most people in 2001—climbing out of a deep economic depression, this seemed a bizarre result. But then this aggressive anti-American stance was most pronounced among the better-educated, more-well-off respondents. This was the position of the newly emergent elite—the men in uniform and the neotraditionalists whom the Putin presidency had elevated.[3]

IN THE ABSENCE of political institutions such as parties or established electoral preferences, and in the absence, too, of political experience, the new elite came to rely heavily on people who called themselves "political technologists." They were like Western political consultants magnified to the point of caricature. They created presidents, parties, and platforms from scratch. They employed small armies of people who produced logos and websites, photo ops and miles of political jargon. Many, though not all, of the soldiers and officers of these armies were very young—often still at university. Together and separately, they made a lot of money.

Neither the political technologists nor the politicians they represented had many—or sometimes any—ideas of their own, and part of the technologists' task was to find and incorporate ideas generated by others. The top political technologist of them all, Gleb Pavlovsky, a former Moscow editor who manufactured Putin's public persona in advance of his election, found Dugin and promoted his ideas. Dugin had a knack for putting the generalized anxiety of the elite into words, and these words sounded smart. After September 11, he said on television, where he was part of a political round table with six other men:

> A deep crisis of the liberal democratic system has been exposed, a crisis of values. The liberal-democratic complex consists of two components: liberalism and democracy. We usually perceive them as synonyms. But if we look at the history of the West, we will see that the democratic component was used actively in the battle against the Soviet Bloc, as a tool of opposition to totalitarianism. But when the Soviet system collapsed, democracy lost its fundamental strategic function. Liberalism retained its function. I believe that liberalism does not have to be combined with democracy. It can mean simply free trade, market mechanisms, which, as we know, can exist perfectly well in the strictest of authoritarian regimes, even in almost totalitarian ones.

He went on to predict that the United States, in the wake of September 11, would abandon its democratic experiment.[4] Dugin was misusing the term "liberalism"—as though it existed solely to denote the opposite of a command economy—and it was not clear what he meant by "democracy" when he claimed that America was on the verge of disposing of it. But his statement perfectly encapsulated the worldview Gudkov's surveys were reflecting. In this picture, the United States defined itself by its relationship to Russia, just as Russia defined itself in opposition to and in comparison with America. In this picture, it made sense for America to give up on democracy now that the Soviet Union was no more. Most important, this picture affirmed the idea that building a market economy and an authoritarian—"almost totalitarian"—regime at the same time was not just possible but also right.

A few months earlier, in April 2001, Dugin had held the founding congress of a new political movement. He had long since split with the National Bolshevik Party; as a political technologist he had helped to shape Putin's Unity Party and a short-lived Kremlin-backed spoiler party called Russia, but now he decided to start a movement of his own. The congress was held at a supper-club-like establishment called Honor and Dignity, which belonged to the counterterrorism shock-troop arm of the FSB, called Alpha. Several Alpha veterans were elected to the new movement's board, and many more men from the uniformed services were in attendance at the congress.

Dugin called the new movement Eurasia, and the event stressed its ties to the Kremlin. There were two large banners in the room. One said, "Russia Is a Eurasian Country. V. V. Putin." The other said, "Eurasia Above All." Predictably, one of the newspaper reports on the congress—all the papers wrote about it—was called "Eurasia über Alles."

"Eurasia above all," repeated Dugin at the conclusion of his address to the congress. His speech had been devoted to the idea that the world, or at least Russia, was being pulled apart by opposing forces: Eurasian and Atlanticist. Even Yeltsin had started to see the futility of the Atlanticist way back in the 1990s, said Dugin, but "it was the rule of Putin that spelled the true victory of Eurasianist ideas." For that reason, he said, "We support the president totally, radically. That places us at the total and radical center."

It was an incomprehensible and mesmerizing phrase, like the "violets blooming on the lips" line he had used on Evgenia a decade and a half earlier. The new movement's youngest member, Igor Nikolaev, from remote Yakutia, spelled out the Eurasian self-perception more clearly in his presentation, which he said had started out as a high school essay. "Individualism and the independence of opinion are traits characteristic of Europe, where we don't belong," he said. "Obedience and love for one's leader are the traits of the Russian people."[5]

"CAN EURASIANISM SAVE RUSSIA?" was the title of a political round table that aired on television in June 2002. Dugin had graduated from discussant to headliner, and Eurasianism from a fringe political movement to a universal solution. It offered an alternative view of Russian history, in which a century and a half of Mongol-Tatar rule had been not an age of destruction but, on the contrary, a vital cultural infusion that set Russia on a special path, distinct from Europe's. Explaining Eurasianism to the broad public, Dugin referred to a 1920 book by Nikolai Trubetskoy, a Russian prince in exile. Trubetskoy, a linguist (he was one of the founders of structural linguistics), focused on what he called "the magic of words." He argued that by using words like "humanity," "universality," "civilization," and "progress," Europeans—or, more precisely, Germans—had fooled the world—or, more precisely, Slavic nations—into buying the cosmopolitan idea. In fact, argued Trubetskoy, by "humanity" Germans meant themselves and those who were like them, and their concepts of "universality," "civilization," and "progress" were equally solipsistic—or, as Trubetskoy put it, "egocentric." By buying into the cosmopolitan idea, therefore, Slavs risked losing their identity and culture.[6]

Trubetskoy's book was called *Europe and Humanity*, and summarizing it for a television audience eighty-two years later, Dugin said that the prince had deemed Europe a threat to humanity. Since then, he explained, things had changed: Europe was not a threat to humanity any longer, but the United States was. "The Western-society project is being forced onto all other nations," said Dugin. "The Eurasianists will continue to oppose the West as long as the West persists in its pretensions to the universality of its own values, in forcing those values onto people, and in attempting to dominate, whether by means of colonization or by means of neo-colonization, which is what globalization is."[7]

This rang true to the broad television audience. The West was expanding. Even as Russia grew disillusioned with all things American, its neighbors began, unexpectedly, to edge westward. In 2003, a bloodless revolution led by young Western-oriented political activists brought down the government of Georgia. There was no love lost between Putin's Kremlin and the ousted Georgian president, Eduard Shevardnadze, who had once served as Gorbachev's foreign minister, but the revolution was nonetheless disturbing for Moscow. Putin dispatched his foreign minister to the Georgian capital to help negotiate the transfer of power, but he, and the Russian media, insisted on calling the events there a "coup" rather than a revolution. Speaking to his cabinet, Putin issued an indirect warning to the new Georgian leadership by stressing, "Russia has had a brotherly relationship with the people of Georgia for many centuries."[8] In fact, Georgia had been a part of the Russian Empire for centuries, except for three years of independence between 1917 and 1920, and the dozen years since the collapse of the Soviet Union. The phrase "brotherly relationship" harked back to the Soviet "friendship of the peoples" rhetoric, as it was meant to. It was also meant to remind the Georgians that Russia was still "first among equals" on its old stomping ground.

Twelve years after the end of the USSR, Russia still perceived its former subjects as parts of itself. Unlike clearly distinct foreign countries, former Soviet republics were referred to as the "near abroad" (Helsinki and Vienna are closer to Moscow than Kiev and Tbilisi, but the designation referred to psychic and political rather than physical distance). Relations with the "near abroad" were not even part of the foreign ministry's purview: they were handled by the presidential administration itself. This was perhaps the most striking example of a Soviet institution that had been claimed by Russia in 1991 and preserved against the logic of time and space. "In essence, this maintained the Soviet system in which the Union republics reported to the Central Committee of the Communist Party," Russian journalist Mikhail Zygar has written. "And since the presidential administration occupied the very same building in Staraya Square as the Central Committee of the Communist Party had, it so happened that the tradition had been maintained for decades, even though the Soviet Union no longer existed."[9] The tradition was one of exerting control over the nominally independent constituent republics (which were no longer constituent) and of appointing their leadership from Moscow.

In 2004, the year after the Georgian revolution, Moscow firmly took control of elections in Ukraine. Russian political technologists flooded Kiev, the Ukrainian capital. Their job was to prevent the election of the pro-

Western challenger to the current regime, which Moscow had found agreeable. Three days before the election, the pro-Moscow government staged a parade to commemorate the sixtieth anniversary of Kiev's liberation in the Second World War (the actual anniversary was nine days later, but they could not wait that long). Putin came, and took his place in the stands next to Leonid Kuchma, the outgoing president, and Viktor Yanukovych, his handpicked successor, whom Moscow was backing. The Victory Flag—the red flag that Soviet soldiers had placed on the Reichstag in 1945—was brought to Kiev for the occasion.[10] Putin was lending the pro-Moscow Ukrainian candidate his own authority, Russia's chief national myth, and the most important physical symbol of the myth.

None of it worked. Yanukovych lost at the polls. He still claimed victory, but this did not work either: Ukrainians took to the streets. They set up camp in Kiev's central square and refused to disperse, braving the November cold and then the December cold until Ukraine's supreme court stepped in and ordered a revote. Viktor Yushchenko, who positioned himself as pro-Western and entirely independent from Moscow—and who was even married to a Canadian woman—was elected president.

MASHA FOUND YUSHCHENKO UNLIKABLE and his anti-Moscow rhetoric personally insulting. She was surprised to discover that she cared so much. "Darn, this is the first time I've been so worked up about other people's elections," she wrote on her blog in November 2004. "I'll say more. This is the first time I've been worked up about any election anywhere."

"It's just that in Russia and in Moscow all the elections of our age have had a foregone conclusion," a friend wrote in the comments.[11]

This was true. At twenty, Masha had been old enough to vote in just one local, one parliamentary, and one presidential election, and the outcome had been known each time. Putin could not have lost his bid for reelection in 2004; Moscow's mayor, who had been in office since Masha was in primary school, was similarly entrenched; and Putin's United Russia party would, it seemed, be in control of parliament forever. Masha did not even know that she or anyone she knew could be passionate about elections these days—until Ukraine showed her.

All Russia was transfixed by the spectacle in Kiev. The year before, the Georgian revolution had drawn relatively little attention here, but now the Ukrainian revolution made people suspect—or hope for—a pattern. Could it happen in Russia too? The imagination ignored key differences between the two countries. In Ukraine, for example, electoral institutions had been developing while Putin had eviscerated Russian ones during his first term in office. And in Ukraine there was a functional, independent supreme court to step in to resolve the standoff, whereas the Russian equivalent, the Constitutional Court, had been effectively subsumed by the executive branch.

Boris Nemtsov was inspired by the turn of events in Ukraine. Since losing his parliamentary seat in December 2003, he had been at loose ends. It was the first time he had been defeated in an election since he entered politics in 1990—indeed, he had once been used to landslide victories. He had taken an executive-level job at a bank, well-paying and dull. But now there was Ukraine, with real political battles and actual high-stakes activism. He started shuttling back and forth to Kiev. He took a volunteer position as an adviser to Yushchenko. He wore a scarf the color of the revolution—orange—and spoke in the square on the first day of the protests. A few days later, in a television interview in Moscow, he held up Ukraine as an example for Russia:

> In the past, people in Kiev used to look to Moscow. And now an awful lot of Muscovites, and not only Muscovites, Russians in general, will probably be looking to Kiev to see how people are fighting for their rights, fighting for truth and freedom.[12]

The political technologists who had been dispatched to deal with Ukraine returned to Moscow and explained their failure: it was the Americans' fault. The Americans—by which they generally meant the United States government and George Soros—had been financing and organizing

Eastern European revolutions beginning with the overthrow of Slobodan Milošević in Yugoslavia in 2000, the story went. Then they hit Georgia, followed by Ukraine. Here it was: every fear of the American expansion was confirmed.

Putin had long been speaking about an external threat to Russia. Most recently he had mentioned it in the wake of the siege of a school in Beslan, a town in the Russian Caucasus, where more than three hundred people— most of them children—had died in September 2004. Less than two weeks after the attack, for which Chechen terrorists were held responsible, Putin announced new sweeping changes to Russia's political system. Governors would from now on be appointed rather than elected. All the seats in the lower house of parliament would from now on be apportioned to political parties based on their percentage of the vote nationwide (before the announcement, half the seats had been distributed among parties while the other half went to popularly elected representatives of 225 territorial districts). Putin explained that these measures would consolidate political institutions, creating the cohesion needed to protect the country from external threat—of which the school siege was the unlikely example. Like most of his earlier reforms, these measures affected formal political institutions and had consolidation as their aim. But to counter the perceived threat of an American-run, Soros-sponsored popular revolution, the Kremlin needed to focus on the public sphere, which it needed to mobilize for the preservation of the regime. A few years later, Australian political scientist Robert Horvath coined a term to describe this process: "preventive counter-revolution."[13]

AS IF TO AFFIRM the Kremlin's fear of a revolution, mass protests broke out in cities across Russia in the winter of 2005. Tens of thousands of people were protesting a new series of measures called the "monetization of entitlements," whereby people who received public assistance—women over fifty-five, men over sixty, early retirees, and the disabled—would no longer have access to unlimited public transportation and other in-kind benefits but would receive fixed sums of money instead. This was a cost-cutting measure, and aid recipients perceived, accurately, that despite what they were told, the money was not equivalent to the value of their old benefits. They were losing assistance that, for many, was essential for survival.

The Kremlin had not expected this backlash. The protests were the stuff of nightmares. The protesters were the elderly and the feeble, and the state could not use force against them even when they were blocking roadways, as they did in cities across the country, or when they set up tents in the streets, as happened in St. Petersburg.

Nor were the retirees the only people protesting. A slew of youth organizations seemed to appear out of nowhere. Some were radical, like the National Bolshevik Party, which had been rejuvenated by an influx of young people all over the country; they were demonstrating alongside or on behalf of the pensioners. Others were youth spin-offs or splinter groups of conventional political parties; these tended to model themselves, aesthetically, on Otpor ("Resistance"), the Yugoslav youth movement that had been instrumental in toppling Milošević. They staged small guerrilla-theater actions.

Finally, chess champion Garry Kasparov, one of the best-known people in the entire country, announced that he was quitting the sport to devote himself to political struggle. He formed an organization called the United Civic Front, an umbrella coalition that could unite the pensioners, the Otpor imitators, and the National Bolsheviks and their ilk, simply because they all opposed Putin and the authoritarian regime he was building. Together, they staged marches, which they called the Marches of the Dissenters.

It was during the Ukrainian elections that Masha had started blogging on livejournal.com, a platform that in America was popular among teenagers but in Russia was spontaneously repurposed to become a rudimentary social network (though the term was not yet in use). By spring 2005, Masha had her bearings on the network and was reading and talking to several people involved with the youth political groups. She went to a couple of meetings of Oborona ("Defense"), a group formed by a young man named Ilya Yashin. Oborona was designed to resemble Otpor in every way, including the sound of its name. Then Sergei objected: he did not want his wife involved with political hoodlums. By the end of the year, Masha was pregnant, and she complied.

Only a small number of people took part in the protests or even knew about them. With the exception of the National Bolsheviks, who had created a wide network of local activists, each of the youth groups counted just a handful of active members. The protesting pensioners were relatively numerous. But Russians who did not desperately need state assistance were mostly occupied with their own lives, which were very, very good. Thanks to skyrocketing oil prices, in 2005 Russia entered its sixth year of unprecedented economic prosperity.

Money was what the Kremlin used to defuse the protests of the disenfranchised: pensions were raised dramatically, and Putin declared a new commitment to social-program spending. Then the government cracked down on the young protest organizers, and on civil society in general. A law placing onerous registration and reporting requirements on nongovernmental organizations was passed. Civil society groups fought the law as well as they could, and the United States Congress even expressed concern about the law, in a nonbinding resolution—thereby affirming the Kremlin's view that Russian nongovernmental organizations were agents of Western subversion. In response to the push-back, the legislation was softened slightly: provisions that would have made it impossible for foreign organizations, such as USAID or Soros's Open Society Foundations, to function in Russia were removed. Still, the bill that Putin signed in January 2007 condemned nongovernmental organizations to useless paperwork designed to sap their resources.

The Marches of the Dissenters faced a physical crackdown rather than a paper one. Police began rounding up activists hours or days before a planned march. Those who managed to attend were first beaten by baton-wielding riot police and then detained. Activists braved these battles for a couple of years, but in early 2008 the marches ceased.

As the Kremlin forced out of the public sphere those people and organizations that it saw as threatening, it stuffed the empty space with supporters. Back in the Soviet era, public space had been monolithic, filled with the

Communist Party and its age-appropriate subsidiaries. Instead of non-governmental organizations, it had entities like trade unions run by the state trade union authority. Now political technologists began manufacturing organizations that created an illusion of plurality. The Kremlin instituted its own foundation, which would give grants to organizations of its choosing. In itself, a system of government grants is not necessarily an instrument of repression—many European countries have civil-society sectors that are primarily funded by the state—but the explicit assumption here was that Kremlin-funded groups would do the Kremlin's bidding. Political technologists cranked out youth groups designed to protect the Kremlin, including fighting for it in the streets if it came to that. They had names like Nashi ("Us," as opposed, clearly, to "Them") and the Young Guard, a name borrowed from a mythologized group of Soviet teenage anti-Hitler guerrillas. A group of students in Moscow put out a few issues of a newspaper called *Aktsiya* ("Action"); the new manufactured groups responded with a newspaper that had offices, a well-paid staff, and a regular print schedule. They called it *Reaktsiya* ("Reaction"). The new groups had training camps and cool T-shirts, and in some smaller cities they organized dances and other leisure activities for young people where none had been available. They staged street actions, including an unironically named March of the Consenters to counter the March of the Dissenters. Fifteen years earlier, a prominent perestroika politician, historian Yuri Afanasyev, had called this "the aggressively obedient majority."

In this context, Dugin's promise of creating a "total and radical center" began to make sense. He now positioned himself as a leader in the fight against the "orange menace," which he described as part of the Atlanticist plot against Eurasia and even an American jihad against Russia. The Eurasian movement spawned a youth wing, the Eurasian Youth Union, which placed itself in the vanguard of the Anti-Orange Front, an entity that Dugin claimed included twenty-five thousand people. What Russia really needed to prevent an orange revolution, said Dugin, was a new *oprichnina*, the reign of terror for which Czar Ivan IV was remembered as the Terrible.

In the process of reengineering the public sphere, the Kremlin changed the calendar. One of the four big public holidays of the year—along with New Year's Eve, May Day, and Victory Day—had been November 7, the anniversary of the Bolshevik Revolution. Yeltsin had renamed it Reconciliation and Agreement Day. Now Putin, apparently concerned that revolutionary organizations might be tempted to use the day to stage protests, abolished the holiday. Russians would still get a day off in November, but it would now be on the fourth of the month and it would mark an event that had not been part of Russia's historical imagination: the expulsion of Polish occupiers from Moscow in 1612. As the intellectual and the historian among the leaders of the "preventive counter-revolution," Dugin took ownership of the new holiday. On November 4, 2005, the Eurasian Youth Union led a march through central Moscow. They called it the Russian March. Eurasian Youth activists walked in the vanguard, carrying a banner emblazoned with the words "Russia Against the Occupiers!" The Eurasianists were joined by several other groups, whose slogans were explicitly racist: "We need a Russian Russia!" one speech concluded. "Glory to Russia!" Another declaimed: "How long are we going to put up with this vermin, with all these 'Latvias,' 'Polands,' and 'Georgias'? We declare this the day of the people's anger. Russians, rise up!"[14]

"By giving a green light to the [Eurasian Youth Union's] anti-Western xenophobia, the authorities had created opportunities for adherents of more extreme variants of ultranationalism," writes Horvath. "As the moderate opposition was driven to the margins, ultranationalists gained admission to Russia's public sphere."[15]

"I HAVE A BRILLIANT IDEA!" Boris shouted into the phone when he called Zhanna in Portugal in the summer of 2005. "You should run for office." His logic was simple: he had met Oborona activists, and the events of that year so far had convinced him that young—very young—people were the future of politics. His daughter had a leg up on everyone else because she carried his famous last name, to which he now referred as a brand.

Zhanna was not interested. She was not interested in much, frankly: she still, or once again, lacked ambition. She had just graduated from the Institute of International Relations, where she had done well enough, despite minimal engagement either with her studies or with fellow students. For much of her time in college her social life had revolved around a group of slightly older gay men—the people who had the best time at the best new clubs in town. Then, during the winter of her last year of studying, she got a call from a friend of her mother's: "Come on over, I'll introduce you to a very cute banker." The banker's name was Dmitry, he was indeed very cute, but he was also fifteen years older than Zhanna and on his second marriage. By spring, though, he was separated and he and Zhanna were living together. Dmitry was worldly, attentive, a good cook, and a great entertainer. Zhanna's friends loved him, and so did her parents—Dmitry had a way of making people feel important. The only wrinkle in their relationship was Dmitry's love of all things glamorous—he wished to see Zhanna in expensive dresses and imposing high heels at all times. But he had a trait that far outweighed her discomfort in high heels: he liked all Zhanna's ideas. This was why they were in Portugal now. Zhanna had taken Portuguese as her second foreign language at the Institute, and she wanted to spend the summer after graduation practicing it among native speakers. It was the best place and the best summer, and Boris was intruding with his insane suggestion.

"Margaret Thatcher ran for office for the first time at age twenty-two," was Boris's ultimate argument, and, unreasonably, it succeeded in convincing Zhanna. She returned to Moscow and declared her candidacy for the city legislature. She and Boris told everyone that the idea was hers and that her father had misgivings about seeing her seek office. Zhanna told reporters that she was "more moderate" than Boris, which journalists generally took to mean that she was not a die-hard opponent of Putin.[16] It seemed that Boris believed the legend himself: he told Zhanna that she had to raise her own money. He did lend her about $20,000 to cover the "electoral collateral"—money that went into escrow pending election results. If she got less than 5 percent of the vote, the state would keep it.

Zhanna talked a college classmate into being her campaign manager. A friend of her mother's, Olga, joined too. Olga was very good at talking to people. Dmitry, supportive as ever, paid for a photo shoot. The photo of Zhanna in a wholesome white blouse, airbrushed to make the candidate look not quite so ridiculously young, went up on billboards. Her tagline was "Zhanna Nemtsova: The United Candidate." The billboards listed five political organizations that had lent Zhanna their support. All of them were pro-democracy groups at some stage of the transition from the mainstream to the margins.

It was not much of a political platform. Her father was fond of talking about what he called "democratic values," but this seemed hopelessly old-fashioned to Zhanna. Nor did "democratic values" seem to be what concerned the residents of her district in northern Moscow. Zhanna studied conscientiously, meeting with residents and the single long-term local politician who had not been washed out by the wave of Putin's new nomenklatura. Chief concerns here were transportation—the Metro did not reach this far north, and buses were unreliable—and housing stock. Thousands of people were living in dilapidated buildings that had once been planned as temporary.

Boris connected Zhanna with Mikhail Prokhorov, co-owner of the metals giant Norilsk Nickel. Maybe he would want to contribute to the campaign. Prokhorov spent an hour bombarding Zhanna with quiz-like questions designed to draw out her political views. Then he said that he would be willing to give her money if she changed districts. He was bank-rolling a ruling-party candidate in southern Moscow, and he would pay for Zhanna to challenge him. He wanted to be entertained. She was indignant. He called Boris and said, laughing, "Your daughter is a socialist."

There was no single moment when Zhanna realized that the game was fixed. By the time the vote came about, she felt like she had always known it. The incumbent, a nondescript man with an unmemorable name, would win because he belonged to Putin's party, United Russia. On election day Olga observed the vote at one of the precincts and saw soldiers bused in to stuff the ballot boxes. This was one way it was done. Another was saturation: the United Russia candidate's name and likeness were everywhere, even if no one really knew who he was. If it had been an honest contest, Zhanna figured she probably would have lost to the Communist Party candidate. As it was, the Communist came in second and Zhanna was third—with 10 percent of the vote, enough to recover her "electoral collateral." Zhanna was proud of this, especially because Boris was. But he said that he had now realized something else: "A name is not enough—a politician has to have a biography. You've got to work."

———

This is all nothing but strange games, an imitation of democracy. The candidates are copying each other's platforms. You can tell ahead of time what they are going to say. What they are really doing is creating a one-party system, which is the road to authoritarianism. We'll probably see parties that will pretend they are the opposition, or the quasi-opposition, and they will by turn kowtow to the government and criticize it. But their true function will be to prop up the one-party system. If the Bolsheviks had been smarter, they would have done this themselves—created a dozen such little bedbugs that will run up and down the body of society.

ALEXANDER NIKOLAEVICH YAKOVLEV had never before let himself sound so testy in public. But in April 2005 he had just finished a lecture tour that had taken him across Russia, sapping his will and his wish to sound civil. "We are laying down a nationalist future for ourselves," he told a journalist. The word "nationalist" remained one of the most damning in his vocabulary. "I am seeing Stalin's mug displayed everywhere, every day, and people are eating it up. It is the face of a nationalist, a chauvinist, a murderer. But we are being told that if we look into it, he wasn't so bad."

"Are you sorry that you and Gorbachev did not disband the secret police?" asked the journalist.

Back in the day in the Central Committee we used to pretend that we were in charge. But it was the CheKa,* the KGB who were always really in command. We couldn't even go abroad without their permission. Take me—I was a member of the Politburo. I was watched over by fifteen KGB agents. Two cooks and the housekeeper had the rank of officers. . . .

Has the center of power moved from the Kremlin to the FSB?
It was there all along. . . .

Why do so many people idealize the past?
It's the "leader principle."† It's a disease. It's a Russian tradition. We had our czars, our princes, our secretaries-general, our collective-farm chairmen, and so on. We live in fear of the boss. Think about it: we are not afraid of earthquakes, floods, fires, wars, or terrorist attacks. We are afraid of freedom. We don't know what to do with it. . . . That's where the fascist groups come from, too—the shock troops of tomorrow.

Is the orange revolution possible here?
We are not going to be like Ukraine. . . . We still live with a simple trinity. The state is on top, and we keep making it stronger. Society is suspended somewhere beneath the state. If the state so wishes, the society will be civil, or semicivil, or nothing but a herd. Look to Orwell for a good description of this. And the little tiny individual is running around somewhere down at the bottom.[17]

This was Alexander Nikolaevich's last major interview. He died in October 2005, a few weeks short of his eighty-second birthday. His son

*CheKa, or Chrezvychaynaya Komissiya, was the original name of the Soviet secret police.
†Yakovlev used the word *vozhdism*, sometimes translated as the German *Führerprinzip*.

continued to work with the documents Alexander Nikolaevich had been publishing. Forty-three books had come out, but many more remained to be compiled and edited. This project, too, had become a source of frustration for Alexander Nikolaevich, because a new kind of response had become prevalent: people were writing letters saying that the stories told by these documents could not possibly be true. But the books had to continue coming out, especially because many of the documents had once again been made inaccessible in the archives.

Seryozha, though, felt that he no longer had an obligation to help. With his grandfather gone, he was free to go anywhere he wanted. He picked Ukraine. There was a girl there, and Kiev happened to be the place everyone wanted to live now.

AFTER LOSING HER ELECTION, Zhanna reverted to the state of having no ambition. This was fine: she was newly married, and with Dmitry's income she did not need to work.

Everyone around her was making money and then more money with that money. Her father and her mother, separately, had started playing the market; her mother proved particularly good at it. Dmitry was the vice-president of a bank, and most of his friends were in finance. After watching them for about a year, Zhanna decided to try for herself. She got a job at an investment firm, and learned to buy and sell. Making money was the easiest thing in the world. All the Russian market did was grow, and finding the stocks that would grow fastest was a fun game.

Starting in 1999, the growth curve of oil and gas prices had roughly the same shape as the curve of Putin's popularity rating in fall 1999: a vertical straight line. The Russian economy did not become more efficient—in fact, if anything, it became less efficient—but it grew sharply nonetheless. The "virtual economy" problem described by Clifford Gaddy was not solved: about half of Russian industry continued to lose value. But these companies were not represented on Russia's tiny stock market, which was dominated by oil and gas companies—so the stock market grew and grew. By 2005, the oil and gas rents far exceeded the needs of the federal budget, which allowed money to be deposited in a reserve fund, which, in turn, could be used in an emergency—like when the fires of the pensioners' protest had to be put out.[18]

MASHA GAVE BIRTH to a boy in September 2006. They named him Alexander, Sasha for short. When the baby was five days old, Masha started hemorrhaging. She was taken to a hospital by ambulance. A burly nurse examined her—it hurt more than giving birth had, and Masha screamed.

"I bet it didn't hurt when you were fucking!" shouted the nurse.

Masha spent the next two weeks in one of the worst hospitals in a city full of bad hospitals. Her roommates numbered between three and five, placed on sagging metal cots in a room with no dividers. The hospital had only the most rudimentary medicines and equipment that dated back to the middle of the twentieth century. One of Masha's roommates had a pregnancy that had become nonviable at twenty-six weeks, but the drugs used to induce labor were ineffective or insufficient and she lay in the room for days, struggling to give birth to her dead baby.

After a few days, Masha figured out that she was part of the hospital's corrupt survival strategy. Russia had instituted a system of mandatory health insurance, a state-run policy that reimbursed hospitals. But this was a facility that no one would voluntarily choose, so at night, ambulances would deliver policyholders to this hospital in exchange for kickbacks. This was what had happened to Masha. Once she was hospitalized, the doctors placed her under an infectious-diseases quarantine, making it impossible to transfer to another facility.

Back at home, something strange happened to Sergei. Instead of doing what any normal husband would do in this situation—asking his mother or Masha's grandmother to come and take care of the baby—he bonded with his son. When Masha came home, she got the sense that Sergei was now more of a parent than she was. He let her join in, and they stayed home for the next year, mothering their baby and running their website.

After that Masha went to work for a distribution company. This was a bit of a misnomer: the line of business she entered probably should have been called "corruption facilitation."

Putin had responded to the pensioners' protests by announcing mammoth government investment in social services. The investment was divided into four different "priority national projects." The first year, Russia invested about $2 billion in the four projects, and the following year the amount went up. The largest share of the money went to National Project Health. It was designed to radically modernize Russian medicine.[19]

Health care and research institutions began importing vast amounts of medical equipment and the chemicals and parts required for it to function. Because the funds were federal, all purchases had to go through the health ministry, where kickbacks accounted for 80 to 90 percent of the expenditures. But foreign suppliers, bound by their national laws, could not accommodate the kickback schemes or pay the bribes at customs. This was where the "distribution company" stepped in. It was Masha's job to ensure that the corruption premiums were paid but the paperwork looked clean. She got an excellent salary.

thirteen

ALL IN THE FAMILY

THE FIRST TIME Lyosha saw another gay man was in December of his first year at university. The man had come to visit one of the girls at the dorm. His name was also Alexei, he was also from Solikamsk, and it was all such a wonderful coincidence that Lyosha immediately fell in love.

He also immediately moved in with Alexei. After that, all was not exactly as Lyosha had expected. Alexei was older—twenty-one to Lyosha's seventeen—and a college dropout. His tiny apartment was filthy. Lyosha spent the first couple of days scrubbing it down and setting it up for domesticity: Alexei had apparently never cooked. The apartment was very close to Perm's lone gay club, and many of Alexei's friends were used to crashing there after a night of drinking, alone or with someone. There was a lot of drinking. Some of Alexei's friends had cirrhosis of the liver. Someone died of it. Someone else committed suicide. The sex was rough and painful, and Alexei had sex with other people too. Still, the most important thing was that Lyosha had a boyfriend.

Now was the time to come out to his mother. When Lyosha went home to Solikamsk for New Year's, he got right to it.

"Mama, we have to talk."

They sat down at the kitchen table.

"Mama, I love you," said Lyosha, and started sobbing uncontrollably. Galina waited for him to collect himself. He could not.

"Are you trying to tell me that you like boys?" she asked finally.

"Yes."

"I must have done something wrong," she concluded dispassionately.

Galina said nothing else for three days, but at family holiday gatherings on each of those days she would down three shots of vodka in quick succession. Normally, she did not drink.

Things were difficult for the next six months, though Galina had resumed speaking to Lyosha and continued giving him money for rent. He knew that she had stared down the choice between Lyosha and society, and had chosen her son. Now she was acclimating to the consequences of that choice. Among family, whenever someone tried to engage her in teasing Lyosha about his not having a girlfriend yet—at the ripe old age of eighteen now, when other young men were considering marriage and children—she cut the conversation off with a stern, "He'll do what he wants when he decides it's time." She also made it clear to him that she did not want to know any of the details: she asked no questions, welcomed no confidences, but also never said anything pejorative. Still, things felt a bit better after Lyosha broke up with Alexei. Galina seemed to breathe a sigh of relief.

What had happened was that Alexei had brought someone home when Lyosha was there. Lyosha had reluctantly agreed to an open relationship, but this was unbearable. Lyosha ended the relationship, but he also made a promise to himself to rid himself of jealousy. It was an unproductive emotion. If he ever had a boyfriend again, he would be mindful of the need for a variety of experiences and would be tolerant of indiscretions as long as the boyfriend did not fall in love with another person. The relationship with Alexei had made Lyosha wiser. Back in the dormitory now, he became a bit of a love guru: female students came to him for advice, and so did the mother of one of his female classmates.

Lyosha met Sasha during one of his visits to Solikamsk. Actually, he did not meet him, but he saw him: Sasha sold music CDs and VHS tapes from a permanent stand at Orbita, the new shopping center. It was perhaps a quarter of the size of the shopping malls that had opened up in Perm, but it had the same blinding neon lights and slippery tiled floors. Someone told Lyosha that Sasha had had a lover, an older and perhaps wealthy man. Someone else told Lyosha that Sasha wanted to meet him.

Lyosha started spending time at Orbita. He came to Solikamsk for all school breaks and some weekends, and he loitered. He met all his friends there, and when they were not available, he went to Orbita alone. Sasha would walk over and ask for a light, but he always did it with a girl on his arm or when Lyosha was speaking to someone else. Technically, they still had not met.

Finally, Lyosha found himself at a birthday party where Sasha was also a guest, and someone introduced them to each other. Sasha asked Lyosha specific questions about his studies and a recent trip Lyosha had taken to a conference in Moscow: Sasha had clearly done as much research on Lyosha as Lyosha had done on him. Lyosha, for his part, already knew that Sasha came from a struggling family, that his parents drank and he had a half-dozen siblings, and that he had tried and failed two or three times to get into Perm Polytechnic. They were, by now, a couple of years into their strange courtship.

They left the party together, with a young woman. They walked her home, and then Sasha walked Lyosha home, explaining that the streets were rough and he himself had such a long way to go to his apartment on the outskirts that the detour made no difference. There was no physical contact: Lyosha was cool, open but not rash. He regretted it the next morning.

Nothing changed after the party. Lyosha still took the bus, five hours each way, to hang out at the mall almost every weekend, and Sasha still asked him for a light. Lyosha finally devised a plan to talk to Sasha alone. He waited at the bus stop outside Orbita until Sasha left work and boarded the bus. Lyosha got on the same bus without being seen—the crowd and the winter darkness made this easy. He got off at Sasha's stop and caught up to him on foot after a short distance.

"Sasha, we have to talk."

Sasha did not seem at all surprised. He did seem to have his answer prepared in advance.

"You shouldn't give in to your fantasies," he said. "Don't believe what people say."

Lyosha poured his heart into a letter and had a mutual friend hand it to Sasha at the mall. Sasha called. This time, he did not tell Lyosha not to believe what people say. He did not even say that he was not gay. All he said was, "I can't," over and over, for an hour and a half.

Lyosha decided that what they needed was to speak in person, not in the mall or in the street, but in private. Sasha just needed to feel safe. Lyosha found a classified-ad newspaper in which people offered apartments for rent by the day. He called, he paid, he picked up the key and called Sasha with the address. He cooked supper and waited. Sasha came.

He said, "I can't."

He said, "I'm sorry. I should not have let this go on. I can't. I hope you can forgive me."

Lyosha said, "Don't ask me to forgive you. I just hope you can forgive yourself."

Lyosha thought it was all too much like a movie, and a very long one: somehow, it took them four hours to say those things to each other. Then Sasha left, and Lyosha left too, because the last thing he wanted now was to spend the night in this apartment.

IT WAS JANUARY 2006 when the Sasha story ended. In the three years since his gay life began, Lyosha had had sex with one man, loved two, and had explored the entire range of options available to him: the closet and the gutter. Or at least those were the options available to his gay body and his gay heart. His gay mind could still soar. He decided that he would be gay in the academy.

The following year Lyosha defended his senior thesis, titled "Sexual

Minorities as a Political Issue." Getting the topic approved by the department was difficult, but he managed, and then went to Moscow for research. At the Russian State Library, which everyone still called by its old name, the Lenin Library, the repository of every periodical ever legally published in the country, Lyosha saw gay and lesbian magazines from the early 1990s. It turned out that there had once been people who wrote in Russian about gay rights, the movement, legislation, a political agenda. They sounded freer and better-informed than anyone Lyosha knew now. They seemed to inhabit a public space that Lyosha could barely imagine, to be connected to efforts that trusted their own importance—this was particularly true of a woman named Evgenia Debryanskaya, a lesbian activist so outspoken the whole country seemed to have heard of her back when Lyosha was in first grade. She was now an entrepreneur, like several other activists of old; others had left the country, and a couple had died.

"The threat of social divisions based on sexual orientation in contemporary Russian society is no less relevant than the threats of the spread of racism, xenophobia, and nationalism," Lyosha wrote in the introduction to his thesis. He wrote that acceptance of sexual minorities, though it had increased in the 1990s, was on the wane—this was more of a hunch than something that he could support with evidence, so he might have skipped a footnote here.[1] He pointed to legislation that had been proposed in 2003— two parliament members had wanted to ban "propaganda of homosexuality."[2] The bill failed, but Lyosha argued that it signified an anti-gay backlash. The thesis might have struck Lyosha's professors as a bit alarmist and perhaps solipsistic—it seemed hard to observe a backlash against something they barely believed existed—but it was one of the most erudite, best-argued theses they had seen.[3] As an outstanding scholar, Lyosha was offered the opportunity to stay at the department for graduate study.

There was a caveat: Lyosha had to broaden his subject. He could, for example, include other minority groups in his research. He had to agree, especially because the entire class was fretting about its future: in previous years graduates had found work as political technologists, but with the withering of public politics, demand had plummeted. Still, during his first year

Lyosha proposed the following research topic: "Sexual Minorities in Political Discourse."

"I like it very much," his adviser said. "But you must understand that our academic council is very conservative, some members are very religious, so I'm afraid they won't allow you to dissertate on this topic." She spoke in jargon to him, because he was now a member of the academic club. They finally settled on "Minority discourse in public politics." Lyosha would be looking at sexual and ethnic minorities, and at women as a minority group in politics.

Lyosha started teaching, helping a slightly older friend who taught the university's lone seminar on gender theory. He started publishing: the department's annual included his paper on women as a political minority. His research was exhilarating. He discovered the word "queer," wrote a paper on the evolution of the concept, and decided that it applied to him.

In the fall of 2009, Lyosha presented his dissertation for preliminary review. In the end, his adviser's demand that he broaden his topic had served a subversive purpose she hardly could have intended: Lyosha wrote about different minority groups as though they were equal to one another. He did point out that homosexuals in Russia had been granted only the bare minimum of legal rights—the right not to be treated as criminals—and had not yet reached full equality with the majority. Still, he wrote about gay people the same way that he wrote about women and ethnic minorities and his dissertation stressed the assumption that he was describing a process of inexorable legitimation and institutionalization of the various groups, all of which would eventually realize their potential to become not only the objects but also the subjects of politics.[4]

Lyosha spoke for twenty minutes and then faced an unprecedented hour and a half of questions from the twelve-member committee.

"Are you aware that homosexuality is a taboo topic in our country?" asked one.

"But it exists," responded Lyosha.

This was the only question that concerned Lyosha's actual topic. A lone committee member, whom Lyosha thought to be a closeted gay man, made

a helpful suggestion on sources. The rest were anxious free-association queries. Members of the committee sounded angry with Lyosha, so angry that
they could not or would not bring themselves to engage with his work.
Their comments showed that they did not think a study like this should
exist.

"I just attended a conference in St. Petersburg where they said that gender was no more," said one.

"What are 'minority groups' anyway?" asked another.

Lyosha sweated and used every trick he could think of to keep his rage
from showing.

A few weeks later, he heard that the professor who had been helpful
during the defense had been seen waving a copy of Lyosha's dissertation
summary booklet during his own seminar, shouting in outrage, "This is
ideological propaganda! This is propaganda of sodomy!" Lyosha was almost
shocked a few weeks later to learn that the committee had cleared him for
his defense.

The defense was, by all accounts, brilliant. The vote was unanimous.

Lyosha's academic triumph immediately translated into administrative
power. He took over the one gender studies course he used to help teach,
and redesigned it to include an LGBT component. Older faculty who had
shunned him earlier were now polite, and made a production of welcoming
his input. He sensed that they were vicious in what they said about him
behind his back, but he chose to interpret this as a symptom of their power-
lessness in the face of his newfound authority.

IT WAS A GREAT TIME to be a young academic in Perm, for reasons that
originated in Moscow. In 2008, Putin had handed the presidency to Dmitry
Medvedev. Putin had served the two consecutive terms the Russian constitution allowed, and did what authoritarian rulers the world over do in such
situations: he ceded the post without ceding the power. Putin became prime
minister, and Dmitry Medvedev, a longtime member of his staff, became

the country's nominal president. The center of power shifted to the cabinet, now run by Putin. Overnight, the president's office became ceremonial: Medvedev had only a tiny staff and no practical means to wield the power that was granted to him by the constitution. Still, Medvedev's office obliged him to maintain a public presence. "For Vladimir Putin and Dmitry Medvedev, Russian citizens are not voters, but an audience," Russian journalist Maxim Trudolyubov wrote in 2009. "The big difference between Mr. Putin and Mr. Medvedev is that they work with different audiences." Putin played to the majority: middle-aged and older, middle-income and poorer, the broad audience of the television channels. Medvedev addressed the better-educated, better-off minority that had been largely ignored during Putin's two terms.[5] Starved for attention, this audience responded to Medvedev's overtures with enthusiasm ranging from cautious to ecstatic. They quickly dubbed the new era "the Thaw."

The term referred to an earlier epoch, the Soviet Union of the late 1950s and early 1960s—the period between Nikita Khrushchev's speech denouncing the cult of Stalin and the Party coup that deposed Khrushchev himself. That had been the time the first *fortochkas* opened: some previously banned writing was published and a small degree of open discussion and an even smaller degree of self-organization were allowed. The term "Thaw" now betrayed low expectations: the original Thaw had not brought about fundamental change—it had merely made the system somewhat less brutal. It had also been followed by the Brezhnev freeze, which did not return the terror of Stalinism but which put an end to any civic initiatives and, more important, any hope for change. The term "Thaw" reflected the belief that the Putin system of one-party rule and ever-shrinking space for civil society, media, and protest was entrenched. That made whatever short-term opportunities the new Thaw did present all the more precious.

Perm happened to produce such an opportunity. The capital of an oil-producing region, it had seen its fortunes rise exponentially during the boom of the 2000s. It also had a governor possessed of Western-style ambition. A Putin appointee, Oleg Chirkunov came to politics from the KGB by way of the retail business. He had worked in Switzerland, and his family stayed there even after he became a public official.[6] He was a quintessential representative of the Medvedev audience: moneyed, Western-oriented, and with a taste for art and culture as Europe understood them. Federal reform undertaken by Putin during his first term deprived Russia's constituent regions not only of much of their political independence but also of their money. A resource-rich region like Perm was handing an ever-increasing share of its tax revenues to Moscow. Quality of life, as a result, dragged far behind regional economic growth. When Garry Kasparov first went on a speaking tour as a politician, this issue—the center's sucking the regions dry—was a major part of his message. But Chirkunov was not looking for a way to confront Putin: he was looking for a way to improve Perm's quality of life and create an alternative source of income *without* confrontation with Moscow. When oil prices took a dive in 2007, his search for a solution became urgent. He decided that culture would be Perm's salvation.[7]

Chirkunov's partners in his culture project were two wealthy art lovers from Moscow. One was Sergei Gordeev, who had made a billion or more in Moscow real estate. His passion was contemporary architecture: he had paid generously to preserve Moscow's Constructivist landmarks. Chirkunov appointed Gordeev one of the two senators from Perm. Putin's new system, in which all high-level regional officials were appointed rather than elected, lent itself to these kinds of transactions. Chirkunov could give Gordeev power, at least symbolically, and influence, in exchange for his investment in the Perm project. Gordeev never lived in Perm or even learned much about it: when he visited the city, he stayed at a hotel. One night, four years into his senate term, he spent four hours wandering the city because he could not get his bearings and could not hail a cab either, for all he had in his wallet were five hundred-euro notes.[8] Still, he promoted Perm faithfully and showed up for high-profile events in the city.

The other Muscovite who came to Perm was Marat Guelman, an art dealer turned political technologist. He had played a key role in creating Putin's public image in 1999–2000, and he had stayed an insider. But with the near-extinction of electoral politics, political technologists were no longer in demand. The market for Russian art, too, collapsed during the financial crisis of 2007–2008. Perm, where life and real estate were cheap and the regime was friendly, offered Guelman a perfect Thaw-style cultural-political-economic opportunity. The three men pooled their—and the region's—influence and money in the hope of multiplying both. They promoted what they were doing unironically as a "cultural revolution." Their avowed goal was to have Perm chosen as a European Cultural Capital, a title bestowed by the European Union but available to cities that are not located in a European Union member country. The title would bring tourism to the city and money and fame to the men.

Gordeev invested, and Guelman curated. A museum of contemporary art opened in a hastily renovated old river port. An experimental theater followed, and a rejuvenated opera theater. At the center of it all stood a summer festival, an entire month of exhibits, performances, and panels that reached far beyond the arts into media and economics. Almost every night, police cars with flashing lights escorted buses ferrying dozens of visiting dignitaries from the Perm airport, where they had been delivered on a chartered plane from Moscow, to newly renovated hotels. The festival, called White Nights, was "overwhelming by design," wrote American anthropologist Douglas Rogers, who spent twenty years studying Perm.

> At the center of White Nights in Perm was a fenced-in Festival Village erected in front of the Regional Administration building on Perm's esplanade. Just over three hectares in size, the Festival Village included two small and one large outdoor stages for concerts and other performances; numerous alleys for small shops and displays; two restaurants and two cafés; and a Festival Club for nearly fifty planned discussions and presentations. In order to cope with inevitable summer muddiness, boardwalk-style walkways were constructed to funnel crowds from space to space; they were repainted white nearly every night. Booths arranged alongside these walkways provided spaces where folk artisans and other culture producers could display and sell their wares, and the grassy spaces between the walkways hosted small-scale performances and exhibitions, from clowns to

blacksmiths. Everywhere there were nooks and crannies—many of them in two massive towers at one end of the Festival Village—where little exhibits or performances sprang up. Most stunningly to many observers, there was even a "festival beach": a large circular pool, suitable for dozens of children at a time, erected within a raised platform that could accommodate hundreds of sunbathers. Showers and changing rooms were located in a sandy area beneath.[9]

It was as if the entire city was, without changing location, transported from its eerie everyday identity as a former military-industrial city closed to outsiders to some shiny Europe of the imagination. In exchange, Europe would someday put Perm on its map—as a capital, no less. This frantic ambition was contagious, especially because Chirkunov and his people made it clear that their vision reached beyond the arts: the governor promised to forge a new "economy of the intellect, where we will create not with our hands but with our heads."[10]

The university, too, developed a vision of itself as a European institution. Lyosha knew that he fit in it well. His own vision was that he would soon be running Russia's only LGBT Studies program. For now, he and Darya, the friend who had been teaching the one gender studies course, launched a gender studies center. It helped that Darya's father was the dean of another department at the university. Darya and Lyosha got some funding for hosting conferences and publishing the proceedings. Their publications had no official status in the university, but this meant that they did not have to face an academic-review board.

Lyosha was lucky. He had heard that a legal scholar in Novosibirsk had not been allowed to defend her dissertation on LGBT rights.[11] In 2010, Lyosha presented at a conference at Moscow State University. His paper was titled "Gender Gaps in Political Science." Only one person—a professor from St. Petersburg—had a question for him.

"Are you aware," she asked, "that there are no lesbians in Russia?"

"I've also heard," said Lyosha, "that there was no sex in the Soviet Union. Yet you are here."

When the conference collection was published in book form, his paper was omitted.

———————

PEOPLE DID NOT SAY those sorts of things at Moscow State—not what Lyosha said to the professor from St. Petersburg, nor what he had said in his paper. The social sciences here sounded very different.

Back in the early 1990s, when the department of sociology was first established at Moscow State, its founders reached out to Western colleagues far from the liberal academic mainstream. One person they sought out was Allan Carlson, an American historian who taught at ultraconservative Hillsdale College in Michigan. Carlson was a follower of Pitirim Sorokin, one of the Russian thinkers exiled on the Philosophers' Ship in 1922. Sorokin went on to found the sociology department at Harvard. His prolific writings included doomsday warnings about the descent of Western civilization into decadence, and it was on these ideas that Carlson had based his own thinking. Carlson's books numbered half a dozen, all had the word "family" in the title, and each argued that the family was the bedrock of civilization and the sole key to the continued survival of humankind.[12]

Carlson visited Moscow State University in 1995, a year when the topic that dominated the social sciences—and much of the media—was Russia's demographic crisis. The country's population had been declining for half a century. People were having fewer children and dying earlier. Male life expectancy was among the lowest in Europe—by the early 1990s, it was in the mid-sixties—and it would stay at that level for a decade and a half.[13] This meant that most adult Russian men living in the 1990s and 2000s would not live past age sixty-five.

American economist Nicholas Eberstadt has written extensively about Russian demographics. A chapter in his book on the Russian population crisis is titled "Russia's Ominous Patterns of Mortality and Morbidity: Pioneering New and Modern Pathways to Poor Health and Premature Death." He showed that no modern country had ever seen people die at the same rate in peacetime. According to 2006 figures, wrote Eberstadt, male life expectancy at age fifteen in Russia compared unfavorably with that in Ethiopia, Gambia, and Somalia. Two things appeared to be killing Russians disproportionately: diseases of the cardiovascular system, and external causes, such as injuries and poisoning, including suicide.

Eberstadt scrutinized all the usual suspects: poor diet, smoking, lack of exercise, environmental pollution, economic shock and subsequent poverty, and, of course, vodka. But none of these factors explained enough of the problem, and even together they added up to barely half an explanation. True, Russians ate a fatty diet—but not as fatty as that of Western Europeans. Plus, Russians appeared to overeat less. Yes, Russia had taken abominable care of its environment, but it was seeing only a few more deaths from respiratory diseases than did Western Europe—and fewer deaths of diseases of the kidneys, which would be expected to result from pollution. Russians had lived through severe economic upheaval, but there was no indication that economic shock in a modern society leads quickly, or at all, to increased mortality—the Great Depression, for example, did not. Nor would a sudden drop in health-care services offer an explanation: Russia's health-care spending was roughly comparable to that of less-affluent Western European countries. Russians smoked a lot, but not as much as Greeks and Spaniards did while living on average as long as other Western Europeans. Russians did drink a lot, but not as much as Czechs, Slovaks, and Hungarians, whose life expectancy started improving soon after they broke off from the Soviet Bloc.[14] Vodka and other alcohol played an important role in the high rates of cardiovascular, violent, and accidental deaths—but not a large enough role to explain the Russian demographic predicament. In fact, while vodka was the most popular explanation, it was also the most contradictory. Some studies actually showed that Russian drinkers lived longer than nondrinkers.[15]

Another scholar of Russian demographics, American anthropologist Michelle Parsons, suggested an explanation for the apparent vodka paradox: for what it is worth, alcohol may help people adapt to realities that otherwise make them want to curl up and die. Parsons, who called her book *Dying*

Unneeded, argued that Russians were dying early because they had nothing and no one to live for. Eberstadt also ultimately concluded that the explanation had to do with mental health. He used longer-term statistics to demonstrate that what Russians were calling a "demographic crisis" had in fact been going on for decades—birthrates and life expectancy had been falling for most of the second half of the twentieth century. Only two periods stood out as exceptions to this trend: Khrushchev's Thaw and Gorbachev's perestroika, the brief spells when Russians anticipated a better future. The rest of the time, it seemed, Russians had been dying for lack of hope.

Allan Carlson's explanation was entirely different: Russians were dying because what he called the "natural family" was on the wane. During his visit, he and members of the sociology department decided to organize a conference to discuss what Russia and other countries could do to resist the attack on the family waged by the decadent West. The conference would be called the World Congress of Families. The gathering, held in Prague in 1997, drew about seven hundred people. Western participants were primarily representatives of conservative religious organizations mobilized against advances in gay rights. Eastern European participants came from newly independent nation-states, some of them very small and all of them struggling with cultural and economic change; they were driven by existential panic—and so were the Russians.

Inspired by the turnout, the organizers turned the World Congress of Families into a permanent organization dedicated to the fight against gay rights, abortion rights, and gender studies. The headquarters of the new organization was in Illinois, but its spiritual center was in Russia, at the sociology department of Moscow State University.[16] Over the next decade the Russians, who had started out as Carlson's disciples, became the senior partners in the organization: with the backing of the government and the Russian Orthodox Church, they could deliver the political muscle.

In his 2006 state-of-the-federation address, Putin called depopulation the country's most pressing problem. "I am going to speak about the most important thing now," he said. "What's the most important thing? At the defense ministry they know what it is." In Putin's language of macho humor,

the phrase was supposed to signal that he was about to speak about something that soldiers—real men—think about all the time.

> Yes, I am indeed going to talk about love, about women and children.
> About the family. And about contemporary Russia's most acute prob-
> lem: demographics. . . . You know that our country's population
> shrinks, on average, by seven hundred thousand people a year. We
> have talked about the issue many times, but have yet to do anything
> of substance about it.[17]

Putin proposed a financial solution: more money to National Project
Health (the one where Masha was facilitating the payment of 80-to-90-
percent kickbacks), more money for birthing clinics, and, most important,
more money for mothers. He instituted a onetime payment of the equivalent
of over $8,000 to any woman who gave birth to a second child (Russian
women were having an average of 1.3 children[18]). The "maternal capital," as
it became known, would remain an act of unparalleled generosity on the
part of the Russian state toward its citizens, showing just how highly the
president valued his subjects' willingness to reproduce.

In the 2000s, the World Congress[19] established positions for what they
called ambassadors—lobbyists at various international and European organizations, including the United Nations. The jobs went to Russians, who
used the weight of the Russian delegation's backing to organize informal
coalitions to press for anti-gay initiatives and oppose measures that advanced
LGBT rights.[20] In the United States, the Southern Poverty Law Center
designated the World Congress a hate group.[21]

BACK AT THE SOCIOLOGY DEPARTMENT at Moscow State, students received
a steady diet of ultraconservative rhetoric—and nothing else. "As a graduate
of the department, I can tell, based on my own experience, that the education students received there could never stand up to either academic or prac-

tical scrutiny," a 1996 graduate said in a 2007 interview. The graduate, Alexandre Bikbov, did what Moscow State students had done back in the Soviet period if they wanted to learn: he educated himself, as Gudkov and Arutyunyan had done one or two generations earlier. "Back then it was possible to go to the library or to another department in the university in order to compensate for the lack of knowledge that the sociology department systematically produced," said Bikbov, speaking about the 1990s. "And then, at the crucial moment of the exam, I could almost always count on unassailability if I could demonstrate that I knew the subject well." In the 2000s, though, said Bikbov, things deteriorated. "Now there is open anti-intellectual censorship at exams: when students show that they 'know too much,' they get lower grades and are threatened with more severe punishment. The same thing happens during seminars, when some faculty tell students not to read [French sociologist Pierre] Bourdieu or when they cut off any and all discussion in the most demeaning manner."[22]

Bikbov was unusually persistent in studying the sociology that Moscow State University did not want to teach him. He taught himself French and translated Bourdieu's *Distinction: A Social Critique of the Judgment of Taste*, a classic of modern sociology, into Russian. He started publishing internationally. He became a professor—not at the sociology department of Moscow State, which was no place for someone like him, but in the philosophy department of Russian Humanities University, a much smaller and far younger institution that did not have its own department of sociology. There he launched his own standing seminar, which, like Levada's seminar in the 1960s, '70s, and '80s, served to give young sociologists access to knowledge they were not getting through official channels. Dozens of Moscow State University sociology department students who figured out, soon after matriculating, that the department was, in Bikbov's words, "a commercial enterprise with an extremism complex," came to Bikbov's seminar to learn.

In 2006, Bikbov organized a conference on the sociology of prisons. Two prominent French academics presented, as did Bikbov's seminar participants and several young people who volunteered at Memorial, the organization founded in the 1980s to tell the story of the Gulag. The combination of the subject matter and academics and students and activists in one room proved combustible. The students resolved to demand change at Moscow State's sociology department.[23]

For a semester in 2007, students staged a series of protests. "Education at the department is a lie!" proclaimed their first flyer. The flyer claimed that staff faculty were forbidden to do original research: instead, they had to use multivolume textbooks written by the dean, Vladimir Dobrenkov, as the basis for all instruction.

1. The schedule is full of ridiculous mandatory classes, including religious upbringing!
2. Outside researchers and faculty are not allowed inside the sociology department. The administration does everything in its power to block students' access, practical knowledge and interesting classes!
3. The administration conceals information on any talks given [in Moscow] by foreign scholars and bans student exchange with colleges abroad.

The flyer listed some recent incidents at the department, including:

All students were required to read a brochure distributed by the dean's office. Titled "Why Are Russian Lands Being Cleansed," it accused the Freemasons of "starting world wars and initiating the creation of the atomic bomb" and claimed that "the Zionist lobby . . . determined the foreign policies of the United States and Great Britain, holds in its hands the world financial system, including the printing of dollars, practically controls all the leading mass media and means of communication." Russia is called a "righteous nation" and America a "beastly nation" and The Protocols of the Elders of Zion is quoted earnestly, as a reliable source.[24]

The protests lasted through the spring, becoming the first sustained and highly public protests in Russia since Putin's "preventive counter-revolution."

Such vocal action at the nation's leading university compelled the presidential administration to respond by commissioning a report on the department. A group of experts concluded that the level of instruction at the department was not up to university standards and that Dobrenkov's textbooks were replete with plagiarism.[25]

The other side retaliated. A group called the Union of Orthodox Citizens, which counted several well-known politicians among its leaders,[26] issued a manifesto in defense of the sociology department: "There is no doubt that a concerted effort to foment an 'orange revolution' at Russia's most important university is what stands behind the actions of radical youths and the students they have conscripted," they wrote. Indeed, the sociology department was to provide a "training ground for a youth 'maidan'"—Ukrainian for "square" but referring specifically to Kiev's Independence Square, the geographic center of the Orange Revolution. This maidan would then spread to other institutions of higher learning. Along with Marches of the Dissenters, and, the manifesto added, "parades of sodomites," the student rebellion "has every chance, come fall, to change the color of Red Square, turning it into an all-Russian rainbow 'maidan.'"[27]

The statement was perfectly in keeping with the improbable assertion Lyosha had made in his thesis: a chasm was opening up in Russian society along the lines of sexual identity. The specter of gay liberation had emerged as a bogeyman much like the Freemasons, the Zionists, and the American financiers.

In the fall of 2007, the department cracked down. A half-dozen leaders of the protests were expelled.[28] The following June, the department hosted an international conference titled "Societal Norms and the Possibilities of Societal Development." Dean Dobrenkov opened the conference by warning against the dangers of homosexuality:

> Issues of virtue and morality have to be at the forefront today. Without that, Russia has no future. . . . How can we talk about the rights of homosexuals and lesbians in light of this? All these attempts to organize gay parades, the introduction of sex education in schools—

all of this aims to defile our young people, and we must say a clear and definitive "no" to that! Otherwise, we will lose Russia.[29]

"All these attempts" referred to a single effort, by a young Moscow lawyer, to force a public conversation on LGBT rights by applying for a permit to hold a Pride march in Moscow. The permit was denied, and the lawyer was taking his case through the courts. The handful of people who showed up for Pride in Moscow in May 2007 were first beaten and then arrested; among the detainees was an Italian member of the European Parliament who had come to lend his support.[30]

The star of the conference was American Paul Cameron, who urged Russia to learn from American mistakes. "It is the homosexuals who are bringing about a demographic catastrophe," he said.

> They cause huge and immeasurable harm to society. According to our data, one third of inmates in the state of Illinois are sexual predators or their victims. And twenty to forty percent are homosexuals or their victims. . . . According to official data, thirty to fifty percent of Illinois residents have had sexual relations with children, primarily as a result of their homosexual proclivities. Twenty percent of such crimes take place in adoptive families.

Cameron was citing Illinois because it was his home state and, he pointed out, the home state of then presidential candidate Barack Obama.

> Russia has every chance to avoid the sad fate of Western countries, which have accepted homosexuality as morally normal, and to choose its own traditions and moral values. I want to ask you: Do you want to be as stupid as we have been?[31]

Introduced in Moscow as a prominent American academic, Cameron had been expelled from the American Psychological Association in 1983 and the American Sociological Association in 1986. The latter organization gave the following reason: "Dr. Paul Cameron has consistently misinterpreted and misrepresented sociological research on sexuality, homosexuality, and lesbianism."[32]

In September 2008, the sociology department inaugurated a new research project, to be headed by a new member of the permanent faculty: Alexander Dugin would run the Center for Conservative Studies. Launching the center, Dugin explained what it was not: "It is not a liberal intellectual group, but also not a Soviet-Marxist one." Both the Soviet idea and the liberal idea that had followed it in Russia had failed, he explained. "And yet there is no conservative intellectual or academic center in Russia in the American or the European sense of the word. This despite the fact that both the people and the regime feel conservatively." Now the country's most important university would take on the mission of generating ideas to fit those feelings:

> The goal of the Center for Conservative Studies is to become the center of development of conservative ideology in Russia. . . . We also need to train a conservatively minded academic and government elite, there is no reason to hide this fact. They must be conservative ideologues. And we must place people in power and in positions of authority in the academy.[33]

The college dropout had worked hard to get to this point. He had long ago achieved public prominence and apparent political influence, but he wanted academic credentials. He defended his dissertation in December 2000 in Rostov-on-Don, in southern Russia, and his second dissertation—it is Russian convention to obtain first a sort of junior doctorate and then a senior one—in 2004, at another Rostov-on-Don institution. A German political scientist, Andreas Umland, noted in 2007:

> For an understanding of the Dugin phenomenon, Dugin's eagerness to become a fully accepted member of academia is particularly revealing. It speaks about both, how he understands himself as well as what the long-term prospects of his role in Russian society might be.

Whether Dugin will be in a position to enter the Ivory Tower, make his pamphlets into textbooks and become accepted in scholarly circles are major issues in assessing his project as he himself understands it.[34]

Less than a year after Umland posed this question, Dugin was installed at Moscow State's sociology department. His classes would now be mandatory for department students. The arrangement was profitable all around: Dean Dobrenkov was importing political muscle that accrued to Dugin—no one would touch him now, whatever the official commission might have concluded about his plagiarism and the low quality of education at the department. Dugin, on the other hand, got the intellectual legitimacy and the pulpit he had long been seeking.

COMPARED WITH MOSCOW STATE UNIVERSITY or, really, any other university in Russia, Lyosha's position in Perm might have looked so privileged as to be unsustainable. A realist would have said that it was only a matter of time before a small oasis like Perm State University's political science department was stomped out, the way all difference in Russia was being stomped out. But an optimist would have said that it was at provincial universities and in small, self-contained spaces of experimentation that Russia's future was being made. Lyosha did not stop being an optimist until he went to Ukraine.

In 2011 he won a competition to take part in a three-year seminar for teachers from post-Communist countries. His track was "Gender, Sexuality, and Power." The seminars were funded by Soros's Open Society Foundations, which were no longer functioning in Russia—but this was a regional program, and the meetings would be in Ukraine. They met for the first time in Uzhgorod, a tiny border town in Western Ukraine, and for the first time, Lyosha was with his people. He was not the queer among academics or the academic among the queers—he was with people who were thinking and talking about the same things he was, and feeling some of the same things too. He was alone only in his epiphany: unlike him, the other participants—Brits, Americans, and Ukrainians—lived and worked with others who were like them. Ukraine, he learned, had thirty-seven registered LGBT groups. The number boggled his mind. He had always thought of Ukraine as Russia's simple provincial cousin, but this country had gender studies and queer studies theorists at several of its universities. And they were not revolutionary explorers like Lyosha: they had teachers. Lyosha had Darya, who was just a couple of years older—a peer, and a friend supportive enough that he sometimes forgot that she was the daughter of a dean, and straight. But then he remembered. The people here had mentors who had studied in the West in the 1990s. Lyosha felt not unlike Arutyunyan had felt nearly twenty years earlier, when she attended the training seminar abroad that delivered her "narcissistic blow." Like her, he saw people standing on the shoulders of their predecessors who stood on the shoulders of their predecessors who stood on the shoulders of giants—while Lyosha stood all alone.

He returned to Perm troubled but inspired: he felt he now had a vision of what his work might become. "I'm glad you are going to these seminars," his department chair told him. "It's like a retreat for you. But when you come back, you should be mindful of where you are." This was her way of broaching the subject of Lyosha needing to refocus his research. The 2012 department annual would not include his paper otherwise.

"There is no future here," Lyosha said to himself. He was not sure what this meant he needed to do now, but he knew that the phrase was true.

WHAT LYOSHA HAD SEEN in Ukraine was, contrary to his expectations, a different culture. Yes, his Ukrainian colleagues spoke Russian, most as their first language, but they had a different educational background, different cultural references, and vastly different political expectations than he did. The Orange Revolution had not brought the change that the revolutionaries had demanded—indeed, Viktor Yanukovych, the once failed pro-Moscow candidate, had finally been elected president in 2010—but nevertheless, Ukraine had left the Soviet Union.

Farther west, all three Baltic states had joined both NATO and the European Union in 2004. Several other post-Soviet states, including Ukraine and Georgia, were negotiating with these international organizations with an eye to possible ascension. Russia was moving in the opposite direction. In his state-of-the-federation address in April 2005, Putin stressed that Russia had to "first of all acknowledge that the collapse of the Soviet Union was the greatest geopolitical catastrophe of the century. . . . Tens of millions of our countrymen ended up outside our country's borders." The rest of that speech was a mishmash of familiar rhetoric—including the assertion that Russia was a European country that valued human rights and civil society—but the statement of grand regret framed the speech, and Putin's politics.[35] To soften the impact, the Kremlin's English translators cast the phrase as "a major geopolitical catastrophe of the century,"[36] but in another two years such pretense had been set aside. Speaking in Munich at an international security conference in February 2007, Putin said:

> The format of the conference enables me to avoid superfluous politesse, the need to speak in smooth, pleasant, and empty diplomatic clichés. The format of the conference allows me to say what I really think about international security issues.[37]

Conference participants, who included German chancellor Angela Merkel and U.S. defense secretary Robert Gates, were taken by surprise: it seemed no one had expected a confrontation.[38] Putin railed against NATO's acceptance of new members:

> I think it's obvious: the process of NATO enlargement has nothing to do with the modernization of the alliance itself or with raising the level of security in Europe. Just the opposite: it is a seriously inflammatory factor that lowers the level of mutual trust. And we have a

justified right to ask openly: Who is NATO enlarging against? And what happened to the assurances given by Western partners after the Warsaw Pact was dissolved? What happened to those declarations? No one even remembers them. But I will dare remind the audience of what was said. I'd like to quote from NATO Secretary-General Wörner's speech in Brussels on May 17, 1990. He said then: "The very fact that we are ready not to deploy NATO troops beyond the territory of the Federal Republic [of Germany] gives the Soviet Union firm security guarantees." Whatever happened to those guarantees?[39]

The quote indeed came from a speech by NATO Secretary-General Manfred Wörner, but it had hardly amounted to the promise Putin was saying had been betrayed. First, Wörner had been careful to use vaguely conditional language: he had said that NATO was "ready not to" expand—not that it would never expand. More important, the conditional guarantee he appeared to be extending applied to the Soviet Union, a country that ceased to exist a year and a half later. Russia was now separated from Germany by a double belt: a ring of former Soviet constituent republics—Ukraine, Belarus, and the Baltic states—and then a ring of former Warsaw Pact countries—Poland, Slovakia, Czech Republic, and others. A clear majority of these countries had, in the intervening years, explicitly asked—and sometimes begged and pleaded—for NATO protection.

Documents that were declassified in the United States around the time of Putin's Munich speech provided the context for the Wörner statement. It had been made in the midst of multilateral talks on German reunification, which lasted from February to July 1990. The Soviet Union wanted to see Germany neutral—part of neither NATO nor the Warsaw Pact; NATO and the new German government, elected after the collapse of the Berlin Wall, wanted to see Germany a full NATO member. In the final agreement, Germany became—or, some might say, remained—a NATO member but former East German territory remained free of NATO military presence. Wörner's statement, like the negotiations from which it stemmed, had nothing to do with the issue of NATO expansion to former Warsaw Pact countries, because the participants assumed at the time that the Warsaw Pact would continue to exist (it dissolved a year and a half later, in March 1991).[40] Putin, who was a KGB officer serving in East Germany at the time of reunification talks, probably understood the contract well, but in his recollection the negotiations were the beginning of "the greatest geopolitical catastrophe of the century"—and were part of the story of Western treachery. The message of the Munich speech was that Russia would no longer accept the post-Soviet, post–Warsaw Pact condition.

WITHIN WEEKS of the Munich speech, it became clear what the new disposition meant. The Estonian government unwittingly provided the occasion. On April 30, 2007, it moved a monument known as the Bronze Soldier from central Tallinn to the city's military cemetery. The Bronze Soldier was erected by Soviet authorities after the Second World War—one of dozens of such monuments placed in the capitals of Eastern Europe to commemorate the Soviet victories there. In Estonia's reading of history, however, what the Soviets considered liberation was actually occupation. Estonia based its post-Soviet laws and policies on the premise that the country had been illegally occupied between the years of 1940 and 1991—first by the USSR in accordance with the Molotov-Ribbentrop Pact, then by Nazi Germany, and then by the USSR again. Among other things, this meant that only people who had been Estonian citizens before 1940 and their descendants automatically became citizens of independent Estonia; all others—presumed occupiers and their descendants—would have to pass Estonian language and history exams to become citizens. Even though the noncitizens were treated just like citizens for the purposes of public benefits and even had the right to vote in local elections, most of the country's sizable Russian-speaking minority—about a quarter of the population—considered the citizenship law discriminatory. The disagreement was fundamental: the Russian speakers did not and would not see themselves as occupiers, so to them the difference in treatment appeared based on ethnicity. Russia objected to the citizenship laws, and after Putin's 2005 "geopolitical catastrophe" speech, in which he called out to "our countrymen abroad," the criticism ramped up. The Bronze Soldier in Tallinn became, increasingly, a gathering spot for radical groups—both those who wanted the monument demolished (and frequently defaced it), and those who called for the restoration of the Soviet Union. The government decided to move the Soldier out of the city center.

Riots broke out in Tallinn. In Moscow, Nashi, the Young Guard, and at least two other pro-Kremlin youth groups began a siege of the Estonian embassy, demanding that the ambassador go home. The police did not intervene, and the consulate was forced to cease operations. After a week, the ambassador flew to Tallinn for what was, officially, a vacation. The youth groups proclaimed victory and lifted the siege.[41] "The siege of the Estonian Embassy in Moscow . . . risks becoming a classic example of a violation of diplomatic law that will later be found in textbooks alongside descriptions of other unlawful incidents involving embassies, including ones as serious as the Tehran hostage crisis in 1979–1981," an Estonian defense analyst wrote later that year.[42]

In addition to the riots and the embassy siege, a novel sort of attack took place: a cyber one. A flood of electronic requests designed to paralyze servers—a DDoS attack—shut down all Estonian government ministries, two banks, and several political parties, blocked all credit card transactions, and impaired the functioning of parliament. NATO and European Commission investigators could not definitively trace the attacks to Russia,[43] but two years later Nashi claimed credit for the act of cyberwarfare, which the movement said had been carried out by a mass of volunteers armed with computers.[44] The attacks had hit Estonia's point of particular pride—it was arguably the most computerized society in the world—and transformed it into a vulnerability, showing that the small nation, no matter how modern it had become and how well integrated into Western international organizations, could still be trampled by the large one, with its myriad soldiers.

RUSSIA'S NEXT WAR also involved a cyberattack, but at its core it was conventional and almost old-fashioned. On August 8, 2008, Russia invaded Georgia.

Tensions had been mounting ever since the 2003 Rose Revolution, when an exuberantly pro-Western government took over. In 2006, Russia banned the import of Georgian mineral water and wine—a source of substantial revenue for the tiny nation—and began restricting the supply of gas to Georgia. It also started amassing troops on the border. These and other actions were primarily directed at continuing to inflame longstanding conflicts in two of Georgia's separatist regions, South Ossetia and Abkhazia. Both were self-proclaimed independent republics with close ties to Russia. Both had existed in a state of neither war nor peace, neither independence nor integration, since the early 1990s. Weak, embattled central governments of the 1990s and early 2000s made this stalemate relatively easy to maintain. The new Georgian government, however, tried both carrot and stick to bring the republics back into the fold; Russia retaliated with redoubled support for the regions and intensified hostilities with the Georgian government. One apparent goal was to torpedo Georgia's attempts to join NATO—and in April 2008 Georgia's application was denied, with unresolved conflicts cited as at least one of the reasons. Two weeks later Putin—legally, in his last two weeks as president—signed a decree establishing economic and political relations with South Ossetia and Abkhazia that were essentially similar to Moscow's relations with the regions of Russia. Then, following a summer of assorted skirmishes, a full-fledged war broke out, with artillery fighting on the ground and Russia attacking from the air.

Ten days into the fighting, France and Germany brokered a cease-fire agreement, which Russia promptly violated. By the end of August, when the fighting stopped, Russia effectively controlled a large portion of Georgia and had issued Russian passports to local residents, turning them instantly into "countrymen."[45] On paper, Abkhazia and South Ossetia had declared independence, and Russia had recognized it, as had Nicaragua, Venezuela, and the tiny Pacific island nation of Nauru.[46] The message to Georgia—and any other post-Soviet country that might have wanted to follow its example—was, If you try to ally with NATO, you will lose lives and territory and will be assured NATO limbo in perpetuity.

A separate message was intended for the West and for Russian citizens: South Ossetia and Abkhazia were just like Kosovo, which had seceded from Serbia because it had a closer affinity with neighboring Albania. NATO had intervened on behalf of Kosovo, giving Russia the moral right to intervene on behalf of South Ossetia and Abkhazia. In 2008, Kosovo, which had been a de facto protectorate since 1999, was about to declare independence—and it was clear that the requisite majority of United Nations member countries would presently recognize it as a state. Russia perceived Kosovo's ascendance as an affront, just as it had perceived the 1999 NATO intervention as an insult—and now it was in a position to retaliate. Just days before Kosovo's announcement, Russian officials summoned South Ossetian and Abkhazian leaders to Moscow for talks and the Russian foreign minister issued a statement that said, "The declaration and recognition of Kosovar independence will make Russia adjust its line toward Abkhazia and South Ossetia."[47]

It was right after the invasion of Georgia that Dugin launched his Center for Conservative Studies. He gushed about the war in his opening address: "We have conducted an intervention, and now we are saying that we didn't just conduct it as an exceptional case but we will continue to commit acts of intervention whenever we deem appropriate."[48] Causes for an intervention would include the perceived need to protect "countrymen abroad," the eternal need to resist a unipolar world, and the necessity of asserting Russia's interests in what it considered its sphere of influence.

> If the president says that Russia's friendly regions represent a zone of privileged interest, that means that this zone is under Russian control. And anyone who tries to challenge that is challenging not only that specific country but Russia, with all its nuclear arms.

Dugin claimed to be interpreting and forecasting Russia's foreign policy, and his claim was now credible. That summer, he had gone to South Ossetia and posed in front of a tank with a Kalashnikov in his hands. That summer had also marked the first time he had seen one of his slogans catch on and go entirely mainstream, repeated on television and reproduced on bumper stickers. The slogan was, "Tanks to Tbilisi!"* Dugin had written, "Those who do not support the slogan 'Tanks to Tbilisi!' are not Russians. . . . 'Tanks to Tbilisi!' should be written on every Russian's forehead."[49]

The slogans, and the war, worked: according to Levada Center polls, Putin's popularity rating shot up to 88 percent, its highest point ever. Medvedev's hit 83 percent, also unprecedented.[50]

---

*Tbilisi is the capital of Georgia.

PART FIVE

PROTEST

fourteen
THE FUTURE IS HISTORY

IN MARCH 2008, Seryozha flew to Moscow to vote in the presidential election. He had been living in Kiev for a year, barely following Russian politics,
but he knew he had to vote. His grandfather would have said so. Alexander
Nikolaevich always talked about how lucky Seryozha was to have been
raised with elections. Perhaps this was why Seryozha felt he had to fly to
Moscow and cast a ballot at his local precinct rather than vote at the embassy
in Kiev.

It was an hourlong flight. From Sheremetyevo International Airport,
Seryozha took a shuttle, a rickety minivan, to the nearest Metro stop. The
vans ran one after another, and so did the slower large buses, so the Metro
station was always full of travelers, most of whom looked tired from journeys much longer than Seryozha's had been. Seryozha got in line to the
ticket booth: of course, everyone had just come in from someplace else and
no one had the multiple-ride cards that saved Muscovites time in line. The
Metro station was stuffy and loud, the air full of everyone's travel dust. Bags
made it feel even more crowded than it was. Tired children complained.
Tired adults snapped at them. The line seemed interminable.

Actually, it lasted fifty minutes. If Seryozha was tired by the time he reached the ticket window, what must it have been like for everyone else?

"Sixty rides, please," he said, pushing a thousand-ruble note through the window. According to a typed price list posted on the ticket booth, sixty rides was the highest-denomination ticket available. It cost 580 rubles, or about twenty dollars.

When he had the ticket, Seryozha walked over to the turnstiles and said as loudly as he could:

"I have just stood in this line for fifty minutes! I don't want you to have to stand in line for fifty minutes too, just because you came here from another town! I have purchased sixty rides! Please go through on this ticket."

There was a pause. Many people seemed to have heard him but not believed him. Then one woman walked over. Seryozha fed his ticket into the turnstile, it spat out the ticket and flashed green, and the woman went through. Then one more person went, then a couple, and then a young police lieutenant was pushing his clean-shaven face into Seryozha's.

"You have to come with me."

Seryozha went. The lieutenant led him through one of the black metal doors in the lobby into the station's own police precinct, where a more senior officer sat. His completely bald head was red and beaded with sweat, and though he was sitting there behind his metal desk, he looked and breathed like he had just been climbing stairs. As soon as they entered, the sweaty man started shouting at Seryozha, a barrage of obscenities. No one had ever shouted at Seryozha like this, and it must have shown on his face, because the young lieutenant now led him back out of the room. Out of earshot of the sweaty man, he tried to use his own words to tell Seryozha that what he had done with the ticket was wrong. He could not really make a logical case, or even a coherent sentence, and this made Seryozha want to help him.

"Look," he said, "there was no fraud here. I did get a discount for buying twenty rides at once, but I am not profiting from it and I saved everyone time and trouble—including the cashier!"

"The resale of tickets is illegal," said the lieutenant.

"I wasn't reselling them."

"You could have gotten the cashier in trouble. She could get fired."

"Why would she get fired? She did nothing wrong! No one did anything wrong."

"What do you think you are, God?"

Something changed right then. Seryozha felt a calm and clarity. The word "zen" floated into his mind, followed by a perfectly formed phrase: "This man's mind works in a way that I will never be able to understand."

"I understand," said Seryozha, and walked away from the policeman. He fed his ticket into a turnstile, walked through, and then stuffed the ticket into the hands of the first person to pause long enough in response to Seryozha's "Excuse me, please." Seryozha had no use for the remaining fifty-five rides.

He went directly to his polling place. It was set up in a school: a half-dozen makeshift booths and two transparent plastic ballot bins in the center of the room. He took his ballot and stopped short of entering a booth. The first name and bio on the ballot were:

BOGDANOV, ANDREI VLADIMIROVICH. Born in 1970, resident of Moscow. Place of work: Democratic Party of Russia, political party. Job title: Central Committee Chairman. Place of work: Solntsevo Municipal Council, City of Moscow. Job title: Deputy, part-time. Nominated by: self. Registered on the basis of voter signatures. Party affiliation: Democratic Party of Russia, party leader.[1]

This made Seryozha mad as the lieutenant had not, and his sweaty-headed boss had not, and all their made-up rules had not. This was outright mockery. An independent candidate—one who was not already a member of parliament—was required by new Putin-era laws to submit two million voter signatures in order to be registered as a candidate, with no more than fifty thousand signatures coming from any one region of the country.[2] This demanded either a lot of money or a large nationwide grassroots network of activists—preferably both. Many people had tried that year. Garry Kasparov could not even convene the required public meeting of an initial group of supporters, because no one would rent him space for such a meeting, for any amount of money. Boris Nemtsov had dropped out of the race to help another candidate, former prime minister Mikhail Kasyanov, but Kasyanov's signatures were arbitrarily thrown out.[3]

But here was some guy named Bogdanov, whom no one had ever heard of, who was ostensibly representing a party that had in fact been dormant since the early 1990s, whose political experience consisted of being a part-time member of a tiny powerless municipal council, and even this was probably fake—and Seryozha was supposed to pretend to believe that this clown had collected two million signatures? This felt just like the time when Seryozha thought everyone was crazy suddenly to accept that nobody, Putin, as the president-apparent. Except this felt worse. It was even more of an offense to human intelligence than the spectacle of Putin handing the presidency over to Medvedev like it was his to lend. Seryozha dropped his blank ballot into one of the bins and walked out. He took a cab back to the airport.

The Central Election Commission reported that Bogdanov got 1.3 percent of the vote. Medvedev won in the first round with 70.28 percent. The two perennial candidates—Communist Party leader Gennady Zyuganov and the Liberal Democratic Party's Vladimir Zhirinovsky (who, as members of parliament, were exempt from having to collect signatures to get on the ballot)—split the rest.[4]

BOTH OF THE THINGS that happened to Seryozha that day were examples of what Yuri Levada had once termed "collective hostage-taking," what was once known as *krugovaya poruka*—literally, "circular bail." For centuries, entire communities could be held responsible for taxes owed or crimes committed by any individual. If a resident failed to pay taxes, the property of any of his neighbors could be seized. The threat transformed all members of a given community into enforcers, but not in accordance with codified law— they had to devise their own means of ensuring compliance.

Russia formally abolished *krugovaya poruka* at the turn of the twentieth century, when modernization seemed to mandate recognizing only individual responsibility before the law.[5] The Bolshevik state resurrected *krugovaya poruka* as an instrument of totalitarian control. During the Great Terror, colleagues and family had to publicly denounce those arrested as "enemies of the people" in order to avoid arrest themselves. Conspiracies conjured by Stalin's prosecutors were always based on the ostensible culprits' social and professional networks, making associations as such suspect. As the range of behavior deemed risky or suspicious broadened, citizens grew ever more likely to act as enforcers.

Krugovaya poruka, which is often translated as "solidarity," is, to the Russian ear, a neutral or even positive term, used to urge Soviet children to study harder and be better little Communists. This may be why Levada chose the more jarring term "collective hostage-taking" to refer to one of "the most potent instruments of coercion and intimidation used by the Soviet state." Even after the Great Terror passed, it kept the overwhelming majority of the population passive with the understanding that any action could endanger a larger group. "A moral predicament in which reasonable action runs counter to the well-being of 'one's own kind' is in itself unreasonable and immoral," wrote Levada. "This predicament was cultivated, and reproduced thousands upon thousands of times."

In the case of the Metro queue, the police officer instinctively sensed that it was his job to ensure that all passengers remain in a state of equal misery, and to prevent any attempt at self-organization. At the polling place, the ballot—with the absurd, almost virtual candidate in first place—turned every voter into a co-conspirator. By casting a ballot one affirmed the legitimacy of the exercise. By voting for Medvedev in the absence of a believable alternative, one agreed to pretend to be an active supporter, symbolically entering the circle—*krug* in Russian—on which the system of "circular guarantees" is based. (In previous years the ballot had included the option of voting "against all candidates," but a 2006 law eliminated this option.)

Much earlier, soon after Putin's first election victory, Gudkov had decided that he needed to take time out of analyzing survey results to write about something else: a concept. The concept was totalitarianism. The word had not been used much in the last decade. It had been thrilling, in the late 1980s, to hear Soviet leaders—first Alexander Nikolaevich Yakovlev and then Gorbachev himself—start using the word to describe the Soviet system. These had been moments of epic honesty and openness. But then, after the Soviet regime appeared to have collapsed into a pile of dust, the word became instantly irrelevant: totalitarianism had ended, and the topics of the day were reforms, the economy, and the new system Russia was assumed to be building. Even the few people who stubbornly insisted on reckoning with the past generally chose to focus on one specific period in Soviet history—Stalinism—and one element of the Soviet system: state terror. But since the Levada studies continued to show that Homo Sovieticus was thriving and reproducing and the initial hypothesis about the withering of Soviet institutions had long been debunked, it seemed like a good idea to return to thinking about the nature of the system that had produced the institutions and the man.

The term "totalitarianism" first came into use in the late 1920s, soon after the first totalitarian regimes formed. At the beginning it was simply descriptive, used by both opponents and supporters of regimes that aimed to *totally* transform societies, as did the Soviet, Italian, and later German leaders. In fact, the first person to use the phrase "totalitarian state" may have been Benito Mussolini, in a 1925 speech in which he extolled the virtues of concentrating all of society in a single state entity. At that point, "totalitarian state" was a vision rather than a system, but it was a vision clearly opposed to Western democratic arrangements, which it saw as weak. By implied definition, a totalitarian state would draw its strength from concentrating all power—including the power of every individual's support for the regime—into a single whole. Both the Germans and the Italians saw the Soviet Union as a successful model of achieving such concentration. Before the Second World War, a few thinkers attempted to describe what made totalitarian regimes different from any that had come before. In 1936, Luigi Sturzo, an Italian priest and politician in exile, identified four key characteristics of the totalitarian state:

(a) Administrative centralization is carried to extremes—the suppression not only of all local autonomy . . . but also of the autonomy of all public or semi-public institutions, charitable organizations, cultural associations, universities. . . . The independence of the legislature and judiciary has completely disappeared, and even the government is reduced to a body subordinate to a leader, who has become dictator under the euphemisms of Duce, Marshal, or Führer. . . .

(b) The Party is militarized. Either it dominates the army or the army allies itself with the prevailing power and the two armed forces cooperate or amalgamate. The youth of the country is militarized, collective life is felt to be military life, dreams of *revanche* or of empire, conflicts at home and abroad, penetrate the whole social structure. . . .

(c) Everyone must have faith in the new state and learn to love it. From the schools up to the universities conformity of feeling is not enough; there must be an absolute intellectual and moral surrender, a trusting enthusiasm, a religious mysticism where the new state is concerned. . . . A whole new moral environment must be created in addition to the work of the school. Hence the official textbook, the state inspired and standardized newspaper, the cinema, the wireless, sports, school societies, the grant[ing] of prizes, are not only controlled but are directed toward an end—the worship of the totalitarian state, whether its banner be nation, race or class. The whole of social life is continually mobilized in parades, festivals, pageants, plebiscites, sporting events, calculated to capture the mind, the imagination, the feeling of the populace. And to excite this collective spirit of exaltation the worship of the state or class or race would be too vague in itself. The vital focus of emotion is the man, the hero, the demigod—Lenin, Hitler, Mussolini—whose person is sacred and whose words are the works of a prophet. . . .

(d) It is impossible for the totalitarian state to allow economic freedom to either capitalists or workers. There is no room for free trade unions or free employers' associations. Instead there are state syndicates or corporations, with no freedom of action, controlled and organized within the state and for the state.[6]

After the war, another exile, this one from Germany, published the most detailed and definitive description of totalitarianism. Hannah Arendt's three-volume *The Origins of Totalitarianism* was published in 1951. For Arendt, the key characteristics of a totalitarian state were ideology and state terror. The substance of the ideology, to the extent that ideology has a substance, was unimportant: any ideology could become the basis of a totalitarian system if it could be encapsulated and coupled with terror. The terror was used to enforce the ideology but also to fuel it. Whatever premise formed the basis of the ideology, be it the superiority of a particular race or of a particular class, was used to derive imagined laws of history: only a certain race or a certain class was destined to survive. The "laws of history" justified the terror ostensibly required for this survival. Arendt wrote about the subjugation of public space—in effect the disappearance of public space, which, by depriving a person of boundaries and agency, rendered him profoundly lonely. This, she wrote, was the product of the marriage of ideology and terror. In this model, Mussolini's Italy was no longer considered a totalitarian state, whatever Mussolini himself might have said. Arendt wrote about Nazi Germany and Soviet Russia, though she had much more knowledge of the former.[7]

The first edition of *Origins* was devoted to the roots and causes of totalitarianism, not to describing the resulting state: she wrote the last chapter, "Ideology and Terror," in 1953.[8] That year, another German exile, Carl Joachim Friedrich, speaking at a conference on totalitarianism (at which Arendt was also a speaker), offered a concise five-point definition of totalitarian society:

1. An official ideology, consisting of an official body of doctrine covering all vital aspects of man's existence, to which everyone in that society is supposed to adhere at least passively. . . .

2. A single mass party consisting of a relatively small percentage of the total population (up to 10 per cent) of men and women passionately and unquestioningly dedicated to the ideology and prepared to assist in every way in promoting its general acceptance, such party being organized in strictly hierarchical, oligarchical manner, usually under a single leader and typically either superior to or completely commingled with the bureaucratic governmental organization.

3. A technologically conditioned near-complete monopoly of control . . . of all means of effective armed combat.

4. A similarly technologically conditioned near-complete monopoly of control . . . of all means of effective mass communication . . .

5. A system of terroristic police control, depending for its effectiveness upon points 3 and 4 and characteristically directed not only against demonstrable "enemies" of the regime, but against arbitrarily selected classes of the population.[9]

In another three years Friedrich and his student Zbigniew Brzezinski, an exile from Poland, published *Totalitarian Dictatorship and Autocracy*, a much slimmer volume than *Origins*, that attempted not so much to describe as to define totalitarianism. They added a sixth point to Friedrich's earlier list: a centralized, controlled economy.[10]

Friedrich, like Arendt, stressed that the Nazi and Soviet regimes were essentially similar, which justified placing them in the same category, apart from all the other countries of the world. In the years that followed, most of the concept's critics focused on this very premise. Some, like another German exile, Herbert Marcuse, argued that all industrialized countries carried in them the seeds of a system like Germany's.[11] Others, especially Western Sovietologists who hailed from the Left, argued that a model based on the study of Nazi Germany did not fit the facts of Soviet life very well, and perhaps even existed solely to discredit the Soviet regime. After the fall of the Soviet Union made it easier to study the country that had been, academics began noting how much richer private life had been in the USSR than they had once thought, how inconsistent and how widely disregarded the ideology, and how comparatively mild police enforcement became after Stalin's death. All of this appeared to contradict the model. A group of scholars led by Australian-American historian Sheila Fitzpatrick put together a collection of papers specifically looking at the differences between Nazi and Soviet systems. They called it *Beyond Totalitarianism*.[12]

The concept had fallen out of use not only in Russia but also among those who studied Russia in the West, but Gudkov had the idea that it was time to revisit it. If you thought about it, the problems with the definition of totalitarianism were built in from the start. First, even though all the original scholars of totalitarianism were exiles from the totalitarian countries, they produced their descriptions on the outside. Certain distinctions were inaccessible to them. Looking from the outside in, one cannot see, for example, whether people attend a parade because they are forced to do so or because they so desire. Researchers generally assumed one or the other: either that people were passive victims or that they were fervent believers. But on the inside, both assumptions were wrong, for all the people at the parade (or any other form of collective action) and for each one of them individually. They did not feel like helpless victims, but they did not feel like fanatics either. They felt normal. They were members of a society. The parades and various other forms of collective life gave them a sense of belonging that humans generally need. They were in no position to appraise the risks of non-belonging in comparison with such risks in other societies, to think about the fact that being marked as an outsider in the Soviet Union carried immeasurably greater penalties than being marked as one in a Western democracy. They would not be lying if they said that they wanted to be a part of the parade, or the collective in general—and that if they exerted pressure on others to be a part of the collective too, they did so willingly. But this did not make them true believers in the ideology, in the way Westerners might imagine it: the ideology served simply as a key to unity, as the collective's shared language. In addition, the mark of a totalitarian ideology, according to Arendt, was its hermetic nature: it explained away the entire world, and no argument could pierce its bubble. Soviet citizens lived inside the ideology—it was their home, and it felt ordinary.

It stood to reason that up close the two pillars of totalitarianism— ideology and terror—looked different than they did from a distance. It stood to reason, too, that researchers might overestimate the weight of ideology, because their objects of study were texts, and texts reflected the ideology more than anything else. Intellectuals were always falling into the trap of mistaking the written word for a true mirror of life.

In the Soviet Union, the ideology proved mutable. The official line shifted radically, from internationalism to the "friendship of the peoples," from viewing the family as a bourgeois anachronism to seeing it as the essential unit of Soviet society. What did not change was the importance of mobilization around whatever the ideology was, and the idea that the country was exceptional. What if ideology as such was not quite so important a component of totalitarian society? And what of terror? Arendt wrote her book soon after the Holocaust; Stalinist terror was still claiming hundreds of thousands of people a year. But the Soviet Union survived for decades after mass terror ended in 1953. Perhaps terror was necessary for the establishment of a totalitarian regime, but once established could it be maintained by institutions that carried within them the memory of terror?

Around 2004—toward the end of Putin's first term—Western journalists began, cautiously, to apply the word "authoritarian" to the Russian regime. Arendt had argued that authoritarian regimes were essentially unlike totalitarian ones and more like tyrannies, because they demanded the observance of certain knowable rules and laws rather than total subjugation from their subjects. A different distinction between totalitarian and authoritarian regimes was later proposed by Juan José Linz, a double exile. The son of a German father and a Spanish mother, Linz had left Germany as a child and Franco's Spain as an adult. As a sociologist at Yale, he wrote a book called *Totalitarian and Authoritarian Regimes*, in which he suggested the following three differences: in authoritarian regimes, the boundary between state and society was not diminished; authoritarian regimes had mentalities rather than ideologies; authoritarian regimes, unlike totalitarian ones, had low levels of societal mobilization. The subjects of authoritarian regimes were, according to Linz's definition, passive: they simply accepted one-party or one-person rule. Authoritarian regimes were profoundly apolitical.[13]

This did not seem the right category. Everything had become political. Russia under Putin was mobilizing—the rhetoric, the renewed military parades, and, more than anything else, the Kremlin's youth movements with their training camps—all existed for this purpose. The boundary between state and society, faint as it had once been, was now obliterated: the takeover of the media and the attack on civil society had served that purpose. There was another issue with calling the Russian regime "authoritarian": it did not take into account the Soviet legacy, which Gudkov increasingly thought was key to understanding the nature of the current regime. He also happened to think that, contrary to what many Western Sovietologists believed, Soviet society had in fact been closest to matching the theoretical model of totalitarianism in real life. And as evidence mounted that Soviet social institutions had been preserved and were resurgent, Gudkov began to think of Russia as a permutation of a totalitarian system. To understand it, Gudkov decided to propose his own definition of totalitarianism, based on the Soviet experience. It contained seven points:

1. The symbiosis of Party and state . . . Society is organized in a strictly hierarchical way. It is constructed from the top down. . . . Society is thus turned upside down: the powerful upper layer will sooner or later become the least competent and least informed stratum, devoid of potential to develop or make its work more efficient. Every changeover brings a less active, less competent individual to the top. . . .

2. A forced societal consensus, created through a monopoly on mass media, combined with strict censorship. This creates the conditions for chronic mobilization of the population, always prepared to

carry out the decisions of the party-state. . . . The subjects' attention is focused predominantly on events inside the country, which is isolated from the outside world; hence the sense of exceptionalism, a focus on "us," and a powerful alienation barrier, a refusal to know or understand events "on the other side."

3. State terror, carried out by the secret police, special services, extrajudicial paramilitary structures . . . The existence of the secret police and concentration camps on the one hand and official propaganda and cultural production on the other, create the conditions for "doublethink." . . . The scale and character of the terror can vary greatly, from the Great Terror in 1918–1922 and the 1930s through the 1950s to the persecution, in the late 1970s and early 1980s, of dissidents, whose number and influence were relatively small.

4. The militarization of society and the economy . . . The activities of mobilizational structures that pierce society from top to bottom, from all educational institutions . . . to sporting clubs etc. . . . are intended less to prepare the population for battle against an external enemy than to systematically train the population . . . to carry out any and all of the regime's initiatives, because the "leader knows best."

5. A command, distributive economy and the concomitant chronic, inevitable shortages of goods, services, information, etc. . . . Shortages are not mere deficits but also a way of organizing society through official hierarchical structures of access to goods and services . . . supplemented by informal shadow economy structures.

6. A chronic state of poverty . . . Totalitarianism takes hold under the conditions of increasing poverty—when a large part of the population has no hope for a better future and projects hope on some extraordinary political measures. Totalitarianism is sustained by maintaining a very low standard of living.

7. A static population, strict limits on both vertical and horizontal social mobility except that which is carried out by the state for its own purposes.[14]

Gudkov did not include ideology on his list of characteristics of totalitarianism: he had concluded that ideology was essential only at the very beginning, for the future totalitarian rulers to seize power. After that, terror kicked in. Later, the drive to conform would take a leading role. This produced what Gudkov meant by "doublethink": it was not the bizarre state described by Orwell but rather a habitual, almost passive fragmentation, when people thought different, often utterly contradictory things at different times and in different situations—whatever they needed to think in order to conform at that particular moment. This, more than anything else, guaranteed that no effective resistance was possible in the Soviet Union: fragmented people could not form and sustain relationships of solidarity and could not imaginatively plan for the future, which is essential for any group effort.

The purpose of defining the Soviet totalitarian regime was to gain more clarity on what Russia had inherited. The inventory was long. On paper, one-party rule had been abolished—but the people remained. The old nomenklatura continued to dominate the bureaucracy and the bureaucracy continued to dominate society, maintaining its upside-down structure. If anything, the upheaval of the 1990s had sped up the process of rotation, as a result of which ever less informed and less competent people were brought to the top. Censorship had been abolished, but after a brief period of freedom, mass media were being monopolized by the state. The KGB had been renamed and had lost some of its reach (some functions, like border control, were taken away), but the judiciary continued to serve the executive power, rule of law had not been established, and law enforcement saw its function in protecting the state. To the extent that society had been demilitarized, Putin had reversed this process—indeed, on the day Yeltsin's resignation made him acting president, Putin found the time to sign a cabinet measure reintroducing military training in secondary schools.[15] The economy was no longer ruled by a central planning authority, but it retained its distributive nature: the Kremlin apportioned assets and access during the privatization of the 1990s, and when Putin came to office he got to work redistributing companies and wealth. Lower down the food chain, this distributive way of functioning was usually called corruption, but it was not exactly that, since the issue lay not with any individual bureaucrat but with the very system of limiting and distributing goods and services. This, in turn, rested on the institution of collective hostage-taking—a system that reinforced lowered expectations, like the Metro Seryozha encountered, which was not selling a service but distributing it.

What should the Russian system be called, then? It was no longer the totalitarian regime it had been, but after disassembling some of its totalitarian institutions—like the Party-state or total militarization—it had started re-creating them, or something that resembled them. But these struck Gudkov as being more like imitations of totalitarian institutions. Western journalists were using the word "authoritarianism" because they seemed to think that authoritarianism was totalitarianism-lite, but the regime was not authoritarian either. Gudkov thought it might be called "pseudototalitarianism." One thing was certain: this regime was not going to develop into a functioning democracy. In fact, it did not seem capable of developing at all. It probably could not re-create the old systems of terror and complete mobilization. Its sole purpose, or so it seemed to Gudkov when he was writing about this in 2001, was to stay afloat, to maintain just enough inertia. In this, its main resource was the Russian citizen weaned on generations of doublethink and collective hostage-taking: the Homo Sovieticus.

BACK WHEN SOCIOLOGISTS and political scientists were defining totalitarianism, psychoanalysts and philosophers were trying to understand and explain it. Gudkov had little patience for much of their writing, in part because they were, generally speaking, Marxists, and in part because several of them were German exiles with a mission—to warn the rest of the Western world that it could happen there. They had seen fascism rise to power in a functioning democracy, and they wanted their knowledge to serve as warning. Gudkov's experience was different—at this point he was less interested in how totalitarianism came to be than in how it refused to end—but some of what he was trying to describe when he wrote about Homo Sovieticus had been noticed by psychoanalyst Erich Fromm seventy years earlier.

Fromm had fled Germany in 1934, and in 1941 he wrote an urgent book called *Escape from Freedom*, in which he attempted to describe the psychological origins of Nazism, though he was careful to note that "Nazism is a psychological problem, but the psychological factors themselves have to be understood as being molded by socio-economic factors; Nazism is an economic and political problem, but the hold it has over a whole people has to be understood on psychological grounds."[16]

To make his case, Fromm went back to the Middle Ages, when

> a person was identical with his role in society; he was a peasant, artisan, or knight, not an individual who happened to have this or that occupation. The social order was conceived as a natural order, and being a definite part of it gave a feeling of security and of belonging. There was comparatively little competition. One was born into a certain economic position which guaranteed a livelihood determined by tradition.

This description also fit late Soviet society, which, as Gudkov had observed, used limits on social mobility as one of its most important instruments of control. People generally moved neither up nor down the socioeconomic ladder—nor were they likely to work in a field very different from their parents'. Seryozha, who did not encounter a single child from outside the top level of the nomenklatura until after the Soviet Union collapsed, grew up behind a series of literal walls, but the invisible walls separating other Soviet citizens from members of different groups were just as effective. People who transcended these boundaries, as, for example, Lyosha's mother did when she left the village to go to university, did so through great effort and determination and were invariably exceptions—as Galina was even within her own family. Still, she was able to move but a step up and one sideways from her initial station: she became a schoolteacher in the small town closest to the village where her mother had worked at the collective farm.

Back at the beginning of the Reformation, wrote Fromm, the individual gained the ability to determine his own path—and at the same time lost his sense of certainty in place and self. Fromm divided newfound freedom into two parts: "freedom to" and "freedom from." If the former was positive, the latter could cause unbearable anxiety: "The world has become limitless and at the same time threatening. . . . By losing his fixed place in a closed world man loses the answer to the meaning of his life; the result is that doubt has befallen him concerning himself and the aim of life." Along came Martin Luther and John Calvin with remedies for this anxiety: "By not only accepting his own insignificance but by humiliating himself to the utmost, by giving up every vestige of individual will, by renouncing and denouncing his individual strength, the individual could hope to be acceptable to God." In other words, the individual could in one swoop regain his certainty in the future—it would now be in God's hands—and rid himself of his most unbearable burden: the self.

In Fromm's view, a new kind of character was thus inaugurated and soon became prevalent among the middle classes of some societies. He described this character as someone who by an individual psychoanalyst might be diagnosed as a sadomasochistic personality but on the level of social psychology could be called the "authoritarian personality"—in part because sadomasochistic tendencies in individual relationships are usually understood as a pathology while similar behavior in society can be the most rational and "normal" strategy. The authoritarian character survives by surrendering his power to an outside authority—God or a leader—whom Fromm called the "magic helper." The "magic helper" is a source of guidance, security, and also of pride, because with surrender comes a sense of belonging. The authoritarian character is defined by his relationship to power:

> For the authoritarian character there exist, so to speak, two sexes: the powerful ones and the powerless ones. His love, admiration and readi-

ness for submission are automatically aroused by power, whether of a person or of an institution. Power fascinates him not for any values for which a specific power may stand, but just because it is power. Just as his "love" is automatically aroused by power, so powerless people or institutions automatically arouse his contempt. The very sight of a powerless person makes him want to attack, dominate, humiliate him.

Another key trait of the authoritarian character is his longing for and belief in historical determination and permanence:

It is fate that there are wars and that one part of mankind has to be ruled by another. It is fate that the amount of suffering can never be less than it always has been. . . . The authoritarian character worships the past. What has been, will eternally be. To wish or to work for something that has not yet been before is crime or madness. The miracle of creation—and creation is always a miracle—is outside his range of emotional experience.

Fromm and thinkers who wrote about the threat of totalitarianism after he did—Herbert Marcuse and Theodor Adorno[17]—believed that this character was common in modern societies. Periods of great social and economic upheaval had the ability to make the authoritarian character dominant in society and to carry an authoritarian character to the top. Germany after the First World War was in just such a state. Old certainties were gone, social structures were in disarray, and a chasm appeared between generations:

Under the changed conditions, especially the inflation, the older generation was bewildered and puzzled and much less adapted to the new conditions than the smarter, younger generation. Thus the younger generation felt superior to their elders and could not take them, and their teachings, quite seriously any more. Furthermore, the economic decline of the middle class deprived the parents of their economic role as backers of the economic future of their children.[18]

This passage described the Russian 1990s as precisely as it did the German 1930s, about which it was written. Arendt described this state as "homelessness on an unprecedented scale, rootlessness of an unprecedented depth."[19] A void opened up where certainty had been; the burden of freedom became unbearable. Hitler emerged as a quintessential authoritarian character with a program that appealed to other authoritarian characters. He hated the Weimar Republic because it was weak, just as his audience hated their elders. Fromm did not see the substance of Nazi ideology as important—indeed, he saw no substance in the ideology at all. Arendt also stressed that the premises of Hitler's—and Lenin's—ideologies to outsiders "looked preposterously 'primitive' and absurd."[20] Fromm observed no logic whatsoever in the ideology: "Nazism never had any genuine political or economic principles. It is essential to understand that the very principle of Nazism is its radical opportunism."[21] What Nazi ideology and practice did have, according to Fromm, was ritual that satisfied the audience's masochistic craving:

> They are told again and again: the individual is nothing and does not count. The individual should accept this personal insignificance, dissolve himself in a higher power, and then feel proud in participating in the strength and glory of this higher power.[22]

And for the sadistic side of the authoritarian character, the ideology offered "a feeling of superiority over the rest of mankind" that, Fromm wrote, was able to "compensate them—for a time at least—for the fact that their lives had been impoverished, economically and culturally."[23]

IN THE SPRING OF 2008, the biggest national television channel announced an online contest to choose the greatest Russian who ever lived. It was called the Name of Russia. By mid-July, with nearly two and a half million votes cast, contest organizers announced that they had temporarily put a halt to the voting because someone—or some group—had rigged the results to make Joseph Stalin the winner. Once voting resumed, the results changed dramatically, to make Nicholas II, the last of the czars, come out on top. But then the organizers said that this, too, had been the result of a hacker attack.[24] After a few weeks, the winner was announced: rather than either of the two popular frontrunners, it was Alexander Nevsky, a thirteenth-century prince known to most Russians as a vague memory from the history books and as the leader of Russian troops in the epic ice battle in Sergei Eisenstein's 1938 film *Alexander Nevsky*.

Lyosha was furious. Everyone could see what had happened: the television executives were mortified by Stalin's popular victory and decided to falsify results the same way real voting officials wrote up whatever was required of them. Except they must have gotten their signals crossed: they thought that Russia's last czar was a safe choice, but they failed to consider what he stood for because he had abdicated, giving in to the Revolution. He had been weak, and now he was despised. Worse, Yeltsin had once publicly repented for the Bolsheviks' murder of the czar and his family, admitting a legacy of guilt—and this admission, too, in the new disposition looked like weakness. So Alexander Nevsky, who had not even been in the running, looked like a safe political choice: all anyone knew about him was that he had fought wars.

"What kind of historical hero is he?" raged Lyosha. "He has no place at all in the Russian historiography!"

"But he fought the Germans!" said the other Lyosha. "And won."

The other Lyosha was, it would seem, Lyosha's boyfriend. He had started messaging Lyosha earlier that year on the VKontakte social network. Lyosha played hard to get. He actually was hard to get. His sublimation strategy, implemented two years earlier, was working. He was happy with his research and his friends. He spent all his time working on his dissertation. He shared an apartment with a female friend and her husband. He stayed away from the gay crowd, because it scared him: it felt like the abyss.

The other Lyosha would not give up. After a couple of months Lyosha agreed to meet. Then he relented. He figured he was strong enough now to allow himself to feel something. What he felt, very soon, was flummoxed. The other Lyosha had his own particular way of conducting a relationship. He would come to Lyosha's apartment every day after work. It was all Lyosha could do to prevent the other Lyosha from moving in, but for all purposes the other Lyosha now lived in his apartment. The other Lyosha said they were a family. Lyosha said that he was opposed to the traditional model of family, but the other Lyosha said that he was Russian Orthodox. He wore a cross around his neck, and he talked about tradition. What kind of tradition could two gay men have in a country where they were utterly invisible? The kind of tradition in which Lyosha, who was twenty-three, was expected to be in every way the dominant partner to the other Lyosha, who was twenty. Or so the other Lyosha said—even though it was Lyosha who felt dominated.

They argued all the time. These were strange arguments. The other Lyosha simply contradicted everything Lyosha said. Lyosha soon realized that the other Lyosha goaded him to get attention, but he could not restrain himself, because, more often than not, the other Lyosha picked fights about things Lyosha genuinely cared about and understood. The other Lyosha said that he liked Putin.

"How can you like Putin?" asked Lyosha.

"I am just starting out in my career, and Putin's Plan is an appropriate plan," the other Lyosha responded.

The answer seemed nonsensical on every level. First, there was no such thing as Putin's Plan: it was a phrase used during the parliamentary campaign, but there was no book or even flyer that contained whatever plan this might be. It was like every Russian was supposed to know intuitively what Putin's Plan was, like it was divine providence, like it was the natural law of things. And the other Lyosha said it was an "appropriate" plan like it was a thing that actually existed—and had something to do with his career! The other Lyosha worked as an assistant to a liberal member of the Perm legislature, Nikita Belykh, a leader of the Union of Right Forces Party that Nemtsov had founded. Lyosha considered asking the other Lyosha why, if

Putin's Plan was so "appropriate," he worked for Belykh, but realized that he did not want to know the answer. He figured that the other Lyosha would say that he worked for Belykh for the money, and what was worse, that would be a lie, because his was an unpaid assistantship: in contemporary Russian, "money" could be the polite word for "power." Also, the other Lyosha was a member of the pro-Kremlin youth movement Young Russia— the one that had, among other things, laid siege to the Estonian embassy the previous summer. He and his best friend, a young woman, attended the militarized summer training camps at Lake Seligher.

The other Lyosha never ran out of things to argue about. He picked a fight about Gorbachev, whom he hated for destroying the Soviet Union— and kept arguing, even though he was too young to remember even a day of life under Gorbachev. He called Yeltsin "nothing but an alcoholic." During one of their fights Lyosha lost it. He hauled off and hit the other Lyosha.

He could not believe what he had done, and broke up with the other Lyosha on the spot. But, true to his inexplicable self, the other Lyosha seemed to revel in the incident. For months afterward, he bragged to their mutual friends that Lyosha was a "tyrant."

FROMM WOULD HAVE FOUND nothing mysterious about the other Lyosha: he was a walking caricature of the authoritarian character, right down to his automatic readiness to worship a thirteenth-century military leader.

Gudkov found nothing mysterious or surprising in the Name of Russia contest. The Levada team had been asking respondents to name "the greatest people who have ever lived" from the beginning of the Homo Sovieticus project. Results had differed only slightly over the years. Stalin had risen steadily—from 12 percent in 1989 to 40 in 2003 (he dropped four percentage points in 2008, which may have been related to the discussion of the supposed hacking of the Name of Russia site). Stalin had not made it into the top five in 1989, but in every subsequent survey he was among the leaders, coming in fourth in 1994 and 1999, and third in 2003 and 2008. Others in the top five were, consistently, Peter the Great, Pushkin, and Lenin. Napoleon and Georgy Zhukov, who commanded the Red Army when it entered Berlin in 1945, made appearances in different years, as did Mikhail Lomonosov, remembered as the country's first scientist, and Yuri Gagarin, the first man in space. Putin, who was first named in 2003 by 21 percent of the respondents, by 2008 was at 32 percent, which made him number five among the greatest people who ever lived.[25]

To Gudkov, the list looked bad from the beginning and worse with every passing survey. Russians apparently saw great people as having been almost exclusively Russian—and with the exception of Catherine the Great, they had all been men. By choosing primarily military leaders and heads of state (who were also generally appraised as military leaders), they showed that they equated greatness with power. (Albert Einstein, one of the few foreigners, started out at 9 percent in 1989 but quickly slipped while Hitler gained on him.)

It all fit. The love of power, the focus on Russia to the exclusion of the rest of the world—with an exception made perhaps only for a Napoleon or a Hitler, whose power trumped even their enemy status but who were made relevant by the fact that they had invaded Russia—this and other survey results added up to a totalitarian mind-set. The only consideration that gave Gudkov pause was what seemed like an utter lack of a concept of the future. He had been taught that totalitarianism presupposed the image of a glorious future. But as he researched both Communist and Nazi ideologies, he came to the conclusion that the appeal of the rhetoric in both cases lay in archaic, primitive images: a simple society, a world of "us," a tribe. Fromm, in fact, rejected the very idea of an image of the future in Nazi ideology and stressed the "worship of the past."

IT MAY BE MORE ACCURATE to say that the Soviet system offered not a vision of the future but the ability to know one's future, much as tradesmen did in feudal times, and to make very small-scale, manageable decisions about the future. Arutyunyan thought about this when she researched her family history. How could her great-grandmother, a peasant woman before the Revolution, have imagined her future? How would she have known that all her sons would die from drink but her daughter would become an academic and a member of the Central Committee? So incomprehensible was this future that she could not fully understand it even after it had happened: of her daughter she knew only that she was "an important person."

But by the time Arutyunyan was growing up in the 1960s, the future stretched out before the Soviet citizen like a narrow but relatively well-lit hallway. If one was born to an educated family, like Arutyunyan was, one went to university. Her grandmother had been a historian, her parents were social historians and sociologists, and Arutyunyan received a degree in psychology, worked at the Institute of Sociology, and married a sociologist. There were, however, choices to be made, chief among them: whether to join the Party. Joining promised greater career advancement and possible perks, up to the ability to travel abroad. Not joining seemed to offer a small degree of autonomy. Each professional field had its own sets of minor choices as well. A theater actor from Moscow, for example, could choose to stay in a repertory in the capital or move to the provinces and become the lead at a local theater.

In the 1990s, the narrow hallway exploded into wide-open space. For Arutyunyan, this was exhilarating, the very essence of freedom. True, life became unpredictable and sometimes felt hard—for a few years in the early 1990s Arutyunyan was the sole breadwinner in her family of four adults and two children. Her parents and husband stubbornly stuck to their social sciences even as their colleagues looked for ways to earn money elsewhere. But Arutyunyan was learning to be a psychoanalyst, like she had always dreamed, and she was traveling abroad, like she had barely dared imagine. In Fromm's classification, all she experienced was "freedom to."

In a few years she saw more and more patients who were suffering from the unbearable burden of "freedom from." Much of their pain was regret: the 1990s looked darker in retrospect, and the roads not chosen weighed too heavily. One patient had left academia—he had been a biochemist—to work for a pharmaceutical company. The company went bankrupt, he could not find another job, and now he was driving a taxi for a living. He could not stop thinking about where he had gone wrong. Should he have stuck it out in academia? His former colleagues who had, seemed to have done better.

There was a specific Russian expression: *budushchego net*, "There is no future." As though it could indeed be canceled. People said it when a particular vision of the future collapsed. For many people—many more than Arutyunyan realized at the time, when she was reveling in her "freedom to"—the future ended when the Soviet Union collapsed and the narrow hallway disappeared. Others struggled on, but the anxiety caused by uncertainty rendered them incapable of meaningful action. In the early 2000s, with the arrival of Putin, whose simple rhetoric made the world comprehensible again, and with inflation receding under the force of high oil prices, many of these patients felt better. They could function again. They were sure that Putin had something to do with it. "Stability" was the magic word of the day—the opposite of fear and anxiety.

The naughts were a time of stability for Arutyunyan too. In 2005 she became a fully credentialed member of the International Psychoanalytical Association—one of only eleven Russians with that status. The same year, the Moscow Psychoanalytic Society was authorized to be a study group—taking it one step closer to full membership in the world of psychoanalytic societies—and Arutyunyan became its chairperson. For her, too, the future was acquiring more definite contours—but she had never longed for this, and was only now realizing how much of an outsider this made her in Russian society.

fifteen

BUDUSHCHEGO NET

"THERE IS NO FUTURE HERE," Zhanna said to her mother in the fall of 2008. It had to do with money, and Zhanna and Raisa were, uncharacteristically, fighting, blaming each other for money that had been lost. Money had turned out to be Zhanna's calling. Not in the sense that she wanted to be super-rich. She was like her father that way: they enjoyed good vacations and big parties, and Boris liked his duplex apartment with a view of the Kremlin, and his Range Rover, but compared with his oligarch friends with their yachts and fleets of cars and multistory wine cellars, the Nemtsovs thought of themselves as simple people. Zhanna liked money the way her father liked physics: it made her brain rev up. To make money, you had to be quick and attentive and know when the moment came to bet against majority sentiment. In this sense playing the markets was the opposite of politics, and this was where Zhanna and Boris differed: she liked the one, and he liked the other.

It helped that the work was virtually free of risk. In 2007, when Zhanna went to work for Mercury Capital Trust, the Russian market only grew and grew, and the task was to grow a bit faster than the competition. Zhanna thought about money all the time. She started studying for a chartered financial analyst exam. At the end of 2007, the Russian market reached an all-time high.

In August 2008, Zhanna and Dmitry were on vacation in Thailand. It was late morning there when the markets opened in Moscow. Zhanna would take a look, maybe move a few things around, and go to the beach. On August 8 she saw something that made her think that a computer somewhere must be broken. The Russian stock market was in free fall.

Zhanna had actually seen the market fall once before, just two weeks earlier. That day, Putin held a meeting in Nizhny Novgorod; the subject was the state of the metals industry. One of the metals moguls was absent, and Putin—now officially merely the prime minister—was not pleased. He said that the Federal Antimonopoly Service should check into the activities of Mechel, the company whose majority owner had failed to show up. "Or perhaps even the Investigative Committee of the Prosecutor's Office should look into it," he said. "We have to figure out what's going on." He accused the company of exporting raw materials at below-market prices, causing the state to miss out on tax revenue. Mechel's owner was absent because he had been hospitalized. "Of course, an illness is an illness," said Putin. "But we may have to send a doctor over to him to take care of all his problems."[1]

Putin had not singled out a company or an entrepreneur like that since he jailed Khodorkovsky and took his company. Within hours of the threat, the value of Mechel stock on the New York exchange dropped by a third. The following morning, when the Moscow exchange opened, the company continued losing at home. Other companies followed. The Russian stock market reverted to levels at which it had been four months earlier, while the Moscow currency exchange lost nearly two years' worth of growth.[2]

That had been bad, but Zhanna had figured the market would recover. She even ignored Raisa's advice to unload all metals companies. Now she was ignoring more than that: she knew, in theory, that if the market was in free fall, you had to sell, but she could not believe it was happening. She was not selling. She was just watching the Russian market collapse.

That day, the day the war with Georgia began, the market lost more than 6.5 percent. In another few days, as it continued falling, it became clear that there was no recovery in sight. Western markets were holding steady or growing—despite the unfolding housing crisis in the United States. Oil prices were even. So it was clear that the collapse was a product of the war.[3] The market was falling in reverse proportion to Putin's soaring popularity. It was this that made Zhanna say *Budushchego net*—"There is no future here." This, and the fact that she and Raisa had lost all their money.

Zhanna and Raisa had been a two-person family unit for about six years. On the last day of 2001, that awful year when Zhanna moved to New York and then came home, there had been a phone call. Raisa picked up. The caller introduced herself as Katya Odintsova. Raisa knew who she was—a television personality from Nizhny Novgorod—and she knew what she looked like: long blond hair, long legs. She was about ten years younger than Raisa.

"Do you know?" asked the caller.

"Know what?"

"I have a child with your husband, and I am expecting another."

"So?" asked Raisa.

"So, something must be done."

"Then I suppose you should do something," said Raisa, and hung up. Then she called Zhanna on her cell phone. Raisa was not sure what to do. In her generation and her social circles—among both the slightly bohemian intellectuals of Nizhny Novgorod and the powerful and the rich of Moscow—marriage did not necessarily carry the assumption of fidelity, especially on the part of the men, but indiscretions were supposed to be discreet. The phone call, the fact that there was a first-grader in Nizhny Novgorod who looked like her husband, and the unavoidable conclusion that Boris had been having a relationship for years—all of this broke the unspoken compact. Still, Raisa was proud that she had kept her cool during the phone conversation.

Zhanna, who was seventeen, saw no valor in her mother's reserve, and no two ways to interpret the situation. She rushed directly to her father's office at parliament, barged in, and told him everything she thought of him and his behavior. After she left his office, she realized that she could not remember what she had said, but it had definitely been angry and she had certainly been right. She told her mother to get a divorce. Both of her parents thought it was a bit too radical a step—her father had no desire to go live with the mother of his other children—but Zhanna had words of principle and conviction where her parents had uncertainty and indecision, so she won.

They separated, though they did not bother legally getting divorced, and her father moved into a rental apartment. He left them the large flat on the Garden Ring and a sum of money. Now this money, which Zhanna and Raisa managed together even after Zhanna got married, was gone. They did not even have the money to pay maintenance on the Garden Ring flat. The only possible solution was to rent it out, but with the economy in the state that it was, who would rent an opulent 185-square-meter four-bedroom apartment in the center of the city?

The answer, as it turned out, was someone who worked at a state bank. During the crisis, government banks took over failing smaller private banks. The process provided many opportunities for the well-positioned employee of a state bank: siphoning off funds was made that much easier by the bureaucratic mess of the takeovers and the panic that surrounded them. A state banker rented the apartment in January 2008 for $3,000 a month. Raisa moved back to Nizhny Novgorod. She and Zhanna split the money, and it was enough for each of them for the time being.

Zhanna had learned a lesson: there was no future here. She was not thinking much about the politics of it—the fact that it was the Kremlin that had sent the market tumbling both times—but she was thinking that hers was a country where this kind of thing would happen again and again. She insisted on selling the apartment once it regained its value. That happened in 2010. Boris—who, unlike Zhanna, was very much talking about the politics of it but still insisted that Russia had a future—tried to convince Zhanna to buy a new place in Moscow. She would not hear of it. She held on to the money until she saw an opportunity: as the Eurozone crisis unfolded, Zhanna dispatched Raisa to explore Greece, Spain, and Italy. Then they both traveled to a village on Lake Garda in Italy, where Boris was on vacation. They decided to invest there. In 2013, Zhanna and Raisa invested the money from the large Garden Ring apartment in a smaller one in the lakeside village. Zhanna started studying Italian—this was an investment in her future. Before she learned much, during the first summer she and Raisa spent on Lake Garda, their electricity was shut off because they had not understood the notices. The next-door neighbor came to the rescue, light was restored, and Zhanna and the neighbor became fast friends. Zhanna imagined that someday she might live here. In any case, she and Raisa would be spending their summers here for years to come—this was Zhanna's permanence, her future, even if she continued to work in Moscow.

Other things, besides the Garden Ring flat, ended in 2010 too. Zhanna and Dmitry divorced. She had seen her husband lose interest in other people—his friends and her friends—and go from present to absent like a switch had been flipped. Then she saw his absence happen with her, and she probably should not have waited for him to tell her. But once he did, she moved out that very day. She went to stay at a minihotel—really, a rental room in a converted apartment on a pedestrian street a block from the parliament building where her father no longer worked.

Boris was now a full-time political activist. After he lost office in 2004, everyone, including him, thought that he could have a lucrative career in GR—government relations. He knew everyone, after all, and everyone knew how important it was to know people. The bureaucracy was becoming more powerful by the year, regulations were changing constantly, and someone who could navigate the opaque structures of the Russian government could save a business. Boris took a job as a GR specialist at a bank. But GR required more diplomacy than he could muster. He stuck it out for a year, made a little money, bought his duplex overlooking the Kremlin, and quit.

He teamed up with Kasparov and other people, most of them unknown to the media and the public. In 2008 they cofounded an organization and called it Solidarity, in honor of the Polish anti-Communist resistance from the 1980s. His friends made fun of him. They were men who used to be called oligarchs. Now, under Putin, they had forfeited their political power, and they held themselves up as exemplars of the art and wisdom of compromise. Strategic concessions could save one from landing in jail like Khodorkovsky, or in exile, stripped of your assets. You ceded some access or assets to those whom Putin wanted to advance, gave up a little to retain a lot. If you were smart, these deals were cut in subtle ways, negotiated in indirect language—and the effort enabled Boris's friends to feel clever while yielding to the stronger party. What Boris was doing was precisely the opposite: unsubtle and reckless. They made fun of him for his earnestness and na-iveté. He laughed along, heartily, because, Zhanna knew, he did not want to appear either naive or earnest.

In October 2009, Boris turned fifty. He put Zhanna in charge of organizing the party. He liked delegating. She liked being put in charge. She rented a restaurant with beige walls, white tablecloths, and plush gray chairs. It looked out on the green lawn of a golf club, like this was not Moscow at all. About 150 people came, the rich and the beautiful crowd. A well-known television journalist, Pavel Sheremet, made a half-hour film called *Nemtsov: An Accounting*. The title was a takeoff on Boris's latest occupation: he had started compiling and publishing reports. His first one, printed in February 2008, as Putin was winding down his second presidential term, had been called *Putin: An Accounting*. The slim booklet consisted of nine chapters:

> Corruption Is Eroding Russia
> The Military, Forsaken
> Roads in Disrepair
> Russia Is Dying [on depopulation]
> The Pension System in Crisis
> Corrupt Justice
> Stomping on the Constitution [on the elimination of elections and
>   of Russia's federal structure]
> The Failure of "National Projects"
> Everyone Is an Enemy, Except China[4]

The report did not break new ground—most of what it contained had been reported by other people—but taken together, the information added up to a damning picture strikingly different from the Kremlin's triumphant reports and from the popular picture of a stronger, healthier, wealthier Russia.

Boris's next report was called *Luzhkov: An Accounting*. It detailed the activities of Moscow mayor Yuri Luzhkov, who had turned the megalopolis into a fiefdom. Boris and Solidarity activists handed out the reports near Metro stations. Often they would set up a folding table and Boris would autograph books, writing dedications in sprawling script and basking in the brief moments of the familiar adoration of a crowd.

Footage of these signing sessions was in the film, as was footage of Boris walking down streets, Boris showing off his athletic prowess—using an elliptical machine in the exercise room in his apartment overlooking the Kremlin, kite-surfing on an unidentified ocean, and using the pull-up bar at a country house. The house was where his current girlfriend, Irina, was living with his youngest daughter, Sonya. The film showed all the children—there were now four—but omitted the fact that they had three different mothers. The narrator said, "He has a large family, in a good way." At the end, the narrator reneged on the title of the film. It was too early for an accounting, he said. Boris might become president of Russia yet, perhaps in the year 2025.[5]

Boris's rich and powerful friends praised him in the film: he was fun, he was brave, he was honest. They came to the party too. Then, having paid homage that they might have thought of as their debt of friendship, they faded away. Only one of the wealthy—metals mogul Mikhail Prokhorov—came to Boris's fifty-first birthday party, in 2010. Truth be told, these men had been coming around less and less since Boris left his GR job and became a full-time activist in 2005. The fiftieth birthday had been their last and finest effort. Even Mikhail Fridman, the oligarch who used to have tea in the Garden Ring flat's kitchen several times a week—the one who told Zhanna she was crazy when she came home from New York in 2001, because "there is no future here"—had long ago told Boris that being associated with him was "toxic" for his business. No one, he said, would ever believe that he was not the one bankrolling those "accounting" reports.[6]

Zhanna noticed that her father was more comfortable with the activists than he had ever been with the oligarchs. His old friends carried themselves like they owned the world; his new allies managed to look shy and ready for battle at the same time. They wore cheap clothes and always looked slightly disheveled. One worked with severely autistic children. Another was a scientist who had been on the barricades continuously since the late 1980s. Then there was a crowd of skinny young men with spectacles and terrible haircuts. Boris had endless patience for phone calls with them, for detailed and repetitive planning of protests, to which only they showed up. At some point Zhanna understood that what she thought was patience was, in fact, desire. Boris enjoyed the phone calls, the planning, and the tiny, isolated protests. The process of planning and discussion—the same process that she remembered from the political discussions in their Nizhny Novgorod kitchen before Boris became a politician, and the physics discussions that preceded them—engaged and sustained him more fully than did kite-surfing and excellent wine.

ON DECEMBER 31, 2010, Zhanna went to a protest with her father. For a year and a half now, activists had been gathering at Triumfalnaya Square in central Moscow on the thirty-first day of every month that had thirty-one days. They gathered to demand observance of Article 31 of the Russian Constitution, which guaranteed freedom of assembly. Sometimes they got roughed up, sometimes they were detained for several hours. But recently the police had seemed to let up a bit—perhaps because the previous New Year's Eve they had managed to hurt Ludmila Alekseeva, at eighty-two Russia's oldest and best-known activist. This New Year's, the city even issued a permit for the protest, ensuring that it would be calm and uneventful. Alekseeva was planning to come again, wearing a New Year's costume: she would be dressed as Snegurochka.* It was practically going to be a party.

---

*The Snow Maiden, granddaughter of Ded Moroz, Grandfather Frost, the secular alternative to Santa Claus that had been rolled over from Soviet tradition.

Boris suggested that they go together and then continue to Irina's house in the country, the one where he had been filmed flipping his body over the pull-up bar, for a New Year's celebration. Zhanna put a long puffer coat on over a dress and heels, and so did Angelica, a new friend, an insurance company employee, also newly single, and they went to Triumfalnaya Square.

"Everyone was acting like it really was a party," Boris wrote in his blog later.

Speakers wore red hats, and Alekseeva was in full Snegurochka glory, in a shiny blue embroidered long coat that looked like it weighed more than she did. Her voice shaky, she spoke for only a couple of minutes:

> If you think about it, all our constitutional rights have been taken away, with one exception: the right to leave the country and return. . . .
>
> That is why it is so important to stand up for Article 31 of the Constitution. That is why it is so important that for the second time in a row we are able to assemble here, in Triumfalnaya Square, undisturbed.
>
> This has been accomplished by those who have been coming here stubbornly on the thirty-first of the month, even though they knew that the riot police were waiting for them here.[7]

This time there were no riot police—only a couple hundred protesters and a few dozen police who looked bored and peaceful. Minutes after Alekseeva left, most of the participants were still milling around, chatting in that way people do when they want to make an event feel more substantial than it has seemed. The riot police appeared out of nowhere, and charged the crowd. Zhanna grabbed Angelica's hand and they ran—first just a few yards, to hide behind a kiosk, and then, after Zhanna peeked around it and saw the police tackling people to the ground and dragging them into prisoner transports, they ran like they did not know they could run. They covered a kilometer and a half—the distance to the next Metro station—in five minutes. How had they managed this, in heels?

They took the Metro back to Zhanna's new temporary rental apartment. Zhanna called Irina to tell her that Boris had been detained and they would not be coming. It turned out that Dmitry, Zhanna's ex-husband, was there at the party, with his new girlfriend. Irina had apparently planned some sort of grand family reunion. Now Zhanna was relieved that she was ringing in the New Year lying on her bed, watching the news on television to see if they would report on the protest. They did not.

Boris rang in the New Year in solitary. After two days, he managed to smuggle out a handwritten note:

> The cell is a concrete box about 1.5 meters [5 feet] wide and 3 meters [9 feet] long. It has no windows, no bed or mattress. It's just a concrete floor, and nothing else.
>
> I have been charged, absurdly, under Article 19.3 of the Administrative Code, for supposedly disobeying police orders. It carries a maximum sentence of 15 days in jail. . . .
>
> The authorities have a problem, though: there is a video recording of my arrest, in which you can see the police doing as they wish, ignoring everything: the law, the holiday, and the fact that we had a permit for the protest. I know that they are just trying to scare us. They are trying to scare the opposition, and my family. This was the first time my daughter Zhanna had joined the protest, and that makes me very proud.
>
> I know that the regime is scared. It's furious, and it doesn't know what to do with the opposition. It's scared, it's flailing, and it's bringing shame to itself and to Russia. We have no right to give up now. We will not give up.
>
> Happy New Year, my friends!

Boris was brought to court on January 3. Everyone in Russia was on vacation—it was the dead week between New Year's and Orthodox Christmas, when everything, including the stock exchanges and all banks, shut down—but one judge, a woman about Zhanna's age, had to come to work. Zhanna came, of course, and Angelica came too, even though the experience of it all, and now the sight of activists sitting on the floor in the hallway—chairs had been removed to discourage their presence—was unlike anything Angelica could imagine, even now that she was witnessing it. There seemed to be a general chair crisis in the courthouse: there was only one chair at the defense table, and Boris, who had spent three days inside the concrete cube, now spent four hours standing up, because his defense attorney was elderly and entitled to sit. The judge called more than a dozen witnesses and ignored their answers, and then read out her sentence, speaking so fast and so softly that no one could understand. Boris got fifteen days' jail time.

Zhanna went home to cook for her father. She wanted to spoil him, so she made the fanciest dish she could imagine: chicken sautéed with prunes. But when she brought it to the detention center the next day and an oddly friendly starstruck policeman brought her father down to the lobby to hang out with her, Boris confessed that jail made him want simple stuff: peasant food—meat and potatoes—and junk-food sweets from the Soviet era.

When his sentence was over, Zhanna came to get Boris, bringing with her a change of clothes, and they went directly out to dinner. She listened to his stories about jail. He had spent two weeks in a cell with five other men, three of them violent offenders with long sentences and two who had been picked up for misdemeanors. He had turned all of them on to politics.[8] He was laughing now, reveling in his new hero status. Zhanna told him that she was no hero. She was never going to go to another protest as long as she lived. She would still support his work, of course. She said that from now on she would pay to have his reports published.

When they walked out of the café, a couple of young men charged Boris and tried to catch him in a large scoop-net, the kind used for fishing. Boris twisted around and managed to push one of the attackers away. This sort of thing had been happening for at least three years. Back in 2007, in the Siberian city of Krasnoyarsk, Boris had turned the weapon against his attacker, a skinny, pimply kid who confessed that he had flown all the way from Moscow to try to humiliate the politician. He would not, however, admit to being a member of one of the Kremlin's youth movements.[9] In 2010, in Sochi, three young men threw ammonia in his face. In 2011—a few months after the fishing net—it happened again: a toilet was thrown over the fence onto the roof of his car in Moscow. The police came out but refused to write it up.[10] Zhanna never would have imagined that her father could keep his cool the way he did.

MASHA SAID *budushchego net* in Moscow, when she left a child neurologist's office. Sasha was four years old, and he was not talking. He had had evaluations, brain scans, and all sorts of tests that involved attaching wires to his blond head and all over his tiny body. The doctors said that his brain did not look good. They said they saw fluid, and the parts that should be small looked large and ones that ought to be large were small. Masha sort of believed them, because it was a fact that Sasha was not talking and this was the reason she had brought him in for tests in the first place. At the same time, she did not believe them. Her son was not just her baby: he was her friend. They did things together, like swim in the pool, and when she asked him for something, he was always happy to do it—even when she jokingly asked him to get her a drink from the open bar at an all-inclusive resort in Turkey. She told everybody about it, not just because it was funny but because it definitively proved that there was nothing wrong with her son's brain. So, mostly, she did not believe the doctors.

And now, this famous child neurologist, whom she had spent months trying to get in to see and whom she was terrified of seeing, leafed through Sasha's chart, full of damning test results and specialists' opinions, examined Sasha, and said, "There is nothing wrong with your child." Then she said, "You are doing everything right. Just keep doing what you are doing. And lose this chart." She handed the thick binder back to Masha.

Masha understood perfectly well what the doctor meant. The pile of diagnoses that had been heaped on Sasha meant that he would never be accepted to a regular school. If Masha did not want him shunted to the mentally disabled track, she had to shred his medical records, bribe someone to make him a pristine but believable new chart, and then make sure that by the time he was about to enter first grade, he was speaking like any other six-and-a-half-year-old.

Or maybe she said *budushchego net* a bit later, when Sergei made it clear that he had not signed up for this. A four-year-old kid who could not speak, with all the questions this brought forth from others, and all the exercises and activities that Masha was fishing out of the Internet that were supposedly going to fix this broken boy—Sergei could not take it anymore. He had another woman, and he was going to go live with her now.

Maybe that was not actually when Masha said *budushchego net*. Maybe that was when she said, "Fine. Alimony." She had a very large sum of money saved up—upward of $100,000—and between that safety net and alimony, she could afford to quit her job and start graduate school in pedagogy. She had a plan: she would become a teacher at a good school. That way Sasha could study there too. Her workday would be short, allowing her to give Sasha the attention he needed.

Over the course of the 2010–2011 school year, Sasha learned to speak, but Masha learned almost nothing—except that Moscow was not the place to learn to work with children, even though she was about to be awarded a degree in this area. Other things she did not see happening in Moscow or in Russia: a new husband—she was nearly twenty-seven and had a child, so this was a foregone conclusion—and a good education for Sasha. She devised a plan that Tatiana would have approved, which was probably one reason it felt self-evident. She would go to Oxford to study educational psychology. Then she would become a science teacher in England. But even before that, Sasha would be in the environment he needed in order to develop. She would be in such an environment too—one where a mother like Masha could ask for help instead of having to falsify her child's medical chart to give him a shot at a future. She took all the required tests, and she placed Sasha in an English-language preschool program: he was speaking well enough now that he could start learning a second language.

Sergei said no. He would not sign the papers to allow her to take Sasha out of the country. That was when she thought, *Budushchego net*. There is no future.

sixteen

WHITE RIBBONS

MASHA HAD NOT BEEN ALONE in her plan to emigrate. A friend set her
sights on Humboldt University in Berlin at the same time. Another friend
followed Masha's lead—to be more precise, Masha talked her into applying
to Oxford. In May 2011, the first friend left for Germany and the second for
England. Masha had one other close friend, but they had a falling-out.
When Masha took an accounting of her larger circle of acquaintances, she
realized that most of them had left earlier, for graduate or postgradute
studies at the famous or not-so-famous universities of the West. Even her
ex-husband, Sergei, had done graduate work in America. Now he relented—
partly—and told Masha that he would agree to her going abroad to study,
and taking Sasha with her, as long as it was temporary. Masha signed up for
a sociology summer school in Malta. The school was interesting, the island
country was tiny and crowded, and the military planes overhead, on their
way to drop bombs on Libya day after day, reminded Masha that there was
a big world out there, full of politics, people, and passion—while she had to
return to Moscow at the end of the summer. She had no idea what she was
going to do there. The only thing she knew was that she would not go back
to working as a broker of kickbacks and bribes.

In September, she tried becoming a housewife—a single mother could be one too. Her job was ferrying Sasha to karate, drawing, and violin lessons and the English-language preschool. At karate and drawing the other mothers could spend hours discussing the best container in which to pack lunch for their husbands. At violin, Masha waited alone. The mothers at the English-language preschool were more interesting—several of them were journalists—but the most they would do was chat over a croissant and cappuccino before either disappearing into their laptops or taking off for work, leaving their children for the nannies to collect.

On September 25, the preschool mothers were outraged. The previous afternoon, Putin and Medvedev had made a joint announcement: at the next election, scheduled for March 2012, Medvedev would hand the presidency back to Putin and return to his post as prime minister. "Can you believe this?" the mothers asked one another. "They don't even try to keep up appearances anymore." They meant the appearance of an election. Masha was not exactly shocked. She was devastated. All she could think was, Now everyone is going to leave the country. Every last person.

In the evenings, after Sasha was asleep, Masha hung out with her two closest friends, at Humboldt and Oxford—by Skype. They opened bottles of wine in parallel in front of their web cameras. Masha's friends did their academic work; Masha roamed the Internet.

This was how she learned of the case of Vladimir Makarov. It seemed unbelievable at first. After she read all she could read about it, she knew it was true, but she still found it incomprehensible. In fact, she knew she would never be able to understand it. An innocent man was going to prison for years on charges of molesting his own daughter.

VLADIMIR MAKAROV was a young civil servant. He had moved to Moscow in 2009 to take a job at the transportation ministry. His wife and young daughter joined him once he had fixed up a rental apartment. In the summer of 2010, Makarov's seven-year-old daughter fell off a home climbing wall, fracturing a vertebra. A lab technician thought she saw traces of sperm in the girl's urine sample when she was brought to the hospital by ambulance. A nurse reported it. Later tests of the same sample failed to confirm the results, a physical exam produced no evidence of sexual abuse, and neither the little girl nor her mother nor anyone else gave any testimony that could be interpreted as confirming the charge against Makarov. Nonetheless, he was jailed, held in pretrial detention for a year, and sentenced to thirteen years behind bars for raping his own daughter.[1]

He appealed, and on November 29, 2011, Moscow City Court downgraded the charge from rape to indecent assault and reduced his sentence to five and a half years.[2] This was probably the worst moment in the whole awful story: by removing the rape charge, the court was disavowing the only basis for the entire case—the supposed finding of traces of sperm in the girl's urine. And still this man, who had done nothing wrong and had already spent a year in jail, would be staying in prison for four more. Why?

Because. Ella Paneyakh, an American-educated Russian sociologist who had for years been studying law enforcement, wrote a piece she titled "And Now the Most Frightening Thing of All Has Happened." It began, "And as is its habit, disaster struck where we least expected it." Paneyakh used the term "the Red Wheel" to refer to the force that had plowed Makarov down. *The Red Wheel* was the title of a trilogy by Alexander Solzhenitsyn, in which he described the destruction of the Russian state by the First World War and the Bolshevik Revolution. Paneyakh used the term to refer to Russian law enforcement. Her point was that it, too, was an inexorable disaster.

> It has forgotten what it's like to encounter resistance. It lacks a built-in function for compromise, retreat, even for saying something like "released upon a closer examination of the evidence." All the mechanisms that could have been employed for this purpose have long since rusted out for disuse. In fact, the machine's only possible response to resistance is a crackdown.[3]

Makarov was doomed as soon as he was first suspected, falsely, of having sexually abused his daughter. His attempts to fight the charges—he asked for further tests, mounted a thorough defense, and then appealed his sentence—only made the law-enforcement machine pursue him harder.

This was not a new mechanism. Law enforcement and the courts had functioned this way for a long time—in fact, they had functioned this way in the Soviet era, and the system was never dismantled, only temporarily weakened in the 1990s. But for most of the post-Soviet period, the punitive force had been applied almost exclusively to a few clearly defined groups of people: entrepreneurs engaged in property disputes, select politicians (who were also, more often than not, entrepreneurs engaged in property disputes), and radical political activists. In other words, people risked being crushed by the Red Wheel only after they ventured into the public realm. What had changed now, wrote Paneyakh, was that "the state has once again found the time, means, and energy to insert its tentacles into a person's private life—a lot deeper than the average person . . . is prepared to let it." The process had been under way for some time, but most Russians had not noticed—in part because they had grown accustomed to feeling separate from the state.

While they were not paying attention, the state had begun regulating what people ate and drank, often introducing seemingly arbitrary rules for political reasons, like when it had banned wine imports from Georgia or sprats from Latvia. The regulating agency invariably justified its decisions by the need to protect the population from potentially dangerous products.

The parliament had been discussing restricting abortion. It had hardened drug laws to the point where pain relief had become virtually inaccessible, even for people with documented severe pain. Roughly half of more than a million inmates of Russian prisons were serving time for drug offenses, because even a minuscule amount could land one behind bars. As new laws piled up, political discussion, such as it was, centered on the need to protect children: from drugs, from abortions, and, perhaps most important, from pedophiles. Masha could not remember when she had first heard about the pedophile menace—it seemed like background noise that had always been there.

▬▬▬▬▬

LYOSHA HAD BEEN WATCHING for years as the idea of the pedophile threat took shape. He had written about it in his undergraduate thesis. Prominent Perm factory owner and politician Igor Pastukhov, a United Russia member, was first accused of raping a sixteen-year-old boy in 2003. Soon after, the charges were dropped and the politician's accuser seemed to vanish. But a second teenager came forward in 2005. Rumor in Perm had it that another powerful local businessman had manufactured the case to discredit Pastukhov. But Lyosha met young men who told him that it had happened to them too: Pastukhov's people were in the habit of hunting down very young men in and around cruising areas and either luring or, if that failed, forcing them into cars and delivering them to Pastukhov and his friends, who raped them.

When Pastukhov faced trial, Perm newspaper headlines were: "Perm Has Been Overtaken by the Gay Lobby"; "Faggots Think They Are Above the Law"; and "Administration Had Better Straighten Its Orientation." What little evidence was presented at the trial was circumstantial, and Pastukhov's accuser was never identified. Pastukhov was sentenced to six years' imprisonment.[4] Lyosha struggled with the Pastukhov story in his thesis. On the one hand, the trial was a travesty. On the other, Lyosha was convinced that Pastukhov was guilty of just these sorts of crimes. Then there was the problem of the media coverage, which equated pedophilia and sexual violence with homosexuality. Later, Lyosha learned how to separate these facts and ideas from one another. The Russian courts listened to the prosecutor and accepted thin evidence, bad evidence, or no evidence at all, but this did not mean that everyone they sentenced was innocent—it just meant that no one, including the guilty, ever got a fair trial. In this case, the fact that charges against Pastukhov involved same-sex contact was what had excited the media: similar violence perpetrated against girls and young women was more likely to be seen as a normal attribute of power. For example, a Pskov bank owner and politician, Igor Provkin, was accused of rape by several different young women over the course of six years. He finally faced charges after he lured a young woman into his car in central Moscow and raped her right there. He confessed and was given a suspended sentence of four years. The case drew scant media attention.[5]

By 2008, the year after Lyosha defended his thesis, the pedophile menace was becoming a commonplace of public rhetoric. Dugin called for Russian men to kill pedophiles on sight. In St. Petersburg, a retired boxer, Alexander Kuznetsov, faced charges for killing a nineteen-year-old man whom he said he had caught trying to rape his eight-year-old stepson. No evidence of the attempted rape was ever produced, but the boxer—who, despite a long arrest record, was not placed in pretrial detention—became an instant celebrity. "It is hard for him to walk down the street in Petersburg," reported *Izvestia*. "People stop him to shake his hand and ask for an autograph."[6] Dugin told journalists that he supported Kuznetsov. "He stood up for his child," he said. "I believe that all Russians, all normal people should act in that exact way. If you see a crime like this happening, you should intervene. And if there is a way to kill the lowlife, then it is necessary to kill and then sort it out later. That's the only way we can change public opinion, the only way to get lawmakers to respond."[7] The headline of the article in which Dugin was quoted was, "What Is to Be Done with Pedophiles: The Death Penalty or Castration?" Such were apparently the terms of the proposed debate—and the debate was framed in a way familiar from the Soviet era, when "concerned members of society" demanded restrictive measures against particular groups or individuals (such as members of the worldwide Zionist conspiracy, or the writer Boris Pasternak) and the state apparatus obliged.

Kuznetsov served just over a year behind bars.[8] By the time he was released in 2010, the debate was raging. A group of parliament members filed a bill that would increase penalties for sexual crimes against children. The bill was so hastily drafted that different passages specified different new penalties for the same crimes.[9] This delayed the bill, prompting the chairwoman of the parliamentary Committee on the Family, Yelena Mizulina, to accuse United Russia of harboring a "pedophile lobby." Mizulina herself was a member of A Just Russia, the latest party created by the Kremlin to imitate a populist electoral alternative. United Russia countered that the latest political pedophilia scandal had concerned an A Just Russia member (this was the case of a parliament member's assistant in the city of Volgograd who managed to escape from police who were arresting him). Whichever party was speaking—and whichever party it was blaming—a consensus emerged in parliament: they had in their ranks a "pedophile lobby" that was sabotaging the protection of children. A parliament member from the Communist Party lamented that many of her colleagues had been ensnared by a "secret powerful pervert organization."[10]

The pedophilia accusation became a potent weapon of political warfare. While parliament members were hurling accusations at one another, political scientist Andreas Umland discovered that Russian and Ukrainian media were reporting that he had been charged with sex offenses against children. The reports were full of details about Umland's legal troubles, all of them imaginary. Umland traced the original report to a Russian online news agency, which, in turn, could be traced to IP addresses used by Dugin and his Eurasian Movement.[11]

Dugin's media had been attacking Umland since he wrote his Oxford dissertation, in which he compared Dugin's movement to Nazism. "Most liberal sociologists in Germany are homosexuals," reported one of the articles on Umland. "And as we know, sixty percent of them are infected with HIV. So the question arises: Why are homosexuals with AIDS telling us what's right and what's wrong?"[12] A follow-up piece claimed that "Umland, who has pedophile proclivities, has been fired from Stanford, Harvard, and Oxford for making homosexual advances to his colleagues."[13]

In the Russian parliament the crusading members never managed to clear up the textual contradictions in their bill, so the Kremlin introduced its own. Legislation increasing penalties for sex offenders was passed in the fall of 2011.[14] Repeat offenders would now face life imprisonment—the maximum penalty possible in Russia for any crime—but the crusaders were not satisfied and continued to insist on chemical castration. The new law introduced a new concept: that of a person afflicted with pedophilia. A defendant diagnosed with pedophilia was now subject to compulsory psychiatric treatment. Psychiatrists had to be trained to diagnose "pedophilic sexual orientation."[15] Letters went out to every psychiatric clinic in the land.[16] Large psychiatric hospitals dispatched doctors for training sessions in Moscow at the Serbsky Center for Social and Court Psychiatry, once infamous as the place where Soviet dissidents were sent for punitive treatment. Participants in Serbsky seminars were taught that perversions were often diagnosed together—for example, pedophilia frequently went with homosexuality.[17]

Even while the parliament was debating new anti-pedophile measures, the police redoubled their efforts. In July 2011, the minister of the interior reported that law enforcement was pursuing 128 different cases of online distribution of pornographic images of minors, that this was just for the first three months of the year and the number represented a 20 percent increase over the year before.

Activist citizens began looking for pedophiles too. A twenty-one-year-old college dropout in Voronezh devoted herself to the hunt full-time. Anna Levchenko claimed to have identified the names and IP addresses of eighty pedophiles in the space of six months. "The number of sex offenses against children has nearly doubled in the last year," declared her livejournal.com page. A manifesto full of boldfaced emphasis followed.

> Pedophiles are afraid of nothing and no one. . . . They are everywhere. **They are united. There are hundreds of thousands of them. . . .** They have cast their nets over the entire world. **They challenge our entire society and they are laughing at us.** They are trying to tell us that **no one will ever be able to protect our children from them.** I will prove them wrong. If law enforcement can't deal with it, then society itself must rise up in defense of the children. I identify pedophiles on the Internet and collect evidence against them. **I make sure that criminal charges are filed.** I work with a group of like-minded

people. We write dozens of reports **every week**. Thousands of people read my blog every day. We need your help, too. You can join our team and help us catch those who are killing our children. . . . Only if we unite our efforts will we be able to defeat this threat. Any support you can lend will help us save hundreds of children's lives and prevent new crimes.[18]

Levchenko developed her own entrapment techniques and then trained other young people to use them. She attended the Kremlin youth training camp at Lake Seligher in the summer of 2011 and was granted an audience with Medvedev so that she could tell him about her work. She informed the president that her movement included three hundred volunteers. Medvedev praised Levchenko's efforts and suggested incorporating her group into the Investigative Committee—the federation's central anti-crime unit—by creating a special anti-pedophile project there. The president's children's rights ombudsman, Pavel Astakhov, perhaps fearful of being left out of the loop, immediately offered Levchenko an assistant position, albeit an unsalaried one.[19]

It was in this context that the Makarov case was unfolding.

SERYOZHA WAS NOT SURE when he first heard about the case—it was fairly soon after he moved back to Moscow from Kiev in 2010—but at some point he became obsessed with it. There was no other word for it. He had to know everything. He read every article about the case several times over, to make sure he grasped every detail. This was how he started reading *Novaya gazeta*, a Moscow weekly that specialized in human rights issues and investigative stories. Several of the paper's reporters had been killed—including Anna Politkovskaya, who had been covering Chechnya for the paper—but though he had heard of Politkovskaya's murder, the existence of the paper had not registered with Seryozha until now. He joined an online community called the Makarov Case, downloaded every document that other members made available, and wrote detailed commentary. It did not take long to understand that the charges were bogus, but Seryozha still felt that the documents could shed light on something. There was a genetic study, done by a scientist who had taken part in identifying the remains of the czar's family—that had to count for something, right? The forensic geneticist's conclusion was that there was nothing in the urine sample that indicated sexual contact. The study was not admitted into evidence. In the end the only expert opinion acknowledged by the court came from a young psychologist who had asked the alleged victim to draw a nonexistent animal—a common task in psychological screening tests—and then concluded that the drawing, of a black cat with a disproportionately large and bushy tail, suggested that the girl had been molested.

Seryozha learned what he could about Makarov's family. They were good people. They loved each other and their daughter. Makarov spent more time with his daughter than a typical Russian father. Somehow, this made it feel even more tragic. Seryozha had not seen that many families who seemed simply, intuitively happy, and this one was being destroyed. And the little girl, the girl all the prosecutors and police and the psychologist were supposedly trying to protect—she was being destroyed too.

Once he started reading *Novaya gazeta*, Seryozha became aware that this case was not unusual. The paper was publishing a lot of articles about Sergei Magnitsky, an accountant who had been tortured to death in a Moscow jail in 2009. His former employer, an American-British financier, was running his own investigation, which was making it clear that Magnitsky had inadvertently stepped on the toes of high-powered officials who were embezzling state money. For this, he had been jailed and killed. It was a wrenching story, but it made at least some sense: Magnitsky had stood between men and money. Makarov had not been in anyone's way. His life and his family were being destroyed just because hospital workers had been instructed to be on the lookout for pedophiles, and because, once set in motion, the Red Wheel could not stop, and just because. Seryozha felt exactly like he had when he saw Lars von Trier's film *Dancer in the Dark*, in which a helpless woman is falsely accused of a crime and executed. The movie had left Seryozha physically sick for days. The Makarov case was happening in real life. There had to be a way to do something. Right?

ONE OF THE MEMBERS of the online Makarov Case community wrote that three people were needed to put in a request for a protest. Masha called him—it had taken a bit of investigative work to get hold of his number. She wanted to volunteer her name and her time. It was now late November, she had been a single-mother housewife for nearly three months, and she had to find another way to live. She had hired a nanny and was going to start looking for work, but for now, she could be useful at a protest—even if she and everyone else knew that protest was futile.

That man never followed through on the protest idea. Makarov received his final sentence—five and a half years—on November 29. A week later an old acquaintance, someone who had been involved with the protest youth group Oborona back when Masha wanted to get involved but Sergei said no, called to invite Masha to a protest. It was about the elections rather than the Makarov case, but Masha went.

The parliamentary elections had taken place the day before. It was the usual setup with four parties: Putin's United Russia, the Kremlin's puppet populists A Just Russia, the Communists, and the Liberal Democratic Party. In parliament the Communists and the so-called Liberal Democrats reliably voted with United Russia while A Just Russia, too small to change any outcome, was occasionally critical of the Kremlin—as it was, for example, in the ongoing campaign to protect children from the imaginary pedophile lobby. Any criticism was better than no criticism, and many of the people whose blogs Masha was reading had voted for A Just Russia. By official count, A Just Russia got just over 13 percent of the vote, or 64 out of the 450 seats in parliament. United Russia would continue to hold more than half the seats, though not quite as many as it had had in the previous parliament.[20]

The point was not so much the outcome of the election, which had the usual suspects seated in the usual proportions, as this very predictability.

The Kremlin did not allow any strangers on the ballot, so the election did not need to be fixed. And still it was fixed. Ballot boxes were stuffed, numbers were doctored, phantom precincts reported, and conscripts were bused in to vote early and often. Not that it even mattered who got into parliament, which existed only to rubber-stamp the Kremlin's policies. But the bad theater of it all, in which you were invited up onstage for a millisecond and not allowed to open your mouth, was insulting. The parliamentary election was also a preview of the election scheduled for March 2012, which would rubber-stamp the reversion of the presidency to Putin.

Masha dressed nicely for the demonstration. This was the first social occasion after three months of her single-mother housewifedom, so she put on heels. It was raining, and the ground in the park where the protest was held quickly turned to gross black mush under thousands of pairs of feet. Masha's heels were sinking. She found herself standing with a group of women wearing fur coats. Maybe they had thought it would be colder and they would stand here, chanting—or whatever people did at these things—for hours. Or maybe they had also dressed up. Whatever, it was now raining on their fur coats. No one was chanting. There were speakers, but they could not hear or see them.

"Do you know what we are supposed to be doing?" asked Masha.

"No idea. This is our first time too," answered the wet fur coats.

Now there was a speaker who was finally loud enough. It was Alexei Navalny. Masha had been reading his blog. He wrote about corruption. Many people did, including Nemtsov, but Navalny had a trick. He dug through publicly available information to expose, repeatedly, exactly two shocking kinds of transactions: the absurd amounts the Russian government spent on the simplest and cheapest things—like, say, toilets; and the real estate and cars that Russian officials owned that they could never afford to buy on their official salary. Masha knew perfectly well how this worked, since until recently she had been a link in the corruption supply chain, but she could not get enough of the blog. Sometimes, though, it made her feel two opposing emotions at the same time: outrage, because this was her tax money that Navalny was talking about, and shame, because the system he was describing had included her. He called this system, the one that determined how Russia functioned, the "Party of Crooks and Thieves."

Navalny led the crowd in a chant of "One for all and all for one," or he tried to—only a couple of hundred seemed to pick it up, and it died down quickly. Then he shouted, "Let's march to Lubyanka!"

Lubyanka was the square, a fifteen-minute walk away, that had once held the giant monument to Dzerzhinsky and that still housed the headquarters of the FSB as well as the Central Election Commission. Masha was unsure which of those buildings was Navalny's intended destination, but she was certain that she did not want to march. Not in heels. Masha headed toward the Metro, but there were thousands walking in that direction—it would be worse than rush hour. She turned left, onto Myasnitskaya, the street that led to Lubyanka, and realized that she was now a part of Navalny's march. Rather, she was among the people who had intended to be part of the march. These people were being grabbed by riot police, thrown against walls, or tackled to the ground and then dragged along the wet street. Masha pressed her body into a building wall and crept along it to the next side street, then dived in.

There was a text from Anastasia, the friend who had invited Masha to the protest. She was at a café that happened to be at the end of this particular side street. Now Masha marched. She barged into the café, a low-key hipster joint of the kind she did not even know existed in Moscow.

"Where do I sign up to be an activist!" she announced. It was not a question. "Because what's going on out there is fucked!"

Anastasia said there was talk of another protest being planned for tomorrow, in Triumfalnaya Square.

"I'm going," said Masha, as if she were issuing a threat to Anastasia and her friends.

ZHANNA WATCHED THE PROTEST on television. She knew just how extraordinary this was. She was now working in television herself. When she first became a trader, she started watching RBK, a cable financial news channel. All the traders watched it. The people who worked there were financial geniuses. They could riff off the numbers live, for fifteen minutes on end, and it made Zhanna feel like they knew how the world worked. She wanted to be one of them. When she studied for her chartered financial analyst exam, it was with an eye to getting a job at RBK. She did. At first everyone was sure that she was there only because she was her father's daughter. She actually overheard one of the executives comment to another that stupid celebrity daughters are not known for passing CFA exams. After a few months, she was allowed to go on air live and riff off the numbers. It made her feel like a genius.

RBK was a financial news channel, but it was still part of the television world, and in this world showing protests on the air was unthinkable. But now there they were on Channel 1, the big state channel. Zhanna felt a pang: Why was she not there?

She knew why. That one experience of running away from the police while her father got arrested had been quite enough. Also, she wanted to get married. This had been Zhanna's goal ever since her divorce, and she pursued it as single-mindedly as she had pursued her job at RBK. She started seeing someone within weeks of the divorce, and it was this man that she intended to marry. She told him about this often, whenever she was not talking about having children together. He was impervious, and she was insistent. But also, he was the kind of man who wanted to be where they were at this moment, at a country club outside Moscow, with the television on, and he was the kind of man who would not take kindly to Zhanna's desire to drop everything to rush to the city to join the protest. Eyes on the prize, she chased the thought away.

Her father was there, in the cold rain. It was his organization, Solidarity, that had secured a permit for the protest—like it had for dozens of protests over the last five years. Those earlier ones had drawn a couple of hundred people—on the good days. So when they applied for a permit this time, anticipating two weeks ahead of time that the election would give reason to protest, they wrote that they expected three hundred people. They were being optimistic, despite the miserable weather and the December wind-down, which had already begun. By Boris's estimate, ten thousand people showed up. The police counted three thousand—still ten times as many as the permit said. One of the skinny bespectacled Solidarity activists, Igor Gukovsky, whose name was on the permit, was fined for the discrepancy and then also jailed for fifteen days for good measure. But his arrest drew little attention, even among the people who had come to the protest, because they had never heard of him. The best-known of the protesters, Navalny and Oborona leader Ilya Yashin, were also sent to jail for fifteen days, as were several dozen other people who had been arrested on Myasnitskaya Street. Altogether, the police had made about seven hundred arrests that night. Probably because the courts and holding facilities could not handle that many people at once, a majority were allowed to go home following a night spent in a standing-room-only cell.[21]

SERYOZHA READ about the planned protest on the *Novaya gazeta* website but could not go: he was on deadline for an app he was writing. Once he read about what had happened, though, he decided to go to Triumfalnaya the following day. The regime had to be called to order. Seryozha was a realist, and as a realist he recognized that a certain understanding had taken hold in Russia over the last dozen years. It was an understanding Seryozha's grandfather would not have liked, but it was there. Russians had agreed to live under a sort of dictatorship in exchange for stability. But they assumed that it was a soft dictatorship, which could negotiate if the need arose. Seryozha imagined that this was the way it worked in China, or at least this was how the papers made it look: the Communist Party had all the power, but if, say, peasants in some village rebelled, then the local bosses would be removed. Pressure and restrictions were a given, but the exact amounts could be adjusted. Right now, the pressure seemed excessive to Seryozha, and it looked to him like other people thought so too. The blatant election-fixing was insulting, and the Makarov case was just too painful to watch. So it was time for an adjustment. Seryozha imagined Putin saying, not in so many words, "All right, let's see what we can do here. What do you say I keep my billions and you keep your lives as you know them?" Then the state would pull back where it had overstepped. "Stability" would be a word for everyone just being left alone—everyone including Makarov and people who might suddenly find themselves in his shoes. This was what Seryozha wanted to communicate when he went to Triumfalnaya Square on December 6, 2011.

THERE WAS NO PERMIT for the protest at Triumfalnaya—permits had to be obtained two weeks in advance, with the observance of all sorts of byzantine procedures. This was just a protest staged by people reacting to what they had seen the evening before. These people seemed to fall into two categories: the diehards who had been roughed up and detained on numerous occasions and who simply felt it was their duty to respond publicly to injustice, and those who had no concept of permits and regulations. Between these two groups was a thin layer of well-informed occasional protesters who weighed their risks every time. They had seen others detained by police, or had been detained themselves, and knew that not having a permit meant that the police felt they had license to be as rough as they wanted to be. Which, after the protest and the attempted march the night before, would probably be very rough.

Neither Seryozha nor Masha knew anything about permits. But Masha had now been to one protest, and she felt she had learned a thing or two. When the police moved in, which seemed to happen instantly, she whipped out her iPhone and started shouting into it in English. The police must have taken her for a foreign correspondent or a tourist—they moved on. Masha ran into a nearby park, which had an American-style diner. One of the first such restaurants in the city, it had catered to expats in the 1990s. Masha ran into the diner and plopped onto the first empty seat she saw, in a booth with three young men who were also just pulling off their coats.

The police were not far behind. They started grabbing people from their seats. Masha repeated the trick that had worked minutes earlier: she turned to the table and started speaking English. The men readily picked up. After the police finished, leaving a dozen shiny red leatherette seats empty in their wake, the group switched back to Russian and did the introductions. Masha's new friends were all second-day protesters like she was. All three had been educated abroad—Stanford, MIT, and the London School of Economics. This was probably why they had known to seek refuge in the diner.

They did not know what they were supposed to do now. All pulled out their phones. Masha read on Twitter that Elena Kostyuchenko, a young openly lesbian *Novaya gazeta* journalist, had been detained. The tweet had the address of the detention center where she had been taken. Masha went. There she met a man named Ilya Ponomarev, who told her he was a parliament member from A Just Russia and a protest organizer. Then she met two young women who said they were members of a group she had never heard of. It was called Pussy Riot. Masha liked the name. Masha had been an activist for twenty-four hours, and her social circle had already quadrupled.

BORIS NEMTSOV HAD BEEN WILLING this moment to come for years, but who would have known that it would come now—or what to do with it now that it had happened? People he knew well and some whom he barely knew gathered together now, at the Solidarity office, and said that they would coordinate the protests. But they were not the only ones. A few blocks away, Ilya Ponomarev, the parliament member who had come out of nowhere, held a town-meeting-style gathering to discuss the protests. Groups were popping up on Facebook and VKontakte, with thousands of people expressing their desire to protest some more. The questions were, where, when, and how, exactly?

Virtually none of the new self-identified activists knew that the authorities had long ago placed extensive restrictions on protest. Some of them, like

Masha, had heard about the Marches of the Dissenters, but many more, like Seryozha, had not been paying attention at all. The permit system was just one example of the restrictions—the most pertinent one at this point. In Moscow, a permit could be obtained only within a specific time window, which in practice meant filing an application in the morning of the day twelve calendar days before the planned action. If you asked early, the application would be denied, and if you asked late, you would be told that someone already had dibs on your spot. This meant that activists had to arrive at city hall before daybreak, to ensure that they were physically the first people to walk through the door of the permits-issuing office several hours later, when the city opened for business. Then there would be negotiations with police. If the application was successful and a permit was issued, the police would erect cordons around a space large enough for the anticipated number of people and set up metal detectors at the entrance to this cordoned-off space. The organizers and the police negotiated the specifics of inspection: Would people be able to bring in plastic water bottles? What about placards on wooden planks? What about metal ones? If the applicants turned out to have underestimated the number of participants, they would face not only a fine but also problems in their relationship with the police, so important for the success of future applications.

The newbies did not know any of this and might not be prepared to understand this. They might also be unwilling to wait for a new application to go through—their desire to protest, which had come out of nowhere, might dissipate just as quickly. Nemtsov, Navalny, several other men, and a couple of women who now felt they had to harness this newfound energy gathered to discuss the predicament. There was unexpected good news: someone had already secured a permit for a protest on December 10—less than a week away. The bad news was, the permit was for three hundred people who were expected to gather in a small square across from the Bolshoi Theatre. In theory and symbolically, this was a good location: the Bolshoi was a short walk from Red Square, separated from it by an area called Revolution Square. A larger protest would fit nicely there.

The prospect of tens of thousands of protesters in Revolution Square was evidently not one Moscow authorities were willing to entertain. Nor were they willing to negotiate with the women who had secured the permit. They reached out to Nemtsov and to several other prominent men whom they believed to be associated with the protests, and proposed an alternative: Bolotnaya Square. *Boloto* means "swamp." The square in question used to be just that; now it was an island, separated by the Moscow River from the Kremlin on one side and by a canal from a residential neighborhood on the other. Nemtsov's apartment happened to overlook Bolotnaya Square from across the canal. The police liked Bolotnaya for obvious reasons: it was easy to cordon off; access and egress would be naturally slowed down by the geography of the place. All the men agreed that a demonstration involving tens of thousands of people would be more orderly at Bolotnaya. They shook on it, and even shared a bottle of whiskey.[22] Nemtsov was convinced that the protesters would be safe only if they complied. He wrote an appeal on his blog:

> Dear friends! For me the safety and security of people are more important than Twitter and Facebook. It's not only experienced opposition activists who are planning to come to the protest but also a huge number of people who have never been to a protest before. It would be a low, provocational, and criminal thing to do, to have them end up beaten by riot police. I could never let that happen.[23]

Nemtsov and two other activists also recorded a video putting forth this position and specifying the demands of the upcoming protest at Bolotnaya Square: the release of all political prisoners—they meant the casualties of the last two protests, when nearly nine hundred people had been detained and scores of them had been sentenced to fifteen days in jail—and new elections.[24] Tens of thousands of people were clicking "I'm going" on the social network pages created for the protest, and the activists felt it was important that they go to the right place and make the right demands. It was for their own good.

WHITE RIBBONS | 343
THE NIGHT before the protest at Bolotnaya, Masha was hanging out with

THE NIGHT before the protest at Bolotnaya, Masha was hanging out with her new friends from Starlight Diner and her childhood friend Tolya, whose family had emigrated to Canada almost twenty years before. Tolya was now a computer scientist working for a Russian company in Moscow. Everyone was planning to go to the protest the next day, and no one could understand why they were supposed to go to the island rather than Revolution Square. Consensus was, this would be a wasted opportunity: for the first and quite possibly the last time in their lives, these people, who had been weaned on profound disgust for any sort of collective action, were moved to join one. They naturally assumed this was true of all other newly minted protesters. How could they allow such a chance to be wasted by going to a place where they would be neither heard nor seen, except by one another?

Masha said that she had been reading about Occupy Wall Street, and it was obvious to her that Occupy was the right model. Go to Revolution Square, set up camp, refuse to leave. Or go to the Central Election Commission, which was just a block away from Revolution Square, and occupy that, demanding new elections. In fact, that was what the Ukrainians did in 2004, long before Occupy Wall Street, and it had worked for them.

"When I was a student at Oxford," said one of the young men, and he launched into a long description of the tactics he saw used by student activists there. "But you need a leader to follow for that."

Did they have a leader? The group began tossing names around. Nemtsov was a holdover from a previous era. Yashin was always trying to get people to take him seriously, because they did not. Another self-proclaimed leader, Sergei Udaltsov, had orthodox Soviet views and generally seemed to want to be a 1920s commissar. That left Navalny. They liked Navalny, though his nationalist views and what they called his "Komsomol ways"—including his love of chanting slogans such as "One for all and all for one"—made him less appealing. Still, they would be willing to follow him if he called them to a good protest. But Navalny was still serving his fifteen-day sentence.

"He should make a statement from jail," said someone. But it was too late for that.

"I think you should go and talk to the organizers and tell them they are wasting an opportunity," said someone. Masha realized that they were addressing her. All of them, in fact, seemed to agree that Masha would be a good person to deliver this message. But she did not know how to contact any of the organizers. So the next day they went to Bolotnaya. So did about fifty thousand other people, making it the largest Russian protest since the Soviet Union collapsed.

———

THERE WAS A STAGE, and speakers on it—apparently, people always had this at protests. Looking at them—he could not really hear them—Seryozha realized that he had been to a protest once before, more than ten years earlier. In April 2001, after almost a year of threats, police raids, and court disputes, the journalists of NTV, the independent national television channel, had been told that the company was now under the control of the state gas monopoly. They called for a protest in the street in front of the television tower, where all the broadcasters had their offices. Seryozha wound his way out there—the television tower was far from the Metro, and Seryozha had trouble navigating the buses in an unfamiliar neighborhood of Moscow. Then he stood in the pouring rain, watching his favorite television anchors, people whose faces had been on the screen as long as he had been aware of television news, come out and speak from the temporary stage. Some of them looked like they were crying, though it was hard to tell in the rain. It had seemed like the end of the world.

Since then, one of the anchors had demonstratively quit journalism to take up the traditional dissident occupation of stove-stoker, another had moved to Ukraine and had his own show there, but the rest of those journalists had found some accommodation within the new, entirely state-controlled television world. Some were enthusiastically stumping for Putin, while others confined themselves to culture and apparently innocuous social issues. The city had built a monorail road to the television tower. And Seryozha forgot about that protest. If someone had asked him, the day before he went to Bolotnaya Square, whether he had ever been to a protest, he would have been adamant that he had not. He would have said, in fact, that up until a few months ago, when he first learned of the Makarov case, he had had no argument with the regime.

Now someone very loud on or near the stage began shouting, "Down with Putin!" A few hundred people picked up the chant. Seryozha did not. Something about it made him uncomfortable. He had not come here to bring down Putin. He did not want to think of himself as a revolutionary—to his grandfather, that had been a dirty word. All that had gone wrong, Alexander Nikolaevich believed, had been the result of drastic action taken without forethought. Good change could be only gradual and intentional. Also, Seryozha did not want to chant. Chanting put one in mind of either Communist-era parades, which Seryozha remembered, or perhaps felt like he remembered, or of the Kremlin youth movements, which sought ecstasy in unity and aggression. Seryozha did not want ecstasy. He wanted to register his existence as someone separate and different from the state. For this purpose, he wore a white ribbon. Somehow, over the last few days, white had become the color of this protest. It was a symbol like Ukraine's orange, but also its opposite. White was pure, it was nonaggressive, and it was every color. It was important to Seryozha and to the people he was now meeting here that this was not a protest of any political party or movement. They preferred to think of it as not being political at all.

ALEXANDRE BIKBOV, the sociologist who had been providing an educational alternative for students of Moscow State University's sociology department, now turned his seminar into a mobile survey unit. Their goal was to ask people what they were doing, and why, while they were doing it. Both the Kremlin and the media in Russia and abroad quickly accepted the understanding that the protesters were members of the middle class who opposed

Putin. One commonly used phrase was "angry city dwellers," where "city dweller" implied affluence and youth. The Levada Center conducted surveys that showed that the protesters were not in fact predominantly affluent—they included some poor people, many people of moderate means, and some rich people. Nor were they predominantly young: just slightly more than half were under forty, but 22 percent were older than fifty-five.[25] Bikbov found that they were also not particularly angry. They liked to joke, and they loved a good funny banner, like I DIDN'T VOTE FOR THESE ASSHOLES, I VOTED FOR THE OTHER ASSHOLES, the runaway favorite among the many visual and textual gags held up on handwritten placards at Bolotnaya. The humor, Bikbov concluded, served a dual purpose. On the one hand, it defused the feeling of having been violated: one is less of a victim if one can laugh about it. It also signaled that the protesters were not dangerous. Revolutionaries do not kid around. By cracking jokes the protesters shifted their focus from the Kremlin to one another. The protest seemed like a contest in which like-minded people looked for the wittiest person among them.[26] Afterward, participants combed social networks to see if their particular placard had become an audience favorite.

"White, the color of our protest, is a good symbol," wrote Nemtsov in a euphoric blog post on December 10. "It means that protest participants can harbor no 'dark' thoughts." The blog post began with the words, "I am happy. The 10th of December, 2011, will go down in history as the day of resurrection of civic dignity and civil society. After ten years of hibernation, Moscow and all of Russia have awakened."[27]

It was all of Russia indeed. On or around the same day, nearly a hundred Russian cities and towns—which is to say, all of Russia's cities and towns—saw protest rallies, demonstrations, or marches. In several places, the relative number of participants—the percentage of a town's population that came out to protest—far exceeded that of Moscow.

In his blog post, Nemtsov announced that the protesters had "unanimously adopted" a list of demands. There had been no vote at Bolotnaya, and most of the participants could not hear the speakers, but the last time Nemtsov had attended a protest this large—over twenty years ago—there had been lists and demands. That seemed to be the way these things worked. There were six demands. One was to release "all political prisoners," meaning the people arrested at last week's protests, and five concerned the parliamentary elections—annul the results; fire the chairman of the Election Commission; investigate reports of vote-rigging; allow opposition parties on the ballot; and hold new, open and fair, elections. Putin's resignation was not on the list, nor did the list include any mention of the upcoming presidential election. The demands did not explicitly include Mikhail Khodorkovsky, who had been in jail for eight years, or Vladimir Makarov, unknown to most of the protesters. The demands made no mention of the killings of opposition journalists, or of media freedom at all. The demands were intentionally minimal, apparently easy to carry out. They were modeled on the logic of the late 1980s and early 1990s, when Gorbachev's Politburo, weak and uncertain, might have been open to compromise and reason. The Communist parties of the Soviet Union's satellite countries had sat down to negotiate with protesters in response to similar kinds of demands during the "velvet revolutions" of 1989. To Nemtsov and his co-organizers, Putin's government seemed, suddenly, to be in the same sort of teetering state as those governments had been.

"Suddenly" was the operative word. Then again, those old enough to remember the fall of the Soviet Union remembered that the regime had seemed eternal until one day it did not. But what had happened now? Why had people taken to the streets by the hundreds of thousands, people of different ages and income levels, all over the country? Social scientists who wrote about the protests invariably used the word "mystery."

A Russian-born, Western-educated German sociologist undertook probably the most thorough attempt to crack the mystery. Mischa Gabowitsch based his study on interviews with dozens of protesters all over the country as well as on a close examination of the posters, slogans, and forms of protest. His evidence debunked the idea that this was a middle-class protest or even a protest primarily driven by middle-class values such as the desire to protect private property and receive good government services in exchange for one's tax rubles. Gabowitsch concluded that the critique of corruption, and especially Navalny's narration of it, created the preconditions for protest. Navalny's term "Party of Crooks and Thieves" supplied the language. Protesters talked about many things being stolen from them—not only money and government services but also votes. Nemtsov put a number on it: he claimed that thirteen million votes had gone missing. The most blatant vote-fix of them all—Medvedev's handover of power to Putin—could also be framed as a manifestation of corruption.

At the same time, noted Gabowitsch, seeing the protests as solely a reaction to witnessing the blatant fraud in the parliamentary election would be wrong.

> Compared with the reforms of electoral law and the elimination, intimidation and pre-selection of opposition candidates, the vote-rigging on election day itself may not be a trifle, but they are no more than the last cog in the power vertical's steering mechanism. This distinguishes the situation in Russia in December 2011 from that in Serbia in 2000, in Georgia in 2003, in Ukraine in 2004 or in Kyrgyzstan in 2005. There electoral manipulation had been the decisive tool to prevent the victory of a candidate who was popular or at least supported by a broad coalition. In Russia, by contrast, the preceding reforms had made the emergence of such a candidate or coalition unlikely. Why, nevertheless, was it a rigged election that led to spontaneous mass protest in Russia?[28]

He suggested that part of the answer lay in the ritual of elections, which had been painfully violated. In other words, it was precisely the obscene manner of the rigging, not the fact of it, that caused the outrage—like what had caused Seryozha to throw a blank ballot in the bin in disgust, after flying all the way from Kiev to Moscow to cast it. If the protesters were objecting primarily to what had felt to them like public indecency—not just at the voting booth but also earlier, in September, when Putin and Medvedev publicly shook on the presidency—then it stood to reason that they did not call for Putin to be deposed and did not confront the regime with its gravest crimes. Held on a cordoned-off island, the protest was not confrontational at all. Some of Bikbov's respondents said that they were demonstrating for stability—using the keyword of the Putin era, turning it into their demand. Or their request.

Even though the protesters belonged to different age groups, Putin had now been in power long enough that a majority of them had spent all or most of their adult lives in the era of supposed "stability." Some of them had expected the Putin era to be like the Soviet past they remembered or imagined, the object of national nostalgia. According to these memories, that time was slow, predictable, and essentially unchanging. But in Putin's era of "stability," things refused to stay the same. The markets crashed because Putin said or did something. Innocent, randomly chosen people went to prison just because the government had declared a witch hunt against pedophiles. The spectacle of the Putin-Medvedev handoff and the experience of the farcical election served as reminders of how powerless Russian citizens were to affect any aspect of life. The protests were an attempt to renegotiate, to reclaim a little bit of space from the ever-expanding party-state—and it so happened that the party was the one of crooks and thieves.

ON DECEMBER 15, Putin held his tenth annual hotline, a show during which he answered questions from a carefully screened audience and an equally well-screened selection of callers. Even though Putin had not formally been president for the last three years, these shows, starring Putin, had continued on schedule. Seryozha watched as for the first twenty minutes Putin fielded softball questions about the protests. He seemed a little unnerved at first, but then Seryozha thought that might have been wishful thinking on his part. Putin grew more confident as he talked. He even took credit for the protests: his regime had produced many active citizens. He promised to place a web camera at every polling station to assure the public that there would be no fraud during the upcoming presidential election. This was ridiculous: web cameras would be useless against most of the falsification practices. But at least they had forced him to respond. Maybe he was scared, after all.

The show's host had once been a brave young reporter at NTV. Seryozha remembered seeing him at that protest, when everyone found a way to promise never to give up. Now he was ten years older and twenty kilos heavier, sitting behind a desk at a state-channel studio, tense and eager next to Russia's most powerful man. The host read a question from a laptop screen in front of him:

> **During the protests in central Moscow people put on white ribbons. Those ribbons are almost like the symbol of a looming "color revolution" in Russia. Do you agree with this assessment? . . .**
>
> As far as "color revolutions," I think everything is clear. They are an established practice of destabilizing societies, and I think that this practice did not come out of nowhere. We know what happened during the Orange Revolution in Ukraine. By the way, some of our opposition activists were in Ukraine at that time and held official positions as advisers to then president Yushchenko. They naturally try to transfer this practice to Russian soil. But to be frank, when I saw, on the screen, that some people were wearing something on their chest, I'll tell you honestly, even though it's inappropriate, but I thought that this was AIDS education, that they had, I'm sorry, that they had pinned contraceptives to their chests. I just couldn't understand why they had taken them out of their wrappers. But then I got a closer look.[29]

It got worse. Putin went on to claim that people had been paid to attend the protests and that the "opposition leaders" had humiliated them by calling out, "Sheep, go forth!" But Seryozha barely heard this, because he was already livid—at the obvious reference to Nemtsov, whose work in Ukraine was described as something akin to treason, but more than that, by the stupid condom joke.

From this point on, Seryozha was driven by rage. His rage focused on producing as many white ribbons as possible. There was a shortage. Retail shops all over Moscow had run out of white ribbons. People were wearing ribbons not just to protests but every day, to work and in the streets. They pinned them to their coats, tied them to their bags and to the antennae of their cars. Seryozha found wholesalers and bought large heavy rolls of ribbon, an inch wide and hundreds of yards long. Cutting the ribbon into tens of thousands of roughly six-inch strips was no trivial task. He invented a technique. He wound the ribbon around the back of a bentwood chair, thirty to fifty times over, and then made two strategic cuts—for as many as a hundred pieces at once. Then the ends of the strips had to be singed with a lighter, to keep them from fraying. Before the next planned protest, on December 24, Seryozha set up a workshop at his apartment. Several people he had met at a gathering called the Protest Workshop came to help. They also produced an instruction video and uploaded it to YouTube.

MASHA WENT TO EVERY ACTION, protest, planning meeting, and related social occasion. Within two weeks of becoming an activist, she had started a new job, as press secretary to parliament member Ilya Ponomarev of A Just Russia, who had been speaking at the protests. She had joined the protest art group Pussy Riot. The all-woman open-membership collective staged guerrilla performances and posted videos online. In December, they sang on a garage roof outside the detention center where Navalny and other protesters were held. In January, they sang in Red Square; the song was called "Putin Pissed Himself." That time, like many other times, they were escorted to a police station and allowed to leave after a couple of hours. Next, Masha wanted them to stage an action in the parliament chamber. They would descend from one of the side boxes, in their mismatched multicolored tights and balaclavas, when the parliament was in session.

This action turned out to be harder to organize than Masha could have imagined. On February 21, Pussy Riot performed instead at the Cathedral of Christ the Savior, the gaudy giant wedding cake of a church near the Kremlin. They sang a song called "Punk Prayer," in which they pleaded with the Virgin to "chase Putin out." Their message was directed at the protesters as much as at anyone else. Rather than assemble in cordoned-off spaces, it said, be confrontational—go where you are not supposed to go and say what you are not supposed to say. In this case, they were confronting the church and state where church and state became one. The presidential election was two weeks away. The patriarch of the Russian Orthodox Church was campaigning for Putin.

On March 4, just before the polls opened, two members of Pussy Riot were placed under arrest on suspicion of felony hooliganism, a charge that could carry up to seven years in prison. Masha was not one of them because she had not made it to the cathedral that day.

LYOSHA HAPPENED TO BE IN KIEV the first weekend of March, at a seminar in the Gender, Sexuality, and Power series. The election looked even more bizarre from a distance. Putin declared victory in the first round with 63 percent of the vote, and the white-ribbon crowd in Russia seemed shocked by this predictable outcome.

On March 8, International Women's Day, the participants staged a march down Kiev's main avenue. They marched for gender equality, LGBT rights, and freedom for Pussy Riot. There were maybe 150 of them, twice as many police, and, it looked to Lyosha, four times as many counterdemonstrators. It was the first time Lyosha marched for LGBT rights. It was also the first time he saw police protecting protesters rather than threatening them. He felt oddly inspired, despite having had to march through a tunnel of police in riot gear.

When he returned to Perm, his department chair said nothing about the march. But she did suggest that it would be wise to change the title of the seminar when he put in the paperwork for where he had been.

seventeen

MASHA: MAY 6, 2012

IN THE MORNING Masha went to church. It was Sunday, the day before Putin's inauguration. The city was quiet—in the early days of May, Muscovites tend to their dachas, opening them up for the summer. Masha had borrowed an icon from one of the hundreds of people she had met in the last few months. He was a very wealthy man with good connections, one of many such men who were hedging their bets by helping the protests. They wanted to maintain useful relationships no matter who was in power. They gave generously to the online account opened by the protest organizers, so that after the December 10 Bolotnaya rally there was always good sound equipment and beautifully printed banners. This man kept saying to Masha that he would like to do something together—something, she took it to mean, protest-y. So she asked to borrow an icon from his famous collection of sixteenth-century Russian religious art. The man sent an icon and a bodyguard, who in this case was working as an icon-guard.

Masha took the icon and the guard and walked over to the church at the Monastery of the Holy Mandylion, a small and pretty church just by the Kremlin. She was going to engage in a fairly standard Orthodox practice, whereby an icon is brought to church for communal prayer: others pray to it and kiss it, and then it is, some believe, holier when it is returned to its regular home. While this was happening, a photographer, or a few photographers, were to snap pictures, and then Masha would explain what this was: a Prayer for the Constitution, Against Obscurantism.

People were praying. Masha was waiting for journalists to arrive, but they must have been running late. The owner of the icon called to scream at Masha for not warning him that this was an action related to Pussy Riot: in his calculus of hedging, this was too risky. The phone call meant that news of Masha's action had already leaked. She still did not have a good shot. She would have to consider this an unsuccessful action. Masha felt strangely serene despite her failure and despite being yelled at over the phone. It must be because I'm in church, she realized.

Just then, men in civilian clothing entered. Even the church caretaker recognized them: her lips curled in, changing her expression instantly from blissful to hostile. The men took Masha to the nearest police station, where they started shouting at her.

"You are defending those bitches, those whores who danced naked on the altar with their guitars! You belong with them!"

"Faggots!" Masha shouted in response. "It's faggots like you who are destroying Russia!"

Masha had worked out this technique over the course of five months and seven detentions. The first few times she found herself at a police station, she had tried to reason with her captors. Then one time she lost her cool and saw that shouting right back at them was much more effective. It destabilized the situation. Police officers did not expect detainees to scream at them, and Russian men did not expect women to scream at them, so the shouting broke their pattern. If she shouted in their language, hurling at them the same sorts of insults that they hurled at her, it worked even better.

They stopped shouting, and released her after three hours—the maximum amount of time they could hold her without booking. This was a relief, because Masha had a lot of work to do for the big march and rally planned for the afternoon.

MASHA WAS NOW AN EXPERIENCED, well-known, and occasionally jaded activist. In the winter, she got to observe the workings of the political machine, or what passed for one in Russia. As Ilya Ponomarev's press secretary, she attended the meetings of A Just Russia in parliament. They were still talking about pedophilia. One of the deputies insisted that they needed to continue to push for chemical castration of convicted pedophiles. Yelena Mizulina, chairwoman of the Committee on the Family, was opposed. The other deputy accused her of caving to the pedophile lobby. She responded that she did more than anyone to protect the children. She had been the driving force behind the Law for the Protection of Children from Information That Harms Their Health and Development. The law had been passed back in 2010, but most of its provisions were going into effect later this year. All media, including books, magazines, and films, would need to be marked with a target age group—to prevent children from consuming harmful information. Now Mizulina was working to extend these restrictions and regulations to the Internet. This, and not chemical castration, was what protecting children was all about, she argued. Masha's sympathies were with Mizulina at these meetings.

Masha got to observe how money worked in the parliament. Members were either wealthy or kept. The state budget gave each parliament member 200,000 rubles a month for a staff of five. That worked out to just over $1,000 a month for each staff member, in a city that now prided itself on being among the world's most expensive. Rich parliamentarians paid their extensive staffs out of their own pockets, while the less rich accepted what they called "sponsorship" money for their aides and press secretaries. They were also likely to have a shadow staff of assistants who did not work or draw a salary but paid the parliament member themselves, in exchange for government credentials.

For Masha's boss, politics was the family business. Ponomarev hailed from Soviet nomenklatura stock: his grandfather was a diplomat and his father's brother was a member of the Central Committee leadership. Ilya himself became active in Soviet politics as a teenager, rising to the post of a city-level functionary in the Young Pioneers organization of Moscow. In the 1990s the entire family, including teenage Ilya, went into private business, to return to politics under Putin. Ilya's mother was an appointed member of the upper house of parliament, and Ilya himself got a seat in the lower house in 2007 on A Just Russia's list.

In 2006, Ponomarev carried out a textbook preventive-counterrevolution operation when he staged an officially sanctioned gathering of anti-globalism activists in St. Petersburg during a G8 summit there. The Kremlin feared that protests would disrupt the summit but also did not want to stage an obvious crackdown on that occasion. So the police detained activists when they arrived in St. Petersburg by train and transported them to a suburban stadium, where Ponomarev was chairing the forum. Many of those who were delivered to the stadium were not anti-globalism activists at all, and members of Kasparov's United Civic Front were even ejected for chanting anti-Putin slogans, but for all the world to see—if anyone in the world could be bothered looking—St. Petersburg had a stadium full of anti-globalism activists gathering openly and legally, and Ilya Ponomarev was their leader.

On paper, most of Ponomarev's income came from consulting fees from state-funded institutions. In 2011, he declared an income of about $330,000, and in 2012 it went up to about $370,000.[1] But most of the money that Masha saw was in cash—stacks, piles, and briefcases of it—and it was not going to be reported on any income reporting forms. Ponomarev was surrounded by men Masha never would have taken seriously, especially because they were so impossibly serious themselves about their task: revolution. As far as she could tell, they thought that if they staged one, they would get laid. Some of these men said that they were anarchists, some said that they were hard-core communists, and some insisted that Masha should read a book called *A Blow from Russian Gods*. She looked it up. It was an anti-semitic screed.[2] Masha figured that Ponomarev was spending time with these men because the more visible protest activists, knowing his history as a protest spoiler, tried to avoid him. It was either that or Ponomarev was purposefully siphoning off money and energy from the protests, like when he had started a parallel organizing committee back in December. At one point Masha grew convinced that at least some of the money circulating through the office was coming from the Kremlin. She quit her job in March.

A few days later, a new amendment was proposed to the Law for the Protection of Children from Information That Harms Their Health and Development. This one would ban "propaganda of homosexuality." Now the "pedophile lobby" would finally be vanquished. Ponomarev supported the amendment.

OF COURSE MASHA had not expected that the protests would change the outcome of the presidential election, in which Putin was effectively unopposed. And yet she had. There were many protests in the three months between when she had declared herself an activist and the election. After Bolotnaya there was another rally, even larger than the first one. Then there was the White Ride, when cars decorated with white ribbons circled the Garden Ring, then a march, and then the White Ring, when people stood on the sidewalks of the Garden Ring, encircling the center of town. Then there was the election, which made it all feel useless and embarrassing. The protest held in Moscow on election day felt more like a wake.

People were talking about emigrating again, but Masha realized that for perhaps the first time in her life she wanted to stay in Russia. It was interesting here—even more interesting than doing a degree in educational psychology at Oxford might be. Not that Sergei would let her take Sasha out of the country to live. But her son was doing well in preschool, and Sergei, now that he was remarried, had resumed his parenting responsibilities. After Masha quit her job at Ponomarev's office, she and Anastasia went to India on vacation. They lay on the beach in Goa, but Moscow kept pinging. The multimillionaire with the icon collection wanted to start an organization called Russia for All, and wanted Masha to run it. A friend from Solidarity wanted to organize a protest. Everyone wanted to organize a protest, in fact.

The big one. The one that would finally make a difference. It seemed there was only one chance left for that: the inauguration.

The city issued a permit for a march and rally on the eve of the inauguration. They would allow protesters to walk down Bolshaya Yakimanka, the street that ran from the giant Lenin monument to Bolotny Island, and then to a rally at Bolotnaya Square.* Udaltsov, the guy who seemed to think he was Lenin, named the protest the March of Millions. People around the country were raising money so they could attend, but this was unlikely to make it large enough to justify the name. And what could the organizers do to make this one count, aside from giving it a grandiose name? As it was, they were having trouble convincing people to speak at the rally. "What's there to say?" they heard again and again. Two days before the march, five men—Kasparov, Navalny, Nemtsov, Udaltsov, and Yashin—gathered to discuss. Someone suggested staging a sit-in. Nemtsov and Udaltsov shot the idea down. Nemtsov refused to challenge the ethos of the nonconfrontational protest; Udaltsov frowned on the idea of passive resistance.

Masha's job was to get journalists to the press area in front of the stage. She was good at this: she knew all the reporters, all the reporters knew her, and she had a loud voice. She stood by the stage as people wandered in slowly from the march: there was always this moment of idleness, when everyone was trying to decide whether to stay for the rally or go to a café instead. A few teenagers from the Protest Workshop stationed themselves at the turnout from the street to the island with a couple of megaphones, and shouted out funny rhymed slogans to keep protesters entertained. Then there was commotion to Masha's right, just where the crowd was meant to turn. It seemed big. Or bad. The volunteers' two-way radios stopped working. Cellular networks were either jammed or overloaded—the phone was no use. Masha made her way over.

---

*Russian adjectives are gendered: they change form according to the gender of the noun they modify. For example, because the word for "square" in Russian is feminine, it takes the feminine form of the adjective for "swampy": Bolotnaya. The word for "island" is masculine, and thus takes the masculine adjective Bolotny. The word for "case" (as in "criminal case") is neuter, and takes the neuter form Bolotnoye.

Navalny was sitting on the ground. He was surrounded by journalists with cameras and microphones. This did not suit his purposes. The journalists refused to either sit down or move out of the way. No one could see Navalny's sit-in, so no one was joining in. Masha looked at her iPhone: it was a little after five in the afternoon. The rally was supposed to start now.

Then there were blows. It did not feel serious—Masha had seen worse back in December—but the riot police had their rubber batons out and blows were landing. A baton reached over the shoulders of people standing behind Masha and hit a woman on the head. The woman slumped and crumpled on the ground. Masha heard herself screaming.

"Call an ambulance!"

She turned around to face a helmeted head.

"Call an ambulance!"

A face behind the glass of the helmet came into focus.

"We don't have orders," it said.

Masha started screaming louder.

Someone threw a smoke grenade. How in the world had they managed to bring it in, through the metal detectors, the bag search, and the double cordon? Someone threw another object, which broke on contact with someone else's shoulder. It was a thermos liner, guaranteed to break into a thousand brittle pieces. Police were pushing from the back and from the sides. In front of Masha, Navalny and several other men, including Nemtsov and Yashin, were sitting on the ground. The woman was lying on the pavement. Masha was pushing back in every direction and screaming like she had never screamed before. The line of riot police parted for a moment and Masha was squeezed out to the other side, as the cops carried the unconscious woman out. The police closed ranks behind her. Masha stood in an emptiness. She was no longer screaming, and it was almost quiet.

Behind Masha, behind a ring formed by the riot police, fighting seemed to continue. In front of her, four rows of interior troops—eighteen-year-old conscripts in gray uniforms—stretched across the bridge that led over the Moscow River to the Kremlin. Behind them, orange street-washing vehicles formed another barrier. They were so afraid of the protesters in the

Kremlin apparently that they thought they needed to wage war just to protect themselves. Masha walked toward the interior troops, holding up her iPhone to film them as she got closer.

"Russia has a constitution," she said to the conscripts. "You are violating it. The orders you've been given are criminal. After the Nuremberg trials, generals who gave criminal orders were hanged. And our soldiers hanged German soldiers who had followed criminal orders. That's what happens to people who commit crimes."

"Orders are not to be discussed," said several of the conscripts in unison.

"Oh yes they are," said Masha. "They are too to be discussed, if they contradict the law of the land."

"No talking!"

The voice came from Masha's left. The conscripts visibly clammed up. She was now just a few steps from the front row of soldiers. She stopped and held her iPhone above her head, and kept filming.

"Step forward!" the invisible voice commanded.

The conscripts, arms linked, about 150 across, took a step toward her. Then another. Masha kept talking.

"You are violating your oath. You are just like the czar over there."

Masha became aware that she was being filmed by someone else, apparently a journalist. She could not see him, but she could hear his voice. He was worried for her. "Don't," he was saying. "They won't understand."

She kept talking.

"You guys are so young, much younger than I am, though I am not that old yet. You have no idea how frightening it is to live in this country, with that czar that you are guarding now, when you have a child."

"Step forward!"

"One more!"

Masha still had her arms up in the air, holding the iPhone aloft, and the boys' shoulders were now brushing her bare underarms. She could feel their titillation. She kept talking. She talked for another four minutes straight. The boys stood still and silent. Finally, a lieutenant came up, a blond guy with a heavy jaw, scarcely older than his soldiers.

"What do you want?" he asked.

"Where do you get your information?" Masha asked what seemed at the moment a logical question.

"There," said the lieutenant, and he nodded at the pavement for some reason. "Television," he added a moment later.

"Who controls the television?" This was the journalist with the video camera speaking.

"The authorities do," said the lieutenant.

Masha tried to point out to him that getting information about the authorities from the authorities might not be wise. After a few minutes, he asked the journalist to turn off his camera. Then he told Masha that the truth was found in the book *Blows from the Russian Gods*, the screed that had been recommended to Masha once before. It purported to "uncover the real crimes of the Jews," who had taken over the world. One subsection was called "The Sexual Traits of the Jews." It began with homosexuality: "Not only was homosexuality widespread among the ancient Jews but it was known to take over entire cities, such as Sodom and Gomorrah, for example." The lieutenant told Masha that every soldier in his platoon had received a copy of this book.[3]

MAY 6 WAS A LONG DAY. It began with being dragged in to the police for praying for the wrong things, continued with an intimate conversation with six hundred interior troops, and went on to another police station, where Navalny and Nemtsov had been taken. Some people from the protest had walked here on their own and were milling around outside. One had a megaphone: the Protest Workshop had bought more than a dozen of them at one point. Masha took the megaphone, fished a copy of the Constitution out of her shoulder bag, and began declaiming, starting with Article 31. She was carried right into the station. Nemtsov and Navalny were in the holding cell, and Masha was instructed to wait outside it, in what might have been called the lobby. She put the Constitution back in her bag, fished out a copy of *Time* magazine's "World's Most Influential People: 2012" issue,[4] opened it to the page with Navalny's picture on it, handed it to him, and told him to look serious. It was a good photograph, with Navalny's forearm stuck through the bars, his hand holding the magazine, his face somber and a little wistful. She e-mailed it to her boyfriend, who was a photographer with the Associated Press. The following day the picture was published all over the world.[5]

Maybe the most important thing that had happened to Masha since she became an activist was that she had fallen in love. Sergey was somewhere out there today, documenting the carnage. It went well into the night, when police continued to chase people down side streets. More than six hundred were detained, more than fifty hospitalized, though many more had been injured.[6] The day never ended, in fact. Most people were released, and some continued to protest the following day, all over the center of town. Riot police detained people merely for wearing white ribbons. Groups of police in bulletproof vests and helmets chased groups who seemed merely to be strolling through the town, loaded them onto buses, took them to police stations, released them three hours later without booking, and started all over again. Nemtsov was detained while drinking coffee at a sidewalk café; riot police turned over tables in the process.[7] Masha spent the day riding around on a kick scooter. She read the Constitution to riot police, got detained, gave interviews, got detained. Meanwhile, in the Kremlin, Putin was inaugurated for his official third presidential term.

MASHA WAS IN LOVE. The cat-and-mouse game with the police continued for another couple of weeks. For a few days, people even set up an Occupy-style camp (though without the tents, because that would be illegal), and then that was broken up. And Masha was still in love. She took Sasha to her mother-in-law, who had a dacha a couple of hours outside Moscow, and then she and Sergey went on their first trip together. He was photographing the European Cup, which was held in Ukraine and Poland that year. Masha liked Donetsk, the eastern Ukrainian city where a new stadium had been built for the tournament[8] and the airport had been refurbished.[9] The city looked like a glossy-magazine version of Europe. Masha had a seat in the fan zone. She had never imagined that she would find soccer mesmerizing, but she did. She told Sergey that she could physically feel the release of testosterone all around her. It was an awesome trip.

MASHA FLEW BACK from Poland on June 10, because she was scheduled to attend the summer session of the Moscow School for Political Studies, a gathering of like-minded journalists and social scientists held just outside the city. Masha's phone rang at eight-fifteen on June 11. It was Nemtsov's assistant.

"Everyone's apartment is being searched," she said. Police had come to Navalny's, Udaltsov's, Yashin's, and other activists' apartments. They had come to Nemtsov's, too, but he was out of town.[10] Masha had an excruciating hangover. She had told Aishat, the nanny, not to open the door if anyone rang the bell—even though Sasha was at his grandmother's dacha for the summer, Aishat, who had fled Baku in 1990, when her husband was killed in the pogroms there, always stayed the summer with her employer. Aishat was not picking up. Masha lay on the bed, waves of sleep and nausea floating over her.

Her phone rang again. She did not recognize the number.

"Hello, Maria Nikolaevna. This is Captain Timofei Vladimirovich Grachev from Head Investigative Directorate. You are suspected of inciting, organizing, and participating in a riot. A subpoena has been left at your place of residence, with Baku native Aishat." He pronounced the nanny's patronymic and last name: "Who appears to be residing there without proper registration."

"Go fuck yourself," said Masha, and hung up.

Aishat still was not answering. Masha lay on the bed some more, then sat up and called the investigator back.

"Look, I haven't seen any subpoena. I'll think about whether I want to talk to you after the weekend." It was the Monday of a long holiday weekend—the next workday was two days away.

It was past noon by the time Aishat picked up. She said she was very sorry: she knew she was not supposed to open the door, but the police were banging on it with something heavy and she thought they might break it down. She was very sorry, but she was quitting. Masha said she was very sorry too and would pay Aishat three months' severance.

Masha was most concerned that the police had found her stash of pot. As it turned out, they had not taken it. Nor had they taken any of a number of financial documents that would have been sufficient to slap together a case against her. What they did take: fifteen white ribbons, a bag of black round buttons with pink triangles—activists had started wearing them to signify their opposition to the proposed "propaganda of homosexuality" amendment—a copy of Nemtsov's *Putin: An Accounting*, and an old laptop where Masha stored Sasha's study aids and all the photographs she had taken of him since birth. They took printed photographs too: Masha's pregnancy, Masha's marriage, and every single photo of Tatiana that Masha had.

CAPTAIN GRACHEV WAS a lanky guy around Masha's age, with good hair and a lousy haircut. He had been dispatched to Moscow from the prosecutor's office in the Tver region, three hours away, to help investigate the Bolotnoye case. It was apparently going to be big. He told Masha that he had just arrived in Moscow when he was sent to search her apartment.

"When I saw those pink triangles, I thought it was some children's game or something, and put them back," he said. But there was a more experienced Moscow officer there. "He says, 'Are you kidding? That's the LGBT movement.' I was like, 'What's LGBT?' He goes, 'Just take it.'" A few weeks into their frequent meetings Masha and Captain Grachev were so comfortable with each other that Masha asked him why he had not taken the marijuana as evidence from her apartment.

"We didn't even take cocaine from another search," he explained. "That's not what we were there for. They told us to look for political propaganda."

Masha and Captain Grachev were using the informal pronoun to address each other. He even allowed Masha to visit her son at the dacha. Other defendants in her case—she did not know them, but she knew that they existed—were under arrest, and Masha was lucky simply to be restricted to staying in Moscow. She had been unable to go to a friend's dacha on the tenth anniversary of Tatiana's death: she hated the idea of being alone or with the wrong people that day, but she hated the idea of asking for permission even more. But later she grew more comfortable, and she missed Sasha so much.

Masha's mother-in-law, like Masha's ex-husband, was a chemist. She worked for an applied-science institute that was not high on the academic socioeconomic ladder, which meant that the village where its staff researchers were allotted plots was a fair distance from Moscow, all the way in the Tver region. In fact, the institute ruled over only half the village—the other half belonged to the prosecutor's office. This was how Masha's mother-in-law came to spend her summers next door to a colonel from the Investigative Committee in the city of Konakovo, Tver region. Masha had met the colonel over the course of several summers. Her name was Natalia, she was forty or so, and she took care of her sixty-year-old mother and eighty-year-old grandmother as well as two kids: her own young daughter and a boy Sasha's age, the son of Natalia's sister who had a bad drug problem. Natalia seemed to work like a dog without taking any interest in the substance of her work: she cared only that she had a lot of mouths to feed. When she was not working, she was sleeping. In between, she smoked cigarettes, a habit that she kept secret from her mother and grandmother. Masha was her smoking buddy.

"Hey, you are part of the Bolotnoye case, aren't you?" she asked when they were having a cigarette Masha's first night at the dacha. It was cool and quiet and you could see the stars.

"Yeah," said Masha.

"Who is your investigator?"

"Grachev."

"Ah, Timokha!" Natalia's voice sang with the joy of recognition. "He is one of mine. I had to send three people. It's a big case. He doing his job?"

"Oh, he is doing his job, all right."

"Good. Say hi to him there."

The following morning, when Masha woke up in her loft bed, there were three six-year-old children playing below. She listened to their voices. They were playing with Legos. One of those children is my son and another is the son of the boss of the man who will send me to prison for two years, she thought. It sounded complicated, but it was so simple: she was passing to another side of existence easily, surrounded by familiar faces all the way.

SHE HAD TO REPORT to Captain Grachev's office twice a week, at ten in the morning. He would name names and ask Masha if she knew the person. If she had the person's permission, she would say yes. If not, she would say that she did not recall—and often, she did not. Captain Grachev would give her things to look at: "Please familiarize yourself." Then he would place an object in front of her—like, say, the flag of the Libertarian Party. Why? She did not know, and he probably did not either. Then there was an endless parade of police photographs. Sheet after sheet of typing paper with two or three photographs glued to each. Other people's bedrooms, desks, closets, letters, pictures, other people's white ribbons. They belonged to Masha's co-defendants. The photographs were taken during searches of their apartments. Somewhere else in this building, or across town, a dozen strangers were looking at pictures of Sasha's bedroom and pictures of pictures of Tatiana. Then there were photographs of all the material evidence recovered at Bolotnaya, the debris of thousands of people under attack: broken cigarette lighters, crushed Bic pens, lost passports that had been stomped upon by a thousand feet. Object after object that had no meaning to Masha, in poor resolution, under a flickering neon light. The point of this is to drown me in senselessness, thought Masha.

Starting on December 20, Masha was required to appear at Captain Grachev's office daily. She dropped Sasha off at the English-language pre-school, had coffee with the journalist mothers, and then they went to work while she went to the Investigative Committee. She was no longer living in the apartment where she grew up. There had been many reasons to get out after the search. One was that a woman from social services had come around and told Masha that she had information that Masha was bisexual and therefore an unfit parent. Another was that the logistics of her life no longer allowed her to live so far from the center of the city. At first she stayed with Sergey, but, of course, Sergey had not signed up for this—the constant surveillance, the telephone harassment, and a girlfriend who could not leave the legal limits of the city. So now Masha was renting an apart-ment in town.

She was reading the case, one giant binder at a time. It amused her at first, this experience of viewing what had been her life for six months—the protests and the people in them—through the eyes of people who could not comprehend it. Everything seemed sinister to them. They were scared of white ribbons and Twitter. But this got tired fast. The binders kept coming. The drowning sensation intensified. Masha wanted to sign the forms with-out reading, but the investigator who was in the room with her at all times told her this was not allowed. This guy was a senior lieutenant—one step below Captain Grachev, and a couple of years younger—sent there from Bryansk, in southwestern Russia. Masha's eyes hurt from reading, so she kept talking with him. He and his wife had been trying to get pregnant for years, and it was not working. Now they were on to IVF, and it still was not taking. Masha had had this experience herself. She tried to reassure the senior lieutenant.

At the end of winter her savings ran out. She went to ask Nemtsov for a job. She needed an employer who could understand her unconventional schedule, and she knew that Nemtsov's organization was getting some money from an American democracy-building fund. He said that there was not enough money to hire her but he could introduce her to a friend who ran a restaurant chain. Masha was willing to wait tables, but even at a restaurant she could not make her hours work. She posted in an online community for foreign correspondents in Moscow: "I want to work as a fixer." Many of these people knew her and knew that she spoke English and could get access to anyone and anything. She started getting some work. It was not enough, and friends lent her money too. Once she had watched a few journalists at work, she realized that she could try doing what they did. She started writing for a Moscow city magazine and then for TV Rain, an independent television channel that, since its founding just a couple of years earlier, had assembled an audience of millions even though the channel was available only to cable and satellite viewers.

The trial began on June 2, more than a year after the protest at the center of the case. Masha saw her co-defendants. Ten men, ranging in age from college student to retiree, were squeezed into a plastic aquarium. They stood, holding their hands behind their backs, the way inmates do when they face law enforcement. All of them had spent the last year behind bars. Another co-defendant, eighteen at the time of her arrest, had spent the year under house arrest. Masha felt piercing guilt. How could she have been feeling sorry for herself, feeling like she deserved other people's sympathy and help, when she had been allowed to walk around and see her child every night this last year?

The trial did not feel that different from the investigation. Masha had seen the women of Pussy Riot on trial a year earlier. That had been bizarre, a veritable witch trial, but it had a dramaturgy to it. This trial had no rhythm, no beginning or end. Most days passed in arguments between lawyers and the judge about admissibility, order of admissibility, and the like. None of it seemed connected to the case, absurd as the case was. The defendants' charges ranged from "participation in public unrest" to "use of force against authorities," with potential sentences of up to five years. There were too many defendants and too many lawyers, and they were all too different to be able to coordinate their actions. At first, they tried. When the oldest of the men in the aquarium, Sergei Krivov, declared that he was boycotting the court and refused to answer any questions, the rest of them went silent too. But the next day Krivov broke his pledge without warning.

Journalists soon grew tired of the proceedings—there was nothing to report—and stopped coming. Every so often, Masha would write an outraged Facebook post to the effect that these twelve people had been abandoned, and some journalists and activists would show up for a day or two. Then they would return to their lives.

Sasha started first grade at one of the better public schools in town. Fortunately, the school was on the same Metro line as the court. But then the trial was moved to a courthouse on the outskirts, and the length of Masha's morning commute tripled.

Everyone referred to it as the Bolotnoye case—the "swampy case." Exactly. Even the drowning was protracted and amorphous. Masha's body began to betray her. She developed sores. By November she was throwing up blood. The doctors said they could find nothing wrong with her.

PART SIX

CRACKDOWN

eighteen
SERYOZHA: JULY 18, 2013

AFTER MAY 6, 2012, there was shock, then the fog of the summer and the Bolotnoye arrests—within a few months, more than two dozen people had been charged (their cases were subdivided and they faced trial in smaller groups). It took about six months for the shock to subside and the fog to settle sufficiently for activists to conduct their own investigation of what had happened.

In December 2012, a group of twenty-six people assembled into an investigating committee. They included actors, scholars, a poet, former dissidents, and several journalists. Each was known to be a person of integrity. Their task was to review thousands of pages of documents, including about six hundred eyewitness interviews collected by activists, media reports, amateur and professional video, and the Bolotnoye case itself.

The committee determined that nearly thirteen thousand troops had been assembled in Moscow that day, more than eight thousand of them in and around Bolotnaya Square. This included over five thousand riot police and about twenty-five hundred interior troops; the rest were traffic police or police academy cadets. There were probably three unarmed protesters, at most, for each armed man in uniform. Troops had been brought in from as far away as the Russian Far East.

Unbeknownst to the protest organizers, police had set up a second row of metal-detector frames at the turnoff from the march route to Bolotnaya Square. A large part of Bolotny Island that had been used during past rallies was cordoned off. Between these two measures, the police had created a bottleneck that first slowed the march down and then brought it to a standstill. Speakers could not physically get to the stage. This was why Udaltsov and then Navalny had called for a sit-in.

It was clear from the video footage reviewed by the committee that Navalny was not the only or even the first person to sit down, as it had seemed to Masha; at least a hundred people were sitting down at one point or another, but their actions were not planned or coordinated. They were separated by groups of people who continued standing, and they themselves kept sitting down and getting up, apparently unsure of what was happening and what should be done.[1] But the police had received orders to start arresting people even before the sit-in began—this the committee gathered from one officer's testimony at the Bolotnoye case trial. In other words, contrary to what Masha and many other protesters had thought, they had not brought it upon themselves: the police had acted first. The question was whether the violence had been planned in advance. Many eyewitnesses reported seeing young men who they thought had infiltrated the protest. Some said that these men had been waved through by the police, bypassing the metal detectors and the searches. These young men seemed to be the ones who had brought in the smoke grenades and breakable bottles that helped spark the violence. The committee concluded that the violence had been planned and instigated by the authorities.[2]

ON MAY 7, 2012, as riot police continued to hunt down people with white ribbons in central Moscow, Putin was inaugurated. That day he signed twelve decrees, including one in which he directed the foreign ministry to pursue a policy of vigilance in relationship to the United States and NATO; one in which he directed the cabinet to introduce a mandatory Russian-language and history exam for migrant workers; and one in which he ordered the cabinet "to secure a rise of the cumulative fertility rate to 1.753 by the year 2018."[3] Then Putin met with International Olympic Committee president Jacques Rogge. The meeting, held in the Kremlin, was Putin's first after formally retaking office.

"In spite of what has been happening in our internal politics, I want to reassure you that the presidential administration, the cabinet, and I personally will make preparations for the 2014 Olympic Games our top priority," said Putin. "We consider this very important. Our work together will continue."[4]

Putin had scarcely mentioned the protests in the months since December, but speaking to Rogge he betrayed the fear that to foreigners Russia must appear to have descended into chaos. Putin had personally traveled to Guatemala City back in 2007 to present Russia's bid for the 2014 Winter Games—in English and French. It had been a bizarre speech—following the standard promises of world-class facilities and an emphatic reminder of how popular winter sports are in Russia, Putin had brought up the losses Russia had suffered in history, if not in sports: "Let me point out that after the breakup of the Soviet Union, Russia has lost all sports venues in the mountains. Would you believe it? Even today our national teams have no mountain venues in Russia for training."[5]

Giving the Olympics to Russia, it would follow, was a form of compensation for its losses, a way to restore its physical sports facilities and its national grandeur. The symbolic significance of such a project warranted meeting with the head of the International Olympic Committee before anyone else, as soon as Putin became president again.

Then Putin played hockey. He had taken up this winter sport just a year and a half earlier, but, playing for a team of amateurs against Russia's all-star team, he managed to score two goals and bring his team to victory.[6]

The following day, Putin asked the parliament to confirm Dmitry Medvedev as prime minister. "We did everything openly," said Putin, referring to having declared the intention to swap offices back in September. "There was nothing about it that could be construed as manipulation." He did not mention the protests directly, but his reference to their accusations of electoral fraud and general theft was clear: How could something be crooked if it was obvious? After the parliament confirmed Medvedev, Putin stayed and talked business. Business was mostly the economy and demographics. On the economy, Putin reproached parliament members for proposing legislation that showed a lack of understanding of basic economic facts. On demographics, Putin praised himself, Medvedev, and the parliament for having raised the fertility rate. "This is the result of sensible policies," he said, referring to the cash payments to women for having a second child. He suggested that it might be time to consider paying women in some parts of Russia to have a third child too.[7]

Next day was Victory Day. The podium from which Putin spoke in Red Square was erected closer to the multicolored St. Basil's Cathedral—Putin did not stand on the Lenin Mausoleum as the Politburo used to—but otherwise the look and feel of the Soviet-era military parade had been restored. So had the scale and the symbolism: the parade once again served to demonstrate Russia's might and affirm its right:

> We have the great moral right to be principled and insistent in defending our positions, because it was our country that bore the brunt of the fight against Nazism. . . . The young people of today are the heirs of the true freedom fighters. . . . We will always be faithful to their valor, and that means that we have a future.* . . . Glory to Russia!

Fourteen thousand men shouted "Hooray!" three times in perfect unison, and the Russian national anthem—the restored Soviet anthem—began playing.[8]

The Victory Day Parade had evolved since Yeltsin renewed the practice

---

*Putin used the phrase *budushcheye yest'*—an implied response to the more common idiom *budushchego net* ("there is no future").

in 1999 and Putin took the reins in 2000. In his first parade speech, Putin had focused on the importance of the holiday to all Russians. At his second parade, in 2001, he ended the speech with "Glory to Russia!"—a slogan that until then had been the mark of fringe ultranationalist organizations. As the years wore on, the focus of the speech shifted to the present day, to the need to be vigilant. The number of troops grew, from about five thousand in 2003 to eight thousand in 2008 and fourteen thousand in 2012. In 2007, the year of the Munich speech in which Putin accused NATO of betrayal and aggression, he used his parade speech for the first time to make a transparent reference to the United States. He did not name the country, but said that, just as in the times of the Third Reich, there was a country that has "pretensions to global exceptionalism and command." In 2008, the year of the war in Georgia, a parade of military equipment—a long procession of tanks and rockets—was added to the Red Square pageant for the first time since the Soviet era. This was also the year Medvedev formally became president, so he and Putin now stood together at the podium, microphones distributed to both of them as though both were speaking at the same time. It was Medvedev who gave the speech for the next four years, though. He did not end it with "Glory to Russia," opting for "Happy Day of the Great Victory" instead. In 2010, the sixty-fifth anniversary of victory, foreign heads of state joined in the celebration in Red Square. That day, an air show was added to the parade, the evening fireworks were extended from ten to fifteen minutes, and for the first time an "all-Russian Victory Day Parade" was declared—full military parades were held in nineteen cities and smaller military marches in fifty-two. The air show was repeated every year after that, and so was the all-Russian parade, in an ever-growing number of cities.[9]

The day after Victory Day, Putin flew to the Urals to visit UralVagon-Zavod, a factory that had just received a large new military contract. The factory made armored personnel carriers, tanks, and modified tanks called Terminator, with two guns instead of the usual one plus two grenade launchers, and Terminator-2, with two guns and four rockets on two launchers. Back in December, Putin's marathon televised hotline—the one that began

with his confession that he had mistaken white ribbons for condoms—
ended with a video call-in question from the factory floor of UralVagon-
Zavod. In a colorized re-creation of the Soviet industrial aesthetic, about
sixty men had stood together, wearing identical black-and-orange uniforms,
freshly ironed, and one man standing in the middle spoke for them. He
wore a tie under his uniform jacket.

> I am Igor Kholmanskikh. I am head of the assembly shop. . . . I have
> a question that's causing me heartache. Back when we were having a
> hard time, Vladimir Vladimirovich, you came to our plant and helped
> us. Today . . . we treasure our stability and we don't want to go back
> in time. I want to say something about those protests. If the police
> don't know how to do their jobs, if they can't do anything about the
> protests, then my men and I are prepared to come out in defense of
> our stability.

"Come on over," Putin had said, smiling.[10] The men of the factory had
gone on to form a committee in defense of Putin, who, they wrote in their
manifesto, was under attack from "do-nothings in Moscow."[11] In fact, protests were also under way in Nizhny Tagil, the city of roughly three hundred
thousand where UralVagonZavod was located: between a hundred and a
hundred fifty people had come out on December 10, the day of the first big
Bolotnaya protest in Moscow.[12] Sticking to the narrative that protests were
staged only by the idle rich of the big cities, the men of UralVagonZavod
had planned to mount their tanks and ride to a pro-Putin counter-rally in
the nearest large city of Yekaterinburg. They were asked to leave the tanks
home,[13] but now that Putin was once again president, his first visit outside
Moscow was one of gratitude—to UralVagonZavod. The men at the plant
wished Putin Happy Victory Day, praised his hockey game, and mentioned
the protesters again.

"They are just doing their jobs," said Putin, meaning that protesters were
working for money—state television channels had by this time aired a series

of reports claiming that the protests were bankrolled by the U.S. State Department.

"The country needs stability, and you are certainly the only person who can give it to us," said one of the men.[14] A week later Putin appointed Kholmanskikh his plenipotentiary in the Urals—a miraculous career move for the head of the assembly shop. In the past, only trusted senior officials, a majority of them retired military brass, had been appointed to these posts. Kholmanskikh was now in charge of six Russian regions with a total population of over fourteen million, and their six governors.

On May 10, while Putin was at UralVagonZavod, the parliament was asked to pass a set of amendments to the Law on Public Gatherings. They raised the fines for violating rules on public gatherings to as much as the equivalent of $1,500—backbreaking for most Russians—and they changed the definition of "public gathering" to allow the police to classify any group of people as engaging in one. The bill sped through parliament like probably no piece of legislation ever had. It became law on June 9, three days before a protest march planned to commemorate Russia's 1990 declaration of sovereignty.[15]

The crackdown proceeded swiftly. After the law on public gatherings came a law that required nongovernmental organizations that received foreign funding to register as "foreign agents," which, in turn, would subject them to paralyzing financial reporting requirements and would serve as a scarlet letter: such organizations would have to add "foreign agent" to all their public communications, which would presumably range from business cards to op-ed articles. In August, the women of Pussy Riot were sentenced to two years' imprisonment for "hooliganism," becoming the first people to receive years in jail for peaceful protest. All along, more people were being arrested in the Bolotnoye case. In September, the Law for the Protection of Children from Information went into effect; by this time, it had been amended to extend to the Internet. In November, laws on espionage and high treason were amended so that their wording reverted to that of the 1930s, when thousands of people were executed on trumped-up charges.

Under the new law, working for an international organization whose activities Russia considered to be hostile could open one up to charges of high treason. A month earlier, Russia had ordered the United States Agency for International Development to cease operations in the country—now the new law could conceivably be used against any of the organization's Russian employees or its numerous Russian associates. The new law also made it possible to apply espionage charges to people who obtained classified information without intent to share it with a foreign state, and those who culled information from open sources.[16] In December, ostensibly in response to a new American law introducing sanctions against Russian officials guilty of "gross violations of human rights"—the so-called Magnitsky Act, named for the accountant who was tortured to death in a Moscow jail—Russia passed a law that forbade the adoption of Russian orphans by Americans and also gave the government the right to summarily shut down nongovernmental organizations if they received any funding from American organizations or individuals. The international monitoring organization Human Rights Watch called the developments of 2012 the "worst crackdown since the Soviet era."[17]

The new laws were the perfect tools of a crackdown: vague enough to put millions on notice, they could be applied only selectively. But the laws, and the discussions in parliament and on television that accompanied their passage, served as messages. They signaled that the Kremlin was in charge, that strict order was being reconstituted. They also seemed to signal to the people of Russia that it was time for them to become enforcers. In Yekaterinburg, a group of parents formed a committee to demand that a number of books be removed from stores and their publishers prosecuted. The books included Israeli author David Grossman's young-adult novel *Someone to Run With*, in which one of the characters is a teenage heroin addict; American authors Lynda and Area Madaras's *"What's Happening to My Body?"* books; and three other books about puberty. A court eventually threw the case out, but by this time one of the publishers had pulped the pressrun and the others had spent fortunes on mounting a defense of their books. Similar cases began popping up around the country. To survive, publishers—especially the publishers of children's books, who risked running afoul of the new Law for the Protection of Children from Information, had to stop publishing books for which they might get dragged into court. The new law, among other things, forbade any mention of death in books for children under the age of twelve. "Naturalistic" description of the human body was also off-limits. Publishers, who could be destroyed by one big lawsuit or even a few pulped pressruns, were well-advised to exercise an overabundance of caution. With vigilant citizens throwing fits in the stacks in one city after another, bookstores and libraries also had to err on the side of caution.[18] Self-censorship was collective hostage-taking in one of its purest forms. It had kicked back in.

YURI LEVADA HAD THEORIZED that periodic protests did not change the structure of Soviet society. Gudkov had developed this idea further: periodic protests were in fact essential to maintaining the structure of society. No matter how restrictive the Russian regime was in any given period, after a while some tension would accumulate between institutions of authority and society (for lack of a better word—in a country with a nearly absent public sphere Gudkov wished there were a term for "society" that did not immediately call to mind a Western society). This tension represented society's potential for change. At times like these, argued Levada, society would go from a state of calm to a state of arousal. The regime invariably responded by using force.

Force could be used inside the country, as when people were arrested, institutions shuttered or purged, and laws became more restrictive; or outside the country, when war was waged. The effect was the same either way—society, which had become more complicated, reverted to a radically simplified state: us, them, and our leader, who shoulders all our responsibility and has all our trust. This made society as a whole feel better. Calm was restored. Change was prevented. Troublemakers were stopped. Gudkov started calling the process "abortive modernization." Crackdowns occurred at regular intervals during the Soviet period, as did wars. Gudkov's own research career, and Levada's project of creating a sociology school, were aborted by one such crackdown in the late 1960s—following the protests in Prague and demonstrations of support for them in Moscow. There were only a few arrests then—most people were punished by having to give up or curtail their intellectual work. The rest simply fell into step. This was the way state terror worked after Stalin: it was enough to punish a few to neutralize the many.

The periodic eruptions, followed by use of force that precluded change, continued after the Soviet Union collapsed. Gudkov was now rethinking the history of that collapse. If one viewed the period of perestroika and the first post-Soviet year as a period of societal "arousal," then the show of force occurred in 1993, when Yeltsin shelled the parliament building. It had the effect one would expect: society felt radically simplified, Yeltsin affirmed his role as leader—though the Russian *vozhd'* or even the German *Führer* was really the word Gudkov had in mind—and, as always happens in times of radical simplification, nationalism flourished. This explained the success of Zhirinovsky's party in the 1993 election. The war in Georgia, in 2008, served a similar function. Wars were almost as good as crackdowns because they discredited anyone who wanted to complicate things. This was Gudkov's depressing and, he had to admit, radical idea: the last century could be viewed as a continuity, with periodic bumps of "aborted modernization," and the society he had been studying his entire adult life had stayed essentially the same. What made this idea radical was that no one wanted to hear it.

IF THE PEOPLE who took to the streets all over Russia in 2011–2012 were protesting, whether they used the word or not, the totalitarian essence of the society in which they found themselves living, then the form and slogans of the protests were not as illogical as they had seemed to Masha. If one of the features of a totalitarian regime is that it politicizes every aspect of life, then protest that strove to be apolitical was an appropriate response. If a feature of a totalitarian regime was that it eliminated all space that belonged to people apart from the state, then holding protests in cordoned-off spaces was not such a strange idea: the very ability to negotiate such a space could be a victory. It stands to reason that the crackdown began with the annulment of that negotiation and the physical destruction of the protest space.

Even the use of the word "stability" by both the protesters and their opponents had a long history in the theory and reality of totalitarianism. Arendt pointed out that both the Nazi and the Soviet regimes conducted periodic purges or crackdowns, which she called "an instrument of permanent instability." Constant flux was necessary for the system's survival: "The totalitarian ruler must, at any price, prevent normalization from reaching the point where a new way of life could develop—one which might, after a time, lose its bastard qualities and take its place among the widely differing and profoundly contrasting ways of life of the nations of the earth." Indeed, she wrote, "The point is that both Hitler and Stalin held out promises of stability in order to hide their intention of creating a state of permanent instability."[19]

When protesters were asking for their "stability" back, it was this normalization that they demanded. But when a Putin foot soldier from Ural-VagonZavod said that the protesters must be crushed because only Putin could guarantee stability, he was reaching for the vision of the leader, literally asking to be mobilized by him then and there.

SOCIAL SCIENTISTS both inside Russia and outside it scoffed at the word "totalitarian" as applied to post-Soviet Russia. Even "authoritarian" was controversial. Soon after the crackdown began, the phrase "hybrid regime" came into vogue. The original term, coined by journalist Fareed Zakaria in a 1997 essay, was "illiberal democracy." Zakaria emphasized the distinction between democracy, a way of selecting governments through free and open elections, and liberalism, the political project of safeguarding individual freedoms. The two did not necessarily go together. Political theory had long acknowledged the existence of liberal autocracies, such as the Austro-Hungarian Empire, for example. It was time to recognize that the corollary could also exist. Zakaria cited the examples of Belarus, Kyrgyzstan, and Peru, among others, as countries where democratically elected leaders had consistently violated constitutional limits of power that had been put in place to safeguard individual freedoms. He noted that Russia, too, was at risk:

> In 1993 Boris Yeltsin famously (and literally) attacked the Russian parliament, prompted by parliament's own unconstitutional acts. He then suspended the constitutional court, dismantled the system of local governments, and fired several provincial governors. From the war in Chechnya to his economic programs, Yeltsin has displayed a routine lack of concern for constitutional procedure and limits. He may well be a liberal democrat at heart, but Yeltsin's actions have created a Russian super-presidency. We can only hope his successor will not abuse it.[20]

The obvious issue with the idea of "illiberal democracy" was that, once a democratically elected government began curtailing freedoms, it was unlikely to continue having truly free and open elections—even if, technically, elections occurred at regular intervals. After all, even the Soviet Union had elections, which, according to the constitution, were direct and conducted by secret ballot: "No control over the expression of will of the voter is allowed," said Article 99. And there was never a more literal illustration of Arendt's thesis that totalitarian regimes rob their subjects of will: every candidate on the Soviet ballot invariably ran unopposed.

In Putin's Russia, most elections had been eliminated altogether: governors and senators were now appointed and the lower house of parliament was formed by parties, through a largely depersonalized form of voting. The candidate for president also in effect ran unopposed in every election beginning with the year 2000. Still, there were banners, billboards, concerts, and other accoutrements of a campaign, and there were ballots. It looked more like a Western democracy, but felt more like the Soviet Union. After a while, the term "hybrid regime" supplanted "liberal democracy."

In Russia, the term "hybrid regime" was popularized by Ekaterina Shulman, a young political scientist. She wrote that

> a hybrid regime is the authoritarian regime in the new historical moment. We know the difference between authoritarian and totalitarian regimes: the former rewards passivity and the latter rewards mobilization. A totalitarian regime demands participation: if you do not march the march and sing the songs, then you are not a loyal citizen. An authoritarian regime, on the other hand, tries to convince its subjects to stay home. Whoever marches too energetically or sings too loudly is suspect, regardless of the ideological content of the songs and the direction of the march.[21]

Shulman was reiterating Juan Linz's definition of the difference between authoritarianism and totalitarianism, but omitting his distinction between the all-political nature of totalitarianism and the nonpolitical nature of authoritarianism. Hybrid regimes were fakers, wrote Shulman, but Western observers tend to focus on only one aspect of the fakery: that of democracy. "It's easy to notice that the facade of democracy is made of papier-mâché," she wrote. "But it's harder to understand that Stalin's mustache is glued on." The amount of force applied by the Putin regime, she argued, was negligible by the standards of the twentieth century. A few dozen political prisoners was to totalitarian terror what the quadrennial election of Putin was to functioning democracy. The hybrid regime survived by imitating both democracy and totalitarianism strategically in varied measure, she argued.

Other terms used to describe the Putin regime were "kleptocracy" and "crony capitalism"—variations on Navalny's theme of the "Party of Crooks and Thieves." A Hungarian sociologist named Bálint Magyar rejected these terms because, he stressed, both "kleptocracy" and "crony capitalism" implied a sort of voluntary association—as though one could partake in the crony system or choose not to, and proceed with one's business autonomously, if less profitably. The fate of Khodorkovsky and the exiled oligarchs, as well as of untold thousands of jailed and bankrupted entrepreneurs, demonstrated that this was a fallacy.

Magyar, who was born in 1952, grew up in Hungary, a relatively less repressive Eastern Bloc country. This allowed him to be well educated as a sociologist. But in the late 1970s Magyar became active in underground opposition politics and was duly punished: banned from teaching at the university and banned from traveling to the West. Eastern European societies became his area of specialization. In the late 1980s, as a founding member of the Alliance of Free Democrats—Hungarian Liberal Party, Magyar was part of the democratic transition in his country. In the 2000s, the party gradually lost ground and finally ceased to exist, and Magyar returned to sociology. Under the new regime of Viktor Orbán, he was once again persona non grata at the university, and once again focused on a study of Eastern European societies.

He had an intense dislike for terms like "illiberal," which focused on traits the regimes did not possess—like free media or fair elections. This he likened to trying to describe an elephant by saying that the elephant cannot fly or cannot swim—it says nothing about what the elephant actually is. Nor did he like the term "hybrid regime," which to him seemed like an imitation of a definition, since it failed to define what the regime was ostensibly a hybrid of.[22]

Magyar developed his own concept: the "post-communist mafia state." Both halves of the designation were significant: "post-communist" because "the conditions preceding the democratic big bang* have a decisive role in the formation of the system. Namely that it came about on the foundations of a communist dictatorship, as a product of the debris left by its decay."[23] The ruling elites of post-communist states most often hail from the old

---

*Magyar is referring to the tendency to view the history of these states as having begun with the end of communism.

nomenklatura, be it Party or secret service. But to Magyar this was not the countries' most important common feature: what mattered most was that some of these old groups evolved into structures centered around a single man who led them in wielding power. Consolidating power and resources was relatively simple because these countries had just recently had a Party monopoly on power and a state monopoly on property. This created unique conditions:

> In the case of other autocratic systems, either . . . private property is converted to property quasi belonging to the state, or the formal distribution of property is left more-or-less untouched. . . . However, no historical example can be found of an instance where state property is transformed en-masse on the basis of dubious norms—at least so far as their social acceptance is concerned. When the intention is to create a layer of private owners, it seems as if they were intent on producing fish out of fish soup.[24]

The property and the power these groups were usurping had no other apparent legitimate holders. That made the job particularly easy.

A mafia state, in Magyar's definition, was different from other states ruled by one person surrounded by a small elite. In a mafia state, the small powerful group was structured just like a family. The center of the family is the patriarch, who does not govern: "he disposes—of positions, wealth, statuses, persons."[25] The system works like a caricature of the Communist distribution economy. The patriarch and his family have only two goals: accumulating wealth and concentrating power. The family-like structure is strictly hierarchical, and membership in it can be obtained only through birth or adoption. In Putin's case, his inner circle consisted of men with whom he grew up in the streets and judo clubs of Leningrad, the next circle included men with whom he had worked in the KGB/FSB, and the next circle was made up of men who had worked in the St. Petersburg administration with him. Very rarely, he "adopted" someone into the family, as he did with Kholmanskikh, the head of the assembly shop, who was elevated from obscurity to a sort of third-cousin-hood. One cannot leave the family voluntarily: one can only be kicked out, disowned and disinherited. Violence and ideology, the pillars of the totalitarian state, became, in the hands of the mafia state, mere instruments.

THE POST-COMMUNIST MAFIA STATE, in Magyar's words, is an "ideology-applying regime" (while a totalitarian regime is "ideology-driven"). A crackdown requires both force and ideology. While the instruments of force—the riot police, the interior troops, and even the street-washing machines—were within arm's reach, ready to be used, ideology was less apparently available. Up until spring 2012, Putin's ideological repertoire had consisted of the word "stability," a lament for the loss of the Soviet empire, a steady but barely articulated restoration of the Soviet aesthetic and the myth of the Great Patriotic War, and general statements about the United States and NATO, which had cheated Russia and threatened it now. All these components had been employed during the "preventive counter-revolution," when the country, and especially its youth, was called upon to battle the American-inspired orange menace, which threatened stability. Putin employed the same set of images when he first responded to the protests in December. But Dugin was now arguing that this was not enough.

At the end of December, Dugin published an article in which he predicted the fall of Putin if he continued to ignore the importance of ideas and history.[26] That is, in Dugin's view, Putin's treatment of ideas and history had been so sporadic and inconsistent as to indicate that he thought them unimportant. In February, Dugin was invited to speak at the Anti-Orange Rally, a Kremlin event organized to coincide with a large protest demonstration in Moscow. This was Dugin's most mainstream appearance ever: from a stage mounted at Poklonnaya Mountain, Moscow's repository of monuments to its victories over invaders from Napoleon to Hitler, he addressed tens of thousands of people, at least some of whom had been bused there from other cities and towns:[27]

Dear Russian people! The global American empire strives to bring all countries of the world under its control. They intervene where they want, asking no one's permission. They come in through the fifth column, which they think will allow them to take over natural resources and rule over countries, people, and continents. They have invaded Afghanistan, Iraq, Libya. Syria and Iran are on the agenda. But their goal is Russia. We are the last obstacle on their way to building a global evil empire. Their agents at Bolotnaya Square and within the government are doing everything to weaken Russia and allow them to bring us under total external control. To resist this most serious threat, we must be united and mobilized! We must remember that we are Russian! That for thousands of years we protected our freedom and independence. We have spilled seas of blood, our own and other people's, to make Russia great. And Russia will be great! Otherwise it will not exist at all. Russia is everything! All else is nothing!

This chant was picked up by other men on the stage. They pumped their right fists in the air.

Russia is everything! All else is nothing! Glory to Russia![28]

It was well below zero in Moscow that day. The protesters at Bolotnaya Square still came out, and the "anti-orange" demonstrators were bused in, but the speeches had to be kept short. Still, Dugin's two-minute statement hit the main points of the ideology he was proposing: Russia is great and it is all that stands between the world as we know it and the Global States of America. It contained the "worshipping of the past" that Fromm had believed to be key to fascist ideology. By calling the imagined American empire "evil" (casually reversing Ronald Reagan's usage), the speech hinted at Russia's unique goodness. This idea was expressed more clearly in a document Dugin cosigned a few days later with a dozen other high-profile men, called the "Anti-Orange Pact." It began:

We are united in our understanding of the need to resist the attack of
the Orange, who are targeting our common fundamental values.[29]

The word "values" was new, and it was key. The fledgling ideology now had
all its components: the nation, the past, traditional values, an external threat,
and a fifth column.

———

DUGIN'S PROPOSED FRAME fit the crackdown, uniting the arrests, the "foreign agents" law, and the new, communally enforced censorship. It was all
in the name of rooting out the fifth column and protecting Russian values.
It stood to reason that Pussy Riot, who embodied both the fifth column
and an apparent disrespect for traditional Russian values, were the first people sentenced to imprisonment in the crackdown. They had been arrested
for protest but tried, in effect, for blasphemy. Court testimony centered
on whether they had crossed themselves properly and how much skin they
had exposed in church. There was some discussion of whether they were
possessed.

Here the state described by Magyar met the society described by
Gudkov. When the state used force and ideology as mere tools, society responded as it had over the course of previous generations to both force and
ideology: by mobilizing. Russia had a mafia state ruling over a totalitarian
society.

"Abortive modernization" continued as more and more people were
arrested in the Bolotnoye case. These arrests served the same purpose as
selective arrests had in the Soviet Union: they issued a warning. Bolotnoye
inmates seemed chosen almost at random. None was a protest leader, and
most, in fact, were less known, even in protest circles, than Masha. This
communicated the message that protest was risky for the rank and file. As
always happens in cases of apparently random arrests, people tried to discern
their logic. A common belief took hold that people who had been detained

during other protests, and those who had been captured on video from the Bolotnaya riots, were the ones targeted. A number of young activists fled the country, seeking haven in Ukraine, the Baltic states, and countries like Sweden and Finland. Still, there were hundreds of people with records of police detentions, and hundreds who had been captured on Bolotnaya video, and most of them were not arrested. That is how terror works: the threat must be credible yet unpredictable.

Protest leaders also needed to be neutralized. Here the Kremlin was cautious, perhaps weary of causing more protest by pushing too hard. Udaltsov was placed under house arrest. The terms of his confinement prevented him from communicating with anyone other than his household members, and from using the Internet. Yet, unlike several dozen lesser-known activists, he had the luxury of sleeping on sheets, sharing a bed with his wife. Few people could be roused to protest the treatment of Udaltsov. After more than a year, when Udaltsov had reliably faded from public view, he was convicted of organizing a riot and sentenced to four and a half years behind bars.[30] Kasparov was pressured to emigrate—or face persecution; he moved to New York City. Nemtsov received a barrage of death threats. Navalny became a defendant in a bizarre embezzlement case.

He was accused of having used his position as an unpaid consultant to the liberal governor of the Kirov region to arrange to steal huge quantities of timber from the region's state-run forestry company, causing half a million dollars in losses.* The charges were similar to those lodged against Khodorkovsky when he went up for trial the second time—he was convicted of stealing crude oil from his own company. Navalny was also accused of doing something both impossible and absurd. The state could not even produce evidence that the money ever went missing. But on July 18, 2013, he was convicted and sentenced to five years in prison.

The social networks filled with expressions of outrage and, above all,

---

*The governor happened to be Nikita Belykh, the former Nemtsov ally and Perm legislature member for whom the other Lyosha had worked.

disbelief—even though the case, the conviction, and the sentence conformed to the overall logic of the crackdown. Seryozha had read that people planned to meet at Manezhnaya Square, just outside Red Square, the night of the sentencing. That was what everyone had been calling it: "a people's meeting," like a town meeting. Whoever scheduled it had, of course, anticipated that the court's decision would be unfair. But when news of the actual sentence came, it was shocking. Strange how that worked: something could be unsurprising and shocking at the same time.

Seryozha went to Manezhnaya around six in the evening. He was among the first couple of thousand to arrive. Police sealed off some of the early arrivals on a portion of sidewalk and shut off the nearest Metro exit, but people kept coming from other streets, joining a crowd that was divided into three or four large segments. There were about ten thousand people in all. There was no permit for this "meeting." Everyone there was risking detention and a crushing fine. Seryozha had never seen people act like this. The last time this happened—the last time Muscovites took to the streets, at great potential peril, because they could not stay home and let things happen—had been in August 1991, when Seryozha was nine.

Seryozha had spent so much time thinking about people and protests. After the crackdown began, he took stock. He realized that he had stopped working entirely. He had been cutting white ribbons full-time. That might have been an exaggeration—he also did things like design posters and banners and help out with other projects, and attend the Protest Workshop. He was lucky that he could afford to: he had an apartment he had inherited, and a lucrative-enough profession that had allowed him to save up.

Then the rules changed and protest had become an almost impossibly high-stakes game. Seryozha still believed in protest. Or, he still believed that all a citizen can do, when the right to vote has been perverted and the courts have been usurped—all a citizen can do, and must do, is go out into the streets. But he also felt that he had no moral right to say this. He searched for this right, he dug into his soul for the source of his authority to call on people to take the risk and protest, and he did not find it. For a person to tell other people to risk their freedom, to risk Russian jail, he had to be beyond reproach. Seryozha was not beyond reproach.

But now all these people had come without asking anyone's permission and stayed without asking anyone's direction. It looked like the beginning of a new era. People stood. At first they stood with their arms linked, in a staring contest with a row of riot police in front of them. Then, after an hour or two or three, the protesters relaxed. Some sang songs, including great rousing Russian war songs—one called on people to rise up, which seemed appropriate. One woman took a book out of her bag and stood there, reading. Periodically, chants would start up. "Freedom! Freedom! Freedom!" or "Putin is a thief!" or "We are not afraid!" At one point, news spread that the prosecutor's office had asked the judge to suspend Navalny's sentence, but no one believed it—at least, Seryozha did not believe it—and everyone stayed. They plastered the facade of the parliament building with round red "Navalny" stickers. People climbed onto the ledge of the elevated first floor of the parliament building and stood there, unafraid of the police, or of the fines, or of falling. This protest felt like nothing had ever felt before. This one was not about making jokes or talking to like-minded people or staking out an apolitical space: this one was about fighting. This one was beyond reproach.

Around eleven in the evening the police seemed to get their orders. They began charging the crowd, grabbing people, throwing them to the ground, and dragging them into prisoner transports. They shouted at the rest to disband. Some people walked away. Seryozha was with a group, maybe a hundred people altogether, wedged between lines of police. They resisted happily at first. The riot police pushed them down the street—their batons were painful against one's back—but these people, most of whom Seryozha did not know, laughed and walked, pretending to be out on a summer night's stroll, then doubled back and took up their protest again. But the group kept thinning, and the number of people in the square kept dwindling. A little after midnight Seryozha was the last man standing. But was he beyond reproach?

He went home. The next morning he learned that about two hundred people had been detained and that Navalny was going to be released. What had happened was legally impossible: there was nothing in the law that enabled the prosecutor to ask for a sentence to be suspended after the sentence had been announced, in the absence of an appeal from the defense. On the face of it, the protesters had won. But it did not feel like it. It felt horrible that morning, like there was no future.[31]

LYOSHA: JUNE 11, 2013

IN AUGUST 2012, Lyosha got a call from a university administrator informing him that he needed to obtain a police clearance to be allowed to continue teaching. Everyone was getting these calls, including a friend of a friend who worked in the toy section of a department store. Such were the new rules, the administrator explained, nothing personal.

The Russian labor code had always forbidden convicted felons to teach. It had just never before occurred to local authorities to extend the rules to people who sold toys or taught at the university level. Now a few things had changed: the country was on the lookout for the "pedophile lobby"; in the spring of 2012 the parliament had passed a law adding convictions for "crimes against the state" to the list of reasons to ban someone from teaching; and everyone had become an enforcer.[1] Lyosha went and got himself certified as never having been convicted of violent, sexual, or political offenses.

In August he was feeling all right. A ban on "propaganda of homosexuality" had passed in St. Petersburg in November 2011,[2] but he thought that maybe it would not pass at the federal level. It was not the first such city law in Russia, after all. Still, this was the country's second-largest city, and it was Putin's city. Also, the law had a particularly prominent advocate there, a local legislature member, Vitaly Milonov. As a scholar, Lyosha could not stop watching Milonov. As a gay man, he felt sickened and terrified by him in a way he had never experienced before. Flamboyant and at times effeminate, Milonov read as gay—though, obviously, not to his current audience. Lyosha knew that the world had seen this before. Milonov introduced the St. Petersburg law, which prescribed fines for "propaganda" from roughly $100 to about $1,500, by saying that "the wave of popularity of sexual deviations has a negative impact on our children." His fellow legislators did not simply support him: they immediately wanted to go further. "Children who have been crippled by pedophiles jump out of windows, they commit suicide," said another legislator during the discussion of the bill. "Pedophilia is a threat to a child's life. That sort of propaganda should be punished by at least twenty years in prison." Other legislators picked up from there, making Milonov look like a moderate.[3]

Once the law was passed, Milonov tried to get Madonna fined for alleged propaganda during her August 2012 St. Petersburg concert.[4] Other legislators wanted to ban a chain of drugstores called Rainbow and a popular brand of cheese with a rainbow on the package.[5] Milonov kept raising the stakes. He teamed up with an organization called Parental Control and went hunting—his word—for pedophiles. It was the old entrapment technique: "hunters" posing as teenage boys met men on social networks and scheduled a date, to which they showed up accompanied by television reporters. The mark was made to confirm, on camera, that he had written the messages to the fictional minor, whereupon he was delivered to a police station and written up on "propaganda" charges.[6] Under the new law there was no need to demonstrate that the messages were sexual in nature: as innocuous a message as "It gets better—you can be gay and happy" was plainly a violation. For his next legislative initiative, Milonov wanted to introduce a mandatory psychological test for teachers to weed out the pedophiles—a reasonable enough idea, now that psychiatrists across the county were learning to diagnose "pedophilic sexual orientation."[7]

The ban on "propaganda of homosexuality" was introduced at the federal level in March 2012. Yelena Mizulina, head of the parliamentary Committee on the Family, took up the mantle—and now she, too, finally shot to national fame, edging out Milonov. This would be her project, an amendment to the Law for the Protection of Children from Information.[8] The parliamentary office of legal review seemed dubious about the bill, though: it noted that Russian law did not provide a clear definition of the word "homosexuality."[9] Lyosha thought that maybe this was an elegant legalistic way of scuttling the bill. But then Mizulina fired back with a long letter:

> Propaganda of homosexuality is widespread in Russia today: there are gay parades, demonstrations, and television and radio programs in support of same-sex unions that are broadcast on all channels in the daytime.
>
> Such widespread distribution of propaganda of homosexual relations exerts a negative influence on the development of a child's personality, dilutes his concept of the family as a union of man and woman, and practically creates the conditions for limiting a child's freedom to choose his own sexual preference when he grows up.[10]

Clearly, only the pedophile lobby could advocate delaying the passage of the bill, which in the federal parliament was referred to as a ban on "propaganda that negates traditional family values."

On television, the debate centered not on whether "gay propaganda" should be banned but, as in the St. Petersburg city legislature, on whether this measure would be enough to protect the children.

> It is not enough to fine gays for propaganda to teenagers. We need to ban blood and sperm donations by them, and if they should die in a car accident, we need to bury their hearts underground or burn them, for they are unsuitable for the aiding of anyone's life.[11]

This was one of the country's best-known television hosts, speaking at the beginning of an hour-and-a-half special on the largest state television channel. The show was structured as a debate, or a mock court: two opponents and three witnesses on each side, all of them famous and all of them straight. It also so happened that everyone on the ban-the-gays side was an ethnic Russian while their opponents were two Jews, a Georgian, and an American citizen, the old dissident Ludmila Alekseeva. The pro-ban side rehearsed the proud history of anti-homosexuality laws of the twentieth century. Both Stalin and Hitler persecuted gays, both saw them as probable spies, and both saw them as bringing moral decay to their armies. Anti-gay laws, it seemed, were an attribute of strong state power. A priest on the pro-ban side pointed out that it is indeed easier for an intelligence agency to recruit a homosexual, so the perception of gays as spies was rooted in fact. No wonder West Germany kept the ban, in the form in which the law had been redrafted under Hitler, even after the war—it was sound policy. But Russia had foolishly rushed to get rid of its sodomy ban as soon as the Soviet Union collapsed.

"They are unable to reproduce," said Dmitry Kiselev, the famous TV host and the leader of the pro-ban team. "This forces them to steal children from the healthy majority." Gay propaganda was a tool of this theft.

A lawyer on the pro-ban side read out the Constitutional Court's definition of "propaganda of homosexuality": "information that can cause harm to the physical or spiritual development of children and create in them the erroneous impression of social equality of traditional and nontraditional marital relations." In other words, the ban was explicitly meant to enshrine second-class citizenship in law.

The anti-ban side tried valiantly, but reason was helpless against demagogy. Nikolai Svanidze, a historian and also a prominent television personality, who led the anti-ban team, tried saying that all this talk of homosexuality was a maneuver to draw attention away from important issues.

"Are you saying that children are not an important issue?" the pro-ban side erupted. "We are talking about children! Our children!"

In his closing statement Kiselev said, "This is a time when we especially need to protect the children we have borne. We all want them to be loved, to live a long time, and to bring us the joy of grandchildren. Sexual minorities have a different plan."

Svanidze asked the audience to "imagine that your very own child has a nontraditional sexual orientation. Will you love him less? Will you want him to be bullied?"

Svanidze's vote counter, which had been ticking slower than Kiselev's all along—viewers could call in to vote for one or the other throughout the show—stopped dead. Russian television viewers were not willing to imagine that they had a gay child. Svanidze's side lost, 7,375 votes to 34,951.

Gays were shaping up to be the perfect scapegoat: they were spies, they were bad for the army and dangerous to children, and whatever acceptance they had gained was a mistake made in 1993, under pressure from the West. Banning the gays, or at least shutting them up, was a shortcut to health and power, a rebuke to the West, and a guarantee of a populous and healthy nation.

Still, when the bill lingered in parliament, when there had been no vote on it half a year later, Lyosha convinced himself that it might not pass.

OLEG CHIRKUNOV, the Perm governor, resigned in April 2012: he had been under attack from state television for some time.[12] The funder of his "cultural revolution" project pulled out of Perm: Gordeev faded from view, having resigned his senate seat and sold his companies. Guelman, the art dealer and former political technologist, continued to run the PERMM, the contemporary art museum. For the White Nights festival in 2013 he organized several shows. One, called *Russian Baroque*, was shut down by the city when it was discovered that it featured photographs from the 2011–2012 protests. Another show, *Welcome! Sochi 2014*, satirized the preparations for the winter games. This one was shuttered as soon as it opened. Soon Guelman was fired as director of the museum. A short time later he moved to Montenegro, together with his family and his curatorial projects.[13]

In September 2012, teaching started as usual, except it was harder. Lyosha submitted a chapter to the department's annual. It was called "Queer Identity in Russia and the Discourse of Human Rights." People in the department gave him good notes. Everyone liked it, and Lyosha was happy with it and happy with his colleagues, who were just being good academics, like there was no madness on television. Then there was a review meeting, and all the same people trashed the paper. They said it was politics, not scholarship. Lyosha said that he would be willing to rework the paper, but consensus was that the paper was beyond repair.

The department chair's recommendations to tone down his research became an order. Lyosha would no longer be allowed to travel to LGBT studies conferences, even if the other side paid for the trip—he was free to travel in his personal capacity, that is, but he should not mention the university. The department had a new grant to study social media. Lyosha was welcome to travel to international conferences under the auspices of this project—all he had to do was change his topic. He did. He started writing about social media. Then he went to conferences in Switzerland and Berlin and delivered papers on "social networks as the new closet." Back in Perm, no one said anything. Except once a friend texted him from a conference: she was sitting next to their department chair, who was complaining that Lyosha was exposing the department to risk. "That's what I get for taking a faggot under my wing," the chair said, and the friend put her phrase in her text message.

It was all true. Lyosha was a faggot, and the chair had had him under her wing. She had been very kind to him. She had cared about him, and she had confided in him. He felt like he had been slapped.

He and Darya still had their gender studies center. They still had the money to hold the annual Gender Aspects of the Social Sciences conference, buy tea and cookies for the participants, and print three hundred copies of the collection of conference papers.

That fall he and Darya were called to a department meeting to talk about the work of the center. They decided that Darya would talk about their work in general and Lyosha would talk about its LGBT aspects. He was better at keeping his cool.

"You and I," said Lyosha, addressing fellow faculty members, "we say that we produce knowledge. LGBT people exist. Their experience is a factor in politics."

No kidding. If you so much as turned on the television, you would get the impression that LGBT people were the only factor in politics. The department listened in silence. It was a horrible, angry and sticky silence, but they did not say anything and this meant that the gender studies center continued to exist, for now.

Much of the center's work happened outside the university. Darya and Lyosha had long ago agreed that educating the public about gender was part of their mission. Darya maintained a public page on VK.com, the Russian social network that used to be known as VKontakte. This started to get tricky. People were writing hate messages. Some of these commenters were their former students, who were now accusing Lyosha and Darya of propaganda. Every time this happened, Darya wanted to take down their page. The messages did not scare her—she really was fearless—but they hurt. Lyosha talked her down. This was work. They were producing knowledge.

LYOSHA'S IDEA of "social networks as the new closet" had a connection to his own life, much of which was happening online. Soon after he broke up with the other Lyosha, a man named Mitya wrote to him on VK. They had seen each other once, during one of those big Perm "cultural revolution" events. Mitya had an incomprehensible-sounding job—he was a marketing coach—and an exotic Moscow lifestyle. He meditated, rode his bicycle for exercise, and watched what he ate. He was driven and ambitious, and he pushed Lyosha to seek recognition by entering his poetry in competitions. He also demanded that Lyosha start taking care of his body, especially because Lyosha's kidney problems—the aftereffects of that playground gay-bashing in Solikamsk—had been flaring up. They messaged about everything—what they did, what the world was like, and what love was. They did not see each other, though. More than a year after they started messaging, Mitya invited

Lyosha to spend a couple of days in his native Nizhny Novgorod. It was a great two days and three nights. The weather was brutally cold, but they went for walks anyway. Talking to each other was easy and fun, as was the sex. But then they did not see each other again for about a year, and then another year after that. In between, Mitya sometimes disappeared for weeks or a couple of months at a time, only to pop back up on Skype as though he'd never been gone.

Andrei showed up during one of Mitya's absences. He had graduated from Perm State University the same year as Lyosha. Lyosha had had a crush on him during their first year, but they never really talked: Andrei came from a wealthy family and traveled in different circles. Now he was a lawyer in Geneva. They ran into each other when he was visiting Perm and soon started Skyping every day. Lyosha talked about the pressure at his department.

"What are you still doing there?" asked Andrei, meaning, *What are you still doing in Russia?* "You've got to get out. And you've got to start learning English."

Andrei kept complaining about his girlfriend, who lived in New York, until one day he confessed that this was actually a boyfriend.

"I knew that," said Lyosha.

After that, Lyosha spent a couple of months coaching Andrei through his coming-out process.

Maybe it was not exactly a closet, but Lyosha's social and emotional life was neatly compartmentalized. In Perm, he had his work and a close friend and collaborator in Darya. His romantic life happened in messages, and, during the periods of Mitya's disappearance, in his imagination. His emotional support came from Andrei via Skype.

In the fall of 2012, Lyosha swung by Geneva to visit Andrei after delivering his paper on "social networks as the new closet" at a conference in Basel. He had just arrived back in Perm when he went to meet a friend for dinner. The friend brought another friend, and Lyosha could not stop talking—about the conference, his paper, Geneva. He might have felt self-conscious afterward, had he not heard from his friend's friend immediately. His name was Ilya. He messaged Lyosha that he was impressed.

Ilya was a few years younger, a recent chemistry department graduate working as a waiter. Dating him was easy. There was none of the anxiety, competition, or obsession that Lyosha had experienced in his previous involvements. There was no talk of love. They did not move in together. They just enjoyed each other.

ON JANUARY 25, the parliament took the first of three required votes on the "propaganda" bill. A couple of members, including Masha's former boss Ilya Ponomarev, questioned whether the measure was necessary.

"You shouldn't treat this issue so lightly!" objected Mizulina. "Just two years ago seventy percent of all sexual crimes were committed against girls. Now many of them are committed against boys! Think about why that is!"

In the end, only one parliament member abstained from voting for the bill and one voted against it—although this member, a novice who had just recently been called up to fill an empty seat, soon said that he had accidentally pushed the wrong button. Three hundred eighty-eight voted in favor. Several, including Ponomarev, left the hall to avoid the vote.[14]

At the entrance to the parliament, LGBT protesters were outnumbered by thugs who threw Nazi-style salutes, tossed eggs and excrement at the protesters, and beat them. A protester's nose was broken. The police watched for a while and then arrested the protesters, not the thugs. A small group of supporters stood to the side of the protesters—they had no banners or pink-triangle buttons, and they kept the physical distance necessary to avoid beatings and arrest. One of them, a biology teacher from a prestigious Moscow high school, was caught on camera trying to reason with one of the thugs. The following day, the teacher, who was straight and married to a woman, lost his job.*

In the spring the Levada Center tried to take a measure of public opinion

---

*The teacher was Ilya Kolmanovsky. He was fired from School Number 2, one of Moscow's two schools famous for their outstanding instruction in math and other subjects.

toward LGBT people. Seventy-three percent of respondents said that they wholeheartedly supported the law. The figure was shocking—for more than two decades the Homo Sovieticus surveys had shown the level of aggression toward "sexual minorities" gradually subsiding. What did this 73 percent mean, and what did people think they were supporting? It occurred to Gudkov that his staff did not know what they were measuring. He asked them to take another look at the questions they had been asking. Every phrase used in the survey had been beaten to death on television, and including these phrases in questions predetermined the answers. Gudkov asked the young sociologists to redesign and re-administer the survey. They tried. They brought in advisers—LGBT activists they knew. They got stuck.

There were only so many ways to say "gay." The Homo Sovieticus survey had traditionally used the phrase "sexual minorities," but the advisers were adamantly opposed to it: they thought the term was demeaning. Perhaps more to the point, it dated back to a time before gays became a topic of political conversation in Russia, had fallen out of use, and probably was not the best term to measure current attitudes. "LGBT" would be incomprehensible to most Russians. "Nontraditional sexual orientation" was the term the state used, so it would inevitably frame the question and the answer. By equating "homosexual" with "pedophile" and proposing to burn gay hearts, television had appropriated those terms for the propaganda campaign as well. "Queer" was even more obscure than "LGBT." They could think of no other way to ask the questions: the Kremlin had hijacked the language.

———

ON MAY 9, 2013, Lyosha turned twenty-eight. He cooked dinner for seven or eight friends that evening at his apartment—he had been living alone for over a year now. Ilya was working the late-night shift; he left after the dinner, to return in the wee hours.

That morning Putin shouted "Glory to Russia!" Eleven thousand troops marched through Red Square and across television screens, followed by at least three kinds of armored vehicles and tanks, five kinds of missile launchers, and sixty-eight different helicopters and airplanes.[15] The city of Volgograd also held a parade. Earlier in the year, the local legislature had voted to use the city's old name during the festivities, so that day it was Stalingrad.[16]

All over Russia, there were fireworks that night. The people of Volgograd/Stalingrad watched them from the city's Volga embankment. When the fireworks ended, a little after ten, a twenty-three-year-old named Vlad Tornovoy and his friends left the embankment to start the long trek home to the working-class outskirts. It was after midnight when Tornovoy was drinking beer with two friends on a bench in a playground in their neighborhood. Then his friends killed him. First they beat him and kicked him, then, while he was lying on the ground, they pushed a half-liter empty beer bottle up his anus. Then another. The third bottle went in only halfway. Then they kicked him some more, and one of the bottles popped out of his body. They threw a flattened-out discarded cardboard box on him and set it on fire, but the fire went out quickly. Then one of them picked up a forty-pound boulder and threw it at Tornovoy's head five or six times. Tornovoy died. Then his friends went home and went to sleep.

The killers were arrested the next morning. They explained that they had killed Tornovoy because he was gay. Television reported that the killers said his homosexuality "offended their sense of patriotism." Other news media got hold of a video in which an investigator was interrogating one of the suspects.

> DETECTIVE: Why did you do it?
> SUSPECT: Why? Because he is a homo.
> DETECTIVE: Is that the only reason?
> SUSPECT: Yes.

It turned out that there was an eyewitness, a man who happened on the scene, sat down on the bench, and watched the murder happen. "I don't feel guilty," he told a reporter. "But I do still feel kind of queasy inside. . . . They killed him, you know, because he was gay." The eyewitness faced no charges.[17]

Ilya came to Lyosha's apartment from work in the early hours of the morning, wished him a happy birthday again, and went to bed. Lyosha got up, sat down at the computer, and read about the murder of Vlad Tornovoy. It had been a year since the televised anti-gay campaign began, and many people made the connection. A barrage of posts on social networks asked Mizulina, the backer of the "propaganda" bill, if this was what she wanted.

"If you accuse crime fighters of creating more crime, then we will never be able to defeat crime," she told journalists, responding to the social media storm. "That's just dumb."[18] In other words, Tornovoy was killed because he had been flaunting his sexuality—exactly the thing she was trying to ban. She pledged that she would get the law passed in the next few weeks. Now Lyosha believed it.

THE PARLIAMENT VOTED for the ban in its second and third readings on June 11, 2013. A few dozen activists staged a protest at the entrance to parliament and were beaten by counterprotesters while police looked on. Eventually the police pushed the LGBT protesters onto paddy wagons and drove them to a precinct. The counterprotesters stayed and beat up two young gay men who had been left behind.

Masha was late for the protest: she had overslept. When she got there, she saw the paddy wagons pulling out. She walked to the nearest police precinct—she had spent time there before, so she knew the location and the drill: bring water for the detainees, who might be stuck in an unventilated room for many hours. She saw two plainclothes cops walking out with a man she recognized. He was the thug who had broken a protester's nose back in January. The men turned the corner. She followed them. She was not sure what she was going to do, but she had to do something.

One of the men stopped abruptly and turned around. He was tall and athletic. Then Masha must have passed out. She came to on the ground, on the sidewalk around the corner from the police station. The men were gone. Her abdomen hurt like something huge and hard had been slammed into it.

It was a sunny summer afternoon in the very center of Moscow; office workers were coming back from their lunch breaks. Someone called an ambulance.

At the Sklifasovsky trauma center Masha could not produce a urine sample. She could not pee. The doctors were nice about it: they inserted a catheter. After the X-rays and ultrasounds they said there was no permanent damage and in a day or two she would pee for herself again.

TWO DAYS after the law passed, the parliamentary committees on the family and on foreign relations held a joint session attended by five foreign guests. Brian S. Brown, head of the National Organization for Marriage, formed a few years earlier to pass legislation against same-sex marriage in California, and French National Front activist Aymeric Chauprade were among them. The foreigners had come to praise the Russians and urge them to use their momentum to go further. Said Chauprade:

> You must understand that patriots of countries the world over, those committed to protecting the independence of their nations and the foundations of our civilization, are looking to Moscow. It is with great hope that they are looking to Russia, which has taken a stand against the legalization, the public legalization of homosexuality, against the interference of nihilistic nongovernmental organizations which are manipulated by American secret services, and against the adoption of children by homosexual couples.
>
> Ladies and gentlemen, members of parliament, Russia has become the hope of the entire world. . . .
>
> Long live the European Christian civilization! Long live Russia! Long live France![19]

Gays had become Public Enemy Number One: foreign agents, the foot soldiers of a looming American takeover, a threat to the foundational values

of the European civilization. One hardly had to mention pedophilia anymore to communicate that gays were dangerous. The fight against them, on
the other hand, positioned Russia as the European civilization's bastion
of hope.

The joint committee resolved to pass legislation that would ban adoption
by same-sex couples or single people from countries where same-sex marriage was legal. They stressed that even this measure would be insufficient,
because there was no foolproof way to ensure that Russian children adopted
by heterosexual foreigners would never be re-adopted by homosexuals. After
the meeting, Mizulina told journalists that she would also devise a way to
have biological children removed from same-sex families.[20]

The adoption ban was passed just a week after the ban on "propaganda"—
in time to become law before the parliament went on summer break. Both
bills passed unanimously. A bill to enable the removal of biological children was introduced as soon as the parliament went back into session in
September.[21]

That year Putin hosted his tenth annual Valdai Club, a weekend junket
at which he made his case on a topic of choice to a select group of foreign
Russia experts. This year he spoke about Russian sovereignty and national
identity:

> Russia is facing a serious challenge to its identity. This issue has
> aspects of both morality and foreign policy. We can see many
> EuroAtlantic countries rejecting their own roots, including Christian
> values, which form the foundation of Western civilization. They re-
> ject their own moral foundations as well as all traditional identities:
> national, cultural, religious, and even gender. They pursue policies
> that place large families on an equal footing with same-sex partner-
> ships, and faith in god with satan worship. An excess of political
> correctness has led to the point that there is talk of registering poli-
> tical parties that promote pedophilia. In many European countries
> people are ashamed and frightened to talk about their religious

affiliation. . . . And this is the model that is being aggressively forced onto the entire world. I am convinced that this is the road to degradation and primitivization, a deep demographic and moral crisis.[22]

Satan, pedophilia, American aggression, the death of the Christian civilization, and, of course, a demographic threat: it was all about the gays now.

The following September, it had been announced, the Kremlin and the Church together would host the World Congress of Families, the organization founded at the sociology department back in 1995. Its headquarters were in Illinois, and its meetings had been held in Europe, the United States, and Australia. In the United States, people who monitored far-right organizations perceived it as an American political export.[23] But Russians, with their money and the high stature afforded their cause by the state, were taking leadership roles in the organization,[24] which would now be coming home in high style. Congress sessions were slated to be held in the Kremlin Palace of Congresses, inside the fortress walls, and a small distance away, at the Cathedral of Christ the Savior, the country's largest—where Pussy Riot had staged their "Punk Prayer" in 2012.[25]

LYOSHA WAS IN NEW YORK when the law passed. He and Ilya were on vacation together. They had been seeing each other for more than half a year. It was still the most companionable relationship Lyosha had ever had. Ilya was a bit immature, but he knew his limitations, and both of these traits made him a perfect weekend-and-holiday partner. That, the distance, and the splendor of New York kept Lyosha from spending too much time thinking about the passage of the law.

Teaching began again in September. Budget cuts had led to some changes in the department. When Lyosha was an undergraduate, all students had been required to take a set of core courses common to the given area of specialization in all Russian universities—this was called the "federal curriculum"—and at least one elective a semester, out of a small number on offer: the "regional curriculum." Now the regional curriculum had been cut down to two courses, and in September each student was asked to pick one. The course chosen by more than half the students would be the only one offered—an elective in the sense that there had been an election of sorts. All the students in a particular specialty would be required to take it that semester.

This was how Lyosha ended up with two groups of more than twenty students in his Gender Approaches in Politics course. He was teaching it twice a week, once to international relations majors and once to political science majors (he was also teaching a "federal" course, Political Processes in Contemporary Russia, which met twice a week). The political scientists were a joy, but some of the international relations students made it clear that they did not want to be there. One student rose and left the room every time the subject of sex came up—as when Lyosha had them discuss *The Myth of the Vaginal Orgasm*, the classic feminist essay by the American Anne Koedt. Then there were two young men, both of them straight-A students, who always sat together and took turns standing up to object every time Lyosha made reference to the patriarchy.

"It has been proven historically that men are the stronger sex," one would say. "What you are saying now harms the institution of family."

Lyosha would calmly try to steer them back to the text under discussion.

"But those are Western studies that you are citing," the other would get up and say. "They are always trying to foist their values on us."

Lyosha had the class watch and write about *The Times of Harvey Milk*, a 1984 documentary about the openly gay San Francisco city supervisor who was assassinated by another legislator. One of the two young men in the class turned in a paper arguing that gays, not being real men, could not be politicians. The paper dripped with homophobia, but unlike the comments the same student left on the gender studies center's VK page, it contained no obscenities. Lyosha gave the student an A: within its framework, the paper was well argued.

LATER IN THE FALL Lyosha got a text message from Darya.

"A friend has been entrapped by Occupy Pedophilia." Lyosha had heard something about this. Occupy Pedophilia was the skinhead version of the online entrapment movement. He knew it was operating in different cities, but he did not know about incidents in Perm. Lyosha looked up the Occupy Pedophilia/Perm page on VK.

"Our next safari will take place on Thursday. Open to all. Entry fee 250 rubles."

The group included more than two thousand members. Lyosha recognized many of the names: he had graded their papers.

He clicked on a video. It showed Darya's friend Valeriy*—Lyosha had met him too. He stood against a tiled wall—it looked like a pedestrian underpass or perhaps the basement of a shopping center, flanked by two large young men. At the beginning of the clip he stated his full name, age, and place of work: he was thirty and taught at a trade school.

"We used to treat pedophilia with urinotherapy," one of the thugs said about halfway through the ten-minute clip. "But especially for you, we have chosen the banana treatment. This is a sacred banana."

From that point on, Valeriy stood with a half-peeled banana in his hands.

FIRST THUG: Have you been gay a long time?

VALERIY: Since I was eighteen.

FIRST THUG: What made you that way?

VALERIY: Nothing.

SECOND THUG: How is that possible? Did you grow up with both of your parents?

VALERIY: Yes.

SECOND THUG: Maybe something went wrong for you with a girl?

---

*Valeriy is a common man's name in Russia.

VALERIY: Not really.

SECOND THUG: Do you believe in God?

VALERIY: Yes.

FIRST THUG: What's your religion?

VALERIY: I am Orthodox.

SECOND THUG: What was it that Jesus said?

FIRST THUG: His kind must be stoned.

There was a splice and then you could see Valeriy squatting, as instructed by the thugs, and eating the banana as they guffawed.[26]

In another clip the thugs had filmed themselves barging into the apartment of Mikhail, an older man Lyosha had seen around for years. The clip had been edited down to twelve minutes and fifty-six seconds from what must have been a much longer ordeal. In that time, the man went from telling the thugs sternly to get out to begging for mercy. Lyosha could see repeated flashes of a taser gun. Most of the clip had been filmed through the open apartment door. At one point, someone must have been walking up or down the stairs, because the thugs called out: "Hey, did you know you have a pedophile living here?" That was when Mikhail looked terrified for the first time and said for the first time, not yet pleadingly, "That's enough."

A few minutes later in the clip Mikhail was on the floor. He had been beaten. The words "I'm fag" had been written in ballpoint pen on his bald head. The thugs pulled him up and propped him against the wall because he could no longer stand on his own. Then they took him around the building, knocking on doors and informing neighbors that he was a pedophile. The thugs introduced themselves as representing "the social movement to prevent pedophilia." The neighbors were receptive. One man in a T-shirt and jeans, with a good haircut—he looked like a young banker or maybe a marketing executive—took down the name of the site where he would be able to watch the video. An older woman in a housecoat popped out of her apartment to testify: "I've seen it! He's got young men coming around all the time!"

The clip ended with Mikhail on his knees, promising never to correspond with boys and saying, "Long live Occupy Pedophilia." He also said, "Death to blacks," and "Glory to Russia."[27]

There was also a clip shot on a sunny afternoon on a busy Perm street. Another acquaintance, Andrei, was being held, yelled at, and tasered by two thugs while two more looked on in view of the camera. Andrei kept calling out to passersby, asking them to call the police. No one stopped, it seemed. But Andrei kept refusing to answer questions about his sexual orientation, or about what he thought of people from the Caucasus. The taser gun kept crackling, and he kept saying, in response to every question, "What does it matter." In the end, the thugs called the police themselves. The clip ended with Andrei being pushed into the back of a police car by two officers and two Occupy thugs.[28]

The thugs in each clip were different. They must have taken turns starring. And then there were the people off-camera, who had paid 250 rubles (roughly eight dollars) a pop to watch.

Lyosha got up and checked the door. Living alone had all at once lost all sense of accomplishment and romance. The door was locked, but it looked useless to Lyosha now. It would take but a few minutes to break down this door, and no one would know.

Darya told him that Valeriy went to the police to try to report having been kidnapped and tortured, but the police threatened him with arrest. He resigned his job at the trade school without waiting for the video to be posted online.

THAT FALL the university got a new staff member. He was in his mid-forties, had close-cropped gray hair, and always wore a suit. His job title was Security Adviser. There had been someone in that role before him, a retired military man of advanced age. He had had no presence and, as far as Lyosha knew, no job title. This one was different. "I think we've got our First Department now," Lyosha said to Darya.

"First Department" in the Soviet Union existed in all organizations that had anything to do with state secrets—which, in that country, covered many if not most organizations—as well as organizations engaged in what was called "ideological work," such as the media or any educational institution. First Department staff reported to the KGB rather than the head of the organization where they ostensibly worked.

In October, Darya went on maternity leave. This left Lyosha alone in charge of the gender studies center. It also meant that Lyosha temporarily took over the administrative duties of assistant dean. He was told that in this capacity he needed to have an introductory meeting with the new security adviser, whose name, as it turned out, was Yuri Gennadyevich Belorustev. He had an office in an old dormitory building. Lyosha recognized the office: a wall of shelves crowded with thick binders; stained wallpaper on the other walls; two well-worn chairs with wooden armrests; a not-quite-matching desk; a potted plant; and white lace curtains on the windows. Lyosha's uncle and cousin, military officers both, had identical offices. This one seemed too small for Yuri Gennadyevich. Or too old. Or a stage set.

"Let's use the informal pronoun with each other," said Yuri Gennadyevich. "This is a friendly conversation."

Lyosha waited. You cannot say no when someone older than you proposes switching to the informal pronoun. Yuri Gennadyevich had a peculiarly soft, treacly voice.

"Do you have students in your department who are restless?"

"I'm not sure what you mean."

"You know, nationalists, radical communists, homosexuals—"

"I don't think keeping abreast of students' personal lives is part of my job description."

"Well, you just make sure to let me know."

Yuri Gennadyevich called Lyosha once a week after that. Lyosha tried not to say a word that could be interpreted as meaning anything. That was difficult to manage on the phone. Sometimes, Yuri Gennadyevich asked Lyosha about a particular student, who Lyosha knew was troubled. It was hard not to notice, but Lyosha pretended to be oblivious. "Do you think he needs psychological help?" Yuri Gennadyevich would ask.

Not from you, Lyosha would think. He would say, "I'm not sure what you mean."

He saw Yuri Gennadyevich every day. The old security adviser must have spent his days sleeping in an armchair in his office. Yuri Gennadyevich was everywhere all the time.

In December the gender studies center held its annual conference. Lyosha chaired the panel on queer identity. As he was exiting the room, he bumped into Yuri Gennadyevich.

"What do you have here?"

"Our annual conference."

Yuri Gennadyevich took a printed program. "Looks very interesting."

Two weeks later Lyosha realized that he was under surveillance. When he came home, there were always plainclothes men milling near the building entrance. As soon as he walked up, the intercom would ring, then the landline, then his cell. A man's voice would repeat the same phrase over and over:

"Your kind deserves to die."

Sometimes Lyosha was sure that the omnipresent "security adviser," the men at the door, and the calls were connected. Sometimes he thought he was paranoid. Whichever was the case, he could not survive intact much longer: if he did not get killed, he would go crazy.

"YOU ARE MOVING IN WITH ME," said Stas. He said it as if they had discussed it.

It was a good option for both of them. Stas had just ended a destructive relationship after four years, and nights alone in his apartment were unbearable. But Stas's apartment was in a secure building with a fence, cameras, and guards. Stas was a wealthy executive. He told Lyosha not to tell anyone where he was living, and he had his personal driver ferry Lyosha wherever he needed to go, which was just to work and then back to the apartment in the evening. Stas and Lyosha cooked for each other. Over dinner, night after night, they told each other everything. Stas talked out the details of his awful relationship. Lyosha obsessed about the university and his future. They cried like neither of them had cried before, two grown men terrified of their lives, their hearts breaking for each other. They had sex once or twice, but this clearly was not why they had each other, even though Lyosha's companionate relationship with Ilya had ended: Ilya knew when he was out of his depth, and he left as easily and kindly as he had come. After a couple of months, Lyosha realized that he had a family now, someone who made him feel safe.

IN APRIL 2014, Lyosha was getting ready to go to work when he got a message from a friend, an administrator at the university: "Lyosha, what is this? Yuri Gennadyevich has brought it to the rector's attention."*

Lyosha clicked on the link. It was a VK post called "What Is Perm Thinking? Propaganda of Sodomy at Perm State Research University." The post went on to describe the gender studies center and ended with a call to action:

> How long can this abominable situation go on? Avowed enemies of the Motherland and of morality are using our money to corrupt students in every sense of the word. When will we put an end to this?
>
> Draw community attention to this! Write to the Perm [State] University rector; file complaints with the police! We are Russian patriots! Victory will be ours!

Photos of Darya and Lyosha were pasted below.[29]

"You are going to have to leave," said Stas that evening. Lyosha already had a ticket to New York: he had liked it so much the previous year that he

---

*In the Russian system the rector is the chief executive of a university—roughly the equivalent of the university president in the U.S. system or the vice chancellor in the UK.

wanted to resume that vacation. He started living on two tracks. On one, he submitted his lesson plans for the coming fall semester. He took part in worrying about further budget cuts and lamenting the fact that the state had no interest in political science anymore. On the other track, he was wrapping up research and friendships. The telephone threats continued. Yuri Gennadyevich kept calling too, asking, "Why don't you ever come and see me?"

In May, Stas threw a birthday party for Lyosha and invited all his friends. No one had done this for him before. In June, they packed up Lyosha's stuff. In July, they drove out to Solikamsk to drop off many of his things and tell his mother that he was leaving.

"What are you going to do there?" asked Galina.

"I like that boy," said Lyosha's aunt. "I hope you bring him around again."

Wouldn't you know it: they had finally accepted him.

———

STAS GAVE LYOSHA $18,000.

"It's an investment in my future," he said. "I plan to retire in America. You go and get things ready."

It was enough to pay a year's rent in Brighton Beach, where apartments were cheap and the landlords spoke Russian and did not care if you had a credit history. There were many Russian queers in the neighborhood—mostly men around Lyosha's age, single and in couples. All of them had fled Russia in the last year. Everyone had a story, and they taught Lyosha how to package his into an asylum claim and how to find a lawyer, and how to apply for a work permit when the time came. Then Lyosha helped teach people who came after him.

In August, he wrote to the department: "I had no choice but to leave the country."

The chair responded with a perfectly mixed message: "Did you stop to consider what kind of trouble that would cause here? Now I have to find someone to take over your teaching load. I always knew you were going to do it. I wish you luck."

Then he heard from Darya and another friend: Yuri Gennadyevich had been calling people in for talks, grilling them about Lyosha. The words "foreign agent" were said. Also, they had figured out that the person who wrote that "What is Perm thinking?" post was someone who had attended the Soros-funded seminars in Ukraine with them.

Then he heard from the department chair again: "We have informed the administration that you are obtaining postgraduate education in the United States. Kindly conform to this story."

LYOSHA STARTED putting together his asylum case. He wrote to a close friend, a former student, who had gotten a phone call from the FSB in the spring of 2013.

"Whom do you have in your department at the university who engages in the propaganda of homosexuality?"

"Are you kidding me?" she had responded. "I graduated a million years ago."

Now Lyosha messaged this friend asking if she would put this story in an affidavit.

"Dear Lyosha," she wrote in response. "I don't know what you are talking about. I never got any such call, and you should be aware that libel is a criminal offense."

Lyosha mentally crossed another friend off the list. The rate of attrition was staggering. He still had Andrei in Geneva, and Stas, who had moved to Moscow. For a while, he continued to correspond with Darya. She had shut down the gender studies group on VK. "I have no desire to continue to do gender studies," she wrote. About eight months after Lyosha left the country, they just did not seem to have anything left to talk about.

twenty

A NATION DIVIDED

IN THE FALL OF 2013, Masha spent her days in court and her evenings at cafés and bars, sometimes working on foreign reporters' assignments or on her own, often not. She was almost always angry and often, by the end of the evening, drunk. There were many arguments that she remembered only because her throat felt scratchy in the morning.

The faces at those cafés were familiar from the protests. Now they had all gone back to their regular lives at television channels, advertising agencies, and, in more than a few cases, in government offices. They were often drunk by the end of the evening too—especially the men from the government offices. One night one of them patted the chair next to him with his pudgy hand: he had something to tell Masha. He said there would be an amnesty—nominally tied to the twentieth anniversary of Yeltsin's constitution, but really intended to make Putin look better in advance of the Sochi Olympics. Amnesties always applied to women, especially if they had small children. So Masha's ordeal would soon be over, he said.

She believed him. Her friends told her it was wishful thinking. They pointed out that Putin was not acting like he cared one bit about improving his image for the Olympics. The women of Pussy Riot were still behind bars—one of them had declared a hunger strike to protest starvation rations and sixteen-hour workdays at her prison colony, and though her open letter had been published the world over,[1] the state appeared willing to let her starve to death. The country's most famous inmate, Mikhail Khodorkovsky, was approaching the tenth anniversary of his imprisonment, with no end in sight. And in September, Russian troops in unmarked uniforms had hijacked a Greenpeace ship flying a Dutch flag in international waters, towed it to the port of Murmansk, and deposited its multinational thirty-person crew in jails there.[2] Just because the ruthlessness of Russian law enforcement defied the imagination, these friends argued, was no reason to disbelieve its threats—quite the opposite.

"I am not going to prison," Masha took to saying to them, like a mantra. "I am walking between the raindrops and staying dry." It was an idiomatic expression, customarily used in the third person, but that fall she made it her own. Still, that was the fall when she started throwing up blood.

In December, Western leaders began backing out of going to the Sochi Olympics. German president Joachim Gauck was the first to announce his non-attendance, followed by the presidents of Poland, Estonia, and France, and the prime minister of Belgium. Finally, American president Barack Obama chose his delegation. It included no high-level politicians— something that had not happened in almost two decades—but, in a well-calculated affront, did include two openly gay athletes.[3] The next day came the amnesty: Masha would not go to prison, the women of Pussy Riot would be released, and so would the thirty Greenpeace activists.[4] And at the end of his annual press conference, on December 20, Putin made an announcement that no one, including his inner circle, expected: he would release Khodorkovsky.[5] Within hours, the former oil tycoon was transported out of the prison and out of the country—to Berlin, where his mother lay gravely ill. A clear condition of Khodorkovsky's release was that he would not return to Russia—unless he wanted to be arrested again. With his company and most of his fortune gone, he would have to reinvent himself on foreign soil. He landed in Germany wearing an airport crew jacket that someone had given him en route, to replace his black prison robe.[6]

Masha, on the other hand, was still in her own city, wearing her old clothes. No one was going to transport her to her new life now that she was no longer a full-time defendant in a political trial. What was she supposed to do with herself now?

OVER HER YEAR AND A HALF of living as a de facto political prisoner, Masha had not been paying much attention to the outside world. The most important event in this outside world was the ongoing protest in Ukraine. The president there had backed out of signing a partnership agreement with the European Union, and Ukrainians had been protesting since November. Like the Orange Revolution nine years earlier, the protests united people of vastly different political views. Cosmopolitans who wanted to see their country become a part of the European community came together with nationalists who wanted to break free of Moscow's influence. Once again, protesters occupied the center of Kiev and settled in for however long it was going to take. Just like nine years ago, everyone in Moscow seemed to think of Ukraine solely as Russia's looking glass. A group of more than fifty Russian writers wrote an open letter to the protesters. "We hope that you succeed," it concluded. "For us that would serve as a sign that we in Russia can also win our rights and freedoms."[7]

The Russian parliament unanimously passed a resolution calling for the protesters in Ukraine to disband. Before the vote, the chairman of the parliament's foreign relations committee said that if Ukraine were to sign the association agreement with the European Union, "that would increase the sphere of influence of gay culture, which has become the official policy of the European Union."[8]

Moscow shut down for the interminable winter holidays, but the protests in Kiev continued. Here was an important distinction between Ukraine and

Russia: precisely two years earlier, the Russian protesters had retreated after their biggest demonstration, taking their long-planned vacations or simply commencing the customary two weeks of eating and drinking, as though revolutions kept office hours.

Just as the Russians were waking up from their holiday, the Ukrainian parliament passed a series of laws aimed at designating the protests as illegal; some of these were textually similar to the bills passed at the beginning of the Russian crackdown. The protesters prepared to defend themselves. They built barricades, using car and truck tires, stones, pieces of pavement, and ice that they chopped up with axes and loaded into sacks. They armed themselves with hunting rifles, slings, and Molotov cocktails. The first shots were fired on January 22. Two protesters were killed and one wounded.

It seemed that Masha was a journalist now—she was not anything else, and she was cohosting a popular-science show on TV Rain—and, following the amnesty, she was free to travel. She went to Kiev.

She was the last to arrive. Every other Moscow journalist was already there. Everyone knew everyone else, everyone had a routine and a hangout, and everyone was an expert. The lay of the land was uncomplicated: a couple of blocks of government buildings were sealed off and heavily guarded; the main city square—Maidan Nezalezhnosti (Independence Square), the one referred to simply as the Maidan, was occupied by protesters, as were a couple of adjacent streets. In the rest of the city, life went on as what must have been normal. Everyone spoke Russian. It was hard to believe that this was a different country, especially one where someone had died for its independence from Moscow. Except when Masha was among the protesters, when they stood together, as they did every hour, to sing the Ukrainian national anthem—then she believed, and she very much wanted them to succeed.

All the stories about the Maidan were being written by the self-confident, experienced journalists who had gotten there before Masha. They had cultivated their heroes and their sources among the protesters, and all their stories starred them. The one thing no one was doing was talking to the soldiers who guarded the government—the ones who, everyone said, had fired the shots that killed the protesters the day before Masha arrived in Kiev.

Masha put on heels and makeup. Lots of makeup. She thought of it as war paint. She went to the Maidan, where the barricades constructed of huge old tires had been set aflame. It seemed to her the protesters were trying to make the square look like revolution—the French one, from the movie of *Les Misérables*. Not that there had been tires at the time of the French Revolution, but the stench and the flames fit her mental picture. Masha crossed the protesters' barricades.

She was in no-man's-land now, a strip of snow that separated the Maidan's burning-rubber barricades from the government's police-fence barricades. Men in long black robes—Orthodox priests—stood here. Masha saw the giant gray shape of a cross in the snow—the long shadow of a small cross held up by one of the priests in the yellow light of a streetlamp. Here, where neither side ventured, Masha's heels sank into the snow. The priests, she realized, were praying for life on both sides of the barricades. She knew at that moment that there was a God and that there would be war.

"You can't go through," said an officer on the government side. He was wearing riot gear. "You need a helmet."

"What if I'm a journalist?"

"You'll still get yourself killed."

"Don't worry, the bullets won't get me." She had almost said, "I'll walk between the raindrops."

"All right," he said, pulling back a section of the barrier. "But don't go near Berkut. You'll get yourself killed."

Berkut—"golden eagle" in Ukrainian—were the special forces. People on the Maidan said that it was Berkut who had killed people. On this side too, Berkut were clearly known as the killers. Masha recognized them by their black ski masks. She edged closer to Berkut's bonfire. Everyone had a fire, on both sides of the barricades, and everyone had hot tea, and everyone shared both. Even Berkut.

"What's your name?" asked a black ski mask.

"Masha."

"Mine is Sergei too." The mask laughed, showing two rows of large teeth. He had no way of knowing that Masha's husband and the one man she had loved passionately were both named Sergei—he must have meant simply that they were alike because they had unremarkable Russian names. She had come from the other side wearing war paint, he was wearing a black mask, but they came from the same people.

Berkut did not want to be interviewed. Masha would not leave. By three in the morning they started talking. By five, Masha had what she had come for: she felt she understood. Berkut officers thought they were there to protect the peace. They were convinced that the protesters were a handful of troublemakers. They were not particularly devoted to Ukrainian president Viktor Yanukovych, but they believed in order and strong power. A real leader would never have let riffraff burn tires in the capital's central square. This sort of thing would never happen in Russia, for example. They even mentioned Bolotnaya. Masha tried to tell them that Bolotnaya had been nothing like the Maidan. They said that was a good thing. She was not so sure. But she was certain that whatever was happening here in Kiev would end differently from the protests in Moscow.

"Ukraine is some sort of parallel-reality Russia," she wrote in the conclusion to her dispatch. "Everything is completely different there."[9] TV Rain's online magazine, *Slon*, published the article as submitted: none of the editors objected to referring to Ukraine as a sort of alternative Russia.

MASHA WAS THE ONLY RUSSIAN to have interviewed Berkut. She came back to Moscow a real journalist.

A day after she returned, Masha cursed out loud when she was reading Twitter. Then she made a screenshot and sent it to TV Rain's web editor with a question: "WTF?"

The tweet originated with TV Rain. It said, "Should Leningrad have been surrendered to the Germans if that would have saved hundreds of thousands of lives?"

It was the seventieth anniversary of the end of the Siege of Leningrad. The siege had lasted 872 days and claimed over a million lives. Masha had been around long enough to know how much trouble this tweet could cause: she had seen battles to the death break out in the Russian blogosphere over less. She knew that no question about Soviet conduct in the Second World War ever went unpunished—and this was a question that suggested that the country's greatest and most mythologized sacrifice in that war could and should have been avoided. She also knew that the new social media manager at TV Rain was in his late teens and that he was about to learn one of the hardest lessons of his life.

The tweet was live for all of eight minutes—the time it took for the channel's web editor to come out of the shower at the gym where he happened to be, open his locker, see outraged and worried messages from Masha and countless others, and delete the tweet. It was too late. The firestorm had begun. In the next few days, the St. Petersburg city legislature called for the channel to be shut down. A federal deputy prime minister publicly backed the demand.[10] Putin's press secretary, Dmitry Peskov, declared war on the channel:

> I want audience reaction to be absolutely merciless here. Because the moment we start becoming even the least bit tolerant of such surveys, our nation will begin to erode, our memory will erode, the genetic memory of our people. I am certain that other countries would give an even harder time to a channel that crossed this kind of moral and ethical red line.[11]

When Masha came to work, she was greeted by members of the youth group Nashi, who were picketing TV Rain. They had brought plastic bags filled with excrement, to spread in the channel's courtyard and to toss at the occasional employee.

Less than two weeks later, all the channel's satellite carriers had dropped it and most of its advertisers had canceled their contracts. The channel's director general, who together with her husband owned TV Rain, called a staff meeting. She announced that there would be layoffs and that those who kept their jobs would have to take a 30 percent pay cut. Masha did a quick mental calculation. She could barely make ends meet as it was—a 30 percent pay cut would mean she had to find another job to supplement the income from the journalism that she had originally entered in order to survive as a political defendant. She decided to quit—by leaving on her own, she could at least make the editor in chief's job a little bit easier. The director general was still talking.

"With all that's been going on, I haven't seen my children at all," she said. "So, starting tomorrow, I'll take a short vacation—we had long planned a ski holiday in the Swiss Alps, and this will dovetail nicely with Davos."

The director was not yet finished talking when a camerawoman named Alya sent out an all-staff message: "Does anyone have a couch I can sleep on? Looks like I'll have to move." Masha knew that Alya had a kid Sasha's age who was living with Alya's mother—even on her old salary, Alya, who was not originally from Moscow, could afford to rent only a small room in the city. Masha herself had been renting out her two-rooms-plus-kitchen apartment ever since it was raided, and renting a similar one closer to the center. Who said she and Sasha could not share a room? The director general was still talking. Masha waved to Alya across the room and pointed to herself with two thumbs, then messaged: "I've got a spare room. Enough for you and the kid."

A lot of people moved in the next few days. One TV Rain on-air personality was spotted wheeling his belongings down the Garden Ring in a supermarket shopping cart. His cat sat on top of his clothes. Alya hailed a cab over to Masha's. That evening both of them changed their Facebook relationship status to "in a domestic partnership."

THE SOCHI OLYMPICS opened on the day of that staff meeting. Foreign correspondents flooded the social networks with photos of filthy tap water and descriptions of absurd malfunctions in hotels that were still under construction.[12] But the opening ceremony was spectacular, and Russia garnered the highest number of gold medals: thirteen. If Masha had felt less disoriented and besieged, she would have felt more patriotic.

In Ukraine, there was more bloodshed on the Maidan. More than a hundred were now dead, including several government troops. On February 21, over a hundred thousand gathered in the Maidan to mourn the fallen protesters. By evening, the square was threatening to storm government buildings unless the president resigned. President Yanukovych fled the capital, seeking refuge first in eastern Ukraine and ultimately in Russia. The following day, Masha got a phone call from Kiev: one of the Berkut officers from that night in January was calling to let her know that his partner had been killed. She had interviewed the partner too. It felt strange, almost like she was somehow responsible.

A friend called from Crimea: everyone was there now, and Masha should come. She went. The day after she arrived, she realized that something had changed overnight. The streets were full of armed men in unmarked uniforms. They walked around smiling. Within a few hours, they were joined by ordinary Crimeans, who had come out to take pictures with the men. No one could know for certain, but the sense was, these were Russian soldiers who had come to save the overwhelmingly Russian-speaking Black Sea peninsula from the Maidan. That was what people were saying: "Save us from the Maidan." With men in unmarked uniforms now in the streets, everyone sounded ecstatic and looked radiant.

Moscow journalists, who really were all there, kept filing dispatches that their editors rejected. Moscow had not confirmed that the armed men were under its command, so the journalists' descriptions of what they were seeing could not be published. Masha was not even sure that she was a journalist now—her media career might have ended as soon as it began—and she would be hard-pressed to explain why she was in Crimea. She wrote a column for the American magazine *New Republic*. It began, "Right now in Crimea, the strangest war I've seen in my 30 years is unfolding."[13] She had not actually ever seen a war before, but you did not have to have seen one to know that this one was unlike any other.

On March 1, Putin asked the upper house of the Russian parliament to authorize the use of force beyond the country's borders—and got its unanimous approval the same day. The armed men were already in Crimea by then. The streets of Crimea filled with billboards showing a swastika and barbed wire on the left and a Russian flag on the right, with the caption, "On March 16, we will be choosing between this and this." That day, at a hastily convened referendum, 96.77 percent of Crimeans voted to join the Russian Federation.[14]

THE HISTORY OF CRIMEA had been as violent as that of any part of the former Soviet Union but perhaps more confusing than that of most of them. From the time the empire first annexed Crimea in 1783, it was a part of Russia for nearly two centuries. In 1944, Stalin ethnically cleansed Crimea: Tatars, who had made up a large part of the peninsula's population, were deported, as were the local Armenians, Belarusians, and Greeks. This left the ethnic Russians, the only people Stalin trusted in the wake of the Second World War. Then, in 1954, Khrushchev, who had just been installed as Soviet leader, redrew the borders of constituent republics, assigning Crimea to Ukraine. No explanation was offered at the time and none could be found later—at least none that could be convincingly documented.

Khrushchev had once been the Party boss in Ukraine, and this led to conjecture that he wanted to give the republic a lavish gift—or, conversely, that he was atoning for the sins committed there (he had taken charge after the man-made famine of 1932–1933, but plenty of blood had been shed on his watch). Harvard historian Mark Kramer has suggested that Khrushchev used Crimea to secure control over Ukraine after the war. Soviet Ukraine had been occupied by the German army for nearly three years. The postwar division of Europe allowed the Soviet Union to keep most of the territory it had annexed under the 1939 Molotov-Ribbentrop Pact. What was now the western part of Ukraine had thus been occupied three times: by the USSR in 1939, by Germany in 1941, and again by the USSR in 1944. Soviet rule there was new and uncertain, making the division between the newly occupied western lands and the eastern part of the republic all the more pronounced. Adding ethnically cleansed Crimea to Ukraine may have been a colonizing strategy: the republic gained nearly a million new residents, all of them Russian-speaking ethnic Russians.[15]

Back in 1954, most Russians had no reason to wonder about Khrushchev's motives. For one thing, most acts of the Soviet leadership appeared arbitrary to the citizens and, for another, this one made no difference in everyday life. Russians continued to think of Crimea as their country's most important resort, and to use it. Crimea, in its way, was an equalizer: someone who came from extreme privilege, like Seryozha, spent his summers in an elaborate castle there while Masha's mother could rent an apartment in season and Lyosha's mother could rent a bed for herself and one for her son. Every Russian story began in Crimea: it was the place where childhood friendships were struck, romances were kindled, virginity was lost, drugs were tried, and all sorts of memories were made. Those who had not yet spent a summer there thought that someday they would. It was the universal Russian aspiration. The realization that the all-Russian summer dream could belong to someone else—another country—came rudely in the wake of the collapse of the Soviet Union. Ethnic Russians still made up the majority of the population there, but now they used a different currency and Russian citizens needed foreign-travel passports to enter. Over the years, many Russians discovered that the Black Sea resorts of Bulgaria and Turkey were more comfortable and more affordable, but Crimea remained the symbol of summer and youth.

On March 18, two days after the Crimea referendum, Putin gathered members of both houses of parliament as well as governors and other dignitaries in the Kremlin for an extraordinary address. He spoke for more than forty minutes. He was interrupted repeatedly by applause and by standing ovations. At the end, Putin and three representatives of Crimea—one of them wearing a thick black turtleneck sweater, as though he had just returned from an imaginary Spanish Civil War—signed a treaty conjoining Russia and Crimea, and the men and a few women in the room stood up to the sounds of the Russian national anthem. As Putin and his cosigners exited, the room erupted in yet another standing ovation, and a chant: *Spasibo!*—"Thank you!"—*Spasibo! Spasibo! Spasibo!* It was a chant one might have heard at the end of a rock concert. The roomful of officials was responding not as it might have to a leader who had led the country to victory—that chant would have been "Hooray! Hooray! Hooray!"—but, in keeping with the "mafia state" model, as it would to a patriarch who had just given members of his clan a grand gift.

Putin's speech laid out Russia's case for Crimea. His first argument was historical, and it echoed every other historical claim to territory ever made. Putin said that Crimea was the cradle of Russian civilization (much like Serbia had always claimed that Kosovo was the cradle of its civilization). He acknowledged the ethnic cleansing of Crimea, sort of:

> Yes, there was a time when Crimean Tatars, like some other peoples of the USSR, were subjected to injustice. I'll say one thing: millions suffered from repression in those times, and most of those people were, of course, Russian.[16]

This was not true of Crimea, but the statement was factually accurate for all of the Soviet Union, if for no other reason than that ethnic Russians far outnumbered all other groups. Through this rhetorical sleight of hand, Putin dismissed the pain and fears of Crimea's ethnic minorities and repositioned Russians as the victims:

> What had seemed impossible became a reality, alas. The USSR collapsed. . . . And it was when Crimea suddenly turned out to be part of another state that Russia realized it had been not simply stolen from but robbed. . . . Millions of Russians went to sleep in their own country only to awaken in a different one. Overnight, they had become ethnic minorities in former Union republics. The Russian people became one of the largest, if not the largest, divided nations in the world.

The difference in meaning between the terms "stolen from" and "robbed" was subtle and unclear, but the implication of violence was unmistakable. In the story that Putin was telling, Russia had recognized the post-Soviet borders that made Crimea a part of Ukraine under duress, because it was too weak to object. Later, under Putin, Russia sacrificed its national interests and deep desires for the sake of peace in the region, and did not contest the post-1991 borders. But after being forcibly moved to another country, without physically moving, the Crimean Russians found themselves citizens of an unstable state:

> Russians, like other Ukrainian citizens, suffered from the ongoing political and the permanent government crises that have been seizing Ukraine for more than twenty years.

This was a reference to both the Maidan and the Orange Revolution, and this was the point where Putin's speech turned away from Russia and toward America—or, rather, from what Russia had lost to what the United States had gained. The United States, he said, had funded the Maidan, and once the Maidan won, it would crack down on its opponents:

> Crimea—Russian-speaking Crimea—was the first in line for the crackdown. Because of this the people of Crimea . . . asked Russia to protect their rights and their very lives. . . . Of course, we had to respond to this plea. We could not abandon Crimea and its people to their plights. That would have been a betrayal.

Not only were Russia's actions right, continued Putin, but they were based on precedent created by the United States itself, when it facilitated Kosovo's secession from Serbia. The only difference between Kosovo and Crimea, he argued, was that the former had had the backing of the United States, which felt that it could make the rules in the post–Cold War world. "They had us all with that," he said. In fact, he said *nagnuli*, a crude expression most accurately translated as "They had everyone up the ass," conjuring the clear image of homosexual rape. The Kremlin's translators rendered it in English as "had everyone agree."[17]

Putin continued the litany of grievances against America: after Kosovo "there was an entire chain of 'color revolutions' managed from the outside"—Ukraine's were just two of many. Countries where these revolutions were "orchestrated" were then "forced to accept standards unsuitable for the way of life, tradition, and culture of the people":

> They lied to us time after time. They made decisions behind our backs and then had us face a fait accompli. That's what happened with NATO's eastward expansion, when military outposts were placed at our borders. They kept saying to us that it's none of our business. Easy for them to say.

Russia could no longer take it. "Like a spring that had been wound too tight," it had uncoiled:

> We will clearly face opposition from the outside. We have to decide if we are prepared to stand firm in protecting our national interests or if we are forever going to be giving in, retreating when there is no-where to retreat to. Some Western politicians are already threatening us not only with sanctions but also with problems inside the country. I wonder what they mean: are they placing their hopes in a fifth col-umn, national-traitors of various stripes, or are they figuring that they will be able to have a negative impact on the Russian economy, thereby sparking popular unrest? . . . We must take appropriate action.

This was a war speech, though Putin laughed off concerns about war even as he spoke:

> They are talking about aggression, about some sort of Russian inter-vention in Crimea. That's odd. Somehow, I can't recall any historical

example of an intervention that went off without a single shot being fired, with no casualties.

Really? Gudkov could readily think of such an example. Hitler's Anschluss of Austria in 1938 was one. His takeover of the part of Czechoslovakia known as Sudetenland was another. That involved not a single gunshot—instead, it employed a plebiscite and a speech, among other bloodless tools. In his September 1938 speech Hitler decried the hypocrisy of Western democracies, which he said refused to recognize the true will of the people. He mentioned that France's sole interest in Czechoslovakia was in using it as a base for launching an attack on Germany. Most important, he mentioned the ethnic-German minority in Czechoslovakia, which, he said, was "robbed of its right to self-determination in the name of [Czechoslovak] self-determination." Germany, he said, had put up with this state of affairs—and with borders that divided its nation—first because it was weak in the wake of the First World War and later in the interests of peace and stability in Europe, but this had been "misinterpreted as a sign of weakness." Now, he said, Germany was finally asserting itself by fulfilling its sacred duty to the oppressed Germans of Czechoslovakia.[18]

Most of the elements of Putin's Crimea speech were familiar from his earlier statements: the tragedy of the collapse of the Soviet Union, the hypocrisy of the United States, the treachery of NATO, the idea that America organizes revolutions and then forces its values on traditional cultures, the obligatory below-the-belt reference, which these days also had to be homophobic, and even the enemy within—the "fifth column." But the idea of a divided nation and a moral duty to countrymen abroad that superseded laws and national boundaries had a different antecedent—it recalled Hitler's Sudetenland speech directly. This got Gudkov reading or rereading thinkers who wrote about Nazism. It occurred to him that all this time his thinking about ideology had been wrong. He had been taught that totalitarian ideology had to include a vision of the future. But this was never a key characteristic of Nazism. Its vision had been archaic, and its promise was simplicity, the return to an imaginary past when laws were instincts and the nation was a tribe.

So maybe this was it. Crimea was Russia's ideology. This was why it pulled together every theme that Putin had floated before. And judging from the reaction to Putin's speech, and from survey data, it functioned as an ideology: Crimea mobilized the nation. Levada Center polls showed that 88 percent of the population supported the annexation of Crimea and only 1 percent said that they were "definitely opposed." This fell below the survey's margin of error: it was as if these people—people like Gudkov—did not exist.[19]

Hannah Arendt wrote that an ideology was nothing but a single idea taken to its logical extreme. No ideology was inherently totalitarian but any ideology contained the seeds of totalitarianism—it could become encapsulated, entirely divorced from reality, with a single premise eclipsing the entire world. Totalitarian leaders, she wrote, were interested less in the idea itself than in its use as the driver and justification of action. They derived the "laws of history" from the single chosen idea and then mobilized the people to fulfill these imaginary laws.[20]

Now that there was, apparently, an ideology, Russia checked off all the boxes on any of the traditional lists of totalitarian-society traits—except, perhaps, Gudkov's own list, which included enforced poverty.

Maybe this was how it worked when a totalitarian society was reconstituting itself rather than being shaped by a totalitarian regime: the ideology congealed last. Gudkov thought of Russia's totalitarianism as a recurrent totalitarianism, like a recurrent infection; as with an infection, the recurrence might not be as deadly as the original disease, but the symptoms would be recognizable from when it had struck the first time.

ANOTHER PERSON TO WHOM Putin's speech sounded familiar was Dugin. He recognized himself. It had been just over five years since Dugin declared his intention to become his country's lead ideologue, and it was happening: Putin was using Dugin's words and his concepts, and he was carrying out his predictions. Back in 2009, Dugin had prophesied the division of

Ukraine into two separate states: the eastern portion would be allied with Russia and the west would be forever looking toward Europe. Dugin saw Ukraine as inhabited by two distinct nations—the western Ukrainians, who spoke Ukrainian, and the people of the east, a nation that included ethnic Russians and ethnic Ukrainians who were, nonetheless, Russian in language and culture. The two nations, in Dugin's view, had fundamentally different geopolitical orientations. This meant that Ukraine was not a nation state. It also meant that its division was preordained—the only question was whether it would be peaceful. There might be war, he had warned back then.[21]

This was about much more than Crimea, much more than Ukraine, and Putin's speech made that clear. Dugin had spent years waiting for Russia to claim its place as the leader of the anti-modern world. The idea, like Dugin's other ideas, had been gaining traction, and Dugin had been accumulating powerful allies. When the protests in Ukraine created an opportunity to be heard, one of these allies, a billionaire who had been supporting ultra-conservative groups, delivered a memorandum to the Kremlin. It proposed using the chaos in Ukraine to launch the process of annexing Crimea and southeastern Ukraine. Written before Ukrainian president Yanukovych was deposed, the memo predicted his demise. It also attributed the Maidan to Polish and British Secret Services and proposed that Russia beat the West at its own game: organize unrest on the ground in southeastern Ukraine to justify its intervention. Many of the words and ideas in the memo belonged to Dugin.[22]

In late February, Putin's administration started organizing and financing anti-Kiev, pro-Moscow protests in cities in south and eastern Ukraine. By design, once people could be roused to storm and occupy government buildings, and while there to adopt resolutions asking for Moscow's help, Russian intervention would begin.[23] Top-level Kremlin officials gave orders and doled out money to local organizers; Dugin stayed in contact with activists, advised on strategy, and issued reassurances. Russia would not stop at Crimea, he told his contacts: it would help southeastern Ukraine fight against Kiev. Sitting in a tall black leather chair in his home office, with hundreds of books for his backdrop, he would conduct long Skype sessions with Ukrainian activists. "This is only the beginning," he would say. "Those who think that it all ended with Crimea are very wrong."[24]

In early April, the protesters in Donetsk and Luhansk, two regional centers in eastern Ukraine, began taking over government buildings. Some of them were armed with weapons looted from a local armory.[25] On April 7, protesters convened a government of what they called the People's Republic of Donetsk and passed a resolution asking Russia to intervene. Fighting began with isolated battles in some other eastern cities—Ukrainian government forces were able to prevent the takeover of more government buildings—and then it became war.[26] The United States, which had imposed sanctions on Russia after the occupation of Crimea—including visa and business bans on several businessmen and officials—threatened further sanctions. Europe hesitated.[27] Russia failed to rouse large enough uprisings in the south, but Ukrainian forces failed to restore Kiev's authority in the east.[28]

On April 17, Putin held his annual televised hotline. Before he entered the studio, one of the two hosts set the stage:

> If things were different, I might have said that this will be yet another conversation, but on this day we have a different country listening to us. Russia is now united with Crimea and the City of Sevastopol.* We have been waiting for this moment for twenty-three long years, ever since the Soviet Union fell apart. For this reason every question today will be either directly related to Crimea or will have a subtext colored by Crimea.[29]

The show lasted nearly four hours. A lot was said. The annexation of Crimea was placed in line with Russia's great Second World War victory. Russians who opposed the annexation were condemned as traitors. One

---

*The city of Sevastopol, geographically part of Crimea, was accorded a kind of sovereignty, making its authorities reportable directly to Moscow.

such opponent came to the show to make amends. It was Irina Khakamada, who back in 1999 had been one of only two Union of Right Forces founders to oppose Putin's candidacy for president—Nemtsov had been the other. A month before this show, she had also opposed the annexation. But now she said to Putin:

> I have come to say the following. Crimea has always needed to have a Russian identity. I have often been to Crimea. . . . They always wanted to be a part of Russia. It happened the way it did, so be it. You are the victor. You really did pull off that operation without firing a single shot.

The opposition—the barely perceptible 1 percent—was surrendering. Only one member of parliament—Masha's former boss Ilya Ponomarev—had voted against ratifying the Russian-Crimean union treaty. He had since been forced to leave the country.[30] Now Nemtsov remained the only person with any name recognition who opposed the annexation.

To Dugin, the most important parts of the show were ones in which he recognized his own influence. There were several points when Ukrainians who remained loyal to Kiev were referred to as "nationalists" and even as Nazis—and Putin pointed out that "such was the historical past of these territories, these lands, and these people." The implication was that the west had been permanently contaminated by the German occupation of 1941–1944. The east, on the other hand, he said, was "connected to Russia at the root, and these are people with something of a different mentality." At the conclusion of the show Putin expanded on the idea of this mentality:

> There are certain special characteristics, and I think they have to do with values. I think that a Russian person, or, to speak more broadly, a person of the Russian World, thinks, first, about the fact that man has a moral purpose, a higher moral basis. That is why the Russian person, a person of the Russian World, is focused not so much on his own self. . . .

Putin trailed off and rambled for a bit, revealing to the attentive listener that he had not yet fully assimilated the ideas he was putting forward. But in a few moments he picked up the thread:

> These are the deep roots of our patriotism. This is where mass heroism comes from in war, and self-sacrifice in peacetime. This is the origin of mutual aid, and of family values.

The phrase "Russian World" was Dugin's. It was a geographically expansive concept, the vision of a civilization led by Russia. Putin was right to circle around to "family values"—the idea was precisely that the Russian World, whatever its borders, was united by values. The point that Dugin had been making for years was that the very idea of universal human values is misleading: the West's idea of human rights, for example, should not apply to a "traditional-values civilization." One of Dugin's best phrases was, "There is nothing universal about universal human rights."

At another point in the show Putin referred to something that Dugin had been working on for years: making connections with people and organizations that shared the Russian World's values even though they were located in Europe:

> I think we are indeed witnessing the process of reevaluating values in European countries. What we call conservative values is starting to gain traction. Take Viktor Orbán's victory in Hungary or Marine Le Pen's success in France—she came in third during a municipal election. Similar tendencies are growing in other countries, too. It is obvious, just absolutely obvious.

Absolutely. In the last few years Dugin had revitalized his contacts with the West: he had built bridges with French ultraright activists—ones who were too radical for Le Pen's National Front—and with Hungarians to the right of Orbán, as well as many other groups, including ultraconservative European and Israeli Jewish organizations. What united these activists and groups, disparate as they were in conventional political terms, was their political opposition to Brussels and philosophical opposition to modernity.[31] His work was now effectively recognized by the president. It had attained the status of a national project.

The following day, Dugin was the guest on the country's most popular interview show. He had been interviewed on television many times, but this was a first. The show was run and hosted by Vladimir Posner, a Jew who had once worked in the United States. This was by far the most liberal, pro-Western show on Russian television—and the fact that Dugin was invited meant that he had acquired the kind of political weight that made him an essential, unavoidable guest. The tone of the interview was antagonistic—Dugin even told Posner at one point that he thought that he, Posner, should be banned from television—but it provided a platform for conveying his views to the widest possible audience. Dugin was able to say that the events of the last couple of months—Crimea and, now, a war in eastern Ukraine—constituted a Russian renaissance, a "Russian Spring." "We are starting to feel pride in our country," he went on. "Russians are beginning to realize that they exist in the world not only as passive objects but as subjects of history. And the more we show that we care about the Russians and Russian speakers outside Russia, the stronger we make our society, the more we emerge from a sleeping state to a state of mobilization. . . . Look at the people who have come from Crimea: this is an entirely different sort of people than our officials or Ukrainian ones. These are people of a new generation, a new brand."

> POSNER: Are you saying that these people are making our nation healthier?

Dugin concurred. Then Posner asked him to expand on a phrase he had seen in Dugin's recent writing: "Greater Russia."

> DUGIN: Greater Russia is the Russian World, the Russian civilization. I think the territory of Greater Russia roughly coincides with the

territory of the Russian Empire and the Soviet Union, give or take. . . .

POSNER: So let me ask you. Is the Caucasus a part of it? Georgia, Armenia, Azerbaijan?

DUGIN: Certainly, of course. These are parts of Greater Russia. But that does not mean that—

POSNER: What about Central Asia?

DUGIN: Central Asia—of course, certainly.

POSNER: The Baltics?

DUGIN: I don't think so. I think perhaps parts of the Baltics and western Ukraine, under certain circumstances—

POSNER: But everything else is—

DUGIN: Greater Russia. Look, civilization doesn't have those kinds of borders.

It devolved into an argument on civilizational exceptionalism. Posner was a difficult interviewer. Still, there it was, an hour-long interview for one of Russia's largest television audiences on the idea of the Russian World. Dugin also mentioned traitors and, pressed by Posner, said that they should be annihilated, and, pressed further, he said their names: Navalny, Nemtsov, Kasyanov, Ryzhkov.* He said what he believed to be true of them, and what he believed all Russians should know: that these men were employed by the Americans.[32]

Dugin was giving many interviews and writing many articles—the urgency of the situation amplified his already superhuman efficiency. He was writing that America was waging war against Russia, that Russia was finally stepping up to the challenge, and that the entire world might be on the verge of erupting into its third giant war.[33] But by the end of May, he was growing impatient and even disappointed with Putin. Rather than embark

---

*Mikhail Kasyanov was prime minister of Russia in 2000–2003 but later declared his opposition to Putin and joined forces with Nemtsov. Vladimir Ryzhkov was a former member of the Russian parliament, and a cofounder, with Nemtsov and Kasyanov, of a right-liberal opposition party.

on an open, all-out war, the Kremlin seemed intent on creating a quagmire. What was the point of that? It was true that a slow war in the east would serve the purpose of destabilizing Ukraine, sapping its strength and weakening its new government, but these were petty, tactical goals. Dugin wanted Putin to invade Ukraine openly, using regular troops, and to aim for a glorious victory that would expand Russia. Indeed, it would be only the beginning of Russia's expansion. But when this failed to happen, Dugin knew the reason: Putin was being held back by his moderate, fundamentally pro-Western advisers. He invented a term for them: "sixth column." If the "fifth column" were people like Nemtsov, who Dugin believed were working directly for the United States, then the "sixth column" were traitors to their civilization, not their country. They hid in plain sight, in the Kremlin.[34]

Dugin had always told his supporters, "We seek not power but influence." Now he used the same juxtaposition to assuage their disappointment. "Our power is negligible," he said, "but our influence is immense."[35] This became something of a slogan among his closest allies. It helped that they kept hearing their words repeated by top Russian officials: the evidence of their influence was there for all to witness, if they knew what to listen for. The fact that Putin's actions were not keeping up with their words should only strengthen their resolve.

Outwardly, Dugin's status shifted too. His right-hand man, Valery Korovin, became a member of the Presidential Civic Chamber, the body created to rule civil society. Dugin was no longer a fringe activist. Even if he now found himself used as a foil to make Putin's views and actions look moderate, this served to legitimize Dugin's own positions too.

IN LATE APRIL, Khodorkovsky gathered about three hundred people in Kiev for what he called a "dialogue." It was a strange list of names: famous writers, not-so-famous activists, and people who were important to Khodorkovsky. Masha was invited, probably because she had been charged in the

Bolotnoye case and because she had corresponded with Khodorkovsky when he was in prison. Behind bars, he had become something of a village elder: people wrote to him with their questions and their grievances. Masha had had grievances: she had felt betrayed and abandoned. Khodorkovsky's response emphasized the virtues of patience, of rising above the fray, and of taking the long view. Masha no longer remembered what she had written, but Khodorkovsky must have, since he invited her.

In his opening address at the congress, Khodorkovsky emphasized the long view again:

> People have been asking me, What's the point of this conference? . . .
> I give my usual answer, one that saw me through my ten long years
> [behind bars]: Do what you must and come what may. . . . I have
> learned over the last ten years to think long-term and to remember
> that darkness will always cede to light and dreams that seem most
> unrealistic today will become reality tomorrow.[36]

As far as Masha could tell, everyone at the congress had the same dream: to get onto Khodorkovsky's payroll. Word was, he wanted to bankroll an entire shadow society. Everyone got in line. Masha decided that she wanted no part of what everyone wanted. She actually had a scheduled appointment with Khodorkovsky, but it was at ten in the morning, following a night she had spent drinking, so she canceled. But Khodorkovsky sought her out himself, in the hotel lobby. They talked. She liked him more than she had expected, a lot more. They were oddly alike—and unlike most of the people at the congress. They were both reluctant dissidents. Masha thought Khodorkovsky really wanted to be the establishment—he wanted to be the president, not the president's Enemy Number One. Most people who fight tyrants do not seek power themselves. Khodorkovsky did, and Masha liked this about him. She would have liked to be a general in his army, or at least an official in his administration.

A couple of weeks later Khodorkovsky's people invited her along to the

Donetsk region to see what was happening there. It was terrifying. She had liked Donetsk when she was there in another life, two years ago—when Sergey the photographer took her along for the European Cup. The beautiful airport was still here—all of Donetsk was still here, in fact—but in place of the measured traffic of everyday, there was hectic motion now, and clumps of tense, angry, armed men. Here in Donetsk they had not fired a shot yet, but you knew that they would.

In and outside the city, men were building checkpoints, placing flags on them. The men had tremors, which Masha recognized, as any Moscow bar regular would: amphetamines. The men stayed up on speed. Masha talked to men on both sides. They spoke the same language, and they hated each other. Each side thought the other was less than human. Their guns were loaded and had no safety catches.

Masha called her mother-in-law to tell her that she was in Donetsk: the older woman had grown up there. The mother-in-law launched into an anti-Kiev tirade. As far as she was concerned, the new government was made up of Nazis.

Two weeks after Masha left Donetsk, anti-Kiev fighters seized the airport. The Ukrainian army took it back after a day of fighting. Four months later, it was attacked again—and then, after weeks of fighting, it belonged to the separatists. But all that was left were ruins: mountains of rubble, chunks of aircraft, and many dead bodies.[37]

Masha finally took a job with Khodorkovsky's organization. She would coordinate his work with political prisoners. Her new colleagues at a clandestine office in Moscow were working on a news site and on educational seminars. The seminars, coordinated by Vladimir Kara-Murza, a guy around Masha's age, were innocuous stuff: basic civics education. But because they were backed by Khodorkovsky, the seminars drew too much attention. Local officials shut them down, pressured venues into canceling rental agreements, and even had the power to a venue cut one time. Masha hated the idea that she had now become a professional political prisoner, or at least a political-prisoner professional, but she liked the fight.

THE EUROPEAN UNION, Canada, and several other Western countries followed the United States in imposing sanctions on Russia. They banned certain Russian state companies from financial markets, embargoed exports of high-tech oil equipment to Russia, and banned the sale to Russia of military and dual-use technology. In addition, a number of Russian politicians were effectively declared personae non grata. The road for this kind of personal sanction had been laid by the Magnitsky bill back in 2012—and Masha's new colleague Kara-Murza had been in Washington lobbying for the sanctions back then.

Businesses got nervous. Western investors began pulling out for fear of the sanctions and of the effect of the sanctions. The Russian economy had slowed down precipitously even before the war, but now it seemed to be going into a tailspin. Others were scared too. The World Congress of Families got cold feet about its planned grand gathering in September—the one slated for both the Kremlin and the Cathedral of Christ the Savior. Everyone, or almost everyone, still came and praised Russia for its brave opposition to the LGBT lobby and talked about the dangers of "gender ideology" and the specter of "demographic winter," but, in apparent deference to the sanctions, the event was billed as Russian-organized and the World Congress name was not used.[38] The patriarch of the Russian Orthodox Church spoke at the opening, as did a vice-speaker of parliament and the minister of culture, among others. John-Henry Westen, a Canadian right-to-life activist and journalist, gushed in an article: "Imagine a land where life, family, faith, and culture are promoted by the official government. Where large families are treated, not as a blight on the planet, but indeed as the 'future of humanity.'"[39]

With the sanctions in place, the forum took on added importance for the Kremlin. Some of the Western guests were elected officials in their countries—and however marginalized their parties might be, they had the potential to disrupt the process of imposing and extending sanctions. So far, even Russia's closest European allies, such as Hungary, had joined the sanctions, but eventually the monolith would have to crack. Here too Dugin had a chance to wield his influence, capitalizing on his contacts with far-right parties in Greece, Finland, France, Austria, and, especially, Italy.[40] He was able not only to be a guest—he continued to lecture abroad even as he seemed to devote all his energies to eastern Ukraine—but also to play host. He invited some of his most daring foreign friends to the Donetsk region in June 2014, to show them how history was made, and to fantasize about a future Greater Russia.[41]

The Western powers introduced sanctions step by step, building on the premise that Putin could be pressured to change his country's behavior—to avoid even greater damage to the Russian economy. But to a Russia that believed that it was at war with the United States, this gradual ratcheting up of pressure looked like nothing but escalation. By the end of the summer Putin responded with sanctions of his own: Russia banned the import of foods from Western countries. Kremlin media estimated that the ban applied to $9 billion worth of imports—the message was that hostile foreign countries would lose this amount of money while Russian food producers would benefit.[42] What actually happened was that food prices grew 10 percent in a single month while the range of food available at supermarkets dropped noticeably. Most cheeses disappeared, for example. Russia once again became a place where food made the best gift: visitors or travelers returning from the West invariably came bearing cheese.

Gudkov made a chart that contained just two curves: Putin's approval rating and the Levada Center's consumer perceptions index. The index was derived from answers to five questions: (1) How has your family's economic situation changed in the last year? (2) How do you expect it to change in the next year? (3) Do you expect the next twelve months to be good or bad for the country's economy as a whole? (4) What about the next five years? (5) Is now a good or a bad time to make large purchases, such as furniture, a television, a refrigerator?[43] They had been tracking the index since 1995, and had been asking the current set of questions since 2008. Soon after Putin's approval rating headed vertically up, the consumer perceptions index began its descent. The economic slowdown had been evident before the Olympics, then there had been a brief moment of optimism, but two months after the invasion of Ukraine, the decline became precipitous.[44] By the spring of 2014, layoffs were epidemic. The ruble, which had held steady for more than a dozen years, began losing ground against the dollar. Sanctions weakened it, the countersanctions pushed it further down, and in the fall of 2015 declining oil prices sent it tumbling. In December, after the ruble spent a day acting like a yo-yo and finally settled 11 percent down against the dollar, Russians rushed to dump their currency on durable goods. Car dealerships ran out of inventory and electronics stores ran out of large-screen televisions.[45]

Gudkov studied his divergent curves. Putin's popularity stayed steady at the anomalously high level that was apparently no longer anomalous. The consumer perceptions index kept declining. This was impossible. Eventually, these curves would have to break and head toward each other.

Or not. Gudkov himself had once added poverty to the definition of totalitarianism: he had come to the conclusion that scarcity was essential for the survival of a totalitarian regime. So perhaps in a case of recurrent totalitarianism, a totalitarianism that was being created from below at least as much as it was being imposed from above, the state and society were cooperating in creating a sense of scarcity.

People found ways to circumvent the sanctions, of course. They labeled food products as being something other than what they were or originating somewhere other than where they originated. One could now buy seafood from landlocked Belarus. In the summer of 2015—a year after countersanctions were first introduced—Putin signed a decree ordering the destruction of all foodstuffs deemed to be contraband. The cabinet then published rules dictating that banned foods should be destroyed "by any available means" in the presence of two impartial witnesses and the process must be captured by photo or video. There was talk of crematoria and of mobile incinerators. Some people were taken aback. A government plan to destroy vast quantities of food—edible food, food that was undeniably in demand—would probably be bizarre in any country, but in Russia it might have seemed particularly shocking. This was the country of the man-made famines that had killed millions, the country of the Siege of Leningrad, of the postwar hunger, of the catastrophic shortages of the 1980s, and of the salary arrears and subsistence off tiny plots of land of the 1990s. The president's own mother had nearly died of starvation during the Siege of Leningrad—this had been the obvious subtext of the outrage over TV Rain's tweet—and now the president was ordering the destruction of food. Over a hundred fifty thousand people signed a petition asking the government to give banned products to the poor instead, and a few officials expressed support for the idea.

Then 114 tons of pork were annihilated in Samara, a city on the Volga. The pork had been labeled as Brazilian but was exposed as hailing from the European Union. Twenty tons of cheese in the Orenburg region were next in line. Then there was more pork, this time in St. Petersburg, and three truckloads of illegal nectarines.[46] Now nothing was too horrible or too bizarre to be believed.

twenty-one

ZHANNA: FEBRUARY 27, 2015

THE SOCHI OLYMPICS ENDED on February 23, 2014. The following day, a Moscow court sentenced eight of the Bolotnoye case defendants. Weeks earlier, when the sentencing was scheduled, it had been clear that setting it for the first day when Putin would not be concerned with projecting a temporarily gentler image boded ill. The Bolotnoye case might be the Kremlin's chance to avenge the humiliation of having been forced to release Khodorkovsky.

Only one of the defendants, a nineteen-year-old woman who had already spent more than a year under house arrest, was given a suspended sentence. The rest—seven men, all of whom had been in pretrial detention—were sentenced to between two and a half and four years behind bars.[1] A small crowd gathered outside the courthouse on the day of the sentencing, and there were arrests—police loaded 234 people onto buses and took them away. Later in the day, people began gathering in Manezhnaya Square in the center of Moscow, the same square where thousands had come to protest Navalny's sentence seven months earlier. This time, there were only 432, and they were all arrested.[2]

Nemtsov was standing on the sidewalk being interviewed by a French television crew when a police officer approached him and said, "Please come to the bus with me." Nemtsov excused himself and followed the policeman. Time was, he would have refused to go, demanded to know on what grounds he was being detained, and made the police work to drag his large body onto a bus. But six months earlier Nemtsov had reentered electoral politics—such as remained in Russia. Only some mayors and municipal-council members in some cities were still elected directly. Nemtsov had been elected to the city legislature of Yaroslavl, a town of roughly half a million people about two and a half hours' drive from Moscow. He took the job seriously—he was now spending roughly half his time in Yaroslavl, where he had become a public figure. He dove into issues of local corruption and promoted local sports. As an elected official, he could not simply be detained by the police: there was a special court procedure for people like him. So he strolled to the bus, his city-legislature credentials in hand—and found himself arrested.

He and Navalny spent that night in a two-person cell.[3] The following day, Navalny was sentenced to seven days' arrest and Nemtsov to ten. Several other activists were sentenced to between one and two weeks. All of them had been found guilty of disobeying police.[4] The message was clear: with the Olympics over, the crackdown would intensify. Protest would be punished. Nemtsov was a fool to think that any Russian law would protect him.

WHILE NEMTSOV WAS LOCKED UP, Russian soldiers in unmarked uniforms invaded Crimea. Nemtsov wrote a short blog post and had it sent to Echo Moskvy, the radio station where he was a regular on the air and had his own blog on the website. Echo sent a message back: he needed to tone down the post. Specifically, they wanted him to remove the phrases "fratricidal war," "mentally unstable secret-police agent," and "the ghoul feeds on the people's blood." Nemtsov refused and put up the post on his Facebook page instead.

> Putin has declared war on Ukraine. This is a fratricidal war. Russia
> and Ukraine will pay a high price for the bloody insanity of this men-

tally unstable secret-police agent. Young men will die on both sides. There will be inconsolable mothers and sisters. There will be orphaned children. Crimea will empty out, because no one will vacation there. There will be billions, tens of billions of rubles taken from the old and the young and thrown into the fire of war—and then even more money will be needed to support the thieves in power in Crimea. He must see no other way to hold on to power. The ghoul feeds on the people's blood. Russia will face international isolation, the impoverishment of its population, and political crackdowns. God, what have we done to deserve this? And how long will we continue to put up with it?[5]

The same day, six people came to Manezhnaya Square and unfurled a banner that said "For Your Liberty and Ours." It was a double quotation: a Polish slogan adopted in the nineteenth century by Russian supporters of Poland during its struggle for independence, it had been used again in 1968, by the seven dissidents who came to Red Square to protest the Soviet invasion of Czechoslovakia. All seven had been arrested then, and sentenced to prison terms and Siberian exile. This time, the six protesters were arrested as soon as they unfurled their banner.[6] Later that day more people went to Manezhnaya and others went to the Defense Ministry building—no one really knew where to go, in no small part because Nemtsov, Navalny, and several of the activists who had for years taken care of the where and the when and of getting the word out were in jail. By the end of the day, 362 people had been arrested.[7] This was the day the parliament approved use of force abroad and Nemtsov and other Russians who were paying attention realized that their country had started a war with Ukraine.

There was also a hastily organized march in support of the invasion—the parliamentary newspaper described it as a march "in support of the people of Ukraine and against the provocateurs who have usurped power in Kiev."[8] Pro-Kremlin youth organizations advertised for participants on social networks:

RALLY AND CONCERT, 500 RUBLES FOR 1 HOUR

Rally connected with current events in Ukraine. Meet up at 15:00 at Pushkinskaya Metro station, in the center of the hall. 50 young people needed. Apply here with two photographs, name, last name, age, and phone number, or call 89104465285, ask for Maxim. Cash payment upon completion.[9]

The ad spoke more to the youth movements' standard organizing practices than it did to the need to pay people to celebrate the occupation. The outpouring of joy was massive and genuine. Zhanna felt it happening all around her. Everyone had lost their minds. Zhanna experienced political outrage—political passion even. She had never felt it before, not even when her father was arrested on New Year's Eve 2009, certainly not when she was running for office. All these years, her support for her father's causes had been intellectual: she had agreed that he was right on the merits of his arguments, and even that was not true all the time. But now she felt like she was staring into an abyss. How could people—intelligent people like her grandmother or the people she worked with—not understand that war would bring disaster? How could people whose opinions on the economy she respected not understand that the economy would now go from sluggish to death-bound? She realized, quickly, that they too felt gripped by passion, and that passion had nothing to do with intelligence. She also realized that refusing to share her nation's joy made her a pariah at her office and in her country.

She wanted to talk to her father about it, but he was in jail again. She brought him food. It was a newly renovated jail building this time, with shiny slippery tile floors and plastic window frames, and, as it turned out, bizarre food rules: tomatoes were allowed but cucumbers were banned.

She talked to him as soon as he was released.

"We have to leave," she said. "This country is finished."

He listened.

"I want to quit my job," she said. "What's the point of debating the future of the gas monopoly when the country itself has no future?"

"Don't quit," he said. "Find another job first."

"I want to go to Ukraine."

"Then go."

Zhanna went to Kiev, knocked on all the doors of all the television stations and found nothing. Boris suggested that he could call Petro Poroshenko, his friend who was now running for president in Ukraine, and ask him for help in finding a job for Zhanna.

"Though it wouldn't be a good look for me, to have you living in Ukraine," he added. Now that Russia was at war with Ukraine, his ties to that country, and to the Orange Revolution, were mentioned ever more frequently. He had become the very image of a traitor.

"No, don't call," said Zhanna. It was not because of what he had said about his reputation—she was worried about hers. She had worked too hard to be seen as her own person.

"Then you have to keep doing your job at RBK as long as they'll let you."

RBK belonged to former metals magnate Mikhail Prokhorov, a friend of Boris's who had himself dabbled in politics. He was the one who had once offered to bankroll Zhanna's campaign while also funding her opponent. Prokhorov tried to at least appear independent of the Kremlin, so his media outlets took more liberties than most. Zhanna had a job in journalism in which she was not forced to broadcast outright lies—this was a luxury. Soon, Zhanna and her father both knew, having a job at all might feel like a luxury.

AS SOON AS Boris and the other Solidarity activists were released from jail, they filed for a permit to hold a peace march. About fifty thousand people came on March 15—a stunning turnout. If the polls were right and only 1 percent of Russians opposed the war, then in Moscow, nearly all of this opposition would seem to have come out for the march. On the other hand, perhaps the polls reflected the fact that only members of the die-hard, risk-everything opposition were willing to express a dissenting opinion anymore, even to a survey taker. Boris marched at the very front, in the middle of a row of people holding a banner that said "Hands Off Ukraine." Behind them, many of the signs said "For Your Liberty and Ours."

Nemtsov was the first speaker at the rally. He talked not so much about Ukraine as about Putin.

> He is a sick man. . . . But he is not merely a sick man: he is also a cynical and dishonest man. He has occupied Crimea because he wants to rule forever![10]

Zhanna went to the march—the first time she had joined her father in the streets since she had found herself running away from police that New Year's Eve back in 2009.

A few days after the march, Nemtsov heard that he would be charged in the Bolotnoye case. Considering what had happened to the other protest leaders, he was not surprised. Udaltsov was in jail; Navalny had escaped prison only because thousands had taken to the streets, but now he was facing new trumped-up fraud charges; Kasparov had left the country after being threatened with prosecution. Boris told Zhanna that he wanted to talk.

"I don't know if I could survive a ten-year sentence," he said. "I'm fifty-five, you know."

He worked out every day. He windsurfed. He loved pictures of himself at the beach. He wore tight blue jeans and white shirts unbuttoned to show off his pecs. His last two or three girlfriends had been younger than Zhanna—Zhanna, in fact, appreciated the current one, a long-legged, dirty-blond-haired young woman from Kiev, for never inserting herself into grown-up conversations, like the one they were having now.

"I'll always support you," said Zhanna. Family could make the difference between surviving in a Russian prison and not.

"You'll lose your job."

"You know I don't care."

"In that case, if they lock me up, will you mention it live on air?"

"You got it."

<hr />

ON MARCH 26, the fourteenth anniversary of Putin's first election, Zhanna turned thirty. Boris called her in the morning.

"I'm sorry I can't come tonight," he said. "I'm in Israel. Will you come visit me?"

Zhanna bawled. They had never missed each other's birthdays. They always had big parties. "I think this is the last time I have a party," she told Raisa. Everyone else came, and everyone noticed Boris's absence, but no one asked about it.

Zhanna flew to Tel Aviv the following week. Boris picked her up at the airport looking like Al Pacino in *The Godfather*, when his character had the permanent black eye. Except Boris had two.

"I had the bags under my eyes removed," he explained. "I needed a doctor's note."

He was referring to the Yaroslavl city legislature's mandatory attendance policy. But what was he thinking? That he could be here on indefinite medical leave? That the Investigative Committee would change its mind about the probe if he waited them out? Was he planning to stay in Israel?

He said he was staying. He also complained about not feeling at home in Israel. Zhanna said she agreed. It was too dense, too hot, and too humid.

"There are other countries," she suggested. "With better weather."

Her father said nothing.

They walked on the beach, and he talked about his life as though he needed to sum up his accomplishments. He seemed old—something he had never seemed before. He did not seem like a superhero. He kept suggesting they go shopping. He wanted to buy her things. She demurred.

Before she left, he told her not to tell anyone where he was. He was not hiding: he was hiding the fact that he was not in Russia. Zhanna told no one. Even when her boss asked her directly if her father was in Israel, she said, "What are you talking about?"

Zhanna's grandmother knew he was abroad, of course, and she was thrilled. To ensure that he stayed abroad, she decided to publish an open letter to her son on the Echo Moskvy website. She sent it to Boris's cousin to arrange publication. The cousin sent it to Zhanna. Zhanna sent it to Boris.

> I have only one thing to ask you, to beg of you—you can call it
> my will and testament, if you like. Don't go to prison. It will
> do no one any good. I mean the people who love you and peo-
> ple of good will in general.

How was Dina Yakovlevna suggesting that he avoid prison? She was a woman born and reared in the Soviet Union, so she could not openly recommend emigration: for most of her life, émigrés were condemned as traitors to the Soviet cause. Still, everyone would know that when she begged him not to go to prison, she was asking him to emigrate. Since this was an open letter, she addressed the obvious concern, that her son, were he to emigrate, would be perceived as unpatriotic.

> I would like to add that my father, Boris's grandfather, was,
> from a young age, a member of the Bolshevik party, a sincere
> believer in Leninism, and he personally saw Lenin speak. He
> was later honored by the Soviet Union in retirement, so he
> was a most honorable man. Boris's ill-wishers fail to under-
> stand that all his thoughts and actions are driven by *honesty
> and his love for Russia*. These are not just words. By the way,
> this is something that he shares with Putin: *a love of Russia*.
> When Crimea joined Russia, I was euphoric like everyone
> else. I thought justice had triumphed. I talked about it with
> my son-in-law, and we both came to the conclusion that Putin
> had secured his place in history. We are simple people. We

didn't know how this was all going to turn out. We didn't see the flip side of the coin.

But now I realize. I think that maybe Putin isn't so thrilled with all of this himself anymore. My daughter says that maybe his advisers weren't all in favor of this scenario. Some of them are probably smarter than others.

Getting back to Boris now. I remember reading in some newspaper that Khodorkovsky was asked, "How did you, being such a smart man, end up in prison when you could have avoided it?" And Khodorkovsky said, "There are smart men and then there are wise men."

Borya, please be wise.

Love, your mother,
16 April 2014

Boris was livid. The idea of being addressed through an open letter by his own mother, the naive attempt to manipulate his will and his image by appealing to Soviet concepts of honor, but most of all, the comparison to Putin—the assertion that they had their love of Russia in common—made him incensed. Still, Zhanna felt that he railed excessively that day on the phone. He seemed to be overreacting a lot these days.

Around the same time, a former socialite who was now an anchor on TV Rain tweeted, "Turns out Nemtsov is in Israel. Probably not returning to Russia, because of criminal probe."[11] When they discussed this on the phone, Boris sounded hurt: he had thought this woman was his friend.

He was a terrible émigré: his heart was not in it. The successful ones ran to save their children or their fortunes. He was running to save his life, but his life was in Russia.

A few days later he went to Khodorkovsky's congress in Kiev, and from there he flew to Moscow. He took a selfie at the airport and posted it on Facebook with a reference to the TV Rain anchor's two-week-old tweet. He was back.[12]

BORIS WAS on borrowed time now, so he worked twice as furiously. He published a report on corruption and fraud in the lead-up to the Sochi Olympics. The report focused on, among others, Vladimir Yakunin, head of the Russian railroads monopoly and a key funder of Russian Orthodox "traditional values" activism. His wife ran an organization called Sanctity of Motherhood and was a fixture of World Congress of Families gatherings. Born in 1948, Yakunin had been a KGB officer in Soviet times. He had been a member of the Putin clan since the 1990s.[13] Nemtsov's focus, however, was not on Yakunin's life but on the business he had done in Sochi, including a contract to build a forty-eight-kilometer* stretch of highway at a cost of more than $50 billion. Nemtsov was certain this was a world record. He called this chapter "The Most Expensive Project of the Most Expensive Olympics in History."[14] That spring Yakunin started dragging Nemtsov into court: he sued him for libel, demanding 3 million rubles—the equivalent of nearly $100,000 when the suit was first filed but worth only about half that amount by the time the case was finally on the docket late the following winter.[15]

Nemtsov also began assembling a report on Putin's war in Ukraine. It would include proof of the use of Russian troops in both Crimea and eastern Ukraine. It would include body counts, which the Kremlin had classified. It would include proof that the missile that shot down a Malaysian Airlines plane in July 2014, killing 298 people, was fired from a Russian-made launcher located on territory controlled by Russians and the Ukrainian separatists they backed. It would include information about peace negotiations held in Minsk in the fall of 2014—like the fact that Russia appended its signature (it was represented by Moscow's ambassador to Ukraine, Mikhail Zurabov) to the accords reached there, thereby acknowledging that it was a party to the conflict.[16]

Nemtsov led a second peace march in Moscow on September 21, 2014—

---

*About thirty miles.

about twenty-five thousand people came.[17] That day one of the buildings along the route featured a two-story-tall square banner bearing the words "March of the Traitors." Beneath images of the U.S. flag and the White House, the banner showed the faces of six people—two writers, a rock musician, and three activists, including Nemtsov.[18] At least half of these people were spending all or most of their time outside Russia. Nemtsov's face had appeared on a similarly large poster that had been hung on a building in the center of the city back in April, when he was in Israel. That one was captioned "The Fifth Column. Aliens Among Us." The group was almost entirely different, but Nemtsov's face was a constant.[19] He appeared again in January 2015, on the largest banner yet—this one covered three and a half stories of a high-rise apartment building. "The fifth column insisted on sanctions against their own country. By supporting sanctions, they are causing incomes to fall and prices and unemployment to grow." A quote from Nemtsov's blog appeared next to his face: "The sanctions that have been imposed may destabilize the country. Putin will be facing a crisis and chaos in Russia."[20]

On New Year's Eve 2015, Alexei Navalny and his brother Oleg were found guilty of defrauding a company whose representative testified that it had not in fact been defrauded. Alexei was sentenced to three and a half years of house arrest—the authorities were apparently trying to avoid another mass protest—but Oleg got three and a half years in prison. He was a hostage now.[21]

With Navalny sentenced, Udaltsov in prison, and Kasparov and Ponomarev in exile, Nemtsov was now the only one of the prominent protest organizers left walking around Moscow (and Yaroslavl). After the winter holidays, he began organizing a third march, timed for the anniversary of the invasion. This time he could not get a permit to march in the center of the city. Nor could he get much support, even among fellow activists, for the march itself. His allies argued that Russians were now concerned more with their own economic problems than with the war. Nemtsov compromised on both counts: the march would be held on the outskirts of the city—an hour's

Metro ride from the center—and it would be called "The Spring March Against the Crisis."

Ten days in advance of the scheduled march, on the anniversary of the day when Ukrainian president Yanukovych was deposed, a government-sanctioned march was held in central Moscow. It inaugurated yet another pro-Kremlin youth movement, the Anti-Maidan, with the prevention of a "color revolution" in Russia its sole declared goal.[22] About thirty thousand people came, many of them carrying flags and preprinted banners bearing slogans such as "The Maidan Brings War and Chaos." A giant black banner carried by more than a dozen people at once read, in white lettering, "Clean Out the Fifth Column." A single poster, copies of which were carried by dozens of the marchers, featured a black-and-white photograph of Nemtsov in an orange frame. The caption said, "Organizer of the Maidan."[23]

ZHANNA WAS NOT PLANNING to go to the march out in the suburbs. She had no use for the euphemism in its name: she wanted to march against the war, or not at all. She was going on vacation to Italy instead—the first week of March, when it always felt like Moscow winter would never end, was the right time to get away. Raisa would come too—she came to Moscow from Nizhny Novgorod on February 27 to spend the night before they flew out together. On the way home Zhanna stopped by Boris's building and left an envelope containing $10,000 in cash with the doorman. This was money for the report on Putin's war in Ukraine. It was about to go to the printer's.

Zhanna said good night to Raisa at half past eleven, went to her bedroom, and turned off the lights and her phone—she always followed this mental-health rule. Raisa was sleeping in the living room.

Zhanna woke up because Raisa was screaming. Zhanna knew it was her mother screaming, yet it was a voice she had never heard before, a voice of terror. Zhanna must have forgotten to lock the door, there must be an intruder.

Raisa was in the living room alone. She was sitting on the couch screaming. She held her phone in her hand.

"They killed him," she said.

Zhanna turned on her phone and the television. There were text messages and news stories. Her father had been shot on a bridge not fifteen
minutes from here. Raisa was having trouble breathing.

"It's okay," said Zhanna. "We'll go there now."

It was pouring rain. She hailed a car.

"Take us to the Moskvoretsky Bridge, please."

"What do you need there?"

"They killed Nemtsov there."

The driver looked at her for the first time. His face, lit by a streetlamp,
looked angry.

"What do you care?"

"Well, maybe you don't care that a world-renowned man was just shot to
death in the center of Moscow, but he happens to be my father."

The police had sealed off the bridge. Zhanna went from officer to officer, showing her press credentials and her passport. "I'm press. We are family. I'm press." It took forever.

The first person they saw on the other side of the barrier was Vladimir
Kara-Murza, Boris's young friend, a co-organizer of the peace marches who
was now working for Khodorkovsky.

"The body is in the ambulance," he said. "I'll follow it to the morgue."

There was no point in driving all over town now.

"We have to think about how to tell Grandmother," Zhanna said to
Raisa.

They called Boris's sister and his cousin in Nizhny, and they went to
Dina Yakovlevna's house to wait for morning. She was bound to turn on the
television or radio as soon as she awoke, and they needed to be there to tell
her the news themselves.

"I want to go to Moscow," the old woman said.

The next day Dina Yakovlevna led a march in Moscow. It was not a
peace march or a "spring march." It was a march of mourning. Fifty thou-

sand people walked through central Moscow without a permit. They carried Russian flags and portraits of Nemtsov and a giant banner with the words "Heroes Don't Die." No one stopped them.[24]

───────

THERE WERE DOZENS of unanswered calls on Zhanna's phone. Everyone wanted an interview. She called her own station.

"I want to talk to you first," she said.

"Sure, let's get you on tape," the editor in chief said.

"I want to be live," said Zhanna.

"I can't do that."

She hung up.

She talked to a BBC reporter instead. She said that she held Putin personally responsible for her father's death. She was merely stating the obvious. Boris was killed on a bridge across the Moscow River, with the Kremlin as the backdrop for the murder. The Kremlin was so close that the bridge was under constant surveillance—as any television journalist who had ever tried to film a stand-up there knew: the Presidential Guard would have been on top of them in seconds. But Boris's body had lain on the bridge for at least ten minutes, with no Presidential Guard in sight. Not that it mattered where the killing happened: Putin had been portraying Zhanna's father as a traitor for so long, and as an enemy combatant for the last year—their fears of prison seemed naive now.

There was a funeral. Pavel Sheremet, the journalist who had made the film for Nemtsov's fiftieth birthday, emceed the memorial service. They miscalculated and had to cut it short—not everyone who had come to pay respects had been able to enter the building by the time the funeral procession left for the cemetery.

Zhanna and Raisa did go to Italy, but the BBC found her there again, and this time Zhanna said even more. Russian police had arrested a Chechen man, a police officer, for Boris's murder. But she said that she had no trust in any Russian investigation.

You keep asking me if my father posed a threat to the regime. Of course he did. You have such a two-dimensional view of the world. Look wider. Study the totalitarian regimes of the world. The dissidents are either in exile—look at how many people have left Russia, like Kasparov—or else they are in prison or under house arrest, or they are killed. . . . Anyone who thinks differently poses a threat to a totalitarian regime. . . .

Are you afraid to return to Russia?
Not really, I'm not. I'm going back.

Did your father's murder change your views of—
You know, I was always a pessimist, but this turned my whole world upside down. Not that I had any illusions. But I certainly didn't think that it's possible at all—I still can't believe that they killed my father. I don't consider myself an activist. But I am an honorable person and I love my father very much, and I want everyone to know the truth. And the truth is what I'm saying—that we'll never get the truth from the authorities in Russia. But I just want to say that what I'm saying now means that the authorities will now view me as an activist. That's all I have to say.[25]

Zhanna did return to Moscow. She figured it was a matter of time before she lost her job—the people at RBK were surely just waiting for an excuse to cut her loose.

Boris's friends—the activists who had been by his side for the last ten years, in Solidarity, at marches, and in jail—set up a memorial on the bridge. After the first time the authorities removed the flowers and Russian flags, they set up a round-the-clock vigil. Vladimir Kara-Murza was one of the half-dozen people who went there every day, to stand in memory and on guard.

In late May, the University of Bonn invited Zhanna to give a talk in memory of her father. She woke up in a slightly worn German Modernist hotel on the three-month anniversary of Boris's death. She read the news. Vladimir Kara-Murza had been hospitalized with multiple organ failure as the result of an unknown toxin. So this was how it worked. The famous got a bullet in the heart and the less famous got poison in their tea.

The hotel, it turned out, had a monthly rate. She could stay there while she looked for an apartment. The family who ran the hotel restaurant spoke Italian—she could communicate with them, even if she knew no one else in this town. It did not occur to Zhanna to go anywhere else. Bonn was quiet and clean and safe, as good a place as any. She was never going back to Russia.

twenty-two

FOREVER WAR

AFTER THE PROTEST following Navalny's sentencing in July 2013—after several of the best hours he could remember, when he and the people all around him were doing what had to be done, asking no one's permission to do it—after the police finally dispersed the crowd, Seryozha found himself standing in the square across the street from the Bolshoi Theatre. Everyone was gone. Some people had been loaded onto police buses. Most had gone home. A few had settled in at nearby bars. The night was warm, and the terrace bars on the pedestrian mall around the corner were serving Cuba Libres. Seryozha still felt the spot where a policeman's baton had poked at his back as he and his little group were pushed along the sidewalk, away from the protest site. He still felt hoarse from shouting out to other protesters when he wanted them to break away from the cops, then double back and take their stand again. Too few of them had heard him. He went home.

The next day, after Navalny had been released from prison, Seryozha read on Facebook that a woman had gone back to the square to continue the protest. He knew her—not well, but he knew her name and he had often gone to a café she managed. She kept writing the same thing on her page, calling on people to come and stand with her, to refuse to leave until all charges against Navalny were dropped and until the Bolotnoye prisoners were released. She wrote comments on her friends' pages—she had a lot of friends—demanding that they come and join her. Sometimes they did, for an hour or two, and then they went back to their lives. She stayed. Every day for three weeks she stood in the square, beneath a clock that was counting down the days and hours to the start of the Sochi Olympics. She held a handwritten sign in Russian and English: "Free All Political Prisoners." For the first few days, she was surrounded by dozens of police officers and several paddy wagons—they clearly expected the protesters to return. But then they left, and the woman stood alone. Every day she posted a picture of herself beneath the clock, which was counting days in reverse, as prisoners do.[1]

Seryozha knew that he should go, but he did not. He felt the cloud coming back down on him again, heavier than before. All he could think about was that he, Seryozha, was not beyond reproach. If he was not beyond reproach, then he had no right to call on other people to act, like he had the other day. He had to act himself. But acting involved other people, and he had no right to involve them. So he was not acting. Not acting was shameful. The shame about his inaction combined with the shame he now felt about his pride, his unwarranted claims to other people's attention, and this double shame, this shame that kept doubling back on itself, paralyzed him.

The paralysis let up briefly in March. After the occupation of Crimea, the outside world became so loud that it broke through the cloud. Seryozha got in touch with a couple of men he had met at the protests in 2011–2012. Together they printed out and laminated portraits of the more than a hundred men and women who had died in the Maidan. They took them to the Ukrainian embassy and set them in a row along the fence, in a linear memorial.[2] A few hours later the police asked the embassy to remove the pictures. They explained that a rally celebrating the annexation of Crimea was happening nearby and there could be trouble. The embassy complied. After that, the cloud descended again.

Seryozha went to see a psychiatrist that spring. He explained what was happening to him. He had no friends. He was not working. Most days, he was not leaving the house. He was a useless, worthless human being.

The psychiatrist prescribed antidepressants. A few days after Seryozha started taking them, he felt no different except that his whole body itched. At least he was feeling his body—maybe this was a good thing, the beginning of recovery. Then he could think of nothing but the itch. By the time he realized that he needed medical attention, by the time he told a doctor that he felt like his skin was coming off, that he felt like he was dying, he really was dying. He had a condition called toxic epidermal necrolysis, a rare side effect of the antidepressants.[3] Some of the damage was permanent. After that, when Seryozha struggled to get out of bed in the morning, it was hard, usually impossible, because of what the depression was doing to him and what the antidepressant drugs had done.

WHEN ARUTYUNYAN LOOKED at her clients, she almost found herself missing the early Putin years. For her, that had been a time when things started shutting down—when a world in which, for a decade or more, opportunity had seemed limitless, began closing in. But she had known even then that she was in the minority. Most of her clients craved "stability," whatever that meant. It had all been too much for them for years. Their anxiety had been intolerable: what Arutyunyan had experienced as "freedom from" the constraints of the totalitarian state, many of her clients experienced as "freedom to"—find a way, measure up, do as well as the others. When the first constraints began snapping back into place, to the beat of the "stability" drum, they had felt calmer. One client had finally felt grounded enough to start her own business—something that she had wanted and feared for years. She, and the business, did well for a while. In fact, even now the business was doing well enough. But the client was having panic attacks. So many laws had changed without warning, so many unwritten rules had gone into effect, that she was constantly unsure whether she had missed something. One day, in February 2016, she stepped outside in the morning to discover that overnight all the low-rise commercial buildings on her street—the shops that sold flowers and bread and soda and cigarettes—had been torn down.

Altogether, ninety-seven buildings in Moscow were demolished that night. The city said that their papers were not in order.[4] But they had stood there for years, in many cases well over a decade—surely their owners thought their papers were good. The woman's own business rented space in an old-construction high-rise, but what was it that she was missing? She had a strong sense—she got signals—that she should be cultivating connections and giving bribes, but she did not know how and, more to the point, she felt strongly that she should not. The signals she was getting about what was right came into conflict with her own inner sense of what was right. If only the law were clear and permanent and applied to all equally.

If only the law were clear and permanent and applied to all equally, Arutyunyan's job would be easier. She would guide her client to understand that her fears were projections—which they were, by definition, yet how was she to draw the line between the woman's fear of a collision with her superego and her fear of a collision with Russia's so-called law enforcement? The client's world did not just feel unpredictable: it was unpredictable by design.

It was not just this client who was living in a state of constant anxiety: the entire country was. It was the oldest trick in the book—a constant state of low-level dread made people easy to control, because it robbed them of the sense that they could control anything themselves. This was not the sort of anxiety that moved people to action and accomplishment. This was the sort of anxiety that exceeded human capacity. Like if your teenage daughter has not come home—by morning you have run out of logical explanations, you can no longer calm yourself by pretending that she might have missed the last Metro train and spent the night at a friend's house and her phone battery had died, and you are left alone with your fear. You can no longer sit still or reason. You regress, and after a while the only thing you can do is scream, like a helpless terrified baby. You need an adult, a figure of authority. Almost anyone willing to take charge will do. And then, if that someone wants to remain in charge, he will have to make sure that you continue to feel helpless.

The whole country felt helpless. You could see it if you turned on the television, which Arutyunyan rarely did. Everyone on television was screaming all the time. There were debate shows—this was what they were called, that is—in which two or more people ostensibly representing two sides of an issue yelled at each other for an hour and a half at a time. "America wants to see us weak!" yelled a politician who happened to be the grandson of Vyacheslav Molotov, the Stalin-era foreign minister who signed the Soviet-Nazi pact. "What is Russia supposed to do?" yelled back his nominal opponent, whose side was supposed to argue for peace with the United States but who was only there to project anxiety. While both debaters yelled in fear, the moderator, who wore all black to every show, yelled in order to scare the participants and the audience.[5]

Newscasts and morning shows ran cookie-cutter anxiety-producing segments. A news report would focus on the dangers of drugs, or of sexual predators. Then a person introduced as an activist would enter the studio and explain that the government was not doing enough to confront the danger. There should be the death penalty for drug dealers! Pedophiles should be castrated! By the end of the monologue, the hosts—usually a man and a woman—would be in a panic, screaming that no one was protecting their children from drugs and pedophiles. The format harked back to a Soviet tradition, in which it was always the imaginary "ordinary people" who supposedly begged the Party for ever more restrictive and punitive laws, but its main purpose was to maintain a constant pitch of high anxiety.

What options did this frightening country offer its intolerably anxious citizens? They could curl up into total passivity, or they could join a whole that was greater than they were. If any possession could be summarily taken away, no one felt any longer like anything was truly their own. But they could rejoice alongside other citizens that Crimea was "theirs." They could fully subscribe to the paranoid worldview in which everyone, led by the United States, was out to weaken and destroy Russia. Paranoia offered a measure of comfort: at least it placed the source of overwhelming anxiety securely outside the person and even the country. It was a great relief to belong, and to entrust authority to someone stronger. The only thing was, belonging itself required vigilance. One had to pay attention: one day Ukraine was where the important war was being fought, the next day it was Syria. In the paranoid worldview, the source of danger was a constantly moving target. One could belong, but one could never feel in control.

TRAUMA IS, as one American theorist has phrased it, "a historical experience of survival exceeding the grasp of the person who survives."[6] It is the experience of having come into contact with a danger so great that it, and the fact of having escaped it, refuse to fit in one's mind. Freud first wrote about trauma in the context of survivors of the First World War and then again as he struggled to understand the Nazi persecution of Jews. In his 1920 essay *Beyond the Pleasure Principle*, Freud introduced the idea of a death drive, a destructive force fueled by trauma, which has made survival intolerable. The death drive compelled repetition, an endless return to loss. Many of Freud's followers later rejected the idea of the death drive, and Freud himself, in his later work, broadened the concept to include outwardly directed aggression. But some later scholars focusing on trauma linked the idea of the death drive to the high rate of suicide among survivors of concentration camps or the Vietnam War.[7]

After the Second World War, American psychiatrist Robert Jay Lifton, who had also trained in psychoanalysis, studied survivors of Chinese internment camps, survivors of the atomic bomb explosion in Hiroshima, and the doctors who became killers in Nazi concentration camps. His aim was to "identify psychological experiences of people caught up in historical storms," he wrote.[8] He spent a lifetime developing clinical and theoretical approaches to trauma. He described phenomena specific to survivors. He called one "psychic numbing"—a sort of emotional shutdown in response to unconscionable events.[9] In his study of Nazi doctors, he identified a psychological principle he called "doubling," defined as "the division of the self into two functioning wholes, so that a part-self acts as an entire self."[10] He described what he believed to be a specifically twentieth-century experience: that of "lifelong immersion in death."[11]

Lifton's work began a conversation about trauma experienced not only by individuals but by groups, including entire societies, which in some cases passed their experience of surviving the unimaginable from generation to generation. Like people, societies could fragment in response to trauma, could go numb, perhaps, as Nicholas Eberstadt suggested when he looked for an explanation for Russia's excessive death rates—an entire society could become depressed. If Eberstadt had been trained as a psychoanalyst rather than an economist, he might even have considered that an entire society could be seized by the death drive.

Traumatic experiences that affect entire societies could include natural disasters, catastrophic wars, genocide, revolution, and lives spent in a situation of chronic oppression. In cases where the trauma was extended in time—as with ongoing oppression or state terror—change, even apparently positive change, wrought further trauma. When familiar social structures stopped functioning, it could be as traumatic as when physical structures collapsed in the case of a natural disaster. Strategies of adaptation that worked under the old order were no longer useful. Therapists working in Kosovo in 2000, for example, discovered that people who had for years been victimized by being told what to do now longed to be told what to do. Liberian refugees in the United States, encouraged by well-meaning American therapists to seek support in their own community, re-created patterns of corruption and exploitation: becoming victims of familiar abuse was indeed comforting.[12]

Arutyunyan's mentors had frowned on the word "trauma"—too much of a wastebasket. The word would make it seem as if people were passive recipients of whatever happened to them, and as if terrible things on the outside produced predictably terrible results on the inside. This sort of thinking was antithetical to psychoanalysis, which Arutyunyan had, after all, chosen because it saw the many and varied conflicts that raged inside a person's psyche all on their own. Arutyunyan had met psychoanalysts who really believed that all of a person's fears and anxieties were always projections, that nothing was external. She wished she could think that way herself.

A British analyst once said that he preferred depression brought on by big bad events to depression that was apparently spontaneous: tragedy increased the chances of recovery. Too bad this logic held only in cases when you could expect the big and bad to end.

―――

IN OCTOBER 2015, Putin convened his annual meeting of international scholars and journalists who specialized in Russia. This year, the gathering was held in Sochi, where facilities built for the 2014 Winter Olympics had fallen into disuse. A month earlier, Putin had flown to New York to address the seventieth General Assembly of the United Nations. He proposed forming an international antiterrorist coalition "like the anti-Hitler coalition."[13] The offer, in other words, was to join forces in fighting ISIS in exchange for Russia's unhindered reign in Ukraine and elsewhere in the region—just like participation in the anti-Hitler coalition had allowed the Soviet Union to keep the spoils of its earlier alliance with Hitler. When the United States snubbed the offer, Russia began bombing Syria. Now Putin convened international guests for a discussion titled "Societies Between War and Peace."

"Peace, a life at peace, has always been and continues to be an ideal for humanity," he said. "But peace as a state of world politics has never been stable." In other words, peace was an anomaly, a fragile state of equilibrium that, he said, was exceedingly difficult to sustain. The advent of nuclear arms helped, he said, by introducing the specter of mutually assured destruction, and for a while—from the 1950s through the 1980s—"world leaders acted responsibly, weighing all circumstances and possible consequences." This was a variation on the usual Soviet nostalgia rhetoric: casting the Cold War as the golden era of world peace.

> In the last quarter century, the threshold for applying force has
> clearly been lowered. Immunity against war acquired as a result of

two world wars, literally on a psychological, subconscious level, has been weakened.[14]

He went on to blame this state of affairs on the United States and to justify Russian intervention in Syria, but the key point of his speech was that only at war could his Russia feel at peace. Or, as Erich Fromm had written of Nazi Germany seventy-five years earlier, "It is fate that there are wars."[15] Arendt, writing about Hitler, had described a nostalgia for the First World War, which had satisfied a "yearning for anonymity, for being just a number and functioning only as a cog. . . . War had been experienced as that 'mightiest of all mass actions' which obliterated individual differences so that even suffering, which traditionally had marked off individuals through unique unexchangeable destinies, could now be interpreted as 'an instrument of historical progress.'"[16] The concept of historical progress—of perpetual motion—was, in turn, key to Arendt's understanding of how totalitarianism took hold.

Russia's official rhetoric was evolving in full accordance with Gudkov's diagnosis of "recurrent totalitarianism." Following this inexorable logic, in September 2016, the justice ministry classified the Levada Center itself as a foreign agent. Gudkov had been expecting this for months, and he knew it spelled the end of his life's work. The law on "foreign agents" required organizations to identify themselves as such in all communications with the public. How would Levada sociologists ever conduct a survey again if they had to present themselves as "foreign agents"?[17]

YEARS EARLIER, Arutyunyan's son, who was born in 1980, told his parents that he had realized they had raised him "in an oasis." The home where he had grown up—Arutyunyan's grandmother's giant Academy of Sciences flat, where four generations had now lived—had been largely shielded from the privations of the 1980s, the fears of the 1990s, and even from much of the sense of shutting down that pervaded the 2000s. These days, though, Arutyunyan found it difficult to stay in her oasis.

Not only had the country changed politically—now the city around her was changing physically. The low-rise stores and cafés had been razed, eliminating the eye-level urban environment that had appeared in the 1990s. The city returned to its totalitarian scale. In Arutyunyan's neighborhood, the streets were eight lanes wide, the sidewalks could fit twelve people across, and the buildings had archways seven stories high. In the absence of the low-rise stores, people once again became mere specks.

Then the city ripped up the asphalt on the sidewalks throughout central Moscow and replaced it with pavement tiles. The first freeze showed that the ice that formed on these tiles stayed smooth and clear, unlike most of the ice on asphalt. People fell. Some days, the streets looked like scenes from slapstick comedy. Pedestrians kept slipping and falling, and slipping and falling. It was hard not to laugh, even as people were breaking arms and hips all around you. Then it was time to marvel at the regime's insistence on turning its own metaphors literal: it was determined to break its people.

In the summer of 2016, the city ripped up the sidewalks again, all over central Moscow. For weeks, it felt like the city was at war with itself. Walking to the store or to the Metro became difficult and unpredictable—people had just formed new routines after the disappearance of the low-rise stores, and now ditches, fences, and dead ends appeared unpredictably in their way, forcing pedestrians to step into the streets, zigzag, and, most important, constantly pay attention. The state of low-level dread became a characteristic of being outside in the city, at any time of day or night.

Finally, more tile was laid down. The city now created a series of bike paths—though these were generally short segments that connected two dead ends. There was a sort of architectural-rendering symmetry and beauty in Moscow's new look. But like a first-year architecture student, someone had forgotten to put trees in these renderings. The city's streets had been stripped of all that had been growing there. Everything was made of stone and right angles. Moscow had acquired the geometry and texture of a graveyard.

Maybe Freud was right about the death drive in the first place. And maybe a country could indeed be affected by it just like a person could. Maybe this energy had been unleashed in Russia. Maybe it was bent on destruction for the sake of destruction, war for the sake of war. Maybe this city and this country were burying themselves alive. The more Arutyunyan thought about it, the less fanciful the idea seemed to her. Entire civilizations in history had ceased to exist. How had life in them felt in the last decades and days? Russia and the Russians had been dying for a century—in the wars, in the Gulag, and, most of all, in the daily disregard for human life. She had always thought of that disregard as negligence, but perhaps it should be understood as active desire. This country wanted to kill itself. Everything that was alive here—the people, their words, their protest, their love—drew aggression because the energy of life had become unbearable for this society. It wanted to die; life was a foreign agent.

At least, that was what Freud might say. At least Arutyunyan had read him. Future generations of Russians might not be so lucky—if there were any future generations of Russians, that was.

She stubbed out a cigarette and lit another.

EPILOGUE

JUNE 12, 2017, was the twenty-seventh anniversary of Russia's declaration of sovereignty, whatever that had meant. It was the twenty-sixth anniversary of Boris Yeltsin's election as Russia's president. It was a national holiday. For its first decade, the holiday was known as the Day of the Passage of the Declaration of State Sovereignty, but in 2002 the name was changed to Russia Day. The declaration of sovereignty—Russia's first step toward separating itself from the Soviet project—was no longer an event to be celebrated. The holiday had to be depoliticized without sacrificing its spirit of patriotism. Over the years, the festivities employed folk music, pop music, and theater productions on historical topics. In the end, the holiday became a cacophony.

One thousand seven hundred twenty people were arrested on Russia Day 2017—the largest wave of arrests in decades. Alexei Navalny had called them to the streets, and tens of thousands had come out in cities from Kaliningrad to Vladivostok, the most geographically widespread protest in Russian history. Most of the detainees were released within hours; many were sentenced to fines and between five and thirty days behind bars; a few would probably face several years in a prison colony. After about a week it emerged that some of the detainees in Moscow had been tortured, and that jailers in St. Petersburg had pumped noxious gas into the cells where protesters were held.

In Moscow, some of the more than eight hundred detainees had to spend the night on benches in a precinct courtyard because there was no room for them inside, but the scene in the city that day had been less tragic or frightening than absurd. This year's Russia Day had been turned over to historical reenactments. No particular period had been chosen, but a medieval bent was in evidence. A few kids were wearing red silky costumes vaguely reminiscent of the Young Pioneers' kerchiefs, but most grown men were dressed in chain-mail armor and carried shields and swords. Still others wore Second World War–era uniforms and milled around barricades made of sand-filled burlap sacks. At one point, a man dressed as a twentieth-century peasant—a costume that in a different context could easily have been taken for hipster getup—climbed a wall of sacks with a sign that said, in English, "Putin Lies." As he climbed, he shouted, in Russian, "Putin is a thief!" When he reached the top, a man in the uniform of the NKVD—the Second World War–era secret police—gave chase up the sacks. The protester tumbled down, into the arms of two other men in period secret-police uniforms, and these men handed him over to two contemporary policemen.

The bizarre spectacle of it all was too much for foreign correspondents, who tried to avoid scenic but incomprehensible shots of knights in shining armor literally shielding a teenage protester from the police. Instead, the reporters focused on the teenagers among the protesters. Everyone seemed to agree that the new face of Russian resistance was barely pubescent: a boy in shorts being tackled by police in riot gear, a girl charging a police line, a paddy wagon full of adolescents. One Russian Facebook user posted a photograph of the teenagers in the paddy wagon with the caption "Russia has a future." He posited that "every mass arrest of young people strengthens youth protest," which, in turn, was sure to bring about the end of the regime.

The poster was Georgy Satarov, a sixty-nine-year-old political scientist.

Satarov was the man who, more than twenty years earlier, had been tasked by Yeltsin with articulating the new Russian national idea—and failed. Now he was shifting responsibility to the teenagers. It was yet another iteration of Levada's old concept: the next generation, free of the fear, envy, and doublethink of Homo Sovieticus, would usher in a new era of freedom. The next generation kept getting younger. The first generation of people who had no memory of Stalin's terror had not succeeded in overcoming the totalitarian legacy; the first post-Soviet generation—those born into perestroika and reared in the 1990s—had been the face of the protests of 2011–2012, but they no longer embodied hope; now it was up to the generation of kids born under Putin.

Masha was amused that a photograph of her being dragged off by police was captioned "Teenage girls among hundreds arrested at Russia protests." She was detained briefly and released—she was still winding her way between drops of rain—and as soon as she got out, she went to work arranging representation for those who had been arrested. She was still doing this work under the auspices of Mikhail Khodorkovsky's organization, but he had cut back on the funding—or, more accurately, he had set limits, while the Russian government was doing the opposite. The number of arrests continued to grow exponentially, and Khodorkovsky's money would not keep up. Fund-raising became a part of Masha's job, and then an increasingly important part. And there was no end in sight; there would be more arrests, more fund-raising, and no possibility of a vacation. She decided to quit. She even announced it in a blog post: she would raise the money, she would make sure everyone who had been arrested on June 12 had representation, she would see those cases through to completion, and then she would quit. She would have another life.

Masha's life as an activist had lasted five and a half years. In 2016, she had run for office—there was an open seat in parliament. There was no hope of winning—even getting on the ballot was an exceedingly difficult task—but Khodorkovsky had the idea that it was important to acquire campaign experience. Masha agreed, but the experience proved more bruising than she could have predicted. She cleaned up her act, quit drinking and doing recreational drugs, and began dressing in button-down shirts and blazers at all times, yet she was still criticized by the very people she was trying to court. The intelligentsia found her language too harsh and cynical. Many of them preferred to vote for a history professor who opposed the war in Ukraine but made no secret of his virulently homophobic views. The history professor did not win, either: not one anti-Putin candidate made a dent in the polls anywhere in the country. Khodorkovsky's project of creating a shadow society looked much better on paper than it felt in real life.

Still, compared with the other Bolotnoye case defenders, Masha was leading a life of glamour. Most of the others had been sentenced to time in prison colonies. Some had been released after serving their two or two and a half years; others remained in prison, and still others were awaiting trial— they had been arrested later. The state continued to add defendants to the five-year-old case.

ZHANNA WAS SETTLED IN BONN. She had a job with Deutsche Welle, the taxpayer-funded broadcasting service. Like the Russian-language services of the British Broadcasting Corporation and the American Radio Free Europe/Radio Liberty, DW used to broadcast on short-wave frequencies during the Soviet period, was granted access to AM frequencies under Yeltsin, and lost it under Putin. It was now a Web-based broadcaster with modest audience numbers, but Zhanna became its star interviewer. At DW, no one told her not to delve into politics.

Zhanna started a foundation named for her father. She convened a board that awarded an annual prize to someone who demonstrated courage and determination in fighting the Putin regime. Remarkably, there was stiff competition for the award, and the board argued long and passionately. In June 2017, Zhanna made it public that her father had planned to run for president in 2018—though, she figured, he would have stepped aside if Alexei Navalny had decided to run. Navalny was running now, for what it was worth. For the time being, he was locked up for thirty days after calling for the June 12 protests. He was also facing ever-mounting trumped-up charges of fraud that could land him in prison for years. In an earlier trial, which ended on New Year's Eve 2014—to ensure that most Russians were properly distracted when the verdict was delivered—Navalny was sentenced to house arrest, and his brother, Oleg, to three and a half years in a prison colony. The intention was clear: house arrest looked like a relatively humane measure, so this time there would be no mass protests. Navalny himself would be kept in line by his brother's sentence: Oleg was a hostage. Navalny refused to play. With his brother's permission and encouragement, he persisted with his investigations. He also refused to recognize his own sentence, because Russian law does not actually provide for house arrest as punishment. He walked the streets. The state asked him to desist, and he refused. The state gave up. And now Navalny was leveraging his ability to keep assembling people in the streets for his freedom—and his life.

In July 2017 a Moscow court sentenced five men to between eleven and twenty years in prison for the murder of Boris Nemtsov. All five were from Chechnya; an ostensible sixth accomplice was killed when the police attempted to detain him in Chechnya. The court spent next to no time trying to determine the men's motives: the prosecution's story seemed to be that they had organized the murder for no apparent reason. Zhanna and her legal team had insisted on summoning highly placed Chechen officials, but these were never interrogated. In the end, the murder would remain effectively unsolved.

Boris's old activist friends—the scruffy lot with whom he worked after he left parliament—maintained a living memorial on the bridge where he was gunned down. The city had declined requests to name the bridge for Nemtsov or to create a permanent memorial there. Instead, every couple of months, and sometimes every few days, city workers descended on it and hauled away the flowers and placards. The next day, time after time, activists replaced them. They kept vigil. Though they were powerless to prevent the removal of the memorial, they made sure that a living friend of Boris was present at the site of his death every minute of every day.

IN NEW YORK, Lyosha found himself talking about Chechnya all the time. In the spring of 2017, news came that gay men there were being rounded up, interned, tortured, and, in some cases, killed. Chechen and Russian officials laughed off questions about the disappearances. In Moscow and St. Petersburg, LGBT activists refused to believe the reports at first, simply because they seemed too awful to be true, but soon the evidence was overwhelming. Chechnya had taken the Kremlin's anti-gay policies to their logical extreme, making Occupy Pedophilia—the vigilante group of the sort that had haunted Lyosha back in Perm—into a state enterprise. The lucky gay men from Chechnya were those who managed to escape to other Russian cities, to attempt eventually to flee to the West.

Lyosha was granted asylum status in the spring of 2017. In the nearly three years that he had been in the United States, he had not been able to find a job in his field—academic positions, even temporary ones, turned out to be prohibitively difficult to come by—but he had learned English and become an increasingly visible activist. He was named co-president of RUSA LGBT, an organization of Russian-speaking queer people helping new asylum seekers. Eventually, he found a job at an AIDS non-profit.

He was still living in Brighton Beach, the Russian enclave and one of the few neighborhoods in New York City that went to Donald Trump in the 2016 presidential election. Lyosha often faced incredulous questions from American friends: How could people who fled the Soviet Union and Putin vote for someone like Trump? But, of course, these were not people who fled totalitarianism. Most of them had arrived around the time the Soviet empire began disintegrating. If anything, what had driven them out was the fear of the Soviet collapse. They longed to return to their imaginary past, which would have made them Putin voters if they had stayed in Russia. Instead, they became Trump voters.

They were also blatantly and sometimes aggressively homophobic.

Though many of the new queer asylum seekers rented apartments in Brighton Beach, they lived their gay lives in Manhattan. Lyosha, on the other hand, decided to organize Brighton Beach Pride. In May 2017, about three hundred people marched along the boardwalk from Coney Island, chanting against homophobia in both Russian and English.

SERYOZHA HAS NOT RESPONDED to my messages and phone calls since June 2015.

THE LEVADA CENTER was deemed a "foreign agent" and fined for not registering as one. The center added a line at the bottom of its website, saying that Levada had been "forcibly added to the registry of noncommercial organizations acting as foreign agents." At first, Lev Gudkov panicked. How were researchers going to continue their work if they had to introduce themselves to potential respondents as "foreign agents"? But it ended up being less of an impediment than Gudkov had thought. He realized that for some people, the "foreign agent" designation had become something of a badge of honor. Potential respondents did not appear to be put off by the designation. In June 2017 the center finished analyzing its "most outstanding person of all time in the entire world" survey. Joseph Stalin came out on top, as he had in the previous survey, in 2012. For the first time ever, Putin took second place, sharing it with Pushkin.

IN 2015, the Moscow Psychoanalytic Society advanced to the status of a "component society" within the International Psychoanalytic Association. There were now twenty-three psychoanalysts who were full members and thirty more who were candidates—essentially, psychoanalysts in training who could work with patients. That made for fifty-three psychoanalysts—one for more than every two hundred thousand Muscovites.

In 2016, Arutyunyan's son, Dmitry Velikovsky—the child who once thanked his parents for having raised him in an oasis—became one of three Russian journalists who worked on the Panama Papers, the giant trove of information on offshore accounts. The most surprising story in the Russian part of the Papers concerned cellist Sergei Roldugin, one of Putin's closest friends from his university days, who had apparently amassed a fortune—or was safeguarding it for someone else. In the spring of 2017, Dmitry was among the more than four hundred journalists from around the world who shared a Pulitzer Prize for their work on the project. In Russia, however, the story had barely made a ripple and was soon forgotten.

In the spring and summer of 2017, the sidewalks (and much of the pavement) in central Moscow were ripped up again, for the third year in a row, to be replaced with ever more perfectly laid geometric tiles that had so reminded Arutyunyan of tombstones. The city also announced a plan to raze between four and a half and eight thousand buildings, including many structurally sound and architecturally interesting ones, and replace them with high-rise developments.

ALEXANDER DUGIN ENJOYED a period of international fame of sorts as a Putin whisperer: for a couple of years some analysts and journalists believed that he was the mastermind behind Putin's wars. Dugin continued to insist that he had great influence but negligible power. Still, his star rose ever higher in unexpected ways. With the election of Donald Trump in the United States, the neo-Nazi movement known as the "alt-right" gained public prominence, as did its leader Richard Spencer, an American married to Nina Kouprianova, a Russian woman who served as Dugin's English translator and American promoter.

THE REMAINS of Czar Nicholas II, his wife, and three of their daughters, which were interred in St. Petersburg in 1998, were exhumed in 2015 at the request of the Russian Orthodox Church. The Church, it was said, wanted to know whether the remains of two more people, found separately, also belonged to the czar's family. These had been found in 2007 and had been positively identified by geneticists as belonging to the czar's only son and one of his daughters. The Church, however, insisted on a comparative study of all remains. Once that was completed, there would certainly be a new burial ceremony, which would erase the memory of the earlier one and of Yeltsin's speech, the one time a Russian leader apologized for the atrocities of the Soviet regime. But nearly two years after the exhumation, the remains were still unburied, perhaps because 2017 was the centennial of the Russian Revolution and neither the Church nor the Kremlin could find a way to handle the symbolism.

MIKHAIL PROKHOROV, the oligarch who once suggested to Zhanna that he could fund both her and her electoral opponent in order to watch the race, made a few other attempts to dabble in politics. The Kremlin kept showing him his place, and he kept not getting the message. Finally, when the print arm of a news outlet he owned—RBK, Zhanna's old workplace—published an investigative piece on Putin's daughter's lucrative real estate concession in Moscow, Prokhorov was forced not only to sell RBK but to divest from Russia entirely. He moved to New York, where he had for several years owned the Brooklyn Nets basketball team.

MIKHAIL FRIDMAN, THE oligarch who said Zhanna was insane for returning to Moscow and who later stopped seeing Boris in order to protect his own status, continued to run a successful bank in Russia. During the 2016 U.S. presidential campaign, the name of his bank, Alfa, surfaced twice in stories about alleged Russian meddling. One report claimed that the Trump campaign had established a back channel for communicating with Alfa-Bank—though a later report said there might be an innocuous explanation. Then Alfa came up again, in an unverified intelligence dossier published by BuzzFeed. Fridman sued BuzzFeed for libel.

NIKITA BELYKH, the member of the Perm legislature who had employed the other Lyosha, was appointed governor of the Kirov region while Dmitry Medvedev was president. For a few years, he enjoyed the reputation of Russia's only pro-democracy governor. In June 2016, Belykh was arrested during a sting operation at a bar in Moscow. He was accused of accepting bribes. He was still in pretrial detention a year later.

PAVEL SHEREMET, the television journalist who made a film for Nemtsov's fiftieth birthday, moved to Kyiv.* Soon after Nemtsov's murder, Sheremet launched a show on Ukrainian television. In July 2016, Sheremet was assassinated by a car bomb in Kyiv.

VLADIMIR MAKAROV, the young civil servant accused of molesting his own daughter, served his five-and-a-half-year sentence. He repeatedly applied for parole and was denied. He was released in 2016. The European Court of Human Rights refused to hear his case, demonstrating that the accusation

---

*"Kyiv" is the non-Russified spelling of the name of the city, preferred by independent Ukraine.

of pedophilia was the perfect persecution vehicle. Many more people have been brought up on child-sex-abuse charges since. In 2017, Memorial activist Yuri Dmitriev, who had discovered the sites of numerous Stalin-era mass executions, was arrested on child-pornography charges.

ILYA PONOMAREV, the parliament member who employed Masha during the protests, was accused of embezzlement. He fled the country, living for a time in California before settling in Ukraine.

ALL OF THE PROMINENT ORGANIZERS of the 2011–2012 protests faced a stark choice between exile and prison—or worse. Garry Kasparov, the former chess champion, moved to New York after he was threatened with criminal charges in 2013. Sergei Udaltsov, the radical-left organizer, was serving four years behind bars. Nemtsov was dead. Only Ilya Yashin and Navalny were still functioning out in the open. In the spring of 2017, Navalny lost most of the vision in one eye when an attacker threw acid at him.

THE MOSCOW SCHOOL FOR POLITICAL STUDIES, where Masha was on that Russia Day weekend she got a phone call about a search at her apartment, was declared a foreign agent and was forced to cease operations.

NEMTSOV'S ASSISTANT OLGA SHORINA, who called Masha that day, left the country. She lives in Bonn and helps Zhanna run the Boris Nemtsov Foundation for Freedom.

MARAT GUELMAN, the gallerist and political technologist who ran the contemporary art museum in Perm, left Russia in 2013 and settled in Montenegro, where he now runs a contemporary arts festival. He might have thought that Montenegro, with a total population of less than a million, was a backwater destination, but in 2017 it emerged that Russia had been plotting a coup there—because Montenegro wanted to join NATO.

VLADIMIR KARA-MURZA, the first person Zhanna saw when she came to the site of her father's murder, survived his poisoning in 2015. He was in a coma for five days. Eventually, he was airlifted to the United States, where he underwent rehabilitation. He returned to work for Khodorkovsky's foundation in Russia. He also made a film about Nemtsov. He screened it in Yaroslavl, the town where Nemtsov had held his last elected post, in February 2017. Less than forty-eight hours later, he was once again hospitalized with total organ failure. The doctors, fortunately, knew how to treat him, and this time the coma did not last as long.

ACKNOWLEDGMENTS

CONVERSATIONS WITH TWO PEOPLE inspired me to begin work on this book. Chitra Raghavan surely had no idea that her lecture on the psychology of trauma would prompt me to write more than five hundred pages about the aftermath of the Soviet experience. Anand Giridharadas, on the other hand, knew exactly what he was doing when he told me, at our first meeting, that I should go write this book—but I don't believe it occurred to him that I would follow his advice. I thank them anyway.

Research for and much of the writing of the book were made possible by the Carnegie Corporation, where I was an Andrew Carnegie Fellow in 2015–2016.

In the summer of 2016, I was fortunate, once again, to be a guest of the Institute for Human Sciences in Vienna, where I wrote nearly half of the book. I enjoyed the support and intellectual company of other Institute guests and fellows: Anton Shekhovtsov, Mark Lilla, Tatiana Zhurzhenko, and Tim Snyder and Marci Shore.

I am grateful for the generous support of Mal Jones of Up the River Endeavors, and of Vladimir Radunsky, who sent me notebooks when I needed them.

I am grateful to my editor, Rebecca Saletan, who encouraged the unusual structure of the book and didn't blink at the word count until the very end, when she asked me to keep the acknowledgments brief. Team Riverhead made it possible for this book to emerge in certainty and style. Thank you, Jynne Dilling, Al Guillen, Karen Mayer, and Anna Jardine.

I am lucky to have Elyse Cheney and Alex Jacobs as my agents.

I am grateful to the people—friends, family, colleagues, and a few almost unsuspecting near-strangers—who talked to me, argued with me, read parts of the book as I wrote, and otherwise helped me move through the process: Roger Berkowitz, Carol D'Cruz, David Denborough, Robert Horvath, Nicholas Lemann, Istvan Rev, Jack Saul, Vera Shengelia, Cheryl White, and my partner through the last seven books, Darya Oreshkina.

My largest debt, though, is to the protagonists of this book, who allowed me into their lives and engaged with endless hours of my unreasonably detailed questions. Thank you, Maria Baronova, Alexei Gorshkov, Sergei Yakovlev, Zhanna Nemtsova, Marina Arutyunyan, and Lev Gudkov.

NOTES

Lyosha, Masha, Seryozha, and Zhanna—their real names—told me their lives over the course of about a year. I spent hours asking them to recall events and places, conversations, feelings, movies, newscasts, and ideas. I used various sources to corroborate dates, times, and descriptions of, say, television footage, and if contradictions arose, I resolved them (or, in one case, noted the discrepancy between recollection and factual chronology). At the same time, my main interest was in personal perceptions. For this reason, all conversations—unless they were recorded—are relayed as they were recounted to me by just one of the participants (and, in one case, as had been recounted by someone else). Our recollections of conversations are rarely precise, but they are precisely what we live with.

Arutyunyan and Gudkov spent dozens of hours each talking with me for this book. Dugin declined to be interviewed but delegated his right-hand person to talk to me; I also interviewed his other associates and studied his copious writing and lectures.

Beyond these sources, I relied on a wealth of scholarship, both Russian and Western. Sources are noted for all information that does not come from interviews with the principal characters and is not the product of firsthand reporting.

one BORN IN 1984

1 Detailed information on Molniya is found on its website: http://www.buran.ru/htm/molnianp.htm, as is information on the space shuttle: http://www.buran.ru/htm/mtkkmain.htm, accessed October 28, 2015.
2 Steven Merritt Miner, *Stalin's Holy War: Religion, Nationalism, and Alliance Politics, 1941–1945* (Chapel Hill and London: University of North Carolina Press, 2003), p. 33.
3 Ibid., pp. 32–33.
4 Ibid., passim.
5 Yves Hamant, *Alexander Men': Svidetel svoyego vremeni* (Moscow: Rudomino, 1994), pp. 104–106.
6 Jennifer Utrata, *Women Without Men: Single Mothers and Family Change in the New Russia* (Ithaca, NY, and London: Cornell University Press, 2015), pp. 126–127.
7 Olga Kryshtanovskaya, *Anatomiya rossiyskoy elity* (Moscow: Zakharov, 2005), p. 180, http://www.telenir.net/politika/sovetskii_soyuz_poslednie_gody_zhizni_konec_sovetskoi_imperii/, accessed October 28, 2015.

8 Anya von Bremzen, *Mastering the Art of Soviet Cooking: A Memoir of Food and Longing* (New York: Crown, 2013), pp. 166–167.

9 Articles 87 and 88 of the Criminal Code of the Russian Soviet Federated Socialist Republic, *Ugolovniy kodeks RSFSR ot 27 oktyabrya 1960 goda*, http://avkrasn.ru /article-2004.html, accessed October 28, 2015.

10 Yelena Bonner, *Postskriptum: Kniga o gorkovskoy ssylke* (Moscow: Interbook, 1990).

11 Boris Nemtsov, *Ispoved' buntarya* (Moscow: Partizan, 2007).

12 A. D. Sakharov, "Intervyu B. Nemtsovu," October 13, 1988, http://www.sakharov -archive.ru/Raboty/Rabot_20.htm, accessed November 2, 2015.

13 *1984*, translated by Viktor Golyshev, was published in *Novy mir*, 1989, nos. 2, 3, 4.

14 Andrei Amalrik, *Prosushchestvuyet li Sovetskiy Soyuz do 1984 goda?* http://www.vehi.net /politika/amalrik.html#_ftnref17, accessed October 31, 2015.

15 Andrei Amalrik, "Posledneye slovo," http:// profilib.com/chtenie/31354/andrey-amalrik -stati-i-pisma-1967-1970-lib-7.php, accessed October 31, 2015.

16 http://antology.igrunov.ru/authors/amalrik/, accessed November 3, 2015.

17 Alexander Galich, "Posle vecherinki," http:// www.bards.ru/archives/part.php?id=4156, accessed November 3, 2015.

18 Mikhail Aronov, *Alexander Galich: Polnaya biografiya* (Moscow: Novoye literaturnoye obozreniye, 2015).

19 Alexander V. Razin and Tatiana J. Sidorina, "The Philosophers' Ship," *Philosophy Now*, no. 31 (March/April 2001), https:// philosophynow.org/issues/31/The _Philosophers_Ship, accessed October 31, 2015; Paul R. Gregory, "The Ship of Philosophers: How the Early USSR Dealt with Dissident Intellectuals," *The Independent Review* 13, no. 4 (Spring 2009), pp. 485–492.

20 Konstantin Sonin, blog posts "'Udovol'stviye byt' sirotoy,'" July 8, 2015, http://ksonin .livejournal.com/574202.html, and "Drugaya zhizn'," April 2, 2013, http://ksonin .livejournal.com/490977.html; both accessed October 31, 2015.

two **LIFE, EXAMINED**

1 Author interview with Evgenia Debryanskaya, New York City, December 1990 (for publication in *Out/Look Magazine*).

2 Author interview with Evgenia Debryanskaya, Moscow, December 2014.

3 M. Heidegger, "Ucheniye Platona ob istine," *Istoriko-filosofsky ezhegodnik* (Moscow: Nauka, 1986), pp. 255–275.

4 Milovan Djilas, *The New Class: An Analysis of the Communist System* (London: Thames & Hudson, 1957), pp. 4–5.

5 http://www.psy.msu.ru/about/history /history2.html, accessed November 10, 2015.

6 http://www.psy.msu.ru/about/history/history .html, accessed December 10, 2015.

7 Aleksandr Etkind, *Eros nevozmozhnogo: Istoriya psikhoanaliza v Rossii* (Moscow: Gnozis-Progress-Komplex, 1994), pp. 15–40.

8 Ibid., pp. 112–113.

9 Ibid., pp. 115–116, 127.

10 Ibid., p. 177.

11 Ibid., p. 179.

12 Ibid., p. 183.

13 Ibid., p. 208.

14 Ibid., p. 205.

15 Ibid., pp. 129–168.

16 Ibid., p. 206.

17 A. A. Leontiev, "The Life and Creative Path of A. N. Leontiev," *Journal of Russian & East European Psychology* 43, no. 3 (May–June 2005), pp. 8–69.

18 Lisa Yamagata-Lynch, *Activity Systems Analysis Methods: Understanding Complex Learning Environments* (New York: Springer Science+Business Media, 2010), p. 20.

19 Etkind, *Eros nevozmozhnogo*, p. 206.

20 Oliver Sacks, foreword to A. R. Luria, *The Man with a Shattered World: The History of a Brain Wound* (Cambridge, MA: Harvard University Press, 1987), pp. vii–xix.

21 N. Bukharin, *Teoriya istoricheskogo materializma* (Moscow, Leningrad: Gosudarstvennoye izdatel'stvo, 1925), viewed at http://www.scribd .com, November 15, 2015, p. 11.

22 G. Batygin, "Preyemstvennost rossiyskoy sotsiologicheskoy traditsii," in V. A. Yadov, ed., *Sotsiologiya v Rossii* (Moscow: Izdatel'stvo Instituta sotsiologii RAN, 1998).

23 Stephen F. Cohen, *Bukharin and the Bolshevik Revolution: A Political Biography, 1888–1938* (New York: Vintage Books, 1975), p. 310.

24 Batygin, "Preyemstvennost rossiyskoy sotsiologicheskoy traditsii."

25 "Postanovleniye Politburo TsK KPSS 'Ob Organizatsii Instituta Konkretnykh Sotsial'nykh Issledovaniy Akademii Nauk

SSSR,'" May 22, 1968, and "Postanovleniye Sekretariata TsK KPSS 'Ob Osnovnykh Napravleniyakh Raboty Instituta Konkretnykh Sotsial'nykh Issledovaniy AN SSSR,'" December 10, 1968, http://cdclv.unlv.edu//archives/Documents/iksi_establish.html, accessed November 17, 2015.

26 D. N. Shalin, "Garvardskoye intervyu s Yuriyem Levadoy," *Sotsiologicheskiy zhurnal*, no. 1 (2008), pp. 126–153.

27 Aleksei Levinson, "Uroki Levady," *Neprikosnovenny Zapas* 6, no. 50 (2006), http://magazines.russ.ru/nz/2006/50/lev30.html, accessed November 18, 2015.

28 Shalin, "Garvardskoye intervyu s Yuriyem Levadoy."

29 D. N. Shalin, "Yuri Levada: Ya schital, shto bylo by neyestestvenno vesti sebya kak-to inache," *Sotsiologicheskiy zhurnal*, no. 1 (2008), pp. 155–174.

30 The Federal Statistics Service website used to provide population divorce figures, but these appear to have been deleted. A remnant is found at http://www.bad-good.ru/2013/december/marriage-divorce.html, accessed November 20, 2015.

three **PRIVILEGE**

1 http://samlib.ru/w/wagapow_a/yesen.shtml#Im_tired_of_living, trans. Alec Vagapov, accessed November 25, 2015.

2 "O kulte lichnosti i yego posledstviyakh," Nikita S. Khrushchev's presentation at the Twentieth Congress of the Communist Party of the USSR, http://www.hrono.ru/dokum/195_dok/19560225hru.php, accessed November 29, 2015.

3 Alexander Yakovlev, "Protiv antiistoritsizma," originally published in *Literaturnaya gazeta* in 1972, reproduced at http://left.ru/2005/15/yakovlev132.phtml, accessed November 29, 2015.

4 A. N. Yakovlev, *Gorkaya chasha: Bolshevizm i reformatsiya v Rossii* (Yaroslavl: Verkhne-Volzhskoye knizhnoye isdatel'stvo, 1994), pp. 9–12.

5 Ibid., p. 21.

6 Ibid., pp. 211–212.

7 Denis Romodin, "'Tsarskoye selo' v Kuntsevo—premium-klass epokhi SSSR," Proekt Sovetskaya Arkhitektura, http://sovarch.ru/273/, accessed November 29, 2015.

8 Map of industrial plants in Moscow at http://www.subcontract.ru/Docum/DocumShow _DocumID_728.html; map of air quality at http://www.moscowmap.ru/imap_eco.shtml; both accessed November 25, 2015.

9 Mervyn Matthews, *Privilege in the Soviet Union: A Study of Elite Life-Styles Under Communism* (London: George Allen & Unwin, 1978), p. 20.

10 Ibid., pp. 59–90.

11 Ibid., pp. 91–92.

12 Ibid., p. 20.

13 Alexander Galich, "Za semyu zaborami," http://www.bards.ru/archives/part.php?id=4162, accessed November 26, 2015.

14 http://solikam-sk.narod.ru/index/0-3; http://www.memo.ru/history/NKVD/GULAG/r3/r3-175.htm; both accessed November 27, 2015.

15 "15 novykh nezavismykh gosudarstv: Chislo abortov na 100 zhivorozhdeniy, 1960–2014," *Demoskop weekly*, no. 663–664 (November 16–29, 2015), http://demoscope.ru/weekly/ssp/sng_abo.php, accessed November 28, 2015.

16 Sergei Zakharov, "Brachnost v Rossii. Istoriya i sovremennost'," *Demoskop weekly*, no. 261–262 (October 16–29, 2006), http://demoscope.ru/weekly/2006/0261/tema02.php, accessed November 28, 2015.

17 D. Zhdanov, Ye. Andreev, and A. Yasilioniene, "Polveka izmeneniy rozhdaemosti v Rossii," *Demoskop weekly*, no. 447–448 (December 13–31, 2010), http://demoscope.ru/weekly/2010/0447/tema03.php, accessed November 28, 2015.

18 Mie Nakachi, "Replacing the Dead: The Politics of Reproduction in the Soviet Union, 1944–1955," doctoral dissertation, University of Chicago, 2008, p. 191.

19 *Venok slavy*, 12 vols. (Moscow: Sovremennik, 1987).

four **HOMO SOVIETICUS**

1 "Postanovleniye Politbudo TsK KPSS i zapiska A. N. Yakovleva ob izdanii serii 'Iz istorii otechestvennoy filosofskoy mysli,'" in A. A. Yakovlev, ed., *Aleksandr Yakovlev, Perestroika: 1985–1991: Dokumenty* (Moscow: Mezhdunarodny fond "Demokratiya," 2008), pp. 203–205.

2 Valeria Novodvorskaya, *Nad propastyu vo lzhi* (Moscow: AST, 1998); Dmitry Volchek, "May 1988-go: Vospominaniya o pervom s'yezde DS," program aired by Russian Service of Radio Liberty, May 21, 2008;

transcript: http://www.svoboda.org
/content/transcript/448783.html, accessed
December 10, 2015.

3 Volchek, "May 1988-go."

4 Novodvorskaya, *Nad propastyu vo lzhi*,
p. 22.

5 Ibid.

6 Ibid., p. 19.

7 Aleksei Alikin, "Vy slovno khodite po
lezvuyu nozha," *Russkaya planeta*, May 28,
2014, http://rusplt.ru/society
/debranskaya-10104.html, accessed December
11, 2015.

8 Walter Laqueur, *Black Hundred: The Rise of
the Extreme Right in Russia* (New York:
HarperCollins, 1993), pp. 204–209.

9 "Otvety A. N. Yakovleva na voprosy
slushateley Vysshey partiynoy shkoly v
Moskve," in Yakovlev, *Aleksandr Yakovlev,
Perestroika*, p. 424.

10 Laqueur, *Black Hundred*, p. 208.

11 Alexander Dugin, *Puti absolyuta*, http://
modernlib.ru/books/dugin_aleksandr/puti
_absolyuta/read/, accessed December 12,
2015.

12 Anton Shekhovtsov, "Alexander Dugin and
the West European New Right, 1989–1994,"
in Marlene Laruelle, ed., *Eurasianism and the
European Far Right: Reshaping the Europe-
Russia Relationship* (Lanham, MD:
Lexington Books, 2015), pp. 35–54.

13 I. L. Solomin, "Lichnostnyi oprosnik MMP:
Metodicheskoye rukovodstvo," http://reftrend
.ru/396397.html, accessed December 17,
2015.

14 L. N. Sobchik, SMIL-566-MMPI-test.
Metodika Minnesotskij Mnogoaspektnyj
Lichnostniy Oprosnik-Standartizirovanniy
mnogofaktorniy metod issledovaniya
lichnosti, http://psycabi.net/testy
/472-smil-566-mmpi-test-metodika
-minnesotskij-mnogoaspektnyj-lichnostnyj
-oprosnik-standartizirovannyj
-mnogofaktornyj-metod-issledovaniya
-lichnosti-sobchik-l-n, accessed December
22, 2015.

15 John M. Reisman, *A History of Clinical
Psychology*, 2nd ed. (New York and London:
Brunner-Routledge, 1991), p. 367.

16 Ruth Sanford (with additions by Irina
Kuzmicheva), "The Other Part of the Soviet
Story," http://ruthsanford.tripod.com/the
_other_side_of_the_soviet_story.htm,
accessed December 17, 2015.

17 Carl Rogers, *The Carl Rogers Reader*, ed.
Howard Kirschenbaum and Valerie Land
Henderson (New York: Houghton Mifflin,
1989), p. 484.

18 Ibid., p. 486.

19 Ibid., p. 492.

20 *Virginia Satir in the USSR 1988*, film
produced by Dr. Bob Spitzer and L. B.
Johnson, https://www.youtube.com
/watch?v=I36XM6_vsf4, accessed December
17, 2015.

21 Boris Grushin, "Na dal'nikh i blizhnikh
podstupakh k sozdaniyu VTsIOMa," polit.
ru, December 10, 2007, http://polit.ru
/article/2007/12/10/vstiom/, accessed
December 18, 2015.

22 Tatiana Zaslavskaya, "Kak rozhdalsya
VTsIOM," in Boris Dubin, Lev Gudkov, and
Yuri Levada, eds., *Obshchestvennyi razlom in
rozhdeniye novoy sotsiologii* (Moscow: Novoye
izdatel'stvo, 2008), pp. 8–14.

23 Yuri Levada, ed., *Sovetsky prostoy chelovek:
Opyt sotsial'nogo portreta na rubezhe 90-kh*
(Moscow: publisher unknown, 1993), p. 11.

24 Ibid., p. 23.

25 Ibid., p. 14.

26 Ibid., p. 16.

27 Ibid.

28 Hannah Arendt, *The Origins of
Totalitarianism* (New York: Harcourt Brace
Jovanovich, 1976), pp. 465–466.

29 Ibid., p. 475.

30 Levada, *Sovetsky prostoy chelovek*, pp. 18–19.

31 Ibid., p. 22.

32 Ibid., p. 286.

33 Ibid., p. 288.

34 George Orwell, *1984* (New York: Signet
Classics, 1961).

35 Levada, *Sovetsky prostoy chelovek*, pp. 30–31.

36 Ibid., pp. 292–293.

37 Ibid., pp. 274–276.

five **SWAN LAKE**

1 V. V. Lebedinsky and N. P. Chesnokova,
"Oktyabryata," *Bolshaya sovetskaya
entsiklopediya*, 3rd ed. (Moscow, 1974), vol.
18, pp. 1080–1081; "Chto v SSSR delali
pionery, kak prinimali v komsomol i kto
takiye oktyabryata?" *Argumenty i fakty*, May
19, 2014, http://www.aif.ru/dontknows
/eternal/1170643, accessed December 28,
2015.

2 Image of back cover of Soviet primary-school
notebook at http://bigpicture.ru/wp-content

/uploads/2014/01/sovietschool02.jpg, accessed December 28, 2015.

3 Mikhail Zoshchenko, "Grafin," in *Rasskazy o Lenine*, http://lib.ru/RUSSLIT /ZOSHENKO/r_lenin.txt, accessed December 28, 2015; A. I. Ulyanova, *Detskiye i shkolniye gody Ilyicha*, chap. 3, http://libelli .ru/works/chapter1.htm, accessed December 28, 2015. (In fact, the chronology of writing, and the appearance of the image of a broken vase in an entirely different, earlier, recollection by Ulyanova, make the entire story appear fictional, but for the purposes of mythology this is irrelevant.)

4 Serhii Plokhy, *The Last Empire: The Final Days of the Soviet Union* (New York: Basic Books, 2014), p. 31.

5 "Sostav rukovodyashchikh organov Tsentral'nogo komiteta Kommunisticheskoy partii—Politburo (Prezidiuma), Orgburo, Sekretariata TsK," *Izvestia TsK KPSS*, no. 7 (1990), http://vivovoco.astronet .ru/VV/PAPERS/HISTORY/KPSS /HISTORY.HTM, accessed January 2, 2016.

6 The Politburo member in question was Andrei Gromyko. Mikhail Gorbachev, *Zhizn' i reformy* (Moscow: Novosti, 1995), vol. 1, p. 408.

7 Ibid., p. 409.

8 Stephen Kotkin, *Armageddon Averted: The Soviet Collapse, 1970–2000* (New York: Oxford University Press, 2008), p. 21.

9 I describe this in detail in *The Man Without a Face: The Unlikely Rise of Vladimir Putin* (New York: Riverhead Books, 2012).

10 Ronald Reagan, remarks delivered at the Annual Convention of the National Association of Evangelicals, in Orlando, Florida, March 8, 1983, http://www .reaganfoundation.org/bw_detail .aspx?p=LMB4YGHF2&lm=berlinwall&a rgs_a=cms&args_b=74&argsb=N&tx=1770, accessed January 3, 2016.

11 Peredovaia, "RSFSR," *Pravda* 31 (February 1, 1936), cited in Terry Martin, *The Affirmative Action Empire: Nations and Nationalism in the Soviet Union, 1923–1939* (Ithaca, NY, and London: Cornell University Press, 2001), p. 452.

12 Peredovaia, "Privet izbrannikam velikogo naroda!" *Literaturnaya gazeta*, no. 3 (January 15, 1937), cited in Martin, *The Affirmative Action Empire*, p. 455.

13 1936 Constitution of the USSR, http://www .hist.msu.ru/ER/Etext/cnst1936.htm, accessed January 3, 2016.

14 1977 Constitution of the USSR, http://www .hist.msu.ru/ER/Etext/cnst1977.htm#iii, accessed January 3, 2016.

15 1978 Constitution of the RSFSR, http:// constitution.garant.ru/history/ussr -rsfsr/1978/red_1978/5478721/, accessed January 3, 2016.

16 A. A. Yakovlev, ed., *Aleksandr Yakovlev, Perestroika: 1985–1991: Dokumenty* (Moscow: Mezhdunarodny fond "Demokratiya," 2008), p. 165.

17 Ibid., p. 166.

18 Thomas de Waal, *Black Garden: Armenia and Azerbaijan Through Peace and War* (New York and London: New York University Press, 2003).

19 Kotkin, *Armageddon Averted*.

20 Yakovlev, *Aleksandr Yakovlev, Perestroika*, pp. 321–351.

21 "Vystupleniye na pervom syezde narodnykh deputatov SSSR," in Andrei Sakharov, *Mir, progress, prava cheloveka* (Leningrad: Sovetskiy pisatel, 1990), pp. 111–116.

22 M. R. Zezina et al., *Chelovek peremen: Issledovaniye politicheskoy biografii B. N. Yeltsina* (Moscow: Novy khronograf, 2011).

23 Yakovlev, *Aleksandr Yakovlev, Perestroika*, pp. 361–362.

24 Ibid., p. 381.

25 Zbigniew Brzezinski, *The Grand Failure: The Birth and Death of Communism in the Twentieth Century* (New York: Collier Books, 1990).

26 Plokhy, *The Last Empire*, p. 38.

27 Yakovlev, *Aleksandr Yakovlev, Perestroika*, pp. 602–605.

28 Soobsheniye Tsentral'noy komissii referenduma SSSR Ob itogakh referenduma SSSR, sostoyavshegosya 17 marta 1991 goda, http://www.gorby.ru/userfiles/file /referendum_rezultat.pdf, accessed January 6, 2016.

29 Yakovlev, *Aleksandr Yakovlev, Perestroika*, pp. 620–634.

30 A. A. Yakovlev, ed., *Aleksandr Yakovlev, Izbranniye intervyu: 1992–2005* (Moscow: Mezhdunarodny fond "Demokratiya," 2009), p. 382.

31 Yakovlev, *Aleksandr Yakovlev, Perestroika*, pp. 659–681.

32 Yakovlev, *Aleksandr Yakovlev, Izbranniye intervyu*, p. 37.

33 Yakovlev, *Aleksandr Yakovlev, Perestroika*, p. 823.

34 Ibid., p. 689.

35 Ibid., pp. 690–695, 824.

36 Zakon SSSR ot 20.05.91 no. 2177-1, http://www.lawrussia.ru/texts/legal_178/doc17a990x543.htm.In fact, the exit-visa requirement would not be phased out fully until 1993: "Vyyekhat' za rubezh poka ne legche, chem ran'she," *Kommersant,* January 11, 1993, http://www.kommersant.ru/doc/7029, accessed January 8, 2016.

37 GKChP, "Obrashcheniye k sovetskomu narodu," http://dok.histrf.ru/20/zayavlenie-gkchp/, accessed January 8, 2016.

38 GKChP press conference, August 19, 1991, https://www.youtube.com/watch?v=TVxH4e3Rfes, accessed January 10, 2016.

39 Boris Yeltsin's address to the public, August 19, 1991, https://www.youtube.com/watch?v=JpoOkFZsPT8, accessed January 10, 2016.

40 Footage of Mikhail Gorbachev returning to Moscow, August 22, 1991, https://www.youtube.com/watch?v=1cnkbL6KV6o, accessed January 10, 2016.

41 Mikhail Gorbachev's press conference, August 22, 1991, http://rutube.ru/video/985c0f40c9416286f1a91d20b6bd8961/?bmstart=4133; Mikhail Gorbachev's televised address to the nation, August 22, 1991, https://www.youtube.com/watch?v=0qB16clLmN4; both accessed January 11, 2016.

42 Yakovlev, *Aleksandr Yakovlev, Perestroika*, p. 695.

43 Vadim Bakatin, *Izbavleniye ot KGB* (Moscow: Novotni, 1992).

44 Petr Akopov, "Sud'ba komissarov," *Izvestia,* August 23, 2001, http://izvestia.ru/news/250769, accessed January 11, 2016.

45 Gorbachev to reporters, December 12, 1991, https://www.youtube.com/watch?v=mCWzf1Ze2tk, accessed January 11, 2016.

46 Gorbachev's resignation speech, December 25, 1991, https://www.youtube.com/watch?v=lHjrmckJiMk, accessed January 11, 2016.

six THE EXECUTION OF THE WHITE HOUSE

1 Serhii Plokhy, *The Last Empire: The Final Days of the Soviet Union* (New York: Basic Books, 2014).

2 Zbigniew Brzezinski, *Grand Failure: The Birth and Death of Communism in the Twentieth Century* (New York: Collier Books, 1990), pp. 41–102.

3 Stephen Kotkin, *Armageddon Averted: The Soviet Collapse, 1970–2000* (New York: Oxford University Press, 2008).

4 Alexei Yurchak, *Everything Was Forever, Until It Was No More: The Last Soviet Generation* (Princeton, NJ: Princeton University Press, 2005).

5 Hannah Arendt, *The Origins of Totalitarianism* (New York: Harcourt Brace Jovanovich, 1976), p. 465.

6 Ibid., p. 391.

7 Wendy Z. Goldman, *Women, State and Revolution: Soviet Family Policy and Social Life, 1917–1936* (Cambridge, England, and New York: Cambridge University Press, 1994).

8 Dan Healey, *Homosexual Desire in Revolutionary Russia: The Regulation of Sexual and Gender Dissent* (Chicago: University of Chicago Press, 2001).

9 Viktoriya Sakevich, "Chto bylo posle zapreta aborta v 1936 godu," *Demoskop Weekly,* no. 221–222 (November 7–20, 2005), http://demoscope.ru/weekly/2005/0221/reprod01.php, accessed February 7, 2016.

10 Mie Nakachi, "Replacing the Dead: The Politics of Reproduction in the Soviet Union, 1944–1955," doctoral dissertation, University of Chicago, 2008.

11 Sakevich, "Chto bylo posle zapreta aborta v 1936 godu."

12 I was one of the two lesbians mentioned by the *Moskovsky Komsomolets* article; the other was Julie Dorf, an activist from San Francisco. At the time, I witnessed some of the negotiations because Colette Shulman called me from the Central Committee. She recounted the events to me on January 25, 2016, in New York City.

13 Yegor Gaidar, *Dni porazheniy i pobed* (Moscow: Alpina, 2014), pp. 58–59.

14 Ibid., p. 93.

15 Zaklyucheniye Komissii S'yezla narodnykh deputatou SSSR po rassledovaniyu sobytiy, imeushykh mesto v g. Tblisi a aprelya 1989 gola, sobchak.org/rus/docs/zakluchenie.htm, accessed May 3, 2017.

16 Vadim Bakatin, *Izbavleniye ot KGB* (Moscow: Novotni, 1992), pp. 75–82.

17 "S'yezd narodnykh deputatov i Verkhovny soviet RSFSR/Rossiyskoy Federatsii (16 maya 1990–4 oktyabrya 1993)," http://www.politika.su/gos/ndrs.html, accessed February 10, 2016.
18 Gaidar, *Dni porazheniy i pobed*, pp. 97–98.
19 Ibid., p. 123.
20 Ibid., p. 156.
21 Ibid., p. 209.
22 "Federativniy dogovor" (Moscow, March 31, 1992), http://constitution.garant.ru/act/federative/170280/#100, accessed February 13, 2016.
23 Nikolay Andreev, "Voyna na territorii Rossii—real'nost': Yeltsin vvodit chrezvychaynoye polozheniye srokom odin mesyats po Severnoy Osetii i Ingushetii," *Izvestia*, November 2, 1992 (Moscow evening edition), p. 1, http://yeltsin.ru/uploads/upload/newspaper/1992/izv12_15_92/index.html, accessed February 13, 2016.
24 Gaidar, *Dni porazheniy i pobed*, p. 212.
25 "Chernomyrdin, Viktor, premier-ministr Rossii v 1992–1996 godakh" (biographical article), lenta.ru, https://lenta.ru/lib/14161208/, accessed February 13, 2016.
26 Mikhail Berger, "Glava rossiyskogo pravitel'stva obeshchayet strane rynok bez bazara," *Izvestia*, December 15, 1992 (Moscow evening edition), p. 1, http://yeltsin.ru/uploads/upload/newspaper/1992/izv12_15_92/index.html, accessed February 13, 2016.
27 Gaidar, *Dni porazheniy i pobed*, p. 281.
28 "Iz obrashcheniya k grazhdanam Rossii prezidenta Borisa Yeltsina," *Moskovskiye novosti*, March 28, 1993, p. A2, http://yeltsin.ru/uploads/upload/newspaper/1993/mn03_28_93/FLASH/index.html, accessed February 13, 2016.
29 "Vserossiyskiy referendum 1993 goda. Spravka," RIA, April 25, 2011, http://ria.ru/history_spravki/20110425/367914805.html, accessed February 13, 2016.
30 "Zakon no. 4901-1, O vnesenii izmeneniy i dopolneniy v Ugolovnyi kodeks RSFSFR, Ugolovno-protsessual'nyi kodeks RSFSR i Ispravitel'no-trodovoy kodeks RSFSR," http://base.consultant.ru/cons/cgi/online.cgi?req=doc;base=LAW;n=3934;fld=134;dst=100070;rnd=0.1744973356835544, accessed February 13, 2016.
31 Vasily Kononenko, "Prezident Rossii nachal obeshchanniye peremeny oglasheniyem proekta novoy Konstitutsii," *Izvestia*, April 30, 1993, p. 1, http://yeltsin.ru/uploads/upload/newspaper/1993/izv04_30_93/FLASH/index.html, accessed February 13, 2016.
32 Veronika Kutsyllo, *Zapiski iz Belogo doma: 21 sentyabrya–4 oktyabrya 1993 g.* (Moscow: Kommersant, 1993), p. 19.
33 Gaidar, *Dni porazheniy i pobed*, p. 304.
34 Ibid., pp. 300–313; Kutsyllo, *Zapiski iz Belogo doma*, pp. 111–155.
35 Author interview with Evgenia Debryanskaya, Moscow, November 2013.
36 Vladimir Zhirinovsky, *The Destinies of Russia* (Moscow: RAIT, 1997), p. 144.
37 Alexander Dugin and Yuriy Vorobyevsky, author-producers, *Tayny veka: Mistika Reikha: 1. Ahnenerbe.* https://www.youtube.com/watch?v=hFHKwKNmYoY, accessed February 14, 2016.
38 Andrei Sidorchik, "Odurevshaya Rossiya: Kak Vladimir Zhirinovsky pobedil na vyborakh," *Argumenty i fakty*, December 12, 2013, http://www.aif.ru/politics/russia/odurevshaya_rossiya_kak_vladimir_zhirinovskiy_pobedil_na_vyborah, accessed February 14, 2016.

seven **EVERYONE WANTS TO BE A MILLIONAIRE**

1 Alessandra Stanley, "Nizhny Novgorod Journal: Camelot on the Volga, with 2 Bold Antagonists," *The New York Times*, April 29, 1994, http://www.nytimes.com/1994/04/29/world/nizhny-novgorod-journal-camelot-on-the-volga-with-2-bold-antagonists.html, accessed February 20, 2016.
2 Howard Witt, "Capitalism Is a Pain in Russian Market," *Chicago Tribune*, September 10, 1992, http://articles.chicagotribune.com/1992-09-10/news/9203220563_1_reforms-heart-attacks-infarction, accessed February 20, 2016.
3 Margaret Thatcher, *Statecraft: Strategies for a Changing World* (New York: HarperCollins, 2003), pp. 65–68.
4 Stanley, "Nizhny Novgorod Journal."
5 Boris Nemtsov, *Ispoved' buntarya* (Moscow: Partizan, 2007), pp. 38–39.
6 John-Thor Dahlburg, "Yeltsin Withdraws Honor Guard from Lenin's Mausoleum: Moscow: The Soldiers' Ritual Was a Red Square Fixture," *Los Angeles Times*, October 7, 1993, http://articles.latimes.com/1993-10

-07/news/mn-43289_1_honor-guard, accessed February 26, 2016.

7 Charles J. Abbott, "Bush, Gorbachev Agree on U.S.-Soviet Grain Pact," UPI, June 2, 1990, http://www.upi.com /Archives/1990/06/02/Bush-Gorbachev -agree-on-US-Soviet-grain -pact/9662644299200/; Andrew Rosenthal, "The Trade Decision: Bush, Lifting 15-Year-Old Ban, Approves Loans for Kremlin to Help Ease Food Shortages," *The New York Times*, December 13, 1990, http://www .nytimes.com/1990/12/13/world/trade -decision-bush-lifting-15-year-old-ban -approves-loans-for-kremlin-help-ease.html; Nadia Arumugam, "The Dark Side of the Bird," *Slate*, January 26, 2011, http://www .slate.com/articles/life/food/2011/01/the _dark_side_of_the_bird.html; all accessed February 23, 2016.

8 Solikamskbumprom website, http://www .solbum.ru/eng/company/, accessed February 23, 2016.

9 "Lyonya Golubkov: vse reklamniye roliki," https://www.youtube.com/watch?v=VzFi-bN XHMo&ebc=ANyPxKrdpUczITDhf4Swmr GHlzXMlbGCbnLsG1fiu5jLmt4to4D2F2X uzxj07BEt3srIoSipg3f-jcL5whgQzm2JBQ JJsyuksQ, accessed February 23, 2016.

10 "Hoper Invest 1994 god, reklama," https:// www.youtube.com/watch?v=SKcIjMncME0, accessed February 24, 2016.

11 Vasily Fedorov and Aleksei Ivanov, "Anatoly Chubais: Nu vot ya i v Khopre!" *Kommersant-Dengi*, December 14, 1994, http://www .kommersant.ru/doc/18410, accessed February 24, 2016.

12 Dmitry Butrin, "Itogi kapitalisticheskoy desyatiletki," *Kommersant-Vlast'*, March 3, 2002, http://www.kommersant.ru /doc/312965, accessed February 24, 2016.

13 Andrei Shleifer and Daniel Treisman, "A Normal Country: Russia After Communism," *Journal of Economic Perspectives* 19, no. 1 (Winter 2005), pp. 151–174.

14 L. D. Gudkov and M. V. Pchelina, "Bednost i zavist: Negativny fon perekhodnogo obshchestva," *Informatsionny bulleten' monitoringa*, November–December 1995, pp. 31–42.

15 Yegor Gaidar, "Ot chernogo vtornika k kommunisticheskomu subbotniku," *Otkrytaya politika*, January 1995, pp. 25–31, http://

gaidar-arc.com/file/bulletin-1/DEFAULT /org.stretto.plugins.bulletin.core.Article /file/4346, accessed February 24, 2016.

eight GRIEF, ARRESTED

1 Fred S. Koch, *The Volga Germans: In Russia and the Americas, 1763 to the Present* (University Park: Pennsylvania State University Press, 1977).

2 Alexander Etkind, *Warped Mourning: Stories of the Undead in the Land of the Unburied* (Stanford, CA: Stanford University Press, 2013), pp. 8–9.

3 Gorbachev described this in a conversation with me and a small group of others gathered to discuss a plan for creating a museum of the Gulag in February 2008.

4 A. Lipsky, "Vlast' opyat' sporit s istoriyey," *Novaya gazeta*, May 5–11, 2005, in A. A. Yakovlev, ed., *Aleksandr Yakovlev, Izbranniye intervyu: 1992–2005* (Moscow: Mezhdunarodny fond "Demokratiya," 2009), pp. 372–374.

5 N. Rostova, "Vozhdi ochen' toropilis', kogda rech shla o rasstrelakh," *Nezavisimaya gazeta*, October 26, 2001, in Yakovlev, *Aleksandr Yakovlev, Izbranniye intervyu*, pp. 311–314.

6 Lidiya Chukovskaya, *Procherk* (Moscow: Vremya, 2013), p. 259.

7 Anya von Bremzen, *Mastering the Art of Soviet Cooking: A Memoir of Food and Longing* (New York: Crown, 2013), p. 126.

8 Rostova, "Vozhdi ochen' toropilis', kogda rech shla o rasstrelakh."

9 Lipsky, "Vlast' opyat' sporit s istoriyey."

10 "O khode raboty po rassmotreniyu voprosov, svyazannykh s reabilitatsiyey grazhdan, neobosnovanno repressirovannykh v period 30-40-kh i nachala 50-kh godov," memo from A. N. Yakovlev to the Central Committee of the Communist Party of the USSR, December 12, 1989, http://www .alexanderyakovlev.org/almanah/inside /almanah-doc/76205, accessed March 19, 2016.

11 N. Zheleznova, "Osvobozhdeniye pravdy," *Literaturniye vesti*, July–August 1998, in Yakovlev, *Aleksandr Yakovlev, Izbranniye intervyu*, pp. 256–262.

12 Ibid.

13 "O snyatii ogranichitel'nykh grifov s zakonodatel'nykh i inykh aktov, sluzhivshikh osnovaniyem dlya massovykh repressiy i posyagatel'stv na prava cheloveka,"

presidential decree no. 658, June 23, 1992, http://www.bestpravo.ru/rossijskoje/rf-instrukcii/c2v.htm, accessed March 19, 2016.

14 Camila Domonoske, "Polish Institute: Files Show Lech Walesa Worked with Communist-Era Secret Police," npr.org, February 18, 2016, http://www.npr.org /sections/thetwo-way/2016/02/18/467209160 /polish-institute-files-show-lech-walesa -worked-with-communist-era-secret-police, accessed March 20, 2016.

15 Nadezhda Nekrasova, "Mekhanizm rassekrechivaniya, slozhivshiysya v seredine 1990-kh godov . . . dolzhen byt' otmenen," polit.ru, June 3, 2008, http://polit.ru /article/2008/06/03/memorial/, accessed March 7, 2016.

16 Joshua Rubenstein, *The Last Days of Stalin* (New Haven: Yale University Press, 2016), pp. 61–140.

17 Letter from L. F. Timashuk to the presidium of the Twenty-third Party Congress, March 31, 1966, http://www.alexanderyakovlev.org/fond /issues-doc/69205, accessed March 20, 2016.

18 Rostova, "Vozhdi ochen' toropilis', kogda rech shla o rasstrelakh."

19 Jacob D. Lindy and Robert Jay Lifton, eds., *Beyond Invisible Walls: The Psychological Legacy of Soviet Trauma* (New York and London: Routledge, 2013), p. 131.

20 Ibid., pp. 132–136.

21 Ibid., p. 139.

22 Ibid., p. 11.

23 *Bolshaya sovetskaya entsiklopediya*, 2nd ed. (Moscow, 1950), vol. 5, pp. 21–24, and letter to subscribers, undated.

24 Yevgeniya Ginzburg, *Krutoy marshrut: Khronika vremyon kul'ta lichnosti* (Moscow: Sovetskiy pisatel, 1990).

25 Naum Korzhavin, "Tan'ka," in Naum Korzhavin, *Vremya dano* (Moscow: Khudozhestvennaya literatura, 1992), pp. 189–197.

26 Victor Serge, *Memoirs of a Revolutionary*, ed. Richard Greenman, trans. Peter Sedgwick with George Paizis (New York: The New York Review of Books, 2012), p. 243.

27 Roberto Bolaño, *2666*, trans. Natasha Wimmer (New York: Farrar, Straus and Giroux, 2008), p. 716.

28 B. I. Belenkin, "Repressirovanniye trotskisty—organizovannaya politicheskaya gruppa levogo soprotivleniya stalinskomu rezhimu (1927–1938): Bor'ba kak norma

zhizni. Na materialakh sledstvennykh del G. Ya. Yakovina," in *Problemy istorii massovykh politicheskih repressiy v SSSR* (Krasnodar: Ekoinvest, 2010), pp. 352–367; Boris Belenkin, "'Tan'ka! Tanechka! Tanya!...' Zametki na polyakh poemy Nauma Korzhavina i biografii Anny Mikhailovny Pankratovoy," in *Pravo na imya: Biografika XX veka: Sed'miye chteniya pamyati Veniamina Iofe* (St. Petersburg: Memorial, 2010), pp. 14–32.

29 Etkind, *Warped Mourning*, p. 137.

30 Ibid., p. 158.

31 A. Gubanov, "Plokhoy chinovnik vsegda sovetskoy shineli," *Rossiyskiye vesti*, January 20, 1998, in Yakovlev, *Aleksandr Yakovlev, Izbranniye intervyu*, p. 240.

32 Ukaz Prezidenta Rossiyskoy Federatsii ot 07.11.1996 g. no. 1537, "O Dne soglasiya i primireniya," http://www.kremlin.ru/acts /bank/10231, accessed March 18, 2016.

33 "Obyavleniye amnistiy v Rossii: Dosye," TASS, http://tass.ru/info/841359, accessed March 18, 2016.

34 A. Gubanov, "Yesli by gosudarstvo moglo priznat' svoye ugolovnoye proshloye," *Rossiyskiye vesti*, October 30, 1997, in Yakovlev, *Aleksandr Yakovlev, Izbranniye intervyu*, p. 233.

35 Gubanov, "Plokhoy chinovnik vsegda sovetskoy shineli," pp. 239, 435.

nine **OLD SONGS**

1 Hannah Arendt, *The Origins of Totalitarianism* (New York: Harcourt Brace Jovanovich, 1976), pp. 466–468.

2 Yuri Levada, "'Chelovek sovetskiy' pyat' let spustya: 1989–1994 (predvaritel'niye itogi sravnitel'nogo issledovaniya)," *Monitoring obshchestvennogo mneniya*, no. 1 (1995), pp. 9–14.

3 Richard Stites, *Russian Popular Culture: Entertainment and Society Since 1900* (Cambridge, England, and New York: Cambridge University Press, 1992), p. 189; Yulia Larina, "Krasno-belo-goluboy ogonyok," *Kommersant*, December 26, 2005, http://kommersant.ru/doc/2296344, accessed March 25, 2016.

4 *Stariye pesni o glavnom 1* aired on ORT on December 31, 1995, http://www.1tv.ru /cinema/fi=8630, accessed March 25, 2016.

5 Oleg Orlov and Alexander Cherkasov, eds., *Rossiya-Chechnya: Tsep' oshibok i prestupleniy* (Moscow: Memorial, 1998).

6 Kirill Rodionov, "Byli li chistymi prezidentskiye vybory—1996?" Gaidar Center, July 30, 2015, http://gaidar.center /articles/transparent-election-1996.htm, accessed March 27, 2016.

7 Footage of Yeltsin's August 1994 visit to Nizhny Novgorod in Alexander Gorski, "On mog byt' prezidentom!" https://www.youtube .com/watch?v=IjtIQJZ9Kbk, accessed March 27, 2016.

8 Boris Nemtsov, *Isproed' buntarya* (Moscow; Partizan, 2007); Ludmila Telen', "Soprotivleniye materiala: Boris Nemtsov pytayetsya sovmestit' zhizn' s politikoy: Obe soprotivlyayutsya," *Moskovskiye novosti*, June 18, 2002, http://nemtsov-most .org/2016/03/29/the-resistance-of-the -material-interview-part-i/, accessed April 2, 2016.

9 Viktor Yaroshenko, "Yegor i Boris: Kommentariy k zabytomu telereportazhu," Fond Yegora Gaidara, February 26, 2016, http://gaidarfund.ru/articles/2541, accessed March 27, 2016.

10 Yegor Gaidar, *Dni porazheniy i pobed* (Moscow: Alpina, 2014), pp. 383–384.

11 Boris Nemtsov, *Provintsial*, manuscript completed 1996; publication information unavailable; PDF obtained online, p. 78.

12 Yeltsin's 1996 campaign videos can be viewed at https://www.youtube.com/watch?v=kAnpi kvpZSI&index=24&list=PLsyd8Y6Pb3j3IuK cRm_dYfOVYUHBUNbgS and https:// www.youtube.com/watch?v=XYddyATMuT M&index=33&list=PLsyd8Y6Pb3j3IuK cRm_dYfOVYUHBUNbgS, accessed March 27, 2016.

13 Timothy J. Colton, *Yeltsin: A Life* (New York: Basic Books, 2008), pp. 389–390.

14 "Boris Yeltsin ishchet natsional'nuyu ideyu," *Nash sovremennik*, no. 5 (1997), p. 248.

15 Yelena Tregubova, *Bayki kremlyovskogo diggera* (Moscow: Ad Marginem, 2003), p. 69.

16 "Tsarskiye pokhorony: Rech Yeltsina," RTR report, July 17, 1998, https://www.youtube .com/watch?v=LQJDMp_OR1A, accessed March 28, 2016.

17 "Prezident Rossii Boris Yeltsin na tseremonii zakhoroneniya ostankov chlenov semyi imperatora Nikolaya II v Sankt-Peterburge," http://yeltsin.ru/archive/video/51553/, accessed April 3, 2016.

18 Boris Yeltsin, *Prezidentskiy marafon* (Moscow: AST, 2000).

19 Igor Sulimov, "Istoriya voyennykh paradov na Krasnoy ploshchadi," *Voyennoye obozreniye*, May 9, 2013, http://topwar.ru/27770 -istoriya-voennyh-paradov-na-krasnoy -ploschadi.html; Bernard Gwertzman, "Yeltsin to Alter Parade on V-E Day to Draw Clinton," *The New York Times*, March 17, 1995, http://www.nytimes.com/1995/03/17 /world/yeltsin-to-alter-parade-on-v-e-day-to -draw-clinton.html?pagewanted=all; Mark Matthews, "Clinton Agrees to Meet with Yeltsin in Moscow," *The Baltimore Sun*, March 21, 1995, http://articles.baltimoresun .com/1995-03-21/news/1995080017_1 _clinton-moscow-50th-anniversary; "Victory Day: The World to Celebrate in Moscow," *The Moscow Times*, April 15, 1995, http:// www.themoscowtimes.com/news/article /victory-day-the-world-to-celebrate-in -moscow/340359.html; all accessed March 30, 2016.

20 Sergei Lavrov, *Lev Gumilev: Sud'ba i idei* (Moscow: Airis-Press, 2007).

21 Mark Bassin, "Nurture Is Nature: Lev Gumilev and the Ecology of Ethnicity," *Slavic Review* 68, no. 4 (Winter 2009), pp. 872–897; Mark Bassin, "Lev Gumilev and Russian National Identity During and After the Soviet Era," in Athena Leoussi and Steven Grosby, eds., *Nationalism and Ethnosymbolism: History, Culture and Ethnicity in the Formation of Nations* (Edinburgh: Edinburgh University Press, 2006), pp. 143–160; Alexander S. Titov, "Lev Gumilev, Ethnogenesis and Eurasianism," doctoral dissertation, University College of London, School of Slavonic and Eastern European Studies, 2005.

22 Poem no. 1, *Requiem*, from Anna Akhmatova, *Selected Poems Including "Requiem,"* trans. A. S. Kline, http:// www.24grammata.com/wp-content /uploads/2014/08/Akhmatova-selected -poem-24grammata.compdf.pdf, p. 141.

23 Author interview with Garry Kasparov, Moscow, July 2005.

24 Sergei Novikov, "Matematiki—gerostraty istorii? (Ne pogibnet li rossiyskaya matematika?)," http://hbar.phys.msu.ru /gorm/fomenko/novikov1.htm, accessed April 20, 2016.

25 Alexander Dugin, *Konservativnaya revolutsiya* (Moscow: Arktogeya, 1994).

26 Alexander Dugin, "Metafizika natsional-bol'shevizma," in *Tampliery proletariata* (Moscow: Arktogeya, 1997).

ten **IT'S ALL OVER ALL OVER AGAIN**

1 Lev Gudkov, Boris Dubin, and Yuri Levada, *Problema "elity" v segodnyashney Rossii: Razmyshleniya nad rezul'tatami sotsiologicheskogo issledovaniya* (Moscow: Fond Liberal'naya Missya, 2007), p. 27.
2 Boris Nemtsov, *Provintsial*, manuscript completed 1996; publication information unavailable; PDF obtained online, p. 33.
3 Ibid., p. 60.
4 Ludmila Telen', "Soprotivleniye materiala: Boris Nemtsov pytayetsya sovmestit' zhizn' s politikoy: Obe soprotivlyayutsya," *Moskovskiye novosti*, June 18, 2002, archived at https://nemtsov-most.org/2016/03/29/the-resistance-of-the-material-interview-part-i/, accessed April 24, 2016.
5 Boris Nemtsov, *Ispoved' buntarya* (Moscow: Partizan, 1997), p. 28.
6 Ibid., p. 24.
7 Ibid., p. 23.
8 "Nemtsov s prostitukami," clip from 1998 Dorenko program, undated, https://www.youtube.com/watch?v=11e-i3e80EA, accessed April 24, 2016.
9 Nemtsov, *Ispoved' buntarya*, p. 23.
10 Telen', "Soprotivleniye materiala."
11 B. Generalov, "Ya s temi, kto chesten do kontsa," *Otkrytaya politika* 7, no. 9 (November 1995), http://www.alexanderyakovlev.org/fond/issues-doc/1009799, accessed April 26, 2016.
12 Clifford G. Gaddy and Brian W. Ickes, *Russia's Virtual Economy* (Washington, DC: Brookings Institution Press, 2002).
13 Tiffany C. Bloomfield, "Former Russian Official Advocates Tax Reform: Nemtsov Gives First of Three Presentations," *The Harvard Crimson*, February 9, 1999, http://www.thecrimson.com/article/1999/2/9/former-russian-official-advocates-tax-reform/, accessed April 27, 2016.
14 "Krizis v Kosovo i rossiyskoye obshchestvennoye mneniye—Issledovaniye VTSIOM," polit.ru, March 31, 1999, http://polit.ru/article/1999/03/31/477071/, accessed April 27, 2016.
15 "Voyenniy parad v Moskve (9 maya 1999 g.)," https://www.youtube.com/watch?v=Q6t8EbHIXuU, accessed April 28, 2016.

16 Robert Burns, "Russia, U.S. Announce Agreement on Troops, Ending Impasse," AP, June 19, 1999, http://amarillo.com/stories/1999/06/19/usn_russia.shtml#.VyLITTArI2w, accessed April 28, 2016; "Confrontation over Pristina Airport," BBC News, March 9, 2000, http://news.bbc.co.uk/2/hi/europe/671495.stm, accessed May 4, 2016.
17 *TASS upolnomochen zayavit'* (Mosfilm, 1984).
18 *Mertvyi sezon* (Lenfilm, 1968).
19 "Indeksy: Odobreniye deyatel'nosti Vladimira Putina," Levada Center, http://www.levada.ru/old/indeksy, accessed April 29, 2016.
20 Yuri Levada, "'Chelovek sovetskiy' 10 let spustya: 1989–1999 (predvaritel'niye itogi sravnitel'nogo issledovaniya)," *Monitoring obshchestvennogo mneniya* 3, no. 41 (May–June 1999), pp. 7–15.
21 Max Weber, *Economy and Society: An Outline of Interpretive Sociology*, ed. Guenther Roth and Claus Wittich (Berkeley: University of California Press, 1978), chap. 14.
22 Arkady Strugatsky and Boris Strugatsky, *Trudno byt' bogom* (Moscow: AST, 2015).
23 Lev Gudkov and Boris Dubin, "Rossiyskiye vybory: Vremya 'serykh,'" *Monitoring obshchestvennogo mneniya* 2, no. 46 (March–April 2000), pp. 17–29.

eleven **LIFE AFTER DEATH**

1 "Yeltsin: Ya ukhozhu i proshu u vas proshcheniya," https://www.youtube.com/watch?v=Tp9FS3OdoAQ, accessed May 6, 2016.
2 "Yeltsin vedyot Putina v Kreml'," https://www.youtube.com/watch?v=plDG_85gCo0, accessed May 6, 2016.
3 O. Solomonova, "Lovushka dlya prezidenta," *Trud*, July 13–19, 2000, http://www.alexanderyakovlev.org/fond/issues-doc/1010066, accessed May 6, 2016.
4 Steven Erlanger, "71 Die When Two Jets Collide High Above Southern Germany," *The New York Times*, July 2, 2002, http://www.nytimes.com/2002/07/02/international/02CND-CRAS.html, accessed May 11, 2016.
5 Olga Kryshtanovskaya, "Rezhim Putina: Liberal'naya militokratiya?" *Pro et contra* 7, no. 4 (Fall 2002), pp. 158–180.
6 Yuri Levada, "2000 god: Razocharovaniya i nadezhdy," *Moskovskiye novosti*, December 25, 2000, archived at http://www.levada

.ru/2000/12/25/2000-god-razocharovaniya
-i-nadezhdy/, accessed May 9, 2016.

7   "Vzglyad na sobytiya Nord-Ost mesyats
spustya . . . ," Levada Center, December 4,
2002, http://www.levada.ru/2002/12/04
/vzglyad-na-sobytiya-nord-ost-mesyats
-spustya/, accessed May 9, 2016.

8   L. A. Sedov, "Yanvarskiy opros: vyborochnyi
analiz," Levada Center, February 10, 2003,
http://www.levada.ru/2003/02/10/yanvarskij
-opros-vtsiom-vyborochnyj-analiz/, accessed
May 9, 2016.

9   "Rezul'taty vyborov deputatov Gosdumy,"
Rossiyskaya gazeta, December 9, 2003, http://
rg.ru/2003/12/09/rezultaty.html, accessed
May 11, 2016.

10 Boris Nemtsov, *Ispoved' buntarya* (Moscow:
Partizan, 2007), pp. 66–69.

twelve **THE ORANGE MENACE**

1   "Zhanna Nemtsova prolila krov' za
Ameriku," *Komsomol'skaya Pravda*, October
19, 2001, http://www.kompravda.eu
/daily/22658/12897/, accessed May 26, 2016.

2   Ibid.

3   Lev Gudkov, "Otnosheniye k SShA v Rossii i
problema antiamerikanizma," *Monitoring
obshchestvenogo mneniya* 2, no. 58 (March–
April 2002), pp. 32–48.

4   *Chto delat'? Vyzhivet li mir posle sobytii 11
sentyabrya v Soyedinennykh Shtatakh?* This
TV program originally aired December 1,
2001, archived at http://trueinform.ru
/modules.php?name=Video&sid=46746,
accessed May 28, 2016.

5   Grigory Nekhoroshev, "Yevraziytsy reshili
operet'sya na Vladimira Putin," *Nezavisimaya
gazeta*, April 24, 2001, http://www.ng.ru
/events/2001-04-24/2_support.html; Igor
Maltsev, "Yevraziya über alles: Sozdano
novoye obshchestvenno-politicheskoye
dvizheniye," *Kommersant*, April 20, 2001, p. 9,
http://www.kommersant.ru/doc/254580;
Eurasia Movement's discussion forum on its
own congress, http://arctogaia.org.ru
/FORUMS/messages/47/622
.html?993838577; all accessed May 28, 2016.

6   N. S. Trubetskoy, *Yevropa i chelovechestvo*
(Sofia: Rossiiskobolgarskoe knigoizdatel'stvo,
1920), text reproduced at http://www
.philosophy.ru/phil/library/vehi/nstev.htm,
accessed May 28, 2016.

7   *"Chto delat'? Yavliayetsya li Yevraziystvo
spaseniyem dlya Rossii?"*

8   "Putin: perevorot v Gruzii proizoshel iz-za
oshibok prezhney vlasti," lenta.ru, November
24, 2003, https://lenta.ru/vojna/2003/11/24
/putin/, accessed May 28, 2016.

9   Mikhail Zygar, *Vsya kremlyovskaya rat':
Kratkaya istoriya sovremennoy Rossii* (Moscow:
Intellektual'naya literatura, 2016), p. 107.

10 Ibid., p. 113.

11 http://ponny1.livejournal.com/6806.html.

12 Robert Horvath, *Putin's Preventive
Counter-Revolution: Post-Soviet
Totalitarianism and the Spectre of Velvet
Revolution* (London and New York:
Routledge, 2013), pp. 33–34.

13 Ibid. While I personally reported on most of
the events described in the following section,
I am indebted to Horvath for the conceptual
framework.

14 Nataliya Kholmogorova, "Probuzhdeniye:
Russkiy March 4 noyabrya," specnaz.ru,
http://www.specnaz.ru/article/?808, accessed
March 16, 2017.

15 Horvath, *Putin's Preventive Counter-
Revolution*, p. 121.

16 "Doch Nemtsova zaregistrirovana
kandidatom v deputaty Mosgordumy,"
newsru.com, October 31, 2005, http://www
.newsru.com/russia/31oct2005/nemcova
.html; Mikhail Tul'skiy, "Iz zhizni Zhanny i
Mashy," *Vzglyad*, August 31, 2005, http://vz
.ru/politics/2005/8/31/5272.html; both
accessed May 30, 2016.

17 A. Samarina, "Rodonachal'nik glasnosti—o
kontrreformak," *Nezavisimaya gazeta*, April
19, 2005, archived at http://www
.alexanderyakovlev.org/fond/issues
-doc/1010283, accessed May 30, 2016.

18 Glifford G. Gaddy and Fiona Hill,
"Doubling GDP and the Illusion of Growth,"
The Moscow Times, November 12, 2003,
archived at http://www.brookings.edu
/research/opinions/2003/11/12russia-gaddy,
accessed June 3, 2016; Clifford G. Gaddy and
Barry W. Ickes, "The Virtual Economy
Revisited: Resource Rents and the Russian
Economy," outline for speech delivered at
Renaissance Capital 4th Annual Equity
Conference, New York, October 20, 2005,
text at http://www.brookings.edu/~/media
/research/files/speeches/2005/10/20russia
-gaddy/gaddy20051020.pdf, accessed June 3,
2016.

19 Mikhail Mel'nikov, "Ne chokayas':
vspominayem prioretetniye natsproekty,"

Russkaya planeta, October 21, 2015, http://
rusplt.ru/society/ne-chokayas-vspominaem
-prioritetnyie-natsproektyi-19327.html,
accessed May 30, 2016.

thirteen **ALL IN THE FAMILY**

1 This Levada Center survey belies his
conclusions: Masha Plotko, "Strakh drugogo:
Problema gomofobii v Rossii," Levada
Center, December 3, 2013, http://www
.levada.ru/old/12-03-2013/strakh-drugogo
-problema-gomofobii-v-rossii, accessed June
10, 2016.
2 Vita Lukashina and Yelena Rudneva, "Duma
snimet s golubykh rozoviye ochki," gazeta.ru,
September 10, 2003, http://www.gazeta.ru
/parliament/articles/52010.shtml, accessed
June 14, 2016.
3 Alexei Gorshkov, "Transformatsiya
otnosheniya k seksual'nym men'shinstvam
kak politicheskaya problema sovremennogo
rossiyskogo obshchestva," senior thesis, Perm
State University, 2007.
4 Alexei Gorshkov, "Instituonalizatsiya
men'shinstv v pole publichnoy politiki,"
doctoral dissertation, Perm State University,
2009.
5 Maxim Trudolyubov, "Who Runs Russia,
Anyway?" *The New York Times*, November 19,
2009, http://www.nytimes.com/2009/11/20
/opinion/20iht-edtrudolyubov.html?_r=0,
accessed June 14, 2016.
6 Douglas Rogers, *The Depths of Russia: Oil,
Power, and Culture After Socialism* (Ithaca,
NY, and London: Cornell University Press,
2015), pp. 289–290.
7 Ibid., p. 291.
8 I happened to be with Gordeev on that walk.
He had invited me to the theater and then to
a party afterward, but we could not make it
from one to the other because he didn't know
where he was, didn't have any Russian money,
and could not let me, a woman, pay for the
cab.
9 Rogers, *The Depths of Russia*, pp. 309–310.
10 Ibid., p. 299.
11 On September 16, 2010, Ksenia Kirichenko
wrote the following post on her VK page:
"Dissertation on Family Law: Looking for
Advice and an Adviser. Here is the story: I
have written a dissertation on family law while
in graduate school but denied an adviser. Now
I am looking for a defense opportunity. . . . I
have tried to do this on my own, but I don't

want to pay a bribe and that's the only option I
have found so far." https://vk.com/topic-
215303_23501181, accessed June 14, 2016.
12 See, for example, Allan Carlson, *The
"American Way": Family and Community in the
Shaping of American Identity* (Wilmington,
DE: Intercollegiate Studies Institute, 2003);
Allan C. Carlson, *Family Questions:
Reflections on the American Social Crisis*
(Piscataway Township, NJ: Transaction,
1989); Allan C. Carlson and Paul T. Mero,
The Natural Family: A Manifesto (Dallas:
Spence, 2007).
13 World Bank data, http://data.worldbank.org
/indicator/SP.DYN.LE00.IN/countries
/RU—XR?page=1&display=default, accessed
June 14, 2016.
14 Nicholas Eberstadt, *Russia's Peacetime
Demographic Crisis: Dimensions, Causes,
Implications* (Seattle: National Bureau of
Asian Research, 2010).
15 Michelle A. Parsons, *Dying Unneeded: The
Cultural Context of the Russian Mortality Crisis*
(Nashville: Vanderbilt University Press,
2014), pp. 135–138.
16 Author interview with Allan Carlson, Tbilisi,
May 16, 2016.
17 "Poslaniye Federal'nomu Sobraniyu
Rossiyskoy Federatsii," *Rossiyskaya gazeta*,
November 5, 2006, https://rg.ru/2006/05/11
/poslanie-dok.html, accessed June 14, 2016.
18 World Bank fertility rate data, http://data
.worldbank.org/indicator/SP.DYN.TFRT
.IN?page=1, accessed June 14, 2016.
19 For some of these activities the WCF uses a
legal stand-in that it admits is virtually
identical in composition and agenda. This
other organization is the Howard Center.
20 The representatives were Alexei Komov at
the UN and Pavel Parfentiev at the European
institutions. See "FamilyPolicy.ru CEO Pavel
Parfentiev Appointed World Congress of
Families Ambassador to the European
Institutions," familypolicy.ru, March 2, 2013,
http://en.familypolicy.ru/read/231, accessed
June 16, 2016.
21 Cole Parke, "Natural Deception: Conned by
the World Congress of Families," Political
Research Associates, January 21, 2015,
http://www.politicalresearch.org/2015/01/21
/natural-deception-conned-by-the-world
-congress-of-families/#sthash.DJXMcOU7
.a9bkcdgH.dpbs (also published in *The Public
Eye*, Winter 2015), accessed June 16, 2016.

22 Anait Antonyan, "Sotsfak MGU: Kommercheskoye predpriyatiye s ekstremistskim kompleksom," polit.ru, March 16, 2007, http://www.polit.ru /article/2007/03/16/bikbov/, accessed June 18, 2016.

23 Author interview with Alexandre Bikbov, Paris, November 11, 2015.

24 "O situatsii na sotsiologicheskom fakul'tete MGU im. M. V. Lomonosova," flyer distributed February 28, 2007, archived at http://www.klubok.net/article2147.html, accessed June 18, 2016.

25 V. V. Radaev, "Zaklyucheniye o prepodavatel'skom sostave i uchebnykh materialakh otdel'nykh kafedr fakul'teta sotsiologii MGU im. M. V. Lomonosova," polit.ru, July 18, 2007, http://www.polit.ru /article/2007/07/18/radaev2/, accessed July 1, 2016.

26 V. P. [Vladimir Pribylovsky], "Soyuz pravoslavnykh grazhdan (SPG)," Antikompromat, undated, http://www .anticompromat.org/s_pg/spr_spg.html, accessed June 19, 2016.

27 "Advokaty gey-parada boryatsya s pravoslavnymi ideyamii v stenakh MGU," statement by Union of Orthodox Citizens, March 24, 2007, pravoslaviye.ru, http://www .pravoslavie.ru/21471.html, accessed June 19, 2016.

28 Bikbov interview; author interview with Ekaterina Tarnovskaya, Moscow, June 10, 2016.

29 "Vladimir Dobren'kov: 'Glavnoy zadachey vlasti dolzhno stat' vozrozhdeniye chelovecheskikh dush,'" Russkaya liniya, June 18, 2008, http://rusk.ru/newsdata .php?idar=177296, accessed June 19, 2016.

30 "Arrests at Russian Gay Protests," BBC News, May 27, 2007, http://news.bbc.co .uk/2/hi/europe/6695913.stm, accessed March 16, 2017.

31 "Pol Kameron: 'Neuzheli vy khotite stat' takimi zhe gluptsami kak i my?'" Russyaka liniya, June 18, 2008, http://rusk.ru /newsdata.php?idar=177294, accessed June 19, 2016.

32 "Paul Cameron Bio and Fact Sheet," Dr. Gregory Herek's blog, University of California, Davis, website, http://psc.dss .ucdavis.edu/rainbow/html/facts_cameron _sheet.html, accessed June 19, 2016.

33 "Rech Dugina na nulevom zasedanii TsKI," Tsentr konservativnykh issledovaniy, September 16, 2008, http://konservatizm .org/speech/dugin/310109151801.xhtml, accessed June 19, 2016.

34 Andreas Umland, "Post-Soviet 'Uncivil Society' and the Rise of Aleksandr Dugin: A Case Study of the Extraparliamentary Radical Right in Contemporary Russia," doctoral dissertation, Trinity College, Cambridge University, 2007.

35 "Poslaniye Federal'nomu sobraniyu Rossiyskoy Federatsii," Kremlin website, April 25, 2005, http://kremlin.ru/events /president/transcripts/22931, accessed June 21, 2016.

36 "Annual Address to the Federal Assembly of the Russian Federation," Kremlin website, April 25, 2005, http://en.kremlin.ru/events /president/transcripts/22931, accessed June 21, 2016.

37 "Vystupleniye i discussiya na Myunkhenskoy konferentsii po voprosam politiki bezopasnosti," Kremlin website, February 10, 2007, http://kremlin.ru/events/president /transcripts/24034, accessed June 21, 2016.

38 Stephen J. Cimbala, "Nuclear Arms Control After a Time of Troubles," in Mark Galeotti, ed., The Politics of Security in Modern Russia (London and New York: Routledge, 2016), p. 108.

39 Manfred Wörner's words are quoted from "The Atlantic Alliance and European Security in the 1990s," address to Bremer Tanaks Collegium, Brussels, May 17, 1990, NATO website, http://nato.int/docu /speech/1990/s900517a_e.htm, accessed June 21, 2016.

40 Mark Kramer, "The Myth of a No-NATO-Enlargement Pledge to Russia," The Washington Quarterly 32, no. 2 (April 2009), pp. 39–61.

41 "Dvizheniya 'Nashi' i 'Mestniye' prekrashchayut blokadu posol'stva Estonii," RIA, May 3, 2007, http://ria.ru /society/20070503/64852572.html, accessed June 22, 2016.

42 Kadri Liik, "The 'Bronze Year' of Estonia–Russia Relations," Estonian Ministry of Foreign Affairs Yearbook, 2007, http://www .vm.ee/en/yearbook-2007, p. 71.

43 Stephen Herzog, "Revisiting the Estonian Cyber Attacks: Digital Threats and Multinational Responses," Journal of Strategic Security 4, no. 2 (Summer 2011), pp. 49–60.

44 "'Nashi' priznalis' v organitsii hakerskikh atak na estonskiye saity," lenta.ru, March 12, 2009, https://lenta.ru/news/2009/03/12 /confess/, accessed June 22, 2016.

45 Svante E. Cornell, Johanna Popjanevski, and Niklas Nilsson, "Russia's War in Georgia: Causes and Implications for Georgia and the World," policy paper, Central Asia–Caucasus Institute and Silk Road Studies Program, Johns Hopkins University, August 2008.

46 Andrei Fedyashin, "Skol'ko v mire 'gosudarstv na sokhranenii'?" RIA, August 26, 2010, http://ria.ru /analytics/20100826/269199864.html, accessed July 2, 2016.

47 C. J. Chivers, "Russia Warns It May Back Breakaway Republics in Georgia," *The New York Times*, February 16, 2008, mobile .nytimes.com/2008/02/16/world/europe /16breakaway.html, accessed July 2, 2016.

48 "Doktrina Med vedeva: Pyat' printsipov rossiyskoy vneshney politiki," Tsentr konservativnykh issledovaniy, September 16, 2008, http://konservatizm.org/speech /dugin/011009193240.xhtml, accessed June 23, 2016.

49 Anton Shekhovtsov, "Aleksandr Dugin's Neo-Eurasianism: The New Right à la Russe," *Religion Compass* 3, no. 4 (2009), pp. 697–716.

50 "Odobreniye organov vlasti," Levada Center, running indices, http://www.levada.ru /indikatory/odobrenie-organov-vlasti/, accessed June 24, 2016.

fourteen **THE FUTURE IS HISTORY**

1 Image of 2008 presidential election ballot at http://pachkov.ru/wp-content /uploads/2008/03/bulleten_2_marta.jpg, accessed July 2, 2016.

2 "Vybory prezidenta Rossiyskoy Federatsii," RIA, March 1, 2008, http://ria.ru /spravka/20080301/100371195.html, accessed July 2, 2016.

3 "Boris Nemtsov otkazalsya uchastvovat' v prezidentskikh vyborakh," *Rossisykaya gazeta*, December 26, 2007, https://rg .ru/2007/12/26/nemcov-anons.html; Polina Matveeva, "Poslali Kasyanova i ushli v otpusk," gazeta.ru, January 21, 2008, http:// www.gazeta.ru/politics/elections2008/2008/0 1/28_a_2606841.shtml; both accessed July 2, 2016.

4 "Danniye o chisle golosov izbirateley, poluchennykh kazhdym iz zaregistrirovannykh kandidatov na dolzhnost' prezidenta Rossiyskoy Federatsii," https:// cdnimg.rg.ru/pril/21/38/55/4608_1a.gif, document downloaded from the Central Election Commission website July 3, 2016.

5 Alena V. Ledeneva, *How Russia Really Works: The Informal Practices That Shaped Post-Soviet Politics and Business* (Ithaca, NY: Cornell University Press, 2006), 91–99.

6 Luigi Sturzo, "The Totalitarian State," *Social Research* 3, no. 2 (May 1936), pp. 222–235.

7 Hannah Arendt, *The Origins of Totalitarianism* (New York: Harcourt Brace Jovanovich, 1976).

8 Hannah Arendt, "Ideology and Terror: A Novel Form of Government," *The Review of Politics* 15, no. 3 (July 1953), pp. 303–327.

9 Carl J. Friedrich, "The Unique Character of Totalitarian Society," in Friedrich, ed., *Totalitarianism* (New York: Grosset & Dunlap, 1953), pp. 47–59.

10 Carl J. Friedrich and Zbigniew K. Brzezinski, *Totalitarian Dictatorship and Autocracy* (Cambridge, MA: Harvard University Press, 1965).

11 Herbert Marcuse, *One-Dimensional Man*, 2nd ed. (Boston: Beacon Press, 1991).

12 Mark Geyer and Sheila Fitzpatrick, eds., *Beyond Totalitarianism: Stalinism and Nazism Compared* (Cambridge, England: Cambridge University Press, 2008).

13 Juan J. Linz, *Totalitarian and Authoritarian Regimes* (Boulder, CO: Lynne Rienner, 2000).

14 Lev Gudkov, "'Totalitarism' kak teoreticheskaya ramka: Popytka revizii spornogo ponyatiya," *Monitoring obshchestvennogo mneniya* 5, no. 55 (September–October 2001), pp. 20–29, and 6, no. 56 (November–December 2001), pp. 13–30.

15 "Postanovleniye Pravitel'stva Rossiyskoy Federatsii no. 1441 ot 31.12.199, Ob utverzhdenii Polozheniya o podgotovke grazhdan Rossiyskoy Federatsii k voyennoy sluzhbe," http://pravo.gov.ru/proxy/ips/?docb ody=&nd=102063823&rdk=&backlink=1, accessed May 3, 2017.

16 Erich Fromm, *Escape from Freedom* (New York: Henry Holt, 1994), p. 206. The passages quoted below on this text page and the two following are from pp. 41, 62, 81, 166, and 169, respectively, of Fromm's book.

17 T. W. Adorno, Else Frenkel-Brunswik, Daniel J. Levinson, and R. Nevitt Sanford,

The Authoritarian Personality (New York: W. W. Norton, 1969).

18 Fromm, *Escape from Freedom*, p. 214.

19 Arendt, *The Origins of Totalitarianism*, p. vii.

20 Ibid., p. 471.

21 Fromm, *Escape from Freedom*, p. 218.

22 Ibid., p. 231.

23 Ibid., p. 219.

24 Susanna Al'perina, "Zaigralis'," *Rossiyskaya gazeta*, July 17, 2008, https://rg.ru /2008/07/17 /imena.html, accessed July 7, 2016.

25 Boris Dubin, "Vydayushchiyesya ludi vsekh vremyon i narodov v rossiyskom obshchestvennom mnenii," Levada Center, August 31, 2008, http://www.levada .ru/2008/08/31/vydayushhiesya-lyudi-vseh -vremen-i-narodov-v-rossijskom -obshhestvennom-mnenii/, accessed July 7, 2016.

fifteen **BUDUSHCHEGO NET**

1 "Putin prigrozil 'Mechelu' zachistkoy," Interfax, July 24, 2008, http://www.interfax .ru/business/23352, accessed July 8, 2016.

2 "Zayavleniye Putin obrushilo aktsii 'Mechela': Takikh zayavleniy ne bylo so vremyon YuKOSa," newsru.com, http://www.newsru .com/finance/25jul2008/mechel.html#7, accessed July 8, 2016.

3 "Voyna v Yuzhnoy Osetii vyzvala obval rossiyskogo fondovogo rynka," newsru.com, August 11, 2008, http://www.newsru.com /finance/11aug2008/rtsobval.html, accessed July 8, 2016.

4 *Putin: Itogi*, February 2008, http://www .putin-itogi.ru/putin-itogi-pervoe-izdanie -doklada/, accessed July 9, 2016.

5 *Nemtsov: Itogi*, film by Pavel Sheremet, https://www.youtube.com /watch?v=f0QEUBLkxcE, accessed July 9, 2016.

6 Mikhail Fishman, "Mikhail Fridman: 'Ne tak mnogo ya vstrechal lyudey, kotoriye mne blizki v zhizni," *Slon*, undated, https://slon .ru/special/nemtsov/fridman, accessed July 9, 2016.

7 Boris Nemtsov, "Novyi God v odinochnoy kamere," *Echo Moskvy*, January 2, 2011, http://echo.msk.ru/blog/echomsk/738807 -echo/, accessed July 9, 2016.

8 Boris Nemtsov, "S Rozhdestvom!" blog post, January 7, 2011, http://b-nemtsov.livejournal .com/2011/01/07/, accessed July 10, 2016.

9 "Okhota nachinalas' s sachka: Boris Nemtsov v Krasnoyarske, 2007 g.," https://kinostok.tv /video/490936/ohota-nachinalas-s-sachka -boris-nemtsov-v-krasnoyarske-2007, accessed July 9, 2016.

10 Andrei Polunin, "Boris Nemtsov: Mne plesnuli nashatyr' v glaza, no ya uspel dobezhat' do umyval'nika," Svobodnaya pressa, March 23, 2009, http://svpressa.ru /politic/article/6227/; "Na avtomobil' Nemtsova brosili unitaz," lenta.ru, June 10, 2011, https://lenta.ru/news/2011/06/10 /unitaz/; both accessed July 9, 2016.

sixteen **WHITE RIBBONS**

1 Svetlana Reyter, "Prezumptsiya vinovnosti," *Bolshoi Gorod*, August 11, 2011, http://bg.ru /society/prezumpciya_vinovnosti-8944/, accessed July 11, 2016.

2 "Obvinyayemiy v pedofilii Makarov priznan sovratitelem, a ne nasil'nikom," RIA, November 29, 2011, http://ria.ru /justice/20111129/501520452.html, accessed July 11, 2016.

3 Ella Paneyakh, "A vot teper' nachalos' samoye strashnoye," inliberty.ru, October 28, 2011, http://www.inliberty.ru/blog/255-a-vot-teper -nachalos-strashnoe, accessed July 11, 2016.

4 Alexei Gorshkov, "Transformatsiya otnosheniya k seksual'nym men'shinstvam kak politicheskaya problema sovremennogo rossiyskogo obshchestva," senior thesis, Perm State University, 2007.

5 "V Moskve eks-senator, iznasilovavshiy 'na radostyakh ot rozhdeniya rebyonka' vypusknitsu, otelalsya uslovnym srokom," newsru.com, January 25, 2011, http://www .newsru.com/crime/24jan2011 /senatorrapestudsnt.html, accessed July 12, 2016.

6 Yuri Snegirev, "'Delo piterskogo pedofila': Aleksandr Kuznetsov dvazhdy popadalsya na narkotikakh . . . ," *Izvestia*, February 4, 2008, http://izvestia.ru/news/332974, accessed July 12, 2016.

7 Igor K., "Chto delat's s pedofilom: kaznit' ili kastrirovat'?" pravda.ru, April 10, 2008, http://www.pravda.ru/society/family /pbringing/10-04-2008/262947-0/, accessed July 12, 2016.

8 "Bokser Kuznetsov, zabivshiy nasmert' nasil'nika svoyego pasynka, vyshel na svobodu dosrochno," newsru.com, August 24, 2010, https://www.newsru.com

/crime/24aug2010/boxermpedofreeomsk
.html, accessed July 12, 2016.

9 Pravitel'stvo Rossiyskoy Federatsii, "Ofitsial'niy
otzyv na proekt federal'nogo zakona 'O
vnesenii izmeneniy v Ugolovniy kodeks
Rossiyskoy Federatsii v tselyakh usileniya
otvetstvennosti za prestupleniya seksual'nogo
kharaktera, sovershayemiye v otnoshenii
nesovershennoletnikh,' vnosimiy deputatami
Gosudarstvennoy Dumy N. V. Gerasimovoy,
A. M. Babarovym, Ye. B. Mizulinoy,"
February 2, 2010, document 357ЛΙ-ΙΙ4.

10 "Glava komiteta Gosdumy po delam semyi
obvinila Yedinorossov v ukryvatel'stve
pedofilov," newsru.com, November 3, 2010,
http://www.newsru.com/russia/03nov2010
/mizulina.html, accessed July 12, 2016.

11 Andreas Umland, "Kak Dugin izobrazil
menya 'pedofilom,'" *Ukrainskaya pravda*,
November 9, 2010, http://www.pravda.com
.ua/rus/columns/2010/11/9/5554710/,
accessed July 12, 2016.

12 Dmitry Yefremov, "Sosiski über alles!"
Evrazia, February 7, 2008, http://evrazia.org
/article/303, accessed July 12, 2016.

13 Ilya Dmitriev, "Zakasnykh del master,"
Evrazia, March 19, 2008, http://evrazia.org
/article/368, accessed July 12, 2016.

14 For the history of the passage of
Zakonoproekt no. 577813-5, "O vnesenii
izmenenij v Ugolovnyj kodeks Rossijskoj
Federacii i otdel'nye zakonodatel'nye akty
Rossijskoj Federacii v celjah usilenija
otvetstvennosti za prestuplenija seksual'nogo
haraktera, sovershennye v otnoshenii
nesovershennoletnih," see http://asozd2
.duma.gov.ru/main.nsf/(Spravka)?OpenAgen
t&RN=577813-5, accessed July 12, 2016.

15 Pedophilia is considered a mental disorder
outside Russia too, though in recent years
Western psychiatrists have stressed that it is
not a sexual orientation but is, rather, a
paraphilia; see, for example, http://www
.medscape.com/viewarticle/813669.

16 Serbsky Center, "Informatsionnoye pis'mo,"
Document UDK 616.89 BBK 56.14 T48,
http://serbsky.ru/index.php?id=
120&Itemid=91&option=com
_content&view=article, accessed July 12, 2016.

17 Author interview with Serbsky training
seminar participant, Moscow, 2012.

18 "Operatsiya 'Spaseniye': Ostanovim nasiliye
nad det'mi vmeste," originally posted at
agatacrysty.livejournal.com, but all history of

the anti-pedophilia campaign seems to have
been subsequently removed from that blog. I
have found numerous contemporaneous
reposts, including http://maxpark.com
/community/129/content/769725 (July 13,
2011) and http://russobalt.org/forum/topic/992
-operatciia-spasenie-ostanovim-nasilie-nad-det
/ (July 2, 2011), accessed July 12, 2016.

19 "Medvedev predlozhil sozdat' v SK
tsentr po bor'be s detskoy pornografiyey,"
RIA, July 7, 2011, http://ria.ru
/society/20110707/398540485.html;
"Devushka, vychislivshaya v Internete 80
pedofilov, budet pomogat' Astakhovu," RIA,
July 7, 2011, http://ria.ru
/society/20110707/398576027.html; both
accessed July 12, 2016.

20 "Rezul'taty vyborov v Gosdumu po
regionam Rossii," RIA, December 6,
2011, http://ria.ru/infografika/20111206
/508314920.html, accessed July 17, 2016.

21 "Zaderzhanniye na marshe," eyewitness
account by blogger Zhertva1211, December
6, 2011, http://zhertva1121.livejournal
.com/104729.html; Boris Nemtsov, "Miting:
Chistiye prudy: Bespredel," blog post,
December 6, 2011, http://b-nemtsov
.livejournal.com/2011/12/06/; "Navalny i
Yashin poluchili 15 sutok za nepovinoveniye
politsii," RIA, December 6, 2011, http://ria
.ru/riatv/20111206/508165390.html; all
accessed July 13, 2016.

22 Yevgenia Albats, Zoya Svetova, Yegor
Skovoroda, Yulia Chernukhina, and Nikita
Sologub, "Dekabr' 2011-go," *New Times*,
December 3, 2012, http://newtimes.ru
/articles/detail/60591/, accessed July 17, 2016.

23 Boris Nemtsov, "O zavtrashnem mitinge,"
blog post, December 9, 2011,
http://b-nemtsov.livejournal
.com/2011/12/09/, accessed July 14, 2016.

24 "Video: sovmestnoye zayavleniye
organizatorov o mitinge 10 dekabrya na
Bolotnoy," December 9, 2011, https://www
.youtube.com/watch?v=kVumeUpaoYM,
accessed July 14, 2016.

25 "Opros in prospekte Sakharova 24 dekabrya,"
Levada Center, December 26, 2011, http://
www.levada.ru/old/26-12-2011/opros-na
-prospekte-sakharova-24-dekabrya, accessed
July 17, 2016.

26 Alexandre Bikbov, "Metodologiya
issledovaniya 'vnezapnogo' ulichnogo
aktivizma (rossiyskiye mitingi i ulichniye

lagerya, dekabr' 2011—iyun' 2012),"
Laboratorium, no. 2 (2012), pp. 130–163.

27 Boris Nemtsov, "Mirnaya belaya revolutsiya," blog post, December 10, 2011, http://b-nemtsov.livejournal. com/2011/12/10/, accessed July 15, 2016.

28 Mischa Gabowitsch, *Protest in Putin's Russia* (Cambridge, England, and Malden, MA: Polity Press, 2017).

29 "Razgovor s Vladimirom Putinym 2011 (polnaya versiya)," https://www.youtube.com /watch?v=mTDGhhcBKdI, accessed July 15, 2016.

seventeen **MASHA: MAY 6, 2012**

1 V.P. [Vladimir Pribylovsky], "Ponomarev Ilya Vladimirovich," dossier, Antikompromat, http://www.anticompromat.org /ponomarev_i/ponom01.html; Ilya Ponomarev's income declarations, archived by Transparency International Russia, http:// declarator.org/person/84/; Oleg Kashin, "Mnogolikiy Ponomarev," *New Times*, October 29, 2012, http://newtimes.ru/articles /detail/58866; all accessed July 18, 2016.

2 V. A. Istarkhov, *Udar russkikh bogov* (Kaluga, Russia: Oblizdat, 1999), copy found at http:// www.libros.am/book/read/id/352959/slug, accessed July 17, 2016.

3 "6 maya: Chto dumayut po 'tu' storonu barrikad," video shot by unidentified journalist, https://www.youtube.com /watch?v=CumgZqEMwZs, accessed July 18, 2016.

4 "The World's 100 Most Influential People: 2012," *Time*, April 18, 2012, http://content .time.com/time/specials/packages /completelist/0,29569,2111975,00.html, accessed July 19, 2016.

5 Maria Baronova's photo of Navalny holding *Time* magazine: http://www.thetimes.co.uk /tto/multimedia/archive/00292/106154947 _navalny_292144b.jpg, accessed July 19, 2016.

6 *Doklad Komissii "Kruglogo stola 12 dekabrya" po Obshchestvennomu rassledovaniyu sobytiy 6 maya 2012 goda na Bolotnoy ploshchadi* (Moscow, 2013), p. 9.

7 "Moskva: 7 maya OMON ustroil pogrom v Zhan-Zhake," Radio Liberty footage, http:// truba.com/novosti-politika/video/moskva_7 _maya_omon_ustroil_pogrom_v_kafe_zhan -zhak-335414, accessed July 19, 2016.

8 "Donbass Arena Ready to Open," Donbass Arena website, July 2, 2009, http://donbass

-arena.com/en/news/?id=9922, accessed July 19, 2016.

9 "Cyborgs vs. Kremlin," undated report, Ukraine Today, http://cyborgs.uatoday.tv/, accessed July 19, 2016.

10 "Politsiya s utra vedyot obyski v kvartirakh oppozitsionerov," *Novaya gazeta*, June 11, 2012, http://www.novayagazeta.ru /politics/53021.html, accessed July 19, 2016.

eighteen **SERYOZHA: JULY 18, 2013**

1 Video of sit-in, published April 21, 2013, https://www.youtube.com/watch?v=0vWRH ahkgoo&feature=youtu.be, accessed July 20, 2016.

2 *Doklad Komissii "Kruglogo stola 12 dekabrya" po Obshchestvennomy rassledovaniyu sobytiy 6 maya 2012 goda na Bolotnoy ploshchadi* (Moscow, 2013), pp. 52–67.

3 "Ukaz o merakh realizatsii vneshnepoliticheskogo kursa," May 7, 2012, http://kremlin.ru/events/president /news/15256; "Ukaz ob obespechenii mezhnatsional'nogo soglasiya," May 7, 2012, http://kremlin.ru/events/president /news/15240; "Ukaz o merakh po realizatsii demograficheskoy politiki," May 7, 2012, http://kremlin.ru/events/president /news/15257; all accessed July 21, 2016.

The fertility rate had been rising since 2006, from 1.3 births per woman to 1.6 in five years. The odd figure—1.753—was likely calculated by assuming that the fertility rate would continue growing at the same rate at which it had been in the year before the decree. But after the decree, the Federal Statistics Service reported a sudden jump to the required rate. Fertility rate, total, Russian Federation, The World Bank, http://data .worldbank.org/indicator/SP.DYN.TFRT .IN?locations=RU, accessed July 21, 2016.

4 "Vstecha s prezidentom MOK Zhakom Rogge," Kremlin transcript, http://kremlin .ru/events/president/news/15235, accessed July 21, 2016.

5 Putin's speech in Guatemala City, RT footage, July 5, 2007, https://www.youtube .com/watch?v=_aNo3DxWaW4, accessed July 21, 2016.

6 "Vladimir Putin prinyal uchastiye v gala-matche lyubitel'skoy hokkeynoy ligi," Kremlin report, May 7, 2012, http://kremlin .ru/events/president/news/15260, accessed July 21, 2016.

7 "Plenarnoye zasedaniye Gosudarstvennoy Dumy," Kremlin footage, May 8, 2012, http://kremlin.ru/events/president /news/15266/videos, accessed July 21, 2016.

8 "Voyenniy parad v chest' 67-y godovshchiny Velikoy Pobedy," Kremlin footage, May 9, 2012, http://kremlin.ru/events/president /news/15271, accessed July 21, 2016.

9 Footage of Victory Day parades by year: 2000, https://www.youtube.com /watch?v=A6xWUqW5e0o; 2001, https:// www.youtube.com/watch?v=PZzUNq6kkFE; 2002, https://www.youtube.com /watch?v=oiuT-3jeDoc; 2003, https://www .youtube.com/watch?v=-I_VwGnCXBk; 2004, https://www.youtube.com /watch?v=SUVMmOwDCZI; 2005, https:// www.youtube.com/watch?v=OZW1vtc-euY; 2006, https://www.youtube.com/watch?v=k -WZCmqvkRY; 2007, https://www.youtube .com/watch?v=YA3Z0VsHemI; 2008, https://www.youtube.com/watch?v= y1_5Fr6xc38; 2009, https://www .youtube.com/watch?v=n8_Q2aB3WhM; 2010, https://www.youtube.com/watch?v=- 7Nv9a7ODxQ; 2011, https://www.youtube .com/watch?v=W2zK-ihbCF0; all accessed July 24, 2016.

10 "Razgovor s Vladimirom Putinym 2011 (polnaya versiya)," https://www.youtube.com /watch?v=mTDGhhcBKdI, accessed July 15, 2016.

11 "Rabochiy klass Urala! Trodovoy narod Rossii!" appeal from Putin defense committee at UralVagonZavod, December 29, 2011, http://www.uvz.ru/news/3/128, accessed July 21, 2016.

12 "Vybory: Aktsiya 'za chestniye vybory' v g. Nizniy Tagil," December 10, 2011, http:// kushvablog.ru/vibory/2828-akciya-za -chestnye-vybory-v-gniznij-tagil.html, accessed July 21, 2016.

13 "Rabochikh Uralvagozavoda ne pustyat na tanke v Yekatirenburg," grani.ru, January 16, 2012, http://graniru.org/War /Arms/m.194881.html, accessed July 21, 2016.

14 "Poseshcheniye nauchno-proizvodstvennoy korporatsii 'Uralvagonzavod,'" Kremlin report, May 10, 2012, http://kremlin.ru/events /president/news/15282, accessed July 21, 2016.

15 For the history of the passage of Zakonoproekt no. 70631-6, "O vnesenii izmemneniy of Kodeks Rossiyskoy Federatsii ob administrativnykh pravonarusheniyakh i Federal'niy zakon 'O sobraniyakh, mitingakh, demonstratsiyakh, shestviyakh i piketirovaniyakh' (v chasti utochneniya poryadka organizatsii i provedeniya publicnykh meropriyatiy, prav, obyazannostey i otvetstvennosi organizatorov i uchastnikov publicnhykh meropriyatiy)," see http:// asozd2.duma.gov.ru/main.nsf/%28SpravkaN ew%29?OpenAgent&RN=70631-6&02, accessed July 21, 2016.

16 Petr Orlov, "K Bondu ne khodi," *Rossiyskaya gazeta*, November 14, 2012, https://rg .ru/2012/11/13/taina-site.html; "Russia Expels USAID Development Agency," BBC News, September 19, 2012, http://www.bbc .com/news/world-europe-19644897; both accessed July 21, 2016.

17 "Russia: Worst Crackdown Since Soviet Era," Human Rights Watch, January 31, 2012, https://www.hrw.org/news/2013/01/31 /russia-worst-crackdown-soviet-era, accessed July 21, 2016.

18 Masha Gessen, "Russian Purge: The Horror Story of Publishing Children's Books in Russia," *The Intercept*, February 17, 2016, https://theintercept.com/2016/02/17/the -horror-story-of-publishing-childrens -books-in-moscow/, accessed July 24, 2016.

19 Hannah Arendt, *The Origins of Totalitarianism* (New York: Harcourt Brace Jovanovich, 1976), pp. 390–391.

20 Fareed Zakaria, "The Rise of Illiberal Democracy," *Foreign Affairs*, November/ December 1997, pp. 22–42, https://www .foreignaffairs.com/articles/1997-11-01/rise -illiberal-democracy.

21 Yekaterina Shulman, "Tsarstvo politicheskoy imitatsii," *Vedomosti*, August 15, 2014, http:// www.vedomosti.ru/opinion /articles/2014/08/15/carstvo-imitacii, accessed July 22, 2016.

22 Author interview with Bálint Magyar, Budapest, June 13, 2015.

23 Bálint Magyar, *Post-Communist Mafia State: The Case of Hungary*, trans. Bálint Bethlenfalvy et al. (Budapest: Central European University Press, 2016), p. 68.

24 Ibid., p. 69.

25 Magyar interview.

26 Alexander Dugin, "Gorizonty bolotnoy revolutsii," *Evrazia*, December 23, 2011, http://evrazia.org/ article/1873, accessed July 23, 2016.

27 "Serdtsu ne prikazhesh," lenta.ru, February 5, 2012, https://lenta.ru/articles/2012/02/04/poklonnaja/, accessed July 25, 2016.

28 "Alexander Dugin na Poklonnoy . . . ," video footage of rally, February 4, 2012, http://hlamer.ru/video/234949-Aleksandr_Dugin_na_Poklonnoiy-Rossiya-vse_ostalnoe-nichto04_02_2012, accessed July 23, 2016.

29 "Zapis' zasedaniya Antiorangevogo komiteta of 10.02.2012," video footage, https://www.youtube.com/watch?v=sL0e1BVIRwk, accessed July 23, 2016. The text of the pact is no longer accessible on the Web, but it is read in its entirety in this video.

30 "Sergei Stanislavovich Udaltsov," biography, gazeta.ru, http://www.gazeta.ru/tags/udaltsov_sergei_stanislavovich.shtml?p=bio, accessed July 23, 2016.

31 Masha Gessen, "Alexey Navalny's Very Strange Form of Freedom," newyorker.com, January 15, 2016, http://www.newyorker.com/news/news-desk/alexey-navalnys-very-strange-form-of-freedom; Masha Gessen, "That Blunt Russian Force," *The New York Times*, July 22, 2013, http://latitude.blogs.nytimes.com/2013/07/22/that-blunt-russian-force/?_r=0; both accessed July 23, 2016.

nineteen **LYOSHA: JUNE 11, 2013**

1 Article 331 of the Labor Code: Trudovoi kodeks Rossiyskoy Federatsii, http://kzotrf.ru/; "Federal'niy zakon ot 1 aprelya 2012 g. N 27-FZ 'O vnesenii izmeneniy v statyu 22 Federal'nogo zakona "O gosudarstvennoy registratsii yuridicheskikh lits i individual'nykh predprinimateley" i stat'i 331 i 351 Trudovogo kodeksa Rossiyskoy Federatsii,'" *Rossiyskaya gazeta*, April 4, 2012, https://rg.ru/2012/04/04/a602462-dok.html; both accessed July 25, 2016.

2 "V Peterburge deputaty zapretili propagandu gomoseksualizma," lenta.ru, November 16, 2011, https://lenta.ru/news/2011/11/16/gayban/, accessed July 25, 2016.

3 "ZakS pochti yedinoglasno podderzhal zapret na propagandu netraditsionnoy seksual'nosti," *Fontanka*, November 16, 2011, http://www.fontanka.ru/2011/11/16/050/, accessed July 25, 2016.

4 "Peterburgskiy sud podtverdil otkaz v iske k Madonne," lenta.ru, February 6, 2013, https://lenta.ru/news/2013/02/06/madonna/, accessed July 25, 2016.

5 "'Vesyologo molochnika' obvinili v poddesrzhke geyev," lenta.ru, September 28, 2012, https://lenta.ru/news/2012/09/28/milkman/, accessed July 25, 2016.

6 "Deputat Milonov vnov' vyshel na okhotu na pedofilov," *Fontanka*, June 19, 2012, http://www.fontanka.ru/2012/06/19/188/, accessed July 25, 2016.

7 "Milonov khochet proverit' pedagogov na pedofiliyu," BBC Russian Service, October 8, 2012, http://www.bbc.com/russian/society/2012/10/121008_milonov_paedophilia, accessed July 25, 2016.

8 For the history of the passage of Zakonoproekt no. 44554-6, "O vnesenii izmeneniy v statyu 5 Federal'nogo zakona 'O zashchite detey ot informatsii, prichinyayushchey vred ikh zdorovyu i razvitiyu' i otdel'niye zakonodatel'niye akty Rossiyskoy Federatsii v tselyakh zashchity detey ot informatsii, propagandiruyushchey otritsaniye traditsionnykh semeynykh tsennostey," see http://asozd2.duma.gov.ru/main.nsf/%28SpravkaNew%29?OpenAgent&RN=44554-6&02, accessed July 25, 2016.

9 M. V. Demenkov, "Zaklyucheniye po proektu Federal'nogo zakona no. 44554-6," November 21, 2012, retrieved at http://asozd2.duma.gov.ru/main.nsf/%28SpravkaNew%29?OpenAgent&RN=44554-6&02, July 25, 2016.

10 Ye. B. Mizulina, "Zaklyucheniye po proektu Federal'nogo zakona no. 44554-6," undated, retrieved at http://asozd2.duma.gov.ru/main.nsf/%28SpravkaNew%29?OpenAgent&RN=44554-6&02, July 25, 2016.

11 *Istoricheskiy protsess—gosudarstvo i chastnaya zhizn'*, Rossiya 1 program, archived at https://www.youtube.com/watch?v=oyvE16z6FrI, accessed July 25, 2016.

12 "Samootvod: Oleg Chirkunov dosrochno pokinul post permskogo gubernatora," lenta.ru, April 30, 2012, https://lenta.ru/articles/2012/04/30/perm/, accessed July 26, 2016.

13 "M. Gelman otrkyl skandal'nuyu vystavku Welcome! Sochi-2014," RBK, June 11, 2013, http://www.rbc.ru/society/11/06/2013/861464.shtml; Marat Guelman, untitled blog post, Facebook, October 24, 2014, https://www.facebook.com/marat.guelman.9/posts/883560208322048; both accessed July 26, 2016.

14 Nikita Girin, "Gey, slavyane i OMON," *Novaya gazeta*, January 9–28, 2013, http://www.novayagazeta.ru/politics/56444.html; for Ponomarev's voting record, http://vote.duma.gov.ru/?convocation=AAAAAAA6&from=25.01.2013&to=25.01.2013&number=44554-6&deputy=99111031&sort=date_desc; both accessed July 29, 2016.

15 "Voyenniy parad v chest' 68-y godovshchiny Velikoy Pobedy," Kremlin website, May 9, 2013, http://kremlin.ru/events/president/news/18089, accessed July 26, 2016.

16 "Volgograd v pamyatniye dni stanet Stalingradom," lenta.ru, January 31, 2013, https://lenta.ru/news/2013/01/31/stalingrad/, accessed July 26, 2016.

17 "Volgogradskiye ubiytsy pokazali, kak zabivali i nasilovali priyaetlya—'geya,'" Tsentral'noye Televideniye, NTV, May 19, 2013, http://www.ntv.ru/novosti/597456/; Daniil Turovskiy, "Stal geyem, chtoby ottuda sbezhat'," lenta.ru, May 23, 2013, https://lenta.ru/articles/2013/05/23/volgograd/; both accessed July 26, 2013.

18 "GD namerena do serediny leta prinyat' zakon o zaprete gey-propagandy," RIA, May 14, 2012, http://ria.ru/society/20130514/937227420.html, accessed July 26, 2016.

19 "Vystupleniye Emrika Shoprada" (Russian version), http://www.komitet2-6.km.duma.gov.ru/site.xp/052057124053057048.html, accessed July 26, 2016.

20 Report on the joint session of Committee on the Family, Women, and Children and the Committee on International Affairs, June 13, 2013, http://www.komitet2-6.km.duma.gov.ru/site.xp/052057124053057048.html; "Deputat Mizulina predlozhila otbirat' detey u rossiyskikh geyev i lesbiyanok," Gay Russia, June 14, 2013, http://www.gayrussia.eu/russia/6814/; both accessed July 26, 2016.

21 "Duma okonchatel'no odobrila zapret na usynovleniye odnopolymi parami," lenta.ru, June 21, 2013, https://lenta.ru/news/2013/06/21/siroty/; Olga Pavlikova, "Aleksey Zhuravlev: 'Gomoseksualist ne dolzhen vospityvat' rebyonka," *Slon*, September 5, 2013, https://slon.ru/russia/aleksey_zhuravlev_gomoseksualist_ne_dolzhen_vospityvat_rebenka-987035.xhtml; both accessed July 26, 2016.

22 "Zasedaniye mezhdunarodnogo diskussionnogo kluba 'Valdai,'" Kremlin website, September 19, 2013, http://kremlin.ru/events/president/news/19243, accessed July 27, 2016.

23 "Everything You Need to Know About the Anti-LGBTQ World Congress of Families (WCF)," Southern Poverty Law Center, October 21, 2015, https://www.splcenter.org/news/2015/10/21/everything-you-need-know-about-anti-lgbtq-world-congress-families-wcf; Cole Parke, "Natural Deception: Conned by the World Congress of Families," Political Research Associates, January 21, 2015, http://www.politicalresearch.org/2015/01/21/natural-deception-conned-by-the-world-congress-of-families/#sthash.DJXMcOU7.a9bkcdgH.dpbs (also published in *The Public Eye*, Winter 2015); both accessed July 30, 2016.

24 The WCF's Russian-language website lists seven top officials of the organization: three Americans and four Russians, http://worldcongress.ru/; the American site lists only American staff: http://worldcongress.org/team.php; both accessed July 30, 2016.

25 "On to Moscow World Congress of Families VIII, September 10–12, 2014," *World Congress of Families News* 7, no. 4 (June/July 2013), p. 5.

26 "Okkupai-Pedofilyai Perm': Vypusk #7," https://new.vk.com/video124656711_165196696, accessed July 27, 2016.

27 "Okkupai-Pedofilyai g. Perm': Vypusk #3: 'Krepkiy oreshek,'" https://new.vk.com/video139331747_169305187, accessed July 27, 2016.

28 "Okkupai-Pedofilyai g. Perm': Vypusk #7: 'Razmorozhennaya pilotka,'" https://new.vk.com/video232045782_169269590, accessed July 27, 2016.

29 "Kuda smotri Perm'?" VK post by Genderniye Issledovaniya: Traditsionniy Podkhod, March 29, 2014, https://new.vk.com/wall-54973617_558, accessed July 27, 2016.

twenty **A NATION DIVIDED**

1 Nadezhda Tolokonnikova, "Pussy Riot's Nadezhda Tolokonnikova: Why I Have Gone on Hunger Strike," *The Guardian*, September 23, 2013, https://www.theguardian.com/music/2013/sep/23/pussy-riot-hunger-strike

-nadezhda-tolokonnikova, accessed May 10, 2017.

2 Masha Gessen, "Northern Exposure: Protest, Petroleum, and Putin's Dream of a Russian Arctic," *Harper's*, June 2014, https://harpers.org/archive/2014/06/northern-exposure/2/.

3 Masha Gessen, "Putin, Snubbed: The Russian Leader May Release Mikhail Khodorkovsky to Distract Attention from Western Leaders' Decision to Skip His Olympics," *Slate*, December 19, 2013, http://www.slate.com/articles/news_and_politics/foreigners/2013/12/mikhail_khodorkovsky_how_obama_s_snub_of_putin_s_sochi_olympics_may_lead.html, accessed May 10, 2017.

4 "Postanovleniye Gosudarstvennoy Dumy ot 18 dekabrya 2013 g. no. 3500-6 GD 'Ob obyavlenii amnistii v svyazi s 20-letiyem prinyatiya Konstitutsii Rossiyskoy Federatsii,'" *Rossiyskaya gazeta*, December 19, 2013, https://rg.ru/2013/12/18/amnistia-dok.html, accessed May 10, 2017.

5 Vladimir Putin's press conference, December 19, 2013, Kremlin transcript, http://kremlin.ru/events/president/news/19859, accessed May 10, 2017.

6 Masha Gessen, "The Putin Nemesis Plotting a Post-Putin Russia," Vanity Fair Hive, July 19, 2016, http://www.vanityfair.com/news/2016/07/mikhail-khodorkovsky-putin-russia, accessed May 10, 2017.

7 "Rossiyskiye pisateli–Evromaydanu," colta.ru, December 1, 2013, http://www.colta.ru/news/1364, accessed May 10, 2017.

8 Olga Pvlikova, "'Assotsiatsiya s YeS oznachayet rasshireniye sfery gey-kul'tury,'" *Slon*, December 10, 2013, https://republic.ru/russia/assotsiatsiya_s_es_oznachaet_rasshirenie_sfery_gey_kultury-1032020.xhtml, accessed May 10, 2017.

9 Maria Baronova, "'Vot oni khotyat Klichko: Klichko—on debil, on boksyor, po golove poluchal," *Slon*, January 27, 2014, https://slon.ru/world/baronova_na_maydane-1048640.xhtml, accessed August 19, 2016.

10 "V skandal vokrug 'blokadnogo' oprosa 'Dozhdya' mozhet vmeshat'sya Yu. Chayka," RBK, January 29, 2014, http://www.rbc.ru/spb_sz/29/01/2014/5592aab69a794719538d19a2, accessed August 21, 2016; "Zdes' i seychas: Natalya Sindeyeva: Ya khochu izvinit'sya pered lud'mi, kotorykh eto deystvitel'no zadelo, takiye lyudi byli i vnutri telekanala," TV Rain, January 29, 2014, https://tvrain.ru/teleshow/here_and_now/natalja_sindeeva_ja_hochu_izvinitsja_pered_ljudmi_kotoryh_eto_dejstvitelno_zadelo_takie_ljudi_byli_i_vnutri_telekanala-361621/, accessed August 21, 2016.

11 "Zdes' i seychas: Dmitry Peskov: Ya ne vizhu smysla zakryvat' telekanal, no oni narushili bol'she, chem zakon, pereshli krasnuyu liniyu," TV Rain, January 29, 2014, https://tvrain.ru/teleshow/here_and_now/dmitrij_peskov_o_situatsii_s_dozhdem_ja_ne_vizhu_smysla_zakryvat_telekanal_no_oni_narushili_bolshe_chem_zakon_pereshli_krasnuju_liniju-361620/, accessed August 21, 2016.

12 Caitlin Dewey, "Journalists at Sochi Are Live-Tweeting Their Hilarious and Gross Hotel Experiences," *The Washington Post*, February 4, 2014, https://www.washingtonpost.com/news/worldviews/wp/2014/02/04/journalists-at-sochi-are-live-tweeting-their-hilarious-and-gross-hotel-experiences/, accessed August 31, 2016.

13 Maria Baronova, "No One Has Done More for Ukrainian Nationalism Than Vladimir Putin," *New Republic*, March 3, 2014, https://newrepublic.com/article/116841/bolotnaya-prisoner-maria-baronova-putins-ukraine-occupation, accessed August 21, 2016.

14 "Referendum v Krymu o statuse avtonomii," RIA compilation, March 16, 2015, http://ria.ru/spravka/20150316/1052210041.html, accessed August 21, 2016.

15 Mark Kramer, "Why Did Russia Give Away Crimea Sixty Years Ago?" Cold War International History Project E-Dossier no. 47, March 19, 2014, https://www.wilsoncenter.org/publication/why-did-russia-give-away-crimea-sixty-years-ago, accessed August 22, 2016.

16 Vladimir Putin's address in the Kremlin, March 18, 2014, Kremlin transcript, http://kremlin.ru/events/president/news/20603; official English translation, http://en.kremlin.ru/events/president/news/20603; both accessed August 23, 2016.

17 http://en.kremlin.ru/events/president/news/20603, accessed August 23, 2016.

18 Adolf Hitler's closing speech at NSDAP (Nazi Party) congress, Nuremberg, September 12, 1938, http://der-fuehrer.org

/reden/english/38-09-12.htm, accessed August 23, 2016.

19 "'Maidan,' Krym, sanktsii," Levada Center, December 30, 2014, http://www.levada .ru/2014/12/30/majdan-krym-sanktsii/, accessed August 23, 2016.

20 Hannah Arendt, *The Origins of Totalitarianism* (New York: Harcourt Brace Jovanovich, 1976), pp. 470–474.

21 "Expert: Raspad Ukrainy neizbezhen," russia. ru, October 8, 2009, http://tv.russia.ru/video /diskurs_5615/, accessed August 26, 2016.

22 "Predstavlyayetsya pravil'nym initsiirovat' prisoyedineniye vostochnykh oblastey Ukrainy k Rossii," *Novaya gazeta*, February 23, 2015, http://www.novayagazeta.ru /politics/67389.html, accessed August 26, 2016. The newspaper attributed the white paper to Konstantin Malofeyev, known as the Orthodox Billionaire. But the logic and, especially, the vocabulary of much of the text point strongly to the possibility that Dugin had coauthored it. Specifically, the repeated use of the word "geopolitical" and, even more important, the term *gorodskaya guerrilya*— "urban guerrilla"—which, in Russian, seems to appear only in encyclopedias and, frequently, in Dugin's writing. The existence of an ongoing working relationship between Malofeyev and Dugin is well documented. See, for example, "Chorniy Internatsional: Malofeyev i Dugin," blog by Russian hacker Shaltay Boltay, November 27, 2014, https:// b0ltai.org/2014/11/27/%D1%87D0%B5%D1 %80%D0%BD%D1%8B%D0%B9-%D0%B8 %D0%BD%D1%82%D0%B5%D1%80%D0 %BD%D0%B0%D1%86%D0%B8%D0%BE %D0%BD%D0%B0%D0%BB%D0%BC%D 0%B0%D0%BB%D0%BE%D1%84%D0%B 5%D0%B5%D0%B2-%D0%B8- %D0%B4%D1%83%D0%B3%D0%B8/, accessed August 26, 2016.

23 "Dokazi prichetnosti vladi RF do poasyaganiya na teritorial'nu tsilisnist' Urkainy," telephone recordings published by Prosecutor General's Office of Ukraine, https://www.youtube.com/watch?v=l6K1 _vHrJPU, accessed August 26, 2016.

24 "A. Dugin i Ye. Gubareva obsudili budushcheye Donbassa i Ukrainy," recording of Skype conversation, March 29, 2014, https://www.youtube.com/watch?v= -jP0yebodlM, accessed August 26, 2016. The channel on which the video was published

belongs to Pavel Gubarev, but he was in jail at the time, so I assume the call was recorded and published by Yekaterina Gubareva herself.

25 "Pro-Russian Crowds Storm Government Buildings in Eastern Ukraine," from "The Ukraine Crisis Timeline," Center for Strategic and International Studies (CSIS), April 6, 2014, http://ukraine.csis.org/east1 .htm#45, accessed August 26, 2016.

26 "People's Republic of Donetsk Calls for Russia to Send 'Peacekeepers,'" from "The Ukraine Crisis Timeline," CSIS, April 7, 2014, http://ukraine.csis.org/east1.htm#46, accessed August 26, 2016.

27 "US, Others Support Ukraine but Europe Divided on Sanctions," http://ukraine.csis .org/east1.htm#58; "Pro-Russian Forces Seize APCs as Ukrainian Operation Falters," http://ukraine.csis.org/east1.htm#59; April 15–16, 2014, "The Ukraine Crisis Timeline," CSIS, accessed August 27, 2016.

28 "Ukraine, Pro-Russian Protestors [*sic*] Square Off in East," April 8, 2014, http://ukraine .csis.org/east1.htm#48; "Pro-Russian Forces Seize Additional Facilities," April 12, 2014, http://ukraine.csis.org/east1.htm#53; "Ukrainian Military, Pro-Russian Forces Clash as 'Anti-Terrorist Operation' Begins," April 15, 2014, http://ukraine.csis.org/east1 .htm#57; all from "The Ukraine Crisis Timeline," CSIS, accessed August 26, 2016.

29 *Pryamaya liniya s Vladimirom Putinym*, April 17, 2014, Kremlin transcript, http://kremlin .ru/events/president/news/20796, accessed August 27, 2016.

30 Yuri Maloveryan, "Gosduma utverdila prisoyedineniye Kryma k Rossii," BBC Russian Service, March 20, 2014, http:// www.bbc.com/russian /russia/2014/03/140320_ukraine_crimea_ duma_ratification; Ilya Ponomarev, "In Exile, but Ready to Save Russia," *The New York Times*, April 15, 2015, https://www.nytimes .com/2015/04/16/opinion/in-exile-but-ready -to-save-russia.html?_r=0; both accessed May 12, 2017.

31 Marlene Laruelle, ed., *Eurasianism and the European Far Right: Reshaping the Europe- Russia Relationship* (Lanham, MD: Lexington Books, 2015).

32 "21 aprelya v programme 'Pozner'— Aleksandr Dugin," April 18, 2014, http:// pozneronline.ru/2014/04/7669/, accessed August 27, 2016.

33 Alexander Dugin, "Nakanunye voyny—2," *Malorossiya*, April 21, 2014, http://maloros .ru/new/4120-aleksandr-dugin-nakanune -vojny-2.xhtml, accessed August 28, 2016.

34 Alexander Dugin, "Putin, vvodi voyska!" *Malorossiya*, May 28, 2014, http://maloros.ru /new/4687-aleksandr-dugin-putin-vvodi -vojska.xhtml; Alexander Dugin, "Russkiye zemli to suzhayutsya, to rasshiryayutsya," *Malorossiya*, May 27, 2014, http://maloros.ru /new/5019-aleksandr-dugin-russkie-zemli -to-suzhayutsya-to-rasshiryayutsya-video .xhtml; Alexander Dugin, "Shestaya kolonna," *Vzglyad*, April 29, 2014, http:// www.vz.ru/opinions/2014/4/29/684247.html; all accessed August 28, 2016.

35 Author interview with Natalya Makeeva, Moscow, May 22, 2015.

36 Mikhail Khodorkovsky, "My mozhem i khotim reshat' samiye slozhniye zadachi, kotoriye stavit pered nashimi narodami zhizn'," khodorkovsky.ru, April 24, 2014, http://old.khodorkovsky.ru/news/2014 /04/24/18768.html, accessed August 28, 2016.

37 Alan Taylor, "A Year of War Completely Destroyed the Donetsk Airport," *The Atlantic*, February 26, 2015, http://www .theatlantic.com/photo/2015/02 /a-year-of-war-completely-destroyed-the -donetsk-airport/386204/, accessed August 28, 2016.

38 Cole Parke, "Natural Deception: Conned by the World Congress of Families," Political Research Associates, January 21, 2015, http://www.politicalresearch.org/2015/01/21 /natural-deception-conned-by-the-world -congress-of-families/#sthash.DJXMcOU7 .a9bkcdgH.dpbs (also published in *The Public Eye*, Winter 2015), accessed August 29, 2016.

39 John-Henry Westen, "Conference Promoting Large Families in Russia Amazes Westerners," lifesitenews.com, September 10, 2014, https://www.lifesitenews.com/news /conference-promoting-large-families-in -russia-amazes-westerners, accessed August 29, 2016.

40 Anton Shekhovtsov, *Russia and the Western Far Right: Tango Noir* (Abingdon, England: Routledge, 2017).

41 Author interview with Johann Beckman, Moscow, June 2014.

42 "Rossiya zapretila import prodovol'stviya na $9 mlrd v otvet na sanktsii," TASS, August 7,
2014, http://tass.ru/ekonomika/1367515, accessed Sept. 4, 2016.

43 "Indeks potrebitel'skikh nastroyeniy," explication, Levada Center, undated, http:// www.levada.ru/indikatory/sotsialno -ekonomicheskie-indikatory/indeks -potrebitelskikh-nastroenii/, accessed September 4, 2016.

44 "Index potrebitel'skikh nastroyeniy," graph, Levada Center, undated, http://www.levada .ru/indikatory/sotsialno-ekonomicheskie -indikatory/, accessed September 4, 2016.

45 Masha Gessen, "The News in Moscow," newyorker.com, December 27, 2014, http:// www.newyorker.com/news/news-desk/news -in-moscow-russia-ruble, accessed September 4, 2016.

46 Masha Gessen, "A Country Haunted by Starvation Burns Its Food," newyorker.com, August 11, 2015, http://www.newyorker .com/news/news-desk/russia-haunted-by -starvation-burns-its-food, accessed September 4, 2016.

twenty-one **ZHANNA: FEBRUARY 27, 2015**

1 "Prigovor po 'delu vos'mi' oglashen," OVDInfo, February 24, 2014, https:// ovdinfo.org/express-news/2014/02/24 /prigovor-po-delu-vosmi-oglashen, accessed September 6, 2016.

2 "Na Manezhnoy zaderzhali 423 cheloveka," OVDInfo, February 24, 2014, https://ovdinfo .org/express-news/2014/02/24/na -manezhnoy-zaderzhali-423-cheloveka, accessed September 6, 2016.

3 Yelena Masyuk, "Nepovinoveniye zakonnomy rasporyazheniyu kosmonavta. Statya 19.3," *Novaya gazeta*, March 3, 2014, http://www .novayagazeta.ru/politics/62480.html, accessed Sept. 6, 2016.

4 "V Tverskom sude vynosyat prigovory oppozitsionnym politikam," OVDInfo, February 25, 2014, https://ovdinfo.org /express-news/2014/02/25/v-tverskom-sude -vynosyat-prigovory-oppozicionnym -politikam, accessed September 6, 2016.

5 Boris Nemtsov, "Voyna—eto bezumiye, eto protiv Rossii," blog post, March 2, 2014, http://b-nemtsov.livejournal.com /2014/03/02/, accessed Sept. 8, 2016.

6 "Shest' chelovek zaderzhany na Manezhnoy ploshchadi za rastyazhku 'Za nashu i vashu svobodu,'" OVDInfo, March 2, 2014, https://

ovdinfo.org/express-news/2014/03/02/shest
-chelovek-zaderzhany-na-manezhnoy
-ploshchadi-za-rastyazhku-so-slovami,
accessed September 8, 2016.

7 "Kak minimum 362 cheloveka zaderzhali segodnya v Moskve," OVDInfo, March 2, 2014, https://ovdinfo.org/express -news/2014/03/02/kak-minimum-362 -cheloveka-zaderzhali-segodnya-v-moskve, accessed September 8, 2016.

8 "V Moskve proydiot shestviye v podderzhku naroda Ukrainy," *Rossiyskaya gazeta*, March 2, 2014, https://rg.ru/2014/03/02/podderjka -anons.html, accessed September 9, 2016.

9 Screenshot of ad, reproduced in journalist Andrei Malgin's blog, March 3, 2014, http://avmalgin.livejournal.com /4376564.html, accessed September 9, 2016.

10 Yuri Maloveryan, "'Marsh mira' v Moskve sobral desyatki tysyach uchastnikov," BBC Russian Service, March 15, 2014, http:// www.bbc.com/russian/international /2014/03/140315_ukraine_moscow_rallies, accessed September 9, 2016.

11 Ksenia Sobchak, tweet, April 14, 2014, https://twitter.com/intent/like?tweet _id=455701786901639169&ref_src=twsrc% 5Etfw&original_referer=http%3A%2F%2Fp erebezhchik.ru%2Fslukhi%2F366 .html&tw_i=455701786901639169&tw _p=tweetembed, accessed September 9, 2016.

12 Boris Nemtsov, Facebook post, April 26, 2014, https://www.facebook.com/boris .nemtsov/posts/619540304782240:0, accessed Sept. 9, 2016.

13 Sergei Mel'nikov, "10 vydvizhentsev KGB," *Ogonyok*, November 7, 2011, http://www .kommersant.ru/doc/1802255, accessed September 9, 2016.

14 Boris Nemtsov and Leonid Martynyuk, *Zimnyaya olimpiada v subtropikhakh: Nezavisimyi Ekspertnyi Doklad* (Moscow: Self-published, 2013), p. 14.

15 Sergei Goryashko, "Vladimir Yakunin reshil nakazat' Borisa Nemtsova rublyom," *Kommersant*, May 28, 2014, http://www .kommersant.ru/doc/2481601; "Sud perenyos slushaniye po delu RzhD k Nemtsovu na 10 fevralya," life.ru, December 10, 2014, https://life.ru/t/%D0%BD% D0%BE%D0%B2%D0%BE%D1%81%D1% 82%D0%B8/146712; both accessed Sept. 9, 2016.

16 Boris Nemtsov, Facebook post, Sept. 6, 2014, https://www.facebook.com/boris.nemtsov /posts/683165751753028:0, accessed Sept. 9, 2016.

17 "Skol'ko cheloek prishli na shestviye v Moskve i chem otlichilsya Milonov na peterburgskom 'Marshe mira': Itogi 21 sentyabrya," TV Rain, September 21, 2014, https://tvrain.ru/teleshow/here_and_now /skolko_chelovek_prishli_na_shestvie_v _moskve_i_chem_otlichilsja_milonov_na _peterburgskom_marshe_mira_itogi_21 _sentjabrja-375624/, accessed March 14, 2017.

18 "Marsh predateley," *Glavplakat*, Sept. 21, 2014, http://glavplakat.ru/article/319, accessed Sept. 9, 2016.

19 "Chuzhiye v gorode," *Glavplakat*, April 11, 2014, http://glavplakat.ru/article/147, accessed September 9, 2016.

20 "Desyatimetrovyi banner Glavplakata na Novom Arbate," *Glavplakat*, January 23, 2015, http://glavplakat.ru/article/424, accessed Sept. 9, 2016.

21 Masha Gessen, "The Bitter Education of Alexey Navalny," newyorker.com, Dec. 31, 2014, http://www.newyorker.com/news /news-desk/bitter-education-alexey-navalny, accessed Sept. 13, 2016.

22 "Manifest," Antimaidan, https://antimaidan .ru/page/9, accessed September 13, 2016.

23 Yevgeni Feldman, "'Antimaidan' v Moskve: Tridtsatitysyachnoye shestviye to Petrovke," *Novaya gazeta*, February 21, 2015, http:// www.novayagazeta.ru/photos/67368.html, accessed September 13, 2016.

24 "Tysyachi lyudey prinyali uchastiye v marshakh pamyati Nemtsova," BBC Russian Service, March 1, 2015, http://www.bbc .com/russian/russia/2015/03/150301 _nemtsov_march_moscow, accessed September 13, 2016.

25 "Zhanna Nemtsova: 'Putin politicheski vinovat v smerti ottsa,'" BBC Russian Service, March 12, 2015, http://www.bbc .com/russian/russia/2015/03/150311_janna _nemtsova_interview, accessed Sept. 13, 2016.

twenty-two FOREVER WAR

1 The protester was Varvara Turova. Photo of her taken August 4, 2013, https://www .facebook.com/photo.php?fbid=10200597542 444759&set=a.2095488550548.2107528.134

5351749&type=3&theater; July 29, https://
www.facebook.com/photo.php?fbid=1020056
8078068168&set=a.1019614374366.2003635
.1345351749&type=3&theater; July 28,
https://www.facebook.com/photo.php?fbid=1
0200561390820991&set=a.2095488550548.2
107528.1345351749&type=3&theater; July
27, https://www.facebook.com/photo.php?fbi
d=10200555923604314&set=a.20954885505
48.2107528.1345351749&type=3&theater;
July 25, https://www.facebook.com/photo.ph
p?fbid=10200541214356592&set=a.2095488
550548.2107528.1345351749&type=3&thea
ter; July 24, https://www.facebook.com
/photo.php?fbid=10200534708553951&set=a
.2095488550548.2107528.1345351749&type
=3&theater; July 23, https://www.facebook.
com/photo.php?fbid=10200529133734584&s
et=a.2095488550548.2107528.1345351749&t
ype=3&theater; July 22, https://www
.facebook.com/photo.php?fbid=10200521098
493708&set=a.2095488550548.2107528.134
5351749&type=3&theater; July 21, https://
www.facebook.com/photo.php?fbid=1020051
3454662617&set=a.2095488550548.2107528
.1345351749&type=3&theater; July 20,
https://www.facebook.com/photo.php?fbid=1
0200508703623844&set=a.2095488550548
.2107528.1345351749&type=3&theater; all
accessed Sept. 21, 2016.
2 Sergei Yakovlev, Facebook post, March 10,
2014, https://www.facebook.com/photo.php?
fbid=519913491459009&set=a.519916641458
694.1073741825.100003210891158&type=3
&theater, accessed September 21,
2016.
3 Marta Herstowska et al., "Severe Skin
Complications in Patients Treated with
Antidepressants: A Literature Review,"
Postepy dermatologii i alergologii 31, no. 2
(2014), pp. 92–97, http://www.ncbi.nlm.nih
.gov/pmc/articles/PMC4112250/, accessed
September 21, 2016.
4 Masha Gessen, "Moscow Just Razed Its
Small Businesses and Became Even Blander,"
newyorker.com, February 10, 2016, http://
www.newyorker.com/news/news-desk
/moscow-just-razed-its-small-businesses-and
-became-even-blander, accessed September
22, 2016.
5 Vyacheslav Nikonov versus Nikolai Zlobin,
on *Poyedinok*, hosted by Vladimir Solovyev,
April 21, 2016, https://www.youtube.com
/watch?v=WiKWoy3RPI4, accessed
September 22, 2016.
6 Cathy Caruth, *Unclaimed Experience: Trauma,
Narrative, and History* (Baltimore: Johns
Hopkins University Press, 1996), p. 66.
7 Ibid., p. 63.
8 Robert Jay Lifton, *Witness to an Extreme
Century* (New York: Free Press, 2011), p. 28.
9 Ibid., p. 127.
10 Robert Jay Lifton, *The Nazi Doctors: Medical
Killing and the Psychology of Genocide* (New
York: Basic Books, 1986), p. 418.
11 Lifton, *Witness to an Extreme Century*, p. 151.
12 Author interview with trauma psychologist
Jack Saul, New York City, December 23, 2015.
13 "70-yz sessiya General'noy Assamblei OON,"
Kremlin transcript, September 28, 2015,
http://kremlin.ru/events/president
/news/50385, accessed September 26, 2016.
14 "Zasedaniye mezhdunarodnogo
diskussionnogo kluba 'Valdai,'" Kremlin
transcript, October 22, 2015, http://kremlin
.ru/events/president/news/50548, accessed
September 26, 2016.
15 Erich Fromm, *Escape from Freedom* (New
York: Henry Holt, 1994), p. 168.
16 Hannah Arendt, *The Origins of
Totalitarianism* (New York: Harcourt Brace
Jovanovich, 1976), p. 329.
17 Lev Gudkov, "Zayavleniye direktora Levada-
tsentra," Levada Center, September 9, 2016,
http://www.levada.ru/2016/09/09/14393/,
accessed September 26, 2016.

INDEX

Brilliant, brave, and eloquent, Masha Gessen writes books that crystallize—and transcend—our time.

Masha Gessen is internationally renowned not only for courageous, impeccably researched reporting, but for work that pushes beyond the bounds of category—history, biography, science, current events—to become nonfiction classics: enduring accounts of lives, nations, and ideas in flux. A Russian immigrant with startling grace in English and uncanny fluency in American culture, Gessen gains access other journalists only dream of and is unparalleled in the ability to translate seemingly incomprehensible events and attitudes into human and recognizable terms. Uncompromising in the pursuit of sometimes shocking and discomfiting realities, this essential writer speaks truth to power and illuminates our most necessary stories.

© Tanya Sazansky

WORDS WILL BREAK CEMENT
Masha Gessen

The Story of Pussy Riot, who resurrected the power of truth in a society built on lies

In February 2012, five young women entered the Cathedral of Christ the Savior in Moscow and performed a "punk prayer" beseeching the "Mother of God" to "chase Putin out." The incident captured international headlines and galvanized people around the world who recognized in the prayer a fierce act of political confrontation as well as a brave and inspired work of art. Drawing on exclusive access to Pussy Riot, their friends, and their families,

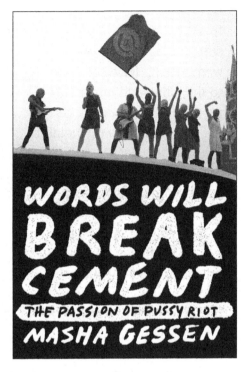

Masha Gessen reconstructs the personal journeys that transformed a group of young women into artists with a shared vision and the courage and imagination to express it unforgettably.

"Urgent...damning...Much here will be new to the American reader. All of it is infuriating." **—Alexander Nazaryan,** *The New York Times*

"Remarkable...Gessen [is] one of the most important activists and journalists Russia has known in a generation....Disquieting, moving, and closely reported." **—David Remnick,** *The New Yorker*

THE MAN WITHOUT A FACE
Masha Gessen

A chilling portrait of one of the most feared figures in world politics

In 1999, the "Family" surrounding Boris Yeltsin went looking for a successor to the ailing and unpopular president. They settled on the almost unknown Vladimir Putin, a "faceless" creature they believed they could mold in their own image. Soon, with ruthless efficiency, Putin dismantled the country's media, destroyed the fragile mechanisms of democracy, and drove his rivals and critics into exile or the grave. Masha Gessen has given us a spellbinding, terrifying, and enduring account of Putin's rise and reign.

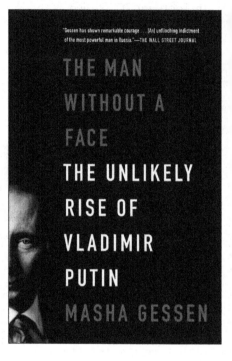

"[An] unflinching indictment of the most powerful man in Russia."
—*The Wall Street Journal*

"Fascinating, hard-hitting reading." —*Foreign Affairs*

THE BROTHERS
Masha Gessen

How the American Dream went disastrously wrong for two immigrants, and the nightmare that resulted

On April 15, 2013, two homemade bombs exploded near the finish line of the Boston Marathon, killing three people and wounding more than 264 others. In the aftermath, Tamerlan Tsarnaev died and his younger brother, Dzhokhar, was captured and brought to trial. Yet even after the guilty verdict and the death sentence, what we didn't know was why such a nightmare came to pass. Acclaimed Russian-American journalist Masha Gessen masterfully reconstructs the struggle between assimilation and alienation that played out in each of the brothers, a split in identity that resulted in a new breed of homegrown terrorist with feet on American soil but sense of self elsewhere.

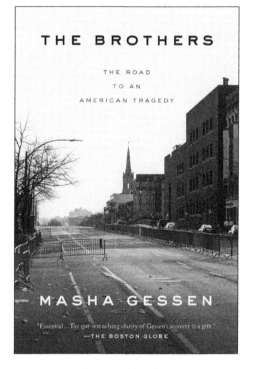

"Remarkable...That [Gessen] makes the case with grace and passion, while also basing it on rigorous reporting, is the triumph of the book." —*Los Angeles Times*

"Essential...The gut-wrenching clarity of Gessen's account is a gift."
—*The Boston Globe*

Made in the USA
Las Vegas, NV
25 March 2022

46250941R10302